Early Childhood Education and Care in Canada

contexts, dimensions, and issues

Margie I. Mayfield

University of Victoria

Prentice
Hall

Toronto

Canadian Cataloguing in Publication Data

Mayfield, Margie
      Early childhood education and care in Canada : contexts, dimensions, and issues

Includes bibliographical references and index.

ISBN 0-13-080039-2

1. Early childhood education – Canada. 2. Child care services – Canada. I. Title.

LB1139.3.C3M39 2001   372.21'0971   C00-931674-4

ISBN 0-13-080039-2

Vice President, Editorial Director: Michael Young
Editor-in-Chief: David Stover
Acquisitions Editor: Andrew A. Wellner
Signing Representative: Katie McWhirter
Developmental Editor: Lisa Phillips
Production Editor: Sherry Torchinsky
Copy Editor: Kelli Howey
Production Coordinator: Peggy Brown
Page Layout: Christine Velakis, Debbie Kumpf
Photo Research: Susan Wallace-Cox
Art Director: Mary Opper
Interior and Cover Design: Sarah Battersby
Cover Image: Scott Harman-Heath

30 16

Printed and bound in Canada.

Statistics Canada information is used with permission of the Minister of Industry, as Minister responsible for Statistics Canada. Information on the availability of the wide range of data from Statistics Canada can be obtained from Statistics Canada's Regional Offices, its World Wide Web site at http://www.statcan.ca, and its toll-free access number 1-800-263-1136.

Dedication

To my mother and friend – Dorothy A. Mayfield.

Brief Contents

Contents

PREFACE

Anne Morrow Lindbergh once wrote, "A preface is perhaps more for the writer than for the reader" (1935/1963, p. vii). This may be true as the standard approach to a preface is for the author to explain, to those readers who choose to read the preface, what the book is about, its overall purpose, why it was written, and how it is organized. However, one hopes that this preface is really for both the readers and the author.

Early childhood education and care has evolved and grown greatly in the past nearly 400 years to be the dynamic and exciting field it is today. Basically, this book seeks to tell the fascinating, and sometimes surprising, story of past and present early childhood education and care in Canada.

If you too believe that education is a life-long process, early childhood education and care is a great field to be in. When I began writing this book, I realized that I have spent almost my entire life in education. I began in early childhood education as a five-year-old child attending public school kindergarten and primary grades. I returned to early childhood education and care as a seventeen-year-old university student enrolled in education courses. I have been in this field ever since. As you can see, early childhood education and care has been a large part of my life and I hope my enthusiasm, respect, and appreciation of this field, its profession, and its people (both adults and children) are evident throughout this book.

This book is an outgrowth of the many years I have taught introductory, history, philosophy, and theory courses in early childhood education and care. My motivation for actually writing this book was the same as many authors of textbooks in many fields: There was not a textbook that met the needs of my students and I became tired of waiting for someone else to write one.

Early childhood education and care in this text refers to the standard definition of the programs and services for children from birth to age 9 and their families. I have tried to make this textbook comprehensive enough in order to reflect and portray the breadth and complexity of early childhood education and care both in the present and in its evolution and development. Because of this approach, the book could easily be used as the textbook for more than one college or university course in early childhood education and care. This would help provide continuity across courses while reducing the costs for the students. Of course, no book can include everything the educated early childhood professional needs or wants to know.

This book was written for a wider than usual audience. Although it will be useful for both present and prospective early childhood educators, it is intended for anyone who wants information, background, and resources on early childhood education and care in Canada. It is also relevant for students and professionals in related fields such as social work, nursing, family studies, and human services as well as people in other countries wishing to know more about early childhood education and care in Canada. It can also be used as a reference and information source for parents, administrators, and anyone else interested in young children. An additional aspect of this book is that because it describes the diversity and types of early childhood programs, it presents possible career options for present and prospective early childhood educators.

The subtitle of this book is Contexts, Dimensions, and Issues. Early childhood education and care does not, and never could, exist in a vacuum. It exists in multiple contexts (e.g., socio-cultural, historical, theoretical, demographic, political, economic, and global). This aspect of the book recognizes and describes these contexts and their implications for children, families, educators, and programs.

There are three dimensions that make up the three major sections of this book:

- The People and the Profession (Chapters 1-4)

- The Roots and Theories of Early Childhood Education and Care (Chapters 5-7)

- Early Childhood Programs (Chapters 8-13).

A more detailed overview of the organization and content of this book is provided in Chapter 1.

Many of the issues facing early childhood education and care today are described in the last section of the chapters. The purpose is to describe the issues, provide information, and permit the reader to draw his or her own conclusions. Of course, contexts, dimensions, and issues in early childhood education and care are all interrelated and interwoven.

Throughout the text are key features to assist the reader. One of these is **For Reflection**. The **For Reflection** pieces present questions or materials (e.g., cartoon, quotations, etc.) to help the reader to reflect on the material just read or the section to be read next. It is important to call the reader's attention to these pieces. Even though the **For Reflection** pieces are located in the margins, they are integral to the text.

In addition, in Chapter 6, key principles for each of three major curriculum models based on child development theories appear in the margins next to the relevant sections of a program description. The purpose of these is to help the reader more easily make the connection between theory and application in early childhood programs.

Another key feature of this book is the **Focus** pieces throughout the book. These describe programs, individuals, ideas, or issues. Some are written by early childhood educators, some are interviews of early childhood educators, some are based on my research, and some are descriptions.

At the end of the chapters are **Key Terms** to help the reader review concepts presented in that chapter. The **Resources** sections provide sources for additional information. These include resources for both adults and children. I know the frustration of students when they cannot get a particular reference in their local library. Therefore, I hope the inclusion of useful Web sites will help in obtaining additional information more easily.

Although Anne Morrow Lindbergh believed that the preface is for the author, I hope you and others will see this book as being useful and informative for the readers.

MIM
October 2000

Acknowledgments

Writing is usually a solitary task. However, no book is ever entirely the endeavour of just the author. This book is no exception. Many people have most generously given their support, encouragement, and time to me and this endeavour.

Firstly, I'd like to acknowledge and thank the friends and colleagues who so kindly read and responded to drafts of chapters: Mimi Davis, Robert Fowler, Kathy Ollila, Lloyd Ollila, Alison Preece, Terry Rennie, Beverly Timmons, and Ulah Watson. Thank you also to the following reviewers: Deborah Collins, St. Lawrence College; Ingrid Crowther, Loyalist College; Malcolm Read, Medicine Hat College; Lois Rennie, Capilano College; Judy Wainwright, Mount Royal College; and Carolyne Willoughby, Durham College. My special thanks to Terry and Bob who listened, read, and responded kindly to ideas – good and bad – while captive at 37,000 feet over the Pacific Ocean, over meals in China, and at other similar inopportune times; and for Terry's invaluable, efficient, and cheerful help with the reference list. And to Kathy and Lloyd for their always kind and practical advice and support including their help with the photographs for this book. And to Beverly and Ulah for more than 20 years of support as well as listening and responding to ideas and questions during countless telephone conversations and while doing Meals on Wheels on Monday mornings. My thanks and gratitude to you all.

Secondly, I'd like to acknowledge and thank the early childhood professionals who so graciously and kindly wrote or were interviewed for Focus pieces: Edna Aedy, Margery Anderson, Barbara E. Corbett, Wanda Kellogg, Karen King, Ethel King-Shaw, Linda Kusz, Karen Letsche-Biemiller, Karin Marks, Susan Riddell, Elsie Stapleford, Joyce Waddell-Townsend, Otto Weininger, and Mary J. Wright. And also my thanks to the individuals and professional organizations who permitted the use of their materials in this book. I have always told my students that one of the benefits in being part of the early childhood education and care profession is that there are so many nice people. The above people and many others I talked with about the topics in this book truly do exemplify that statement.

My deepest thanks to my family for their encouragement, support, listening, and practical advice – Dorothy, Jack, Robin, Margaret, Megan, Andy, and Cissi.

In our high tech age, I don't think any book could be written without the support of technical experts. I have been fortunate to be able to call upon Stephen Kagan, Perry Plewes, and Marc Thoma at the University of Victoria. As many chapters in this book were written while I was in Asia, I wish to thank the staff of the business centres at the Miramar Hotel in Hong Kong, the Shangri-la Hotel in Singapore, and the Dusit Mangga Dua Hotel in Jakarta for their assistance, technical expertise, and enthusiastic interest in this project – and for the endless cups of tea.

Also, I wish to recognize the staff at Prentice-Hall and Pearson Education Canada for their contribution to making this book a reality. My thanks to: Katherine McWhirter and Cliff Newman for their confidence and encouragement to undertake this book; to Laura Forbes, Sharon Loeb,

Lisa Phillips, David Stover, Joe Zingrone, and Sherry Torchinsky for their editorial work, design, and formatting of this book; and to Kelli Howey for her expert copyediting, cheerfulness, and equanimity in communicating from Waterloo with an author in rural Indonesia and other locations.

And, of course, my very special thanks to the children, families, and colleagues who have taught me so much over the years. Thank you all!

Part One

The People and the Profession

This dimension focuses on the most important factors in early childhood education and care—the people.

Chapter 1—Overview of Early Childhood Education and Care

Early childhood education and care is a dynamic, broad, and varied field. This chapter is an introduction that defines early childhood education and care, describes a variety of types of programs, and surveys some aspects of the field today.

Chapter 2—Children in Canada

What better and more appropriate topic to begin a book on early childhood education and care than children in Canada? This chapter examines who are the children of Canada, the determinants for their optimal development, the changing concept of childhood, children's rights, and some of the issues facing children in Canada today.

Chapter 3—Canadian Families Today

Families have changed in many ways in the past few decades. This chapter defines and describes the Canadian family, outlines why and how families can be included in early childhood programs, and discusses family stressors.

Chapter 4—Early Childhood Educators: Their Roles and the Profession

Early childhood educators are the key to high-quality early childhood programs. This chapter examines the roles, stages of development, professionalism, ethics, and career development of early childhood educators. It concludes by discussing some current issues and future directions for Canadian early childhood educators.

Overview of Early Childhood Education and Care

That was the best time of my life.
—*An eight-year-old boy reflecting about his day-care experience from ages two to five*

Early childhood education and care is a diverse and dynamic field. The field is expanding, and the following examples illustrate its current variety.

- Every school-day morning, Cyndy takes the bus to high school with her infant son. While Cyndy attends class, her son attends the school's infant day-care program.

- Noriko eagerly runs out to the car because this morning her dad is going with her to kindergarten to help with a special project.

- Kirstin and Carl are parents of four-year-old Matti, who attends a parent cooperative nursery school. Because they are both nurses working different rotating shifts, Kirstin and Carl can split the required parent-duty days.

- The Singh family was happy to find a family day-care home that was able to take both their ten-month-old and their four-year-old, as the family wished the children to be together.

- Maria-Carlotta has recently moved to another province. She was pleased to find that there was a family resource centre in her new neighbourhood. She plans to take her son Juan there to play and she hopes to make some new friends for herself and Juan.

- Tim is a provincial-government employee who takes his two-year-old daughter to work every weekday. She attends the on-site child-care centre in his office building.

- Bradley and his grandfather spend every Wednesday together. One of their first stops is the local toy library, where three-year-old Bradley chooses a toy to borrow. Then Granddad and Bradley return the children's books they borrowed last week and select two more.

- Eight-year-old Jeanne meets her brother Pierre every afternoon at his kindergarten classroom, and they both go to the school-age child care program in their school until 5 p.m.

· Helen has been telling stories in her grandchildren's nursery school on their reserve for the past five years. She thinks it is important for elders to share traditional Aboriginal stories with young children.

· Beth and her stepson Isaac go to Kindergym every Thursday at the local recreation centre. Isaac is learning to do a forward somersault and walk the balance beam.

What do all of these children and their families have in common? They are participating in an early childhood program. A general trend in Canada in the past 30 years has been the increasing number and type of early childhood programs. At the beginning of the twentieth century, early childhood programs were basically a few kindergartens, nursery schools, and day cares. However, at the beginning of the twenty-first century, more children *and* families are participating in a much greater variety of early childhood programs.

Take a look at the above examples and identify which of these programs were available in your community when you were a young child. Which ones are available in your community now? Early childhood education and care has gained a much higher profile in most Canadian communities over the past 30 years. And in more recent years, the field has received more and continually increasing attention from families, media, governments, and business than ever before (Kagan, 1999b).

Here are some questions to think about while you read this chapter:

· How is early childhood education and care typically defined?

· What are some rationales for early childhood education and care?

· What types of early childhood programs are found in Canada today?

· What are some potential career opportunities for you in early childhood education and care?

· What are some of the major issues facing contemporary early childhood programs and early childhood educators?

What Is Early Childhood Education and Care?

As can be seen from the previous examples, early childhood education and care is diverse and varied. This means that its definition must be broad and encompassing. **Early childhood education and care** is typically defined as "programs and services for children from birth to age nine and their families." It includes day care, nursery school, kindergarten, and primary grades as well as other types of programs such as family support programs. This definition is a very general one. However, the term *early childhood education and care* can be clarified by examining its component parts.

Early childhood is the most formative period of children's development. During the first eight years of life, great growth and development occur and the foundations are set for further growth and development. Therefore, it is important that programs for young children are quality programs that will foster their development and positively influence their lives.

Chapter 2 describes the evolution of the concept of childhood.

Childhood, as we think of it, is historically a relatively recent concept. Hundreds of years ago most people did not think of childhood, much less *early childhood*, as a specific stage of development in a person's life. Due to high infant and child mortality rates at that time—still a factor in some parts of the world—many children did not survive their early years, so childhood was fleeting.

Education and care refers to the comprehensive focus of early childhood programs. Both education *and* care are essential for the optimal growth of children. Young children need experiences and opportunities that foster cognitive and social stimulation. They also need nurturing and attention to their physical needs such as health, safety, and nutrition. Early childhood programs provide for the needs of the whole child—physical, emotional, social, and intellectual. How these areas are balanced in an early childhood program can depend, in part, on the developmental level of the child. For example, an infant typically requires more care, such as feeding and diapering, than will a four-year old. However, they both need social interactions, cognitive stimulation, and emotional support. Some people have suggested the use of the term *educare* to reflect this integration. However, this term has not become widely used in Canada.

Rationales for Early Childhood Education and Care

Because early childhood education and care encompasses so many types of programs and a range of ages, there can be many rationales for why it is important. Which rationales are presented often depends on the context and type of program. Landers (1990) has identified eight major rationales or arguments for early childhood education and care, as follows:

- *Demographic argument*—Changes in the population and family structure, for example the increasing numbers of mothers in the paid labour force, necessitate early childhood programs.

Recent research on the scientific argument is presented in Chapter 2.

- *Scientific argument*—Research has shown that the early years are critical for children's development.

- *Human rights argument*—Children have the right to develop to their full potentials and early childhood programs are part of that right.

- *Program efficiency argument*—Because of the comprehensive nature of early childhood programs, they are an efficient means to provide for a variety of needs (e.g., nutrition, screening for special needs, and resources for families).

- *Social-economic argument*—Quality early childhood programs can foster children's optimal development and thereby reduce later costs to health care and educational systems. Prevention is usually less costly than remediation.

- *Social equity argument*—Early childhood programs can help to ameliorate some of the negatives of poverty, such as poor nutrition and health risks.

- *Moral-social values argument*—A society transmits its values through the education of its children and this process begins at a young age.

- *Political argument*—Young children and families seem to go in and out of political fashion. Therefore, this rationale is typically more prominent at some times than others (e.g., near elections).

Rarely is only one rationale cited for early childhood education and care. Multiple arguments are often used in different combinations depending on the type of program, its sponsor, the children and families being served, the social and political climate, and the beliefs of the individuals involved.

The long-term effects of early childhood education and care are discussed in Chapter 6.

Contexts of Early Childhood Education and Care

Children, families, educators, and programs all exist in a variety of contexts. To understand fully and appreciate early childhood education and care, it is necessary to recognize and be familiar with these contexts. A variety of contexts have impacted and continue to affect early childhood education and care in Canada, including

- The demographic context
- The socio-cultural context
- The historical context
- The theoretical context
- The political context
- The economic context
- The global context

The Demographic Context

Demographics is the study of human population trends. While one can debate whether "demographics explain about two-thirds of everything" (Foot, 1998, p. 8), it is nonetheless important for understanding our field and planning for its future.

One obvious demographic variable is the number of children and the predictions for their numbers in the future. For example, in recent years there has

The key demographics relevant to better understanding children and families in Canada are presented in Chapters 2 and 3.

been a general trend of declining numbers of children per family. This might lead one to predict that there would have been less need for early childhood programs. However, demographics is complex and trends interact. So while it is true that women in Canada over the past 30 years have had fewer children and family sizes have decreased, at the same time many women have joined the paid labour force. Therefore, the end result has been an increase in the need for early childhood education and care programs.

The Socio-Cultural Context

The socio-cultural context is a broad and pervasive one. It encompasses areas such as how we as a society view children and families, the effects of technology on our lives and on early childhood education and care, and the increasing diversity of the Canadian population.

A demographic trend that has changed the cultural and ethnic context of Canada over the past 100 years is increased immigration. The resulting multicultural heritage is reflected in early childhood education and care programs, for example in the variety of languages and cultural backgrounds of children and families that can be seen in an early childhood program. In some highly multicultural areas, such as Toronto and Vancouver, it is not unusual to have half a dozen or more first languages spoken by the children and families using an early childhood program.

A social trend that has had significant effect on early childhood education and care is the women's movement. Women have had an active and highly influential role in the growth and development of early childhood programs since the mid-1800s. Feminism has long been part of early childhood education and care—this has not just happened in the past 30 years. Many of the originators and promoters of early childhood programs have been women. Indeed, women have had a higher profile and more influence in early childhood education than at any other level of education.

Some of these women and their contributions are described in Chapter 5 and later chapters.

The Historical Context

The history of a field can help explain much about the current practices and programs of a profession, and early childhood education and care is not an exception. Our field has a rich and long history going back to the seventeenth century and even beyond that to the ancient philosophers. The origins and evolution of early childhood programs and how they developed in Canada can explain much about the programs we have today. For example, in Canada **kindergarten** is most typically a program for five-year-old children in the public schools, and **day care** and **nursery schools/preschools** are programs for younger children outside the public system. In China, as well as some other countries, kindergarten typically means government-funded programs for children from three to six; there is no distinction between kindergarten and day care.

Chapter 5 presents the history and evolution of early childhood education and care.

The Theoretical Context

Every early childhood educator and every early childhood program has theories and philosophies. These may or may not be clearly articulated. They may even be unconscious, but we all have certain beliefs about how young children develop and learn that influence how we interact with children and the types of programs we plan. As reflective early childhood educators, it is important that we are aware of what our beliefs are, where they come from, and how they influence what we do or do not do.

The major theories in early childhood education and care and examples of program models reflecting these theories are presented in Chapter 6.

The early childhood educator as reflective practitioner is described in Chapter 4.

The Political Context

The political context of a country influences early childhood education and care in that country. The political context varies across countries. For example, Sweden has achieved almost universal child care because this has been a goal of the national government for decades. However, this is not the case in Canada. In some countries, the regulations governing early childhood programs are the same across the entire country because these are federal regulations.

In Canada, as in some other countries, individual provinces and territories set the regulations for most early childhood programs. Therefore variations exist across Canada. This is not to say that this approach is a bad thing or a good thing; each side can be argued. However, the reality is that the political context impacts programs for children and families. The political priorities and resources of a country, province/territory, or municipality also affect children and families. For example, the availability of recreational facilities from parks and playgrounds to recreation centres for families depends on the political priorities of local communities and their resources.

Policy issues and early childhood programs are discussed in Chapter 12.

The Economic Context

Quality early childhood programs are not inexpensive. Not every family can afford to pay the fees for private programs. The economic cycles of the global community and Canada affect early childhood programs. In recent years, economic circumstances have led to cutbacks in public spending that have affected programs for children and families.

Limited economic resources raise serious questions such as which areas or groups get funding—education or health, seniors or young families, urban or rural areas, prevention programs or crisis intervention? The questions of who receives which programs and when in times of limited resources are difficult decisions.

A very significant economic factor in the lives of many Canadian children is growing up in poverty. Poverty puts children's growth and development at risk. For example, children who do not receive adequate nutrition and health care may not develop to their optimal potential.

The effects of poverty on children and families in Canada are presented in Chapters 2 and 3

The Global Context

We are all citizens of the global community as well as our own individual countries and communities. What happens in one part of the world—be it ash in the atmosphere from the eruption of a volcano, or the collapse of foreign economic markets—influences what happens in Canada.

Early childhood is a global phenomenon. I find it fascinating to investigate early childhood programs in other countries and this is why one of my research interests has long been comparative early childhood education and care, which examines the programs and services other countries provide for young children and their families.

The seven contexts identified above all interact with and influence each other. It can be difficult to attribute certain conditions to one or even two specific contexts. In addition, because we are ourselves embedded in these contexts, maintaining perspective and objectivity can be more difficult.

Some of my observations and experiences are shared throughout this book, especially in Chapter 13.

Dimensions of Early Childhood Education and Care

This book examines three broad dimensions of early childhood education and care: the people and the profession, historical roots and theories, and early childhood programs and services. The three major parts of this text correspond to these three dimensions:

Chapters 2, 3, and 4 focus on the people and the profession.

The People and the Profession considers children, families, and educators. The profession part examines the status of the early childhood education and care profession and some of the issues facing it.

Chapters 5, 6, and 7 examine historical roots and theories.

Historical Roots and Theories examines the development and growth of early childhood education and the theoretical supports for early childhood programs.

Chapters 8 to 13 discuss early childhood programs.

Early Childhood Programs describes a variety of Canadian programs from the long-established day care, nursery school, and kindergarten programs to more recently developed programs such as toy libraries, family resource centres, and intergenerational programs. In addition, some of the issues for these programs now and in the future are discussed.

By examining different aspects of these three dimensions, the scope and nature of early childhood education and care in Canada today can be clarified and elaborated.

Dimension 1—The People and the Profession

Five aspects for this dimension are:

- Acknowledgement of the importance of early childhood education and care
- Achievements in early childhood education and care
- Advancement of the profession
- Advocacy and action
- Ages served

Acknowledgement of the Importance of Early Childhood Education and Care

Early childhood education and care is important for children, families, educators, and society. This past century has seen a growing and impressive body of knowledge and research about the importance of the early years, how young children develop, and the factors that assist or hinder this process. The early years of birth to age nine are truly formative ones. Moreover, what occurs during those years can have lasting effects. This is one reason why the United Nations Convention of the Rights of the Child states that children should have first priority for a nation's resources.

The Convention of the Rights of the Child is described and discussed in Chapter 2.

Early childhood education and care is also important for families. The focus of early childhood programs has been expanding from typically a primary focus on the child to the inclusion of the parents and more recently to the inclusion of the entire family. Indeed, families too can benefit from quality early childhood programs. For example, it may be the peace of mind that a parent has knowing his or her child is well cared for in a safe environment. Or it may mean the parenting strategies family members learn from watching skilled early childhood educators interact with young children. Quality early childhood programs can benefit entire families, not only the young children enrolled in the program.

Early childhood education and care is obviously important to early childhood educators. Because we recognize the value and role of our field, we have the additional responsibilities that accompany this acknowledgement. For example, because we are aware of how young children develop and what their developmental needs are, we have the responsibility to defend the children's right to their childhood and to protect them from risky situations and inappropriate practices.

Society is also slowly recognizing the role and importance of early childhood education and care. Although we may wonder why it has taken so long to understand what this profession has believed for nearly 200 years, the support base for early childhood programs has broadened in the past decade. One now hears and reads of policy-makers, business people, the media, and professionals in other fields commenting on the value of providing children with quality experiences to foster their early-years development. This increasing recognition of the role and importance of early childhood education and care is one of our achievements.

Will Faller

There are now more early childhood program options than ever before.

Achievements in Early Childhood Education and Care

The passing of a millennium naturally seems to promote reflection. When we as early childhood educators reflect about early childhood education and care, we need to identify and celebrate our achievements as well as make plans for further strengthening our field.

There have been many achievements in early childhood education and care in the past 50 years. For example, the number and types of programs available to families in Canada has increased substantially. Fifty years ago there were relatively few public-school kindergartens across Canada. Today, there is almost universal kindergarten enrollment of five-year-olds in Canada even though kindergarten enrollment is not compulsory.

While not every child or family who needs or wants an early childhood program has access to one, the situation is more positive than it was just a few decades ago. There is now more subsidized child care for families with limited incomes. Fifty years ago the only option for a working single mother of preschoolers might have been to place her children in an orphanage during the week and take them home only on weekends (Varga, 1997).

Advancement of the Profession

One achievement that deserves to be singled out is the advancement of the profession. Early childhood educators have traditionally had a strong sense of mission and commitment to their profession (Silin, 1987). We as early childhood professionals have come to "better understand our field by seeing how it, like other organizations or individuals, has become a distinctive institution within society"(Spodek, 1985, p. 3).

I have seen a growth of professionalism in early childhood education and care in the past 25 years. For example, there has been an increase in both the number and size of early childhood professional organizations in Canada. There are now professional organizations at the local, provincial, and national levels. Moreover, there seems to have been a decided shift in this profession from being primarily reactive to being proactive on a wide variety of issues and concerns affecting young children and families. I see more and more people taking the time and making the effort to become knowledgeable about issues, taking a stand, and defending that position.

Advocacy and Action

Early childhood educators have an important role as advocates for children, families, and our profession. We are committed to the welfare and optimal development of young children because they are not able to protect, defend, or lobby for themselves. Therefore, we need to be able and ready to respond on their behalf. An example of this is the response of individual early childhood educators—as well as local, regional, and national and professional organizations—to the federal government's request for feedback on its proposed National Children's Agenda.

> *Advocacy is discussed in more detail in Chapters 2, 4, and 7.*

> *The National Children's Agenda is described and discussed in Chapter 2.*

In addition, early childhood educators are frequently front-line resources for families. For example, some families may not be aware of possible resources in the community or may not know how to access these. Their children's early childhood program is often their starting point. Therefore, early childhood educators need to be knowledgeable about the resources, programs, and services available in their communities. And thirdly, as discussed above, we are also advocates for our profession. We need to be alert and aware of societal, economic, social, and other changes and trends that affect children, families, and our profession.

Ages Served

Another aspect of contemporary early childhood education and care is the range of ages served. Despite their name, early childhood programs can involve people in every age range, from babies to senior citizens. Early childhood programs can be an antidote to society's "age ghettos" (Boyer, 1993, p. 56), where seniors live in special communities, college students rarely encounter young children, and infants attend programs with other infants. It seems our society tends to separate people by age.

> *Chapter 11 includes examples of community-based early childhood programs that include individuals of various ages.*

While the largest age group using early childhood programs is young children from three years of age, a strength of early childhood education and care is its ability to include a range of ages. For example, intergenerational programs can have seniors as adopted grandparents for young children, young children interacting with seniors in adult-care facilities, and seniors being e-mail pen pals for children in the primary grades.

> *Intergenerational programs are described in Chapter 11.*

A growth area for early childhood education and care in the past decade has been infant (0–18 months) and toddler (19–35 months) care. As more parents have entered the paid labour force, there has been an increased need and demand for out-of-home care for younger children. Although there are not sufficient programs for all of the families that want them, the number of spaces has been generally increasing in most regions. Another age group in need of care while their parents work are young school-aged children: school-age care provides a safe and stimulating environment before and after school hours for children from six to nine or ten years of age who otherwise might be left on their own as "latchkey children."

Dimension 2—Historical Roots and Theories

Four aspects of early childhood education and care for this dimension are

- Appreciation of the past

- Attention to the present

- Applications of theory to practice

- Approaches to early childhood programs.

Appreciation of the Past

Chapter 5 traces the development and growth of early childhood education and care from ancient times to this century.

Early childhood education and care has a long and rich history, as presented in Chapter 5. It is important that early childhood professionals be aware of and knowledgeable about this history. Not only does one gain a perspective and appreciation, but also one can gain an understanding of where our field has come from and why it has developed in the way it has. For example, "during the 200-year history of early education, practices, policies, and philosophies have been woven and rewoven in a series of movements" (White & Buka, 1987, p. 83). These movements have included the social reform movement, the kindergarten movement, the mental hygiene movement, the child welfare movement, the women's movement, and the compensatory education movement. Of course, an appreciation of our past should not preclude our attention to the present.

Chapters 8, 9, and 10 include the development of day care, nursery school, and kindergarten in Canada.

Attention to the Present

We live in dynamic, ever-changing times. However, these times of accelerated changes can subject societies and families to significant stress (Hamburg, 1995). As early childhood educators, we need to be aware of these changes and their possible implications for early childhood education and care.

Some of the most significant changes for families in the past few decades (as discussed in Chapters 2 and 3) include

- Changing family structures

- Increased number of working parents

- Fewer children and smaller family size

- Later marriages, increased divorce, and more single parents
- Increasing immigration and culturally diverse population
- Increasing number of families living in poverty
- Aging of Canadian society

Applications of Theory to Practice

Theory influences everything we do in an early childhood program. This influence can be seen if we take play as one example. The application of theory to practice can be seen in one's responses to the following questions:

Play is discussed in Chapter 7.

- Why do you think children need to play?
- How would you include play in your early childhood program?
- What would be your role in fostering children's play?
- How much time would you provide in the daily schedule for play activities? and
- What do you consider essential components in a play environment?

Your answers to these questions reflect theories and your beliefs about play and young children. The applications of theory to practice are also seen in the basis of programs, their philosophies, goals, and content; in other words, the approaches of programs to serving young children and their families.

Approaches to Early Childhood Programs

The theories that have influenced early childhood programs have changed over time. For example, the predominant theory observed in the operation of nursery school programs in the 1950s was psychoanalytic theory (Katz, 1996). On the other hand, the original and earliest kindergartens in Canada were Froebelian. Yet neither is true of today's nursery schools and kindergartens. It is important that, as an early childhood professional, you know the major child development theories and their applications.

These theories and the program models derived from them are described in Chapter 6.

The structure and content of early childhood programs is also influenced by other factors such as the participants and their needs, location, licensing regulations, and funding restraints. For example, kindergartens are typically half-day programs but in rural or isolated areas the need for busing has made full-day or alternating-day kindergartens more practical. There is no agreed-upon single approach to early childhood programs. There are many questions and issues; for example, What is a child-centred program?

Licensing and funding are discussed in Chapter 12.

Child-centred programs are discussed in Chapter 6.

Dimension 3—Early Childhood Programs and Services

Seven aspects for this dimension are:

- Adaptability of early childhood education and care to changing contexts

- Array of available programs and services

- Alternatives for participants

- Appropriateness

- Assessing and assuring quality

- Awareness of issues

- Accountability

Adaptability of Early Childhood Education and Care to Changing Contexts

Just as Canada has changed dramatically in the past 150 years, so too has early childhood education and care. Although some things, such as the need for child care for children whose parents are working, have remained the same as they were when the Grey Nuns began their early childhood programs in Montreal in the 1850s, much has changed. One hundred and fifty years ago Canada had many fewer people, was more rural, and had a more homogeneous population. Even just 25 years ago, AIDS was not known and computers were found in research facilities, not homes. Both of these societal changes have had implications for early childhood education and care. That our field can and does adapt successfully to a host of changes is to its credit. As Saracho and Spodek (1991) noted, "there is a dynamism to the field of early childhood education and a willingness to respond to continuous societal transformations" (p. 230).

While one cannot predict *what* changes are coming in this new century, one can predict that there *will be* changes. The task of early childhood educators is to modify programs and develop new ones to meet the needs of children and families resulting from these changes.

Chapter 13 looks at possible future directions.

One of the ways in which the field of early childhood education and care has met changes in the past is by developing a wide array of programs for young children and their families.

Array of Available Programs and Services

An array of program and service options is important because there is not one type of early childhood program that fits all. Centre-based day care will not meet the needs and wishes of all families with young children. As illustrated by the examples at the beginning of this chapter, there are currently many options available. Today there are more early childhood programs, more types of programs, and more diversity across programs than at any previous time in the history of our field. A characteristic of a field that is dynamic, active, and developing is that new and expanding services are created (Spodek, 1990). This has certainly been true for early childhood education and care.

The following four types of programs and services are described in this book (only a brief definition is given here, as each is described in detail in later chapters).

Core Programs

The first group includes the *core programs*. These are the ones that have the longest history, that are the best known, and that are the most widely used.

Day care—Typically out-of-home, full-day care for children from infancy through elementary school age in a group setting. It is usually used by working families. There are several types of centre-based child care. The following are some brief examples:

- **Infant-toddler day care**—For infants (0–18 months) and toddlers (19–35 months).

- **Campus day care**—Centre-based programs that provide child care for students, faculty, staff, and sometimes community families at post-secondary institutions. They also often serve as observation and practicum sites.

- **School-age care**—Centre (or home-based) programs for school-aged children (i.e., 5 to 12 years) to provide care for the hours before and after school, on school professional days, summer holidays, and other times school is not in session.

In addition to the above types of centre-based care, there are:

- **Family day-care homes and networks**—Child care for a small number of children from infancy through school age (out-of-school care) provided by a non-relative in a caregiver's home. Several or more homes are sometimes organized under an umbrella agency to create a network or supported family day care.

Kindergarten—Usually for children the year before beginning grade 1 (also called senior kindergarten in some provinces). Kindergarten may have half-day, full-day, or alternating-day schedules and are usually part of the public school system, but may be private programs.

- **Junior kindergarten**—Kindergarten programs for children two years before they begin grade 1 (i.e., four-year-olds). These programs are not available in all provinces.

Nursery schools—Typically half-day (i.e., two- to three-hour) programs for two- to five-year-old children. The original name was nursery school; preschool is now the name used for these programs in some provinces. Some specific types of nursery schools are:

- **Parent cooperative nursery schools**—A type of nursery school that is operated by a parent board. Typically an early childhood educator is assisted by two or more parents each session. The program may be daily or two to three mornings or afternoons a week.

- **Laboratory/demonstration nursery schools**—Programs that are affiliated with a university, college, or institute for the purposes of observation, practicum placements, and research. These are typically

See Chapter 8 for descriptions and discussion of centre-based child care.

See Chapter 10 for descriptions and discussion of kindergarten.

See Chapter 9 for descriptions and discussion of nursery school.

Stone

A wide variety of children and families participate in many different types of early childhood programs.

nursery school and kindergarten programs but may also include elementary school (e.g., the Institute for Child Study at the University of Toronto).

Special-Group Programs

The second type of programs includes programs designed for specific groups (e.g., teen parents, families of children with special needs, families with an incarcerated parent, First Nations families, etc.). Some of these *special-group programs* include:

Teen-parent programs—Typically centre-based programs and services located in or near high schools to provide child care, and often parenting education, to enable parenting teens to complete their education.

Infant-development programs—Home visitors go to the homes of families with young children who have special needs to provide therapy for children and advice and support for families.

See Chapter 8 for descriptions and discussion of work-related child care.

Work-related child care—Programs or services provided, in whole or in part, by employers for the children of employees.

See Chapter 11 for descriptions and discussion of parent education.

Parent education—A wide variety of programs and services (e.g., workshops, courses, support groups, lectures, or print materials) to assist families with children by providing information on child development, parenting strategies, local resources, and other information wanted by families.

Intergenerational programs are described and discussed in Chapter 11.

Intergenerational programs—Programs that target young children and adults (often older adults) together for their mutual benefit. One example of an intergenerational program is *family literacy programs.* These programs promote the literacy of all family members through an intergenerational focus.

Head Start–type compensatory programs—Programs designed and developed for children and families usually from economically poor backgrounds.

Examples of this type of program are described in Chapter 5.

Family resource centres—Community-based programs typically in informal neighbourhood settings providing support and resources for families with young children.

Toy libraries—Programs that promote play and provide play materials and other related resources for families with young children.

Toy library programs are described in Chapter 11.

Play therapy programs—Therapeutic programs for young children that use a play approach to treat a variety of children's emotional and psychological problems.

See Chapter 7 for more on play therapy.

Information and resource services—These are typically community-based agencies that provide families with information about resources, programs, and services in their local community. They are also known as information and referral services or resource and referral services.

See Chapter 11 for more on information and resource services.

The above are only a few examples of programs designed and developed for specific groups. It is unfortunately beyond the scope of this book to describe all of the types of interesting early childhood programs that have been developed for special groups in Canada.

Historical Programs

The third type of early childhood programs available can be termed *historical programs.* These programs are based very closely on the philosophies and methods of earlier theorists, specifically Friedrich Froebel and Maria Montessori. There are relatively few of these programs in Canada today. Two examples are

Froebel kindergarten—A program for three- to seven-year-old children based on the teachings of Friedrich Froebel, who founded kindergartens in 1837.

See Chapter 5 for details on Froebel.

Montessori nursery school/kindergarten/primary school—A program that follows the philosophy and method of Italian educator Maria Montessori. These programs are most typically full-day early childhood programs, although several Montessori elementary schools exist in Canada.

See Chapter 5 for details on Montessori.

Recreational Programs

The fourth type of early childhood programs available in Canada can be broadly termed *recreational programs.* These are community-based programs for young children and their families with a recreational, rather than an educational, focus. These are often offered through local parks, recreation centres, YM/YWCAs, or community centres. Some examples of this program type are:

Margie I. Mayfield

Playgrounds are a common recreational resource.

Children's museums—A museum or a section of a larger museum designed for children from preschool through the teen years. Emphasis is on hands-on, interactive exhibits geared to children's interests and varied levels.

Drop-in programs—Short-term child-care programs. Some are located in shopping malls or ski resorts for occasional use by families with young children. Others are used on a regular basis (e.g., while parent is participating in an exercise class at a fitness centre or having kidney dialysis at a clinic). These are sometimes called *child-minding programs.*

Playgrounds—Community-based play facilities designed for children. There are traditional, creative, and adventure playgrounds. Some playgrounds have regularly scheduled programs for children and families.

Playgrounds are described and discussed in Chapter 7.

Alternatives for Participants

One positive outcome from this wide array of available early childhood programs is the variety of possible alternatives or options for children, families, and early childhood educators. The above section described the correspondingly increasing program alternatives available. An important implication is the increasing variety of career alternatives available to early childhood educators. One of the goals of this book is to make you aware of these possible career options. Although the core programs of day care, nursery school, kindergarten, and family day care are the most numerous, there are many other alternatives. For example, you might choose to work in a family resource centre, a recreation program, a children's museum, an information and resource service, a licensing agency, or as an early childhood advocate or consultant.

My career so far in early childhood education and care is a good example of the alternatives possible. I began my career in the primary grades, then shifted to kindergarten, nursery school, and day care. Later I was the acting director of a demonstration laboratory nursery school and also coordinated experimental kindergarten to grade 2 programs in public schools. Most recently I have taught early childhood education at the post-secondary level and done research on topics such as kindergarten, toy libraries, family support programs, programs for children with special needs, family literacy programs, and early childhood programs in other countries. While the specific alternatives I have pursued are unique to me, the variety in my career path is not unusual. It might be interesting for you to ask early childhood educators you meet what they've done in the field and why they changed or have not changed programs.

Career ladders and lattices are described in Chapter 4.

Appropriateness

Appropriateness is a word you'll see and hear frequently in early childhood education and care. It may be used in reference to programs, curricula, or practices. It may be part of the terms *developmental appropriateness, age appropriateness, individual appropriateness, cultural appropriateness,* or *community appropriateness.* Although the concept of appropriateness has long been part of early childhood education and care, these more specific terms are of relatively recent origin (Kagan, 1999a).

Developmental appropriateness is the umbrella term and includes the concepts of age, individual, cultural, and community appropriateness. A program, curriculum, or practice is typically considered developmentally appropriate when it is "based on what is known about how children develop and learn" (Bredekamp & Copple, 1997, p. 8). Developmentally appropriate can be considered the match between children and the program or the experiences provided (Kessler, 1991). An example of an issue in this area is the question, What place does teaching reading have in early childhood programs; in other words, at what stage in young children's development is the formal instruction of reading developmentally appropriate?

The developmental use, misuse, and criticisms of developmentally appropriate practice are discussed in Chapter 12.

Age appropriateness is a narrower concept than developmentally appropriate. It is based on the idea that there are certain developmental experiences and growth sequences that occur during the early years. The term refers to what is suitable for children of a specific chronological age and reflects a long-established tradition in early childhood education. An example of age appropriateness is the rating system used for films. Children are admitted to or excluded from specific films based on their ages. For example, a child must be over 14 years to see some films. This does not recognize or consider that the maturity, knowledge, and experience levels of two 14-year-olds can be quite different, so what would be an "appropriate" film for one may not be suitable for another; this is an example of **individual appropriateness.** As another example, an educator addressing a child in that child's first language of Spanish might be individually appropriate; addressing a child who speaks only English in Spanish is generally not individually appropriate. Individual appropriateness recognizes and accommodates the individual child's unique combination of interests, strengths, abilities, past experiences, and development level.

The role of reading instruction is discussed in Chapter 10.

Community and **cultural appropriateness** have gained more recognition in recent years. These components of appropriateness refer to the specific characteristics of a local group or community. This has been referred to as "following the community's vision for its children" (Ball & Pence, 1999, p. 47). The community and cultural contexts may or may not be the same. For example, a practice may be generally acceptable within a community but is not usual within a particular group within that community (e.g., although a family may visit the local fast-food restaurant, their religion does not permit eating beef hamburgers). Likewise, a practice may be part of the culture of a group wherever individuals of that group are living (e.g., Aboriginal families living on- or off-reserve). Some of the community-based programs described in Chapter 11 have been developed as grassroots programs to address and meet a community's specific, sometimes unique, needs and wishes. Appropriateness is part of the larger issue of assessing and assuring quality early childhood programs and services.

Assessing and Assuring Quality

Quality is the subject of Chapter 12.

What is a quality early childhood program? What does it look like? What are its contents? Are there universal or generic indicators of quality that apply to all programs? What is the role of licensing and accreditation? These are only some of the questions that can be asked related to assessing and assuring quality. Although the provision and maintenance of quality early childhood programs is an obvious and important goal, how this is done and how quality is determined are long-standing areas of debate. In your observations of early childhood programs, you might keep a mental or written list of examples that you think exemplify quality in early childhood programs.

Chapter 13 concludes this book with a discussion of some possible issues for early childhood education and care in the future.

There are many issues and important questions that you will need to address during your career in early childhood education and care. The following section provides a small sample of some of the issues discussed in this book. The last section of each chapter focuses on a few key issues related to the topic of that chapter. In addition, throughout the following chapters there will be periodic *Focus* and *For Reflection* boxes, which will present additional issues or questions for you to think about. One important responsibility of being an early childhood professional is to be aware of and reflective about the issues in our field.

Awareness of Issues

Early childhood education and care has always had plenty of issues sparking debates; this was true 100 years ago and it is true today. Some of the issues may have changed, but the need to understand and discuss the issues has not. One of the goals of this book is to help you become familiar with some of the issues in early childhood education today. Of course, it is impossible to discuss or even raise all of the possible current issues in early childhood education and care. Moreover, there may be issues that are specific to your community that you may need to examine.

Three prominent contemporary issues are availability, accessibility, and affordability. These three terms are often used together and refer to the need for early childhood programs that are of sufficient number (*available*), are available where and when families need and can use them (*accessible*), and are financially possible for families to access and are areas in which early childhood educators can afford to work (*affordable*). Affordability is also raised in discussions about the need for early childhood programs and services from a cost–benefit perspective. In other words, Are the benefits of early childhood programs worth their costs? Early childhood advocates often rephrase this question to Knowing there can be positive benefits for young children and their families, can we afford *not* to provide these programs and services? A related issue debated in early childhood education and care is accountability.

Accountability

Accountability is shorthand for the question, Who is responsible? It applies at several levels. For example, accountability for an early childhood program may mean that it must document and make a case that it is meeting certain standards or goals. Accountability can also be applied to individuals. As a professional, one has certain responsibilities and is held accountable for meeting these. For example, ongoing professional development is a recognized characteristic of a professional and many licensing and professional organizations require periodic proof of professional development activities. At another level, accountability can mean, Who is responsible for the provision and supervision of early childhood programs? The answer here is important because that group sets standards, grants licenses, and monitors and assesses programs. Although this group is usually a government body in Canada, there has been an ongoing debate within provincial and territorial governments as to which ministry or ministries should have jurisdiction over (i.e., be responsible for) early childhood programs. At various times, early childhood programs have been the responsibility of ministries of health, social services, education, children/families, or others. On the other hand, some people have argued that professional organizations or individuals, and not government agencies, should be responsible for program accountability.

These topics are discussed in more detail in Chapters 4, 6, 8, and 12.

Professional development is discussed in Chapter 4.

Policy issues are discussed in Chapter 12.

What's Ahead for Early Childhood Education and Care?

What will be the issues in early childhood education and care in the twenty-first century? We know that every century in the past has had its particular concerns. For example, in the mid-1800s the establishment of kindergarten was an issue. Now key issues for kindergarten are the length of the day and the role of an academic curriculum. In the mid-1900s, a prominent issue was how important the early years are for children's education and when this education should begin (Clarke-Stewart, 1988). Today this issue has evolved into asking what types of programs are most appropriate for which children and at what stage in their development.

As well as some continuing twentieth-century issues, such as the place of computers and technology in early childhood programs, new issues we haven't foreseen are sure to emerge. The twenty-first century will be at least as interesting as the previous centuries.

Summary of this Chapter

This chapter introduces and provides an overview of the contents of this book. It is organized around three broad dimensions:

- The People and the Profession (Chapters 2–4)

- Historical Roots and Theories (Chapters 5–7)

- Early Childhood Programs and Services (Chapters 8–13)

Each of the following chapters expands on these dimensions, provides information, and identifies some of the issues relevant to the topics in that chapter. The next chapter examines children in Canada.

Key Terms

age appropriateness, 19
community and cultural
    appropriateness, 20
day care, 6
demographics, 5
developmental appropriateness, 19

early childhood education and
    care, 3
individual appropriateness, 19
kindergarten, 6
nursery schools/preschools, 6

2

Children in Canada

*Children are people with needs as real as, if different from, our own, and
with an equal right, as citizens like us, to have them met.*
—Penelope Leach, Children First

Canada has children—millions of them. Indeed, "Canada has never been a
childless nation," not even in its earliest days (Ashworth, 1993, p. 9). And
children have always had developmental needs. How and how well these
needs are being met is, in great part, a reflection of how society perceives
children, childhood, and children's rights. Meeting the needs of Canada's
children is the subject of this chapter.

Chapter 1 presents a general overview of early childhood education and care.
Now this chapter builds on Chapter 1 by exploring the status, contexts, needs,
and issues facing young children in Canada today. The next chapter continues
and expands this examination in the context of the family. But first, we need to
look at children in Canada.

Here are some questions to think about while you read this chapter:

· What does it mean to be a child in Canada?
· What do children need to be healthy and happy?
· What is childhood and how has this concept changed over time?
· Do young children have rights?
· How can we support children and their rights?
· What are some issues facing children in Canada today?

The next section is an overview of the demographics of children in Canada
today. This information provides important background for understanding
current issues and concerns for young children.

Demographics of Canadian Children

While the number of children in Canada has increased over the past 40 years, their percentage of the population has been decreasing. Thus, now there are proportionately fewer children in Canada than at any other time since the Second World War (Canadian Council on Social Development, 1996). This trend is expected to continue.

Child Population

Population projections for 2016 are for children under the age of nine to comprise 11 percent (4.1 million) of the Canadian population as compared to 13 percent today (Statistics Canada, 1998d). There is a declining percentage of children in all provinces and territories. Table 2.1 shows a summary of the change in the percentage of children under 15 in Canada from 1971 to 1996.

See Chapter 3 for more on changing family structures.

Nearly three-quarters of children live in families with married parents. Moreover, the number of children living in families increased 6.3 percent between 1991 and 1996 (Statistics Canada, 1997e). However, there was no increase for married-couple families, and a big increase in children living in common-law and lone-parent families.

Urban Living

In Canada, the population of urban areas has been increasing since the 1960s. More than four-fifths of Canadian children under 12 live in urban areas, and

---

TABLE 2.1

Changes in Child Population under Age 15 1971 and 1996

	1971	1996
CANADA	30%	20.5%
NEWFOUNDLAND	37%	20%
P.E.I.	32%	22%
NOVA SCOTIA	30.5%	20%
NEW BRUNSWICK	32%	20%
QUEBEC	30%	19%
ONTARIO	29%	21%
MANITOBA	29%	22%
SASKATCHEWAN	30%	23%
ALBERTA	32%	23%
BRITISH COLUMBIA	28%	23%
YUKON	35%	24%
N.W.T.	43%	33%

Source: Based on data from Statistics Canada, *The Daily*, July 29, 1997.

almost half in urban centres with more than 500,000 population (National Longitudinal Survey of Children and Youth, 1996). This pattern is part of a larger worldwide trend: "the trend toward urban living is well established around the world as societies have moved from agriculture-based economies to industrial-based economies over the course of the twentieth century. Families have migrated to the cities to pursue economic opportunities. As a result, fewer children live on farms or in small rural communities" (National Longitudinal Survey of Children and Youth, 1996, p. 17). However, that does not mean that early childhood programs and services are not needed in rural communities. The children who do live in rural areas are most likely to be in the Maritime provinces. The majority of children nine and under live in Ontario or Quebec (Vanier Institute, 1996).

The Canadian city with the highest percentage of children under 15 is Oshawa (23.7 percent), and the lowest is Victoria (16.6 percent) (Statistics Canada, 1997c). The cities with the highest percentage of preschoolers are

- Oshawa (8.2 percent)
- Saskatoon (7.5 percent)
- Kitchener (7.3 percent)
- Toronto, Calgary, and Regina (7 percent)
- Edmonton, London, and Ottawa–Hull (6.9 percent).

(Foot, 1998)

In *The Progress of Canada's Children*, the Canadian Council on Social Development (1996) commented, "city life provides these children and their families with many advantages—cultural diversity, a broad range of social and health services, and a concentration of economic activity and job creation. City living is also associated with the trend toward smaller families, higher divorce rates (which can lead to increased family stress and economic insecurity), and a diminished sense of community" (p. 9).

These trends are discussed further in Chapter 3.

Diversity

Another trend in Canada is that of increased ethnic diversity. The ethnic origins of children in Canada are summarized in Figure 2.1. The recent increase in immigration has meant that many early childhood programs have more children and families from a wider variety of ethnic backgrounds.

Immigration is discussed in Chapter 3.

A significant component of Canada's multi-ethnic, multicultural diversity is the three percent of the population composed of Aboriginal peoples. The Aboriginal child population under age 10 makes up 24 percent of the total Aboriginal population, nearly twice that of the general Canadian population (Statistics Canada, 1998f). The Aboriginal population of Canada is also younger than the general population: 53 percent of all Aboriginal peoples are under age 24 (Canadian Council on Social Development, 1998).

(*figure 2.1*)   ETHNIC ORIGINS OF CHILDREN IN CANADA

Ethnic origins of children aged 0 to 11 years, 1994–1995

ETHNIC ORIGINS	RESPONDENTS REPORTING EACH ETHNIC ORIGIN[a] (%)
CANADIAN	51.9
BRITISH[b]	35.3
FRENCH	27.4
EUROPEAN[c]	25.1
NORTH AMERICAN INDIAN, MÉTIS OR INUIT	4.3
CHINESE OR SOUTH ASIAN	3.2
BLACK OR AFRICAN	1.4
OTHER	18.1

Note: The ethnic origins of the child are based on the response given by the PMK.
[a] Total will add to more than 100% because some respondents reported more than one ethnic origin.
[b] Includes English, Scottish and Irish.
[c] Includes Dutch, German, Italian, Jewish, Polish, Portuguese and Ukrainian.

Source: National Longitudinal Survey of Children and Youth, 1996, p. 19

Still another trend in Canada is increasing linguistic diversity. Most children speak English (68.6 percent) or French (22.2 percent) as their first language; however, many have a different mother tongue. For example, as shown in Table 2.2, in the territories more than one-quarter of the children under 12 speak a language other than English or French (Canadian Council on Social Development, 1998). In addition, as shown in Figure 2.2, 15.1 percent of Canadian children are fluent in two languages, and 1.2 percent in three or more (National Longitudinal Survey of Children and Youth, 1996). Many early childhood programs have several families for whom English or French is not a first language.

Mobility and Housing

The 1996 census reported that the majority of Canadians had not moved in the previous five years. Of those who did move, the majority of families remained in the same area (Statistics Canada, 1998h). This means that Canadians have become less mobile than in previous times.

Nearly three-quarters of children under 18 live in homes owned by their parents, while approximately one-quarter live in rental accommodation (Canadian Council on Social Development, 1996). However, children in lone-parent families were three times more likely to live in rental housing. Overall, families in Canada are "well-housed" (Canadian Council on Social Development, 1996, p. 29). However, an exception is the housing situation of many Aboriginal families in Canada. Two-thirds of housing on reserves does not meet

TABLE 2.2

Most Frequently Spoken Non-Official Language as First Language

PROVINCE/TERRITORY	FIRST LANGUAGE
NEWFOUNDLAND	MONTAGNAIS-NASKAPI
PRINCE EDWARD ISLAND	DUTCH
NOVA SCOTIA	MI'KMAQ
NEW BRUNSWICK	MI'KMAQ
QUEBEC	ITALIAN
ONTARIO	CHINESE
MANITOBA	GERMAN
SASKATCHEWAN	GERMAN
ALBERTA	GERMAN
BRITISH COLUMBIA	CHINESE
YUKON	GERMAN
NORTHWEST TERRITORIES	INUKTITUT

Source: Based on data from Statistics Canada, 1996 Census, Nation tables

figure 2.2   LINGUISTIC BACKGROUNDS OF CANADIAN CHILDREN

Distribution of children aged 0 to 11 years by language spoken, 1994–1995

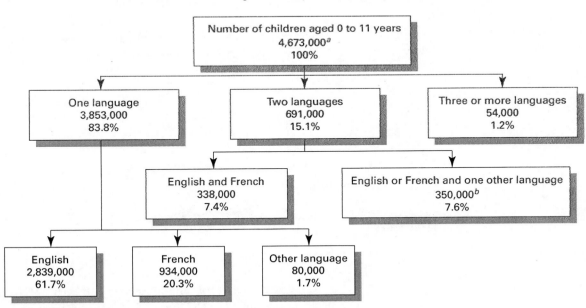

[a] *Includes 75,000 (1.6%) children for whom no information was available on the languages(s) in which they could converse.*

[b] *Does not include 3,000 (0.1%) children who speak two languages, neither of which is French or English.*

Source: National Longitudinal Survey of Children and Youth, 1996, p. 20

Homeless families are discussed in Chapter 3.

FOR REFLECTION

Bouchard (1996) writes, "Our children are living in a time of great risks and great opportunities" (p. 177). What do you think are the greatest risks and greatest opportunities facing Canadian children today?

at least one of the government's housing standards, while a third of off-reserve families are in housing need (Canadian Council on Social Development, 1996). In addition, many families are kept from returning to their reserves to live because of housing shortages. Housing has also become a problem for other families. Recently, housing affordability has become more of a problem for young and lone-parent families especially when combined with the cessation of social housing construction in most provinces (Canadian Council on Social Development, 1998).

Determinants of Children's Development

If you ask families expecting a child what they wish for that child, their answer is almost always: "For my/our child to be healthy and happy." Families, early childhood educators, society in general, and children themselves want children to be healthy and happy. There are many factors that contribute to or mitigate against the well-being of young children. According to a recent Health Canada publication, "researchers are beginning to understand what it takes for a child to grow up healthy and happy. Those needs are called the determinants of healthy development" (Guy, 1997, p. xvi).

What are the determinants for the optimal development of young children? There is not yet a definitive answer. However, researchers and theorists believe that the early years lay the foundation for subsequent development and that this development is influenced by interconnected biological, social/emotional, economic, familial, and environmental factors (Tipper, 1997). Exactly how all these factors interact and are interconnected is not yet fully understood. What we do know is that there seem to be certain broad areas that are particularly important in the early years. Five of these areas are

- Health
- A safe physical environment
- Social and emotional security
- Cognitive stimulation
- Economic security

Health

There seems to be agreement among experts that Canada's children are basically healthy. For example, the Canadian Council on Social Development (1997), which tracks the well-being of children, reported that "Canadian children are very healthy, and their level of health has improved considerably over past decades" (p. 36). This is not to say that *all* children in Canada are healthy and happy or that the health of Canada's children could not be improved. For example, some countries have higher child immunization rates than does Canada (UNICEF, 1998).

Prenatal Factors

One major factor in the health of very young children is their health as a fetus. This is related to the mother's health and health practices during pregnancy. As the National Longitudinal Survey of Children and Youth succinctly phrased it, "the importance of good prenatal care cannot be stressed enough" (p. 37; for more on the National Longitudinal Survey of Children and Youth, see Focus 2.1). Factors contributing to a healthy pregnancy include access to prenatal care; avoidance of smoking, alcohol, and substance abuse; good nutrition; age of the mother (adolescent and older mothers are at higher risk); income; emotional health and education of the mother; housing conditions; and social support (National Longitudinal Survey of Children and Youth, 1966; Tipper, 1997).

The most frequent adverse factor affecting the prenatal health of children in Canada is maternal smoking during pregnancy. About one in four newborns (23.6 percent) were born to mothers who smoked during pregnancy. Smoking during pregnancy can result in low birth weight, stillbirth, prematurity, nicotine withdrawal by the newborn, and respiratory problems by the newborn (National Longitudinal Survey of Children and Youth, 1996).

The advice given on alcohol use during pregnancy is straightforward: Don't. It is generally considered that there is no "safe" amount of alcohol that can be consumed during pregnancy. The period of greatest risk is at conception and during the first trimester, before many women realize they are pregnant.

Focus 2.1

The National Longitudinal Survey of Children and Youth

In this chapter, you may have noticed the references to the National Longitudinal Survey of Children and Youth (NLSCY). The purpose of this study is to follow children's development for many years. It began in 1994 by gathering information on 23,000 children from birth to age 11 across Canada. The NLSCY hopes to follow these children to adulthood to gain a better picture of Canada's children. The NLSCY is done by Statistics Canada and Human Resources Development Canada, and their publication *Growing Up in Canada** reports some of the initial data and interpretive reports. The NLSCY will be a valuable source of information for early childhood educators because, as Keating and Mustard (1996) have commented, "a society needs usable information about how its population is faring and where problems are occurring. This monitoring must occur at the national, provincial, and community levels because important patterns emerge at each. The key to an effective system is a national framework, which is what the NLSCY can provide" (p. 11).

> *The National Longitudinal Survey of Children and Youth was published in 1996 by the Minister of Industry under the title *Growing Up in Canada* (ISBN 0-660-16470-1). The survey is referenced throughout this text as National Longitudinal Survey of Children and Youth, 1996.

Alcohol consumption during pregnancy can result in fetal alcohol syndrome (FAS) or fetal alcohol effects (FAE). FAS can result in serious neurological damage, birth defects, low birth weight, and subsequent developmental delays or even death. It is estimated to be the leading cause of developmental problems in young children in Canada (Canadian Council on Social Development, 1996). FAE children have normal intelligence but have behavioural and learning problems. It is estimated that between one and three children per 1,000 will be born with FAS, while the rate for FAE is thought to be several times higher (Canadian Council on Social Development, 1998). In the National Longitudinal Survey of Children and Youth, 83 percent of the mothers reported that they did not drink any alcohol during their pregnancy.

Nearly all mothers in the National Longitudinal Survey of Children and Youth (1996) reported receiving prenatal care from either a physician (92.4 percent), a nurse (2.9 percent), or a midwife (1.4 percent). In addition, there are numerous educational and support programs for pregnant women and new parents in Canada. These programs include breast-feeding support groups, post-partum depression groups, parenting and nutrition programs for pregnant teens, young moms/dads programs, mentoring, and home-visitor programs (see Chapter 11).

Infants' Health

Most babies (90 percent) in Canada are born healthy (Canadian Council on Social Development, 1996; Nault, 1997). Only five percent of parents in the National Longitudinal Survey of Children and Youth (1996) rated their babies' health as fair or poor, which is also the approximate percentage of low-birth-weight newborns (Canadian Council on Social Development, 1996; Nault, 1997). (For more on the effects of low birth weight, see Focus 2.2.) The Yukon had the lowest percentage of low-birth-weight births (4.1 percent) while the Northwest Territories (7 percent), Ontario (6 percent), Quebec (5.9 percent), Alberta (5.9 percent), and Nova Scotia (5.9 percent) were above the Canadian average of 5.8 in 1995 (Nault, 1997).

Child Mortality

Although infant mortality (i.e., death of children under one year of age) decreased in Canada in the twentieth century, the decline has slowed in the past decade because of the increase in the incidence of low birth weight (Nault, 1997). In 1995, Prince Edward Island had the lowest infant mortality rate, while the Northwest Territories and the Yukon had the highest (Nault, 1997). Almost three-quarters of infant deaths since 1975 have occurred in the first 27 days of life, due primarily to respiratory conditions, short gestation, low birth weight, and maternal complications of pregnancy (Nault, 1997).

One of the stated Year 2000 goals of the 1990 World Summit on Children was the reduction of infant and child mortality rates. The under-five mortality

Children's safety is discussed later in this chapter.

> **Focus 2.2**
>
> ## Why Is Low Birth Weight Significant?
>
> Low birth weight (i.e., less than 2,500 grams or 5.5 pounds) is an internationally used indicator of young children's health. It is the key indicator of poor health at birth (Canadian Council on Social Development, 1996). Low birth weight is related to premature birth or prenatal problems and is linked to infant death, health problems, and later learning and behavioural problems. The factors contributing to low birth weight are complex and include "broad determinants of health, such as socioeconomic status (poorer women have a higher rate of low birth weight), social discrimination, social support, access to health services and the beliefs and values of society. They also include behavioural factors such as nutrition, work, smoking and alcohol use, and biological and genetic factors." (Canadian Institute of Child Health, 1994, p. 38).

rate for Canada in 1996 was seven deaths per 1,000 live births, compared to four for Singapore, Finland, and Sweden (UNICEF, 1998). Overall, the leading cause of death for children in Canada from one to nine years of age is injuries (Canadian Institute of Child Health, 1994).

Immunization

Immunizations are readily accessible in Canada and are promoted by medical and public health professionals. According to the Canadian Council on Social Development (1996) polio has been eliminated in Canada and there have been no recent reported cases of tetanus or diphtheria. A current Canadian goal is the elimination of measles by 2005 (Health Canada, 1996). However, in Canada, two percent of children under age one are not yet immunized against measles (UNICEF, 1998). While this is a level many countries envy, other countries such as Jamaica, Argentina, Kuwait, Gambia, and many European countries immunize a higher percentage of their children against measles (UNICEF, 1998). However, according to Health Canada, "even in areas of good coverage, pockets of poor coverage may exist" (1996, p. 1). Not everyone is aware of the importance or availability of immunization, and some people do not believe in it for philosophical, religious, cultural, or personal reasons (Waxler-Morrison, Anderson, & Richardson, 1990). In these days of rapid transportation, mobile populations, and epidemics in other parts of the world, any country cannot afford to become complacent about immunizing its children. Therefore, to raise awareness of this issue, National Immunization Week has been set as an annual event held in late October (information is available from the Canadian Immunization Awareness Program, the Canadian Paediatric Society, and Health Canada; addresses are at the end of this chapter).

Nutrition

Good nutrition for children is essential, not only for their optimum growth and development but also because nutritional habits learned in the early years "have a strong impact on future eating habits and health" (Canadian Paediatric Society, 1992, p. 299). This fact is of particular relevance for early childhood programs, as many children in Canada eat a significant portion of their daily food intake in an early childhood program. According to the Canadian Paediatric Society, early childhood professionals "are in an ideal position to create a foundation for the child's health by encouraging the development of good eating habits that children will practise for the rest of their lives. Because preschool-age children are very interested in all aspects of food—how it is grown, purchased, prepared and served—they are receptive to learning and developing good food habits" (1992, p. 299). Early childhood curricula typically include nutrition, cooking, and safe eating practices.

Good nutrition requires an adequate intake of nutritious foods. Not all children in Canada get adequate food. For many young children and their families, hunger is an ongoing problem.

> Hunger is discussed with poverty later in this chapter.

Dental Care

Although young children in Canada have access to the health-care system regardless of income, the same is not true for dental care. Not all provinces and territories have comprehensive, free public dental programs for children. The Canadian Council on Social Development reported that poor children had less access to dental care than children from higher-income families, and the majority (56 percent) of poor children under age 12 did not see a dentist in 1993 (1997). Medical and early childhood organizations recommend that young children see a dentist when they are three years old or have their 20 primary teeth (Canadian Paediatric Society, 1992; Kendrick, Kaukmann, & Messenger, 1988).

Exercise

Another component of good overall health is physical activity. The print and electronic media are full of programs and commercials promoting physical fitness and advice, equipment, and materials to help adults exercise. It seems that much less media time and space is devoted to promoting young children's fitness. As with nutrition, good physical fitness habits as a child can continue as a person ages. According to Belfry (1996), the benefits of physical activity can include happy children, healthy bodies, better sleep, more nutritious eating, positive self-esteem, better school performance, social time, parent–child bonding, and alternatives to unhealthy lifestyles that include drugs, alcohol, and tobacco. The early signs of arteriosclerosis can be seen in children at about five years of age (Poest, Williams, Witt, & Atwood, 1990).

Children need at least 30 minutes of physical activity every day; however, they are 40 percent less active than they were 30 years ago (Belfry, 1996).

Preschool boys tend to be more physically active than girls are by approximately four more hours a week (Canadian Council on Social Development, 1997). The top three physical activities for preschoolers are running and kicking games, swimming, and biking; one-quarter participate in gymnastics, other movement games, and skating (Canadian Fitness and Lifestyle Research Institute, 1998). However, Canadian children become less active as they age. For example, while children from one to four spend about 22 hours a week in physical activity, elementary and high-school children spend only 14 (Canadian Fitness and Lifestyle Research Institute). This finding has implications for program planning in school-age child-care programs.

Lack of exercise is a major factor in obesity, according to the Canadian Medical Association, and obesity in 6- to 11-year-olds has increased more than 50 percent in the past two decades (Lechky, 1994). Early childhood programs typically include both informal and scheduled physical activities for children. The families of young children also have a role to play. For example, a study by the Canadian Fitness and Lifestyle Research Institute found that parents who were active and believed in physical activity strongly affected their children's physical activities (i.e., children of highly active parents were also more active). In addition, most parents believe that physical activity helps promote children's "growth and development, build their self-esteem, self-image, and concentration, and promote learning, sharing, and cooperating" (Canadian Council on Social Development, 1997, p. 38). Likewise, early childhood educators need to actively promote physical exercise by providing the needed materials, time, and curriculum, as well as by being models for children.

FOR REFLECTION

Poest, et al. (1990) advise to "Plan daily fitness activities for you and the children. Including regular fitness activities and participating eagerly with the children provides a positive model for the children and a good stress-reducer for you" (p. 8). What are five fitness activities you could do with a group of young children?

Health in the Early Childhood Curriculum

Good health is essential for optimal development. Early childhood professionals can serve as information resources, and encourage families and children to pursue healthy practices. For example, health and safety topics such as nutrition, dental health, safety, and personal hygiene can be included in the curriculum in addition to implementing and modelling healthy practices.

The early years are a prime time for fostering the attitudes, understandings, and habits for a healthy and happy lifestyle.

A Safe Environment

Garbarino poses a key question: How do we answer when a child asks us, "Am I safe?" (1995, p. 63). Safety is an essential component of a child's healthy development and happiness and encompasses physical safety, a safe environment, and personal security.

Air Pollution and Respiratory Problems

Respiratory problems are the leading cause of hospitalization of children up to age 14, with the younger children having higher admission rates (Canadian

Institute of Child Health, 1994). Although the number of Canadians with asthma has doubled in the past 15 years (Canadian Council on Social Development, 1997), the number of *children* with asthma has quadrupled (Arnold, 1999). It is now the most common chronic illness of children in industrialized countries; 13 percent of Canadian children have asthma (Canadian Council on Social Development, 1997). Atlantic Canada has the highest incidence of childhood asthma, and the Prairies the lowest (Arnold, 1999).

Many health professionals attribute the increase in childhood respiratory problems, at least in part, to air quality—both indoors and outdoors (Bueckert, 1999). Air pollution has a greater effect on children than on adults because children inhale more air relative to their body size than adults do, and at a faster rate; they therefore inhale more pollutants. The air quality in Canada improved between 1974 and 1992 because hazardous air toxins such as sulphur dioxide, nitrogen dioxide, lead, dust and smoke declined. However, internationally Canada is one of the highest per capita producers of air pollutants (Canadian Council on Social Development, 1996). In 1994, Halifax had the fewest number of days rated poor or fair for air quality, while Toronto and Vancouver had the most (Canadian Council on Social Development, 1996).

Also of importance for young children is the air quality of their indoor environments. One major source of indoor air pollution is smoke. According to the Canadian Institute of Child Health (1994), 46 percent of preschoolers live in a home with at least one smoker. In addition to decreasing the quality of the air those children breathe, living with a smoker also increases the likelihood that they will become smokers and therefore be at greater risk for all of the health problems associated with smoking (Canadian Council on Social Development, 1996). In addition to smoke and second-hand smoke, other indoor pollutants can include pesticides, herbicides, fungicides, lead-containing blinds, asbestos insulation, solvents, and other chemicals.

Ultraviolet Radiation

Another physical-environment risk factor for young children is ultraviolet radiation, which has become an increasing danger in the past few decades with the decrease in the ozone layer. Research has shown that high exposure to ultraviolet rays as a child or youth is one of the most significant factors in the later development of skin cancer (Canadian Council on Social Development, 1997). A child born in Canada in 1997 has "a one-in-seven chance of developing non-melanoma skin cancer and a one-in-120 chance of developing malignant melanoma" (Canadian Council on Social Development, 1996, p. 23). Skin cancer rates are highest in British Columbia, Nova Scotia, and Prince Edward Island (Owens, 1998). One role in health promotion for early childhood educators is encouraging the use of sun hats and sunscreen for children and assisting the children in applying these prior to outdoor activities. In 1994, almost 70 percent of parents reported that their children used sunscreen (Canadian Council on Social Development, 1996).

Accidents and Injuries

Young children's physical safety is a major concern and responsibility of early childhood programs. Although no one wants any child to be hurt, accidents or injuries are the leading cause of death for children over age one in Canada (Canadian Council on Social Development, 1997). For children from ages one to four, car accidents accounted for 38 percent of these injury deaths; for children from ages four to nine, it was 54 percent (Canadian Council on Social Development, 1996; Canadian Institute of Child Health, 1994). One reason for these rates is that, although the majority of children under age ten were using car seats or seat belts in 1997, Transport Canada reported that only 68 percent of children from under one to age four were properly restrained; this figure rose to 89 percent for five- to nine-year-olds (Canadian Council on Social Development, 1998). Bicycle helmet use in Canada has increased in recent years, especially in those provinces with compulsory helmet laws (Canadian Council on Social Development, 1998). However, of the children under nine years of age injured in bicycle accidents in 1994, fewer than 30 percent were wearing helmets (Canadian Council on Social Development, 1996).

Safety risks related to violence, poor housing, and poverty are discussed later in this chapter.

Playground safety is discussed in Chapter 7.

For every death due to injuries, 75 preschool children were admitted to hospital and another 100 sought medical attention (Canadian Institute of Child Health, 1994). The leading cause of injury requiring hospitalization of children from 1980 to 1990 was falls for both one- to four-year-olds (29 percent) and five- to nine-year-olds (42 percent) (Canadian Institute of Child Health, 1994). Centre-, school- and home-based early childhood programs need to be safe environments for young children. Accident and injury prevention topics should also be part of the early childhood curriculum throughout the year (e.g., observing Fire Prevention Month every fall and discussing summer safety in June).

In Sweden, a child safety shop called Akta ("be careful" in Swedish) was established in 1974. It specializes in products for the prevention of child accidents and injuries. Its employees include a research team, a journalist, and a public health coordinator who works closely with pediatric centres, the Red Cross, and health and consumer agencies. In addition to wholesale and retail, the company invents new products (Childhood Accident Prevention, 1987).

Social and Emotional Security

Another determinant for children's health and happiness is social and emotional security: "stable, supportive relationships with loving and responsive parents and other caregivers" (Canadian Council on Social Development, 1996, p. 39). For young children, this begins at birth, with bonding by the newborn with his or her mother and then other caregivers. A mentally and physically healthy mother is more likely to successfully bond with her child and to initiate the emotional and social security that a young child needs for optimal development.

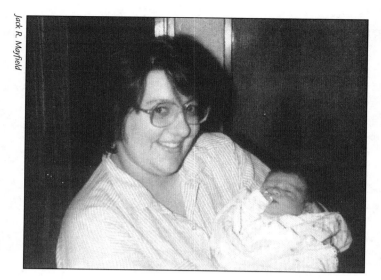

Jack R. Mayfield

Attachment is important for children's social and emotional security.

Attachment

A key concept in social and emotional security for children is **attachment**. Attachment is a long-term process in which young children and their primary caregivers develop a relationship. According to the Canadian Institute of Child Health (1994), two critical areas for emphasis in promoting and improving young children's healthy development are the prevention of low birth weight and the promotion of the healthy attachment of mothers and babies.

Attachment is an important factor in children's subsequent development. According to a leading researcher in this area, studies show that "without intervention or changes in family circumstances, attachment patterns formed in infancy persist. At age two, insecurely attached children tend to lack self-reliance and show little enthusiasm for problem solving. At three and a half to five years, according to their teachers, they are often problem kids, with poor peer relations and little resilience" (Karen, 1990, pp. 36–37). Other child disturbances linked to insecure attachment include excessive aggression, clinginess, withdrawal, and inability to attend to schoolwork (Karen, 1994). Secure attachment has been linked positively to motivation, peer relationships, self-concept, trust, security, and positive expectations by children that supports their exploration of the world and subsequent development (Kerns, Cole, & Andrews, 1998; Raikes, 1996).

Alice Honig considers attachment theory to be "possibly the most powerful new tool that ethological theorists have provided us with in recent decades" (1993, p. 70). Attachment theory and the accompanying research are an interesting story. John Bowlby, considered to be the father of attachment theory, researched homeless children in Europe after the Second World War. He found that early prolonged separation of a young child from the mother negatively affected the child's subsequent development (Bowlby, 1982). Then in the early 1960s, Canadian psychologist Mary Ainsworth furthered attachment theory with her studies of infants and their mothers in home and "strange" situations. She identified "secure attachment" between infants and mothers who were warm, responsive, and dependable. She postulated that this secure attachment was very important for children's psychological development (Ainsworth, 1978). Subsequent research has shown that securely attached young children were friendlier, more independent, more empathic, had better social skills, and were perceived as more likeable and competent by their teachers (Sroufe, Egeland, & Kreutzer, 1990; Sroufe, Fox, & Pancake, 1983).

Attachment theory has been influential in early childhood education and care, especially infant care. For example, key characteristics of successful attachment for children are that it is established early, is consistent, and is stable over time (Guy, 1997). The interpretation of attachment research has resulted in some researchers questioning full-time child care outside the home, especially for infants. For example, Jay Belsky concluded that more than 20 hours per week of non-maternal care could risk a baby's development of secure attachment to the mother (Belsky, 1988; Belsky & Rovine, 1988). This idea has been hotly debated in the field of infant day care.

Another area of contention is the overall importance of attachment for children's development. Attachment theory is not universally accepted. Some child psychologists argue that too much attention is given to the long-term effects of children's early experiences, and that children are more resilient than many researchers and theorists think (resiliency is discussed later in this chapter). Some feminists take issue with attachment theory for its focus on the child's relationship with only the mother. Others claim attachment is defined differently across cultures. Still other critics include behaviourists, who believe behaviour is learned, as well as those who support a more genetic or hereditary approach in which the child is thought to develop based on an innate "schedule." Probably, most psychologists would agree with Paul Steinhauer's statement that "to say a child has an insecure attachment is not saying that that child already has a disorder; having an insecure attachment is a risk factor for difficulties later on" (1999, p. 18). It is, however, not a certainty.

Infant day care is described in Chapter 8.

Temperament

We have speculated about individual differences in temperament and their causes since the days of the ancient Greeks and Romans (Kagan, 1994). *Temperament* is commonly defined as "an individual's characteristic style of behaving in and responding to the world" (Guy, 1997, p. 67). More specifically, temperament is "individual differences in behavioral tendencies that are present early in life and are relatively stable across time and a variety of situations" (Martin, 1994, p. 120). From your experience you have probably known babies who are friendly, happy, and outgoing, as well as babies who are fussy, teary, and withdrawn.

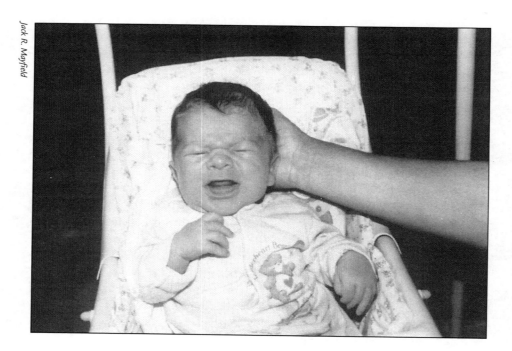

Jack R. Mayfield

Babies have varied temperaments: Some are more fussy and cry more than others.

Temperament is thought to influence how a child meets new challenges, interacts with others, deals with change, behaves in school, perseveres, expresses emotion, and copes with stress (Martin, 1994; Prior, 1992). The National Longitudinal Survey of Children and Youth (1996) has begun to look at children's temperament and its influence on children's development over time. Early NLSCY data suggest that "babies perceived to be more difficult were from families in which overall family functioning was lower, parents were hostile to their baby, and the mother was young or depressed postpartum" (p. 60). It is necessary to also recognize that research indicates temperament is bidirectional and interactional; in other words, parents influence their children and children influence their parents (Collins, Maccoby, Steinberg, Hetherington, & Bornstein, 2000).

Sources of Stress for Young Children

Young children's lives are not always easy or without problems. Stress affects children as well as adults. **Stress** can be defined as "the state that results when people cannot cope with either internal or external demands" (Jewett, 1997, p. 172). According to the National Longitudinal Survey of Children and Youth (1996), one-third of children under 12 had experienced significant stress, according to their parents. (See Table 2.3 for the common sources of children's stress.)

Parental stress can also negatively affect children. For example, a depressed parent tends to be less responsive to his or her children (Shore, 1997). Moreover, depressed parents often have children who are depressed: if one parent is depressed, there is a 15–17 percent likelihood their child will be; this figure

TABLE 2.3

Sources of Stress for Young Children

THE MOST COMMON SOURCES OF STRESS FOR CHILDREN UNDER AGE **12** WERE:

DEATH IN THE FAMILY	27%
PARENTS' DIVORCE OR SEPARATION	25%
FAMILY MOVE	8%
FAMILY MEMBER'S ILLNESS OR INJURY	8%
CHILD'S ILLNESS OR INJURY	6%
CONFLICT BETWEEN PARENTS	6%
HOSPITAL STAY	5%
ABUSE OR FEAR OF ABUSE	4%
SEPARATION FROM PARENTS, EXCLUDING DIVORCE	4%
DEATH OF A PARENT	3%
ALCOHOLISM OR MENTAL HEALTH DISORDER IN THE FAMILY	2%
A STAY IN A FOSTER HOME	1%
OTHER	29%

Source: Based on data from Canadian Council on Social Development, 1997, p. 38

jumps to 45–50 percent if both parents are depressed (Marshall, 1999). Incidents of child depression are important to treat so the condition does not become ongoing.

Children's temperament can affect how they respond to stressful situations. Two important factors in the effect of stress are its duration and intensity. Stress can be brief or ongoing, with chronic and ongoing stress having the most serious, and potentially permanent, effects on children (Jewett, 1997). Stressors can also have a cumulative effect if they are multiple and simultaneous.

Resiliency in children is discussed later in this chapter.

Social Competency

Another part of children's social and emotional well-being is their relationships with people outside their own families, including other children. Research has shown that children who have positive relationships with the caregivers in their lives have positive peer relationships as well (Howes, Hamilton, & Matheson, 1994). *Socially competent* young children are "those who engage in satisfying interactions and activities with adults and peers and through such interactions further improve their own competence" (Katz & McClellan, 1997, p. 1). According to Katz and McClellan, the components of **social competence** are

- Emotional regulation (e.g., dealing with frustration or fear)
- Social knowledge and understanding (e.g., social customs of the peer group, or ability to communicate intentions to play partners)
- Social skills (e.g., ability to enter an existing play situation, or contribute to an ongoing discussion)
- Social dispositions (e.g., a pattern of behaviour such as being cooperative or empathetic).

Many children experience common social difficulties at some time in preschool and kindergarten, such as not taking turns, or negotiating conflicts with peers, or being able to communicate their intentions sufficiently clearly. However, between 5 and 27 percent of children have more serious socio-emotional problems by age three, including physical aggression, separation anxiety, anti-social behaviour, emotional disorders (e.g., depression, excessive crying, etc.), and hyperactivity (Canadian Council on Social Development, 1996).

Implications for Early Childhood Programs

The research on infants and young children's attachment, temperament, and social development has important implications for early childhood programs, including

- Provision for continuity and stability of caregivers, especially for the youngest children

- Recognition and accommodation of differences in temperament and personality of even very young children

- Facilitation of children's transitions from home to other care settings so children feel safe and secure

- Use of predictable daily routines and experiences to provide security

- Importance of being responsive to children's needs (e.g., holding infants, comforting a frightened child, etc.)

- Importance of helping children to develop coping strategies for both social and stressful situations

- Fostering of genuine interaction and communication with even the youngest children (e.g., talking to a baby while diapering)

- Provision of assistance for families to understand the importance of children's early development, beginning prenatally.

Young children's social and emotional security forms the "bedrock" for their subsequent "cognitive adventures" (Szanton, 1998, p. 67). (See Focus 2.3 for an example of one province's coordinated approach to fostering children's development.)

Cognitive Stimulation

Another determinant of young children's optimal development is cognitive stimulation. The early years are considered to be crucial for later cognitive development (Canadian Institute of Child Health, 1994; Doherty-Derkowski, 1995; Guy, 1997; Shore, 1997). Given the great strides made in research on the brain in the past two decades, more attention is now being paid to the cognitive development of children beginning from birth.

Ontario's Better Beginnings, Better Futures Project

The Better Beginnings, Better Futures project was begun in response to a 1983 report on children's health that reported one in six children had an emotional or behavioural disorder. This project is a 25-year longitudinal prevention policy research demonstration project funded by the Ministries of Community and Social Services, Health, and Education of Ontario, and the federal Department of Indian and Northern Affairs and the Secretary of State. It was designed to be preventive, comprehensive, high quality, and to meet local needs and wishes.

Its three main goals are to:

· Prevent physical, cognitive, social, emotional, and behavioural problems in young children

· Promote healthy child development

· Enhance capacities of economically and socially disadvantaged communities.

This project targets children from birth to eight years living in 12 communities across Ontario. There is a prenatal/infant development model integrated with preschool for children up to age four and a preschool model integrated with primary schools for children from four to eight years. The program components vary with the needs and wishes of the communities but generally include home visits, classroom and child-care enrichment, parent/family programs, as well as community and other child-focused programs. These programs are delivered by community members using local resources whenever possible. Interagency cooperation is encouraged.

Sources and for more information: You can find information on Better Beginnings, Better Futures online at www.opc.on.ca/bbbf and www.crime-prevention.org/ncpc/database/models. See also the *Canadian Journal of Community Mental Health*, Fall 1994, 13(2).

Brain Research

The role of the brain in the development of human beings has long been a topic of interest and speculation. However, only recently, with the advent of magnetic resonance imaging (MRI) and positron emission tomography (PET), have neuropsychologists and other scientists gained a clearer and more impressive picture of how the brain develops and functions.

A one-pound fetus has 100 billion brain cells, called *neurons* (Shore, 1997). However, at birth the infant's neurons are not yet linked to form a connected network. An analogy used frequently is that the newborn's brain is like a computer that has yet to be programmed (Tipper, 1997). To do this programming, or make the connections needed to form the network, the brain requires input to stimulate and activate the neurons to create connections with other neurons.

Each neuron can be connected to as many as 15,000 other neurons. These connections are called *synapses*. A parent playing patty-cake with his infant is stimulating the child's brain through sight, touch, and sound. This seemingly simple activity is actually stimulating the child's neurons to make new connections and to strengthen existing connections.

The infant's brain produces many more neurons and synapses than are necessary. In fact, a three-year-old has twice as many synapses as an adult (Shore, 1997). It is children's early experiences that provide the stimulation to the brain that determine which synapses remain and which are eliminated. The brain is very efficient about not keeping synapses that are not being used. In the first three years of life, the brain is rapidly establishing synapses; this then continues at a steady pace until approximately age 10, when production and elimination of synapses is about balanced. By early adolescence, elimination of synapses dominates production. It is important to know that more connections do not mean that a child is more intelligent, and that eliminating excess synapses is a necessary function. In fact, both abnormally low and high synaptic densities cause mental deficiency and there is no direct relationship between the number of synapses and intelligence (Bruer, 1998).

Research has shown that the early years are a crucial period for brain development and that the environment and experiences of these years can affect a child for the rest of his or her life. This raises the concept of **critical periods**, *prime times*, or *plastic periods* in children's development. These are times when the brain is particularly receptive to specific kinds of learning. For example, at one month of age, the sensory-motor functioning area in the brain is very active (Shore, 1997). Some critical periods are lengthy; for example, the one for learning the grammar of a language continues to approximately age 16 (Bruer, 1998). Although critical periods may mean that it is easier for the brain to establish certain connections, it does not mean that it is a now-or-never situation. These "windows of opportunity do not close completely" (Steinhauer, 1999, p. 16). Furthermore, the noted psychologist Jerome Kagan (1998) argues that "the doctrine of infant determinism ignores the many powerful influences that affect the profile of adolescents and young adults after the second birthday" (p. 130).

It is important to remember that children's cognitive development is complex and that many factors influence it. Scientists have discovered that "throughout the entire process of development, beginning even before birth, the brain is affected by environmental conditions, including the kind of nourishment, care, surroundings, and stimulation an individual receives" (Shore, 1997, p. ix). Some factors (e.g., trauma, abuse, malnutrition, etc.) may have negative, and potentially lasting, effects.

Exciting and promising though the recent research is, many well-respected scientists warn about overenthusiastic application of this research. For example, John Bruer (1998) stated, "well-founded educational applications of brain science may come eventually, but right now, brain science has little to offer educational practice or policy" (p. 14). Despite such cautions (see also Kagan, 1998), recent research on young children's development, including brain

FOR REFLECTION

In the wake of the brain research has come commercially developed educational materials, kits, parent books, and other materials to supposedly foster infants' and young children's brain development. According to Puckett, Marshall, & Davis (1999), "products based on brain research must not be allowed to raise the hopes of unsuspecting parents and educators, without cause. As professionals, we must support parents in resisting trends toward 'neuromania,' and we must recognize programs and experiences based on accurate interpretations of emerging research" (p. 11). Therefore, when parents of a newborn who have been reading about the recent research on infants' brain development ask you for advice, what would you tell them?

research, has been used as a significant part of the rationale for political and policy decisions such as the federal government's proposed National Children's Agenda and some recent provincial proposals. Perhaps a realistic assessment is that of Newberger (1997): "the findings affirm what many parents and caregivers have known for years: (1) good prenatal care, (2) warm and loving attachments between young children and adults, and (3) positive, age-appropriate stimulation from the time of birth really do make a difference in children's development for a lifetime" (p. 4).

The National Children's Agenda is discussed in Chapter 12.

One of the implications of these cautions for early childhood educators is the need to "critically read and analyze the [brain] research in order to separate the wheat from the chaff" (Wolfe & Brandt, 1998, p. 10). A second implication is for early childhood educators to be resources for parents and others who wonder what the "new brain research" means for them and their children.

Economic Security

Another determinant of children's health and happiness is having economic security. Simply, this means that the child has adequate nutritious food, medical and dental care, standard and safe housing, appropriate clothing, and so on. Unfortunately, poverty prevents many Canadian children from experiencing these conditions. When asked what being poor means, eight-year-old Ashley replied, "You can't buy food. You don't have a place to live. You can't have nice clothes . . . . You can't go to the movies . . . . You can't do what you want to do" (Baxter, 1993, p. 42).

One in four Canadian children under the age of six (i.e., 1.3 million children) was living in poverty in 1996. (Ironically, 1996 was the International Year Against Poverty.) Although Canada has consistently been rated number one in quality of life by the United Nations in recent years, it has the second highest rate of child poverty of the industrialized countries (Chisholm, 1997). Moreover, the rate of child poverty has increased in every province since 1989 (Campaign 2000, 1998). By 1996, the provinces with the highest rates of increase were Ontario (+85 percent), Nova Scotia (+50 percent), and British Columbia (+49 percent). The lowest rates were Saskatchewan (+12 percent) and Newfoundland (+13 percent) (Campaign 2000, 1998).

For more information, see the suggested readings in the Resources section at the end of this chapter.

Child poverty as part of the larger problem of family poverty is discussed in Chapter 3.

Poverty puts children, especially in the early years, at risk for a wide variety of problems that can affect their entire lives. One federal government report on child poverty commented:

> For children, living in poverty affects what and how often they eat, what they wear, where they can live and how safe that environment is, their health status, what recreational activities they can participate in, their emotional well-being, and how successful they will be in school and in life. (Sub-Committee on Poverty, Standing Committee on Health and Welfare, Social Affairs, Seniors and Status of Women, 1991, p. 7)

According to the Vanier Institute of the Family, in 1998 it cost approximately $160,000 to raise a child from birth to 18. This was an increase of $4,000 since 1995 (Canadian Council on Social Development, 1998). The biggest percentage was child-care costs (33 percent), followed by shelter (23 percent), food (19 percent), and clothing (10 percent). Manitoba Agriculture puts the figure at $200,000. If there are two children in a family, the figure increases by 1.69, and 2.24 for three children (Olson, 1983). Do you agree with those who say children are becoming a luxury item in Canada?

Research has shown that the duration of poverty in childhood is an even more significant factor than its timing (e.g., Duncan, Brooks-Gunn, & Klebanov, 1994). As Huston (1991) has noted, "children living in persistent poverty are at risk for problems in health, cognitive and social development, school achievement, and future job prospects. The word *risk* is used to signify that not all poor children have poor health, low school performance, and other negative outcomes" (p. 290).

Effects of Poverty on Child Health

The possible effects of poverty on children's health can begin before their birth. Mothers with inadequate prenatal nutrition are more likely to have low-birth-weight babies who are therefore at greater risk for infant mortality, later health problems, and lower life expectancy (Sub-Committee on Poverty, 1991) (see Focus 2.2). Children born into or living in poverty are also more likely to experience

- Chronic health problems, such as bronchitis, asthma, and anemia
- Digestive problems
- Hearing and vision impairments (not corrected)
- Physical disabilities
- Lower immunization rates
- Speech and language delays
- Inadequate dental care.

(Campaign 2000, 1998; Halpern, 1987; Ryerse, 1990; Sub-Committee on Poverty, 1991; Weissbourd, 1996)

In addition to their own health problems, poor children are more likely to have parents with health problems, which may result in separation due to hospitalization and disruption of family life.

Children living in poverty are also at risk for reduced nutrition due to the family's inability to afford nutritious food. This is especially important in the early years because even mild forms of malnutrition, especially over time, can negatively affect children's development (Pollitt, 1994).

Hunger is a reality for many Canadian children. Statistics on hunger are difficult to calculate accurately; however, the use of food banks is a frequently used indicator of hunger. According to the Canadian Council on Social Development, more than 250,000 children received food from food banks in Canada. One study of mothers using food banks in Metro Toronto found that the majority of mothers reported going hungry and 27 percent reported their children had (Canadian Council on Social Development, 1998). Aboriginal children are reportedly four times more likely than non-Aboriginal children to have experienced hunger (Turner, 1998).

Effect of Poverty on Children's Education

Poverty can have serious implications for children's cognitive and social development. Children living in poverty are more likely to experience

- Developmental delays due to inadequate nutrition

- Learning problems

- Lower grades

- Remedial classes

- Hyperactivity

- Aggression/anti-social behaviour

- Low self-esteem

- Lateness due to lack of alarm clocks in the home

- Absences from school due to illness and truancy

- Difficulties concentrating due to hunger and health problems

- Fewer opportunities to participate in school, extra-curricular, or recreational activities that require additional costs.

(Baxter, 1993; Canadian Council on Social Development, 1998; Ryerse, 1990; Sub-Committee on Child Poverty, 1991; Weissbourd, 1996)

I remember numerous times when I was working with young children, in both North America and Europe, when a child would come to the day-care centre or school without having had breakfast (and sometimes no meals since their snack the previous afternoon), no mittens or boots, clothes too small or too large, tired because the child couldn't sleep well due to lack of heat in the house, or with a chronic cough. For some children, a good early childhood program is essential for their health and development.

Implications for Early Childhood Programs

Early childhood programs promote and foster the optimal development of young children. They also function as prevention and protection for young children. Early childhood programs can provide support, comfort, respite, and services for young children and their families. Some early childhood programs helping to meet the needs of children and their families are

These programs and others are described in subsequent chapters.

- Prenatal and postnatal health care

- Parenting education/support

- Family support programs

- Child-care programs that make quality care accessible and affordable

- Community kitchens and nutrition programs

- Mentoring programs

- Counselling

FOR REFLECTION

On November 24, 1989, the Canadian House of Commons passed a resolution to seek to abolish child poverty in Canada by 2000. Since that time, the number of poor children has risen by 58 percent to almost 1.5 million children (Campaign 2000, 1997). What three suggestions would you give Parliament for abolishing child poverty in Canada?

- Clothing and toy exchanges

- Information and resource services

- Family literacy programs

- Recreational and activity programs

- Family resource and drop-in centres.

In summary, research has linked poverty and negative consequences for children. Poverty puts children at risk for poorer health, lower levels of educational achievement, more illness and injury, and "over the long term . . . significantly endangers a child's opportunity to grow and to develop into a healthy, self-reliant adult" (Lochhead & Shillington, 1996, p. 9).

As well as being informed about the current status of children, it is important for early childhood professionals to be familiar with the history of childhood and to consider how society views children. This insight can provide a valuable perspective for examining current issues.

Views on Children and Childhood

If you were a visitor to Canada from another planet, how would you complete the sentence: *In Canada, children are thought of as* _____.

How did you complete the sentence? Why did you give the response you did? Some ways I've heard that statement completed include

individuals	part of society	a duty
our future	important	a precious resource
human beings	a big expense	vulnerable
valuable	a joy	the continuity of the family
tomorrow's workforce	an investment	dependent
deserving our care and attention	animals with superior brains	members of families
the foundation of our society		

How a person completes the above statement reflects their view of children and their concept of *childhood*.

The concept of **childhood** has been of interest and debate to historians, philosophers, anthropologists, sociologists, educators, psychologists, and economists for many, many years. At various times throughout history, the child has been thought of in one or more of the ways described below. Which of the following concepts do you think exist in Canada today?

- *The child as miniature adult*—This view perceived children as being like adults, only smaller; a very small human being. Matthews (1994) terms this "the little person theory of childhood" (p. 22). For example, in pre-Renaissance European paintings, such as those by Brueghel the Elder depicting children's games, the children are not proportioned accurately as children but rather are shown as small adults with adult body proportions (Cleverley & Phillips, 1986). However, some artists of that time did portray children more realistically (Fuller, 1979). This view of children can still be seen in the line of greeting cards that portrays children as miniature adults.

- *The child as property*—Another historical view of children considered them to be property; this view was exemplified during the Middle Ages and in later societies that practised slavery. In Canada, children were not mentioned in the British North America Act and were considered to legally come under the section on property.

- *The child as toy or pet*—In some of the paintings from Restoration England, one sees elaborately clothed and coiffed adults with children and small dogs at their feet. The children give the appearance of being some type of exotic pet. The word *pet* is still considered a term of endearment by some people (as in "Oh, you're such a dear little pet"). A recent example of pairing children and pets is the no children/no pets policy of many rental accommodations in Canada.

- *The child as sinner*—During the fourteenth to eighteenth centuries, children were perceived as sinners. At this time, many people believed in the doctrine of original sin and thought that unless steps were taken (e.g., baptism and religious instruction), children would die sinners. Within this view, children's behaviour and discipline became very important. An example of this is the "spare the rod and spoil the child" idea (Proverbs 29:15 says, "The rod and reproof give wisdom, but a child left to himself brings shame to his mother"). According to Cleverley and Phillips (1986), under this philosophy "good habits were developed under a strict regime of controlled sleeping, fasting between meals, whispered requests for food at table, regular family prayers, and the judicious application of corporal punishment" (p. 29). This was also seen in schools in the corporal punishment of children for relatively minor misbehaviour.

- *The child as cheap labour*—In the days of predominantly agrarian economies and during the Industrial Revolution, even young children were seen as workers in the fields or factories. Robert Owen began his infant schools in the eighteenth century to provide an alternative to the mills for young children (see Chapter 5). Today, in subsistence agriculture societies, children as young as six or seven are expected to work in the fields to help feed their families. Some people include the existence of today's migrant worker families, child prostitution, and teens working in the service sector—for example, in fast-food restaurants—under the view of children as cheap labour (Morrow, 1995).

- *The child as blank slate*—This view sees children as neither good nor bad. They are thought of as blank slates (*tabla rasa*) to be inscribed through instruction, or as empty vessels to be filled. The underlying theory here is that there is no innate genetic code or predisposition and that children are shaped by the environment and their experiences. John Locke, a philosopher prominent in the seventeenth century, was a leading proponent of this view.

- *The child as a growing plant*—This is a frequently used analogy by early childhood theorists such as Froebel and Comenius (see Chapter 5). The idea was that children, if given the proper conditions, would unfold or grow like plants. This view of children and their development is seen in the maturationist philosophy (see Chapter 6) and is still a widely used analogy in the popular press.

- *The sensual child*—This concept was derived in large part from the work of Sigmund Freud, who believed that even young children have sexual feelings and that these feelings should be given expression rather than be repressed. This concept is represented in psychodynamic theories (see Chapter 6). For example, some early childhood educators interpreted this concept to mean that children should have lots of access to materials such as clay and water and that they should be encouraged to use these in any way they wished, including throwing them.

- *The conditioned child*—The work of the early behaviourists, such as Watson, Thorndike, and, later, Skinner, influenced psychologists, educators, and parents' perceptions of children. The basic tenet was that "the environment provided by the parents [and later the school], including the way they rewarded and punished the child, determined the subsequent development of behavior" (Cleverley & Phillips, 1986, p. 120). Examples of behaviourism can be seen in most early childhood programs in varying degrees. Practices and strategies such as positive reinforcement, time outs, and stickers reflect this view of the child.

- *The adaptable child*—This twentieth-century view of children is credited to the work of early anthropologists such as Margaret Mead, Ruth Benedict, and Kingsley Davis, who saw children as "plastic and adaptable in contrast to adults, who are rigid and unadaptable" (Elkind, 1993, p. 7). This is not to say that young children can learn anything and everything. As Elkind comments, "there is a time and place for everything, and early childhood education is not the time nor the place to teach children computer programming, the threat of nuclear war, or, for that matter, the dangers of AIDS" (p. 9).

- *The child as investment in the future*—This view of children and childhood has existed since the Middle Ages. The child is perceived as an investment for the family or the nation; a recent term is *human capital*. In some societies, where there are no social insurance or pension plans, the resources of one's children determine the quality of one's old age. In these societies, there is a high birth rate in order to guarantee that some children survive to support their parents and grandparents. In the rhetoric of today, one often hears politicians, policy-makers, and advocacy groups referring to children as "our future." One needs to consider what view of children such statements imply; as Blitzer (1991) has commented: "more references are made to children as an investment in the country's future than to the importance of educating children for the present so that they can lead rich, productive lives while they are still young" (p. 18).

FOR REFLECTION

Gaile Sloan Cannella (1997), among others, has questioned the lack of children's participation in the construction of our concepts of children and childhood. She wrote, "younger human beings are limited to the possibilities that fit our constructions of them" (p. 64). Do you agree with this view? If yes, what does this mean for your personal views of childhood?

- *The priceless child*—"Priceless" refers to children's emotional value. The view of the emotionally priceless child became popular in the late nineteenth and early twentieth centuries, especially in the middle and upper classes (Zelizer, 1985). It was a very sentimental view of children that can be seen in some of the children's literature of that time. In many countries, young children are still necessary, contributing members to the family's economic resources. And in some countries with a high infant mortality rate, sentimentality about children and childhood is considered a luxury.

- *The competent child*—This view grew out of the work of psychologists such as Hunt, Bloom, and Bruner, who, in the 1960s, postulated that the early years were a period of rapid and great development and therefore should be emphasized in education. This belief led to an increased focus on the development of young children, especially the cognitive development of infants. The work of these psychologists and others was sometimes misinterpreted and overgeneralized to mean that if optimal growth did not occur during this time, there would be irreparable harm done to the child. There was a subsequent growth in programs to teach infants and toddlers reading and mathematics. On the other hand, the legal system still sees young children as more incompetent than competent; for example, the courts are not usually required to ask children for their opinions in decisions that affect them. As Leach (1994) notes, "in the best interests of the child" can sometimes mean paternalism and authoritarianism.

- *The superchild*—The "superchild" concept originally referred to so-called child prodigies such as Mozart. In the late twentieth century and today, the term has been used as synonymous with the "hurried child," whose childhood is eroded or has disappeared due to the good intentions of parents and educators to provide children with "the best." For some children this has meant being overscheduled and stressed from going to school, ballet class, music lessons, sports, and other activities to the point where the child is being deprived of a childhood.

The hurried child phenomenon is discussed later in this chapter.

Some early childhood theorists see the concept of children and childhood from a predominantly evolutionary perspective (e.g., Ariès, 1962; Elkind, 1993). In this view, childhood is a "social construction" (Hoyle & Evans, 1989, p. 19);

it is a product of its time, place, and culture. However, others argue that the concepts of children, childhood, and child-rearing have not changed substantively over time (e.g., Pollock, 1983).

It is also important to recognize that the above concepts of children and childhood are basically Eurocentric/Western ideas. *Childhood* has different meanings in different cultures (Kessen, 1981). And Canada has many cultures, including Aboriginal cultures. Moreover, these differences can be fundamental and profound. For example, "the Buddist/Confucian conception of childhood is very positive. Young children are like angels who have come to earth for a period of time, and our purpose is to try and convince them to stay . . . . In Asia, childhood is a period of indulgence" (Emblen, 1998, p. 34).

Richard Louv (1990) asked third-grade children "What is a childhood?" Some of their responses were:

- "How you live, when you're a baby to when you're grown."

- "What you do when you're little and what you do with your life."

- One boy said simply, "What your life is" (p. 17).

Another revealing question to ask children and youth of different ages is, When does childhood end? Some of the children's responses I've heard are that it happens when one

- gets a driver's licence

- begins high school

- finishes high school

- gets a job

- can legally drink alcohol

- can vote

- leaves home

- gets married.

While children may think that childhood should end sooner, Morrow (1995) points out that "what is frequently overlooked is the fact that the age at which one is considered to be 'a child' (at least in terms of social and economic dependency) has gradually increased during this century as a result of a range of social policies" (p. 224). On the other hand, there are societal and sometimes familial pressures for children to grow up sooner (Elkind, 1981).

Do you think an extraterrestrial being would agree with Kessen (1979) that "no other animal species has been catalogued by responsible scholars in so many wildly discrepant forms, forms that a perceptive extraterrestrial could never see as reflecting the same beast" (p. 815)?

How we perceive children and childhood is also reflected in what we think about children's rights.

Children's Rights

Do children have rights? Do even very young children have rights? If so, what are these rights? And who is responsible for seeing that these rights are available to all children? These are some questions early childhood educators have raised regarding children's rights. Children's rights are not the same as adults' rights, because children are more dependent on their families and society as they are more vulnerable and less able to protect themselves.

After the devastation of the First World War, various groups became active in promoting children's welfare including children's rights. The League of Nations established a Committee on Child Welfare in 1919. At about the same time, Save the Children was founded by Eglantyne Jebb (and her sister) in response to her work with children in the wartorn Balkans. Jebb advocated a set of rights for all children and protection of children even during armed conflicts (Edmonds & Fernekes, 1996). In 1923, she wrote a Children's Charter that in 1924 was adopted by the League of Nations as the Declaration of the Rights of the Child. This declaration has been the basis for subsequent efforts to articulate and promote children's rights internationally.

The International Year of the Child in 1979 focused the world's attention on children. One result was the Polish government's proposal for a convention for children's rights to replace the Declaration of the Rights of the Child (a declaration is not legally binding). A working group was appointed, and after ten years of work the United Nations General Assembly adopted the final draft on November 20, 1989. It became international law in September 1990 when the twentieth country ratified it, which was the fastest ratification of any human rights treaty in the history of the United Nations. The Convention on the Rights of the Child is especially significant "not only because it represents an enforceable legal consensus of world experts and over 175 nations, but also because it is the highest international legal source for the basic principles and standards constituting the rights of the child" (Edmonds & Fernekes, 1996, p. 10).

The specific rights listed in the Convention on the Rights of the Child (United Nations, 1991) are often summarized and grouped as the Three Ps: Provision, Protection, and Participation.

Provision means children have the right to possess, receive, or have access to certain things and services including

- Life (Article 6);

- A name, birth registration, and nationality (Article 7);

- Preservation of that name, family relations, and nationality (Article 8);

- Family reunification (Article 10);

- Privacy (Article 16);

- Access to information (Article 17);

- Child-care services and facilities (Article 18);
- Adoption in the best interests of the child (Article 21);
- Special care if disabled (Article 23);
- Health care (Article 24);
- Periodic review of treatment or placement (Article 25);
- Benefits of social security (Article 26);
- An adequate standard of living (Article 27);
- Education to develop the child's full potential (Articles 28 & 29);
- Respect for the child's culture (Article 30);
- Adequate rest, leisure, and play (Article 31);
- Rehabilitative care and reintegration after abuse, neglect, exploitation, torture, cruel treatment, or armed conflicts (Article 39); and
- In judicial proceedings, the right to be presumed innocent, a speedy trial, non–self-incrimination, and to be dealt with in an appropriate manner (Article 40).

Protection means the right of children to be shielded from harmful practices and acts such as:

- Discrimination of any kind (Article 2);
- Separation from parents (Article 9);
- Violence, injury, abuse, neglect, maltreatment, and exploitation (Article 19);
- Economic exploitation (Article 32);
- Illicit drug use and activities (Article 33);
- Sexual exploitation and abuse (Article 34);
- Abduction, sale, or trafficking (Articles 11 & 35);
- All forms of exploitation (Article 36);
- Torture, cruel treatment, capital punishment, and life imprisonment (Article 37);
- Participation in armed conflicts (Article 38); and
- Special protection and assistance if a refugee or without a family (Articles 20 & 22).

Participation means the right of children to participate in society and in decisions affecting their lives:

- The best interests of the child are a primary consideration in all actions concerning the child (Article 3);

- The right to express their views in matters affecting themselves (Article 12);

- Freedom of expression (Article 13);

- Freedom of thought, conscience, and religion (Article 14); and

- Freedom of association and peaceful assembly (Article 15).

Some criticisms of the Convention on the Rights of the Child are that (a) it does not go far enough because it was drafted by consensus and is therefore a minimum standard, (b) it is unnecessary to have a separate rights document for children, (c) it lacks enforcement provisions, (d) it reinforces the status quo, (e) it needs updating to include issues such as environmental rights, and (f) not every country ratified it in total. For example, Canada ratified the Convention with reservation, claiming that it could not guarantee that incarcerated children would be detained separately from adults (Australia, Japan, the Netherlands, New Zealand, and the United Kingdom filed the same reservation). An additional criticism is that the Convention undermines the rights and authority of the family, especially parents.

Because the Convention on the Rights of the Child is a legal document, ratification by a country means that country is then "legally accountable to the international community for creating conditions to satisfy the rights of children" (Khaki, 1994, p. 24). Part of this accountability is the requirement that each country report its progress to the United Nations Committee on the Rights of the Child within two years of ratification and then every five years thereafter. This committee of ten members monitors the convention, questions countries about their reports, provides advice and suggestions, and reports the results to the United Nations General Assembly. In 1995, this committee criticized Canada for (a) its treatment of children under the Immigration Act, which permitted their separation from families when parents are deported, (b) the fact that children could not apply for family reunification until they were 19, (c) the fact that children were detained with adults in prisons, (d) the fact that teachers and parents were permitted to use corporal punishment, and (e) the fact that a high percentage of Aboriginal children were living in poverty (Schlein, 1995).

More recently, Canada has been criticized on some of these same points by another United Nations Committee, the Committee on Economic, Social, and Cultural Rights, which monitors the United Nations Declaration of Human Rights. The Committee pointed out that although Canada has consistently ranked number one by the United Nations for standard of living in recent years, the following were concerns:

- The rising levels of poverty and homelessness;

- The treatment of Aboriginal people, especially women;

- The lack of social and economic rights in the Canadian Human Rights Act;

FOR REFLECTION

Gerison Lansdown (1996) has written, "If we care about the welfare of our children, we must be prepared to listen to them" (p. 81). This implies not only listening but seeking and encouraging their input. In Denmark, a Ministry of Social Affairs policy is that "children should be included in the planning and execution of activities in daytime child care facilities, according to their age and maturity" (quoted in Partners in Quality, *Kaiser & Rasminsky, 1999, p. 10). Do you agree with this policy? If yes, what are some examples of how four- and five-year-olds could be included in the planning of their program?*

- Fighting the deficit at the expense of social and economic programs;

- Poverty among women and children; and

- The increasing use of food banks.

(McCabe & Beltrame, 1998)

The first implication of the Convention on the Rights of the Child for early childhood educators and families is children's right to be listened to respectfully and to be consulted (i.e., a responsibility on the part of adults to actively seek their views). This right not only affects processes, but also has the potential for making programs less authoritarian and more participatory. Focus 2.4 shows a resource sheet from the Canadian Child Day Care Federation that outlines some children's rights in an early childhood setting.

Focus 2.4

The Child's Rights in a Preschool Setting

Introduction

"By setting out the rights of children, one can determine on an on-going basis whether children's needs are being met. Children's rights should be sufficiently elaborated so that the family and the community will have certain rights they can insist upon in seeking services for their children."*

Note: The term preschool refers to all group settings for children five and under.

Emotional Rights

A child in the preschool setting shall be entitled to the right to:

1. encouragement to help foster a sense of self-esteem

2. opportunities for independence, success and fun

3. have his/her feelings fully accepted whether negative or positive

4. freedom to develop his/her own unique creativity

5. a sense of order, routine and consistency

6. realistic expectations, clear limits and positive guidance

7. opportunities to meet special individual needs

8. respect for individual ethnic and cultural differences and a culturally integrated curriculum which stresses pride in each child's own heritage as well as pride in being a Canadian

9. special attention for children with English as a second language

10. courtesy and support for his/her parents

11. opportunities for input from his/her parents

12. access for his/her parents to parent education relating to child growth and development and parenting skills.

*Mr. Justice Berger, *Social Work*, Spring 1979.

Social Rights

A child in the preschool setting shall be entitled to the right to:

1. play
2. freedom to interface with peers along with wise adult intervention
3. companionship
4. an environment in which a cooperative spirit is encouraged
5. opportunities for group experience
6. know the rules of the centre
7. discipline and guidance with encouragement toward self-responsibility for actions
8. clearly conveyed boundaries which are enforced and followed through with consistency
9. constructive criticism of inappropriate behaviour
10. appeal decisions
11. flexibility
12. choose solitude
13. express his/her ideas, views and opinions and to have real input into the program
14. freedom from pressure-coercion to be busy and/or participating at all times
15. ample play materials to alleviate sharing problems
16. teachers who serve as good role models
17. freedom from sex-role stereotyping
18. teachers sensitive to his/her individual developmental needs.

Intellectual Rights

A child in the preschool setting shall be entitled to the right to:

1. a well-qualified, thinking teacher who is warm, practical, and involved, and has patience and a sense of humor while maintaining a professional approach
2. a quality education geared to his/her developmental level based on learning through play
3. a varied and challenging program in which he/she is exposed to thorough coverage of all the traditional curriculum areas: science, math, social studies, language and literature, music, art, and physical education
4. an opportunity to explore in depth an area in which he/she has shown a real interest
5. a balance of individual, small group, and large group learning activities
6. a program which incorporates spontaneous self-chosen play exploration and some teacher planned and organized activity

continued

continued

7. a comfortable, relaxed atmosphere conducive to positive learning

8. every opportunity to be intellectually challenged, to progress at his or her own rate, to reach his/her fullest potential.

Physical Rights

A child in the preschool setting shall be entitled to the right to:

1. close supervision to ensure safety at all times

2. comforting, when necessary

3. freedom from physical or psychological abuse

4. privacy when toileting, if desired

5. active and quiet individual and group play opportunities

6. conditions which promote good health: (e.g. sanitary conditions; good nutrition; etc.)

7. a comfortable, inviting, spacious playroom with all the standard interest areas: block corner, playhouse, science area, library, music corner, art area, manipulating area, large muscle equipment

8. a well-designed, aesthetic playroom set up to provide an enriched sensory experience (not overstimulating)

9. adequate playspace outdoors adjacent to the playroom which has climbing, digging and running space, and is aesthetically pleasing

10. private quiet spaces for play

11. a large open space indoors if possible (e.g. gym or hall)

12. comfortable space for sleep time, if applicable.

Canadian Child Day Care Federation, 1985
Resource Sheet #3

The second area of implication is the curriculum. An early childhood program has a responsibility to help children become aware of their rights and the rights of others in a developmentally appropriate way. A few suggestions from Waters (1998) for doing this include

- Discussing *rights*, not *rules*, with the children;

- Encouraging individual and group decision-making;

- Providing opportunities for children to make decisions;

- Incorporating the vocabulary of rights into conversations with the children (e.g., *respect, privacy, fair, caring,* etc.);

- Reinforcing that each child is unique and special;

- Using children's names frequently and encouraging them to use each others' names; using games to teach the children's names;

- Helping children identify their feelings through puppets, masks, art media, drama, stories, and so on;

- Helping children develop an awareness of other people's feelings;

- Practising group problem-solving, including the use of consensus and seeking others' opinions;

- Including stories/books in the library centre and items from a range of cultures in the dramatic play centres; and

- Displaying pictures of children and their families.

The third area of implication is the role of the early childhood professional in publicizing the Convention on the Rights of the Child to families in the program and to the larger community. For example, the child's right to play is one of the rights stated in the Convention. One way to promote the right to play might be to use posters or displays about children's rights in the program or by discussing children's rights with families at meetings or periodically in newsletters (see Waters, 1998).

Play is discussed in Chapter 7.

Advocacy for Children

Advocacy for children is a concept, an attitude, and a professional responsibility. A simple definition of child advocacy is "standing up for children and their needs" (Goffin & Lombardi, 1988, p. 1). Advocacy is also "a state of mind that guides action" (Westman, 1991, p. xxi). It is one of the roles of an early childhood educator. According to Goffin and Lombardi (1988), "our caring cannot be restricted to our classrooms or offices if we truly want to improve the lives of children" (p. 2). This willingness to protect children and their rights has been called "a moral litmus test of any decent and compassionate society" (Children's Defense Fund, 1989, p. 36).

Other roles of early childhood educators are discussed in Chapter 4.

Advocacy activities can include

- Protecting and promoting children's rights

- Determining children's needs

- Identifying and suggesting ways to meet these needs

- Educating families and the community about children's rights and needs

- Encouraging support for projects for and by children

- Acting as a resource and catalyst

- Lobbying policy-makers, politicians, and administrators on behalf of children and their families.

Norway was the first country to appoint a government advocate who had powers to speak and act on behalf of children. This *Barneombud* was established in 1981 and has been a model for national children's ombudspersons in many other countries since then. The appointment of a federal commissioner for children has been proposed for Canada and is being discussed in Parliament. However, many provinces and some municipalities already have child advocates.

An important concept for children's rights and advocacy is **First Call**. This principle was elucidated in the preamble to the Declaration of the Rights of the Child (1959), which states, "Whereas mankind owes to the children the best it has to give," and in Principle 8: "The child shall in all circumstances be among the first to receive protection and relief." This means that children should have first claim on the resources of a nation, especially in times of natural or political disaster.

Advocacy for the world's children seems a daunting task. However, there are many things that one person can do to improve the lives of children in Canada and elsewhere. One person can make a difference. The history of early childhood education and care has many examples of individuals who made a difference (see Chapter 5). Some actions that one person can do for children's advocacy are provided below.

- Find out if your municipality/province/territory has a child advocate or ombudsperson for children (see the Web sites listed at the end of this chapter); if there isn't one, you can lobby to get one!

- Support early childhood, charitable, and national/international organizations that work with children and families.

- Write or telephone your provincial/territorial representatives and member of parliament about issues that affect children and families.

- Share information with other professionals.

- Educate families in your program and people in your community about issues facing young children.

- Become a community resource (e.g., by speaking to local community groups, writing articles for the local newspaper, etc.).

- Ask candidates for elected office about their positions on issues affecting children and families.

- Be a volunteer for community coalitions affecting children (e.g., lobbying for children's play spaces as part of urban renewal planning, developing position statements with other groups, etc.).

An individual needs to be active, alert, and available to use opportunities to promote the rights and welfare of young children. (For specific steps and processes in advocacy work, see Goffin & Lombardi, 1988.)

FOR REFLECTION

If early childhood professionals will not speak up and be advocates for young children, who will? There are many ways to be an advocate for children. What are three ways you could advocate for young children in your community?

Issues for Canadian Children

There are many issues facing Canada's children at the beginning of the twenty-first century. How we as individuals and as a society respond to these issues reflects our value of and commitment to children. Four contemporary issues discussed in this section reflect how we as individuals and as a society perceive children, childhood, and children's roles for the future. These issues are violence in the lives of children, the resiliency of children, consumerism and children, and hurried and pressured children.

Violence in the Lives of Children

Even though Canada may be considered to be a very good place for children to live, this does not mean that there are no serious issues impacting young children in Canada. One serious issue that, unfortunately, is common to children around the world is violence.

We have all been saddened and horrified at reports of young children being killed or seriously injured at the hands of their parents or other children. Even though provincial and federal governments point out a declining overall crime rate, parents and professionals are concerned about children's safety in their homes, early childhood programs/schools, and communities.

Violence is not an isolated, independent phenomenon. It is associated with adverse factors such as poverty, unemployment, family disruption, substance abuse, inadequate housing, and social isolation (Canadian Council on Social Development, 1996; Hashima & Amato, 1994; Isenberg & Brown, 1997; Jenkins & Bell, 1997; National Crime Prevention Council, 1997; Zeanah & Scheeringa, 1997). Trauma or abuse in the early years can negatively affect a child's development resulting in poor attachment and socialization, aggression, impulsiveness, and a predisposition to violence (Perry, 1997; Renken, Egeland, Marvinney, Mangelsdorf, & Sroufe, 1989; Shore, 1997). In addition, factors are cumulative, so that repeated exposure to violence or violence combined with other adverse factors may be even more devastating for the young child (Garmezy, 1993; Jenkins & Bell, 1997). Any violence can affect a child, but the impact can vary (Perry, 1997). Some factors that influence the effect of violence on a child are

- The type of violence

- The child's relationship to the victim or victimizer

- The child's developmental level

- The child's previous experience with violence

- Other stressors in the child's life (e.g., poverty, illness, etc.)

- Presence of supportive adults.

(Jenkins & Bell, 1997; Perry, 1997)

Television, including its relation to violence, is discussed in the section on media and technology in Chapter 13.

Violence affects children, whether they experience it as witnesses or victims. Some effects on children include anxiety, sleep disturbances such as nightmares, eating problems, avoidance of adults or clinging to adults, toileting problems, temper tantrums, anger, aggression, fear, withdrawal, poor attention, phobias, and regression of behaviour (Marans & Adelman, 1997; Osofsky, 1997).

Children can experience three general types of violence:

- community,

- media, and

- family.

(Zeanah & Scheeringa, 1997)

Community Violence

Children under age 12 are less likely to be victims of violence than are older children. In 1994, only 6 percent of all crime victims were children under 12; children under 12 are 16 percent of the total population (Canadian Council on Social Development, 1996). While community violence may be a concern of Canadian society as a whole, parents in the National Longitudinal Survey of Children and Youth (1996) did not have many concerns about *their own* communities. The majority (88 percent) agreed that it was safe for their children to play outside during the day and that there was no big problem in their neighbourhood with burglary (61 percent), young people (73 percent), drugs (86 percent), or public drinking (87 percent).

A growing concern of schools is bullying. According to data from the National Longitudinal Survey of Children and Youth, 1 in 7 boys (ages 4–11) bullied other children, and 1 in 20 was a victim of bullying; for girls, the figures are 1 in 11 and 1 in 14, respectively (Canadian Council on Social Development, 1998). Many schools and school districts have instituted anti-bullying and violence prevention programs in the past few years. See Focus 2.5 for one community's way of reducing the problem of bullying.

Family Violence

Family violence is of particular concern to early childhood educators and other professionals because the family is such a crucial context for young children's development. According to Statistics Canada's national Violence Against Women survey, one in three women in Canada has been assaulted by her partner (Rodgers, 1994). In marriages with violence, 39 percent of the children witnessed violence against their mothers. Moreover, in 52 percent of these cases, it was a very serious form of violence where the mother feared for her life (Rodgers, 1994). Children's reactions to violence are greatest when the violence involves a parent as victim or victimizer (Osofsky, 1997). Although violence can be intergenerational, "the majority of neglected children never become violent. The majority of traumatized children never become violent" (Perry, 1997, p. 139). However, repeatedly witnessing violence and living in

Focus 2.5

The KidSafe Program

KidSafe is a project in Vancouver schools designed to give children a safe place during school holidays and breaks. It grew from the beating of an eight-year-old boy as he walked home from school in 1983. Four local school principals and representatives from the *Vancouver Sun* Children's Fund initiated the project. Four schools are safe havens for 300 children from 5 to 13 years of age. The children receive breakfast, lunch, and an afternoon snack while participating in arts and crafts activities, a recreational program, a reading program, and field trips. There is also a community kitchen program for families. KidSafe is funded by private and government groups. Past users still return to the program—according to one journalist from a national magazine, "there is hardly a better barometer of success in the struggle to give children the things they need the most" (Chisholm, 1997, p. 45).

> Sources: Canadian Council on Social Development, 1998; Chisholm, 1997; KidSafe staff, personal communication, 1999.

threatening circumstances can have long-term detrimental effects (Slaby, Roedell, Arezzo, & Hendrix, 1995).

Child Abuse and Neglect

Perhaps the most horrific form of violence towards children is child abuse. There is no one agreed-upon definition of child abuse (Gargiulo, 1990). Abuse has many dimensions. In addition, abuse is a cultural concept (Korbin, 1981)— what is abusive in one culture is not necessarily considered abusive in another. We might consider some initiation practices in other cultures to be abusive; on the other hand, other cultures consider the practice of time out or making a hungry child wait until a specific time for lunch to be abusive. Cultures that value children and childhood typically have a low incidence of child abuse (Archard, 1993).

Child abuse can be defined as "the physical, psychological, social, emotional, and sexual maltreatment of a child whereby the survival, safety, self-esteem, growth and development of the person are endangered" (Meston, 1993, p. 5). Child abuse and neglect can take many forms. The following are all examples of child abuse I have read about in newspapers over the past couple of years:

- An infant locked in a car on a hot summer's day

- A child not sent to school regularly

- A toddler sexually abused by her stepfather

- A child told repeatedly by his parents that he was no good and never would be

- Parents not seeking medical help for their seriously ill child
- A baby shaken and brain damaged by a foster mother.

The above are all examples of maltreatment: neglect, physical abuse, sexual abuse, and emotional abuse.

The incidence of child abuse in Canada has to be estimated because of the difficulty in getting accurate data. The most frequent estimates are that one in every 13 or 14 children per 1,000 children is abused (Canadian Institute on Child Health, 1994; National Crime Prevention Council, 1997). The actual number of incidences is thought to be greater than those reported, and there is general agreement that the incidence of reported child abuse has increased in the past 20 years. No matter what the actual statistics may be, even one child per 1,000 abused is too many.

Implication of Violence towards Children for Early Childhood Educators

Violence is an interdisciplinary problem, and prevention and treatment require the involvement of many professionals. Professionals have important roles in identification, prevention, and protection. Early childhood educators need to know the signs of child abuse and neglect and the local reporting procedures. It is a legal requirement to report child abuse and neglect.

Identification of behavioural problems at a young age is also important, as research has shown that disruptive behaviour at age five is a predictor of adolescent juvenile delinquency (Tremblay, 2000). In addition, the early childhood professional can be a supportive adult, which is a protective factor for children (this concept is discussed along with resiliency later in this chapter) as well as a positive role model for both children and parents. A good early childhood program can be a safe haven and a respite for abused and neglected children. Early childhood professionals can foster children's self-esteem, coping skills, and conflict resolution and problem-solving strategies. They also can have a referral function for families to parenting programs such as Nobody's Perfect (developed by Health and Welfare Canada) or Parents in Crisis (a support group for abusive or potentially abusive family members).

Unfortunately, there is no easy quick fix to violence affecting children. According to Isenberg and Brown (1997), "curbing violence requires a systemic approach that includes changes in families, neighborhoods, and schools and requires a critical mass of people working together to change the structure and policies that frame children's lives" (p. 36). Early childhood professionals are part of that critical mass.

Resiliency of Children

Over the years, many researchers and psychologists have pointed out that not all children who have faced trauma, stress, disadvantages, or crises in their lives

FOR REFLECTION

Some countries, such as Denmark, Sweden, Finland, Austria, Norway, Cyprus, and Latvia, have made the practice of spanking children illegal. Quebec's Commission for Human Rights has proposed that Ottawa repeal Section 43 of the Criminal Code that allows parents and teachers to use "reasonable force" to discipline children (Cherney, 1999). Do you support this proposal? Why or why not?

are dysfunctional. Most of these children are healthy people (Rutter, 1985; Weissbourd, 1996). This is not to say that anyone would wish children to suffer, but the reality is that not all children experience a happy, healthy, and safe childhood. Children are not invincible or invulnerable. All children experience stress, disappointments, and negative events in their childhood. In addition, some children experience trauma, grief, serious problems, or multiple difficulties simultaneously or cumulatively.

The effects of life experiences and how individuals respond varies considerably (Rutter, 1985). We can all probably think of a friend or relative who experienced trauma in their childhood yet is a healthy, happy adult. We can also probably think of another person who has never recovered from a similar childhood trauma. Why some children have adverse reactions and others do not has been an area of research for the past 50 years. Researchers have termed this concept *resiliency*.

Resiliency is defined as the "successful adaptation in the individual who has been exposed to biological risk factors or stressful life events, and it also implies an expectation of continued low susceptibility to future stressors" (Werner & Smith, 1992, p. 4). It is the "capacity to bounce back or recover from a disappointment, obstacle, or set back" (Demos, 1989, p. 3). Resiliency is an appealing, optimistic concept, as it places the emphasis on the positive. Some psychologists and therapists think there has been too much emphasis on weakness and the negative and not enough on why children succeed and how they cope with stressors (e.g., Pipher, 1996). This latter orientation has led researchers to look at why some children who experience adversity and a difficult childhood grow up to be healthy, functioning adults.

Perhaps the most widely known research is the longitudinal study by Emmy Werner and her colleagues (Werner, 1989; Werner & Smith, 1982, 1992). This study has followed children on the Hawaiian island of Kauai since 1955. The children were from primarily Japanese, Filipino, and Hawaiian backgrounds. Most of their fathers were unskilled or semi-skilled plantation workers, and 54 percent of the children grew up in poverty. The children were followed from birth to age two and then at ages 10, 18, and 32 (505 individuals were still in the last study).

Overall, Werner and Smith (1992) found that there were "large individual differences among high risk children in response to chronic adversity in their lives" (p. 189). One in three of the high-risk children (10 percent of the total group) "grew into competent, confident, and caring adults whose educational and vocational accomplishments were equal to or exceeded those of the low risk children in the cohort who had grown up in more affluent, secure, and stable environments" (p. 192). Werner and Smith stated that when disadvantages and stress increased and were cumulative in the lives of the children, more protective factors were required to provide for positive developmental outcomes. Three types of *protective factors* identified were

- Individual attributes (e.g., temperament, intelligence, etc.)

- Family factors (e.g., close ties to parents or parent substitutes such as grand-parents or siblings)

- External community factors (e.g., school, church, youth groups, etc.).

Other researchers investigating children's resiliency have also investigated and identified protective factors (e.g., Brooks, 1994; Clark, 1983; Garmezy, 1991, 1993; Osborn, 1990; Rutter, 1985; Silva-Wayne, 1995). These factors include:

Individual attributes of children:

- Good self-esteem and self-efficacy

- Persistence

- Good problem-solving ability

- Sense of hope

- Independence/self-reliance

- Sociability, cheerfulness, responsiveness

- Easy temperament

- Goal-directed

Family factors in children's lives:

- Family as a secure base

- Warm, affectionate bonds

- Family cohesion

- Good supervision and appropriate discipline

- High expectations by parents

- Clean, uncluttered, uncrowded home

- Infrequent family conflict

- Well-defined parent and child roles

- Learning and education promoted

- Mother not depressed

- Responsive and supportive adults

- Children's participation in the family

- Parents aware and respectful of children's individuality

- Child-centred parenting.

Fostering Resiliency

Perhaps the most significant community organizations experienced by most young children are early childhood programs and elementary schools. These programs have been called "safe havens" or "refuges" for children. They can definitely be protective factors for young children and help foster resiliency. Some things that early childhood educators and programs can do are

- Be role models who are friendly and caring

- Have high expectations of children (e.g., not assuming that because children are poor or from difficult home situations, they cannot learn)

- Provide emotional support (i.e., educators as friends, confidants) and teach social skills

- Foster self-esteem (e.g., by recognition of each child's special qualities, praise of children's competence, displaying children's work, etc.)

- Provide developmentally appropriate situations where children can develop and practise independence, self-efficacy, and responsibility

- Provide opportunities for sports, art, music, and field trips that may not be available in the home

- Provide a good physical environment that is clean, well organized, and uncluttered

- Include families in the program (see Chapter 3)

- Recognize and accommodate the variety of family structures (e.g., grandparents as parents).

(For more ideas, see Novick, 1998; Weinreb, 1997. For a description of the child and family resiliency research program at the University of Alberta, see Kysela, McDonald, Drummond, & Alexander, 1996 or www.srv.ualberta.ca/educ/centres/cfrrp/cfrrp.htm.)

Consumerism

In my local grocery store, there are miniature grocery carts for young children and each cart has a flag stating "Customer in Training." While one's first response might be that it's cute or it's nice the store is giving children some way to occupy themselves while shopping with a parent, the deeper question to be asked is: Are we encouraging children to be consumers at ever-younger ages?

The child as consumer, or the target of consumerism, is not a new topic in Canada. In 1978, the Canadian Council on Children and Youth published a report, *Admittance Restricted*, on the status of children in Canada. One trend identified was the view of the child as "a consumer market to be ruthlessly exploited" (p. 154). Another report the next year by the Canadian Commission for the International Year of the Child stated:

> Current manufacturing and advertising practices are frequently at odds with the best interests of children, as evidenced by violence-oriented toys, massive television advertising campaigns using sophisticated marketing techniques and so on. (p. 41)

One wonders what these authors would say about the current state of child consumerism more than 20 years later.

Authors such as David Elkind (1981) have expressed concern that young children are being treated as adult consumers who can accurately assess advertising claims and make informed choices. Lorna Marsden, a former senator and researcher on social change in Canada, has written about our market culture: "By and large, the values we express are framed by the priorities of surrounding adults . . . . These priorities focus on what we think society needs, or our economy needs, or we need; none focuses on the social, emotional and developmental needs of our children" (1996, p. 229). The child as consumer reflects how today's society sees children and perceives their rights. Observation of children's use of consumer goods can cause adults to reflect on the effects of a material culture in their own lives (Seiter, 1993).

A recent child-consumer trend has been the production of series of toys that encourage young children to become collectors (e.g., beanbag toys, action figures, and cartoon characters). These toys are advertised on children's television shows and given away in fast-food restaurants. Therefore, one is not surprised to read that children are considered full-fledged consumers by the time they are three years old (Holst, 1999).

Oppenheim (1987) poses the question of how we can teach children to live in a consumer society. The values of a consumer society, both obvious and implied, are not the ones many parents and educators wish children to espouse. Many early childhood programs I have visited in recent years very directly and explicitly model and teach the values of recycling and reusing.

Families are concerned about the effects of consumerism on children, the need to teach their values to their children, and the financial burden consumerism places on a family. As early childhood educators, we need to be aware of how difficult it is to raise children in today's consumer-oriented society, and provide parents with support and ideas.

One of the most frequently requested presentations I give to parent groups is called Toys from the Kitchen and Basement, which gives dozens of ideas for play materials that parents and children can make at home. This presentation promotes the idea of developmentally appropriate play materials that parents can make at no or little cost while modelling and teaching children to recycle and reuse and spending fun time with their children. Another useful presentation to share with families just before the holiday buying season is called Characteristics and Examples of Good Toys for Children. I think it is important to stress good play materials that are inexpensive, such as crayons and a big pad of paper; that are makeable, such as playdough; and that are open-ended, such as a collection of felt figures and a flannel board. Can you think of some items

Source: Adrian Raeside, *Victoria Times-Colonist,* 1998

you would put on a "good gifts for children" list? (An excellent resource for information on play materials sold in Canada is the Canadian Toy Testing Council's annual *Toy Report,* published every November.)

Older preschoolers are able to begin to understand the nature of consumerism. An interesting discussion with children is what makes a good gift and what gifts you could make for a friend. Diane Levin (1998) suggests that some key questions might be (p. 110):

Addresses and more information on CTTC is povided in the Resources at the end of this chapter.

- How do you decide what to give for a gift?

- What makes a good gift?

- How can you tell if someone will like a particular gift?

- What gifts can you give that don't cost any money?

- What kinds of things can you make as a gift?

- Are there things you can *do* for others as a gift?

Another topic to discuss with children is their experiences with advertising and the actual product. One six-year-old who wanted a particular doll was very disappointed when her mother refused to buy it for her. When asked why it was so important, the child said, "I want Rainbow Brite because her song on TV says she can make you happy even when you feel sad" (Oppenheim, 1987, p. 54). A few weeks later, after her grandmother had bought her the doll, the child said, "I like Rainbow Brite—a lot. But it's not true. She doesn't make me

If Carly were a child in your kindergarten class and her mother came to you for advice, what would you suggest she do?

happy when I feel sad; she doesn't brighten up my day. That's just a song." This child has learned about truth and reality in advertising.

Hurried and Pressured Children

In a recent Canadian parenting magazine, a mother wrote: "My daughter Carly burned out at the tender age of five. The problem? She spent three days a week in daycare, and I had her enrolled in three programs: ballet after kindergarten on Monday, and gymnastics and skating on the weekends. It didn't seem like a lot to me, especially given the busy schedule of many of her friends. I reasoned that she needed opportunities to learn with people who were better teachers than my husband and I" (Cornell, 1998, p. 51).

David Elkind has used the phrase *hurried children* as the title to his modern classic on the subject of overextended and pressured children. He identifies two forms of **hurrying**: developmental and energic. *Developmental hurrying* occurs when children are asked or expected to do activities or behave or understand in ways that are more suitable for older children. *Energic hurrying* is more a quantitative idea of asking children to do too much to the point of unhealthy fatigue or stress.

A study by the Institute for Social Research at the University of Michigan found that the leisure time of children 3 to 12 years old had decreased from 40 percent of their time left after sleeping, eating, personal hygiene, and school/day care in 1981 to 25 percent in 1997 (Labi, 1998). One of the reasons for the decline was the 50 percent increase in participation in organized sports activities. While physical activity is necessary and desirable for young children's healthy development, many educators, psychologists, and parents question the place of organized sports for young children. According to Elkind (1981), "the pressure to engage in organized competitive sports at camp and at home is one of the most obvious pressures on contemporary children to grow up fast" (p. 9).

Several years ago, after giving a presentation in downtown Montreal, I was taking a taxi to the airport and the driver and I got to talking about this topic. He said that the previous month he had driven his 15-year-old to the hockey rink for his usual early morning practice and his son refused to get out of the car. When the father asked what was wrong, the child replied, "I've played hockey for you for the past 10 years. Can I please quit now? I don't like hockey." The father said he felt terrible because he had not realized his son didn't like playing hockey. Many of us can remember doing an activity, such as dance class, music lessons, or sports, because we thought it would make our parents happy. And many parents pay for expensive lessons because they think it will make their children happy and more proficient, well-rounded people.

Pressuring and stressing young children can produce negative results such as sleep disturbances, fatigue, eating problems, headaches, depression, hyperactivity, apathy, withdrawal, and learning and behavioural problems. With older children and youth, the accumulation of both developmental and energic hurrying can lead to self-destructive behaviours such as drug and alcohol use and suicide attempts. Teens comment on "their stress and fatigue originating in childhood. If one has juggled the responsibilities of adulthood since age seven, physical and psychological manifestations of stress and fatigue during one's adolescence should surprise no one" (Kincheloe, 1997, p. 47).

The second most frequent cause of death of Canadian teens from ages 15–19, after motor vehicle accidents, is suicide (Canadian Institute of Child Health, 1994). This rate increased 400 percent between 1960 and 1991 (Canadian Council on Social Development, 1998). And the suicide rate for Aboriginal youth is five times the rate for all other Canadians (Canadian Council in Social Development, 1998).

Hurrying children can also be seen in the academic area. Many early child-hood educators have felt pressured by parents, administrators, and sometimes children to begin formal instruction of reading before it is developmentally appropriate. In my experience, the rationale behind these requests is usually that today's children need a "head start" if they are to be successful in today's high-tech, high-demand world. However, hurrying children does not guarantee suc-cessful children. Stressed for success is not an appropriate or healthy situation for children. Such hurrying threatens the concept of childhood and the right of children to have a childhood.

Celebrating Children

The International Year of the Child in 1979 was proclaimed by the United Nations for the purpose of focusing attention on the world's children and their needs, and what could be done to meet those needs. Many worthwhile proj-ects (e.g., global immunization of children), facilities (e.g., playgrounds and recreation centres), services (e.g., clean water and sanitation), and initiatives (e.g., the Convention on the Rights of the Child) resulted from this year-long celebration of children.

An annual celebration of children is National Child Day on November 20. This date was selected because it was the day in 1959 when the Declaration of Human Rights was adopted by the countries of the United Nations, and it was also the day in 1989 when the Convention on the Rights of the Child was adopted. National Child Day was established as "a special day just for children [to] reflect the growing recognition that children are important and valued members of society" (Health Canada, 1997, p. 4).

In addition to celebrating National Child Day, many communities in Canada stage events throughout the year with a focus on children. For exam-ple, the Northern Saskatchewan International Children's Festival is an annual summer event held in Saskatoon.

For more information about National Child Day, see the address given in the Resources section.

FOR REFLECTION

What activities would you plan to celebrate National Child Day with the children, parents, and staff in your early childhood program?

Summary of this Chapter

The title of this chapter suggests the question, Who are Canada's children and how are they doing? Perhaps a good answer to that question comes from the National Longitudinal Survey of Children and Youth (1996):

> They [Canada's children] come from varied ethnic, religious and linguistic backgrounds; they live in different types of families and households; and they are growing up in families with disparate levels of social and economic resources. At the end of the twentieth century, the lives of children in Canada have never been more complex, the life chances of many of them never more uncertain. (p. 17)

Early childhood educators and programs have an essential role to play in the lives of Canada's children in the twenty-first century.

The key themes in this chapter are the:

* Importance of the early years for children's healthy development
* Demographics of Canadian children, including the decreasing percentage of children and increasing diversity
* Factors necessary for the optimal development of children: health, a safe physical environment, social and emotional security, cognitive stimulation, and economic security
* Health of Canadian children; our children are by and large healthy, although serious problems do exist for some
* Differing views of children and childhood, both historical and contemporary
* Issues facing today's children, including violence, consumerism, and hurrying
* Remarkable resilience of many children
* Rights of all children, which are outlined in the Convention on the Rights of the Child
* Role of the early childhood professional as an advocate for children and families
* Importance of celebrating children.

Key Terms

attachment, 36
childhood, 46
critical periods, 42
First Call, 58

hurrying, 68
resiliency, 63
social competence, 39
stress, 38

Resources

For Sharing with Children

Some books you might want to share with children are:

Fitch, S. & Labrosse, D. 1997. *If you could wear my sneakers!* Toronto: Doubleday Canada. A lovely collection of animal poems related to specific children's rights. Fitch is an award-winning author from Halifax; Labrosse is a past Governor-General's Award winner. My two favourite poems are the ones about bats (protection from abuse) and beavers (child labour).

Kindersley, B. & Kindersley, A. 1995. *Children just like me.* Bolton, ON: Fenn Publishing Ltd. in association with UN Children's Fund. Includes photos of children from 31 countries including Canada, and descriptions of their daily lives. A companion book is *Celebrations!*

Berenstain, S. & Berenstain, J. 1992. *The Berenstain Bears and too much pressure.* New York: Random House. The characters in a popular series of children's books suffer the effects of trying to do too much.

For Further Reading

For more information about the demographics of children in Canada, take a look at the National Longitudinal Survey of Children and Youth. 1996. *Growing up in Canada.* Ottawa: Statistics Canada. The first publication on the longitudinal study that started in 1994. Lots of useful information and statistics.

Another useful resource that's updated yearly is Canadian Council on Social Development's *Progress of Canada's Children.* A summary can be found on their Web site at www.ccsd.ca. The address for ordering is given at the end of Chapter 3.

For children around the world, try Woodhead, J. & Woodhead, M. 1990. *All our children: A window on the world of childhood.* Crow's Nest, NSW: ABC Enterprises for the Australian Broadcasting Company. This book describes the lives of about 55 children in many countries in text and photos.

UNICEF/United Nations Children Fund's annual *The Progress of Nations,* available free from local UNICEF offices, ranks countries on their progress in achieving goals for children. The publication includes yearly focus areas (e.g., birth registration, immunization, and poverty).

For more information on the history of childhood in Canada, try Ashworth, M. 1993. *Children of the Canadian mosaic: A brief history to 1950.* Toronto: OISE Press.

A recent publication on areas of children's development is Shore, R. 1997. *Rethinking the brain: New insights into early development.* New York: Families and Work Institute (visit their Web site at www.familiesandwork.org or phone

212-465-2044). A relevant and readable 91-page summary of the latest on the fast-moving field of brain research.

The title of this one says it all: Katz, L.G. & McClellan, D.E. 1997. *Fostering children's social competency: The teacher's role.* Washington, DC: National Association for the Education of Young Children.

For information and debate on the latest brain research, take a look at these four books:

Bruer, J. 1999. *The myth of the first three years.* New York: The Free Press.

Eliot, L. 1999. *What's going in there? How the brain and mind develop in the first five years of life.* New York: Bantam Books.

Gopnik, A., Meltzoff, A.N., & Kuhl, P.K. 1999. *The scientist in the crib: Minds, brains, and how children learn.* New York: William Morrow and Company.

Kagan, J. 1998. *Three seductive ideas.* Cambridge: Harvard University Press.

A selection of stories and interviews from Canadian children living in poverty is found in Baxter, S. 1993. *A child is not a toy: Voices of children in poverty.* Vancouver: New Star Books Ltd.

Three personal favourites on children and families in today's society are:

Weissbourd, R. 1996. *The vulnerable child: What really hurts America's children and what we can do about it.* Reading, MA: Addison Wesley Longman. Good title; good suggestions.

Pipher, M. 1996. *The shelter of each other: Rebuilding our families.* New York: G.P. Putnam's Sons. A family therapist talks about children, families, and communities. The author also wrote *Reviving Ophelia.*

Louv, R. 1990. *Childhood's future.* New York: Doubleday. Discusses a broad range of issues.

If you'd like to do more reading on children, children's rights, and advocacy, try Elkind, D. 1981. *The hurried child: Growing up too fast too soon.* Reading, MA: Addison Wesley Longman. A modern classic. If you like this book, try his *Miseducation: Preschoolers at risk,* and *All grown up and no place to go: Teenagers in crisis.* Another recommended book is Lundy, C. 1997. *An introduction to the Convention on the Rights of the Child.* Sparta, ON: Full Circle Press.

Also of interest related to children's rights and advocacy is Hatch, V., Hegstad, H. Heimgartner, N. Izumi, W., Konrad, K., & Miller, B. 1992. *Human rights for children: A curriculum for teaching children's rights to children ages 3–12.* Alameda, CA: Hunter House, a project by the Human Rights for Children Committee of Amnesty International USA.

Children's rights and advocacy are also explored in the readable and practical Goffin, S.G. & Lombardi, J. 1988. *Speaking out: Early childhood advocacy.* Washington, DC: National Association for the Education of Young Children.

Useful Addresses and Web Sites

For general information, lots of good links, and excellent places to begin looking for information or organizations, try Child and Family Canada and Health Canada. Child and Family Canada's Web site, located at www.cfc-efc.ca, has links to dozens of non-profit organizations and information on a variety of topics. Health Canada's site, at www.hc-sc.gc.ca, has links to many organizations. There, you can link to the site for National Child Day, which has ideas for activities and suggestions for organizing National Child Day. You can also write or fax for more information to:

National Child Day
Health Canada
Jeanne Mance Building, PL 1909C2
Ottawa, ON K1A 1B4
Fax: 613-952-1556

Other relevant Web sites are:

Canadian Council on Social Development, www.ccsd.ca. This site is operated by the independent, national, non-profit research organization that publishes the annual *Progress of Canada's Children*.

Canadian Immunization Awareness Program, www.ciap.cpha.ca. This site provides information and answers questions on immunization. See also their links to other health organizations.

Canadian Institute of Child Health, www.cich.ca. This site provides information on children's health topics from an institute that has been an advocacy group for children's health and development issues for more than 20 years. Or, you can write, phone, fax, or e-mail the Canadian Institute of Child Health at:

512-885 Meadowlands Dr. E.
Ottawa, ON K2C 3N2
Telephone: 613-224-4144
Fax: 613-224-4145
E-mail: cich@igs.net

Canadian Toy Testing Council, www.toy-testing.org, is a not-for-profit charitable organization that has been evaluating toys (and recently software) for almost 50 years. The Council publishes an annual *Toy Report*, and also gives annual awards for Children's Choice, Best Bet Toys, and Excellence. To write, phone, or fax the Canadian Toy Testing Council:

22 Hamilton Avenue North
Ottawa, Ontario K1Y 1B6
Telephone: 613-729-7101
Fax: 613-729-7185

The Childwatch International Web site, childhouse.uio.no/childwatch, is an international research network for issues related to children's development and well-being, including children's rights and the Convention on the Rights of the Child. To write, phone, fax, or e-mail their office in Norway:

PO Box 1132
Blindern
N-0317 Oslo, Norway
Telephone: 47-22-85-43-50
Fax: 47-22-85-50-28
E-mail: childwatch@uio.no

The National Clearing House on Family Violence's Web site at www.hc-sc.gc.ca/nc-cn provides information on topics related to violence within the family including child abuse, violence against women, elder abuse, and research; the clearing house's information resources include videos, print information, and a directory referral service. Write, phone, or fax them at:

Health Canada
Address Locator 1907D1
Jeanne Mance Building
Tunney's Pasture
Ottawa, ON K1A 1BA
Telephone: 1-800-267-1291
Fax: 1-888-267-1233 or 613-941-7285

Another useful Health Canada Web site is their Childhood/Youth Division site (www.ch-sc.gc.ca/childhood-youth); e-mail to children@hc-sc.gc.ca. Information on safety, nutrition, health, parenting, and child development.

Other useful resources include Canada Youth in Care, www.youthincare.ca, which has links to other groups including child advocates, and ResilienceNet's Internet site (resilnet.uiuc.edu), which has information on resiliency. The contact information for the Canadian Coalition for the Rights of Children (www.cfc-efc.ca/ccrc) is:

Suite 339
180 Argyle Avenue
Ottawa, ON K2P 1B7
Telephone: 613-788-5085

Two sites for information about poverty in Canada are Campaign 2000 (www.campaign2000.ca), and Campaign Against Child Poverty (www.childpoverty.com).

Finally, for statistical information about Canada's children and families, be sure to visit Statistics Canada's Web site at www.statcan.ca. It's an excellent source for accurate and current information on children and families. You can also find a toll-free telephone number in the blue pages of your local telephone directory.

chapter

Canadian Families Today

Everyone you know lives in a family. Every family is a different group of people . . . there are all kinds of families.
—Gretchen Super, What Kind of Family Do You Have?

The above quote encapsulates the themes of this chapter: the importance of families for young children, the universality of families, and the current diversity of families in Canada. This chapter builds on the previous chapter, about children in Canada. Knowledge of families is also a prerequisite for being an educated and informed professional (see Chapter 4) and for understanding and developing programs for families (such as those described in Chapter 11).

Here are some questions to think about while you read this chapter:

· What is a family?
· What are families like today in Canada?
· How are today's families the same and different from your family when you were a young child?
· What stressors face families and what are the implications of these for early childhood programs?
· How do families participate in early childhood programs?
· How can families' participation be facilitated?

Families are key in children's development. The family is the primary environment for children's earliest growth and development. Indeed, the family is the child's first and most influential teacher. Family members are also important participants in an early childhood program.

What Is a Family?

The term **family** should be an easy one to define. After all, everyone has been in a family and knows lots of families. However, the difficulty in defining family is that there are so many different kinds of families and families have so many different functions.

For the International Year of the Family in 1994, the United Nations concluded that "the family unit constitutes the basic unit of society and therefore warrants special attention." And "families assume diverse forms and functions from one country to another, and within each national society" (United Nations Proclamation, 1994, p. 5). However, this is a rather general description of families. The Vanier Institute of the Family considered the role and functions of families when it defined family as:

> any combination of two or more persons who are bound together over time by ties of mutual consent, birth, and/or adoption/placement and who, together, assume responsibilities for variant combinations of some of the following:
> - physical maintenance and care of group members;
> - addition of new members through procreation or adoption;
> - socialization of children;
> - social control of members;
> - production, consumption, and distribution of goods and services; and
> - affective nurturance—love.
>
> (Vanier Institute, 1994, p.10)

Family is obviously not an easy term to define. The above statements illustrate that families can be described or defined by their structure, by the functions they perform, or by how they define themselves. There is no one universal or agreed-upon, or universally applicable, definition of family (Che-Alford, Allan, & Butlin, 1994; Emlen, 1995; Levin & Trost, 1992). Family may mean one thing to some people and something quite different to others. As the quote at the beginning of this chapter said, "every family is a different group of people" (Super, 1991, p. 52). It is important for anyone working with children and families to be aware of this diversity and not to judge or expect all families to look or act like our own family. In addition, it is necessary to recognize that the families we work with also have their own concepts of what a family is, which may or may not be the ones we have.

Before looking at today's Canadian families, find some friends or think of your own family members and complete the following Scavenger Hunt on Families.

Harold C. Mayfield

Does this family look like your family?

Scavenger Hunt on Families

1. Is an only child _____
2. Has/had five or more siblings _____
3. Has a relative who has been divorced _____
4. Has an adult relative who has never married _____
5. Has a friend or relative with both children and stepchildren _____
6. Is a parent in a two-parent family with both parents in the paid labour force _____
7. Uses child care outside of the home _____
8. Has/had four grandparents born in Canada _____
9. Speaks a first language other than English or French at home _____
10. Is 34 to 36 years old _____
11. Lives in an urban area _____
12. Has/had a grandparent who lived past age 90 _____

Trends Affecting Today's Families

Were you able to name someone for every item in the Scavenger Hunt on Families? Which items were the most difficult for you to complete? These were probably ones where the Canadian family has changed the most in recent decades (e.g., because of the declining birth rate, there are fewer families with more than three children).

Some of the major recent demographic changes in Canadian families that have implications for early childhood education and care are

- Lower birth rates and smaller family size
- Declining marriage rates and increased divorce rates
- More lone-parent (i.e., single parent) families
- More families living in poverty
- More mothers in the paid labour force
- Varied family structures
- Increasing diversity.

Each of these trends and its implications will be examined in the following sections.

Lower Birth Rate and Smaller Family Size

Even though the number of families in Canada has increased in the past 25 years (from 5.1 million in 1971 to 7.8 million in 1996) *and* 65 percent of

(*figure 3.1*)   **DECLINING FERTILITY RATES**

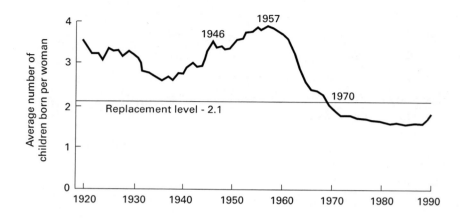

Total fertility rate, 1920 to 1990

Source: Statistics Canada, Catalogue 84-204, in McKie, 1993, p. 3.

families have children at home, family size has decreased (Statistics Canada, 1998a; Vanier Institute, 1996). One major reason for today's smaller Canadian families is the declining birth rate (see Figure 3.1).

Births in Canada

The Canadian birth rate has been falling for more than a century (Baker, 1993). For example,

- in 1921, the average woman in Canada gave birth to 3.5 children in her life;
- by 1960, this rose to a high of 3.9 children;
- but by 1987 it had dropped to the lowest level of 1.6 children (this is also the figure for 1996).

(Baker, 1993; Statistics Canada, 1998k; Vanier Institute, 1994)

In 1995–96, there were 3.2 percent fewer babies born in Canada than the previous year, and this marks the sixth consecutive yearly decline of births and the greatest decline since 1972. Moreover, according to Statistics Canada (1998k), "this trend shows no sign of reversing" (on-line). In addition, fewer women are having three or more children, and having seven or more children has "virtually disappeared" (Grindstaff, 1995, p. 14) (see Figure 3.2).

This decline in births is attributed to a variety of factors including

- The shift from an agrarian to an industrialized society earlier this century,
- The increase in the numbers of working parents,

figure 3.2   CHILDREN AND THEIR SIBLINGS

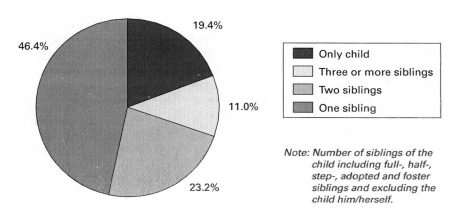

**Distribution of children aged 0 to 11 years by
number of siblings in household, 1994–1995**

- Only child
- Three or more siblings
- Two siblings
- One sibling

*Note: Number of siblings of the
child including full-, half-,
step-, adopted and foster
siblings and excluding the
child him/herself.*

Source: National Longitudinal Survey of Children and Youth (1996) p. 30.

- Increased educational and career opportunities for women,
- Later child-bearing by women,
- Higher costs of living and raising children,
- More women opting not to have any children,
- Fewer infant deaths, which reduces the need to have more children, and
- Improved contraception methods.

The replacement rate for a country (i.e., the number of children that must be born per woman to maintain a steady population) is 2.1 children. As shown in Figure 3.1, the fertility rate in Canada has not been above this level since 1970. Therefore, Canada has become dependent on immigration for maintaining its population (immigration trends are discussed later in this chapter). However, Statistics Canada (1998k) predicts that "unless there is an immediate and significant recovery of the fertility rate (which is highly unlikely) the decline in the number of births will continue before stabilizing at a relatively low level" (on-line). In the 1995 General Social Survey, Statistics Canada reported that nearly half of 20- to 39-year-old Canadians plan to have two children, and a quarter three or more (Dupuis, 1998). (For information on using Statistics Canada as a resource, see Focus 3.1.)

Family Size

The size of the average Canadian family has also decreased in the past 25 years, and "the days of large families appear to be over" (National Longitudinal Survey

Focus 3.1

Statistics Canada: A Resource

In this chapter you may notice that Statistics Canada and the 1996 Census are often cited as a source of information. Statistics Canada is the federal agency responsible for conducting a census every five years. The first census in Canada was done in New France in 1666. The British North America Act of 1867 required a census be done every 10 years; the first was done in 1871. The Canadian census is now done in mid-May every five years; the next ones are scheduled for 2001 and 2006. Data from a census are typically released in phases, beginning about 12 months after the census is completed. This information is available on the Statistics Canada Web site (www.statcan.ca) and in hard copy in public and university libraries. There is also a toll-free telephone number for statistical information (see the blue pages of your local telephone directory). The census and other surveys initiated or conducted by Statistics Canada provide a wealth of fascinating and useful information. The National Longitudinal Survey of Children and Youth described in Chapter 2 is one of Statistics Canada's current projects.

of Children and Youth, 1996, p. 31). In 1971, the average family was 3.7 people, and since 1986 it has been basically stable at 3.1 (Statistics Canada, 1998a). Provincially, the figures are:

3.0 PEOPLE
NOVA SCOTIA
NEW BRUNSWICK
QUEBEC
BRITISH COLUMBIA

3.2 PEOPLE
PRINCE EDWARD ISLAND

3.1 PEOPLE
NEWFOUNDLAND
ONTARIO
MANITOBA
SASKATCHEWAN
ALBERTA
YUKON

3.6 PEOPLE
NORTHWEST TERRITORIES

Based on data from Statistics Canada, 1998c

Age of Mothers

One of the reasons for both a reduced birth rate and smaller family size is the growing number of women who are not only having fewer children, but are having them later. Many women delay both marriage and especially children until they finish their education or establish careers (LaNovara, 1993). The average age of mothers having their first baby in 1971 was 23.3 years; this increased to 26.6 years by 1992 (NLSCY, 1996;). In the recent National

Longitudinal Survey of Children and Youth, the average age of parents of children under 11 was 33.8 years for mothers and 36.6 years for fathers.

Teen parenthood is not as prevalent in Canada as the media and popular press might lead us to believe. In fact, only 0.4 percent of children (20,700 of 4.67 million children) live with teen mothers (NLSCY, 1996). There has been a general decline in teen child-bearing in Canada since the 1970s (Bibby & Posterski, 1992; Vanier Institute, 1994). Interestingly, the fathers of the majority of babies born to teen mothers are not teens but in their 20s or older (Millar & Wadhera, 1997). In the 1960s and 1970s the majority of teen mothers placed their babies for adoption; this trend has reversed and the majority of teen mothers now raise their babies (Baker, 1993; Millar & Wadhera, 1997). The children of teen, lone-parent mothers are more likely to be raised in poverty than children in two-parent families are.

Implications of Birth Rate and Family Size

There are several implications of declining birth rates and smaller families for early childhood programs. One of these is that although there are fewer children per family, there are also fewer family members to care for them. This, coupled with more parents in the labour force (discussed later in this chapter), has resulted in the need for child care outside of the nuclear family and the home.

One contributing factor to smaller family sizes is the growing proportion of families without children. In 1996, more than a third of Canadian families had no children in the home, although the majority of these were "empty nest" families (Statistics Canada, 1996). One possible implication of fewer families with children is the potential for less interest in and support by the general public for issues affecting young children, such as day care and children's rights.

Another implication of the declining birth rate is the smaller number of people available for the labour force and paying taxes. In times of limited resources, competition for funding increases among groups providing programs and services. The Vanier Institute (1994) concluded, "clearly, lower fertility is at the heart of many of the social and economic questions that bedevil business people, communities, planners and lawmakers" (p. 54).

Yet another implication of the reduced birth rates and family size is a reduction in the number of siblings a child has. There are relatively few families with even three children (see Figure 3.2). Children born today are likely to be only children or to have just one sibling. For many children, their socialization and experiences with other children will occur primarily in early childhood programs rather than in the family.

In China, the one-child policy, which limits most families to having only one child, means that many children will never have a sibling, cousin, aunt, or uncle. It does mean that there are four grandparents and two parents for that single child ("the 4–2–1 syndrome"). What possible implications might this have for young children and early childhood programs? How is this situation similar to or different from the situation in Canada?

Marriage and Divorce and Families

Other recent demographic trends that have affected overall family size in Canada are decreasing marriage rates and increased divorce rates.

Marriage in Canada

Marriage is becoming less common and is more likely to end in divorce in Canada than it was 25 years ago. In 1996, there were 5.8 million married-couple families in Canada, which was a decreasing proportion in every province and territory (Statistics Canada, 1997e). However, the proportion of children living in lone-parent and common-law families had increased. For example, in 1971 the marriage rate was 8.9 marriages per 1,000 population; only 20 years later it was down to 6.4, the lowest figure since the 1930s (Che-Alford, Allan, & Butlin, 1994; Statistics Canada, 1993). In 1996, 73 percent of Canadian children lived in married-couple families, which was a decrease from the previous census (Statistics Canada, 1997e).

One reason why marriage rates have decreased is the dramatic increase in common-law relationships. Some Canadians live in these relationships prior to marriage and some as a permanent arrangement (Che-Alford, Allan, & Butlin, 1994). Between the 1991 and 1996 censuses, the rate of common-law couples increased 28 percent and the number of children living with common-law couples increased 52 percent. Fourteen percent of all children in Canada under the age of six were living in common-law families. These data resulted in Statistics Canada concluding, "of all family structures, growth was strongest among common-law couple families" (Statistics Canada, 1997e, on-line). One in seven couples in Canada is living common-law, with 43 percent of all these families living in Quebec and the fastest growth reported in New Brunswick and the Northwest Territories (Statistics Canada, 1997e).

Of those marrying, there is a trend for later ages of first marriage for both men and women. The average age for first marriage

- in 1971 was 22.6 years for women and 24.9 for men;

- in 1990 was 26 years for women and 27.9 for men;

- in 1997 was 27.4 years for women and 29.5 years for men.

(LaNovara, 1993; Vanier Institute, 1994; Statistics Canada, 1999e)

In addition, a growing percentage of the adult population are choosing not to marry at all. For example, the percentage of never-married people aged 20 to 24 has increased from

- 56% in 1971, to

- 85% in 1991, to

- 89% by 1996.

(Statistics Canada, 1997e)

Divorce in Canada

Another significant trend for Canadian families in the past 25 years has been the increased divorce rate. Canada is not unique, as many industrialized countries have experienced the same trend (Baker, 1993). The divorce rate

- in 1966 was 0.5 divorces per 1,000 people,

- in 1971 was 1.4

- in 1991 was 2.7, and

- in 1995 was 2.6.

(Dumas, 1997; Statistics Canada, 1993)

Since 1996, the overall divorce rate has declined slightly (Statistics Canada, 1999). In 1997, divorce rates were highest in the Yukon, Alberta, and British Columbia, and lowest in the Northwest Territories, Newfoundland, and Prince Edward Island (Statistics Canada, 1999a). The current projection is that 35 percent of Canadian marriages will end in divorce within 30 years (Statistics Canada, 1999a).

There are many reasons why people divorce and why divorce rates increased. Some frequently suggested reasons are that

> many people now view marriage as a contract which can be broken under certain circumstances. Growing individualism has discouraged couples from staying together out of duty or concern for family reputation. The logistics of divorce become easier with fewer children per family, and as more women work for pay, divorce is more economically feasible for both men and women. The liberalization of divorce in Canada in 1968 and 1985 has further contributed to rising divorce rates. (Baker, 1993, p. 9)

However, young Canadians are still optimistic about marriage. In a survey of teens, Bibby and Posterski (1992) found that at least 84 percent of the high-school students surveyed plan to marry and have children and a lifelong marriage. It is interesting that while less than half of Canadian women said they'd stay in a bad marriage for the sake of their children, almost 60 percent of men said they would (Frederick & Hamel, 1998).

Implications of Divorce for Early Childhood Programs

The increased divorce rate has meant that the number of young children experiencing marital breakup has tripled in the past 20 years (National Longitudinal Survey of Children and Youth, 1996). Of the children born in 1987–88, 15 percent experienced their parents separating before they were six years old; for those born in 1983–84, 13 percent saw the breakup of their parents' marriage before they were six, and 19 percent before they were ten (Fine, 1999c). For children born to common-law parents, 63 percent of their families break up by the time the children are ten (Marcel-Gratton, 1999). Therefore, the average early childhood program will likely have several children who have experienced—or who are experiencing—their parents' separation or divorce. Such significant upheaval in a young child's life can manifest itself in a variety of behaviours and emotions often observable by early childhood educators.

Parents with joint custody of their children typically both wish to be informed about and included in their children's early childhood program (Frieman, 1998), for example by each parent receiving newsletters and messages and participating in parent conferences and class or centre activities. On the other hand, in some divorces, one parent is denied access to the child or access is restricted. Therefore, early childhood programs need to be informed of these situations so steps can be taken to protect the child. For example, some early childhood programs require official documentation and request a photograph of anyone not permitted contact with a child.

Yet another implication of declining marriage rates and increasing divorce rates has been "the continuation of the upward trend over the past 25 years in the number of lone-parent families" (Statistics Canada, 1997e, on-line).

More Lone-Parent Families

Due to divorce and other factors, the number of lone-parent families increased 19 percent from 1991 to 1996 to number more than 1.1 million families (Statistics Canada, 1997e). This meant that almost one in every five children in Canada was living with a **lone parent** in 1996. For four out of five of these children the lone parent was female, as the number of female lone parents has increased more rapidly than male lone parents. (The term *lone parent* is used rather than *single parent*, as the latter term may imply that the parent has never married and is therefore "single." A lone parent may be never married, divorced, or widowed; it is the more comprehensive term and the one used by Statistics Canada.)

Although "the proportion of lone-parent families is not unprecedented, the dominant reason for the creation of such families has changed. Historically, most lone parents were widows or widowers. Until the early 1970s, more than 60 percent of lone parents were widowed" (Che-Alford, Allan, & Butlin, 1994, p. 17). In 1996, the proportion was only 20 percent widowed because "divorce, separation, or common-law arrangements are key factors in lone parenthood" (Statistics Canada, 1997e).

A National Longitudinal Survey of Children and Youth (1996) diagram reflects the changing look of family types (see Figure 3.3). The authors pointed out that "the figure that stands out is the number of children 0–11 years who are living with one parent" (p. 29). In 1961, the number was 11 percent of families; in 1991 it had nearly doubled to 20 percent. The same study concluded that most of the children in lone-parent families show no problems and that most parents are doing a good job raising their children.

Perhaps the most significant implication of the increase in female-headed lone-parent families is the higher incidence of low income than for male-headed lone-parent families (Statistics Canada, 1997e). This means that more young children are living in poverty.

Additional child-care issues facing families with young children are discussed in Chapters 8 and 12.

FOR REFLECTION

Early childhood programs have traditionally assisted children in making Mother's Day and Father's Day cards and gifts. What would you do about this activity in your program if there were two children who lived with their mothers but never saw their fathers, a child in the custody of her grandmother with no parental access permitted, a father in prison in another province, and a child whose mother had died of cancer in the past year?

figure 3.3   CHILDREN BY FAMILY TYPES

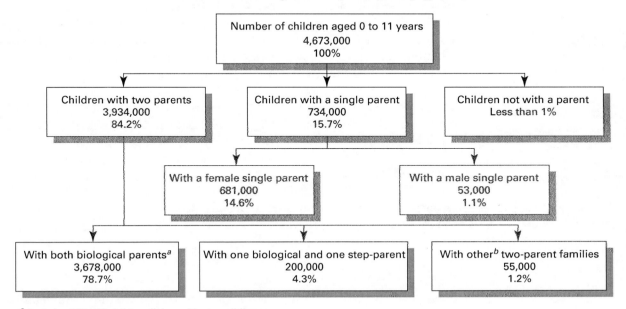

Distribution of children aged 0 to 11 years by family type, 1994–1995

Number of children aged 0 to 11 years
4,673,000
100%

Children with two parents
3,934,000
84.2%

Children with a single parent
734,000
15.7%

Children not with a parent
Less than 1%

With a female single parent
681,000
14.6%

With a male single parent
53,000
1.1%

With both biological parents[a]
3,678,000
78.7%

With one biological and one step-parent
200,000
4.3%

With other[b] two-parent families
55,000
1.2%

[a] *Includes 182,000 children living with step-siblings.*

[b] *Includes children with two adoptive parents, one biological and one adoptive parent, two foster parents, two step-parents, and one adoptive and one step-parent.*

Source: National Longitudinal Survey of Children and Youth (1996), p. 29.

More Families Living in Poverty

Given the recent economic restraints and cutbacks in Canada, the increasing number of families living in poverty is a well-known fact. For example, the number of food banks in Canada increased from 75 in 1984 to more than 625 in 1998 (Tieleman, 2000). According to the Vanier Institute of the Family (1994), the conditions under which poverty thrives include high divorce and unemployment rates, low wages (especially for women), inadequate education and lack of child care and social programs.

Family income declined from 1980 to 1985, recovered in the late 1980s, and then declined 4.8 percent since 1990 (Statistics Canada, 1998i). Poverty has increased in every province since 1990. From 1990 to 1995, the percentage of families below the low-income cut-offs increased from 13 percent to 16 percent (Statistics Canada, 1998i). (Although social policy analysts, editorial writers, child/family advocacy groups, politicians, and others use the low-income cut-offs to measure poverty, "Statistics Canada does not claim that these lines

Child poverty and its effects are discussed in Chapter 2.

FOR REFLECTION

A common recommendation in the preparation of early childhood professionals is that they need to know how to work with children and families in poverty (e.g., Isenberg & Brown, 1997). Do you agree that working with these children and families is different than working with other families? If yes, how is it different and what do you personally need to learn to better work with children and families living in poverty?

measure poverty. Rather, they define a set of income cut-offs below which people may be said to be living in straitened circumstances" [Lochhead & Shillington, 1996, p. 2].)

Although most poor children in Canada live in two-parent families, the poverty rate is higher among lone-parent families, especially if the parent is a woman. A smaller percentage of lone parents, both mothers and fathers, were in the paid labour force in 1996 compared to 1981 (Statistics Canada, 1998i). In addition, there are fewer Canadians working full time and more working part time. Specifically, women in Canada are more likely to work part time than men are; even if working full time, women average only 71 percent of what men earn (Statistics Canada, 1998i). Moreover, the average income for female lone-parent families declined 6.5 percent between 1990 and 1995 (Statistics Canada, 1998i). About 36 percent of visible minorities and 44 percent of the Aboriginal population live in poverty, compared to 20 percent of the general population (Statistics Canada, 1998i). Also, the longer a family remains in a low-income situation, the less likely it will be to escape (Laroche, 1998). Thus, both changes in family composition (e.g., due to divorce) and employment situation can result in young children being raised in a low-income household.

More Mothers in the Paid Labour Force

Many demographers and social historians consider the increase in the number of mothers in the paid labour force during the past 25 years to be one of the most significant demographic trends in the twentieth century. Demographers often refer to *women in the paid labour force.* This is a somewhat awkward phrase to use instead of the more common *working women.* However, it is meant to recognize that women work inside the home as mothers and homemakers and that some women are self-employed and do paid work from their homes. For these women, the terms *women who work* or *women who work outside the home* are not accurate—hence the phrase *women in the paid labour force.*

Canadian women have always worked both in and outside the home. For example, in 1871 42 percent of the individual workforce in Montreal was female, as was 33 percent in Toronto (Nett, 1979). The Canadian Families Project found that in the 1901 census, the category "living on their own" was disproportionately female and included widows, lone parents, and other female heads of households (i.e., no male breadwinners) (Sager, 1998).

The biggest increases of women in the paid labour force in Canada occurred in the 1970s and 1980s. There are several reasons given for the increase of women, especially mothers, in the paid labour force, including

- higher educational levels of women,

- delayed marriage and child-bearing,

- increased career opportunities,

- the necessity of two incomes,

- fewer children at home needing care,

- increased maternity and parental leaves and benefits,

- changing gender roles, and

- improvements in birth control.

The number of fathers staying at home and caring for children has increased from one to six percent in the past 20 years (Marshall, 1998b). While some of this may be by choice, much may be due to economic hard times and resulting job loss or cutback of hours.

Dual-earner families are now the norm in Canada. Specifically, the percentage of dual-earner families with children under six increased from 38 percent in 1981 to 56 percent in 1996. However, for female lone parents with preschoolers there was a decrease from 41 percent in the paid labour force in 1981 to 38 percent in 1996 (Statistics Canada, 1998j). Almost three-quarters of women with children both under and over six years of age are employed (Statistics Canada, 1996). Although the percentage of mothers in the paid labour force increases with the age of their children, a recent trend has been the relatively quick return of new mothers to the labour force. Nearly nine out of ten mothers of newborns return to work within a year, and many of those return sooner than 12 months (Statistics Canada, 1999b). One implication of this is the need for infant care.

Another significant trend that will be discussed further in the section on work-related child care in Chapter 8 is the variety of work patterns and arrangements of Canadian families. For example, parents with children under six are least likely to work a traditional Monday to Friday daytime schedule (Marshall, 1998a).

Implications of the trend of more dual-earner families in the labour force are the need for and use of out-of-home care for young children, the subsequent challenge of finding accessible and affordable child care for the times when it is needed, and the task of balancing family and job responsibilities.

This topic is discussed later in this chapter under the heading Stressors Facing Today's Families.

Varied Family Structures

Diversity is also a characteristic of the structures of families today. "There are all kinds of families" is a true statement for Canadian families. While the statistics and demographics given above are useful in providing a general, overall picture of today's families, it is important to remember that there is no one type of family—there are many, many types. According to Mirabelli and Glossop (1997), "for some years now, families have come in so many different forms that it would be misleading to paint a picture of one type of family and label it 'The Canadian Family'" (p. 6).

If you think of your own family, you may be able to quickly identify several different family patterns. For example, if my family had a reunion and all my cousins came, there would be individuals who are married with children, never married, divorced with children, married with no children, remarried with children and stepchildren, divorced with no children, and married with grand-children. Here are seven family patterns—and I have only nine cousins!

Sociologists have long examined the different patterns of families. There are nuclear families, blended families, lone-parent families, joint-custody families, adopted families, foster families, extended families, common-law families, gay/lesbian families, relatives as guardians, communal families, and other varia-tions. One study of families identified 196 patterns (Petzold, 1994). Statistics Canada has stated that "the profile of Canadian families is one of growing diver-sity" (LaNovara, 1996, p. 7). Moreover, it is expected that this trend of family diversity will continue.

The structure of families changes over time, as seen in the demographic trends discussed in this chapter. The structure of individual families also changes as children are born, grow up, leave home, and begin families of their own. In just one class of four- and five-year-olds that I taught, the parents ranged in age from late teens to early sixties; some children had no siblings, others had infant, school-aged, or teen siblings, and one child was an uncle—at age four!

As shown in Figure 3.4, children in Canada live in a variety of family structures. According to the Vanier Institute of the Family (1993), "less than a

figure 3.4　　CHILDREN AND THEIR STEPFAMILIES

Distribution of children aged 0 to 11 years by step-family type, 1994–1995

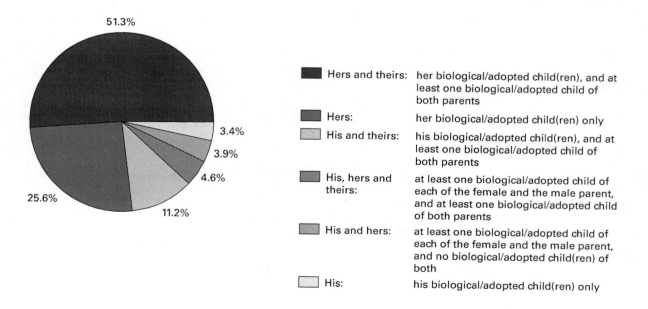

Source: National Longitudinal Survey of Children and Youth (1996), p. 30

lifetime ago, the majority of Canadian families were composed of two adults in a permanent union that produced three to five children. All other kinds of families were the exception. Today, the exceptions are the rule" (p. 2). One implication of the above statistics is that many children will experience more than one of these settings before they are adults, including many children in early childhood programs.

Another implication for early childhood professionals is the need to be aware of the potential for diverse family structures as well as to be knowledgeable about different types of family structures. For example, some ethnic and cultural groups may be more likely to have extended families than others might. In the children's book *First Nations Families* (Clark, 1996), a variety of extended family patterns are described and illustrated. Members of the extended families portrayed in this book include stepfathers and stepmothers, stepsisters and stepbrothers, half-brothers and half-sisters, grandmothers and grandfathers, aunts and uncles, cousins, great-grandmother, sister's boyfriend, cousin's spouse and children, and cousin's girlfriend. Clark concludes the book with the statement "There are many kinds of First Nations families" (p. 40).

Another family pattern is families headed by gay/lesbian parents. Although it is estimated that one in ten people are gay or lesbian (Boyd, 1999), these families are not a homogeneous group. For example, some individuals may have been in a previous heterosexual relationship, and some may be openly gay/lesbian and others not. However, gay/lesbian families generally perceive themselves as similar to other parents, particularly single or divorced parents (Clay, 1990). An issue for a gay/lesbian family can be how others respond to its non-stereotypical structure. An implication of this issue for early childhood educators is to be aware of the possible biases of other adults and children. For example, all children should feel comfortable and secure drawing, displaying photos of, and discussing their own families.

FOR REFLECTION

The children in your program have been painting pictures of their families for an upcoming open house. One of the children points to Jessica's painting and asks, "Why does Jessica's picture have two mommies and no daddy?" You know that Jessica's parents are a lesbian couple. How do you reply to the child who asked that question? How would you reply to a parent who asked about Jessica's parents?

Increasing Diversity

The Canadian population is becoming more diverse. This fact is evident in the variety of ethnic and cultural groups across the country. A multicultural population is not new for Canada. Historically, Canadian settlers were "multicultural, multi-ethnic, and multi-racial" (Eichler & Bullen, 1986, p. 9). Canada has long been a nation of immigrants. In fact, immigration has been responsible for approximately 20 percent of Canada's population growth since the beginning of the twentieth century (Vanier Institute, 1994).

Immigration

Immigration to Canada increased 14.5 percent in the five years from 1991 to 1996, while at the same time the Canadian-born growth rate was only 4 percent (Statistics Canada, 1997f). Canada's population growth is dependent on the average annual 235,000 immigrants because of the below-replacement birth rate. Immigrants made up 17 percent of the Canadian population in 1996, which was the largest percentage in more than 50 years. However, the number of immigrants in 1998 declined 20 percent and was the lowest level since 1988 (Duffy, 1999).

One significant trend has been the shift in the sources of immigration. In 1981, 67 percent of all immigrants to Canada were born in Europe. However, by 1996, European immigration had declined to 47 percent while immigration from Asia and the Middle East had increased from 14 percent to 31 percent (Statistics Canada, 1997f). The most frequent countries of origin for recent immigrants were Hong Kong, the People's Republic of China, India, the Philippines, and Sri Lanka. Ontario, British Columbia, and Quebec became home to most of these recent immigrants (Statistics Canada, 1997f).

In 1996, 85 percent of all immigrants lived in metropolitan areas, especially Toronto, Vancouver, and Montreal (Statistics Canada, 1997f). Toronto has the largest immigrant population of any city in Canada, and this population increased from 38 percent in 1981 to 42 percent in 1996 (Statistics Canada, 1997f).

Toronto is the preferred destination, with 42 percent of all new immigrants to Canada settling there; 18 percent go to Vancouver and 13 percent go to Montreal. These numbers are not surprising, as urban life is typical for more than three-quarters of *all* Canadians (Statistics Canada, 1996). In Montreal, recent immigrants are most frequently from Haiti, Lebanon, and France (Statistics Canada, 1997f). In Vancouver, the majority of recent immigrants are from Asia, especially Hong Kong, China, and Taiwan. The recent increases in immigration have been responsible for British Columbia having the highest provincial growth rate (Statistics Canada, 1997f). This immigration is one of the reasons why it is estimated that in 2001 Chinese will replace French as the second most common language spoken outside Quebec (Klotz, 1999).

Aboriginal Peoples

National Aboriginal Day is June 21. See Resources for contact information.

Aboriginal peoples made up three percent of Canada's total 1996 population of approximately 30 million people. The 1996 census reported that

- 35 percent of all Aboriginal people were children under age 15 (this number was 20 percent for Canada as an average);

- The Aboriginal population was 10 years younger than the general population (25.5 years vs. 35.5);

- Four in five Aboriginal people lived west of Quebec;

- Ontario had the most North American Indians;

- Alberta had the largest Metis population;

- The Northwest Territories had the largest Inuit population;

- The average Aboriginal person's income was 34 percent below the national average;

- 30 percent lived on a rural reserve;

- One-quarter had an Aboriginal language as a mother tongue, most frequently Cree, Inuktitut, and Ojibway;

- 54 percent of Aboriginal people over the age of 15 did not have a high-school diploma (compared to 35 percent of non-Aboriginals); and

- 4.5 percent had a university degree (compared to 16 percent of non-Aboriginals).

(Statistics Canada, 1998f)

> *Aboriginal Head Start is described in Chapter 11.*

Aboriginal people live in all parts of Canada. There are many different Aboriginal groups, and it is not accurate or appropriate to generalize from one group to another. For example, an Aboriginal family living on Baffin Island is not the same as a family living in Regina or a family living on-reserve in Ontario.

A Greying Canada

Another demographic trend that is affecting Canada is the increasing number of older people. The 1996 census confirmed the "aging trend in Canada's population. The working-age population is graying, and there are more seniors than ever before" (Statistics Canada, 1997c, on-line). This trend is due to a combination of the aging of the baby-boom generation (people born between 1946 and 1966) and the increasing life expectancies of Canadians.

The population profile for Canada is shifting as the population ages (see Figure 3.5). Note particularly the changes for the age groups over 60 in 1995 compared to the projections for 2016. The number of senior citizens is currently increasing at double the rate of the general population (Statistics Canada, 1997c). The Canadian population is definitely getting older and will continue to do so. For example, the median age of Canadians

- in 1891 was 21.4 years;

- in 1991 was 33.5 years; and

- in 1996 was 36.1 years for women and 34.5 years for men.

(Statistics Canada, 1997c)

Moreover, by 2026 the median age is projected to be 43 to 44 years (Statistics Canada, 1998d).

Not very long ago, it was rare to hear of anyone reaching his or her one-hundredth birthday. Now this seems like a much more common occurrence. In fact, one of the fastest growing groups in Canada is the over-90-year-olds. Moreover, the number of people over 90 is projected to nearly triple by 2016, while the population of children under nine years of age is projected to increase only slightly (Statistics Canada, 1998d). Three- and four-generation families will become more common (Che-Alford & Hamm, 1999). However, this does not

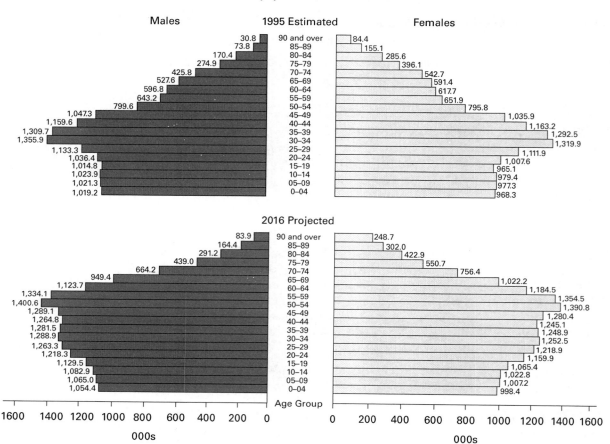

figure 3.5   CANADA'S POPULATION PYRAMID

Canada's population, 1995 and 2016

Source: Statistics Canada, Catalogue nos. 91-213-XPB and 91-520-XPB, 1994

Intergenerational programs are described in Chapter 11.

FOR REFLECTION

What are some possible implications for early childhood programs of the increasing population of senior citizens in Canada?

necessarily mean three or four generations living together. Currently, less than three percent of all Canadian households are three-generation. Their number has been increasing, due, in part, to the increase in Asian immigration and their culture's tradition of extended families living together (Che-Alford & Hamm, 1999).

Senior citizens today and in the future are healthier and more active than many were able to be in the past. More grandparents are functioning as parents for their grandchildren on a full-time or part-time basis (Smith, Dannison, & Vach-Hasse, 1998). In addition, many early childhood programs have included seniors in their programs as volunteers, resource people, members of an advisory board, and in other roles.

Seniors play active roles in many families.

An implication of the changing nature of Canadian society is the need to be knowledgeable about the diversity of today's families, as well as accepting, respecting, valuing, and honouring this diversity. Early childhood educators need to recognize that they cannot generalize from their own families and their own childhood experiences to the children and families with whom they work. Flexibility and accommodation can result in greater inclusion of all families in the early childhood program. For example, for lone parents who work days, a conference or meeting at their child's early childhood program during the day may be difficult or impossible to do; however, evenings may be possible, especially if child care is provided. For other parents who work evening or night shifts, a day meeting or appointment may be more convenient. Sometimes only one parent might come to a meeting or program at the day-care centre; with other families, several members of the extended family might come. For some children, their "parent" is actually their grandparent or an older sibling. Recognizing this diversity can enrich an early childhood program. For more on diversity, see Focus 3.2.

Cultures, Families, and Child-Rearing

Culture is "a very powerful force in young children's lives, [that] shapes representations of childhood, values, customs, child rearing attitudes and practices, family relationships and interactions" (Rodd, 1996, p. 326). Raising children is one of the primary roles of families across cultures; however, there are cross-cultural differences in child-rearing practices and beliefs (e.g., Bhavnagri & Gonzales-Mena, 1997; Bornstein, 1991; Clark, 1981; Harrison, Wilson, Pine Chan, & Buriel, 1990; LeVine, Miller, & West, 1988; McGillicuddy-DeLisi & Subramanian, 1996). There is no one "right" way to raise children; and likewise, there is no one "right" way to care for and educate children.

Child-rearing reflects and is part of a culture. Given the increasing diversity of Canada's population, early childhood educators are more and more likely to have families from different cultures in their programs. Therefore, early childhood professionals need to be aware of the child-rearing beliefs and practices of the families with whom they work. One infant development worker commented

> There are differences in how caregivers respond to crying, how much face-to-face interaction occurs with babies, the extent to which babies are calmed or stimulated, whether children are carried a lot, how much parents talk to children. There's a lot of variety in age-related expectations of children, including at what age a child is considered capable of being self-regulating and responsible for his or her own behaviour. (from Kellerman, 1996, p. 23)

Differences in child-rearing beliefs and practices are also seen for preschool and primary-aged children. For example, some families stress children's obedience, respect for elders and authority, diligence, and deference to the group (Chen & Uttal, 1988; Lin & Fu, 1990; Scarcella, 1990). In some cultures, there is an emphasis on the extended family and a reliance on kinship groups for resources, advice, support, and assistance (Salend & Taylor, 1993). In others, there is an emphasis on independence, self-reliance, and assertiveness (Okagaki & Diamond, 2000). For some groups, cooperation, sharing, generosity, and respect for age and traditions are valued highly (Sipes, 1993).

How families use language with their children and how they foster language development may vary across cultures. For example, European and North

American families use frequent verbal interactions with their children, while other cultures do less of this (Richman, LeVine, New, Howrigan, Welles-Nystrom, & LeVine, 1988). For example, Delpit (1990) discusses the strong tradition of oral storytelling among Aboriginal groups and the valuing of oral expression abilities by Afro-American communities.

Another area for potential cultural differences between families and an early childhood program is around basic child-care needs such as feeding, sleeping, toileting, and dressing children. Food can be a particular concern for some families (Bernhard, Lefebvre, Chud, & Lange, 1995). A parent may be justifiably concerned, for religious reasons, that their child is not being fed any pork or products with ingredients derived from pork, such as lard (this is a common ingredient in baked goods). In addition, many young children have definite culturally based food preferences and may not want or like to eat food that is unfamiliar to them. In some cases, children from certain ethnic groups may have difficulty digesting some foods, such as milk products.

On the other hand, food can be an excellent way of sharing and learning about different cultures for both children and their families. A potluck supper where families share their favourite foods can be a popular, enjoyable, and educational occasion. Family members can also be encouraged to come to the early childhood program to demonstrate how to prepare their traditional foods, especially those associated with special occasions and holidays. This family participation helps young children to learn about other cultures and to appreciate new foods. It is also a more authentic activity than the so-called "Tacos on Tuesday" tourist approach. Also, in some communities in Canada, various groups have established Saturday schools to teach children how to speak, read, and write their native language as well as to learn the traditions of their culture. For example, in Victoria, British Columbia, there is a Chinese school located in Chinatown.

Another area for possible cultural differences is curriculum and program philosophy. According to Guild (1994), "there is very little disagreement that a relationship does exist between the culture in which children live (or from which they are descended) and their preferred ways of learning" (p. 17). Some children may prefer more structured learning situations where they can interact with an adult, while others may prefer peer interaction and cooperative work (Chamot, 1988). Some families may place high value on cooperation with the group, sharing, and non-competitive activities (Little Soldier, 1989; Sipes, 1993). Others may place a high value on individualism and independence (Bromer, 1999). Still other families may advocate formal academic instruction combined with the encouragement of perseverance in learning tasks (Tobin, Wu, & Davidson, 1989). Some families may be concerned about the lack of academic and cognitive activities and expect a very structured early childhood program (Bernhard, et al., 1995). An important caution in looking at children's and families' learning styles is not to make the assumption that all members of a particular ethnic or cultural group will necessarily have the same learning styles, preferences, or experiences.

Early childhood professionals can do much to make their programs cultur-ally relevant, appropriate, and accommodating. A first step is to become knowl-edgeable about the diversity of Canada and its families. The professional needs to have time to explore the community and become familiar with the back-grounds, cultures, experiences, and values of its families. One also needs time to seek out the resource organizations and people in a community that can pro-vide information and advice. Understanding, respecting, and honouring the various cultures and backgrounds of children and families can be invaluable in planning relevant and appropriate programs.

A position statement from the National Association for the Education of Young Children (1996) advocates that

> For the optimal development and learning of all children, educators must *accept* the legitimacy of children's home language, *respect* (hold in high regard) and *value* (esteem, appreciate) the home culture, and *pro-mote* and *encourage* the active involvement and support of all families, including extended and non-traditional family units. (p. 5)

An action the early childhood professional can take is to incorporate and integrate an anti-bias curriculum into the early childhood program. **Anti-bias** is defined as "an active/activist approach to challenging prejudice, stereotyping, bias, and the 'isms'"[e.g., sexism and racism] (Derman-Sparks & ABC Task Force, 1989, p. 3). It is a step beyond recognition and accommodation of multi-culturalism. It is more than being non-biased. It means "taking a stand against unfair treatment associated with one of the areas of diversity where bias may exist" (Hall & Rhomberg, 1995, p. 2). According to Hall and Rhomberg, these areas of bias can include appearance, gender, socio-economic status, culture, race, family composition, age, ability, sexuality, and beliefs such as religion. An anti-bias curriculum addresses children's own identities, attitudes, familiarity, and comfort with diversity; abilities to recognize and resist stereotyping and discrimination; and the importance of creating an anti-bias environment.

Another action early childhood professionals can take is to examine the skills and attitudes we bring to an early childhood program. The Consortium on Diversity in Education (1997) has outlined five areas of these skills and attitudes that are considered important for professionals working with multi-cultural and multi-ethnic groups:

- Self-understanding,

- Understanding of others and their cultures,

- Interacting well with others,

- General skills such as accepting ambiguity and change and honouring diversity, and

- Effective cross-cultural communication skills such as accepting silences, avoiding judgments, clarifying perceptions, and monitoring one's own feel-ings and reactions.

FOR REFLECTION

A director of a large day-care centre once told me: "We can't celebrate every holiday, so in our centre we don't celebrate any." What are the pros and cons of this policy?

Recognition, appreciation, and accommodation of the diversity of children and families across Canada today can make for better and higher-quality programs.

Roles of Families in Early Childhood Programs

Just as there is no one family pattern in Canada, there is no one "best" role for families in early childhood programs. Again, diversity is a theme. (The term **family involvement** is used here rather than *parent involvement* in recognition that all family members, not only parents, may participate and be partners in an early childhood program.) There are a variety of roles for family members in early childhood programs. Because of the diverse patterns, interests, talents, and circumstances of families, this variety is both desirable and practical. Some families may have more time available for in-program participation; others may be willing to take on tasks such as making or repairing materials at home, or fundraising with other parents.

The family's involvement in young children's education has long been a part of early childhood education. Many of the early theorists commented on its role and importance (see Chapter 5). Families want what is best for their children and most would like to participate in their children's early childhood program; however, because of constraints such as time, energy, work schedules, lack of transportation, and other family care responsibilities, they may not be able to do so. Therefore, the provision of options for family involvement can enable more families to participate.

Families in early childhood programs can be involved in their children's program through one or more types of family involvement (Epstein, 1996; Gordon & Breivogel, 1976; Greenwood & Hickman, 1991; Olmstead, 1991). They may be an audience (i.e., recipients of information about the program and their child's progress). Or they might participate in the program as volunteers, resource people, or paraprofessionals. Or they might do activities at home with their child such as reading stories or helping their child with "homework" (e.g., looking at home for something round). Or they might participate in the operation of the program by being members of the board or advisory committee or helping to plan or evaluate the program.

Generally, families want to be involved in their children's education; they want to be informed about what their children are doing, and what they can do to help (Cleve, Jowett, & Bate, 1982; Epstein, 1990; Galinsky, 1990; Mayfield, 1990). Studies have shown that family involvement can have positive effects on children, adult family members, and programs. These effects can include

- Recognition of the importance of education,

- Appreciation for the role of families in the education of children,

- More positive attitudes toward education and educators,

- Improved academic achievement by children,

- Better understanding of curriculum by families,

- Increased social network,

- Increased likelihood of seeing their children and themselves as competent,

- Increased self-esteem,

- Improved job-related skills,

- Increased knowledge of child development and parenting strategies,

- Increased knowledge about children and their families,

- Increased appreciation of families as partners,

- More likelihood of reinforcing activities at home with children as well as siblings, and

- More confidence in dealing with schools and other agencies.

(Berger, 1991; Dauber & Epstein, 1993; Eccles & Harold, 1993; Epstein 1991, 1995, 1996; Henderson, 1988; Swap, 1992)

Research has shown that parents want to participate and that they do not have to be middle-income or well educated to do so effectively (Chavkin & Williams, 1989; Coleman, 1997; Epstein & Dauber, 1991). In addition, reviews of the research have reported that (a) there are similarities between parents and educators (e.g., they have the same goals for children), that (b) family involvement programs take time to develop and should continue through high school for maximum effectiveness, and that (c) they should include all families (Epstein, 1991).

The overall and types of effects of family involvement are disputed among researchers. Some researchers claim that "there is consistent evidence that parents' encouragement, activities, interest at home and their participation at school affect their children's achievement, even after the students' ability and socioeconomic status are taken into account" (Epstein, 1991, p. 262). Other researchers claim that "the effectiveness of family involvement programs has not been adequately documented" and we are not able to say unequivocally that family involvement is effective (Coleman & Churchill, 1997, p. 147).

It is logical to recognize that not all family involvement endeavours are necessarily or equally effective, and that some may not be effective at all or may even have negative effects. Family involvement needs to be appropriate, well planned, and of high quality if there are to be positive effects. Some strategies and ideas for providing quality, effective family involvement are discussed in the next section.

FOR REFLECTION

The National Association for the Education of Young Children's Position Statement on Responding to Linguistic and Cultural Diversity— Recommendations for Effective Early Childhood Education states, "Parents and families should be actively involved in the learning and development of their children. Teachers should actively seek parental involvement and pursue establishing a partnership with children's families" (NAEYC, 1996, p. 8). In what circumstances might family involvement not be a good idea? Why do you think so?

Strategies and Ideas for Involving Families

There are many ways to involve families in early childhood programs. As Powell (1998) states, "across all populations and programs, a major challenge is to develop ways of engaging parents that respond to a family's interests and life circumstances" (p. 63). Doing so can be a special challenge given the diversity of today's Canadian families. There are also a few obstacles. There is no one family involvement strategy or activity that is guaranteed to work with all families all of the time.

One strategy to help ensure that the family involvement activities that you plan are appropriate and appealing to families is to provide for options. Having only one option does not provide any choice for families; it's a take-it-or-leave-it situation. When an early childhood educator is just beginning in a new program, perhaps two or three options may be all that one can reasonably plan and implement. However, with experience and time, the number of available options can be increased. A caveat here is that more family involvement is not always better. Appropriate, quality options are preferable to simply lots of poorly planned and implemented options. Some typical options for family involvement include:

- Working with the children in the early childhood program

- Working with their own children at home (e.g., book bag programs, reading to their children, etc.)

- Attending workshops

- Attending family potluck suppers, picnics, parties, or slide shows of the children's activities and projects

- Assisting on field trips or participating in family field trips on weekends

- Making or repairing materials for the program at home

- Collecting scrap or recycled material for the children to use in art and construction activities

- Attending meetings to hear a guest speaker

- Participating in family nights, fathers' Saturday, or other activities

- Attending family–teacher conferences

- Using the school library or parent library

- Planning, attending, or participating in child development or parenting courses

- Participating in adult discussion or support groups

- Reading to children (in the program or at home)

- Helping with craft projects

- Helping assemble booklets of recipes, songs, or fingerplays that the children know

- Being the photographer on field trips, at parties, and other important events

- Fundraising

- Being a computer assistant for children (and educators!)

- Checking and organizing materials for a book bag or activity box/learning packet program

- Being a scribe for children

- Helping to plan or evaluate the program

- Serving on the board or advisory committee of the program

- Being an advocate for children and early childhood education.

These are some ideas—this is not by any means a definitive list of options.

A second strategy that facilitates the provision of appropriate options for family involvement is to assess what is needed and wanted. The early childhood professional, no matter how knowledgeable and experienced, needs to ask the families what they perceive are their needs and what they would like in the way of family involvement. For example, parent cooperatives (described in Chapter 9) have ongoing parent education as part of their total program. These often include evening meetings or workshops on a variety of topics related to young children, their development, care, and education. Doing a brief survey at the beginning of the year and perhaps again during the year will help to ensure that the topics are relevant, of interest, and of use to the parents. An early childhood educator should not presume to know what families need or want.

A third strategy to encourage family involvement in programs is ongoing communication. And the related fourth strategy is to communicate frequently. Much of this frequent and ongoing communication is done in early childhood programs through short chats with families when they drop off or pick up their children or by telephone calls and brief notes to families one doesn't see very frequently. The increasing availability of answering machines, voice mail, Web sites, and e-mail makes communication easier. One useful idea for voice mail is to have one designated number or multiple lines for information of interest to parents (e.g., press 3 for dates of upcoming events; press 4 for the snack and lunch menus for next week; press 5 for a summary of the children's activities for the past week, etc.). (For more information on using voice mail see Cameron & Lee, 1997.)

Not every family has access to electronic technology such as e-mail, so other options for ongoing communication could include

- Weekly newsletters (translated if necessary)

- Monthly calendars of the children's activities (past and/or future) and song–fingerplay–poetry booklets

- A "this is what we're doing now" bulletin board near the main door with photos, samples of children's work, captions or brief explanations written by the staff or dictated by the children

- A welcome letter, telephone call, and/or home visit before a child begins in the program
- Telephone calls to families by staff or telephone trees by volunteers or families
- Videos, slide shows, or photo albums of children's activities (can be shared first at a family night and then made available for home viewing)
- Communication journals or logs that go back and forth between home and the early childhood program (also known as "back-and-forth" books)
- Portfolios of the children's artwork, photos of their activities, audiotapes of their storytelling, copies of dictated stories, songs they know, lists of favourite books, and so on.
- Designated time for telephone calls or drop-in visits when specific staff will be available for conversation, to answer questions, or to provide information
- "Ask me" notes (Berger, 1996) placed in the child's lunch box or pinned to his or her clothes. These tell the family that the child has something special to tell them, such as the first time she managed her boots and mitts all by herself or he went on a visit to the library. For the latter, the note might read, "Ask me where I went today."

In addition, the children themselves are a major source of information about programs for their families (Cattermole & Robinson, 1985).

Another strategy is to actively recruit families to participate in the program. For example, some family members who have been invited to come on a field trip or serve as a resource person (e.g., cooking with the children, demonstrating a craft, etc.) have then continued on. In addition, some have become active in program planning and evaluation. Some educators discuss the options for family involvement in the program at home visits before the child begins the program or during conferences with the parents. It is not unusual for programs with highly successful family involvement to be approached by family and community members willing to volunteer in the program. Word of mouth is a powerful recruitment strategy. Part of a recruitment strategy is to provide a welcoming atmosphere for families. Ways to foster this atmosphere could include posting an explicit policy statement on the value of family involvement; setting up a place for volunteers to hang their coats and have a cup of tea or coffee; greeting volunteers when they arrive; and thanking volunteers for their help every time they finish and perhaps hosting a special recognition activity at the end of the year.

Some programs plan activities that target specific groups of parents or families. For example, one-time or ongoing activities can be planned for fathers and their children (e.g., see McBride & Rane, 1997).

Hoover-Dempsey and Sandler (1997) identified three factors that influence families' involvement in their children's education:

1. Parents' beliefs about their role in their children's lives (these beliefs help determine the types of activities they will do);

2. Parents' feelings of efficacy (i.e., if they have confidence in their own abilities and think they'll be effective); and

3. Parents' perception of whether their involvement is wanted. Active recruitment and a welcoming atmosphere can foster a positive view.

Yet another strategy for encouraging and facilitating family involvement is careful planning. Effective family involvement does not just happen. It is the result of careful consideration and planning. Some points to consider include how the families would like to participate; what types of family involvement are needed in the program; what options are possible; how family needs (e.g., transportation, child care, etc.) can be accommodated; what activities can be provided for families who cannot attend centre-based activities or who can attend only occasionally; what orientation, training, and support should be provided for volunteers working with the children; and how family involvement can be initiated and then perhaps expanded.

Still another strategy is monitoring and assessing family involvement. This process should be ongoing and can be done by observation, interviews, or surveying families. Getting feedback that can help improve the program and family involvement in this is important.

Obstacles to Family Involvement

Planning and implementing family involvement is not without its disappointments and obstacles. Even though families wish to be involved, sometimes they cannot be, for a wide variety of reasons. The obstacles mentioned most frequently by the early childhood professionals and parents with whom I have discussed this topic are

- Work schedules

- Lack of time (for both families and educators)

- Other family members at home who need care (e.g., a younger child or an elderly parent)

- Lack of transportation

- Overextended and exhausted families

- Concern over low literacy skills or limited English or French

- Lack of knowledge about family involvement in general and lack of information about the current options available

- Parental doubts that their participation could make a difference

- Cultural attitudes of awe and deference to teachers and authority figures

- Mistrust due to a previous bad experience

- Parents' own negative school experiences

- Fear of parents/fear of educators

- Negative attitudes of families and/or early childhood educators

- Unwelcoming environment.

Some of these obstacles are easier to overcome than others. Research shows that parents who work full time, lone parents, families with transportation difficulties, and fathers tend to be less involved, on average, unless steps are taken and activities planned to facilitate their participation (Epstein, 1995). Work schedules may be accommodated for some families by scheduling meetings on evenings or weekends. Transportation may be provided or arranged through carpooling or changing the time of a meeting to fit with the local bus schedule. An unwelcoming environment can be made more friendly. One woman who walked her grandson to and from kindergarten every day felt she was not welcome or wanted because "there isn't even anywhere to sit" (Andrews & Sweeney, 1986, p. 3).

Not all families will participate in an early childhood program, even if they would like to do so. Sometimes families face problems or multiple circumstances that preclude their participation. As a social worker in Winnipeg once told me: "To ask some families I know to do one more thing, even if it is something for their kids, would be just the last straw." Knowledge and understanding of the stressors faced by today's families is important for working with families.

FOR REFLECTION

Select one or two of the obstacles to family involvement listed above (or identify others) and think about how these obstacles might be overcome.

Stressors Facing Today's Families

All families experience stressors. There are many stressors for families in today's world. Some, but by no means all, families are affected negatively by these stressors. Also, what is a stressor to one family may not be a stressor for another family. Stressors have affected families in the past as well; although some of today's stressors are the same, some are different. No one can say with certainty that today's stressors are any more or less serious than those in the past.

Over the past two years I have asked groups of early childhood educators to tell me what they think are the major stressors facing today's Canadian families. The list includes five major stressors: poverty, lone parenting, working, the superfamily syndrome, and lack of support for families.

Poverty

Poverty is not a recent phenomenon in Canada. However, poverty has recently become more high profile and solutions to the problem have been much debated in the popular media, among professionals, and by politicians and policy-makers. This debate has not reversed the trend of increasing family and child poverty in Canada. According to one popular magazine, "in recent years the extent and depth of the problem has become a national embarrassment" (Chisholm, 1997, p. 42).

Child poverty is discussed in Chapter 2.

Although poverty is a stressor for families, it does not mean that all poor families are in crisis. Most poor families are healthy and functioning well. This is not to say that poverty is not a problem for those experiencing it and that financial security would not be preferable.

As described earlier in this chapter, poverty can have serious effects for families' functioning and thus for children's development. For example, one negative effect has been the increased number of homeless families, especially women and children, in the past 20 years (Shimoni & Baxter, 1996). As the cost of housing increases and family income decreases, finding adequate and affordable housing becomes more difficult and families must spend a greater percentage of their income on housing. This can be a special difficulty for families, as some places will not rent to families with children. A necessity for all families should be "having a warm, comfortable place to call home, a physically safe place for children to grow up" (Pugh, De'ath, & Smith, 1994, pp. 25–26). However, for some Canadian families, this need is not a reality. For example, almost half of the people using Toronto's homeless shelters in 1996 were families (McCann, 1999). And the numbers using shelters increased by more than 60 percent between then and 1997 (Alston, 1998).

Homeless is an encompassing term that typically includes those who have no shelter and sleep on the streets or in shelters, as well as those who are highly transient and move frequently among friends and relatives (Bruder, 1997; Swick, 1999). Homelessness can put young children at risk for developmental delays, illness, poor nutrition, behavioural and mental health problems, and family stress (Bruder, 1997; Sailor, 1998). Early childhood educators can assist by being resources, liaisons, and advocates for homeless children and their families.

While income is a significant factor in distinguishing functional and dysfunctional families, it is important to remember that the majority of poor families are not dysfunctional (National Longitudinal Survey of Children and Youth, 1996). According to Weissbourd (1996), "poor parents are not typically undisciplined or arbitrary, unable to provide structured, consistent, safe, and stimulating environments for their children" (p. 18). It is a grave mistake to stereotype all poor families as having the same characteristics. Poor families are diverse; what they do have in common is poverty.

Persistent family poverty is particularly harmful to children, especially in the early years (Smith & Zaslow, 1995). However, it is not necessarily a life sentence (Corak, 1998). Early childhood programs and early childhood educators can be valuable supports and resources for all families, including poor families.

Lone Parenting

In recent years the number of lone-parent families in Canada has increased significantly (National Longitudinal Survey of Children and Youth, 1996). Raising children alone can be a stressor. A major consequence for lone-parent families, especially those headed by women, is the increased likelihood of poverty and the risk of the problems associated with poverty such as poor health, depression, isolation, and homelessness.

Again, not every lone-parent family is in difficulty. According to the Vanier Institute (1992), "It is a mistake, however, to think of a lone-parent family as inherently pathological . . . . It is not family structure but rather poverty and isolation that are the crucial factors causing difficulties for lone-parent families" (p. 29). Early childhood educators can serve as a resource and facilitate referrals for families that can benefit from programs and services available in the community. Not all families are necessarily aware of the options available to them or how to access their options. However, not all families need or want such programs.

Work-Related Stressors

Canadian families in the paid labour force also face stressors. In addition to the difficulty of finding employment in an uncertain job market, there is concern about keeping the job. Many people in Canada work two or more jobs to provide for their families. And in many families, both parents are working in order to avoid poverty. The increasing numbers of mothers of young children in the labour force has also contributed to families needing to balance jobs, home, and child care.

The increasing demands on families, especially mothers, have led to a time crunch and more stressors (Fast & Frederick, 1996). A common phrase today is "the 24–7 job" meaning 24 hours a day, seven days a week. Many parents believe that 24–7 applies to them. The average wife and mother in Canada who works a full-time week spends 15 or more additional hours per week on caring for children and another 15 hours or more doing housework (Statistics Canada, 1998g). Fathers, especially single fathers, also report time-crunch problems (Briggs & Walters, 1985; Grover, 1999). In addition, for many parents, there are older members of the family who need care and attention. The current "sandwich generation" woman is predicted to spend 17 years caring for children and 18 years helping an aging relative (Vanier Institute, 1992). For many families, being part of a sandwich generation will be an additional stressor. It is not surprising that Statistics Canada found that severe time stress had increased since 1992; the most time-stressed were mothers employed full time who had children under five years of age (Statistics Canada, 1999f).

According to Statistics Canada, "work demands can impinge on family roles, the quality of family relationships and the well-being of family members. Conversely, family roles can interfere with work performance and/or commitment to one's job" (Che-Alford, Allan, & Butlin, 1994, p. 36).

Some employers in Canada have instituted programs, services, or policies (e.g., flex-time) to assist families with children; however, their numbers are relatively modest.

See Chapter 8 for descriptions of work-related early childhood programs.

The Superfamily Syndrome

Look at the titles of articles in popular press magazines, especially those targeting women, or scan the self-help section in your local bookstore, and you'll see a plethora of articles and books on how families—especially mothers—can do more and more in less time. There are examples of women who are managing a multitude of tasks and roles, seemingly with little effort. However, the actual situation is not as rosy. Indeed, there is widespread recognition among families that the average Canadian family with children is time-stressed from trying to do too much. In fact, in a recent Statistics Canada survey (1999f), one-third of the 25- to 44-year-olds said they were workaholics and the majority worried about having enough time for their family and friends.

Hurried families often produce hurried children. What with the demands on families and the desires of families to provide the best for their children, there seems to be little time left in the day for family time. The superfamily, like the superchild, thinks it has to do it all. A very popular workshop given by one of my colleagues for parents of young children is about stress management. A good companion workshop could explore what young children need to develop to their full potential, which includes time with their parents.

Hurried children are discussed in Chapter 2.

Lack of Support

A need common to all families is support. Not all families need support all the time or even most of the time. And not all families need the same kinds of support. Most of today's families do not have the extended families or kinship groups that traditionally provided support, assistance, and advice. One of the roles of early childhood programs is to help provide support for families with young children.

The key points for early childhood educators to consider when thinking about the stressors facing today's Canadian families are to

1. Recognize that these stressors exist and can impact on families;

2. Realize that most families cope with these stressors most of the time. A relatively small number of families are in crisis; and

3. Investigate what early childhood educators can do to assist families with young children.

Family support programs are described in Chapter 11.

FOR REFLECTION

Select one type of stressor discussed on pages 103–106 and identify resources, organizations, agencies, or sources of information in your community that might be of assistance to those families.

Celebrating Families

There is much to celebrate about Canadian families. Families are essential for children and for Canada. Families are important to both parents and children. A 1999 survey (Invest in Kids) reported that 92 percent of parents agreed that "being a parent is the most important thing I can do." Also recently, Canadian children under 18 selected "the right to have a family to care for us" as the most important right; food and shelter came second (Youth rate families, 1999). Obviously families and their roles are recognized and valued by Canadian families.

Often it seems we hear less about the successful, happy, contributing families than the families who are experiencing problems and suffering. While it is important to be realistic about the stressors and challenges facing Canada's families, it is also important to maintain perspective. Most families are well. This does not mean one should have a sentimental or nostalgic view of the family. As Coontz (1995) stated, "we cannot return to the 'traditional' family forms and expectations that were at least partly mythical in the first place" (p. K18). However, one thing we can do is to be advocates for children and families. One way to be an advocate is to celebrate families.

The International Year of the Family in 1994 focused on the role and importance of families around the world. In Canada, Family Services Canada (a non-profit organization) had instituted National Family Week even earlier, in 1985. The purpose of this week is to celebrate the uniqueness and special qualities of every family, to acknowledge their achievements, and to build family-friendly neighbourhoods and work environments (Family Services Canada, 1998). National Family Week is observed every October during the week before Thanksgiving.

FOR REFLECTION

If you were the director of a large child-care centre, what activities would you plan for the next National Family Week?

Summary of this Chapter

The key themes in this chapter are the:

- Universality of families

- Importance of families

- Diversity of Canadian families

- Ways that today's families may be different from your family

- Ways that recent demographics have affected families in Canada

- Possible roles for families in early childhood programs

- Ways that early childhood educators can involve families in programs

- Stressors faced by today's families

- Importance of celebrating families

Key Terms

anti-bias, 96
family, 76
family involvement, 97

homeless, 104
lone parent, 84

Resources

For Sharing with Children

Some books to share with young children are:

Super, G. 1991. *What kind of family do you have?* Frederick, MD: Twenty-first Century Books. Also by this author is *What is a family?*

Hausherr, R. 1997. *Celebrating families.* New York: Scholastic Press.

We are all related: A celebration of our cultural heritage 1996. Vancouver: G.T. Cunningham Elementary School.

Clark, K. 1996. *First Nations families.* Victoria: Greater Victoria School District, First Nations Education Division.

Dooley, N. 1991. *Everybody cooks rice.* Illustrated by P.J. Thornton. Minneapolis: Carolrhoda Books. Everyone in Carlie's neighbourhood eats rice—but in different dishes from different countries (e.g., Vietnam, Barbados, India, Italy, and Haiti). Recipes included.

Pellegrini, N. 1991. *Families are different.* New York: Holiday House. A child adopted from Korea describes her family.

Graeme, J. and Fahlman, R. 1990. *Hand in hand: Multicultural experiences for young children.* Don Mills, ON: Addison-Wesley. A series of books on topics such as food and celebrations.

A useful resource for children's books, including multicultural/anti-bias ones, is the Canadian Children's Book Centre. Visit their Web site at www3. sympatico.ca/ccbc, or contact them at

35 Spadina Road
Toronto, ON M5R 2S9
Telephone: 416-975-0010
Fax: 416-975-1839
E-mail: ccbc@sympatico.ca

For Further Reading

If you want to know more about demographics in Canada, two popular-press books you might read are:

Foot, D.K. 1998. *Boom, bust, and echo 2000.* Toronto: Macfarlane Walter & Ross.

Adams, M. 1997. *Sex in the snow: Canadian social values at the end of the millennium.* Toronto: Penguin Books.

For more specific information about Canadian families with young children, an excellent resource is:

National Longitudinal Survey of Children and Youth. 1996. *Growing up in Canada.* Ottawa: Human Resources Development Canada and Statistics Canada.

If you want to know more about families and working with diverse families, some suggestions are:

Kellerman, S. 1998. *All in the family: A cultural history of family life.* Toronto: Penguin Books. An excellent and interesting description and discussion of the historical development of families and family life.

Powell, D.R. 1989. *Families and early childhood programs.* Washington, DC: National Association for the Education of Young Children.

Rosenfeld, A. & Wise, N. 2000. *Hyper-parenting: Are you hurting your child by trying too hard?* New York: St. Martin's Press. Advice for the "superparent" and "superfamily."

Shimoni, R. & Baxter, J. 1996. *Working with families: Perspectives for early childhood professionals.* Don Mills, ON: Addison Wesley Longman.

Bisson, J. 1997. *Celebrate! An anti-bias guide to enjoying holidays.* St. Paul, MN: Redleaf Press. Ideas and strategies for an anti-bias approach to holidays, including developing a holiday policy.

Boyden, J. 1993. *Families: Celebration and hope in a world of change.* London: Gaia Books/UNESCO Publishing. International examples.

Denman-Sparks, L. & the ABC Task Force. 1989. *Anti-bias curriculum: Tools for empowering young children.* Washington, DC: National Association for the Education of Young Children. The classic reference on this topic.

Chud, G. & Fahlman, R. 1995. *Honouring diversity within child care and early education.* Victoria: Ministry of Skills, Training, and Labour and the Centre for Curriculum and Professional Development. An excellent, usable resource.

Gonzalez-Mena, J. 1993. *Multicultural issues in child care.* Mountainview, CA: Mayfield Publishing Company. Describes varied child-rearing practices (e.g., feeding, sleeping, play, etc.).

Hall, N.S. & Rhomberg, V. 1995. *The affective curriculum: Teaching the anti-bias approach to young children.* Toronto: Nelson Canada. Another excellent, practical Canadian resource.

Kilbride, K. (Ed.) 1997. *Include me too! Human diversity in early childhood.* Toronto: Harcourt Brace & Company. Diversity from theory to practice.

 ## Useful Addresses and Web Sites

National Canadian organizations:

Campaign 2000
c/o Family Service Association
355 Church Street
Toronto, ON M5B 1Z8
Tel: 416-595-9230, ext. 241
Fax: 416-595-0242
E-mail: popham@web.net
Web site: www.campaign2000.ca

Canadian Council on Social Development
441 MacLaren Street, 4th Floor
Ottawa, ON K2P 2H3
Tel: 613-236-8977
Fax: 613-236-2750
E-mail: council@ccsd.ca
Web site: www.ccsd.ca

Family Service Canada
404-383 Parkdale Avenue
Ottawa, ON K1Y 4R4
Tel: 613-722-9006
Fax: 613-722-8610
E-mail: fsc@igs.net
Web site: www.cfc-efc.ca/fsc

The Vanier Institute of the Family
94 Centrepoint Drive
Nepean, ON K2G 6B1
Tel: 613-228-8500
Fax: 613-228-8007
E-mail: vif@compuserve.com
Web site: www.familyforum.com/Vanier
(Their publications are useful references on Canadian families; for example, the Winter 1999 issue's theme was Family Life: Past, Present, and Future.)

National Aboriginal Day
For more information, see www.inac.gc.ca (Department of Indian Afairs and Northern Development, Ottawa).

Child and Family Canada (www.cfc-efc.ca)

Statistics Canada (www.statcan.ca)

Canadian Parents Online (www.canadianparents.com).
A source for current topics of interest to parents.

4

Early Childhood Educators:
Their Roles and the Profession

*The most important determinant of the quality of children's experiences
are the adults who are responsible for children's care and education.*
—National Association for the Education of Young Children

"Y ou should be a teacher." Did family or friends ever tell you that? I think the first time I heard that statement was when I was about six years old. I was teaching my brother and his best friend next door how to read. And I remember hearing that statement a lot when I was growing up. Thus, I suppose no one in my family was very surprised when I became a teacher; they thought I was doing what came naturally. I have been in this profession, in various roles, for 30 years, and I think I made a good decision for myself. That is not to say it is the best decision for you or for others. You need to decide for yourself if this is the profession for you. Becoming more familiar with this profession, the roles of early childhood educators, and some of the professional issues will help you make this decision.

One of the attractions of early childhood education and care as a profession is its expanding variety. Many of the options available today did not exist even 15 years ago. The future seems to promise just as much, if not more, expansion and variety.

While I was writing this book I heard from a former student who was working as a nutrition educator in Alberta. She said that her early childhood education courses were very useful in her current job. I then thought about other students I've taught and what they are now doing. Their careers are illustrative of this variety: they are educators in non-profit day-care centres, cooperative nursery schools, work-related child-care programs, infant/toddler day-care centres, campus day-care centres, family day cares, primary grades in public and private schools, special-needs centres, family resource centres, early intervention programs, infant development programs, parent education programs, private- and public-school kindergartens, owner-operated day cares, hospital-based programs, colleges and universities, teen-parent programs, government ministries, licensing agencies, support networks, family literacy programs, toy libraries, raising their own children, and working as consultants. One is even a children's author. You can see the wide range of options from just my former students. There are even more possible career options. Which of the above options have you thought about?

Here are some questions to think about as you read this chapter:

- What are the characteristics of good early childhood educators?
- What are the roles of early childhood educators?
- Do early childhood educators experience developmental stages?
- What are the characteristics of a profession?
- Is early childhood education and care a profession?
- What does it mean to be a professional early childhood educator?
- How do the working environment and working conditions affect early childhood educators?
- What are some professional organizations for early childhood educators?

Early Childhood Educators

From the previous list of examples of early childhood educators, it is evident that this term is a very broad one. My preferred term for those of us working in this profession is **early childhood educator**. I like this term because it is both broad and inclusive while still being distinctive. Early childhood education and care professionals, perhaps more than those in other fields, have long debated what we call ourselves. If we can't decide what we should call ourselves, we can't complain that others don't know what to call us.

The nomenclature issue has been quite contentious. I've heard individuals working with children from birth to age nine who say, "Don't call me a caregiver," "Don't call me a teacher," or "Don't call me a practitioner." About the only thing there seems to be agreement on is "Don't call me a babysitter." While it is much more important to be clear about what it is we do and why, nomenclature is important.

Various terms have been suggested in the past, such as *educarer*. The governing legislation and regulations in Canadian provinces and territories contain varied terms and descriptions. However, my preferred nomenclature for this book is *early childhood educator* or *early childhood professional*, defined as "individuals who are responsible for the care and education of children, birth through eight, in centers, homes, and schools, and others who support that delivery of service" (Bredekamp, 1992, p. 52).

Characteristics of Early Childhood Educators

It is a belief in our profession that good early childhood educators are a prerequisite for good quality programs for young children. They are more essential and important than the physical facilities, equipment, length of the day, type of program, staff–child ratios, or any of the other multitude of variables research studies have examined. (This is not to say these other variables are not important.) The early childhood educator is "the most potent predictor" of quality (Phillips & Howes, 1987, p. 2). But what *is* a good early childhood educator?

How would you complete this sentence:

A good early childhood educator _____.

Obviously there are many ways in which that sentence can be completed. When I asked some preschool children to complete that sentence, their answers included *is nice, is pretty, likes me, is helpful, is fun, is happy (laughs and smiles a lot), sings good, fixes things, is fair, pushes swings, wears earrings, takes care of me, knows everything, reads lots of stories, doesn't yell at me, is funny, hugs you when you're hurt,* and *teaches me stuff.*

The children's list generally agrees with what research studies have found. Over the years I have kept an ongoing list of characteristics of good educators from the research and literature:

adaptable	encouraging	knowledgeable
attractive	enthusiastic	moral
buoyant	ethical	open–minded
caring	expressive	organized
cheerful	fair	patient
committed	flexible	personable
competent	friendly	polite
confident	generous	professional
considerate	good listener	punctual
consistent	good-humoured	reliable
cooperative	healthy	resourceful
democratic	helpful	respectful
dependable	honest	responsible
emotionally stable	inspirational	self-disciplined
empathetic	intelligent	sociable

social	sympathetic	trusting
stimulating	tactful	understanding
supportive	task-oriented	warm
		well-groomed

Obviously this paragon of virtues would be difficult to find! Which of the above characteristics do you personally consider to be the most essential for an early childhood educator?

Most of us can probably identify some of the above characteristics that we already have, some we'd like to have, and many that we're working on. Some of the descriptors may not be very clear. Personally, I'm not sure what a "buoyant" educator is! In the end, this type of a list is not really very helpful in understanding specifically the early childhood educator. The bottom line is that it seems preferable for any person working with children to have the above qualities rather than to be uncaring, dishonest, irresponsible, unfriendly, cruel, and morose. Perhaps a more precise and useful approach is to examine the roles of early childhood educators.

FOR REFLECTION

Sally Cartwright (1999) writes that, "A well-balanced, mature, and keenly observant teacher knows in her bones how to be with a child" (p. 6). What do you think of this view?

Roles of Early Childhood Educators

Because the field of early childhood education and care is so diverse, the potential roles for early childhood educators are also varied and diverse. A list of possible roles for today's early childhood educator can be almost as daunting as a list of desirable qualities. The following list of roles was brainstormed by undergraduate students:

administrator	evaluator	motivator
advocate	facilitator	nurse
artist	friend	nurturer
authority figure	guide	organizer
caregiver	helper	participant
co-discoverer/learner	initiator	player
coordinator	inspirer	professional
creator	instructor	referral source
curriculum planner	inventor	repairperson
decision-maker	leader	resource
designer	learner	supervisor
director	manager	supporter
disciplinarian	mediator	teacher
educator	mentor	
entertainer	model	

Can you think of any more roles to add to the list?

This list gives us an idea as to how varied the roles of the early childhood educator are. According to Gestwicki (1997), **roles** refers to "the particular functions and behaviors that teachers are expected to perform and exhibit" (p. 86). The roles expected of early childhood educators by society have expanded as programs have expanded and people have become more aware of the importance of early education and child care. Now, more is often expected of early childhood programs and educators than in the past. Given our continually changing and evolving society, as described in Chapters 2 and 3, the roles of early childhood educators are likely to continue to expand and diversify in the twenty-first century.

The many current roles of early childhood educators can be grouped into seven key role areas:

- Nurturer

- Facilitator, guide, and instructor

- Model

- Program and curriculum organizer

- Observer and evaluator

- Learner and researcher

- Colleague and professional

These roles are discussed in the following sections.

Nurturer

The nurturer is the role that most people seem to associate with early childhood educators. It's a role that has been part of the profession for a very long time (Beach, 1992). It is sometimes typified in the oft-heard statement, "Oh, you must love little children." Early childhood educators are sometimes seen as professional nurturers.

The nurturer role is an appropriate one for professionals who work with young children because, along with the child's family, they have the most effect on young children's development. Early childhood professionals are also important for the young child's developing sense of security, health, and general care.

While there are many similarities between the role of nurturer as an early childhood educator and as a mother, there are also distinctions. Even young children seem to see some similarities. As an early childhood educator, have you ever had a child call you mommy? It's a common occurrence.

The comparison of mother and educator roles is the usual comparison, rather than parent or father roles, because most early educators are women. Early childhood education and care has been called "a notably gendered profession" (Beach, 1992, p. 464). This is not to say that fathers or other family

Men in early childhood education and care are discussed later in this chapter.

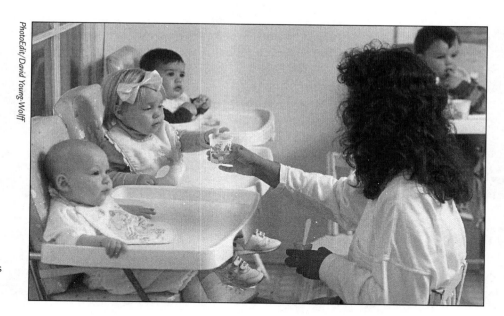

PhotoEdit/David Young-Wolff

Some of the roles of educators and families are similar (for example, feeding).

members cannot be nurturing or do not nurture young children. On the other hand, there are distinctions of the roles and young children can identify different roles for mothers and educators (Klein, 1988).

Katz (1980) has identified distinctions in the nurturing role of mothers and educators that are useful in clarifying the differences. These distinctions are

- *Scope of functions*—A mother is responsible for more aspects of a child's life than an educator is.

- *Intensity of affect*—Mothers are more emotionally involved with their children than educators are, in part because the relationship with an educator is a more temporary one.

- *Attachment*—Mother–infant bonding is highly desirable (see Chapter 2). Educators need to keep a more optimum distance, as one cannot maintain such intense attachments to multiple children concurrently. To try to do so leads to stress and burnout. However, that is not to say that educators do not get attached to children, especially when they have been caring for them for several years.

- *Rationality*—Educators need to be systematic and rational in their analysis and planning for groups of children based on their knowledge and expertise of child development and pedagogy. Mothers can be more individually focused on their own children.

- *Spontaneity*—Educators have the needs of the entire group of children to consider and accommodate. A mother is able to change plans for the day on the spur of the moment, for example by postponing or eliminating nap time. However, this is usually not an option for an infant-care centre.

- *Partiality*—Mothers can advocate for their individual children; an educator supports *all* children. Parents can and should be their children's biggest fans and supporters, but an educator cannot play favourites.

- *Scope of Responsibility*—A mother is responsible for her child only, while an educator is typically responsible for a group of children. When dilemmas arise, the educator has to consider the welfare of the entire group.

A key component of the nurturer role is caring. This means caring for and caring of. Caring *for* can mean taking physical care of a child. The type of nurturing and the scope are determined by the child's needs. For example, infants typically require more assistance with feeding, bathing, and toileting than do older children. However, older children do sometimes need this care, for example in school breakfast programs. It also means tending to children's emotional, social, and cognitive needs—all are important for children's optimal development. Caring *of* includes respecting children. This can mean respecting them for themselves, respecting their space and privacy, and respecting their belongings and creations. For example, a child's drawing or recycle sculpture is their creation and therefore belongs to them. The child's permission should be asked for and obtained before it is moved, their name written on it, or a photo taken of it.

Nurturing is a complex role and involves much more than a simplistic "loving little children." As Lightfoot (1978) has commented, "even those teachers who speak of 'loving' their children do not really mean the boundless, all-encompassing love of mothers and fathers but rather a very measured and time-limited love that allows for withdrawal" (p. 23). Nurturing and caring can also be seen as a moral obligation of society toward its youngest members. It is often said that a society should be judged by its treatment of its most vulnerable members. This statement is applicable to early childhood education and care. A society that does not care for and nurture its youngest and most vulnerable is one that is not likely to prosper and develop.

Facilitator, Guide, and Instructor

These roles recognize the early childhood educator's functions of *facilitation* (i.e., making easier), *guidance* (i.e., assisting), and *instruction* (i.e., teaching). This is a much broader conception of the educator's role than the traditional one of an educator as a transmitter of knowledge.

The early childhood educator as **facilitator** serves as a catalyst or provides assistance. He or she may be a resource who provides a needed piece of material so the child can complete a task. Children require varying degrees of support at different times depending on the task they are doing. Sometimes all that is required is to be the audience for the child who says "Watch me do this." Sometimes just knowing that the educator is there is enough for a child to attempt a challenging task. Sometimes facilitation involves *scaffolding* a task to promote a child's growth.

Scaffolding is the concept that a child learns from attempting something just a bit challenging when there is a more experienced person nearby to provide support (see Vygotsky in Chapter 6). This can be seen, for example, when a child is attempting a more difficult puzzle than usual. When the child seems stumped, the educator may provide scaffolding by saying, "Why don't you try turning that piece around?"

The role of **guide** involves encouraging, motivating, coaching, and perhaps inspiring a child. A child may need specific coaching; for example, we can act as a guide by helping a child to develop the strategies to enter an existing play situation. Guiding is helping; it is not therapy. As the noted child psychologist Anna Freud (1952) observed, "the teacher is neither a mother nor a therapist" (p. 565). Guidance is a traditional role for the early childhood educator. Therapy is a role for trained professional therapists.

See the play therapy section in Chapter 7.

Part of facilitation and guidance is responding. This includes responding to children and adults. It involves listening carefully to what is said and how it is said. It involves asking questions. One responds to children's requests for help and information. One may also need to respond to parents' requests for information about child development, accessing services, or locating resources.

It is important to know where the professional boundaries are. An early childhood educator can be very helpful by referring people to other professionals and agencies for help. However, it is not appropriate to try to deal with some problems (e.g., a parent's medical or marital problems) when one does not have specific qualifications in those areas.

Instruction is perhaps the role most typically associated with educators. Educators educate; teachers teach. While this is true, it is not the only role. Instruction itself can be varied. For example, there is indirect instruction and direct instruction. An early childhood program typically includes both. **Indirect instruction** is seen in the selection of materials, the arrangement of the learning environment, and the routines established. For example, children enter a day-care centre and look for the symbols or names that indicate their cubbies and hang up their coats; this is an example of the environment being structured to teach the meaningfulness of symbols/print. On the other hand, **direct instruction** is not only lecturing children. It includes demonstrating a task, explaining how to do something, teaching specific steps such as in cooking or tying shoes, presenting new information such as reading a book about feeding birds in winter for the new class bird feeder, and teaching songs and fingerplays.

Instruction is not always planned ahead of time. Many times the "teachable moment" is the motivation for an activity. For example, if a child brings in a wasps' nest it is a good opportunity to explore the children's questions about wasps and related insects.

The relative emphasis placed on facilitation versus formal instruction will vary with the type and philosophy of a program. For example, an early childhood educator in an academic-type program (see Chapter 6) will have more of an instructional role than will an educator working with infants.

Model

Because early childhood educators are such significant adults in young children's lives, they can be powerful role models. Have you ever listened to children in the dramatic play centre and been surprised how much they sound and act like their parents—or you? The responsibility to be an appropriate role model is shared by parents and early childhood educators. Many a parent and early childhood educator has learned to eat dark-green vegetables without complaining because they wanted to model that behaviour for a child. As Hillman (1988) has written, "One of the most important things we adults can do for young children is to model the kind of person we would like them to be" (p. 54).

One area that is modelled by early childhood educators is attitudes. Think of different programs you have observed. Sometimes you get a feeling of enthusiasm and other times a feeling that nothing is interesting. The expertise and knowledge of the educators in the program have a lot to do with this feeling, but so do their attitudes. For example, one program I visited had an educator who was very interested in and knowledgeable and enthusiastic about nature, especially plants. Not surprisingly, so were the children. Their interest and enthusiasm carried over into other aspects of the program. They had one of the best discovery/science centres I have seen in an early childhood program. Curiosity and enthusiasm can be contagious.

Another important area for modelling in early childhood education and care programs is speech and language. The early years are a time of tremendous and significant language development (see Chapter 2). Early childhood educators in a child's life can foster this development. It is important to talk to babies even though they cannot yet respond with recognizable language. They need to hear good speech and language models. Children copy what they hear. When I was teaching in England and was reading a story that introduced a vocabulary word the children did not know, they would use my pronunciation of the word at first. They later either figured out the "correct" British pronunciation of the word by themselves or were corrected by others.

Language can also be modelled as a thinking strategy for young children. For example, the use of think-alouds can help children plan and implement their ideas: An early childhood educator can say to the child, "What do we need to have to make playdough? What do we do first? What comes next?" and so on. Activities such as crafts, cooking, and science experiments are good opportunities for modelling think-alouds. Think-alouds can also be used by children to assist in play or other social situations. Modelling can also take the form of demonstrating how to do something, such as making playdough or gluing.

Educators' non-verbal behaviours also provide models for children. Research has shown that children pick up clues to teachers' attitudes, feelings, and expectations from their non-verbal behaviours (Woolfolk & Brooks, 1985). At the beginning of this chapter, I explained how the children noted some non-verbal behaviours, such as smiling, as characteristics of good early childhood

Play-Do-Review is an example of this strategy. It is described in Chapter 6.

educators. Children also pick up on when educators are bored—look at some of the non-verbal behaviour of adults doing playground supervision. An interesting activity is to set up a video camera in the room and let it run. Later, go back and observe the educators' and children's verbal and non-verbal behaviours such as facial expressions, posture, gestures, and movements.

Non-verbal cues can be useful strategies for educators. My cousin in Sweden, who was an early childhood teacher educator, used what she called her "strict eyes" to convey her concern to young children about what they were doing. Another effective strategy is to increase wait time after asking children a question. Many educators do not wait more than a few seconds before expecting an answer, so children who are fast responders get called on to participate. When the educator waits longer, all children have a longer time to think and more will respond. If you ask a question and no one seems to be able to answer it, wait longer. Almost always someone will respond—this works with students of all ages. Even silence communicates a message.

The behaviour one models is the result of a cultural context. It may or may not be the same as the children's. For example, in some cultures people stand and sit much closer to each other than in others. If you move away from a child who is used to closer proximity, they may take this as rejection. In some cultures lack of eye contact is seen as being respectful, in others it is seen as being disrespectful.

One issue in early childhood education and care is that of male role models. The popular wisdom is that because of the number of children from lone-parent families where the mother is the custodial parent, young children are in need of male role models. While it is recognized that children benefit from having both male and female role models in their lives, research shows that most young children do have male role models, even if these are not their fathers (McBride & Rane, 1997). The popular perception that children need male role models *in their early childhood programs* is not supported by the research (Coulter & McNay, 1993). Research has also shown that there is not a gender-specific difference in how men and women work with young children (Bowman, 1990; Robinson, 1988; Seifert, 1988b).

There are relatively few men working in the field of early childhood education and care; one estimate is that about 5 percent of early childhood educators are men (Seifert, 1988b). If approximately half the general population is male, why are there so few men in early childhood education and care? Think about your years in day care, kindergarten, and the primary grades. How many male educators did you have?

There has been recognition of the need for male educators since the 1940s (Bowman, 1990). However, men are still more likely to be visitors and observers in early childhood programs than permanent members of this profession (Seifert, 1988a). A key word here is *permanent*. There is a much higher dropout rate for male early childhood educators than there is for women, with many citing low salaries as the reason (Robinson, 1988). However, in the public elementary schools where teachers are paid the same salary regardless of grade level, there are still relatively few men teaching kindergarten.

Part of the reason there are few male early childhood educators may be that working with young children has traditionally and historically been perceived as a feminine occupation. There is a gender-role tradition in our society that men do not work with young children. Seifert calls this situation "historical inertia" (1988b, p. 114). Although the field of early childhood education and care advocates gender fairness and there is little overt discrimination against men, they report bias from society, parents, other educators, and sometimes themselves (Gestwicki, 1997; Seifert, 1988a, 1988b).

The six key roles discussed earlier apply to men as well as women in early childhood education and care. Men can and do fulfill all of these key roles. Whether the increasing recognition of the role of fathers in child-rearing translates into more men in early childhood education and care in the future remains to be seen.

Program and Curriculum Organizer

Good teaching and good programs look easy. One can use the analogy of watching a championship tennis match: It looks easy; however, trying it yourself for the first time reveals that it is not very easy at all. Developing and operating good-quality early childhood programs is also not easy. It requires organizational, management, and administrative skills to create and operate a healthy, safe, attractive environment and enriching program for young children. Early childhood educators must know what they are doing and why and also be able to articulate this. Some features of this role include curriculum developer, program organizer, decision-maker, and planner. (If you are operating your own early childhood program, you also need to be an entrepreneur and know established practices for small businesses such as budgeting and taxation

The Slide Farm/Al Harvey

Educators plan appropriate and interesting learning experiences for young children.

regulations.) In the area of curriculum, the early childhood educator is responsible for what is included, how it is presented to the children, selecting among program options, providing learning experiences, and evaluating the curriculum and program.

An early childhood educator needs to be organized. Organization includes arranging the physical environment, the materials, and a timetable to meet the needs of the children. Routines need to be determined and taught. Scheduling staff, determining responsibilities and duties for the daily program, locating resources, providing materials, and allocating budget are also organizational tasks.

All of the above require decision-making. An early childhood educator is a decision-maker all day long. Moreover, most of these decisions seem to need to be made immediately! Decisions can range from the relatively trivial such as the colours of the paints on the easel to important ones such as identifying children's individual needs or determining whether to make referrals for children who would benefit from special help. The wide variety of decision-making makes this an interesting and sometimes challenging role.

Observer and Evaluator

The roles of observer and evaluator are very important in early childhood education and care. The most frequently used evaluation technique in our field is observation. It is the number-one way we get information about children so we can provide programs that are appropriate and that meet the needs of individual children. When doing observation of children it is important to record the information so it is accessible and useful in the future. One cannot accurately recall information about many children over a period of time. The invention of Post-it notes was greeted enthusiastically by note-taking educators at all levels. However, each early childhood educator needs to work out a system that works for him or her.

Observation requires that one become familiar with the variety of possible observation techniques and their uses. For example, anecdotal notes of specific occurrences may be appropriate for recording the first time a child goes down the slide without holding someone's hand, while a running record may be more appropriate for detailing a child's group play strategies. Participation charts are useful for tracking who is participating during circle time or who is playing in which activity centres.

Documentation is important for accurate reporting and sharing of information about children. Documentation can include specific examples of the children's work, photos of their activities, audiotapes or transcripts of their conversations, and portfolios of their work. Careful and comprehensive documentation makes report writing or conferences with parents easier and more professional.

More detailed and frequent assessments may be required for children who have disabilities. This information is useful for establishing the child's individual education plan and monitoring the child's progress. Written records are useful for sharing with other professionals who are also working as part of the team for this child, such as physiotherapists or psychologists.

Evaluation also includes early childhood educator self-evaluation. We need to be constantly thinking about what we did and how well it went. It is important to periodically step back and think about what things mean and how we can improve. This process is often termed **reflection** or *self-reflection*. It can be defined as "a natural process that facilitates the development of future action from the contemplation of past and/or current behavior" (Han, 1995, p. 228). It's like a self-conversation or an inner conversation in your mind.

Reflection is characteristic of effective early childhood educators. It helps educators gain better perspective, insight, and understanding. It is critical to developing self-confidence and professional judgment (Duff, Brown, & Van Scoy, 1995). Reflection can be an individual or group process. Some educators keep journals; others participate in peer discussion groups. Some questions for self-evaluation and reflection include:

- Why am I doing this?

- How did it go?

- What does it mean?

- What did I do well?

- How could I have done it differently, better, more effectively, or more efficiently?

- Where do I need to improve? How can I do this?

- How can I better meet the children's needs?

Reflection is important for the early childhood educator at any stage of one's career. It is also an essential part of being a professional (Schön, 1983). Part of being a reflective professional is to continually examine our profession, its practices, and standards and to question the status quo. Especially as a student, you need to ask yourself—and others—why our profession values this, believes that, or does whatever. Being reflective means not accepting current assumptions and practices unquestioningly.

A well-known example of a reflective practitioner is Vivian Paley. She describes her insightful observations of children and her reflections about teaching and learning in a series of books she began writing when she was 50 years old. She taught at the University of Chicago Lab School for many years. Her first book was *White Teacher*, published in 1979 (reissued in 2000). Her latest is *The Kindness of Children* (1999). My personal favourites are *Boys and Girls: Superheroes in the Doll Corner* (1984); *You Can't Say You Can't Play* (1992); and *Kwanzaa and Me* (1995). One of her comments on educators is:

> More and more teachers are accepting as a personal responsibility the
> day-to-day clearing away of the cobwebs of indifference. They attend

endless conferences and study groups and read through piles of curricula and official memoranda, all of which offer solutions to a multitude of problems. But it is the teachers themselves who examine the lives of their own students and try to imagine a better world for them. (1995, p. 114)

Vivian Paley is an excellent example of how we can learn both from and with children through observation and reflection. The observation and assessment of children also raises questions to be answered. Some of these are our questions; many of them come from children. Responding to these questions leads to another role.

Learner and Researcher

An early childhood educator is also a **learner**. The curiosity and questions of young children inspire and motivate adults to learn about all kinds of things one probably never thought of before. Has a young child ever asked you the question, "Why can we sometimes see both the sun and the moon at the same time?" Do you know the answer or how to find out? There is always more to learn and more topics to explore. The oft-heard statement that teaching is a great way of learning is a true one. The concept of a lifelong learner is very appropriate for early childhood educators.

Do you ever get upset when you do not know the answer to a question a child, parent, or colleague asks you? Do you think that you should know all the answers? If so, don't worry—that is a very common feeling of beginning educators. They often get upset when they do not know the answers to questions from children, parents, or themselves. The professional early childhood educator is a specialist and has specialized knowledge, but is not an expert in every area. We each know a lot about our field, but no one knows everything. Teaching is a great way of learning and there is no shame in saying "I don't know but let's find out" to a child, parent, or colleague. Today seems to be the age of the expert. We are constantly bombarded by experts' often-contradictory opinions from magazines on supermarket displays, talk shows on television, conferences, and the education/parenting section of the local bookstore.

I'm sure you've listened to an "expert" and realized you had no or very little idea of what that person meant. When this happens, it's natural to think that we are lacking something because we didn't understand. Sometimes this is the case (for example, I have difficulty understanding computer manuals because I do not have much technical computing knowledge). However, many times it is a problem of the so-called expert being unable or unwilling to make his or her ideas accessible to the audience. Part of being a specialist in early childhood education and care is being able to explain important ideas to others in an easily understandable way. Sometimes we have a problem in talking with parents or others because of the professional vocabulary we use. Every profession has its own vocabulary. For example, a physician talks about *hematomas*;

most of us call these black-and-blue marks. Likewise, early childhood educators speak of the *whole child, individual differences,* or *developmentally appropriate practice* because these terms are part of our professional vocabulary. However, if the listener does not understand the professional vocabulary, they may perceive it as jargon and an impediment to their understanding. Early childhood educators need to be sensitive to the knowledge and understanding levels of their audiences and accommodate these.

The early childhood educator in the *learner* role approaches a problem much as a **researcher** does. For example, if the children have stopped playing in a particular activity centre, what would you do to find out the cause? First one gets a clear idea of the question (or problem); next, one thinks of possible ideas or solutions, which are then examined or tried out and feedback gathered; this information is subsequently analyzed and conclusions are drawn. This is known as **action-research**. It is practical, systematic, field-based research that is undertaken to answer a specific question.

The need to be a lifelong learner has never been more important than it is today. The so-called knowledge explosion has meant that we are finding out more about children, their development and learning, and ways to work with children and families at a rate faster than ever before. It is essential that early childhood educators stay up to date. There are a variety of ways this can be done including reading professional journals and books, being active in professional organizations (see the list in this chapter's Resources section), attending conferences and workshops, discussing professional issues with peers, or doing advanced work at a university or college. The desire to continue learning and finding ways to do this are characteristic of the professional early childhood educator.

Colleague and Professional

Unless you are planning to work one-to-one with an individual child in your home or elsewhere, you'll be working with other adults as well as children. Being a good **colleague** is an important role for the early childhood educator. This role encompasses working with other adults in your program; for example, other educators, parents, volunteers, practicum students, and other staff, as well as other professionals in the community such as therapists.

A frequent analogy for effective collegial interaction and functioning is a team. Like in a team situation, there is cooperation and everyone doing his or her part to reach a common goal, whether that is winning a soccer game or providing quality early childhood programs. Being a team member sometimes means playing one's strength and letting others play theirs. In programs with several educators, it is typical to divide up some tasks so that those who are stronger in one area can use those strengths. For example, an educator who is musical may plan and organize the music part of the curriculum. Another who is good at woodworking may take responsibility for this. In my experience, this can also apply to interactions with parents. When I was a young early childhood educator, I often worked with assistants who were older and more experienced than I was. I quickly learned that some parents preferred to ask advice of the more-experienced assistants. That was fine with me, as the advice they gave was appropriate and often more creative and realistic than what I would have suggested. However, it is important that the most qualified person take on a particular role rather than adhering strictly to some hierarchical arrangement.

Collaboration is also discussed in Chapter 12.

This type of teamwork is often referred to as **collaboration**. Collaboration involves "organizational and interorganizational structures where resources, power, and authority are shared and where people are brought together to achieve common goals that could not be accomplished by a single individual or organization" (Kagan, 1991, p. 3). Collaboration can mean collaboration on a large scale, as in several national professional groups uniting to advocate for quality child care, or smaller-scale collaborations such as the individuals within a single program. The focus of this section is on the latter type of collaboration.

Successful collaboration or teamwork requires that people know and trust each other. It also requires time. I have seen programs where the staff has been very creative in finding time in busy schedules to sit down and talk with each other to plan, resolve problems, and do other collaborative tasks. Time is essential for getting to know one another as well as for discussing ideas and planning. Sometimes a new program can be particularly challenging if none of the people know each other. To make this and all other collaborations successful requires good interpersonal skills of everyone. This is one reason why interpersonal and communication skills training are usually part of the professional education of early childhood educators and other helping professionals.

When a group of early childhood educators really "fits" and its members relate well to one another and the children, the result can be a joy. I have been fortunate in my career to have had many of these experiences (I've also had some less-than-great collaboration experiences). One of the most unexpected ones occurred when I was supervising a practicum student in a different area of the province. I had not met the student or her sponsor previously. Over the course of several weeks, we got to know each other well, liked what we found, and ended up with the three of us team-teaching on Friday afternoons. This was an example of three educators experiencing the joy of teaching and working with other compatible educators. There was no thought of role division based on academic degrees or numbers of years of experience. I think it was a valuable experience for the practicum student, as she has continued to work in team settings.

Early childhood education and care is becoming more collaborative. Even in public-school kindergartens, where traditionally each educator has had his or her own classroom, this has changed. For one thing, more people are involved in young children's lives. Parents are more likely to be found in classrooms as observers, resource people, or volunteers. Other professionals, such as aides for children with special needs, interpreters, and therapists, may be in classrooms for part or all of the day.

Another collegial role you'll probably experience and perform in your career is that of a **mentor**. A mentor is an adviser, guide, and supporter. Mentors encourage reflective thinking, listen and discuss concerns, are confidants, model behaviours, provide additional insights into issues, give advice, and provide personal and professional support and encouragement (Wildman, Magliaro, Niles, & Niles, 1992). A mentoring relationship is a voluntary one for both parties. I have been involved in situations where I have been "assigned" to be someone's mentor and I have found that this rarely works well. An individual needs to identify her or his own mentor. It has to be a mutually beneficial and rewarding relationship if it is to work.

Early childhood educators have each of the above six roles. However, the emphasis or amount of time spent in each role will vary with the type of program and one's position within the program. For example, while all early childhood educators have a professional role, those who work directly with younger children may have a larger nurturer role than those who are administrators. The roles of the early childhood educator can also vary with the type of program, its philosophical and theoretical orientations (see Chapter 6), and the ages and developmental levels of the children. Within a program there can also be differentiation of roles. A familiar differentiation is that of the student educator and the sponsor educator.

The roles of the early childhood educator have changed as the profession has evolved. One hundred years ago keeping the stove lit, fetching water from a well, and cleaning the outhouse were common tasks. No one then had yet imagined being computer literate as a useful skill for an early childhood educator.

FOR REFLECTION

How are the roles of early childhood educators working with toddlers in a day-care centre similar to and different from those working in a public school kindergarten?

The Stages of Educators' Development

The concept of stages of development is long-standing in early childhood education and care. It has usually been applied to the growth and development of children. However, the concept of stages of development has also been applied to early childhood educators. It can be a helpful concept for understanding some of the feelings and challenges facing educators at different stages of their professional lives.

Stages of Student Educators

Caruso (2000) has identified six stages or phases of development in student educators. These phases are

1. *Anxiety/euphoria*—Anxiety and questions about what the practicum experience will be like and the people one will work with are normal. A major task of this stage is to become acquainted with the children and other adults. A frequent worry is: Will I be accepted by the children and adults in the program?

2. *Confusion/clarity*—The student educator is confronted with the complexity of working in a program with a group of children, established routines one does not yet know, an unfamiliar learning environment, locating materials and resources, as well as trying to meet the requirements of the college or university, which all can be confusing until one "learns the ropes." At this stage, the various elements of the early childhood program begin to fit together and make sense.

3. *Competence/inadequacy*—This stage is important for building self-confidence. Student educators appreciate lots of positive feedback and encouragement at this stage. It is not unusual for one less-than-great day or experience to result in doubts about one's ability and choice of career. For example, I closed a car door on a child's fingers on the first day of my first practicum—I went home wondering if I should be in this profession! Another issue at this stage is to resolve one's role as an authority figure. Children often "test" new people in their environment and some student educators think they'll be seen by the children as mean or unkind if they correct or discipline them.

4. *New awareness/renewed doubts*—This is the phase during which the student educator becomes more reflective about him- or herself and others. He or she begins to think of alternatives and to become critical of some of what the sponsor educator or mentor is doing. A frequent sentiment (spoken or unspoken) is, "If this were *my* program, I'd do _____ differently." At this stage, the student educator is becoming more aware and appreciative of some of the subtleties of early childhood programs.

5. *More confidence/greater inadequacy*—At this stage the student educator feels he or she will survive. The student has more confidence in his or her ability to succeed. He or she experiences more successes, which further reinforce self-confidence. Failures are less personally devastating than in Stage 1. This is the stage where the student educator wishes to assume more responsibility. However, that is sometimes more responsibility than the sponsor educator wishes to delegate. Some sponsors are much more cautious than others in delegating responsibility to student educators. It is necessary to remember that the sponsor educator has the legal responsibility for the program and the children.

6. *Loss/relief*—This is the separation stage. All practica come to an end. This means separation for the student educator, the sponsor educator, and the children. Often specific activities are planned, such as a party, a memory book, or the preparation of farewell cards. Combined with this separation is the need to make the transition back to classes and the student role. It is also a time of reflection about the desirability of continuing in this profession.

Recognition of the stages one may experience makes the process more understandable. Students who understand the stages realize that they are not the first to feel like a failure after the first day or first week—or wished they could stay with the children rather than return to coursework.

Stages of Educators

Once the post-secondary education is completed and a person has a position in an early childhood program, their professional development continues. Several people have identified and labelled various stages of professional growth and development (e.g., Berliner, 1994; Huberman, 1989; Katz, 1977; Steffy, 1989; VanderVen, 1988). The four stages identified by Lilian Katz are most often cited for early childhood education and care:

1. *Survival*—This stage is somewhat a revisitation of the anxiety stage of the student practicum experience. One concentrates efforts and energy on getting through the day, and then on getting through the first week. This stage may last for the first year. An issue here for many beginning early childhood educators is first the realization and then acceptance of the responsibility for a group of young children. During a practicum, the thought in the back of one's mind is "If I get into too much trouble, my sponsor educator or supervisor will bail me out." This is no longer an option when one is the early childhood educator in charge. Support, encouragement, and a good mentor can make this stage easier.

2. *Consolidation*—According to Katz, this is the stage where educators are consolidating gains made during the first year and identifying what to learn or master next. There is an increased feeling of confidence. The focus of the early childhood educator is less on him- or herself and more and more on the children and meeting their individual needs.

3. *Renewal*—After several years of working with young children, the educator seeks out new ideas, alternative methods, and new challenges. At this stage, educators look for workshops, conferences, professional groups, peer discussion groups, journals, books, and courses that will expand their horizons.

4. *Maturity*—The early childhood educator is now confident of his or her abilities to do a good job. Katz estimates that this stage may be reached in three years for some people and after five years or more for others. Individuals have now developed their own philosophies and see themselves as committed early childhood educators. It is at this stage that the early childhood educator asks the "big" questions, such as, How does change occur? Why is this or that part of early childhood education and care? and What needs to be done to improve early education and care in our community or nation?

These stages can be seen as ever-widening circles of functions and perspectives as the early childhood educator matures and develops (VanderVen, 1988). While the individual educator is the focus of the survival stage, one's perspectives and interests have broadened greatly by the maturity stage.

Not everyone agrees with the concept of stages of development for educators. The concept has been questioned for assigning "typical" time periods (e.g., Sluss & Thompson, 1998), because some early childhood educators will require more time than others will. In addition, the stage concept may not be broad enough to include the social, political, and cultural variables that impact both programs and their participants. Perhaps the key conclusion to be drawn from the above is that early childhood educators need to be reflective and aware of what they are doing and what is happening to them. All educators can benefit from support and opportunities to expand their knowledge, skills, and competencies throughout their careers.

Professionalism and Early Childhood Education and Care

Early childhood educators believe that what they do is important. Research shows that studies in early childhood education at the post-secondary level is a key factor in quality programs. Yet one of the ongoing issues in early childhood education and care is the perception of the field as a profession—from the perspective of both the public and of early childhood educators themselves. This is an often-contentious issue that has been much debated in the literature in recent years. First, we'll look at what a profession is, and then we'll consider the debate surrounding whether early childhood education and care meets the criteria for a profession.

Criteria for a Profession?

If you were asked to name five professions, which ones would you list? What do those professions on your list have in common? Katz (1987, 1988) has identified eight essential criteria for a profession. As you read through the list, consider if early childhood education and care meets the criteria:

1. *Social necessity*—Is this work essential for the functioning of society?

2. *Altruism*—Is this work service-oriented and client-focused?

3. *Autonomy*—Does the professional determine what is done and how?

4. *Code of ethics*—Is there a specific code of ethics that is accepted by the group? Is ethical behaviour expected and enforced?

5. *Distance from client*—Is objectivity and an optimal emotional distance established? (For example, surgeons do not operate on their own family members.)

6. *Standards of practice*—Are there accepted and agreed-upon standard procedures and practices?

7. *Prolonged training*—Is there a definite period of formal specialized education required? Is this training done by accredited bodies? Is continuing education required?

8. *Specialized knowledge*—Is there a body of knowledge and theory that is relevant and specific to this work that everyone is expected to master?

Other people have included additional criteria such as credentialing/licensing, legal enforcement, a professional culture, a professional organization, public acceptance and respect, control of admission of new members to the profession, and assurance of quality procedures (e.g., Ade, 1982; Fromberg, 1995; Shanker, 1996; Spodek & Saracho, 1988). However, there is no universally agreed-upon set of criteria for a profession.

Do you think early childhood education and care meets the eight criteria outlined above? Is it a profession? Not surprisingly, there is no consensus on this. Some people think it is a profession, others think it is not, and some think it is a semi-profession (or a marginal or developing profession).

Professionalizing Early Childhood Education and Care: A Good Idea?

Some critics of professionalization criticize the idea as being based on concepts from sociology that are outdated and not applicable to early childhood education and care today. Others argue that listing criteria indicates or at least implies that there is consensus across a profession. However, as Ade (1982) has pointed out, "early childhood educators are primarily concerned with the education and care of young children, but beyond that, there is little consensus as to what constitutes the parameters of their work" (p. 26). Because early childhood education and care is such a diverse field, they question whether such consensus is possible. Because of this diversity, it is logical that members would have diverse views, experiences, concerns, and needs. As Shimoni (1991) noted, "it is not at all clear to what extent the commitment to professionalization, as expressed by the leaders in the field of early childhood education, is shared by the majority of those actually working with children in the field" (p. 16).

The advantages most frequently cited for professionalization of early childhood education and care are the increase in status of early childhood professionals, along with increased compensation and improved working conditions (e.g., Bredekamp & Willer, 1993; Spodek, Saracho, & Peters, 1988). Professionalization might also encourage more stated agreement (e.g., on a shared knowledge base and ethical behaviour) and also promote more consistency across settings. Possible disadvantages or risks include an increase of the division between early childhood educators and parents, and the exclusion of people from the profession, which would in turn mean fewer educators and would hamper growth of needed programs for young children and their families. There would also be increased cost due to increased salaries and benefits for early childhood educators, and this cost might be passed on to the families. Finally, it would create a hierarchical system. The fear with this latter point is that such a system is the antithesis of the collegial, teamwork orientation typical of early childhood and care programs.

Bredekamp and Willer (1993) present five challenges facing professionalizing the field of early childhood education and care:

1. The need for everyone to commit to ongoing professional development;

2. The need to link knowledge and competencies to credentials or formal programs of study;

3. The need to ensure that, in building up early childhood education and care, others' roles (e.g., parents) are not devalued;

4. The need to ensure that higher costs do not result in less access to programs for families; and

5. The need to exclude the unethical and incompetent.

Being an Early Childhood Professional

Just as the meaning of *profession* is debatable, so too is *professional*. Not everyone who works with young children should be considered a professional. To do so would include people who should not be working with children or who don't do it well, and this damages both the concept of and others' perceptions of professionalism in our field. Although this approach might perhaps be seen by some as exclusionary, it is so only in the sense that anything less than full inclusion is exclusionary. Yet, if we truly believe that not everyone has the ability, skills, and expertise to be an early childhood educator, then we need to consider carefully the requirements of being a professional. The advancement of the early childhood education and care profession is most effectively served by quality professionals who can deliver quality programs.

From the above discussion about a profession, it is obvious that an early childhood professional is more than someone who works with children. One of the difficulties our profession has historically suffered from has been the idea that anyone can work with young children. Even though formal education for early childhood educators has existed for 200 years, the general public does not seem to be convinced there is a need for formal specialized education.

There is a difference between *training* and *education* that goes beyond the semantic. A person can be trained to mix paints or supervise children on playground equipment to keep them safe. An educated person knows why children use paints, how this helps their development, how to facilitate children's artistic development, and how this relates to other areas of the curriculum. Being a professional educator "relates not only to doing things well, but to doing things at the right time for the right reason" (Spodek, Saracho, & Peters, 1988, p. 8). Therefore, I think the term "early childhood *education*" is preferable to "early childhood *training*." While it may seem a small point, the use of certain words does convey an image to other professions and the public. It also helps to reinforce the idea that not everyone can or should work with young children.

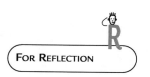

FOR REFLECTION

Some questions you might ask yourself about your professional education and development are

· *Am I learning about the history, theory, and issues of early childhood education and care?*

· *Am I completing my early childhood courses through an accredited program?*

· *Do I act ethically and expect others to do so?*

· *Do I frequently reflect upon what I do, why I do it, and how I can do it better in the future?*

· *Do I have plans for increasing my knowledge, competence, and skills throughout my career?*

· *Am I committed to early childhood education and care as a profession and do I advocate for it whenever possible?*

· *Do I belong to professional organizations?*

· *Do I participate in professional activities (e.g., reading professional journals, attending workshops, going to conferences, etc.)?*

· *Do I assist others in my profession?*

Ethics and Early Childhood Education and Care

A professional early childhood educator is ethical. Having a statement of ethics seems to be the most agreed-upon criterion across professions. Partnered with this is the concept of enforcement of the ethics by the profession and penalties for unethical behaviour.

Ethics is reflective thinking by a profession as a group about its responsibilities, obligations, values, and practices relevant to children, families, other professionals, and society. Ethics illuminate what a profession perceives as valuable and worthy. A **code of ethics** is the statement of these responsibilities, obligations, values, and practices.

A code of ethics does not mean that everyone will now believe the same thing about all issues. That is not realistic, as we are all products of our genes, backgrounds, and experiences. We have each been developing our own senses of right and wrong (i.e., morality) since we were young children. Personal morality encompasses one's individual views of what is right and good and one's beliefs about obligations and responsibilities and how to behave (Feeney & Freeman, 1999). Professional ethics is professional morality. It is what members of a profession recognize as right or wrong in the context of their work based on common agreement across the profession. This is why codes of ethics will vary across professions.

Codes of ethics are typically drafted initially by a small group within a profession and then circulated to the larger group for review, comment, and suggestions. The draft code is then revised. This process may occur several times. Once the code of ethics has been approved by the organization, it is disseminated widely and members are educated about it through articles in professional journals and newsletters, sessions at the organization's conferences, workshops, surveys, and other means.

The code of ethics provides a reference for professionals, support for their decision-making, guidance, and help with the grey areas. These grey areas are not often addressed directly by regulations or by program policy and procedures. For example, a new director of your program wants everyone to teach all three-year-olds to read because it would be an attractive "marketing tool" to the parents; or, a parent asks if her child misbehaved today and you know if you are honest and say yes, the child will be punished physically at home. Examples such as these are the grey areas where a code of ethics can be helpful.

Obviously, no code of ethics is ever comprehensive enough to provide specific guidance for every ethical dilemma. However, Feeney (1991) suggests two general guiding questions in resolving ethical dilemmas:

> Might this decision cause children any harm now or in the future? [and] Which choice is most worth embracing in terms of the core values of early childhood education? (p. 21)

Core values are the values that the profession, as a whole, accepts and promotes. They are typically stated in the code of ethics. The following are a few examples of common core values:

- Each child is unique and has individual strengths.

- Early childhood is an important time in children's growth and development.

- Early childhood educators work collegially with families and other professionals.

- Early childhood programs foster the development of the whole child.

- Early childhood educators respect the confidentiality and privacy of children and families.

An example of a code of ethics for early childhood educators is provided in Focus 4.1. This Code of Ethics by the Canadian Child Care Federation (2000) has eight "Principles of the Code," accompanied by an explanation and a list of standards of practice. Several provincial early childhood professional organizations have also developed Codes of Ethics.

Focus 4.1

Code of Ethics of the Canadian Child Care Federation

Child care practitioners[1] work with one of society's most vulnerable groups—young children. The quality of the interactions between young children and the adults who care for them has a significant, enduring impact on children's lives. The intimacy of the relationship and the potential to do harm call for a commitment on the part of child care practitioners to the highest standards of ethical practice.

Child care practitioners accept the ethical obligation to understand and work effectively with children in the context of family, culture and community. Child care practitioners care for and educate young children. However, ethical practice extends beyond the child/practitioner relationship. Child care practitioners also support parents[2] as primary caregivers of their children and liaise with other professionals and community resources on behalf of children and families.

The Canadian Child Care Federation and its affiliate organizations recognize their responsibility to promote ethical practices and attitudes on the part of child care practitioners. The following principles, explanations and standards of practice are designed to help child care practitioners

monitor their professional practice and guide their decision-making. These ethical principles are based on the *Code of Ethics* of the Early Childhood Educators of B.C. They have been adapted for use by adults who work with children and families in a variety of child care and related settings. They are intended both to guide practitioners and to protect the children and families with whom they work. Professionalism creates additional ethical obligations to colleagues and to the profession.

Eight ethical principles of practice are presented. These principles are intended to guide child care practitioners in deciding what conduct is most appropriate when they encounter ethical problems in the course of their work. Each principle is followed by an explanation and a list of standards of practice that represent an application of the principle in a child care or related setting.

The ethical practice of child care practitioners reflects the eight principles. However, the resolution of ethical dilemmas can be difficult and there will be circumstances in which the ethical principles will conflict. In these difficult situations, it is recommended that child care practitioners carefully think through the likely consequences of giving priority to particular principles. By evaluating the consequences, it may become clear which principle ought to be given more weight. The preferred action should be the one which produces the least amount of avoidable harm. Child care practitioners are also encouraged to consult with colleagues to obtain different perspectives on the problem, always being mindful of confidentiality issues. However, the final decision will be made by the individual practitioner facing the ethical dilemma.

The Principles of the Code

· Child care practitioners promote the health and well-being of all children.

· Child care practitioners enable children to participate to their full potential in environments carefully planned to serve individual needs and to facilitate the child's progress in the social, emotional, physical and cognitive areas of development.

· Child care practitioners demonstrate caring for all children in all aspects of their practice.

· Child care practitioners work in partnership with parents, recognizing that parents have primary responsibility for the care of their children, valuing their commitment to the children and supporting them in meeting their responsibilities to their children.

· Child care practitioners work in partnership with colleagues and other service providers in the community to support the well-being of children and their families.

· Child care practitioners work in ways that enhance human dignity in trusting, caring and co-operative relationships that respect the worth and uniqueness of the individual.

· Child care practitioners pursue, on an ongoing basis, the knowledge, skills and self-awareness needed to be professionally competent.

· Child care practitioners demonstrate integrity in all of their professional relationships.

Child care practitioners promote the health and well-being of all children.

Child care practitioners are responsible for the children in their care. They create environments for children that are safe, secure and supportive of good health in the broadest sense. They design programs that provide children with opportunities to develop physically, socially, emotionally, morally, spiritually, cognitively and creatively. A healthy environment for children is one in which each child's self-esteem is enhanced, play is encouraged and a warm, loving atmosphere is maintained.

In following this principle, a child care practitioner:

· promotes each child's health and well-being;

· creates and maintains safe and healthy environments for children;

· fosters all facets of children's development in the context of the child, their family and their community;

· enhances each child's feelings of competence, independence and self-esteem;

· refrains from in any way degrading, endangering, frightening or harming children;

· acts as an advocate on behalf of all children for public policies, programs and services that enhance their health and well-being; and

· acts promptly in situations where the well-being of the child is compromised.

Child care practitioners enable children to participate to their full potential in environments that are carefully planned to serve individual needs and to facilitate the child's progress in the social, emotional, physical and cognitive areas of development.

Child care practitioners understand the sequences and patterns of child development and cultural influences on those patterns. They

---

1. This code uses the term *child care practitioner* to refer to adults who work in the field of child care including: early childhood educators; family child care providers; family resource program personnel; resource and referral program personnel; and instructors in early childhood care and education programs in post-secondary institutions.

2. This code uses the term "parent" to refer the parent of legal guardian or the adult who assumes the parental role in the care of the child.

continued

continued

use this knowledge to create environments and plan programs that are responsive to the children in their care. Child care practitioners implement programs and use guidance techniques that take into account the ages of the children and individual variations in their development.

In following this principle, a child care practitioner:

· considers cross-cultural variations in child-rearing approaches when assessing child development;

· applies the knowledge that the stages of physical, social, emotional, moral and cognitive development of each child may be different;

· determines where each child is on the various developmental continua and uses that knowledge to create programs that allow for individual differences and preferences; and

· uses developmentally appropriate methods and materials in working with children.

Child care practitioners demonstrate caring for all children in all aspects of their practice.

Caring involves both love and labour. Caring is at the core of early childhood education and is reflected in the mental, emotional and physical efforts of child care practitioners in their inter-actions with all children. Being cared for and cared about is consistently communicated to all children.

In following this principle, a child care practitioner:

· responds appropriately to each child's expressions of need;

· provides children with experiences that build trust;

· expresses warmth, appropriate affection, consideration and acceptance for children both verbally and non-verbally;

· communicates to children a genuine interest in their activities, ideas, opinions and concerns; and

· supports children as they experience different emotions and models acceptable ways of expressing emotions.

Child care practitioners work in partnership with parents, recognizing that parents have primary responsibility for the care of their children, valuing their commitment to their children and supporting them in meeting their responsibilities to their children.

Child care practitioners share joint interest in the children in their care while recognizing that parents have primary responsibility for child-rearing and decision-making on behalf of their children. Child care practitioners complement and support parents as they carry out these responsibilities. Through positive, respectful and supportive relationships with parents, child care practitioners advance the well-being of children.

In following this principle, a child care practitioner:

· promotes considerate relationships with the parents of the children in care;

· respects the rights of parents to transmit their values, beliefs and cultural heritage to their children;

· supports parents with knowledge, skills and resources that will enhance their ability to nurture their children;

· encourages and provides opportunities for parents to participate actively in all aspects of planning and decision-making affecting their children; and

· builds upon strengths and competencies in supporting parents in their task of nurturing children.

Child care practitioners work in partnership with colleagues and other service providers in the community to support the well-being of children and their families.

Child care practitioners recognize that nurturing family environments benefit children. Child care practitioners work with other helping professionals to provide a network of support for families.

In following this principle, a child care practitioner:

- supports and encourages families by developing programs that meet the needs of those families being serviced;
- assists families in obtaining needed specialized services provided by other professionals; and
- advocates public policies and community services that are supportive of families.

Child care practitioners work in ways that enhance human dignity in trusting, caring and co-operative relationships that respect the worth and uniqueness of the individual.

Child care practitioners welcome and cherish children unconditionally. They respect the dignity of children, parents, colleagues and others with whom they interact. They demonstrate respect for diversity by valuing individuality and appreciating diverse characteristics including ideas and perspectives.

In following this principle, a child care practitioner:

- communicates respect by practising and promoting anti-bias interactions;
- supports and promotes the dignity of self and others by engaging in mutually enhancing relationships;
- plans inclusive programs that communicate respect for diversity regarding ability, culture, gender, socio-economic status, sexual orientation and family composition; and
- provides opportunities for all children to participate in childhood activities.

Child care practitioners pursue, on an ongoing basis, the knowledge, skills and self-awareness needed to be professionally competent.

Early childhood professional practice is based on an expanding body of literature and research. Continuing education is essential. In-service skills training and self-awareness work prepare child care practitioners to fulfil their responsibilities more effectively.

In following this principle, a child care practitioner:

- recognizes the need for continuous learning;

- pursues professional development opportunities;
- incorporates into practice current knowledge in the field of early childhood care and education and related disciplines;
- assesses personal and professional strengths and limitations and undertakes self-improvement;
- articulates a personal philosophy of practice and justifies practices on the basis of theoretical perspectives; and
- shares knowledge to support the development of the field.

Child care practitioners demonstrate integrity in all of their professional relationships.

Child care practitioners are truthful and trustworthy. They communicate honestly and openly and endeavour to be accurate and objective. Child care practitioners treat as confidential information about the children, families and colleagues with whom they work. Information may be shared with colleagues and other helping professionals as required for the care and support of the children or as required by law. Child care practitioners acknowledge real or potential conflicts of interest and act in accordance with the principles of this code of ethics.

In following this principle, a child care practitioner:

- communicates with children, parents, colleagues and other professionals in an honest, straightforward manner;
- conscientiously carries out professional responsibilities and duties;
- identifies personal values and beliefs and strives to be objective;
- treats as confidential information concerning children, families and colleagues unless failure to disclose would put children at risk; and
- recognizes the potential for real or perceived conflict of interest and acts in accordance with the principles of the code where dual relationships with colleagues or families exist and/or develop.

A Professional Body of Knowledge

Another criteria usually suggested for a profession is that it has a body of knowledge that is *specific* to the profession. This does not mean a *unique* body of knowledge. Related professions share some common or overlapping knowledge bases. For example, although a pediatrician and an early childhood educator have both taken courses in child development, one has also had courses in medical procedures and diagnosis and the other has had courses in curriculum development and planning. These are *specific* to the profession. One example of a unique part of a knowledge base of a profession is its own history. This history is that of the specific profession and therefore is unique to that profession.

What else do you think should be in the core knowledge base of early childhood education and care? Willer (1994) suggests two key questions for determining core knowledge:

> Is this knowledge or skill required of *every* early childhood professional regardless of level or setting or professional role? . . . [and] Does the sum of this body of knowledge and competencies uniquely distinguish the early childhood professional from all other professionals? (pp. 11–13)

One difficulty with trying to outline a definitive body of knowledge is that both knowledge in general and research related to early childhood in particular are continually evolving and growing. The identification of a core body of knowledge is further complicated by the diversity of early childhood programs. For example, a large day-care centre in Metro Toronto, a combined kindergarten to grade 2 class in a rural school in Saskatchewan, a parent cooperative nursery school in the Yukon, a special-needs family day care in Vancouver, and a school-age program in Newfoundland may require different specific pieces of knowledge. While all early educators might need to have a general knowledge of children with disabilities, an educator working with children who are deaf may also need to know sign language. This raises the problem of determining what is "core" knowledge and what is specific knowledge related to local contexts, cultural variations, or specific programs. The diversity of early childhood education and care has made it difficult to develop a common body of knowledge and agreed-upon formal education.

The concept of a body of knowledge has been criticized on philosophical grounds. Some think that this approach overemphasizes "scientific knowledge," which reflects only a part of early childhood education and care, and that social and economic realities should also be considered (Silin, 1987, 1988). Vander Ven (1997) criticizes the idea of linear, prescriptive, and rigid descriptions of a knowledge base. She believes that in order to reflect the changing world, the knowledge base should be interdisciplinary and advocate interprofessional education in human-services fields. Feminists also critique this idea because they think that "feminine" professions (such as early childhood education and care) have broader dimensions encompassing caring, warmth, and supportive relationships. For example, Noddings (1990) raises the question of how

A summary of the history of early childhood education and care is presented in Chapter 5.

professionalization will actually benefit children. Other critics have raised the issue of a knowledge base from one culture being inadequate for all, and that traditional knowledge is not sufficient to deal with ever-changing realities (Jones, 1993). Still others have questioned the presumption of "experts" determining what novice educators really need to know and are concerned that this may result in a "think-as-experts-think curriculum" (Ott, Zeichner, & Price, 1990, p. 122).

Since 1981, the National Association for the Education of Young Children has been developing comprehensive guidelines for the professional preparation of early childhood educators. They posed the question: What do early childhood professionals need to know and be able to do? According to NAEYC, "one of the hallmarks of a profession is the existence of standards of professional practice. . . . [These] guidelines articulating performance standards for early childhood professionals provide an important framework for building an early childhood professional development system" (Bredekamp, 1995, p. 69). These are

FOR REFLECTION

- Understanding young children

- Promoting child development and learning

- Knowledge of integrated curriculum

- Multiple teaching strategies for meaningful learning

- Reflective practice

- Family partnerships

- Professional partnerships.

(National Association for the Education of Young Children, 1996)

Some educators think that given the variety of individuals and programs in early childhood education and care, it is not possible, realistic, or practical to have a common set of standards such as those listed by the National Association for the Education of Young Children. Do you agree or disagree? Why?

The Canadian Child Care Federation (CCCF) established a national training committee to study professional education issues in 1989. In consultation with the field, this committee developed a series of articles and a discussion paper entitled Issues in Post-Secondary Education for Quality Early Childhood Care and Education. After feedback from "organizations, educational institutions, government departments and interested individuals" (Canadian Child Care Federation, 1994, p. 6), the committee went on to develop the CCCF National Guidelines for Training in Early Childhood Care and Education. These were ratified at the CCCF's annual general meeting in 1995.

The guidelines are based on "certain shared beliefs" about training and education:

- Post-secondary institutions are appropriate places for professional education

- Integration of theory and practice is the foundation

- Diversity contributes to the richness of the education

- Respect and trust are cornerstones of positive relationships

- Innovation and creativity are needed for advancement of professional education

- An educational continuum recognizes personal and professional development.

(CCCF, 1995)

In these guidelines, entry-level early childhood professional education has two key themes: program content, and learning environment. **Program content** is defined as "the study of the knowledge, skills and attitudes that are essential for Professional practice" (CCCF, 1995, p. 7). This is the "core" subject matter that links theory and practice. It includes studies in

- Self-awareness and communication

- Human development

- Family studies

- Foundations (e.g., history, philosophy, research, policy, current issues, etc.)

- Program planning and implementation

- Professional practice (including field experiences)

- Professionalism and community relations.

The second key theme is **learning environment**, which refers to "the human, physical, technological and financial resources, that are critical elements in facilitating the learning process" (p. 6). The six themes in this area are

- Faculty

- Administrators

- Students

- Advisory groups

- Governments and policy-makers

- Shared responsibilities of all.

After reading the above lists of what could be the content of a professional preparation program, you may be wondering how long this program should be. Of course, one could spend decades studying these topics. In reality, provincial or territorial legislation or policies usually determine the length of professional preparation. This results in variation across Canada and across types of early childhood programs. For example, in some provinces a kindergarten educator in the public school system is required to have a five-year degree. In some provinces the professional course for child-care educators is two years, in others it is less.

In recent years, the lengths of programs have been reduced in some provinces, often for budgetary reasons. Moreover, in some provinces a person with no specific early childhood education can work with young children. There

FOR REFLECTION

A recent study of the educational needs of family support workers in Ontario identified the following necessary components for a professional preparation program: community development, adult education, multiculturalism, administration, policy, the child and family, program planning, advocacy, and management (Kellerman & MacAulay, 1998). Do you think there could be a common program for early childhood educators wishing to work in a day-care centre and those wishing to work in a family resource program? What could be the same? What, if anything, would need to be different?

is also variation across post-secondary institutions, even within the same province. This variation has led some educators to call for national standards. The rationale is that other countries (e.g., many European ones) do this, and that having national standards would promote professional development and facilitate educators transferring from program to program and province to province. An argument against such a plan is that the standards set, at least originally, would likely be the "lowest common denominator" (i.e., whatever the provinces or territories with lower standards were doing). Provinces and territories that now require more professional education might reduce funding, or the regulations might be changed because they are considered "no longer necessary" or "too high."

Professional Development and the Early Childhood Educator

Another characteristic of a profession and an early childhood professional is continued education. Professionals typically see education, including their own, as a lifelong process of learning and reflection. For the early childhood educator, education does not stop at the end of the pre-service program. Professional development continues throughout one's career.

Accessing professional development activities is usually easier for those in urban areas. There are more resources available locally and there is less need for expensive travel. In addition, most post-secondary institutions in Canada are located in urban areas. However, recent technological developments have increased the possible options for rural and isolated educators. For example, there are now programs available through interactive video, Internet delivery, multimedia packages, module learning packages, local weekend or summer institutes, videos with accompanying study guides, on-site delivery in rural or isolated areas, specialized programs developed for specific groups such as First Nations communities and then delivered on-site, correspondence programs, local educator resource centres, interlibrary loan programs, and so on. In addition, there are resource and support educators who can assist educators on the job. For example, with the increased inclusion of children with disabilities in early childhood education and care programs, other professionals such as speech and language pathologists, occupational therapists, and physiotherapists provide information and professional education in the classroom environment. There is a range of professional options, from self-study to college or university courses taken for credit. The variety and availability of these options will likely continue to increase in the future.

Professional development needs to be an ongoing process. Professional development activities not only keep the early childhood educator current and up to date, but can sometimes be used to gain additional certification or career advancement. NAEYC has developed a continuum that reflects career-long professional development. This continuum (NAEYC, 1994) has six professional levels for early childhood professionals:

- Level 1 includes people working in an early childhood professional role but under supervision or with support while participating in professional education.

- Level 2 is the completion of a one-year certificate or the equivalent.

- Level 3 is the completion of a diploma/certificate or the equivalent.

- Levels 4, 5, and 6 are the completion of a bachelor's, master's, or doctoral degree, respectively, or the equivalent.

This type of continuum is often seen as a career ladder. In other words, additional qualifications and education enable the individual educator to assume additional or different roles (i.e., moving up the ladder).

Career Ladders and Lattices

There are a wide variety of roles, knowledge, skills, and competencies at differing levels in early childhood education and care. Likewise, there are early childhood educators with varied experiences, education, and qualifications. It is important for the profession to continue to be inclusive of this range of educators. In order to do this, there needs to be provision for and promotion of options for educators to increase their expertise and knowledge, if they wish.

The concept of a **career ladder** is one way to express a continuum of professional development. A career ladder typically has several steps (or rungs) with "predetermined criteria for advancement to a new step, objective evaluation procedures, the opportunity for teachers to take on new roles in the higher steps . . . and stipulations for the training and the certification required for advancement" (Association of Teacher Educators, 1985, p. 12). Given the diversity and range of early childhood education and care, one career ladder is not realistic. Multiple career ladders is a more realistic concept, although potentially complex. A **career lattice** incorporating multiple, interlocking career ladders may be a more easily visualized and articulated framework.

The career lattice concept "provides for the multiple roles and settings within the early childhood profession (vertical strands), each allowing for steps of greater preparation tied to increased responsibility and compensation within that role/setting (horizontal levels), and allows for movement across roles (diagonals)" (NAEYC, 1994, p. 71). An early childhood professional is an educator who is somewhere on a professional path on this lattice (see Figure 4.1 for an example of a career lattice).

In Britain, a similar framework is described as "a multi-dimensional climbing frame rather than a single ladder of qualification. Like a climbing frame there are several different ways of getting on and it is possible to move sideways as well as up" (Hevey & Curtis, 1996, p. 219).

In both of these frameworks, a person who begins working in an early childhood program while doing his or her first professional education courses would advance up the lattice when that formal professional education program is completed successfully. At a later time, this early childhood educator pursues

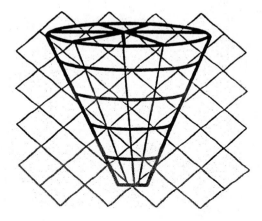

figure 4.1   CAREER LATTICE WITH BODY OF KNOWLEDGE CONE

The cone reflects the expanding knowledge base obtained by participating in a comprehensive, articulated system of professional development.

Source: Bredekamp & Willer, 1992, p. 50

additional professional education through workshops and credit courses and meets the provincial requirements to work with children with disabilities. Still later, this individual has children of her own and operates a family day-care program from her home for a few years. She is still on the lattice but has moved sideways into another type of setting. After her children begin elementary school, she becomes employed for half-days in a parent cooperative nursery school (another lateral move on the lattice). She also takes additional courses at the local college or university and earns a bachelor's degree in early childhood education. In her province this entitles her to a teaching certificate for elementary school. While teaching kindergarten, she takes courses in the evenings and summers and completes a master's degree. She has now moved further up the lattice. Her additional qualifications and experience enable her to get a position with the local municipal government inspecting and providing resources and support for early childhood programs.

Of course, an educator can increase his or her qualifications and remain in the same job. I know of educators with master's degrees who are operating small family day-care programs. However, the lattice framework recognizes that continued professional growth can lead to increased opportunities for movement around the lattice (horizontally or vertically) into diverse roles and positions.

A current dilemma for the early childhood profession is that increased professional development should be rewarded with increased compensation and recognition, and unfortunately this is not always the case. If increased professional development is not rewarded, educators may become discouraged and disinclined to pursue increasing levels of professional development and advancement. It is especially problematic when, because of low salaries, taking credit courses from post-secondary institutions to gain additional formal credentials can itself be expensive as well as time-consuming. Working conditions are closely tied to professional image and development as well as personal satisfaction with one's profession.

Working Conditions in Early Childhood Education and Care

There have been four recent surveys on the working conditions in the field of early childhood education and care: *Caring for a Living* (Canadian Child Day Care Federation & Canadian Day Care Advocacy Association, 1991); *Our Child Care Workforce* (Beach, Bertrand, & Cleveland, 1998); *You Bet I Care* (Doherty, Lero, Goelman, Tougas, & LaGrange, 1999), which replicated the 1991 survey; and *Partners in Quality* (1999), which is a joint endeavour of the Canadian Child Care Federation and provincial professional organizations. All four of these studies identified (a) compensation, (b) image of the profession/lack of respect for the profession, and (c) the need for more professional development and career opportunities to be major areas of concern for early childhood educators. (In interpreting the presentation of the data and results of these studies, it should be kept in mind that the *Caring for a Living* and *You Bet I Care* studies surveyed only educators in licensed group centres; none of the studies included kindergarten or primary-grade educators. Family day-care educators are also not typically included in these surveys. Thus these surveys are not representative of the *entire* field of early childhood education and care in Canada and should be interpreted accordingly.)

Wages and Benefits

Compensation is a big issue for most early childhood educators. Statistics Canada (1998i) reported that the salaries of early childhood educators and assistants in child care were among the 25 lowest paying occupations in Canada. They earned approximately the same income as pet groomers/animal-care workers and taxi/limousine drivers. It is therefore not surprising that early childhood educators in the above surveys felt that their wages did not reflect the value of their work. One of the above studies reported that parking-lot attendants in New Brunswick and Nova Scotia had higher average salaries than child-care educators (Doherty, et al., 1999). As Bloom (1997) commented, "virtually every study examining teacher job satisfaction in early childhood education indicates that child care workers are dissatisfied with the low pay and paltry benefits they receive" (p. 51). (In contrast, kindergarten teachers in public school systems typically have higher salaries and better benefits packages.)

Low wages and lack of benefits have implications for recruitment, as prospective educators may decide they cannot afford to be or stay in the field of early childhood education and care (e.g., see the section earlier in this chapter on men in early childhood education and care). Not surprisingly, these conditions also impact on retention, as "low wages significantly increase the probability of turnover" (Beach, Bertrand, & Cleveland, 1998, p. 90).

Another important component of compensation is benefits. In a recent Canadian working conditions study, benefits were reported to be generally "scarce," with the majority of respondents not receiving sick leave, pensions, or medical benefits (Beach, Bertrand, & Cleveland, 1998, p. 77). However, another study reported that the majority of respondents received overtime, paid coffee breaks, financial assistance for professional development including release time, sick days, maternal/parental leave, extended health care, and dental and life insurance (Doherty, et al., 1999).

Turnover was typically much lower in day-care centres with pension plans (Beach, Bertrand, & Cleveland, 1998). The lack of provision for a pension or retirement savings plan may become a higher-profile issue in the future as members of the early childhood profession age. There is currently a relatively low percentage of early childhood educators over age 40 working in child-care centres (White & Mill, 2000). The question for the future is, Will the currently larger cohort of middle-aged and younger educators remain in the profession without increased wages and benefits such as pensions?

Stability in care is important for young children because of their need for nurturing, ongoing relationships with the significant adults in their lives (see Chapter 2). In addition, the stability of care relationships is an indicator of quality for early childhood programs. Compensation and potential for future career advancement is a strong predictor of turnover in licensed child-care centres (Stremmel, 1991).

A common suggestion for improving the compensation issue is to tie wages to increased professional education. Kindergarten educators in the public school systems in Canada typically receive increases in their wages based on their levels of education and years of experience. These increases and the requirements for them are spelled out clearly and can serve as motivation for further professional development. A difficulty in group and family day care is that wages are heavily dependent on the fees paid by the families (or subsidized fees in cases of need). The potential for a significant increase of public funding for early childhood programs and educators' wages and benefits has been side-tracked by ongoing economic problems and government policies. To increase compensation significantly without prohibitively raising the costs of child care for families who cannot afford increases is the financial and moral conundrum facing the profession, policy-makers, and politicians today.

Compensation in our culture is a tangible sign of the value our society places on an individual's work. It is, therefore, a self-esteem and emotional issue as well as a financial one. Recognition and appreciation are intangible but important.

The Image of the Profession and Public Respect

In *Caring for a Living*, respondents indicated that they felt the general public did not respect what they do and its importance and that they will likely leave the field because of this (CCDCF/CDCAA, 1991). One implication of this perceived lack of value and respect is low compensation: "If the care and education of children were valued in Canadian society, public investment and caregiver compensation levels would be higher" (Beach, Bertrand, & Cleveland, 1998, p. 122). However, this issue is more than a financial one.

Career and Job Satisfaction

Intrinsic aspects of the early childhood profession, such as career and job satisfaction, also affect the working lives of early childhood educators. These aspects are more difficult to measure and assess quantitatively. However, they are important because studies indicate that it is the intrinsic rewards that keep early childhood educators in the profession (e.g., CCDCF/CDCAA, 1991).

The most frequently mentioned intrinsic factor is career and job satisfaction. This satisfaction with one's chosen career is "usually seen as foundational to becoming a self-motivated professional" (Duff, Brown, & Van Scoy, 1995, p. 86). Furthermore, early childhood professionals feel a commitment to their profession and especially the children (Beach, Bertrand, & Cleveland, 1998). Specifically, early childhood educators perceive that the advantages to this profession are

- The nature of the work
- The way they feel about their work
- Their co-workers and the children.

(CCDCF/CDCAA, 1991)

Perhaps the profession and society needs to celebrate the satisfactions while continuing to work on the problem areas. There is also a need to publicize and promote the early childhood profession and celebrate what is valuable and important in the work we do. As long as there are members of the general public who think that early childhood education and care is babysitting, the profession will not get the recognition (tangible and intangible) that it deserves. In 1979, on my first trip to China, a bus driver asked me what kind of work I did. I told him I was an early childhood teacher educator. He immediately shook my hand and said that the early years were the most important and that I must be very happy doing such important and fulfilling work. Some countries and cultures place more value on early childhood education and care than others do.

As James Hymes remarked a quarter of a century ago, "the profession of Early Childhood Education isn't one problem after another. The field offers many deep satisfactions" (1975, p. 65). It is, apparently, these deep satisfactions that keep many of us going.

Work Climate

The organizational climate is important for the individuals working in that environment and contributes to the overall quality of the early childhood program. Have you ever walked into an early childhood program and thought, "This looks like a good place to work"? Have you, on the other hand, ever walked into a program and had the feeling that it was not a pleasant place? **Organizational climate** can be defined as the "distinct atmosphere that characterizes work settings" (Bloom, 1997, p. 1). In a review of the research on organizational climates, Jorde-Bloom (1997) identified ten attributes of positive climates:

1. A strong sense of collegiality

2. Opportunities for professional and personal development

3. Facilitative and supportive administrators

4. Clear policies, procedures, and role responsibilities

5. A reward system

6. Involvement in decision-making

7. Goals agreement

8. Planning, efficiency, and task orientation

9. Effective physical environments

10. Innovativeness and adaptability to change.

A negative organizational climate variable that one seems to hear about more and more today is job-related stress. While all jobs have some stress, excessive and prolonged levels of job stress can cause burnout. Symptoms of **burnout** include "physical depletion, feelings of helplessness and hopelessness, disillusionment, and the development of a negative self-concept and negative attitudes towards work, people involved in the work and life itself" (Pines & Aronson, 1988, p. 9). Burnout is the stage at which some early childhood educators leave the profession. Stress is not just a twenty-first-century problem in this profession. In an early childhood textbook from 1935, Ilse Forest advised readers that "balancing out-of-school life enables [one] to take the inevitable jars and rubs of [one's] professional existence sanely and objectively" (p. 276).

I have asked numerous groups of early childhood educators how they deal with job stress. Their suggestions include talking things over with a colleague, friend, or family member; trying to look at the big picture; going for a walk; having a cup of tea; meditating; exercising; petting a dog or cat; using biofeedback; trying to see a humourous side; eating nutritionally; using self-talk; getting more sleep; leaving problems at work; taking a time-management course; making lists; writing a journal; doing crossword puzzles; imaging; looking forward and back to gain perspective; and focusing on the children. Obviously, what works for you in any given situation is a very individual thing. Thinking about stress, one's reaction to it, and how to cope can be part of a professional's reflective thinking. Career and job satisfaction is an important mitigator of job-related stress (Latham, 1998).

Future Directions for the Profession

The profession of early childhood education and care has come a long way in the past few decades and it is probably safe to predict it will advance even further in the next few decades. Early childhood education and care seems to have always been a dynamic field in transition. Furthermore, our profession will evolve further due to the political, social, economic, and social forces it now faces. For example, the continuing diversification of the population of Canada means that there will continue to be children and families of diverse backgrounds. Diversity will also be seen in the expansion of the types of early childhood programs (the current range is described in Part III of this book). The expansion of early childhood will have implications for career options, which in turn will have implications for early childhood professional preparation and professional organizations. The early childhood professional organizations in North America have grown in both membership and influence in the last 20 years. Their continuing advocacy efforts on behalf of their members, children, and families will be required in the coming years.

The demographics of the aging population may impact on the types of programs, the need for some programs, and the creation of new types of programs. A shortage of early childhood professionals due to the need for increased numbers of professionals for increased numbers of programs, demographics, or the loss of educators to other professions could become a serious problem.

To accommodate the need for professionals and the diversity of programs, there may be increased professional development programs targeting the specific needs and competencies required for different types of programs. On the other hand, continued economic restraint and cutbacks may force a more "generic" professional educational model on all helping or service professions. Another possibility might be the return to a more integrated pre-service professional education model that considers the child from birth to nine rather than dividing at birth to three, three to five, and five to nine as is the current tendency in post-secondary programs in Canada. Depending on conditions in the field, more or less education may be required to work with young children and families. The overall trend within the profession has been a move toward more education at both the pre-service and in-service stages. However, the direction of this trend will depend in great part on the availability of funding and the compensation rewards for early childhood educators for pursuing this increased education.

Additional education or time spent on post-secondary education may need to increase as the knowledge base of the profession widens and expands. This has potential implications for post-secondary education programs for the future and the amount of time necessary to effectively deliver these programs.

Given the expansion and growing diversity of early childhood education and care, the career lattice will need to expand, become more comprehensive, and provide even more options and routes for advancement. The increased use and invention of new technologies will impact on the delivery of early childhood professional development options. The delivery methods will, in turn, impact on the content and the scope of professional development.

Summary of this Chapter

The key themes in this chapter are the:

- Difficulty in defining *early childhood educator* with precision. The roles of early childhood educators are more clearly identifiable.

- Fact that these roles (e.g., nurturer, model, learner, etc.) are wide-ranging. The emphasis placed on specific roles can vary with the type of program, level of the children and other factors.

- Characteristics of being a professional, including professional development and life-long learning.

- Common developmental stages early childhood educators seem to experience, from their initial practica throughout their careers.

- Debatable question Is early childhood education and care a true profession? The field has many characteristics of a profession, such as a code of ethics and ongoing professional development options.

- Ways that major issues in child-care programs including wages, benefits, and working conditions affect the commitment early childhood educators feel to their profession.

- Ways that the profession of early childhood education and care has changed significantly in the past few decades, and how it will likely continue to do so in the future.

Key Terms

action-research, 125
burnout, 147
career ladder, 142
career lattice, 142
code of ethics, 133
collaboration, 126
colleague, 125
core values, 133
direct instruction, 118
early childhood educator, 112
ethics, 133
facilitator, 117

guide, 118
indirect instruction, 118
instruction, 118
learner, 124
learning environment, 140
mentor, 127
organizational climate, 147
program content, 140
reflection, 123
researcher, 125
roles, 115
scaffolding, 118

Resources

For Sharing with Children

The following books can be read with children:

Weiss, L. 1984. *My teacher sleeps in the school.* New York: Puffin Books. Answers every young child's question, "But where is your bed?"

Allard, H. & J. Marshall. 1977. *Miss Nelson is missing.* New York: Scholastic Book Services. What happens when a teacher goes "missing" and is replaced by a most unsatisfactory substitute. A modern classic.

For Further Reading

If you want to know more about being a reflective practitioner and staff development, try Vivian Paley's books: *Kwanzaa and me: A teacher's story* (1995) and *You can't say you can't play* (1992). Both by Harvard University Press, Cambridge, MA. The author is a superb reflective practitioner who makes the reader reflect, too.

For examples of 18 teachers' reflective experiences with developmentally appropriate practice, there is Tertell, E.A., S.M. Klein, & J.L. Jewett (Eds). 1998. *When teachers reflect: Journeys toward effective, inclusive practice.* Washington, DC: National Association for the Education of Young Children. Addresses topics such as play, working with families, and emergent curriculum. See also Jones, E. (Ed.) 1993. *Growing teachers: Partnerships in staff development.* Washington, DC: National Association for the Education of Young Children. Has the personal stories of beginning teachers, what they learned, and how.

On working conditions and improving them, try Bloom, P.J. 1997. *A great place to work: Improving conditions for staff in young children's programs.* Washington, DC: National Association for the Education of Young Children.

For information on the Canadian situation, take a look at Beach, J., J. Bertrand, & G.Cleveland. 1998. *Our child care workforce: From recognition to remuneration.* Ottawa: Child Care Human Resources Steering Committee. This publication is available free of charge; there is also is a short summary document.

The Canadian Child Care Federation has a series of publications on its Partners in Quality Project (with provincial/territorial child care organizations). The first issue looks at various aspects of quality including working conditions.

On ethics: Feeney, S. & N.K. Freeman. 1999. *Ethics and the early childhood educator.* Geared to NAEYC's Code of Ethics, with lots of thought-provoking ethical dilemmas applicable to multiple settings.

On educators' roles: Yardley, A. 1989. *The teacher of young children*. Oakville, ON: Rubicon Publishing. A small book by a well-known British early educator outlining and explaining 13 teacher roles. (This title is out of print but usually available in libraries.)

 ## Useful Addresses and Web Sites

Some of the major national early childhood organizations in Canada are listed below. The best place to begin to access information about these professional organizations in Canada including their addresses and telephone/fax numbers, e-mail addresses, and links is the Child and Family Canada Web site (www. cfc-efc.ca). The site also has lists and links to provincial early childhood organizations.

The Canadian Association for Young Children, www.cayc.ca, a non-profit organization that publishes the journal *Canadian Children* (ages 0–9). Write, fax, or e-mail

> **Membership Services**
> **c/o Rise Bulmer**
> **612 West 23rd Street**
> **North Vancouver, BC V7M 2C3**
> **Fax: 604-984-2861**
> **E-mail: info@cayc.ca**

The Canadian Child Care Federation, www.cfc-efc.ca/cccf, which produces publications including the journal *Interaction* and position papers such as Code of Ethics and National Statement on Quality Child Care.

> **383 Parkdale Avenue**
> **Suite 201, Ottawa, ON K1A 4R4**
> **Telephone: 613-729-5289 or 1-800-858-1412**
> **Fax: 613-729-3159**
> **E-mail: cccf@sympatico.ca**

Child Care Advocacy Association of Canada

> **323 Chapel Street**
> **Ottawa, ON K1N 7Z2**
> **Telephone: 613-594-3196**
> **Fax: 613-594-9375**
> **E-mail: ccaac@istar.ca**

The largest U.S. early childhood organization, the National Association for the Education of Young Children, www.naeyc.org, has a membership of more than 90,000; it offers an extensive publications list, including the journals *Young Children* and *Early Childhood Research Quarterly*. To write, phone, fax, or e-mail:

1509 16th St. NW
Washington, DC 20036-1426
Telephone: 202-232-8777
Fax: 202-328-1846
E-mail: naeyc@naeyc.org

Another large U.S.-based early childhood organization, the Association for Childhood Education International, www.udel.edu/bateman/acei, has an international membership. There are quite a few Canadian members; one of the recent past presidents was Glen Dixon from British Columbia. Their publications include the journals *Childhood Education* and *Journal of Research in Childhood Education*. Write, phone, fax, or e-mail to:

17904 Georgia Avenue, Suite 215
Olney, MD 20832
Telephone: 301-570-2111; 1-800-423-3563
Fax: 301-570-2212
E-mail: aceihq@aol.com

An interesting international professional organization is Organisation Mondiale pour l'Éducation Préscolaire (usually called OMEP or the World Organization for Early Childhood Education). This international organization holds congresses every three years in a different country. A past president is Candide Pineault from Quebec. Publishes the journal *International Journal of Early Childhood*. You can join through OMEP Canada:

569 du Fleuve, Pointe-au-Pere, Quebec
Telephone and fax: 418-723-1401
E-mail: theriaultjacqueline@moncourrier.com
Internet: www.omep.usnc.org

chapter 5

The Roots of Early Childhood Education and Care

Early childhood education has a unique history
—*Jonathan G. Silin, "Authority as Knowledge,"* Young Children

Early childhood education and care has a long history. It did not originate in the 1960s. It did not originate in the United States. And programs such as work-related child care, summer camps for poor children, and junior kindergarten are not inventions of the later twentieth century. Just as people have pondered the concept of childhood for centuries, so too have people speculated what education for young children should be. As shown in Chapter 2, there were early believers in the importance of the early years in children's development. Likewise, there were those who recognized the role of early education and care.

Part of being an early childhood professional is knowing the origins and development of early childhood education and care. The historical context helps us to better understand the

- Reasons for existing early childhood programs,
- Similarities and differences among these programs, and
- Persistence of certain issues (e.g., the content of early childhood curriculum, the role of the family, teacher education, and appropriate teaching strategies).

Knowledge of the history of our field helps us to recognize which ideas and practices have persisted and which "new" ideas are not really new but recursive. Knowing antecedents, contexts, and derivations can help us to evaluate contemporary ideas. Looking backward and examining the rich history of early childhood education and care is a necessity for looking forward in the twenty-first century.

Here are some questions to think about while you read this chapter:

- Who have been the key historical figures in the development of early childhood education and care?
- How is the influence of their ideas reflected in today's early childhood programs?
- How did early childhood programs develop and grow?
- What are the roots of Canadian early childhood programs?
- Why are there day care, nursery school, and kindergarten programs in Canada, and not just one type of program as in some other countries?
- What has been the role and significance of women in the historical and philosophical development of early childhood education and care?

Most of this chapter focuses on key individuals who have shaped, guided, and significantly influenced early childhood education and care. Their ideas were developed within historical, social, economic, political, and cultural contexts and have become part of the foundation of today's early childhood programs. Even though developed in their time, the ideas of these individuals are significant, often transcending time and place and remaining relevant and meaningful for early childhood educators today. Some of these individuals were educators; some were not. However, they all cared about young children and their early development. You may find that many of their historical thoughts and writings sound remarkably contemporary. The next section looks briefly at the ancient roots of early childhood education before continuing on to the modern sources. This approach illustrates that early childhood education and care has been a concern of important thinkers for hundreds of years.

The Early Roots

The first written documentation of discussion on early education and care is found in the writings of the ancient Greeks and Romans. For example, Plato (c. 428–348 BCE) and his student Aristotle (384–322 BCE) recognized the importance of the early years and the development of children before they begin formal schooling. Both men proposed educational systems including the early years. Although this was not early childhood education and care as we know it, the roots of early childhood education and care today can be seen in their ideas.

Plato

Plato was concerned with developing a utopian society with the goal of producing ideal human beings. These ideal people would be virtuous, wise, brave, and just. In order to achieve this ideal state, Plato outlined his ideas on education from young children through adulthood. He thought the early years were important for the development of healthy bodies, the establishment of good habits, and particularly for the early formation of character. This theme of children's character education and moral development continues in early childhood programs today.

Plato wrote that trained nurses should raise infants in communal settings. A modern version of this idea is the infant houses on some Israeli kibbutzim with their *metapelets* (trained child-care workers). From the ages of three to six, children should have opportunities to play with other children under adult supervision, such as with their nurses (Hummel, 1994). Throughout this period of infancy to age six, children should be educated at home by their parents. Plato recommended games, music, art, and literature as the "home curriculum." Storytelling was proposed as the main instructional method. However, he did point out that many of the traditional Greek myths and legends were inappropriate for young children because of the violence and other unsuitable behaviours of the gods in these stories. This question of what is appropriate literature for children and the role of censorship are still issues today.

According to Plato, formal education would begin at age six and include reading, writing, literature, mathematics, gymnastics, art, and music. This education would be compulsory for all children of the elite groups in Greek society. Although he advocated compulsory education, it was *not* universal education. However, one radical notion for that time was Plato's belief that both boys and girls should be educated and indeed educated together in the early years of formal schooling.

Plato raised many of the issues that early childhood theorists and educators would spend hundreds of years debating and operationalizing. Some of these issues are still areas of debate, such as the content of early childhood programs, the role of parents, universal access to early childhood programs, and curricula suitable for very young children.

Aristotle

Aristotle, like his teacher Plato, believed in the importance of the early years, life-long education, infanticide, censorship, education for the elite, and education for virtue. However, he did revise some of Plato's ideas. For example, he did not believe that very young children should be raised in communal settings but rather that, up to the age of seven, children should be taught at home by their mothers or nurses. Aristotle commented that this education was the responsibility of the parents and formal study and physical labour were not appropriate during these years. Thus, he might be seen as the first critic of the "hurried child."

Aristotle also addressed prenatal development. He wrote that mothers should be careful during pregnancy to exercise, eat properly, and stay calm (*Politics*, 1962, VII, xvi, 1335). This is still good advice. He also identified four subsequent stages of development: infancy, early childhood, age seven to puberty, and puberty to age 21. This division at around age seven was also suggested later by Comenius, Piaget, and others. In addition, Aristotle recognized that individual children had different strengths. Therefore, education should be geared to children's individuality and age, a belief that underlies many early childhood programs across Canada.

Aristotle advocated public education for the elite and believed the state was responsible for compulsory education from ages 7 to 21. The content of this education should be "such useful subjects as are really necessary . . . . But this does not mean the inclusion of every useful subject" (*Politics*, 1962, VIII, ii, 1337, p. 334).

Quintilian

Roman educators built on the ideas of Plato and Aristotle. For example, Quintilian (c. 35–95) identified stages in children's learning and believed that there were educational implications for each of these stages. He thought that, given the nature of young children, it was especially important for children under age seven to be exposed to good role models because they learned from example and by imitation. In Quintilian's view, young children lacked the capacity to reason and were impulsive. Moreover, he considered socialization important and advised parents to supervise children's free time and their playmates (Gutek, 1997). Quintilian advocated the use of manipulatives in teaching young children. For example, he constructed alphabet letters from ivory for children to manipulate for learning to read (a precursor of Montessori's movable alphabet in the early twentieth century). Formal education began at age seven, when boys (but not girls) were expected to attend school to learn to read, write, and calculate. He advocated using the best teachers for young children and warned parents to be certain of the teacher's good character and pedagogy.

Montessori's ideas are discussed later in this chapter.

Other Ancient Philosophers

The education of young children has never been an exclusively western European or North American phenomenon. Other ancient societies had formal systems of education; for example, Egypt, Sumeria, India, and Persia, and the Maya, Inca, and Aztec civilizations in the Americas. Likewise, scholars in ancient Asia also pondered what early education should be. One of these scholars was K'ung Fu-tzu, known to us as Confucius (551–479 BCE). He has been called the "most influential philosopher in Chinese history, and, until the Communist revolution in 1949, was the single most important influence on

Chinese thought" (Osborn, 1991, p. 13). Confucius developed ideas similar to those of Aristotle more than 150 years before and half a world away. They shared a belief in the importance of developing virtuous citizens through education and the desirability of moderation in all things. Confucius believed people could improve themselves through education and develop nobility and virtues, thus raising the moral levels of society (Yang, 1993). Although he had little to say specifically about the early development of children, his influence is still seen throughout Asian early childhood programs today; for example, in the emphasis on children's character development and children's place in society.

Confucius's views on teachers would find agreement with most early childhood educators today. He believed that

> A good teacher should first and foremost be passionately and conscientiously committed to his [or her] work . . . . must love his [or her] pupils, know them well, understand their psychological particularities, give thought to ways and means of facilitating their access to knowledge and, to that end, develop an effective methodology. (Yang, 1993, p. 215)

These early philosophers and teachers began the known process of laying out what early childhood education and care could look like. Although what they said and wrote may seem rather obvious and accepted practice for us today, their ideas were often considered radical by their fellow citizens more than 2,000 years ago.

(Note that there were educational philosophers and ideas between the ancients and the seventeenth century, but it is beyond the scope of this text to include a discussion of them here.)

FOR REFLECTION

Which of the ideas of the ancient philosophers can be seen in today's early childhood programs?

For more information about specific individuals, see the resources section at the end of the chapter.

The Modern Roots

While the importance of the early years has been recognized since the ancient philosophers, the following individuals have more recently made significant and lasting contributions, specifically to early childhood theory and practice. Their work and contributions are still recognized and appreciated by early childhood educators today.

Each of the following sections will begin with a brief biography of the individual—who they were. This background helps provide a context for the individual's development and sometimes helps explain their interest in early childhood education and care. Many of these individuals had eventful, dramatic, and sometimes difficult lives and especially childhoods—a few of them of sufficient drama for television movies. Many lived in times of social, religious, and political upheaval (e.g., Comenius and the religious wars of the seventeenth century, Pestalozzi and the French Revolution, Froebel and the Revolutions of 1848, and Montessori and the rise of Fascism). A description of their work and key contributions to early childhood education follows—what they did and said. Each section concludes with an examination of the lasting significance of their work and the implications for today—what their work has meant. A historical timeline is provided in Focus 5.1 as an overview of the rest of this chapter.

Focus 5.1

Historical Timeline for Early Childhood Education and Care, 1628 to 1926

1628
School of Infancy by John Amos Comenius is published

1657
Orbis Pictus (the first picture textbook) by Comenius is published

1762
Émile by Jean-Jacques Rousseau is published

1767
Jean Frederic Oberlin begins a knitting school in France

1800
Adelaide de Pastoret begins an infant-care program in Paris

1801
How Gertrude Teaches Her Children by Johann Pestalozzi is published

1805
Pestalozzi begins his school at Yverdon

1816
Robert Owen establishes infant school at mill at New Lanark

1826
Education of Man by Friedrich Froebel is published

1837
Froebel begins first kindergarten in Germany

1844
Jean Marbeau opens crèche in Paris

1851
Kindergarten banned by Prussian government; Bertha Ronge opens first kindergarten in London

1856
Toronto Public Nursery is established; Marguerite Schurz begins first kindergarten in North America (private, German-speaking)

1858
Sisters of Charity (the Grey Nuns) begin day nurseries in Montreal

1860
Elizabeth Palmer Peabody opens first English-speaking kindergarten in North America

1873
Susan Blow teaches first kindergarten in a public school system in North America in St. Louis

1874
Henriette Schrader-Breymann establishes Pestalozzi-Froebel House in Berlin

1878
Ada Marean opens a private kindergarten in Toronto

1883
First public school kindergarten in Canada begins in Toronto

1885
Kindergarten instruction is offered at Toronto Normal School and Ottawa Normal School; Ontario first Canadian province to approve kindergarten as part of public school system

1887
Montreal Day Nursery is established

1888
Ada Marean Hughes establishes Toronto Kindergarten Association (known today as Toronto Early Childhood Association)

1892
International Kindergarten Union is founded (becomes Association for Childhood Education in 1930, then ACEI in 1946)

1893
Patty Smith Hill becomes director of the Louisville Free Kindergarten Society

1907
Maria Montessori opens first Casa del Bambini in Rome

1911
Margaret and Rachel McMillan establish the Open Air Nursery School in London

continued

continued

1913
Caroline Pratt begins playgroup for poor children in New York City that becomes City and Country School

1915
First cooperative parent preschool begins at University of Chicago

1918
Public funding of nursery schools in Britain is authorized

1921
Patty Smith Hill establishes nursery school at Teachers College, Columbia University, and begins the National Committee on Nursery Schools in 1925 (becomes NANE in 1931, then NAEYC in 1964)

1926
St. George's School for Child Study at the University of Toronto opens (in 1939 becomes Institute of Child Study); nursery school at McGill University begins operating 1927

John Amos Comenius

Comenius' famous statement: "Let the students learn to write by writing, to talk by talking, to sing by singing, and to reason by reasoning" (*The Great Didactic*, 1657/1967, p. 195) could have been made by an early childhood educator today. It was actually said in the seventeenth century by Jan Komenský, known to us as John Amos Comenius (1592–1670). He has been called "the lost founder of early education" and his role in modern times compared to that of Plato in ancient times (Fowler, 1983, p. 67). Comenius may merit this title because he is generally considered to be the first "modern" theorist to truly recognize the importance of the early years and to propose methods for teaching young children.

Background

Comenius was a teacher before and after becoming a bishop in the Protestant Moravian Church of the Brethren in what is now the Czech Republic. Because of the religious wars and subsequent upheavals during his lifetime, he lived, taught, and wrote in many countries and influenced some of the greatest thinkers of his time and since. Unlike most of the ancient philosophers, his ideas were widely known during his lifetime. In books, pamphlets, and lectures, he elaborated principles for early education that would later be expanded by others. For example, his ideas on child development, described in his most important work *The Great Didactic* (1657/1967), were a foundation for those of later theorists such as Pestalozzi, Froebel, Montessori, Piaget, and Dewey. All were familiar with Comenius' writings and, in fact, Jean Piaget (1957) wrote a long introduction on the importance of Comenius' work as part of a three-hundredth anniversary reissue of Comenius' writings and referred to him as "the great Czech specialist in theory and practice" (p. 11).

Key Educational Ideas

Comenius' major lasting ideas concern children's development and learning, teaching methods, and the role of the home. He believed that children's development evolved in a natural way and therefore their education should be appropriate for and follow this "unfolding." Comenius used the analogy of children as plants to explain this concept and referred to children as "celestial plantlets" to be sown and watered so they would bloom and flourish (*School of Infancy*, 1628/1896, p. 11). He believed that children should not be expected to do more than they were capable: "violence is done to the intellect whenever the pupil is obliged to carry out a task which is beyond his capacities" (1657/1967, p. 114).

Comenius advocated sensory learning (i.e., knowledge is derived from experiences of the senses). This idea predated Montessori by 300 years. He stated that children learn best by doing and that it was necessary to appeal to children's senses. An essential for children's learning, according to Comenius, was motivation. He wrote that no teaching should be attempted without first gaining the children's attention and interest. To do this he advocated the use of real objects for hands-on, concrete learning and warned of the dangers of inactivity for children.

One of Comenius' major contributions was his illustrated textbooks written specifically for children. *Orbis Pictus*, published in 1657, was the most famous of his works (Good, 1960). (Today, the award for outstanding nonfiction for children by the National Council of Teachers of English is called the Orbis Pictus Award.) Comenius believed that language was the basis for subsequent learning. Consequently, he developed a textbook that taught children Latin and the vernacular language by using illustrations with accompanying short descriptive passages in each language. Comenius' textbooks helped generations of European children learn to read. He is also credited as the originator of the term "whole language," which is used today to describe a holistic philosophy to teaching reading (Goodman, 1989).

He encouraged parents and teachers to ask children meaningful questions such as, What is this? What does it do? This was a significant shift from an emphasis on rote- or drill-type questioning. He was opposed to corporal punishment of children at a time when this practice was widespread.

Comenius emphasized the importance of the physical learning environment. He wrote that it "should be a pleasant place, and attractive to the eye both within and without," and that classrooms should be clean, bright, and decorated with pictures (1657/1967, p. 131). In addition, there should be a place for play and a garden.

Comenius was a strong believer that every child should attend school. Part of his reasoning for this was his religious belief that all children are precious to God and therefore should all be educated, not just the elite or wealthy. He advocated schools for boys and girls from all social classes and divided schooling into four parts:

• *The school of the mother's knee* (ages 0–6)—Children were taught at home by their mothers or nurses (see below);

• *The vernacular school* (ages 6–12)—The language of instruction was the local language rather than the traditional Latin. The curriculum included reading, writing, mathematics, music, mechanical arts, religion, and morals;

- *The Latin school* (ages 12–18)—Intended for those children who had done well in the Vernacular School. As the name implies, instruction was in Latin, the universal language of that time.

- *University and travel* (ages 18–24)—To broaden and complete the student's education.

Comenius believed that mothers were the best teachers of young children and wrote a handbook for mothers and nurses of children under age six. This handbook, *The School of Infancy*, outlined his suggestions for mothers instructing their children. It was a parenting manual. He discussed and provided advice on children's health, breast-feeding, nutrition, safety, medications, naps, exercise, manners, language development, daily routine, and discipline, as well as spiritual care and religious instruction of the child.

Lasting Significance

Although Comenius' impact on education during his lifetime was slight (Weber, 1984), his work is still studied today. Conferences are still held to discuss his ideas and contributions to early education. Moreover, the Pedagogical Museum of J. A. Comenius in Prague displays his writings and artifacts of his life and work. Unfortunately, when I was in Prague, the museum was closed for maintenance work. However, I was fortunate to speak with Czech educators and realized how important Comenius was to the development of early education and that his significance and contributions are still recognized and appreciated today, as evidenced by the Comenius Institute of Education of the Czech Academy of Science in Prague and the Comenius University in Bratislava in the Slovak Republic (www.education.gov.sk/univ).

For me, Comenius' most significant contributions to early childhood education and care are

FOR REFLECTION

Which Canadian educator should have his or her own museum? What criteria would you use to select this person?

- The promotion of the concept of child development and growth,

- The presentation of active learning as the way young children learn best,

- The textbooks he wrote specifically for children,

- His emphasis on the importance and role of the family and his suggestions to mothers, and

- His advocacy of education for all children.

One educator who built on the ideas of Comenius 100 years later was Jean-Jacques Rousseau.

Jean-Jacques Rousseau

Jean-Jacques Rousseau (1712–1778) articulated a child-centred approach to education and advocated for children's right to be children. His ideas have influenced educators and educational theories since the eighteenth century.

Background

Rousseau was a tumultuous person in a tumultuous time. He was a protester in a time in which there was much to protest. Eighteenth-century Europe saw major political, social, and religious changes including cataclysmic ones such as the French Revolution.

Jean-Jacques Rousseau was born in Geneva, Switzerland, and raised by relatives at the death of his mother shortly after his birth and desertion by his father. Rousseau had varied careers that included being apprenticed first to a lawyer uncle (he was sent back), then to an engraver (he ran away), followed by study and conversion to Catholicism, employment as a servant (he was accused of theft), a footman (he had an affair with his mistress), a tutor, a musical composer (for examples of his work, see www.wabash.edu/Rousseau), secretary to the French ambassador to Venice (he quarrelled with diplomats), a novelist, a political writer, and a social philosopher. In the process he changed his religion twice, was banished from France for his anti-government ideas, and became mentally unstable near the end of his life. This "strange, distorted, undisciplined life" (Braun & Edwards, 1972, p. 39) nonetheless produced some of the most influential educational, social, and political ideas of the eighteenth century, which have had a profound effect on early education.

Key Educational Ideas

Rousseau's most relevant works for early childhood education and care were two novels: *Julie or the New Heloise* (in 1761) and, especially, *Émile* (in 1762). Rousseau thought this latter book was his best and most important work (Soetard, 1994). In *Julie*, he described the ideal family life, in which the mother served as teacher. Later, this idea was further developed by Pestalozzi (see next section). One of the many contradictions of Rousseau was that, although he advocated the importance of the family for children's development, he gave each of his own children to a foundling home at their births. (The odds on a child living to their fifth birthday in a foundling home then were one in four [Cannella, 1997].)

Émile, Rousseau's most significant and famous work, describes the fictitious rearing and education of a child to age 12 in a country setting by a tutor. Rousseau believed that children were naturally good and advocated that young children not be exposed to the evils of society. The famous first sentence in this novel is "God makes all things good; man meddles with them and they become evil" (1762/1993, p. 5). Rousseau felt that a role for adults was to protect children from vice and the evils of society; hence, the raising of Émile away from other people.

Stages of Development

Rousseau believed that the first 12 years of life were the most crucial developmentally. He divided development into five stages:

1. *Infancy* (0–5 years)—Rousseau believed that children's development unfolded naturally and so children should be allowed to develop naturally (e.g., allowed to explore objects in the environment).

2. *Childhood* (5–12 years)—According to Rousseau, this stage should be a "negative" stage in which the child should not be pressured or hurried into doing things, including learning. Rousseau warned "zealous teachers [to] be simple, sensible, and reticent; be in no hurry to act unless to prevent the actions of others" (1762/1993, p. 71). The emphasis during this stage should be on physical activity and sensory training. Rousseau emphasized the importance of play and wrote that Émile did not distinguish work and play, which were the same to him.

3. *Early adolescence* (12–15 years)—It is at this stage that children develop rational thought and can learn concepts such as cause and effect with ease. He stated that only those subjects that are useful, such as science and manual arts, should be studied.

4. *Later adolescence* (15–18)—At this stage, the focus should be on the development of social relationships.

5. *Adulthood* (18–20)—Study should be supplemented by travel to broaden one's perspective of the world at this stage.

In Rousseau's description of the stages of development, one can see his emphasis on children being seen as children and not miniature adults, as was typical at that time (see Chapter 2). He saw childhood as an important time not to be rushed. This view, combined with his concept of stages, led to his pedagogical ideas.

Although Rousseau never established or worked in a school, he had definite ideas on pedagogy. He saw the role of the teacher as a guide. Education should be child-centred, hands-on, and responsive to the child's curiosity and interests, especially in a natural environment. Therefore, there could be no predetermined curriculum. Rousseau believed that the child developed knowledge by interacting with the world, especially through the senses, and that children should learn at their own individual pace—beliefs that underlie many early childhood programs in Canada today.

Rousseau did not emphasize formal subjects. In fact, he was anti-reading and anti-book. He wrote, "Reading is the curse of childhood" (1762/1993, p. 95) and "I hate books; they only teach us to talk about things we know nothing about" (1762/1993, p. 176). For Rousseau, the first book children should read, and the only book for quite a while, was *Robinson Crusoe*. He wrote, "I am pretty sure Émile will learn to read and write before he is ten, just because I care very little whether he can do so before he is fifteen" (1762/1993, p. 96). Thus, Rousseau could be seen as an early advocate of not hurrying young children (see Chapter 2). He advised parents to permit "childhood to ripen in your children" (1762/1993, p. 68).

If Émile was to be educated in an enlightened way, the same was not true for Sophie, the female character in the novel. Rousseau was definitely not a believer in gender equality. He thought women were to be subservient to men as, in his view, they were weak and passive. From childhood they were to be taught the skills and duties of nurturer, homemaker, and pleasant, docile companion.

Lasting Significance

Émile was a popular bestseller in Europe and was in such demand that booksellers rented it out by the hour (Darling, 1994). Not only were Rousseau's ideas widely read and discussed during his lifetime, they had a lasting impact on early childhood education and care. It is for this reason that he is included in most early childhood textbooks. Perhaps his most significant contributions over time have been

- His ideas of children as active initiators of and participants in their own learning.

- The way he matched specific learning and teaching activities to the separate stages, going beyond Quintilian and Comenius, who also identified stage development of children. (This work was a precursor to Piaget and others.)

- His belief that children should be observed to identify their interests.

- His belief in the importance of child-centred curriculum and hands-on learning through the senses, which was later expanded by Pestalozzi, Froebel, Montessori, and others.

On the negative side, Rousseau has been criticized for not really being child-centred and for his anti-feminist views. Overall, however, Rousseau's influence on the development of early childhood education and care has been "enormous and long lasting" (Fowler, 1983, p. 75). One of Rousseau's statements with which you may identify—I do!—is "this early education . . . is only appreciated by the wise" (1762/1993, p. 151). One of the "wise" who did appreciate and expand on the ideas of Rousseau was Pestalozzi.

Johann Heinrich Pestalozzi

There is a statue of Johann Heinrich Pestalozzi (1746–1827) in a small park in Zurich. Several years ago, some friends and I were in Switzerland for an international early childhood conference. We all had our photos taken in front of the statue of Pestalozzi, much to the bemusement of the Swiss office workers who were eating their lunches on the park benches. Who was Pestalozzi, and what did he do that would make Canadian early childhood educators want to have a photo of his statue?

Pestalozzi has been called "the father of modern educational science" (Soetard, 1994, p. 297). He was a very influential thinker and advocate for the education of young children. Unlike his predecessors discussed in this chapter so far, he established schools and taught young children. Pestalozzi's ideas directly influenced Canadian educators and the development of Canadian education in the mid-1800s.

Background

Pestalozzi was born into a Swiss Protestant family of Italian origin. His father, a physician, died when Pestalozzi was five years old, and he was raised by his mother in Zurich. As a child he often visited his grandfather, a pastor in rural Switzerland, who took him on visits to poor families. Pestalozzi hated school as a child but liked university. He tried several careers (e.g., ministry, law, politics, and farming) before he found his true vocation of education.

In 1771, Pestalozzi bought a farm called Neuhof and in 1774 established it as a school for poor children—a radical idea at that time. Unfortunately, the farm and school went bankrupt in 1780 because of financial mismanagement. Undaunted, Pestalozzi directed an orphanage in Stanz from 1798–1799, taught at Burgdorf in 1799, and then went on to establish his famous school at Yverdon in 1805, which attracted visitors from all over Europe. Pestalozzi's ideas on education evolved over time. He derived some of his ideas from the works of Comenius (e.g., the education of the young and the poor) and Rousseau (e.g., the innate goodness of the children, the role of the natural environment in children's development, and sensory training). He was particularly influenced by Rousseau and even tried unsuccessfully to raise his son, named Jean-Jacques, using the ideas outlined in *Émile*. From this experience, and his teaching and running schools and orphanages, he developed his own ideas and outlined these in a novel, *Leonard and Gertrude* (1781). He described how Gertrude educated her children at home in such an exemplary way that she inspired others in her village. This book was a best-seller and won a gold medal. In a subsequent book, *How Gertrude Teaches Her Children* (1801), Pestalozzi set forth his ideas including the importance of the family, children's attachment to their mothers, and the home as a model for the school. This is probably his most influential work and has been called "a classic in education" (Osborn, 1991, p. 40). He also wrote children's books.

Pestalozzi was often described as a father figure. One former student wrote that he was:

> A very ugly man, with rough, bristling hair, his face scarred with small-pox and covered with freckles, a pointed, untidy beard, no neck-tie, ill-fitting trousers, stockings down, and enormous shoes . . . . The man we called "Father Pestalozzi" . . . . We all loved him, for he loved us all. (De Guimps, 1909, pp. 253–254)

Pestalozzi spent the last almost three decades of his life educating teachers in his method. Today his school at Yverdon is a museum and there is a large statue of him in the town square.

Key Educational Ideas

Pestalozzi believed in the education of the whole child. He expressed this as *heart–head–hand*. In other words, *love*, *the intellect*, and *manual training*. Specifically, he saw the goal of education of children as "to live, to be happy in one's station in life, to be useful in one's sphere" (cited in Anderson, 1931, p. 40). Pestalozzi recognized the importance and interrelatedness of children's emotional and cognitive development.

A key concept in Pestalozzi's method was ***anschauung***, perhaps best translated as "the process of active and interactive learning through all the senses." Although Pestalozzi saw this as his greatest contribution to educational theory, other educators found his explanations vague, imprecise, or confusing (Gutek, 1968). Froebel wrote that Pestalozzi's "addresses were very vague, and, as experience showed, were only serviceable to those already in the right way" (1908, p. 80).

Pestalozzi operationalized *anschauung* through the Object Lesson. While others before him, such as Rousseau, had advocated using real objects for instruction whenever possible, Pestalozzi outlined a specific procedure called the Object Lesson. The three stages in the Object Lesson were

1.   What kind of object is it (e.g., how many, type, etc.);

2.   What is it like (e.g., its appearance, form, size, characteristics, etc.); and

3.   What is it called (i.e., name, vocabulary, descriptive words, sentences, etc.).

The Object Lesson was designed to promote the concepts and skills needed for literacy and mathematics.

Just as Pestalozzi built on Comenius' object lesson, so too would Froebel and Montessori further develop Pestalozzi's ideas such as the Object Lesson and sensory training. Later proponents of his ideas, however, turned the Object Lesson into a "mechanistic, rote, catechetical affair in which students replied to a number of previously set questions" (Gutek, 1968, p. 160).

Pestalozzi advocated the use of real objects from the children's environment for teaching. He took children on walks to observe and discuss their environment. Other learning principles Pestalozzi identified were carefully observing children to determine their individual levels, beginning with what the children already know, moving from the concrete to the abstract, and oral language preceding reading and drawing preceding writing.

Pestalozzi's educational ideas incorporated social and humanistic dimensions. He advocated the inclusion of poor children in schools and worked with them in his school and orphanage. He demonstrated that poor children could learn as well as their wealthier peers if conditions were right (Noddings, 1998). From these experiences, he also became convinced of the importance of emotional security and love for children and the need for the school environment to reflect this. He prohibited flogging in his schools. However, this prohibition was not always honoured in later schools purporting to follow his principles. Thomas Dence (1911), the great-grandfather of one of my colleagues, wrote of his experiences in the 1840s at Mr. Ebenezer Prout Newcombe's Pestalozzian School in London:

> It was a mixed school, taking both boys and girls, taught in separate classes of 20 to 50 each. The assistant master was a German, there was also a lady teacher. Mr. Newcombe had a long 6-foot pointer freely used both for demonstration and castigation. (p. 14)

Pestalozzi believed that education began in the home and saw the school as the connector between the home and society. While recognizing that not all home situations were ideal, he stated the importance of mothers as the first teachers of children: "Whoever has the welfare of the rising generation at heart, cannot do better than consider as his highest object, the Education of Mothers" (Pestalozzi, cited in Rusk, 1933, p. 44). Pestalozzi expressed concern over the effects of the industrialization of nineteenth-century Europe on the family (similar to authors today writing on the decrease of family time because of work responsibilities).

Pestalozzi perceived parents as teachers, and teachers as parent figures. He believed that teaching was an honourable occupation (not always the common view at that time) and one that required caring, knowledgeable, moral individuals. Perhaps because of his agricultural experience, he saw the teacher as a gardener—tending the young plants and facilitating their growth through careful attention to all of their needs.

Lasting Significance

Pestalozzi was a well-known writer and educator during his lifetime, and some of his books were translated into other languages. He established schools that were visited by many people, including Froebel, much as the schools of Reggio-Emilia are visited by today's educators. Pestalozzi's schools were considered innovative and advanced with their balanced curriculum that provided for the education of the whole child and included music, art, and outdoor activities. His emphasis on hands-on learning and real objects, progression from the simple to the complex, and the use of domestic tasks were ideas that would later be used by Froebel and Montessori in their approaches. He emphasized the importance of the environment, as did Montessori, and the advantages of outdoor activities, as did the McMillan sisters later on.

Pestalozzi's recognition of teacher education and his training of teachers, including Froebel, at his schools was another lasting contribution to early childhood education. According to Downs (1975), "the idea of professional training of teachers probably originated with Pestalozzi" (p. 89). He was especially concerned with educating teachers to work with younger children and poor children.

Although it has been said that in terms of teaching techniques, "Pestalozzi invented nothing, not even the slate, and that he borrowed what was useful from all and sundry" (Soetard, 1994, p. 303), Pestalozzi made practical and workable many of the ideas of his predecessors, as well as adding his ideas. He influenced many of the early childhood theorists who came after him such as Froebel, Owen, Montessori, and Piaget. One of the deterrents to the spread of his methods was that although many educators were inspired by his ideas, they did not really understand how to apply them.

An example of the international impact of Pestalozzi's ideas was the Home and Colonial School Society, begun in England in 1836 to promote Pestalozzi's ideas. It established a model Pestalozzi school in London and educated thousands of teachers in Pestalozzi's methods (Good, 1960). His ideas would be applied in North America in an infant school in Robert Owen's utopian community in New Harmony (see next section).

Pestalozzi's ideas directly impacted Canadian education. The first super-intendents of schools in Ontario in the mid-1800s were proponents of Pestalozzi's ideas (Phillips, 1957). For example, Egerton Ryerson wrote a report in 1846 advocating the use of Pestalozzi's ideas, including the Object Lesson, in the public elementary schools of Ontario. His influence was also seen in the writing of educators in Ontario, Nova Scotia, Prince Edward Island, New Brunswick, and Quebec throughout the 1800s (Phillips, 1957; Wilson, Stamp, & Audet, 1970).

Pestalozzi's ideas continued to influence early childhood programs. For example, after the Second World War, Pestalozzi villages were established in Switzerland to care for orphans and refugees (much as Pestalozzi had cared for the young victims of war at the orphanage at Stanz). When these villages were closed in the 1960s, the Pestalozzi Children's Village Trust continued its work with child refugees such as Tibetan children in India, as well as other children in India, Thailand, Nigeria, and Vietnam. Currently, the Pestalozzi Overseas Trust provides scholarships for children over age 16 to finish secondary school and attend higher-education institutions in their own countries or abroad (www3.mistral.co.uk).

In summary, Pestalozzi's major contributions to early childhood education are his

- Emphasis on the observation of children,

- Education of the whole child (head–heart–hand),

- Recognition of children's need for emotional security and love as prerequisites to optimal learning,

- Use of active learning and the use of the senses for learning, including the development of the Object Lesson,

- Inclusion of poor children in schooling,

- Recognition of the importance of the home and the need to educate mothers, and

- Application of learning principles such as progressing from the concrete to the abstract and the simple to the complex, and drawing before writing.

Two of the many visitors to Pestalozzi's school were Robert Owen from England and Friedrich Froebel from Germany. Both, in turn, made significant contributions to early childhood education and care and will be discussed in the next two sections.

Robert Owen

An enthusiast of Pestalozzi's ideas was Robert Owen (1771–1858), a self-made industrialist, idealist, visionary, social reformer, social philosopher, opponent of child labour, founder of the cooperative movement, and the originator of

FOR REFLECTION

How were Pestalozzi's ideas similar to those of his predecessors and how are they similar to those of educators today?

employer-supported child care. Owen became concerned about the welfare of young children during the Industrial Revolution in Great Britain, when children seven years old and sometimes even younger worked in factories, mills, and mines for 14 hours a day (Gordon, 1994). It was estimated that almost half the employees in spinning mills in northern England and Scotland were children (Morton, 1962). A contemporary described Owen as being kind and well intentioned, with "an enthusiastic desire to promote the happiness of mankind" (Cole, 1953, p. 72).

Background

Robert Owen began his educational career at age seven when he tutored his sisters and other children. He was apprenticed as a shop assistant to a draper when he was 10 years old. By the time he was 20, he was the manager of a cotton mill in Manchester. By 1800, he was part owner and manager of the largest cotton mill in Scotland, where he improved the working conditions, housing, and health of his employees. He also established an infant school at his mill in New Lanark in 1816 for the children of mill employees and children under 10 who were working in the mill. Visitors from Britain as well as other countries came to New Lanark to observe his reforms. In 1824, after a falling out with his partners, he resigned from the school and left for the United States, where he established a utopian community based on cooperative socialism in New Harmony, Indiana, in 1825. The school was planned as the centre of the community. After this community failed in 1827, he returned to England and spent the rest of his life promoting the cooperative and labour union movements.

Key Educational Ideas

Owen, an "idealistic humanitarian" (Mayer, 1973, p. 292), was influenced by the work of Rousseau and Pestalozzi, among others. He believed education should be egalitarian, universal, early, natural, enjoyable, and should promote happiness. In his educational scheme, there would be no corporal punishment, no scolding, only "unceasing kindness in tone, look, word, and action, to all children without exception" (Owen, 1968, p. 173). He believed character developed from the innate nature of children interacting with the environment. Therefore, a favourable environment was very important for children's development and especially their moral development.

Owen advocated the use of manipulative materials and objects found in the children's environment; however, he echoed Rousseau when he wrote, "booklearning should be postponed until the age of ten" (Owen, 1813/1970, p. 33). His curriculum included physical exercise such as dancing from age two and military drill from age five, music, singing, art, dancing, geography, history, natural science, and mathematics based on Pestalozzi's work. However, this curriculum was more subject-specific than that of Pestalozzi.

While Owen did not develop original educational methodologies, "he was the first to put them into practice on a large scale" (Morton, 1962, p. 102). The infant school at New Lanark had three levels:

- three- to six-year-olds (half day),

- six- to ten-year-olds (from 7:30 a.m. to 5 p.m.), and

- older children and adults working in the mill (evening classes).

Outdoor activities were important and the younger children spent much of their time playing outdoors on the paved playground in front of the school. About half of their school time was spent in lessons. There did not seem to be a specific timetable for the children's activities. No child was required to do an activity, including nap. There was also provision made for using space in the infant school for parent education, for as Owen told parents, "my friends, you are yet very deficient with regard to the best modes of training your children" (1968, p. 89).

Lasting Significance

Robert Owen's most significant contribution to early childhood education and care is written on his tombstone: "He originated and organized infant schools" (Harrison, 1968, p. 1). He popularized this type of school and was responsible for the growth of infant schools in Britain. However, it can be argued that Owen's infant school was not the first of its type. Jean Frederic Oberlin (1740–1826) was a French Protestant pastor in Alsace who, beginning in 1767, organized "knitting schools" (*écoles à tricoter*) for the young children of working parents. He employed young women to teach and play with the children as well as to teach the older children to spin, knit, and sew. However, these knitting schools did not spread beyond France.

Owen's infant schools are considered to be the forerunner of day-care programs. His ideas of lifelong education, especially for poor and working families and their children, were a part of his program of social reform and the creation of a new society. His recognition of the need for these programs and his willingness and ability to do something about it was 200 years before the early childhood poverty programs in North America. A summary of Robert Owen and his work is that he was a good person who did good work for young children and families at a time when the needs of workers and their families were not typically considered by their employers.

Infant schools based on Owen's model were also established in France, Germany, and Italy in the early 1800s (White & Buka, 1987). The infant school concept had also spread to North America by 1825 (Pence, 1990).

Infant Schools in North America

North American infant schools were sponsored by charitable organizations, churches, wealthy individuals, and schools. Many of these groups and individuals saw the infant schools as a means of ameliorating the problems of nineteenth-century urban life. It was hoped that poverty could be eliminated through the education of young children from poor families. The 1960s were not the first time this rationale for compensatory early childhood programs was voiced.

FOR REFLECTION

Robert Owen said that, "the state which shall possess the best national system of education will be the best governed" (New View of Society, 1813/1970, p. 187). Canada does not have a national system of education at the pre-school, elementary, secondary, or post-secondary level. What would be your reply to Robert Owen?

Early childhood poverty programs in North America, such as the Head Start program, are discussed later in this chapter.

The infant schools were found primarily in major cities along the Atlantic coast, from Charlottetown to Savannah. In Canada, they spread to Halifax, Kingston, Montreal, and Toronto (Prochner, 1995). These schools provided for a broader-based clientele than Robert Owen's infant schools. One of the first infant schools in Canada was begun by several women in 1828 for the instruction and care of local poor children (Prochner, 2000). The Montreal Infant School Society established additional infant schools that were used by a cross-section of their local communities.

The Infant School Movement in the United States was relatively short-lived and began to fade in the 1830s, but it continued in Canada until late in that century, especially in New Brunswick and Newfoundland (Prochner, 2000). Nonetheless, the infant schools were one of the roots of day-care centres. Other origins are crèches and day nurseries (described later in this chapter). Infant schools sparked early arguments about early education and its role in dealing with social problems. At that time, it was believed that infant schools "could permanently eliminate poverty by educating and socializing young children from poor families" (Spodek & Saracho, 1994, p. 33). The decline of the infant schools occurred at the same time as the rise of kindergarten.

Friedrich Froebel

Friedrich Wilhelm August Froebel (1782–1852) is called the father of kindergarten. His kindergarten "can be considered the beginnings of early childhood education as it is practiced today" (Williams, 1992, p. 49). This German educator put the ideas of Comenius, Pestalozzi, and others into practice in a school he originally named *kleinkinderbeschäftigungsanstalt* (i.e., "an institution where small children are occupied"); thankfully, this term was later shortened to **kindergarten** in 1840. Kindergarten is a German word meaning "children's garden" (its German origin is why *kindergarten* is spelled with a *t* and not a *d*).

Background

Froebel was the sixth child of a German pastor. His mother died a few months after his birth. Froebel later claimed that this event determined "the external circumstances of my whole life" (1908, p. 3). His stepmother took little interest in him, and at 10 he went to live with an uncle. Even more so than Pestalozzi, Froebel had numerous careers: surveyor, forester, science student, private secretary, architecture student, teacher, mineralogy and crystallography student (he was offered the curatorship of the Mineralogy Museum in Stockholm but declined), and soldier in the Napoleonic Wars. From 1804 to 1807, he worked in a Pestalozzi-type school in Frankfurt, and then as a tutor at Yverdon from 1808 to 1810. As did many others, Froebel found Pestalozzi's method difficult to understand, and wrote in his *Autobiography* that Pestalozzi "could never give any definite account of his idea, his plan, his intention. He always said, Go and see for yourself (very good for him who knew *how* to look, how to hear, how to perceive); 'it works splendidly!'" (1908, p. 57). Froebel must have seen, as he wrote in his *Autobiography*, "I passed a glorious time at Yverdon, . . . critically decisive for my after life" (1908, p. 83).

He founded his first school, the Universal German Educational Institution, in 1816 to educate his three nephews. Froebel outlined his philosophy of education in *The Education of Man* in 1826. The same year, he developed his Gifts and Occupations (described below). He then founded a school specifically for three- to seven-year-old children in Blankenburg in 1837. In 1844, he published his book for mothers, entitled *Come Let Us Live for Our Children. Mother Songs, as well as Songs for Games with Body Limbs and Senses. For the Early and Uniting Care of Childhood. A Family Book by Friedrich Froebel* (more commonly called *The Mother Song Book*).

In 1849, Froebel began to educate kindergarten teachers in his school. The growth of kindergarten in Germany was short-lived, as the Prussian government banned kindergarten in 1851 as an atheistic and politically subversive institution. Froebel died the next year. The banned kindergartens and teacher institute were allowed to reopen in 1861.

Key Educational Ideas

Like Pestalozzi before him, Froebel constructed a philosophy of education on a foundation lain by previous theorists. From Comenius, he stressed the importance of mothers, school for young children, the integrated teaching of reading and writing, and the analogy of the child as a developing plant. Froebel shared with Rousseau a belief in children learning through the senses, the role of play in children's development, and an emphasis on nature. However, Pestalozzi was perhaps the greatest influence on Froebel's educational ideas. This is not surprising, as Froebel taught at Pestalozzi's school. He extended Pestalozzi's ideas, such as the Object Lesson, the educational training of teachers, education in the home, matching tasks to children's levels, and others. As one Froebel scholar wrote, "Froebel developed and perfected Pestalozzi's ideas about 'how to teach' in such a way that it is no longer possible to enter a contemporary classroom without being aware of his influences" (Liebschner, 1992, p. x). Froebel was also influenced by the events and philosophies of his day and life including his Christian faith, his love of nature, and the Romanticism, nationalism, and scientific movements.

Froebel's philosophy of education can be divided into three major areas:

- the nature of children and childhood,
- the concept of unity and connectedness, and
- the role of play.

Froebel, like Comenius and Pestalozzi and others before him, frequently used the analogy of children as plants. He envisioned their development as a parallel to the development of other living things. Like seeds and plants, he believed that children needed a favourable environment and care for continuous growth and development.

Froebel recognized, respected, and encouraged children's uniqueness and creativity and believed that children's natural instincts "were proper and worthy of encouragement" (Downs, 1978, p. 53). Froebel agreed with Comenius and Pestalozzi on the importance of the early years and the influence of the home on children's moral development.

A second key component of Froebel's philosophy was the concept of unity and connectedness. He wrote about the unity of life: "the child's life in and with himself, his family, nature, and God is as yet a unit" (Froebel, 1826/1887, p. 56). His concept of unity included the idea of harmony: in the home, the classroom, and the natural world. He wrote about the connectedness of all things including nature, God, and human beings. He saw school as part of the continuity and connectedness of home, school, and the world. His symbolic use of the circle is seen in his First Gift, circle games, and the use of circle time still seen in programs today.

Visitors to Froebel's schools frequently commented on his play with the children. One of his greatest supporters, the Baroness Bertha Marie von Marenholtz-Bulow, described her first sight of Froebel: "A tall, spare man with long grey hair was leading a troop of village children between the ages of three and eight, most of them barefooted, up a hill where they played and sang" (Froebel-Parker at www.geocities.com). This is not surprising, as play was a cornerstone of his educational theory. Froebel wrote that "play is the highest phase of child development . . . [and] play at this time is not trivial, it is highly serious and of deep significance" (1826/1887, pp. 54–55). He promoted play activities and designed materials, called Gifts, to promote children's purposeful play activities. Although the play activities in the Froebel kindergarten seem rather formal and structured by today's standards, this was very innovative in the 1800s. He distinguished the process-oriented play of young children from the more formal, goal-oriented play and games of older children.

A major contribution of Froebel was the development of materials and activities to encourage children's learning through activity. Many of their derivations are still used today. His three types of materials and activities were:

- Gifts

- Occupations

- Mother songs and plays.

The **Gifts** were hands-on objects to be manipulated by the children to help them recognize and understand the unity and interconnectedness between their lives and the forms, patterns, and laws of the natural world (Liebschner, 1992). Froebel's ten Gifts, grouped by type, are:

- *Solids*—Six yarn balls of different colours (the ball represented the unity of people, God, and nature);

- *Surfaces*—A wooden ball, cube, and cylinder; a two-inch wooden cube divided into eight equal pieces; a two-inch wooden cube divided into six

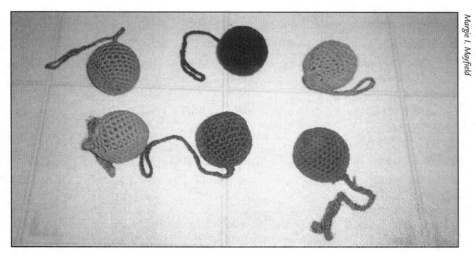

Froebel's first Gift

pieces; a three-inch wooden cube divided into 27 one-inch cubes; a three-inch wooden block divided into 36 pieces; a set of coloured squares and triangles (parquetry);

- *Lines*—A set of wooden sticks of varying lengths (like Cuisenaire rods); a set of rings and pieces of rings one to three inches in diameter;

- *Points*—A set of peas and small sticks.

These Gifts are still being made in Germany and are available in North America (for examples, see www.quincyshop.com/quincy/froebel).

Each child and teacher had his or her own set of Gifts, which were kept in individual wooden boxes with sliding lids. The children were allowed to play with the Gifts as long as they were interested, although the teacher might ask questions similar to Pestalozzi's in his Object Lesson to assist children in seeing similarities and differences. For each Gift, "the child would learn to handle the gift, how to place it appropriately on the specially lined Froebel table, and how to use the many facets of the gift" (Ransbury, 1982, p. 105). The child would also manipulate the Gift, be encouraged to compare it to other objects, name its properties, and build with it or make patterns. Froebel also wrote songs for use with each Gift.

Froebel's Gifts have been credited with some interesting outcomes. For example, Frank Lloyd Wright, the great twentieth-century architect, credited his interest and success in architecture to a set of Froebel blocks his mother purchased at the Centennial Exposition in Philadelphia in 1876. He recalled frequently working at his kindergarten table with the Froebel Gifts and wrote, "Eventually I was able to construct designs in other mediums. But the . . . maple-wood blocks were most important. All are in my fingers to this day" (Wright, 1957/1995, p. 159). Wright's biographer noted, "Indeed, many of Wright's buildings have been said to be derived from basic Froebelian forms.

Wright himself noted that his habit of designing on a modular plan directly paralleled the exercises in which Froebel encouraged children to arrange wooden blocks on a two-dimensional grid to create geometric patterns and structures" (Costantino, 1998, p. 10). I grew up not far from some of Frank Lloyd Wright's famous early houses. Even as a young child, I could see that these were very different from the typical houses in the area. Perhaps their unconscious appeal to me as a child was that they did look like structures that could be made from blocks or Lego.

Whereas the Gifts were concrete materials to be manipulated by the children to learn about their environment, the **Occupations** were complementary activities designed to practise specific skills and developmental areas. They were extensions of the Gifts and included the following activities:

- Perforating (poking holes around a design with a needle)

- Sewing/embroidery

- Drawing

- Weaving with slats

- Paper weaving

- Paper folding (origami)

- Building with peas and sticks

- Folding paper to make three-dimensional structures

- Modelling with clay.

The presentation of the Occupations went from points to solids, the reverse order from the Gifts (see Figure 5.1 for a visual representation of the Gifts and Occupations used in a Froebel training program in Toronto in the 1940s.)

Although the Occupations resulted in a product and were often taken home as a present, the emphasis was still on process, not product (Corbett, 1989). One can see the correspondence of the Occupations with many of the activities in today's early childhood programs. Pestalozzi had children observing nature (e.g., animals, plants, and the land); Froebel added more hands-on activities. For example, children not only observed and collected plants but also

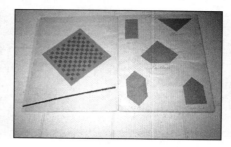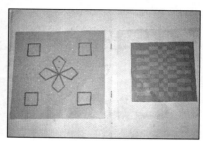

Margie I. Mayfield

Examples of Froebel's Occupations: Embroidery, paper folding, and paper weaving (done by Edna Aedy).

figure 5.1   DIAGRAM OF THE RELATIONSHIP OF FROEBEL'S GIFTS
AND OCCUPATIONS

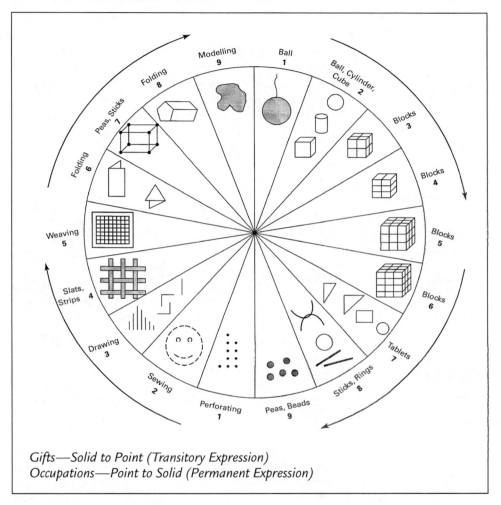

Gifts—Solid to Point (Transitory Expression)
Occupations—Point to Solid (Permanent Expression)

Source: From Edna Aedy's class notes.

grew them. Froebel provided gardening activities in his kindergarten (very appropriate, given the name). Each child had a plot of land for his or her own garden as well as the group garden. Early drawings of the original kindergarten show the gardens to be quite prominent and extensive. This feature of Froebel's kindergarten seems not to have been incorporated by others in many subsequent kindergartens. Susan Blow, an early Froebelian kindergarten teacher, wrote, that the kindergarten was much impaired by not following Froebel's recommendations for including gardening and the care of pets (1894/1910). It is interesting that the care of pets and gardening are considered important activities in today's early childhood programs for fostering children's environmental awareness and appreciation of nature.

Froebel thought the family was important and that the "union of the family and school life is the indispensable requisite of education" (1882/1887, p. 230). Froebel wrote a weekly periodical for families that provided helpful suggestions and ideas. Like Pestalozzi before him, Froebel also wrote a book for mothers to use with their infants and toddlers at home. His *Mother Songs and Plays* was a collection of 50 songs, fingerplays, and games. These were later used in the kindergarten. The purpose of these activities was to encourage physical play between mother and child utilizing motor skills, and the senses, to promote "knowledge about the world around the child and the symbolic meaning of life" (Liebschner, 1992, p. 104). These songs and plays helped develop sensory and perceptual awareness to foster children's thinking—an idea very similar to Piaget's theory. Each of these activities had a story with an illustration accompanied by a song suitable for a fingerplay and a commentary on the activity for the mother. The subjects were the family, daily activities such as gardening, and common objects such as birds, gates, and milk.

An example of a Mother Play is the "Pigeon House." In this Mother Play, there is a picture of a pigeon house with birds flying in and out. There is also a mother bird on a nest in a tree and children walking home from a field. According to Susan Blow (1894/1910), the purpose of this Mother Play is to show the mother how to integrate herself into her child's life with love and sympathy. The child is meant to see home as a dovecote and see self as a dove that flies away but always returns home. There are instructions for a fingerplay. It ends with the line "The world is pleasant, but home is best" (Blow, 1895/1903, p. 44).

A Day in a Froebel Kindergarten

Susan Blow (1894/1910) described a typical day in a Berlin Froebel kindergarten as beginning with a 15-minute conversation time with the children sitting around "their motherly friend" (p. 215). The teacher then took the children in groups of six or seven to look at and discuss one or two illustrations from *The Mother Plays*. The fingerplay and song were then taught. The rest of the children were doing Occupations or were in the garden with an assistant. Table activities were usually followed by active games or exercise, then work with the Occupations (Brosterman, 1997). There were also excursions and stories (often illustrating a moral point, such as the theme of child obedience in "Little Red Riding Hood"). The day ended with a goodbye song.

A contemporary example of a Froebel kindergarten is the Froebel Education Centre in Mississauga, Ontario, which enrolls approximately 50 children from three to seven years of age. Their day begins with Opening Circle, including a greeting song, prayer, and a Bible or inspirational thought for the day that the children discuss and relate to their own experiences. The kindergartner works with eight or nine children around a large table. (See Focus 5.2 for a description.) Activity times for the three- to five-year-olds include Gifts, Occupations, and outdoor play. Those for the six- to seven-year-olds are language arts, theme studies, mathematics, occupations, and outdoor play. Circle time, singing games, stories, music, free play, and snacks are part of the daily program (Corbett, 1990; and personal communication November 1999).

A Froebel Education

By Karen King, Kindergartner, and
Barbara E. Corbett, Director
The Froebel Education Centre,
Mississauga, Ontario

Our Kindergarten is for children ranging in age from three to seven years; a family grouping as Froebel intended. We also use the toys and activities he suggested. To promote their wholesome, creative and knowledgeable growth, Froebel designed toys which he called Gifts and suggested complementary art and craft activities which he referred to as Occupations. These Gifts and Occupations, in the hands of knowledgeable and wise kindergartners, can not only open out the world of things to children but also by the playful spirit employed, children are helped to form positive and healthy attitudes towards learning.

The Gifts are fundamental shapes found in nature. The shapes include spheres, cubes, bricks, geometrical surfaces, lines, rings and points. Using their creative powers and imagination, children can create solid forms, pictures, outlines of forms or straight and curved artistic lines.

An example of one Gift is the round rings. This Gift consists of three whole metal rings (with the largest having a diameter of two inches and the smallest one inch) and six corresponding half rings. At the beginning of the Gift Play the kindergartner might distribute one ring to each of nine children sitting around their table. The children are asked for their observations about the ring. They might comment on what it looks like, what it is made of, what it feels like, what it sounds like, or what it can do. Responses that might be heard from three- or four-year-olds include: "It fits my wrist," "I can twirl it on my finger" or "Look, I can spin it like a top." The children might try to roll it across the table but notice that it falls over and spins. They will call out, "Listen to it ring," as it drops onto the table. The excitement is palpable. For the children the ring can become a steering wheel, a Ferris wheel, the sun, the moon, or even a cat. The children have not only thought about their own idea but also

hear and share in the ideas of eight other children at the table. As these ideas multiply they in turn provide new energy and stimulus for the children's further activity and learning.

The next day they might again be given one large ring but then a half ring will be added to it. Additional rings are added on succeeding days. What are the possibilities with more rings? What idea will each child suggest? What story will a child tell about his or her idea? The only thing the kindergartner can be sure of is that the ideas and stories will come out of the children's own experiences. By pursuing one thought at a time the children discover the possibilities of things and then begin to combine them in new ways that again express their creative and formative instinct. Each child definitely takes the ownership of his construction. The kindergartner listens, observes, and responds with helpful language, interesting conversation, enthusiasm and song. As she talks and sings appropriate songs she is building on the ideas expressed by the children. Thus, Gift Play is a special happy time with each child contributing.

Such an education is vital and meaningful. The children are full of life and interacting in creative ways with their environment. The kindergartner is guiding her little group, talking with them and singing. What could be a happier atmosphere and learning environment? Froebel wrote, "Come, let us live in harmony with our children." Let us live with them by interacting with them and enjoying them. The impressions they form of love and understanding, joy, and companionship, as well as the knowledge gained through experience will be deep and lasting. Only that kind of foundation laid during their early years will bear the structure of the sound education which is to be built upon it.

Teacher Education

Froebel saw the role of the teacher as that of guide or facilitator and believed in teacher education. Teachers came to Froebel's lectures and kindergarten to learn more about his approach, much in the way he went to Pestalozzi's school many years before. He recognized the need for a formal teacher education program and began one in 1849 with eight students. The program lasted up to six months. The teachers were called **kindergartners**, which is a term still used in some Froebel programs.

The students were mostly women. Froebel, especially in his later years, became an advocate and promoter of higher education for women. This may have been because, in part, "he found sympathy and understanding among women, comparatively little among men" (Downs, 1978, p. 45). The man who had been a motherless child with no sisters and who married later in life became supportive of and instrumental in the education of women. His education of liberal-minded women helped the rapid growth of kindergarten and other social programs throughout Europe and to North America in the years following the ban on kindergarten.

During Froebel's time, many saw women educators as a threat. At one conference of educators, Froebel spoke out strongly on the need for women teachers. The male audience laughed at him and one of the education professors asked him, "'Does Herr Froebel mean we shall eventually have women university professors?'—and the minutes record that the assembly once more erupted in hilarious laughter" (Liebschner, 1992, p. 28). Froebel might be gratified to know that today there are indeed women professors of education. In addition, Froebel Colleges exist in London, Dublin, Berlin, Bolivia, and the Canary Islands. In Canada, Froebel teacher education is offered at the Froebel Education Centre in Mississauga. (See Focus 5.2 for a description of the Froebel Education Centre's day.)

Criticisms of Froebel's Ideas

Froebel was heavily criticized both during his lifetime and afterward. Even though his ideas and work were widely known during his lifetime, they were not always understood by his contemporaries and were often interpreted as being radical and even revolutionary. He was criticized for allowing too much freedom and for lack of specific direction. This is ironic as he is now criticized for advocating too much formality and structure in his instruction and for not providing for children's creativity (Piaget, 1970). Moreover, his materials and tasks have been considered as not meaningful for children in the twenty-first century. Froebel originally meant his materials to be "auto-didactic" or self-evaluative (Liebschner, 1992), much in the way Montessori designed her materials. However, many of the followers of Froebel seemed to use the materials in a more rigid, inflexible manner. As early as 1894, Susan Blow was bemoaning the fact that the use of Froebel's materials had become formalized and "consists in attributing a magic power to Froebel's gifts and games, and in expecting blocks and balls, songs and gestures to do the work which can only be accomplished by human insight and devotion" (1894/1920, pp. 213–214).

Froebel's description of children as plants is seen today as being not very comprehensive, with an overemphasis on maturation in that it does not include social, cultural, and environmental factors impacting on children's development. However, perhaps it is unfair to criticize Froebel for his use of the children as plants analogy. He may have emphasized this comparison as it was easy for non-educators to understand and was an analogy that had been used before by earlier theorists such as Comenius and Pestalozzi.

Another area of criticism has been Froebel's Gifts. According to Liebschner (1992), the Gifts were considered to be "too simple for children to play with and at the same time too difficult for teachers to understand" (p. 117). The materials have been criticized as being too narrow in their use and the range of activities (Fowler, 1983). They were also criticized for being overly structured.

Perhaps the most devastating criticism for Froebel himself was the banning of kindergarten in 1851. He did not live to see its return and expansion. Indeed, by 1872, Froebel's method was compulsory throughout the Austro-Hungarian Empire (Brosterman, 1997).

Lasting Significance

Perhaps the most obvious and lasting of Froebel's contributions to early childhood education and care was the name and concept of "kindergarten" and its current presence as part of public education throughout the world. Kindergarten has indeed been an educational success story. However, the ideas that supported kindergarten were also significant. Many of the principles and practices common in today's early childhood programs can be traced to Froebel and his kindergarten. These ideas include:

- A child-centred rather than subject-focused approach and the integration and connectedness of curriculum and activities.

- The use of observation.

- The role of children's play in their learning and development (although this was more structured than today's free play).

- His materials and promotion of using concrete materials.

- His emphasis on activities that are appropriate for the size of the children and their developmental levels.

- The fact that many of the manipulative materials and activities in today's early childhood programs are derivatives of Froebel's Gifts and Occupations.

- The ways that Froebel's mother songs and games and their use in his kindergartens can be seen as the early form of today's circle time with its songs, fingerplays, and group games.

According to Corbett (1990), "Froebel's philosophy and approach to early childhood education . . . have more relevance for us today than they had in his own time" (p. 108). What aspects of contemporary early childhood education and care would be recognized and approved by Froebel?

- His advocacy of universal education and the education of women.

- His support of women as teachers of young children despite his being criticized for promoting feminism and undermining the family.

- His recognition of and support for the role of the family in the education and development of young children; Froebel believed in the interconnectedness of the family/home and the school.

- His publication of a weekly newsletter for families as well as the book *Mother Songs and Plays*.

Froebel influenced many people of his time and later, as well as changing the look of early childhood programs forever. As the father of kindergarten, he left a legacy for early childhood education and care. At the very end of his life, Froebel toyed with the idea of moving his kindergarten to North America. Although he did not live to do this, many of the teachers educated at his kindergartens and his supporters spread kindergartens internationally after 1851.

Women and the Development and Growth of Early Childhood Education and Care

If Rousseau, Pestalozzi, and Froebel are considered to be the fathers of early childhood education and care, then the women who were instrumental in the growth of their programs throughout Europe, North America, and other countries can certainly be considered its mothers. Unlike other levels of education in the late nineteenth and twentieth centuries, women have played more prominent and leadership roles in early childhood education and care. Feminism permeates the history of early childhood education and care. This is seen perhaps most clearly in the growth of kindergarten.

Many of the strongest advocates and promoters of kindergarten were women. In Germany, for example, many of the women who spread Froebel's ideas and kindergartens also participated in the women's movements (Reyer, 1989). Early education in the mid and later nineteenth century was seen as a logical extension of the traditional interests of women—children, the poor, and the sick. The kindergarten movement was one that "urged women to find public applications for the virtues of the private sphere" (Allen, 1988, p. 26).

Froebel's niece, Henriette Schrader-Breymann, used the phrase "spiritual motherhood" to explain that "women's special talent for nurture would benefit not only her immediate family but a society which [was] sorely in need of the enlightened and compassionate female influence" (Allen, 1982, p. 319). This idea was part of the kindergarten movement from its earliest stages. It was used as one rationale for women in kindergarten and teacher education for women (Allen, 1982).

Kindergarten teaching appealed to a variety of women: liberal-minded women, philanthropic and religious women, career-oriented women, and women of all classes. Their motivations seemed to range from altruism to political and social activism to a need for personal and financial autonomy. These women "wrote books, lectured, taught, and trained others in kindergarten pedagogy. They took opportunities that had not previously been available to them" (Cannella, 1997, p. 97). The adoption of kindergartens into public school systems further increased the visibility and role of women in education.

The profiles of the women in the following sections on the kindergarten movement and the development of nursery schools and Montessori programs illustrate the importance of women and their key roles in the growth and development of early childhood education and care.

The Kindergarten Movement

Before kindergartens were banned in Germany in 1851, they had already begun to increase. Before the days of mass media communication, common methods of disseminating ideas were through books and lectures. For example, Froebel wrote and published materials about his program during his life, but he and others also disseminated their ideas through lectures. One of his most energetic disciples was Baroness von Marenholtz-Bulow (1810–1893), who devoted years of her life to educating kindergartners and spreading the word about kindergarten throughout Europe. In addition to individuals, collective efforts were also common, such as those of the German Froebel Society.

Bertha Ronge and Marguerite Schurz

Two German Froebel-trained sisters were responsible for the development of kindergarten in England, from where it came to North America. The banning of kindergarten was part of a greater government crackdown on the growth of liberal thought in Germany and other European countries in the mid-nineteenth century. Many liberal thinkers left Germany and emigrated to other countries; these emigrants included Bertha Meyer Ronge and her sister Marguerite Meyer Schurz.

Bertha Ronge established the first kindergarten in London in 1851. This was a private kindergarten. Ronge was responsible for a demonstration of kindergarten at an international exhibition in London in 1854 that effectively publicized kindergarten and encouraged its growth in Britain. She also began English-language kindergarten teacher education. Ronge advocated public kindergartens and Froebel training for all women (Beatty, 1995). Her sister fulfilled Froebel's dream of taking kindergarten to the United States.

Marguerite Meyer Schurz (1833–1876) established the first kindergarten in North America in 1856. This was a private German-speaking kindergarten for Schurz's two daughters and their four cousins in Watertown, Wisconsin. The house of the original kindergarten is now a museum and its original site (now a parking lot) is indicated by a plaque.

Elizabeth Peabody

A meeting crucial for the future of kindergarten in North America occurred at a social gathering in Boston in 1859, when Marguerite Schurz met Elizabeth

Palmer Peabody (1804–1894), an influential woman with a long interest in education. After meeting Schurz, Peabody read Froebel's *Education of Man*, about kindergarten. At age 54, she became an advocate, promoter, and facilitator of kindergarten in North America. She began an English-language kindergarten in Boston in 1860. In 1863 she and her sister published the first North American textbook on kindergarten, *The Kindergarten Guide*. She also began the *Kindergarten Messenger* professional journal in 1873.

Peabody studied Froebel's methods in Europe and then lectured extensively about kindergartens and is credited with being the first female lecturer in the United States (Osborn, 1991). At one of her lectures, a man from the audience offered to manufacture the Froebel Gifts. His name was Milton Bradley—a name you may recognize from board games you played as a child. He described his initial response to the idea of kindergarten as his "educational awakening" (Shapiro, 1983, p. 69). In 1871, his company became the first one to sell kindergarten materials in North America (Osborn, 1991). He and other manufacturers exhibited Froebel and other kindergarten materials at the Centennial Exhibition of 1876. The sale of these materials to the general public was important in the popularization of kindergarten (Shapiro, 1983). However, Peabody was later to become critical of this commercialization of kindergarten (Beatty, 1995).

Another of Elizabeth Peabody's significant contributions was her effort in introducing kindergarten to the public school system. She wrote repeatedly to William Harris, the school superintendent in St. Louis, to encourage him to introduce kindergarten into the public schools, which he eventually did. She was also instrumental in bringing Maria Kraus-Boelte to New York City to train Froebel teachers. Kraus-Boelte had studied with Froebel's widow Luise and had taught in Bertha Ronge's kindergarten in London; Kraus-Boelte was to educate many North American kindergarten teachers, including Canadian kindergartners.

Susan Blow

Another significant promoter of the Froebelian kindergarten was Susan Blow (1843–1916). In 1873, the first kindergarten in a public school in North America was opened in St. Louis, with Blow as the first kindergarten teacher. She had been trained at the Froebel kindergarten school in New York City by Maria Kraus-Boelte. There is some dispute over the date of the first public-school kindergarten, with some claiming there was one in Boston in 1870 or in New York in 1871 (see Osborn, 1991). Regardless of this minor controversy, Susan Blow was a direct link to the establishment of kindergarten in Canada.

Susan Blow was a strong proponent of play: "What flight and air are to the bird, play is to the child; it is both his distinctive activity and the element in which his life moves" (1894/1910, p. 111). Along with Froebel's Gifts and Occupations, she used stories, literature, storytelling, songs, games, and fingerplays. She included field trips, nature study, pet care, and gardening in her kindergarten program.

Blow taught kindergarten in the mornings (3-1/2 hours) and taught kindergarten teachers in the afternoons. These student kindergartners also worked in the kindergartens in the mornings. An advanced course was given on Saturdays. Blow did home visiting and organized mothers' meetings. She also lectured extensively to public and professional groups about Froebel's methods. Her books, such as *Songs and Music of Froebel's Mother Play* (1895/1903) and *Symbolic Education* (1894/1910), are still found in many college, university, and public libraries in Canada.

Blow's original kindergarten was for three- to five-year-old children, but in 1883 was changed by the school district to include only five-year-olds, with a quarterly tuition of one dollar (Beatty, 1995, p. 67). Kindergartens were considered to be somewhat expensive, as the cost to the school district was $16 per child per year compared to $12 for other grades (Beatty, 1995, pp. 65–66). In St. Louis, the superintendent's cost-cutting solution was to have two kindergarten sessions a day, a common pattern in public school kindergartens to this day. However, this pattern made home visits and mothers' meetings difficult to schedule.

With these changes and increasing poor health, Susan Blow resigned from the St. Louis School District. However, she continued her promotion of and teaching about kindergarten through the International Kindergarten Union and at the Teachers College at Columbia University in New York City.

Blow became concerned over what she considered the inappropriate interpretation and use of Froebel's philosophy and materials. She wrote "It is a sad thing for any one who has mastered Froebel's principles to witness the perverted application so often made of his gifts" (1894/1910, p. 129). She campaigned against the "revisionists" who wanted to modify and "update" Froebel's kindergarten. For example, she chaired the committee of the International Kindergarten Union that in 1913 wrote a report supporting the traditional/Froebel/conservative approach to kindergarten. (Ada Marean of Toronto was also part of that committee.) The chair of the liberal/Progressive committee was Patty Smith Hill. These two women have come to represent the conflict between the traditional (Froebel) and modern (Progressive) views of kindergarten.

The traditional versus modern debate and its implications are discussed in Chapter 10.

Patty Smith Hill

Another significant woman in the kindergarten movement was Patty Smith Hill (1868–1946). She began as a kindergarten teacher, then was a director and teacher educator in Louisville, Kentucky (1889–1905). She later taught at Teachers College, Columbia University until 1925. She came to question some of Froebel's ideas and advocated a less structured approach to the use of the Gifts; elimination of many of the Occupations; inclusion of free expression in play, art, and music; and use of a curriculum relevant to the children's lives and not one developed much earlier and in another country and culture. In 1928, she wrote, "the home and the school are the real centers of little children's lives" (p. 211).

The project approach is discussed in Chapter 6.

Hill was a follower of John Dewey's philosophy of hands-on, active involvement by the child (learning by doing), the use of everyday materials, children's choice of activities, problem-solving, and a play-centred curriculum for young children. Dewey saw the teacher's role as more of a guide compared to the directive role of the Froebel kindergartner. Hill studied with Dewey, applied his ideas to the kindergarten, and became a leader in the Progressive kindergarten movement.

Patty Smith Hill created large wooden blocks (forerunners of the present large hollow wooden blocks), child-sized housekeeping-centre materials, pegboards, puzzles, and wheeled vehicles. She designed a kindergarten report card that listed "desirable" behaviours for children. She and her sister Mildred Hill, also a kindergarten teacher, wrote the song "Happy Birthday," which is copyrighted until 2010 (Rasmussen, 1961). One evening, Hill went to a Broadway play in which "Happy Birthday" was sung. She had not authorized its use, and so sued the producer for violation of copyright and won a large sum of money, which she used to equip new nursery schools and kindergartens in housing projects in New York City.

Hill believed in parent education and the kindergarten's involvement in the community. She referred to parents as "home teachers" and stated her belief that "much that is taught in the school could be more effectively taught in the home if the parents were helped to know *how* to teach and *what* to teach" (1928, p. 212).

Hill was active in professional organizations. She organized a series of meetings in the 1920s of what came to be called the National Committee on Nursery Schools. This group became the National Association for Nursery Education in 1929, changed its name to the National Association for the Education of Young Children in 1964, and today is the largest professional early childhood organization in North America. She was also active in the International Kindergarten Union, which in 1930 became the Association for Childhood Education including nursery, kindergarten, and primary levels. This organization changed its name in 1946 to the Association for Childhood Education International.

Due to the efforts of women such as Susan Blow and Patty Smith Hill, Froebel's wish for kindergartens in North America was fulfilled. According to Allen (1988), the success of the kindergarten movement in the United States was due, in part, to the visibility and power of American women in both professional and political roles.

Kindergarten Comes to Canada

A significant woman in the development of kindergarten in Canada was Adaline (Ada) Augusta Marean (1848–1929). She was born in New York State and attended the Normal School in Albany before she went to study with noted Froebelist Maria Kraus-Boelte in New York City in 1877. Marean established a private kindergarten in Saint John, New Brunswick, in 1878.

(According to Prochner [2000], the first private kindergarten in Canada began in the Wesleyan Methodist Church in Charlottetown in 1870.)

James Hughes (1846–1935), the superintendent of the Toronto public schools, had a great interest in kindergarten and was a lifelong supporter. He had observed a demonstration kindergarten at the Centennial Exhibition of 1876 (where he probably also saw Milton Bradley's display of kindergarten materials). He stopped in New York City on his way back to Toronto to visit Maria Kraus-Boelte. It was on her recommendation that Hughes invited Ada Marean to Toronto to establish a private kindergarten. Hughes liked her kindergarten and sent her to study with Susan Blow in St. Louis in 1883.

In the fall of 1883, the first public-school kindergarten in Canada was established in the Toronto public schools at the Louisa Street School. Marean was appointed the head teacher, with seven trainee assistants and 70 children (Dixon, 1994). Her kindergarten attracted the attention of other educators, and soon other kindergartens were established in southern Ontario. According to Dixon, "these kindergartens were firmly based on Froebelian principles, as were many of the contemporaneous kindergartens in the United States. In fact, the Froebelian movement in North America was characterized by a frequent exchange of ideas and visits back and forth between Canadian and American educators" (Dixon, 1994, p. 6). A schedule in a traditional Froebelian kindergarten in Toronto was:

- Opening exercises with prayers
- Songs
- Exercises
- Gifts and Occupations
- Circle
- Games
- Closing song.

(Dixon, 1994)

Ada Marean married James Hughes in 1888 and continued to promote kindergarten and professionalism to the end of her life. She founded the Toronto Kindergarten Association, which evolved into today's Toronto Early Childhood Association. She was elected the president of the Ontario Educational Association in 1900 and was active in the International Kindergarten Union.

Philanthropy and Early Childhood Programs

Philanthropy was a major force in the growth of all types of early childhood programs in North America in the late nineteenth and early twentieth centuries. Middle-income and wealthy women established programs, organized fundraisers, and kept programs going; men served on the advisory boards of these organizations (Prochner, 1996; Schulz, 1978). These philanthropic groups

The development of kindergartens in Canada is described further in Chapter 10.

FOR REFLECTION

October is Canadian Women's History Month. How could the work and accomplishments of Ada Marean Hughes (and other female Canadian educators) be celebrated?

and a few individuals established hospitals/clinics, orphanages, and day nurseries. The day nurseries benefited particularly from philanthropy: "by far the most important and energetic of the day care providers during the early period were volunteer, philanthropic women's organizations" (Schulz, 1978, p. 140).

Another source of early childhood programs was the social reform movement in Europe and North America. Kindergartens and day nurseries were often part of settlement-house programs (Allen, 1988). This was especially true of North America during the large immigration waves in the early decades of the 1900s (Weber, 1984). For example, Central Neighbourhood House established in 1911 in Toronto had a kindergarten (Jones & Rutman, 1981).

A prototype of this type of program was established in Berlin in 1874 by Henriette Schrader-Breymann (1825–1899), who was Froebel's niece. Schrader-Breymann had been a pupil of Marenholtz-Bulow but decided to work with mothers and children rather than in a kindergarten. She established the Pestalozzi-Froebel House for poor mothers and children. There were several programs operating at Pestalozzi-Froebel House: kindergarten (combined Pestalozzi and Froebel pedagogies), infant day care, school lunch programs, after-school care to age 10, summer camps, mothers' meetings, cooking courses, parenting courses, and nursing. This centre was internationally renowned and today it operates 12 day-care programs for children from birth to 12 years of age, family centres, counselling services, a foster home, and two vocational schools for early childhood educators throughout Germany (Oberhauemer, 1995; and see www.b.shuttle.de/b/pfh).

The early kindergartens in North America followed somewhat of a social-welfare model. The kindergarten educator taught the children in the morning and did home visits in the afternoon. These educators were a source of information and advice and often functioned in a social worker role. In the poorer urban areas, "the kindergarten was frequently the only social agency offering a helping hand" (Braun & Edwards, 1972, p. 75). Many private kindergartens were sponsored by philanthropic and religious organizations.

The Development of Day Nurseries

Day-care programs were also part of the social reform movement in Canada. They are not a recent invention. The effects of industrialization and urbanization resulted in the need for child care for working mothers and their children; the presence of mothers in the paid labour force is also not a new phenomenon. The earliest infant day-care programs were established in Paris to help working mothers with infants: in 1800 by Adelaide de Pastoret, and later in 1844 by Jean Marbeau.

Many families with children were living in poverty with congested housing, inadequate nutrition, and resulting high infant mortality rates. For example, in the Toronto Public Nursery between 1859 and 1866, nine percent of all the children died, including 46 percent of those under two years of age (Prochner, 1996, p. 13).

The day nurseries are an ancestor of today's day-care centres. **Day nurseries** has been defined as "the historical term for agencies whose essential purpose was to provide a place where children could be cared for during the day, while their parents worked or were otherwise unable to provide home care" (Varga, 1997, p. 11). The current term is *day-care* or *child-care centre*. The earliest day-care centres in Canada were established by the Grey Nuns in Montreal in the 1850s. By 1878, they had five day nurseries (Schulz, 1978). Although the Toronto Public Nursery was begun shortly after the Montreal programs in 1856, "day care did not gain a foothold in Canada until the late 1880s" (Prochner, 1994, p. 10). For example, in 1887, the first English-speaking day nursery began in Montreal, followed in 1890 by the Toronto Crèche (now Victoria Day Care Services), and then the West End and East End Crèches.

Philanthropy played a large role in the growth of day nurseries in Canada. For example, philanthropic women began the Montreal Day Nursery and the Toronto Public Nursery. Charitable groups, such as Associated Charities, also established programs (e.g., the Vancouver Crèche at Infants' Hospital Centre in 1910).

Settlement houses often had day-nursery programs. The Jost Mission Day Nursery was begun in 1910 in Halifax, and the Ottawa Day Nursery (now the Andrew Fleck Child Care Centre) was established in 1911. These types of settlement-house-based programs began "as a philanthropic social service to relieve family destitution" (Varga, 1993, p. 119). Some operated employment services for mothers, who were often widows or single mothers and therefore the only wage earner in the family. Other services often included well-baby clinics, food banks, emergency housing, clothing, provision of fuel, cash loans, counselling, and family parties for holidays (Schulz, 1978).

The development of day care in Canada is discussed further in Chapter 8.

The Development of Nursery Schools

The **nursery school** (also known as *preschool*) developed at the same time as kindergartens but from a different context. The roots of the nursery school are in the health and social welfare movements in the early twentieth century. As with kindergartens and day nurseries, the nursery school owes much of its development to the efforts of many women.

Margaret and Rachel McMillan

The individuals most associated with the early nursery school are Margaret McMillan (1860–1931) and her sister Rachel (1859–1917). They were activists and advocates at a time when such activities were often thought of as unladylike and unseemly. The McMillan sisters approached early childhood education and care from a different context than did Rousseau, Pestalozzi, or Froebel. Their emphasis was on children's health and the social welfare of children and their families.

Background

The McMillan sisters were born in New York of Scottish immigrant parents. When their father and younger sister died in 1865, their mother took the children back to Scotland. Although Margaret McMillan originally trained and worked as a governess, she had many careers: journalist, romance novelist, adult educator, school board trustee, socialist, and political activist—not the typical careers of a woman at the turn of the twentieth century.

A special area of concern of the McMillan sisters was children's health. Rachel had been trained as a health inspector and worked as a health visitor in England at a time when there were many homeless, orphaned, ill, and abandoned children living in the streets. A study in 1908 reported that although 80 percent of British babies were born healthy, by the time they began school only 20 percent were healthy (Osborn, 1991). Margaret was elected to the school board in Bradford in northern England at the age of 33. During her time on the school board, she was responsible for the establishment of medical care for children in school clinics. The McMillans were outraged at the local conditions that resulted in one in five babies not living to age one due to poor living conditions, unsanitary housing, and sickness such as tuberculosis. For example, of 1,100 children examined at a local health centre, 500 needed immediate medical treatment (Bradburn, 1995, p. 70). She wrote *Early Childhood* in 1900 outlining her ideas and theories of child development. In 1904, she was asked to be the manager for schools in Deptford, a slum area of London.

Margaret McMillan would warrant mention in histories of early childhood education and care for her work in initiating school clinics, health programs, and being a vocal advocate for children during her entire life. However, what is considered to be her greatest contribution is the establishment of the Open Air Nursery School. She is also credited with inventing the term *nursery school* (Greenberg, 1987).

The Open Air Night Camps for Boys and Girls was established in 1911 with a camp for girls. The purpose of these camps was to provide a healthy place for school-aged children to sleep, away from the overcrowded conditions in the tenements. The children each had their own bed in a tent pitched outdoors and went home after breakfast. The first boys' camp was set up in a graveyard but shortly had to move as the neighbours were concerned about the effects of children on the graves. A school called the Camp School was established to meet the educational needs of these children. This school received favourable reports from the local school inspectors (Bradburn, 1995).

Margaret McMillan soon realized that prevention of health problems should begin with preschool children. She began a day camp where babies could sleep in the fresh air during the day and play in the garden. This developed into the Open Air Nursery School (it was renamed the Rachel McMillan Open Air Nursery School and Training Centre after Rachel's death in 1917). The original Open Air Nursery School benefited from the support of prominent individuals such as the playwright George Bernard Shaw. He described Margaret McMillan as "one of the best women of her time ... but also one of the most cantankerous" (Mansbridge, 1932, p. 131). Others described her as patient, dignified, supportive, hospitable, forthright, and persistent (Mansbridge, 1932).

Key Educational Ideas

The nursery school enrolled children from ages two to seven. Margaret McMillan believed that children needed to be fed and comfortable before they could learn. Her program focused on the whole child and provided baths, clean clothes, food, fresh air, and a place to sleep. The program for three- and four-year-olds included gardening, animal care, cleaning the school, self-help skills, art, music, rhythmic activities, language, arithmetic, science, and water and sand play (Spodek & Saracho, 1994). She also sought to nurture "children's emotional life and development of their imaginations" (Williams, 1992b, p. 53). As many of the children's activities as possible took place outdoors.

An information sheet about the Open Air Nursery School in the late 1920s claims that in the nursery school only seven percent of the children were "delicate and diseased," compared to 30–40 percent in the local elementary schools. In addition, there was no ringworm or impetigo, no uncured rickets, and no deaths due to measles (Braun & Edwards, 1972, p. 128). The same could not be said for other schools in similar areas.

Margaret McMillan also included parents in the Open Air Nursery. She began a Parents' Club to maintain contact between the home and school as well as to foster personal and parenting skills. A mothers' group where child-rearing and parenting topics were discussed met monthly.

In addition, McMillan recognized the need for educating teachers to work in the slums. In 1930, she began a three-year course with a strong practicum component. Student teachers were required to live in the area, as did Margaret McMillan, so that they could better understand the lives and needs of the children and their families. They were also required to do home visits and work in the medical and dental clinic as part of their professional education. Margaret McMillan was a strong advocate for teachers and teacher education programs.

FOR REFLECTION

In her book The Nursery School, *Margaret McMillan stated that the role of teachers was "helping to make a brain and nervous system [in young children], and this work which is going to determine all that comes after, requires a finer perception and a wider training and outlook than is needed by any other kind of teacher" (1919, p. 175). Do you agree with this statement? Why or why not?*

Lasting Significance

Margaret McMillan was thought of as a prophet or pioneer in her lifetime (Mansbridge, 1932). She saw the nursery school as more than a place for children; it was a family and community place. The Open Air Nursery School seems to have functioned rather like a settlement house. She integrated health, welfare, and education in one program. (This integration would be seen again in the original Head Start program in the United States.) She saw the nursery school as a place where families could stay during family crises such as illness.

Other significant contributions of Margaret McMillan included:

Head Start is described later in this chapter.

- The establishment of the Open Air Nursery School, a model for nursery schools throughout Britain and in other countries. The school is still in Deptford and still attracts visitors today.

- The establishment of the Training Centre, which promoted the professionalism of nursery school educators and public recognition. The educators trained by Margaret McMillan were instrumental in the growth of nursery schools in Britain and in other countries.

- The passing of the Fisher Act by the British Parliament in 1918, which is often credited to Margaret McMillan. The Fisher Act permitted the establishment of nursery schools as part of local public school systems. Although nursery schools had expanded during the First World War as part of the war effort, not many were established under this provision due to lack of government funding. However few their number at that time, nursery schools had become part of publicly funded education in Britain. In the early 1970s I worked in nursery schools for three- and four-year-olds in two of the London boroughs for the local educational authorities. One was located in a Victorian-era brick school; the other in a centre that had been built as a 24-hour-care centre during the Second World War for the children of mothers employed in a local war plant.

The more than 80-year history of three- and four-year-olds being part of the public school system in Britain is due, in great part, to the work and efforts of the McMillan sisters.

The Development of Nursery Schools in North America

In the early twentieth century, women were largely responsible for the growth of nursery schools from England to North America. For example, one of the women who worked with Margaret McMillan was Abigail Eliot (1892–1992). She would get her opportunity to have such a program when she became the director of the Ruggles Street Nursery School and Training Center in Boston in 1922. This nursery school was located in a poor area similar to that of McMillan's Open Air Nursery.

Abigail Eliot

Eliot had originally been a social worker before she became interested in nursery schools. She believed that the child's home was the most influential environment. Eliot was generally impressed with the McMillans' nursery school but thought there was too much emphasis on physical hygiene and preferred a program with more emphasis on children's social development and contact with families (Beatty, 1995).

An important feature of her nursery school was the philosophy and practice of supporting and involving parents. She stated that without parents' help and interest "no nursery school can do its work really well" (Beatty, 1995, p. 144). At the Ruggles Street Nursery School, educators made home visits, parents were encouraged to volunteer and observe the program, and informal mothers' meetings for discussion of topics raised by the mothers were organized. The parents did participate, and some of the mothers decided to become nursery school educators. In 1926, the nursery school began one- and two-year nursery education courses. (This teacher education centre later became part of Tufts University, which named it the Eliot-Pearson Department of Child Study. It is still a prestigious centre for early childhood research.)

Caroline Pratt

Caroline Pratt (1867–1954) began an informal playgroup in a poor area of New York City in 1913. It evolved as an experiment and example in Progressive education by 1919 into the City and Country School. This experiment could be judged a success as it is still operating in the same neighbourhood and enrolls approximately 130 children from 2 to 13 years of age (Driscoll, 1995).

Pratt credited watching a friend's son play with inspiring her to design toys for young children; however, this was not financially viable. She believed that children learned through play. She agreed with John Dewey's philosophy of hands-on experiences as the basis for curriculum. Her beliefs are reflected in the title of her book *I Learn from Children*, her use of field trips within the neighbourhood to learn from common occurrences such as garbage pickup, and her open-ended, unstructured play materials. The curriculum was based on the experiences of the children. When Lucy Sprague Mitchell (1878–1967) taught there, she wrote a series of children's books (called "here and now books") about children's everyday activities and objects (e.g., a spoon, going for a walk).

Pratt was concerned about children's play materials throughout her career. She designed the wooden unit blocks that are still found in most early childhood programs. She included small-scaled people and animals to enrich children's block play and to stimulate language, storytelling, and dramatic play. This program is to this day known for having limited, simple, open-ended materials available for the children (Lanser & McDonnell, 1991). Pratt believed in providing open-ended materials such as paint, clay, water, and, of course, blocks. There was also an emphasis on children's creativity and artistic expression that fit well with the emphasis on children's social and emotional development. The educator's role was to support and help the children and to expand on child-initiated ideas.

Pratt, Mitchell, and Harriet Johnson founded the Bureau of Educational Experiments, which became the world-renowned Bank Street College of Education. The lab school there became a model for the original Head Start program in the 1960s (Greenberg, 1987).

Nursery School Comes to Canada

As seen in the above examples, nursery schools were often developed by people from varied backgrounds. There was much more variation in the backgrounds of nursery school initiators than in kindergarten. In addition, philanthropy was important in the establishment of the earliest nursery schools. For example,

FOR REFLECTION

Polly Greenberg (1987) comments that our profession has ignored its numerous heroines and their contributions. She asks the question "What's so great about those old nursery teachers anyway?" (p. 83). What would your reply be?

...ools and the
...nt of nursery
schools in Canada are discussed in
Chapter 9.

Nursery schools are described and
discussed further in Chapter 9.

many of the early nursery schools in North America were originally funded by the Laura Spelman Rockefeller Fund, and some are still in existence today. Two of these were the St. George's School for Child Study (now known as the Institute of Child Study) at the University of Toronto, begun in 1926, and McGill University's Day Nursery and Child Laboratory in Montreal, which operated from 1927–1930.

Nursery schools "had a slow start, and a relatively late start" in North America (Goodykoontz, Davis, & Gabbard, 1948, p. 44). Their development followed a different pattern from kindergartens and infant schools. It is interesting that although the nursery school was originally established for children and families living in poverty, in North America it was "established for educational experimentation, for demonstration of methodology, or for purposes of research, but not for the relief of working mothers or neglected children" (Hewes, 1996, p. 3).

Maria Montessori

Maria Montessori (1870–1952) was a physician, educator, feminist, humanist, and lifelong advocate for children's and women's rights. Her work provides a bridge from the historical roots of our field to the present day. Montessori's contribution to education is honoured in Italy in a unique way. Her portrait is on the front of the 1,000-lira note, which is the most common denomination of Italian currency. If you go to Italy you'll be reminded of Montessori, and hopefully her contributions to early childhood education, every time you open your wallet.

Background

Maria Montessori had a colourful and eventful life. As did other early educators described in this chapter, she came to early childhood education after a variety of life and career experiences. She was born the only child of a well-educated, well-to-do Italian family. Renilde Montessori expected her daughter to knit for the poor, and Maria did so daily from a young age. When she was 12, Maria decided she wanted to be an engineer because she liked math and was very good at it. Although her father wanted her to become a teacher (how prophetic!), she enrolled in technological schools where she was the only female student. After graduating in 1886, she decided she no longer wanted to be an engineer but wanted to study medicine. When she applied to the University of Rome medical school, there were no women in the medical school and her application was refused. However, Montessori was not deterred and later claimed that she gained admittance with the help of Pope Leo XIII. Her medical studies were not always pleasant, as the other students shunned her and she faced discriminatory rules because of her gender. For example, she had to do the required dissections in the morgue by herself late at night. Her mother helped her study for exams when the other students would not. She had high marks and won academic prizes in pathology, medicine, and surgery (Gutek, 1997).

A month after her graduation in 1896, Montessori was selected as one of Italy's delegates to an international women's congress in Berlin. The newspapers reported that this "young, beautiful, and eloquent" woman gave two well-received addresses on equality for women and equal pay for equal work (Kramer, 1988, p. 55). Her struggles and experiences to this stage of her life were probably key in developing her feminist views and advocacy of women's and children's rights.

Montessori practised medicine for 10 years. In 1897 she was on the staff of a psychiatric clinic while doing post-graduate work in psychiatry and worked with the then-called "idiot children." At that time, children who were delayed or who had mental or psychiatric problems were placed in adult psychiatric wards and typically given little treatment. A frequently told story about Montessori is that one day she observed some of these children playing underneath a table with bread crumbs (they had no toys) and decided to help them. She took courses in pedagogy, philosophy, psychology, and anthropology to improve her background for working with children and lectured in anthropology and hygiene at a teacher training college for women.

In 1900, she became the director of the new Orthophrenic School for teacher education and children with disabilities. She worked with these children and formed many of her ideas on education. She modified materials designed by Edouard Seguin and developed her own materials. When these children subsequently passed the national exams designed for normal children, the press was quick to recognize this achievement. Montessori (1912) wondered: "While everyone was admiring the progress of my idiots, I was searching for the reasons which could keep back the happy healthy children of the common schools on so low a plane that they could be equalled in tests of intelligence by my unfortunate pupils!" (p. 39).

In 1906, she was approached by the Roman Good Building Institute, which renovated tenements in the slums of Rome. The developers and investors were concerned about the vandalism on their properties by children left unattended during the day while their parents worked. She opened her first *Casa del Bambini* (Children's House) on January 6, 1907, in the Quarter San Lorenzo, which was known for its beggars, homeless, prostitutes, criminals, and disease (Montessori 1912). She described these children's houses as being "a real house; that is to say, a set of rooms with a garden of which the children are the masters" (Montessori, 1914, pp. 9–10). Each children's house was to be "a school within the house" (p. 44) and include a large main room and if possible a parlour, bathroom, dining room, common room, nap/rest room, and gymnasium. There was also to be a good-sized playground with space for a garden. Like Margaret McMillan, Montessori required that the teachers live in the tenements so they could be accessible to the children and families (Montessori, 1912). The parents were required to send the children to the program washed and in clean clothes, and mothers had to meet weekly with the teacher to discuss their children.

The Casas del Bambini spread through Italy, and by 1908 the houses were found even in the affluent areas of Rome. News of these centres and Montessori's methods spread to other countries. As of 1911, Montessori's methods had been adopted officially in the public schools of Italy and Switzerland and schools were planned in China, Mexico, Korea, India, and Argentina (Kramer, 1988). *The Montessori Method*, a history of her work, how it evolved, and an explanation of her Method, was published in North America in 1912. It was translated into more than 20 languages and the first U.S. edition of 500 copies sold out in four days; more editions were printed and it became the number-two nonfiction bestseller for 1912 (Kramer, 1988). This achievement was followed by her first lecture tour of North America in 1913, which was a huge success and included lectures in Carnegie Hall in New York City. The English translation of *The Advanced Montessori Method* and *The Montessori Elementary Materials* in 1917 extended her Method into the elementary school years.

In 1922, Montessori was appointed government inspector of the Montessori nursery and elementary schools by the Italian government. Although the Fascist government in Italy initially accepted and promoted Montessori schools, it closed all of Montessori's schools in Italy in 1934. Like Froebel, Montessori saw her schools for young children banned by a reactionary government. In the 1920s and 1930s, Montessori was living in Barcelona and conducting teacher education courses in Europe and South America. The Spanish Civil War broke out in 1936 and her schools in Spain were closed. She then moved to the Netherlands. When Italy entered the Second World War, Montessori was in India doing teacher education courses. Although she was technically an enemy alien, the British authorities let her continue to teach and establish schools in India throughout the war.

After the war, Montessori based herself and her *Association Montessori Internationale* in the Netherlands, where her Method had become "most firmly established in the educational institutions of the country" (Kramer, 1988, p. 292). Although she spent most of her time travelling the world establishing programs and educating teachers, Montessori spent little time in North America and none after 1917.

Key Educational Ideas

Maria Montessori developed a comprehensive method of teaching young children. She based her method on the work of those who had come before her, such as Rousseau, Pestalozzi, and Froebel. In addition, she incorporated with her own observations and work the ideas of two doctors, Jean Itard (1775–1838) and Edouard Seguin (1812-1880). She has been aptly called "an eclectic borrower" (Chattin-McNicols, 1992, p. 36).

In her writings she recognized the contributions of others, while at the same time being very clear about where and how she disagreed with some of their ideas (for examples, see Montessori, 1974). She did share Rousseau's, Pestalozzi's, and Froebel's beliefs in the goodness of children, the importance of the early years, the need for children to have freedom, the education of the poor, the use of manipulatives, and building on children's interests and levels of development. One significant difference was the role of the educator. While Pestalozzi and Froebel perceived educators in a more directive role, Montessori saw them as facilitators, demonstrators, and resources. In Montessori programs to this day, they are typically referred to as directors or directresses and not as teachers or educators. Montessori wrote that a directress "moves quietly about, goes to any child who calls her, supervising operations in such a way that anyone who needs her finds her at his elbow, and whoever does not need her is not reminded of her existence" (1912, pp. 346–347).

Montessori's Concept of Children and Childhood

Montessori viewed children with almost a mystical reverence: "A child is mysterious and powerful and contains within himself the secret of human nature" (1966, p. 255). Some of her writings on this topic read very much like Rousseau's. She was deeply religious and recognized the spirituality of children.

Montessori wrote that "respect for the children is of the greatest importance and must be observed in practice" (1976, p. 113). She called for respect for both individual children and their individuality and also promoted their rights as children. Montessori proposed the creation of a ministry of childhood and the creation of an international social party (*Il Partito Sociale del Bambina*) to defend the rights of children in government legislatures in every country. She also encouraged parents to "be concerned with the great social question of the day, the struggle to gain a recognition of the rights of childhood in the world" (1966, p. 263).

Montessori's Concept of Child Development and Learning

Like Froebel, Montessori saw children's development as a natural unfolding. This development occurred through stages, which she termed *sensitive periods*. During these times, children were most receptive to certain types of learning (e.g., language development in the preschool years). Montessori, like others before her, thought the early years were the formative ones and most important. She once told a reporter: "If we can keep the hands of the adult generation off the child from birth until seven, it will have a good chance of growing up as nature intends" (quoted in Kramer, 1988, p. 261).

Montessori's stages of development were ages 0–6 for character and intelligence, 6–12 for culture acquisition, 12-18 for independence, and 18 and over for maturity through work and experience (Turner, 1992). She characterized the early years as the time of the "absorbent mind." By this she meant that children were absorbing sensory information from their environments and trying to bring order to this information. Her method seeks to provide the order and structure that she believed children wanted and needed. It was therefore important for the teacher to observe individual children to determine their stages to provide the most appropriate materials and activities.

A key principle in Montessori's development of materials and her Method is the active involvement of children learning through their senses. Materials and activities should be hands-on manipulatives to provide for sensory learning, as this was essential for children's intellectual growth and independence.

Montessori emphasized the golden rule in her schools and did not believe in extrinsic reward or punishment. She felt that the need to create order, interest, and the success of using materials would be the reward for the children. Discipline was finding the appropriate materials and tasks for each child, teaching him or her to respect their work and the work of others, and perhaps redirecting a child to another activity, if needed.

Montessori's Method

Montessori developed what she termed a method of "scientific pedagogy" applied to child education. Scientific pedagogy was her application of sciences such as psychology, medicine, and pedagogical anthropology to education to develop a systematic approach to early education. This is usually referred to as the Montessori Method (explained in detail in Montessori, 1912).

The most lasting contributions of Montessori's approach to early childhood education and care are found primarily in the Prepared Environment and the materials developed by Montessori. She emphasized the physical environment of the classroom (i.e., the **Prepared Environment**). She stated that it should be homelike and "a place of comfort and peace with full and varied interests. The essential charm . . . is its cleanliness and order, with everything in its place, dusted, bright, and cheerful" (Montessori, 1967/1995, p. 277). The Prepared Environment should include child-sized furniture (tables, not desks), washstands, low cupboards, plants, aquarium, chalkboard, and carefully selected pictures. In other words, it should be attractive, orderly, appropriate, and interesting for the children. She believed that it was important to teach children the skills they needed to function well in the Prepared Environment (see the Practical Life activities below).

Montessori (1914) stated that the technique of her Method could be divided into three components:

- Motor education
- Sensory education
- Language.

Through motor education, the young child was educated in the gross and fine motor movements necessary for activities such as gymnastics, manual work, gardening, rhythmic activities, and care of self and environment. The self-help skills included dressing and undressing, and to facilitate this Montessori developed a collection of frames on which the children practised buttoning, tying, lacing, and snapping. Montessori instructed that, "the teacher, sitting by the child's side, performs the necessary movements of the fingers very slowly and deliberately, separating the movements themselves into their different parts, and letting them be seen clearly and minutely" (1914, p. 22). Gross motor activities included washing and setting the tables, sweeping the floor, and so on. Perceptual motor activities such as serving soup to other children were also part of motor education.

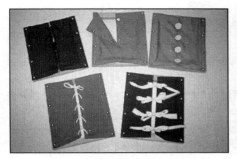

Margie I. Mayfield

Montessori's practical life materials; Montessori's knobbed cylinders

Montessori designed a set of didactic materials for use by young children to foster sensory education. These **sensorial materials** are graduated, self-correcting, facilitate repeated practice, and are the most widely known of the Montessori materials. (See Table 5.1 for a list of the sensorial materials.) The materials were designed to be attractive for the children (e.g., painted colours) and to be *auto-educative* (i.e., self-instructional). For example, with the knobbed cylinders, the child removes the cylinders from the frame; if the child tries to replace a cylinder in the wrong hole, it does not fit and thus the child knows that corrections need to be made.

Some of these materials are similar to some of Froebel's Gifts. Mathematics and geometry were common areas of interest and expertise for Pestalozzi, Froebel, and Montessori. Thus it is not surprising that the materials designed by Froebel and Montessori reflect this interest and expertise.

In line with the emphasis on sensory learning, some of Montessori's materials, such as the smell bottles or the bells, were designed so the child focused on one specific sense. Some of the activities with the sensorial materials were to be done blindfolded in order to heighten the child's sensory awareness.

Language education was considered an important part of the sensitive period of the preschool years. Montessori wrote that the teacher must be careful to pronounce words clearly and completely and recommended songs as a way of improving children's pronunciation. The sensorial activities such as the bells and sound boxes helped develop children's auditory discrimination.

TABLE 5.1

Montessori's Sensorial Materials

PINK TOWER	TEXTILE BOXES
BROAD STAIRS	SMELLING BOTTLES
LONG STAIR/RED AND BLUE RODS	SOUND BOXES/CYLINDERS
KNOBBED CYLINDERS	BELLS
KNOBLESS CYLINDER	GEOMETRIC SOLIDS
COLOUR TABLETS	GEOMETRICAL INSETS
ROUGH AND SMOOTH SANDPAPER TABLETS	GEOMETRICAL CARDS

Montessori outlined the Three Periods Lesson for use with the materials. This lesson has some similarities to the lessons outlined by Froebel and Pestalozzi. Montessori's Three Periods Lesson format assisted children in developing vocabulary as well as concepts such as large and small: Period 1 was termed *Naming*, as in "This is large. This is small." Period 2 was called *Recognition*: "Give me the large _____ . Give me the small _____ ." Period 3 was termed *Pronunciation of the Word*: "What is this?"

Montessori believed that writing preceded reading and that most children would learn to read by age five. Many of the practical life activities and the sensorial materials such as tracing helped prepare children for writing. The children learned how to form the letters by tracing sandpaper letters and hearing the teacher make the corresponding sounds (*look*, *feel*, and *hear*). They then formed words using the letters of the movable alphabet. This process was helped by the fact that Italian is more phonetically regular than English.

Criticisms of Montessori's Ideas

Montessori's educational ideas were criticized as soon as her work became known. For example, Patty Smith Hill went to Italy to see Montessori's program and then criticized it for being overly structured and lacking provision for group activities, cooperation, and socialization (Beatty, 1995). Many of the early criticisms are the same as those made about Montessori's ideas today.

Two common criticisms are the perceived lack of play and lack of creativity in the Montessori approach. Montessori believed that children's work was their play, and that work was an order-producing activity and play was not. Children played as a leisure activity when they had nothing better to do (Montessori, 1966). The didactic nature of the materials and Montessori's instructions for their use led to the criticism that creativity was not encouraged. The lack of play centres and art materials such as paints was seen by critics as deterring children's imaginations and creativity. Montessorians respond that the hands-on, exploratory nature of the materials and the children's choice of activities promote creativity (Humphryes, 1998). Montessori thought that fantasy and fairy tales were inappropriate for young children, as the children could not distinguish real and make-believe. Some Montessorians will argue that the practical life activities can present opportunities for fantasy play (i.e., playing at grown-up tasks) and that pouring activities are a type of water play (Chattin-McNichols, 1992).

Another common criticism was the lack of opportunities for socialization among the children. Part of this criticism was about the role of interaction and play in young children's language development, which some educators thought was weak in the Montessori Method.

During her life and since, educators have questioned whether Montessori's approach was really scientific, as she claimed (e.g., Bruce, 1984; Kilpatrick, 1914; Rohrs, 1994). She stated that "my method is scientific, both in its substance and in its aim" (1914, p. 8). A criticism is that while she tried various techniques and materials, she never "tested" her approach against other ones. In fairness, one should remember that such experimental approaches were not common in educational programs at the beginning of the twentieth century. Related to this criticism is the one that the growth of Montessori programs was not due to their scientific base but more to the personality and efforts of Montessori herself.

Because many of the Montessori programs during her lifetime and afterwards were private schools, the criticism of elitism has been raised. This is ironic, given that Montessori originally developed her program in the slums of Rome. However, the cost of the materials that are manufactured by a company under licence from Montessori's heirs does increase the costs of the program compared to other similar early childhood programs.

Another criticism is that because Montessori kept such tight control of teacher education and was so specific about the use of the materials, her followers have tried to be true to her ideas. As a result, some "modern Montessorians have become trapped in an ossified curriculum" (Bruce, 1984, p. 77). It is important to note that there are several different Montessori groups. Some of these have updated Montessori's ideas for modern times. However, these modifications have caused dissension among Montessorians reminiscent of the divisions over kindergarten between the traditional Froebelians and the Progressives. Today there are many Montessori associations and societies worldwide. In Canada, the two groups that accredit Montessori teacher educator programs are the *Association Montessori Internationale* and the American Montessori Society. There are accredited Montessori teacher education programs in British Columbia and Ontario.

Lasting Significance

Montessori programs are still in existence around the world nearly 100 years after their beginning in Italy. Her books have been translated into many languages and most are still in print. The popularity of Montessori's programs has been more up and down in North America than in Europe. According to Kramer, in her biography of Montessori, the reasons for this were that Montessori was female, Catholic, foreign, autocratic, insistent that her program was a whole package, and criticized by some of the leading educators of her time. It may also be due, in part, to Montessori's concentrating her efforts on establishing programs and educating teachers in Europe. The early growth of Montessori programs around the world at a time when communication was not easy is also noteworthy.

Part of this early growth was the first Montessori program in Canada, thought to be The Montessori School founded in Calgary in 1919 by Margaret and William Potts. Margaret Potts had done a training course given by Maria Montessori in London. The Pottses operated their day and boarding school for children from grades 1 to 12 and educated Montessori teachers. The school is now named the Calgary Montessori School and is administered by the Pottses' granddaughter Alison O'Dwyer. Preschool was added in 1971 and there are now

FOR REFLECTION

If Maria Montessori were to visit an early childhood program in Canada today (not a Montessori one), what do you think she would recognize from her Method? What activities and materials would she like and what would she question? Would she include computers in her program if she were doing it today? Why or why not?

approximately 200 children in the elementary program and 300 in the preschool (Alison O'Dwyer; Terry Gorrie, personal communications, December 1999).

Although Montessori programs increased in North America in the 1920s, they declined in the next two decades. There was a resurgence of Montessori programs in the mid-1960s and again in the mid-1970s and early 1980s (Goffin, 1994). It is perhaps easy to underestimate Montessori's effect on early childhood education and care today because so much of what was innovative for her time is now accepted practice in early childhood programs. Many of her ideas (e.g., children's active involvement with materials) and her materials, or their variations (e.g., tying and lacing dolls) are now part of mainstream early childhood programs.

Just as earlier educators such as Froebel and Seguin influenced Montessori, she too influenced those who came after her. Some of these connections are direct. For example, Piaget did his initial formal observations of young children in the 1920s in a "modified Montessori" program in Geneva and was president of the Swiss Montessori Society for many years (Kramer, 1988, p. 326). Piaget's theory on the interaction of the child and the environment was based on his careful observation of children but went beyond Montessori's ideas. The noted psychologist Erik Erikson's only formal teaching certificate was from a Montessori education program.

As a teacher educator, I think that one of the lasting contributions of Montessori is her contribution to teacher education. One cannot help but admire a person who spent almost 50 years educating teachers around the world. Many years ago, when I first started teaching, I would meet teachers who had been educated by Maria Montessori. They all commented on her dynamic personality, enthusiasm, and commitment to young children and their education. Even though Montessori was criticized during her lifetime and since for being very possessive of Montessori teacher education, that does not lessen her achievement in this area.

Montessori's work has implications for the next chapter of this book, which examines curriculum models in early childhood education. As Goffin notes, Montessori's was the "first curriculum model carefully and intentionally mass-marketed for dissemination and replication" (1994, p. 38). It would not be the last.

Recent Programs for Poor Children and Their Families

The last half of the twentieth century saw interest in providing programs for young children with the hope of ameliorating the potential effects of poverty in the early years. The best known of these programs, and the largest, is **Project Head Start** in the United States. It has grown to influence the field of early childhood education and care in significant and lasting ways. This "model of early intervention has great appeal and has clearly influenced Canadian approaches to early childhood education" (Howe, Jacobs, & Fiorentino, 2000, p. 219). There have been several much smaller-scale and usually localized Head

Start-type programs in Canada such as the Moncton Head Start program, Apprenti-Sage in Quebec City, the University of Western Ontario Laboratory Preschool (described below), and the current Aboriginal Head Start (described in Chapter 11).

Project Head Start

Project Head Start began as an eight-week summer program for poor children and their families in 1965, and by the late 1990s had served almost 17 million children and families (Head Start Bureau, 1998). It has been described as "among the most significant educational and social experiments in American history" (Evans, 1975, p. 72). Ever since its beginning, Head Start has been suggested as a possible model for use in Canada.

Head Start was developed in response to the recognition of the effects of poverty on young children and families. This was also true in the past for other early childhood programs. For example, the McMillans' nursery school in London, Montessori's Casa del Bambini in Rome, and the day-care centres established by the Grey Nuns in Montreal could all be considered programmatic responses to the effects of poverty.

See Chapters 2 and 3 for discussion on the effects of poverty on young children and families.

The idea that education is an important, effective way to solve social problems is long-standing. In theory, lack of education leads to unemployment, which in turn leads to financial hardship/poverty, which can then lead to unhealthy children and families who are not able to benefit from education—and thus the cycle continues. Education has been thought to be an effective way to break the poverty cycle.

The 1960s were a time of social awareness and optimism about solving social problems that may seem rather naïve and overoptimistic now. I remember the feelings of optimism and the conviction that small groups and individuals could make a difference. I was beginning university at this time and my friends and I volunteered in various programs, such as tutoring and recreational programs, established in inner city areas to help ameliorate the effects of poverty on children.

The 1960s were also a time influenced by the push for increased education, especially science and mathematics in the wake of the Soviet Union's launching of the first satellite in 1957. In addition, several cognitive psychologists' and researchers' works coalesced at this time, including the works of Piaget, which became available in English only beginning in 1952 (the original work was published in French in 1926). Bowlby's work on the long-term effects of deprivation on children also contributed to the ethos (Bowlby is discussed in Chapter 2). The writings of environmentalists such as Hunt (1961) and Bloom (1964) outlined their views that children's development, including intelligence, could be improved by improving children's environments. Thus, early childhood programs were seen as one way of providing stimulating, quality environments for young children during the critical formative years of their development. Therefore, Head Start was a reflection of the times both socially and politically. (However, the initiators of Head Start always saw it as a broad-based program and not as a way to raise children's IQs [White & Buka, 1987]).

The health, education, and welfare of young children was a major focus of the War on Poverty, and Project Head Start became a centrepiece. The U.S. federal government authorized $150 million in 1965 for an eight-week summer program. The first summer program had an enrollment of 652,000 children in 2,500 centres, with 41,000 teachers and 250,000 other staff including volunteers (Osborn, 1991, p. 153).

The Head Start programs were to be community-based, to be responsive to local needs, and to involve community members. Although every Head Start program was to reflect the needs of the community, each was to be a comprehensive program including required components (these are still requirements of all Head Start programs):

- *Education*—With priority for children the year before beginning elementary school.

- *Health*—Medical, dental, and nutritional services including screenings, immunizations, and hot meals as part of the program.

- *Social services for families*—Including community outreach, referrals, emergency assistance, and so on.

- *Parent involvement*—Volunteering in the operation, governance of the program, parent education, workshops, and so on (Head Start Bureau, 1999).

The original Head Start summer program was expanded into a nine-month half-day program in 1966. Although originally planned as half-day programs, Head Start has been moving to full-day programs. (See Table 5.2 for a daily schedule from a Head Start program in Florida.)

Project Follow Through was authorized in 1966 to continue the comprehensive programming for children into kindergarten and through grade 3. Head Start also initiated a competency-based training program called the Child Development Associate (CDA) program. Many of the graduates of this program were former parent volunteers, some of whom then continued their formal education and became teachers, directors, and administrators in Head Start and other programs (Zigler & Muenchow, 1992). By 1998, 90 percent of Head Start educators had degrees in early childhood education or a CDA credential (Head Start Bureau, 1998). Almost one-third of the staff were parents of current or former Head Start children. Other spinoff programs have included Head Start Family Day Care, Home Start, Head Start Transition Project (to provide developmental continuity between Head Start programs and elementary schools), and Early Head Start for children under three years of age.

In 1998, Head Start enrolled almost 800,000 children (60 percent of whom were four-year-olds) and had a budget for fiscal 1998 of US$4.66-billion (Head Start Bureau, 1998). At least 20 percent of an individual program's funding must come from sources other than the federal government.

A frequently asked question is, Has Head Start made a difference? Much more than any of the other programs discussed in this chapter, Head Start has

TABLE 5.2

Head Start Daily Schedule

TIME	ACTIVITY
7:30–8:30	BREAKFAST AVAILABLE IN CAFETERIA
8–8:10	TELEVISED ANNOUNCEMENTS
8:10–8:30	ATTENDANCE, LUNCH ORDERS, SOCIAL SKILLS (E.G., SAYING NO; READING OTHERS' FEELINGS), POEM, STORY
8:30–8:45	MOVEMENT ACTIVITY OR GAME
8:45–9	SNACK (E.G., FRUIT, JUICE, COOKIE)
9–9:30	OUTDOOR PLAY
9:30–10:40	PLAN-DO-REVIEW
10:40–11:10	SPECIAL CLASS (I.E., MUSIC, SPANISH, PE, ART, MEDIA CENTRE)
11:10–11:40	SMALL GROUPS
11:40–11:50	LITERATURE (E.G., BOOKS, FINGERPLAYS, ETC.)
11:50–12:20	LUNCH IN THE CLASSROOM
12:20–12:30	BATHROOM AND TOOTHBRUSHING
12:30–1:30	REST
1:30–1:45	AWAKE, PREPARE FOR HOME
1:45–2	DISMISSAL

Source: Margery Anderson, personal communication, July 1999

been scrutinized by the media, government, academics, educators, and the public since its very beginning. Head Start has been "researched extensively" (Ellsworth & Ames, 1998, p. ix), although not always well (Powell, 1994). The common answer often given in reports and in the media is that "Head Start works" (Boyer, 1992, p. 54). This statement is an oversimplification and certainly does not tell the whole story about the effects of Head Start.

The very comprehensiveness of Head Start has made it difficult to assess. Also, although there are national regulatory standards for all Head Start programs, variation has been allowed and encouraged. This in turn makes assessment across programs more difficult. In the early stages of Head Start research,

Research on the long-term effectiveness of the programs developed as part of Planned Variation is presented in Chapter 6 along with a description of some of these programs.

FOR REFLECTION

Zigler, Styfco, and Gilman (1993) question whether instead of looking at the potential long-term gains from Head Start we need to emphasize today's accomplishments rather than the longitudinal effects. They wrote: "Each year over half a million poor children and their families experience an improved quality of life, however fleeting, as a result of their involvement in Head Start . . . . This alone is enough to justify the expenditure; any longer-term benefits are a bonus" (p. 26). Given the current political and economic climate in Canada, how receptive do you think the policymakers and politicians would be to such an argument for a Canada-wide Head Start program for poor families?

the emphasis was on variables that could be measured quantitatively, such as IQ. This meant that other goals of Head Start, such as children's socio-emotional development, were underemphasized in the early research. The focus of research on the effectiveness of Head Start has broadened over time and the continuing research addresses these methodological and design problems.

An early report on the effectiveness of the Head Start Program was the Westinghouse Report in 1969. This report concluded that the summer-only Head Start program had not been effective and that the year-long program was only somewhat effective (Brown, 1985). In addition, the gains in IQ by the children in the preschool years faded during the first years of elementary school (Raver & Zigler, 1991). The report did not address medical and nutritional areas that were also part of Head Start's mandate. A review of studies later showed that programs with strong parent involvement fared better (Bronfenbrenner, 1974). The results from these studies were a disappointment for many at the time who had hoped a relatively short-term intervention would be a permanent "quick fix" for the effects of poverty.

These results were also a disappointment for funding agencies, and what may have saved Head Start in these early days was "a grass roots contingency led by Head Start parents and staff" (Brown, 1985, p. 10). These groups lobbied for continued funding of Head Start. On the major anniversaries of Head Start (e.g., its twenty-fifth year), there are many media reports of past participants and families describing how Head Start had very positive effects on their lives. However, funding agencies tend to discount anecdotal or testimonial data in preference to more controlled research studies.

Over the years, Head Start has been shown to be effective in several areas. For the children the positive effects included better health, more immunizations, improved nutrition, lower absenteeism from school, improved performance on school achievement tests, fewer grade retentions and special-needs placements, and improved socialization and social behaviours (Head Start, 1982; Zigler, Styfco, & Gilman, 1993). For example, nearly 100 percent of the children receive medical screenings, immunizations, and medical treatment; Head Start is the largest single health-care provider to poor children in the United States (Zigler & Styfco, 1993). For families and communities the effects of Head Start include improved parenting skills, more parent participation in the school including decision-making positions, and more employment of parents in the program (Head Start, 1982; www2.acf.dhhs.gov/programs/hsb/index.htm).

Even though Head Start is now generally perceived as a modern success story and is often cited as the darling of U.S. politicians and the media, it has its critics. Some object to it as being too expensive; others criticize it because it does not serve all the children who could benefit from it. Some object to it on more philosophical grounds. For example, Head Start has moved away from its origins as a community action program as it has grown. These critics claim that it has been standardized and, because of regulations, has less flexibility to respond to locally identified needs.

University of Western Ontario Laboratory Preschool

Although Canada did not have a large federal early childhood project such as Head Start, there were "a few isolated compensatory education programs" (Dickinson, 1987). For example, there was one in Moncton, a few in Nova Scotia, and several sponsored by the National Council of Jewish Women (see Ryan, 1972). The best-documented Canadian program was developed at the University of Western Ontario Laboratory Preschool, which opened in September 1973 with Dr. Mary J. Wright as its director. She is Professor Emerita of Psychology at the University of Western Ontario and a former president of the Canadian Psychological Association. See Focus 5.3 for information on the evolution of the university's program, obtained during a recent conversation I had with Dr. Wright. Much of Focus 5.3 is in Dr. Wright's own words.

Aboriginal Head Start in Canada is discussed in Chapter 11.

See Chapter 9 for more information on laboratory nursery schools.

Focus 5.3

The University of Western Ontario's Laboratory Preschool

Mary Wright was a member of the group from the Institute of Child Study at the University of Toronto that went to Britain during the Second World War to establish a training school for child-care workers. The school included a day nursery and served, for the most part, children from low-income families. Wright was greatly impressed by the effects of the nursery school experience on these children.

Years later, at the University of Western Ontario, Dr. Wright lobbied for a laboratory preschool to be included in the building plans for a new Social Sciences Centre. The preschool was specially designed with the assistance of an architect from the Nurseries Branch of the provincial government. It was located on the fifth floor, with a spacious roof playground. It had large playroom, a smaller playroom, two special project rooms, and observation rooms with one-way-vision mirrors and microphones for students, parents, teachers, and researchers. This preschool has been called "the Rolls-Royce of University-affiliated schools in Canada" (Howe, 1994, p. 17).

There were two focuses of the preschool:

1. Research and teaching in child development, and

2. Program development in early education; specifically, a high-quality preschool program for low- and middle-income children.

At that time, there was a need for Canadian research, especially as the results from Head Start at that time were discouraging.

continued

continued

Because of her interest in children who were assumed to have little intellectual stimulation and her experiences in and studies of preschool education, Dr. Wright decided that a primary goal of the program should be to promote the cognitive development of the children. A cognitive-interactionist model was employed, with Piaget's stages in cognitive development used as guidelines for the development of curriculum. This orientation was also applied in the strategies for teaching and the fostering of children's questioning and problem-solving skills. Assessment had shown that the children needed to improve their self-management skills, problem-solving cognitive styles, representational skills, and conceptual abilities. However, the curriculum was broad-based and addressed all areas of development (i.e., personal, social, physical, and cognitive). It was "an individualized active-discovery type of program" (Wright, 1983, p. 26) that was play-oriented. The daily schedule included indoor and outdoor free play, small group teacher-guided activities (e.g., drama and language stimulation), snack, and large group activities such as stories, music, discussions, and games. Participation in circle time was voluntary for the children.

While Wright's research was in progress, the preschool enrolled mainly three- to five-year-olds and, unlike the Head Start program, both low- and middle-income children. The children attended five days a week for 2-1/2 hour sessions.

There were four teachers and a supervisor in addition to the director. There was little staff turnover during the project, and some of the teachers are still at the program today. The role of the teacher was a more active one than was found in the more "traditional" Ontario preschools at that time, but it was a facilitative rather than a didactic role (cf. p. 352 of Wright's book).

One of the purposes of the University of Western Ontario Preschool Project was to assess both the short- and long-term impact of this type of program on the children (i.e., in preschool and into elementary school). In order to see if there were any permanent changes, longitudinal research was done. The low-income children who had attended the preschool and a group of comparable children with no preschool experience were studied for up to four years after their entry into elementary school. The findings were generally positive. The preschool children maintained their cognitive gains and were promoted more often in elementary school than the control subjects. The failure rate in the control group was three times higher than that of the preschool graduate group. The children's language and problem-solving strategies improved, and the children with two years of preschool experience had better social and personal adjustments to school than children with only one or no years of preschool. (For more information, see Wright, 1983.)

The UWO Laboratory Preschool is still operating (see www.sscl.uwo.ca/psychology/preschool), and has the same basic philosophy. The number and types of programs have increased over the years. For example, a program for two-year-olds was added in 1986, and a toddler program in 1988. A resource teacher for children with disabilities was added in 1989 (10–12 percent of the children have special needs). In 1992 a parent-child program was designed with the assistance of the parents. This program meets one morning a week. Its curriculum is sensory-based and includes indoor and outdoor activities. There are weekly reading materials for parents and videos and books are available for loan. In 1995 a junior kindergarten was added, followed by a senior kindergarten in 1999. Local teachers have told the director that they can spot the UWO children in their classes because of their problem-solving skills (personal communication, Mary Lou Vernon, November 1999).

When I asked Dr. Wright what advice she would give the federal government on early childhood education and care for the twenty-first century, she said to make early education universal so all children will have access to it, especially those from low-income families whose parents are unemployed and who now fall through the cracks.

Contemporary Issues in Historical Context

Many of the issues related to Head Start and early childhood education and care today are issues that have historical roots. For example, reducing the effects of poverty on children and families was the impetus for Head Start. It was also the issue that concerned the McMillan sisters. Montessori and Owen also planned programs for poor children. The following section briefly examines a few of the issues from Head Start and other programs that are common to many early childhood programs past and present.

One issue is how uniformity across programs is reconciled with the specific needs and wishes of individual communities. The U.S. government has been criticized both for making Head Start too standardized and not consistent enough across sites. This has been a problem for many program developers in the past. Froebel's kindergarten exponents in North America split into the Traditionalists and the Progressives over how much adaptation was appropriate. Proponents of Montessori programs have also faced this problem. It becomes difficult to keep programs "true" to the original ideas over time and distance. Some will argue this is a positive development, others see it as negative. This is a long-debated topic in early childhood program development.

Head Start is criticized because it is not available to all children who could qualify for and benefit from it, and there is no universal access. Early childhood programs have long wrestled with this dilemma. Despite the call for universal early education from the time of Comenius, this is not a reality in Canada until the child is old enough for the public elementary school. Kindergarten became widely available in Canada only when it became part of the public school systems (and kindergarten attendance is still not compulsory in most provinces and territories).

The kindergarten–grade 1 transition is discussed in more detail in Chapter 10.

Another issue that has faced Head Start is the need for continuity between its program and the elementary school. Montessori resolved this problem by creating an elementary program using her Method. Head Start tried to address this issue through the Follow Through program.

Yet another issue for Head Start and other programs, past and present, has been the need for qualified staff. To address the shortage of qualified staff, Head Start began the Child Development Associate program. This program combines classroom and on-the-job training over variable lengths of time. The successful student is then given a CDA diploma. Montessori, Froebel, and McMillan all included teacher education in their programs in order to provide educators who were "properly" educated in their methodologies.

Parent/family participation in early childhood programs is discussed in Chapter 3.

From its beginning, Head Start has included parent participation as one of its goals. The role of parents in the education of their young children has long been recognized. Many of the early educators discussed in this chapter have provided for parent education through print materials such as Froebel's newsletter and books and Owen's lectures for parents.

Many of today's issues in early childhood education and care are thus not "new." They have roots and antecedents that go back many years. These issues will be expanded upon in subsequent chapters. Chapter 5 has provided the historical context for early childhood programs. Chapter 6 will provide the theoretical context. Both of these contexts have been and continue to be sources of contemporary early childhood programs in Canada and elsewhere.

Summary of this Chapter

The key themes in this chapter are the:

- Roots of early childhood education and care, which can be traced back to the philosophers of ancient Greece and other ancient civilizations.

- Influences of great thinkers throughout documented history who have discussed children and their early education and care. Their ideas came from many sources and, in turn, influenced each other as early childhood programs developed.

- Works of Comenius can be considered the beginning of modern early childhood education and care.

- Works of Rousseau, Pestalozzi, Froebel, and others who built on the work of their predecessors and were, in turn, the precursors for later theorists and educational ideas such as children's developmental stages, children's rights, and teacher education.

- Evolution of kindergarten, day care, and nursery school from different philosophical, ideological, and historical roots and for different purposes and to meet different needs. Some of these differences are still evident today.

- Desire and need to assist poor children and their families that motivated Owen, the McMillans, Montessori, and the compensatory programs of the 1960s.

- Philanthropy and child welfare movements, which contributed to the early development and growth of early childhood programs in Canada.

- Issues in early childhood education and care today that are long-standing or have their origins in the history of the field.

Key Terms

anschauung, 167	nursery school, 189
day nurseries, 189	Occupations, 176
Gifts, 174	Prepared Environment, 198
kindergarten, 172	Project Head Start, 202
kindergartner, 180	sensorial material, 199

Resources

If you wish to know more about some of the people and topics in this chapter, here are a few suggested publications and Web sites.

For More on Friedrich Froebel

My current favourite book on Froebel is Brosterman, N. 1997. *Inventing kindergarten.* New York: Harry N. Abrams, Inc. This is a coffee-table-sized book with beautiful colour photographs of Froebel's Gifts and Occupations and a very interesting part on the influence of Froebel's ideas on well-known artists and architects. Definitely an ask-Santa-for (or your birthday) book!

An excellent scholarly work on Froebel is Liebschner, J. 1992. *A child's work: Freedom and play in Froebel's educational theory and practice.* Cambridge: The Lutterworth Press.

Two good Web sites on Froebel are The Froebel Education Centre in Mississauga (www.froebel.com) and The Froebel Web (www.geocities.com). These sites contain lots of information on Froebel and also some on Pestalozzi and Rousseau.

 ## Other Useful Web Sites

Rousseau (www.wabash.edu); Pestalozzi (www.pgg.grz.th.schule.de); and Robert Owen (cedar.evansville.edu).

For More on Maria Montessori and Other Women

For Montessori's own explanation of her Method and ideas, try *The Montessori Method* (originally published 1912). New York: Schocken Books, 1964.

The best Montessori biography I've read is Kramer, R. 1988. *Maria Montessori: A Biography.* Reading, MA: Addison-Wesley Publishing Company—the fascinating story of a fascinating woman.

For more information about interesting and important women in early childhood education, try Snyder, A. 1972. *Dauntless women in childhood education 1856–1931.* Washington, DC: Association for Childhood Education International. Now out of print, but well worth a trip to the library—and if you ever see it in a used bookstore, grab it. Love the title!

Two books on Margaret McMillan are Bradburn, E. 1989. *Portrait of a pioneer.* London: Routledge, and Steedman, C. 1990. *Childhood, culture and class in Britain: Margaret McMillan, 1860–1931.* London: Virago, 1990.

A book by Caroline Pratt on the early days of nursery school is *I Learn from Children.* New York: Cornerstone Library, 1948/reissued 1970.

For More on Head Start–Type Programs

A comprehensive book with chapters by all the movers and shakers in the original Head Start is Zigler, E., & Jeanette Valentine (Eds). 1979. *Project Head Start: A legacy of the war on poverty.* New York: MacMillan Publishing Company.

A more recent update is Zigler, E., & Sally J. Styfco (Eds). 1993. *Head Start and beyond: A national plan for extended childhood intervention.* New Haven, CN: Yale University Press.

The Head Start Web site is www2.acf.dhhs.gov.

For more information about the University of Western Ontario's Laboratory School, see Wright, M.J. 1983. *Compensatory education in the preschool: A Canadian approach.* Ypsilanti, MI: High/Scope Press. UWO Laboratory School Web site is www.ssci.uwo.ca/psychology/preschool.

For History of Early Childhood Education and Care in Canada

Two good resources are:

Prochner, L. & Howe, N. (Eds.) 2000. *Early childhood care and education in Canada.* Vancouver: UBC Press.

Varga, D. 1997. *Constructing the child: A history of Canadian day care.* Toronto: Lorimer.

6

Theories Supporting Programs

Opinions and ideologies concerning appropriate curricula and methods are argued with great heat and conviction by each generation of parents, educators, and politicians.

—Lilian G. Katz *and* Sylvia C. Chard, Engaging Children's Minds: The Project Approach

Have you ever wondered where early childhood programs come from? Or why two early childhood programs in the same neighbourhood plan quite different activities for children? Sources for curriculum are varied. So far in this text we have looked at how the view of the child, childhood, and families can influence programs. Chapter 5 describes how the historical context and philosophies can impact program development. Now, this chapter examines some of the key theories of the past century that have been and are used as the bases for today's early childhood programs. Theories are a major influence in early childhood education and care. Examples of programs that are applications of the major theories are included in this chapter.

Here are some questions to think about while you read this chapter:

· What are some sources for curriculum for early childhood programs?
· What do I believe about how children develop and learn?
· How are theories applied to practice?
· What do the programs based on different theoretical models look like?
· Is any model better than the others?
· How relevant is the Italian Reggio Emilia approach for Canada?
· What is a child-centred curriculum?
· What are *projects, themes,* and *units*?
· Are early childhood programs cost-beneficial?

One of the educator's roles is developing a curriculum and program (see Chapter 4). What you believe about children and how they learn impacts on your program. Your beliefs influence your teaching strategies, planning, management, response to children, and selection of materials. Even if there are provincial/territorial curricula or guidelines, how these are interpreted and operationalized in your program is your responsibility. I have observed educators who have quite different philosophical beliefs and theoretical orientations create quite different early childhood programs, each complying with provincial/territorial regulations. Curriculum guides themselves usually present a specific theoretical orientation, stated or implied; however, there is still room for interpretation. Part of being an effective early childhood educator is being reflective: thinking about what you are doing *and why*.

Reflecting on Your Beliefs

To help you focus on what some of your beliefs are, please complete the questionnaire in Focus 6.1 before reading further.

What did you learn about your beliefs from doing the questionnaire? If you are like most of my students who have completed this or similar questionnaires over the years, your answers reflect a range of theories about how young children develop and learn. Most of the educators I know have an eclectic personal theory of early childhood education and care. However, eclectic does not mean random. Seifert and Handzuik (1993) found from interviews that "early childhood educators make particular philosophical assumptions about children, and that the assumptions are systematic and therefore akin to formal psychological theories . . . . Theories, it seems, are not the sole property of scholars, but are created by everyone" (p. 21).

The following section is a brief overview of some of the major formal theories of child development. Much of this information may be familiar to you from a previous course in child development or psychology.

Theories of Child Development

How children grow and develop has fascinated people for more than a thousand years. Early childhood education theorists such as Comenius, Rousseau, Pestalozzi, and Froebel wrote on the subject. Maria Montessori applied what she termed a "scientific approach," which included then-known research about children's development, to the development of her Method (see Chapter 5). However, the real growth of the study of child development began at the turn of the twentieth century.

Focus 6.1

What Is Your Ideal Early Childhood Program?

Consider each of the following statements in terms of the ideal early childhood program. Mark the responses that correspond to your personal belief or opinion of what practice should be for the majority of children in the ideal early childhood program for three- to five-year-old children.

1. Much of the day is free play.

    Strongly Agree   **Somewhat Agree**   **Neutral/Don't Know**   **Somewhat Disagree**   **Strongly Disagree**

2. Activities are planned to ensure the children's academic success.

    Strongly Agree   **Somewhat Agree**   **Neutral/Don't Know**   **Somewhat Disagree**   **Strongly Disagree**

3. Activities result from the cooperative planning of the children and the educator.

    Strongly Agree   **Somewhat Agree**   **Neutral/Don't Know**   **Somewhat Disagree**   **Strongly Disagree**

4. There is an emphasis on materials found in the environment (e.g., sand and water).

    Strongly Agree   **Somewhat Agree**   **Neutral/Don't Know**   **Somewhat Disagree**   **Strongly Disagree**

5. Children learn mainly through the use of hands-on and manipulative materials.

    Strongly Agree   **Somewhat Agree**   **Neutral/Don't Know**   **Somewhat Disagree**   **Strongly Disagree**

6. Dramatic play is used as a means of resolving children's emotional upsets.

    Strongly Agree   **Somewhat Agree**   **Neutral/Don't Know**   **Somewhat Disagree**   **Strongly Disagree**

7. The educator provides information by direct instruction.

    Strongly Agree   **Somewhat Agree**   **Neutral/Don't Know**   **Somewhat Disagree**   **Strongly Disagree**

8. Educators provide situations and materials where children can experiment.

    Strongly Agree   **Somewhat Agree**   **Neutral/Don't Know**   **Somewhat Disagree**   **Strongly Disagree**

9. Workbooks and worksheets are used for instruction.

    Strongly Agree   **Somewhat Agree**   **Neutral/Don't Know**   **Somewhat Disagree**   **Strongly Disagree**

10. Children are encouraged to make connections from present events to their past experiences.

    Strongly Agree   **Somewhat Agree**   **Neutral/Don't Know**   **Somewhat Disagree**   **Strongly Disagree**

11. The educator determines the pace of instruction.

    Strongly Agree   **Somewhat Agree**   **Neutral/Don't Know**   **Somewhat Disagree**   **Strongly Disagree**

12. The learning process is self-rewarding for children.

    Strongly Agree   **Somewhat Agree**   **Neutral/Don't Know**   **Somewhat Disagree**   **Strongly Disagree**

13. How the child works/plays is more important than the final product.

    Strongly Agree   **Somewhat Agree**   **Neutral/Don't Know**   **Somewhat Disagree**   **Strongly Disagree**

14. The children initiate and determine the nature of the majority of daily activities.

    Strongly Agree   **Somewhat Agree**   **Neutral/Don't Know**   **Somewhat Disagree**   **Strongly Disagree**

continued

continued

15. Children are encouraged to use materials in creative (although safe) ways.

| Strongly Agree | Somewhat Agree | Neutral/Don't Know | Somewhat Disagree | Strongly Disagree |

16. Children's correct answers/responses are reinforced with external rewards (e.g., tokens).

| Strongly Agree | Somewhat Agree | Neutral/Don't Know | Somewhat Disagree | Strongly Disagree |

17. Children are free to choose their own activities throughout most of the day.

| Strongly Agree | Somewhat Agree | Neutral/Don't Know | Somewhat Disagree | Strongly Disagree |

18. Task completion is important.

| Strongly Agree | Somewhat Agree | Neutral/Don't Know | Somewhat Disagree | Strongly Disagree |

The following questions reflect a behaviourist orientation:

2, 7, 9, 11, 16, and 18.

The following questions reflect a cognitive-interactionist orientation:

3, 5, 8, 10, 13, and 15.

The following questions reflect a developmental-maturationist orientation:

1, 4, 6, 12, 14, and 17.

Review your responses to see if there is a pattern. Do most of your responses agree or strongly agree with one of these orientations? Are your responses split mainly between two orientations? Are they distributed across all three orientations?

Based on Mayfield, Dey, Gleadow, Liedtke, & Probst, 1981

The Child Study Movement and Maturationist Theory

An influential early-twentieth-century researcher in child development was G. Stanley Hall (1826–1924). He used a scientific approach to studying young children's development in order to gather normative data. Hall believed that children developed through an automatic process of unfolding, in which heredity was more influential than the child's environment. He advocated that teachers carefully observe each child. This was not a new idea: Rousseau, Pestalozzi, Froebel, and Montessori had said the same thing. What Hall added to this observation of children was the systematic gathering of data about their development for the purpose of establishing norms (i.e., "averages"). Hall enlisted the help of kindergarten teachers in gathering data in his early studies (Weber, 1984).

The Child Study Movement also influenced the program at the Institute of Child Study in Toronto described in Chapter 9.

Hall wanted the information from his studies to inform curriculum. For example, he studied children's preferences and use of dolls in play and "concluded that the educational values of doll play were enormous" (Weber, 1984, p. 50). Hall criticized Froebel's ideas as being too metaphysical and thought Froebel's Gifts and Occupations needed revision and broadening. He stated that children's gross motor skills should be developed before their fine motor skills, and therefore Froebel's Gifts were not appropriate for young children. Many Progressive kindergarten teachers agreed with him.

A student of Hall's, Arnold Gesell (1880–1961), also supported the **maturationist or normative theory** of child development. He wrote: "the total ground plan is beyond your control. It is too complex and mysterious to be altogether entrusted to human hands. So Nature takes over most of the task, and simply invites your assistance" (1946, p. 6).

The research of Gesell and his associates popularized the **"ages and stages" model** of child development. As I write this paragraph, I can look up at my bookshelf and see a 1976 copy of *Your Four Year Old: Wild and Wonderful* by Louise Ames and Frances Ilg of the Gesell Institute of Child Development. If you look in the parenting section of a bookstore, you'll probably see books such as *Your Two Year Old*, which is an example of the ages and stages approach. The National Film Board of Canada at one time distributed films such as *Terrible Twos and Trusting Threes,* and *Frustrating Fours and Fascinating Fives* (Weber, 1984). Although these types of ages and stages publications have been criticized by more experienced parents and educators as being narrow and not typical of their experiences, many new parents and educators have found these books helpful in providing guidance as to what types of development and behaviour they could expect—or *not* expect—from children at certain ages. Gesell and his colleagues have also been criticized for basing the ages and stages on norms derived from data on predominantly white, middle-class children, which raises questions about the validity of applying the ideas to the development of other children.

The influence of the maturationist theory was seen in the organization of early childhood classrooms. Whereas many of the early theorists such as Froebel and Montessori had multi-age classes, the trend of a single age in a single - classroom was indicative of the ages and stages approach. Another tenet of the maturationist theory was the concept of readiness. Because of children's unfolding development, the idea was that they needed to be "ready" before they could learn certain concepts. This idea was particularly strong in North America in reading and mathematics. It is still common in some parts of North America for children in kindergarten to be given readiness tests before beginning grade 1. When I was in graduate school, I earned money for my tuition by scoring the section of a well-known readiness test that required children to draw a picture of a person. Their fine motor skill and inclusion of detail supposedly helped determine their readiness for grade 1.

The maturationist view has been a pervasive one in early childhood programs throughout the twentieth century and still appeals to many educators (Graue, 1992). Although it has critics, the maturationist theory, with its hands-off approach, is often used as a rationale to support child-centred programs (Hyson, 1996).

Child-centred programs are discussed later in this chapter.

Psychodynamic Theories of Child Development

Another strong influence on early childhood programs has been the **psychodynamic theories** of child development. These theories share some of the concepts of the maturationist theory, such as fostering children's self-expression and the need for a supportive environment. However, psychodynamic theories emphasized children's socio-emotional development. This focus has appealed to the early childhood community since Freud's time. Hyson (1994) stated, "of all the major developmental theories, psychoanalytic theory has placed the greatest emphasis on emotions as contributors to development and has been most specific about how emotions influence children's lives" (p. 31). Two examples of psychodynamic theory are the **psychoanalytic theory** of Sigmund Freud (1856–1939) and the **psychosocial theory** of Erik Erikson (1902–1994).

Freud's theory focused more on adults than children and emphasized the importance of the unconscious and drives in determining people's behaviours. Because he recognized the importance of the early years on personality development and later behaviours, his theory was well received by early childhood educators (Weber, 1984). The importance of a happy, well-adjusted child was a common topic in early childhood education textbooks in the 1930s (e.g., see Forest, 1935; Johnson, 1936).

Erik Erikson studied with Freud's daughter, Anna. He studied and wrote more about children than did Freud. His psychosocial theory of development considered the effects of the social environment on the development of personality. His first book in 1950 was entitled *Childhood and Society*. He identified eight stages of development; each stage has a dilemma that must be resolved by the individual. How these dilemmas were resolved could have either positive or negative effects on the development of the person. The first four stages are relevant to early childhood:

- Basic trust vs. basic mistrust (0–1 year of age)

- Autonomy vs. shame and doubt (2–3 years)

- Initiative vs. guilt (4–5 years)

- Industry vs. inferiority (6–puberty).

(Erikson, 1963)

See Chapter 7 for a description of play therapy.

Briefly, examples of important goals for each of these stages are adult–child bonding in infancy during the first stage, the development of independence by toddlers during the second stage, the development of children's identity and self-concept during the third stage, and the beginning of formal schooling and development of feelings of competence during the fourth stage. In this theory play is important, and play therapy is seen as a way to resolve children's problems.

The influence of psychodynamic theories has fluctuated over the last half century, with Freud's ideas on early childhood now less popular than Erikson's theory. Perhaps Erikson's most consistent and lasting influence in early childhood has been in infant and toddler education and care, especially with the recent increasing attention to children's socio-emotional development. In addition, helping children to resolve conflicts through play and verbalization is part of developmentally appropriate practice (Bredekamp, 1987). It might be said that the encouragement of self-expression and creative activities such as art, movement, and dramatic play has its roots in psychodynamic theories.

Different program models place different emphasis on artistic expression.

Behaviourist Theory

Behaviourism is really more of a theory about learning than development, although it is usually included in discussions of developmental theories. This is not inappropriate, as development and learning are obviously closely tied. For the behaviourists, learning is a key part of development.

The behaviourists believe it is important to carefully observe a child's behaviour before one can change it. At the beginning of the twentieth century, Edward Thorndike observed children to gather objective data about their behaviours; he improved observation studies by using more specific descriptions of behaviours.

Thorndike's work influenced Progressive kindergarten teachers such as Patty Smith Hill, who was his colleague at Teachers College, Columbia University. Perhaps because of this connection, he became interested in kindergarten and young children. In 1903, he wrote that the goal of kindergarten education was "the establishment of worthy habits" (quoted in Weber, 1984, p. 69). This is a similar idea to those expressed by some of the theorists discussed in Chapter 5, but the difference was in how establishing worthy habits was to be achieved. For the behaviourists, it would be accomplished by inhibiting unworthy habits and specifically fostering worthy ones. The behaviourists advocated the use of clear, specific objectives and careful analysis of tasks before teaching them.

Perhaps the person most associated with behaviourist theory is B.F. Skinner (1904–1990). His emphasis was on the actual behaviour of the child and not the internal motivation. For Skinner, the environment was important. He applied behaviourism to education, especially the concept of *operant conditioning*. Examples of early childhood educators using positive reinforcement to increase the frequency of a particular behaviour by a child can be readily seen in early childhood programs. Moreover, Skinner believed that punishment was not a very effective way of changing children's behaviours. He promoted the idea of breaking down a task into smaller sequential steps, teaching those steps in order, and reinforcing the behaviour after the child successfully completes each step. The reinforcement might be a token or some other extrinsic reward. The use of behaviour modification to shape children's behaviour is a legacy of Skinner.

Behaviourist theory has had a somewhat limited impact on mainstream early childhood programs, but a greater impact on special education, including early childhood special education. Many educators react negatively to behaviourist theory because they see it as manipulative and rigid (Hyson, 1996). However, you may recognize from the questionnaire you completed earlier in this chapter that early childhood educators do use behavioural principles such as positive reinforcement.

Behaviourism has also been criticized for being deficient in the social aspects in children's development. Social learning theory addresses this deficiency by recognizing the learning context as including a person's innate characteristics and behaviour, as well as the environment (Miller, 1993). According to social learning theory, these three factors influence each other in reciprocal ways. The concept of factors interacting in children's development is the defining characteristic of interactionist or cognitive development theory.

Cognitive-Interactionist Theories

The **cognitive-interactionist** theories have had the most impact on early childhood education and care in the last half of the twentieth century. They can be seen as a middle position as both the child and the environment are important, and it is the interaction of these factors that promotes learning and development. The child is perceived as an active learner. The two most significant theorists for early childhood education and care are Jean Piaget (1896–1980) and Lev Vygotsky (1896–1934).

Jean Piaget began by studying natural sciences in Switzerland, where he wrote his doctoral dissertation on mollusks. His research interest shifted to children's development during his post-doctoral studies in psychology and philosophy and continued for more than 50 years until his death at age 84. He was appointed director of the J.J. Rousseau Institute in Geneva in 1921 and began publishing his books in 1923. Piaget identified four stages in children's development:

* Sensorimotor (approximately ages 0–2)
* Preoperational (approximately ages 2–7)
* Concrete operational (approximately ages 7–11)
* Formal operational (approximately ages 11–15).

Piaget stated that each of these stages evolves from the previous one, the sequence is fixed, and, although children progress through the stages at different rates, stages are universal across cultures. The interactionist theorists believe that children actively construct knowledge through cognitive processes. According to Piaget, children use assimilation and accommodation to make sense of information and to fit new information into their existing cognitive schemas.

Piaget's theory has been criticized for its stage concept and insufficient recognition of social and emotional factors in children's development. For example, Margaret Donaldson (1978) criticized Piaget for not considering the context of children's thinking. She thought it was necessary to look at children's perceptions of a situation in order to understand fully their thinking. Her research showed that young children were able to appreciate other viewpoints, depending on the context. For example, if they had the background, they could see the problem in a story from the viewpoint of two different characters. Other critics also took exception to Piaget's universal developmental patterns or the methods and design of his research. While recognizing the strengths of Piaget's theory, these and other perceived weaknesses have been addressed in the work of a group of theorists referred to as neo-Piagetians. One of the leading neo-Piagetians is Robbie Case from the University of Toronto. He has postulated a stage concept similar to Piaget's but has integrated information processing with Piagetian theory (see Case, 1985; 1991).

Although Piaget's theory is probably still the most influential one for Canadian early childhood programs, many early educators seem to find Lev Vygotsky's ideas especially relevant and useful. In the past 10 years, there seems to have been an increased interest and discussion of Vygotsky's theory.

Lev Vygotsky was born in Russia the same year as Piaget but, tragically, died early of tuberculosis. I have often wondered what he would have contributed to child development theory if he had lived as long as Piaget; for example, he had plans to study children's emotional development but didn't live long enough to do so. Vygotsky originally studied medicine but graduated with a law degree. He then studied literature (he wrote his dissertation on *Hamlet*), philosophy, art, and, finally, psychology. He taught psychology at a Soviet teachers' college, and because he spoke eight languages including French, English, and German he was able to read widely in psychology and pedagogy (Berk & Winsler, 1995). He read Piaget's work, but until the 1960s his own work was not widely known outside of the Soviet Union because Stalin banned it.

One of the key features of Vygotsky's work is his belief that language plays a major role in cognitive development. In his book *Thought and Language* (1962), the last chapters of which were dictated from his deathbed, Vygotsky states "to understand another's speech, it is not sufficient to understand his words—we must understand his thought. But even that is not enough—we must also know its motivation" (p. 151).

Vygotsky's emphasis on the importance of language in children's development was not new. However, his contribution was the emphasis on the socio-cultural context of language and learning. He believed "development cannot be separated from its social context . . . [and] language plays a central role in mental development" (Bodrova & Leong, 1996). For this reason, Vygotsky's theory is sometimes referred to as a socio-cultural approach. It is also one area where Vygotsky and Piaget differ: Vygotsky placed more emphasis on the role of language and cultural and social contexts in learning than did Piaget.

One of the well-known contributions of Vygotsky is the concept of the **zone of proximal development** (ZPD). Vygotsky identified three levels of behaviour: the first and third zones are independent performance (i.e., the child does a task by him- or herself) and assisted performance (i.e., the child requires assistance from a more skilled individual in order to complete the task); in between is the zone of proximal development (i.e., varying degrees/amount of assistance or support is needed by the child). This assistance or support can take a variety of forms, such as questioning, peer tutoring, demonstrating a task, establishing the environment, or providing hints (e.g., What do you think would happen if you tried _____?). The ZPD is not the same for every child and is constantly changing as the individual child learns to do more and more things independently. As children learn, the new learning in turn enables them to develop to higher levels. The concept of ZPD has been well accepted by early childhood educators, especially those in early childhood special education. This concept also reinforces the long-held principle in early childhood programs of observing the child to determine what they know and can do, and then beginning from where they are.

Another Vygotskian concept relevant to early childhood is the idea of *scaffolding* (i.e., the educator provides just as much support or assistance as the child needs). An example of this is the early childhood educator adapting the amount and complexity of language in one interchange to the child's level, whether he or she is a toddler or an ESL child. Then as the child gains more language, the educator's language becomes more complex and the interchanges longer. Scaffolding is another concept that is also widely accepted in early childhood special education. One question early childhood educators voice about scaffolding is, When is it appropriate to apply scaffolding and when to let the child be? (Seifert, 1993).

Vygotsky's work has been criticized for neglecting non-verbal language and communication (Berk & Winsler, 1995), as well as for not more fully explaining the functioning of ZPD in children (Miller, 1993). However, perhaps one has to temper some of the criticism with the recognition that because of Vygotsky's early death, his was a theory in progress, not a completed work.

Other psychologists, some of whom were Vygotsky's students, have carried on his work. The interest in the past decade in the socio-cultural context and the theories that reflect this orientation have led to a renewal of interest in Bronfenbrenner's work. Vygotsky and Bronfenbrenner could both be termed *contextualists* in that they believed that contexts are critical in children's development. Bronfenbrenner's theory has been called an ecological theory because it focuses on children in the context of their total environment. The child is the centre of four interacting systems (Bronfenbrenner, 1992). These four systems, expanding outward from the child, are:

- The *microsystem* (e.g., child's home, school, friends)

- The *mesosystem* (e.g., link between home and school)

- The *exosystem* (e.g., government, media)

- The *macrosystem* (e.g., culture).

Each of these systems has significance for and impact on young children's development. Bronfenbrenner's theory has not had as much direct effect on early childhood programs as have other theories (Hyson, 1996). It seems more relevant to social policy and the development of comprehensive programs that target the child and family within the context of the community.

Piaget's and Vygotsky's theories of development emphasize cognition. The broadening of developmental psychology to emphasize more than cognition is particularly appealing for early childhood educators as the concept of the whole child has long been a key principle of many programs. Howard Gardner broadened cognition by identifying eight *intelligences*, or "ways of knowing" (1993; 1999):

The application of ecological theory and descriptions of comprehensive programs that target the child and family within the context of the community are presented in Chapter 11.

- Linguistic

- Logical-mathematical

- Musical

- Spatial

- Bodily-kinesthetic

- Naturalistic

- Interpersonal

- Intrapersonal.

FOR REFLECTION

Recall an early childhood program you have observed. Try to think of one or more activities for each of Gardner's eight types of intelligence. How applicable do you think these eight intelligences are for young children?

(Gardner also suggests a possible ninth intelligence, Existential, which is relevant to topics such as the meaning of life and death.)

According to Gardner, all children have these eight intelligences but each child has a unique pattern of strengths (e.g., a child might be highly verbal but not have particularly good spatial awareness, while another same-aged child may be very musical but not have good interpersonal skills). This theory has also been well received by educators working with gifted children (Hyson, 1996).

The **theory of multiple intelligences** has been applied to preschool and early primary levels in Gardner's Project Spectrum, which emphasizes identifying children's areas of strength and using this information as the basis for an individualized educational program (see www.projectzero.harvard.edu; Gardner & Kritchevsky, 1993). Although Gardner's theory has been criticized for lacking specific research support, it has become widely known among educators. Early childhood educators tend to respond to it favourably because it is compatible with educating the whole child and recognizes that each child has individual strengths and weaknesses.

Another trend arising at the end of the twentieth century has been an increasing focus on children's affective development. One example of this is **emotional intelligence** (Goleman, 1995), which includes concepts such as self-awareness, empathy, feelings, motivation, and social competence. These concepts are prominent in the anti-bullying/conflict resolution programs found in many Canadian schools today. Another similar trend is the recently revived interest of child developmentalists in children's moral development and spirituality (Noddings, 1998). Robert Coles' (1990; 1997) work on children's moral intelligence and spirituality and the virtues movement (e.g., Popov, 1997) are popular examples.

Critique of Child Development Theories

Child development theories as the bases of models for programs can be critiqued on three points. The first is the weaknesses inherent in each individual theory itself, as discussed above.

The second point concerns child development theories in general. One of the implications of a theory is universality. The more we come to know about children, especially in the global context, the more the universality of theories is questioned. A second characteristic desirable in theories is reliability and predictability—what the theory describes holds true across situations. There are many potential mediating factors in young children's development. For example, the experiences of children from different cultures and societies may be quite diverse. Most theories reflect the mainstream culture and context of their time, and thus may not be applicable to children in other countries, cultures, or times. For example, researchers have noted that three- and four-year-old children in China often do activities such as origami that require fine motor skills more advanced of what educators would expect of children the same age in North America (Gardner, 1989; Mayfield, 1994). The application of child development theories based on norms from white, middle-class children to all children has been criticized (e.g., Berhard, 1995; Charlesworth, 1983).

In addition, as shown in Chapter 2, there can be different perceptions of children and childhood across time, cultures, and theories. For example, behaviourist theorists have been criticized for perceiving children as objects to be manipulated (Polakow, 1989). A paradox in the field of early childhood education and care is our continual desire to find commonalties and predictability, while also recognizing and honouring diversity and individual differences. Some of the neo-Piagetians emphasize the unevenness of children's development. New and Mallory (1996) have suggested that perhaps "different theories of development and learning are necessary for different children" (p. 152). Perhaps the desire for a one-size-fits-all child development theory is no longer realistic.

A third point for critique is the use and misuse of child development theories. Theorists are not responsible for how their theories are used or misused in program development and implementation. For example, Piagetian theory has been a major influence in early childhood programs in the past 50 years, yet

Piaget himself said relatively little about the direct application of his theory to educational programs. Even Montessori, who controlled the education of Montessori teachers and the growth of her programs, was not able to keep programs from developing that claimed to use the Montessori method but did not. Another misuse of child development theories occurs when what is described in a theory as "normal" is translated into what is desirable—which, then, influences or determines evaluation techniques (Goffin, 1996). One of the difficulties with the normative approach is that many children, such as children with disabilities, are considered to be outside the "norm." A theory may tell us more about what children *can* do, but is unable to tell us what they *ought* to do.

Another concern is theories reinforcing the status quo (Stott & Bowman, 1996). Theories can be "fashionable" at particular times. Lilian Katz (1996) has commented on how psychodynamic theory was the "in" theory when she was teaching preschool in the 1950s. Throughout my own teaching career it has been the interactionist theories, especially Piagetian theory. Despite these and other concerns, "child development knowledge has been so foundational to the field of early childhood education that erasing it would seem to leave us in a meaningless limbo in which everything is relative and nothing matters" (Lubeck, 1996, p. 158).

What is the future for child development theories? Will one be *the* theory for the twenty-first century? It of course remains to be seen which one, if any, it will be. Perhaps we'll see more synthesis and reconciliation of existing theories. Perhaps the ever-growing research on children's early development, especially in infancy (see Chapter 2), will significantly modify theories or lead to new theories of development and learning. Or perhaps we'll continue with the eclectic model that seems to be prevalent in early childhood programs today. You may have found from completing the questionnaire at the beginning of this chapter that you exemplify an eclectic model. But eclecticism also has its critics!

The issue of a theory telling us more about what children can *do, while remaining unable to tell us what they* ought *to do, is expanded upon in the discussion of developmentally appropriate practice in Chapter 12.*

FOR REFLECTION

Respond to John Morss' statement "the problem with orthodox, psychological approaches to development is quite simple—they are too developmental" (1996, p. 1).

From Theories to Programs

Chapter 5 traces the historical development of early childhood programs to the early twentieth century. According to Spodek and Brown (1993), "early childhood curriculum development remained dormant from the 1930s to the 1960s" (p. 95). This is probably not surprising, as many of those years were times of economic collapse and war. However, the 1960s and 1970s were a dynamic period of program growth and experimentation in early childhood education and care. While kindergartens, Montessori programs, day care, and traditional nursery school programs already existed, other options were being tried. Researchers often developed these programs as alternative models, as seen in Head Start and Follow Through Planned Variation, to try to discover the most effective curriculum model for early childhood programs. This interest has continued, and current interest in *curriculum models* "has materialized, in part, because of demand for consistent program quality and accountability" (Goffin, 1994, p. 32).

Head Start and Follow Through are discussed later in this chapter.

A **curriculum model** has been defined as

> an educational system that combines theory with practice. A curriculum model has a theory and knowledge base that reflects a philosophical orientation and is supported, in varying degrees, by child development research and educational research . . . . Curriculum models are central to any discussion of early childhood programs. (Epstein, Schweinhart, & McAdoo, 1996, pp. 9–10)

Curriculum models are derived from ideas about how children learn and develop. They are useful because "every educator knows that a valid curriculum model provides both the theoretical framework and the practical information and procedures needed to operate an early childhood education program" (Schweinhart & Epstein, 1996, p. 4).

Contemporary early childhood programs reflect a range of theories. A useful visual construct to illustrate this is a continuum with two end points and the various curriculum models and the programs they represent strung out along this continuum. Figure 6.1 illustrates one possible continuum.

There are, of course, gaps and overlaps of programs. Two programs that have a similar philosophical or theoretical base can look quite different in practice. For example, although both Montessori and Reggio Emilia programs originated in Italy and are considered to be cognitive-interactionist programs, they are not the same and indeed have many significant differences.

The following sections will present four different curriculum models as examples of how theory translates into practice in planning and implementing early childhood programs. The four programs are Direct Instruction, the High/Scope curriculum, the British infant school, and the Reggio Emilia approach. These four programs were selected because they are good examples of the application of theory to practice and all are different from each other.

figure 6.1   CONTINUUM OF PROGRAM MODELS

DESCRIPTORS:		
STRUCTURED		UNSTRUCTURED
FORMAL		INFORMAL
TEACHER-INITIATED		CHILD-INITIATED
ACADEMIC/SKILLS EMPHASIS		SOCIO-EMOTIONAL EMPHASIS
THEORIES:		
BEHAVIOURIST	COGNITIVE-INTERACTIONIST	DEVELOPMENTAL-MATURATIONIST
PROGRAMS:		
DIRECT INSTRUCTION	HIGH/SCOPE	ORIGINAL HEAD START
	MONTESSORI	BRITISH INFANT SCHOOL
	REGGIO-EMILIA	

Most typical early childhood programs today are "hybrids": they reflect an eclectic approach, which makes it more difficult to see clearly the application of a specific theory to practice. Therefore the programs selected for discussion in the next part of this chapter are those that are based on specific theories and designed specifically to operationalize those theories. The four programs are well-known examples of their type, and have existed for many years. Each program is described using the following framework: background, educator's role, curriculum and program organization, physical environment, assessment of children, and critique. (Key principles and characteristics are found in the margin next to the relevant paragraph. These are included to help the reader better make the connection between theory and application in an early childhood program.)

Behaviourist Program

I have chosen to begin with the structured, formal end of the continuum (see Figure 6.1) because I find that the behaviourist principles are the easiest to recognize in application. The behaviourist program described here is Direct Instruction.

Background

This program is probably the best-known behaviourist program in early childhood education. It had its beginnings in 1964 in a behaviourist curriculum model developed by Carl Bereiter (now at OISE-University of Toronto) and Sigfried Engelmann. This was a preschool program known as the Bereiter-Engelmann Model. When Wesley Becker replaced Bereiter the name was changed to the Engelmann-Becker Model. When the model became part of Head Start/Follow Through Planned Variation, it was extended to a preschool–grade 3 program. This program is named Direct Instruction, and its materials have been marketed under the name DISTAR (Direct Instructional System for Teaching Arithmetic and Reading). The program has been used in various parts of Canada, but is now used primarily with children with special needs.

Educator's Role

The educator is very important in this program because it is a teacher-directed program (i.e., the educator makes almost all the decisions). Educators are referred to as "instructional engineers or educational arrangers" (Peters, Neisworth, & Yawkey, 1985, p. 91).

As might be expected in a teacher-directed program, how things are taught is very important. Educators are advised that to make the program succeed, they must "follow the program" (Engelmann & Osborn, 1976a, p. 12). In order to help ensure this, detailed instructions are provided. They also receive pre- and in-service training in using Direct Instruction, because a thorough knowledge and understanding of behaviourist principles is essential. In addition, the educators need to be able to use techniques such as prompting (e.g., using hand signals to

■ Teachers model behaviour

■ Most behaviour is learned

cue children's responses). In the original program, trained aides were used to do some of the small-group teaching.

Curriculum and Program Organization

■ Academic emphasis

The focus of the Direct Instruction program is on academics. Its developers believed that what children from poor areas who participate in programs such as Head Start needed was a program specifically focused on academic subjects to help them "catch up" (Bereiter & Engelmann, 1966). The main areas of this program are arithmetic, language, and reading. Direct Instruction divides each of these areas into three levels, which are further sub-divided into individual lessons.

In a behaviourist program, lesson planning typically involves the following steps:

■ Learning is hierarchical

1. Identifying the learning objective

■ Task analysis breaks down concepts into small steps

2. Identifying the key parts of the concept to be taught

3. Doing a task analysis

4. Sequencing steps

■ Steps are sequenced

5. Planning instructional strategies to teach the objective (Fueyo, 1999).

In the DISTAR materials, the individual lessons are very detailed and are done as scripts that indicate what the educator is to say and what the desired responses from the students are. An example of this, from DISTAR Language, level 1, is seen in the following excerpt from a lesson on Polars. The children are asked to look at four lines of different lengths. The teacher's edition instructs

■ Uses prompts and reinforcement of behaviour

> Look at these lines. Let's find the lines that are long. Point to each line and ask: Is this line long? [The children respond yes or no. Then the teacher repeats by saying] Is this line long? [if the children answer with one word, they are told] Say the whole thing [i.e., This line is not long. The above pattern is repeated for each of the four lines. The scripted lesson ends with the instruction] When all the children's responses are firm say: Now you know which lines are long. (Engelmann & Osborn, 1976b, p. 64)

■ Uses fast-paced lessons and drill techniques

■ Formal lessons typically follow a set pattern

The above lesson is done at a fast pace, and hand signals are given for the children to cue their response, much of which is in unison. The children are seated in a semi-circle around the educator so that they can clearly see each other. The DISTAR program emphasizes repeated verbal response. Instruction of the children is to be done "in a business-like, task-oriented manner" (Bereiter & Engelmann, 1966, p. 59). Routine is considered to be important. The educator is instructed to "adhere to a rigid repetitive presentation pattern" (Berieter & Engelmann, 1966, p. 111).

■ Uses small-group instruction

In Direct Instruction, the children are divided into small groups for lessons. Small groups maximize the amount of response by the children and allow the educator to assess which children have mastered the concepts. These groups are determined by the children's abilities and the concepts to be taught, and DISTAR materials include placement tests. Each group has a lesson in each of the three core subjects. These lessons last approximately 15 minutes. In between the lessons the children have semi-structured activities that may include games or puzzles to reinforce the concepts being taught. The timetable also includes periods for music and unstructured activities as well as lunch, rest, snack, toileting, and cleanup. Play is not part of this program because it would take time from the academic subjects.

The materials in DISTAR are didactic. In addition to the teacher's guides, which suggest the scripts for each lesson, there are workbooks and worksheet pages to provide additional practice. Take-home workbooks with exercises for parents to do with their children provide additional reinforcement of the skills.

Physical Environment

In the original program model, there was one large room (the "homeroom") and three small rooms that were used for small-group instruction. These rooms were to be clearly delineated and have minimal visual distraction. Charts with stars to reward children for desired behaviour were deemed appropriate. Bereiter and Engelmann (1966) wrote that "sterilizing the environment is a firm requirement of the work-oriented preschool" (p. 72).

Assessment

The children's progress is evaluated by frequent criterion-referenced tests. These tests are used to determine if the individual child has mastered the concept and is therefore ready for the next level.

Critique

In my experience, the behaviourist programs are the ones that early childhood educators react to most strongly—positively or negatively. The Direct Instruction program and its forerunners may be the most hotly debated early childhood programs in the past 35 years. These programs are most frequently criticized for their content, instructional strategies, materials, and role of the educator. Many early childhood educators are critical of the lack of provision for play and creativity. Bereiter and Engelmann addressed this point in stating that "concepts of creativity and self-expression have only a very vague status in the context of early childhood education," and that, because children are not in school all day, they can be creative during the "ten other hours of the day" (1966, p. 62). The behaviourist programs are also criticized for the emphasis on academics and the lack of attention to the arts. In the case of programmed materials the content of the curriculum is determined by individuals who do not know the children or the community. The instructional strategies have been criticized as being repetitive, redundant, and overly predictable. Some educators see extrinsic reinforcement as manipulation or bribery of children and think it can be an oversimplification of the learning process (Evans, 1975).

- Follow a set timetable each day

FOR REFLECTION

How would cleanup time be done in a behaviourist program?

- Reinforcement of skills is important

- Instructional materials teach basic concepts and skills

- Children learn from their environment

- The physical environment is structured

- Develops children's self-esteem through academic success

- Uses continual evaluation by teachers to determine children's progress

Cognitive-Interactionist Program

Cognitive-interactionist programs (also called constructivist programs) are based on the theories of Piaget, Vygotsky, and other constructivists. From your answers to the questionnaire at the beginning of this chapter, you'll have noticed how much—or little—of your own philosophy is compatible with the cognitive-interactionist view. In one survey of 671 early childhood programs in the United States, the most frequently used model was an interactionist one (Epstein, Schweinhart, & McAdoo, 1996).

One curriculum model that is based on Piagetian theory is the High/Scope curriculum. It has been in existence for almost 40 years and has been widely disseminated. According to Hyson, "the most direct and widespread influence [on program models in early childhood] has come about through the Piaget-influenced High/Scope curriculum" (1996, p. 57). This program is also noteworthy because of the systematic documentation and research it has done.

Background

The High/Scope curriculum grew from the efforts of David Weikart, who, when he was special education director for a public school district in Michigan, "turned to the preschool years as a way of reaching children before they fell into the traditional school patterns that spawned their failure" (Weikart & Schweinhart, 1993, p. 196). In 1962, he established the Perry Preschool for three- and four-year-olds (named for its location—the Perry Elementary School in Ypsilanti, Michigan). This program was originally part of a school district and not a Head Start program. When the program became part of Follow Through Planned Variation, it was extended into the primary grades. In 1970, the High/Scope Educational Research Foundation was established. It is the administrative body that now operates the High/Scope programs.

In the late 1970s, the High/Scope curriculum was adapted for children who have special needs and for Spanish-speaking children and their families. The curriculum now covers preschool and primary levels as well as an adolescent residential program. While the program's major basis is still Piagetian, other theories have influenced the curriculum over the years. The High/Scope curriculum has been used in the laboratory nursery schools at the University of Waterloo and at Ryerson Polytechnic University. The recently approved Quebec curriculum *Jouer c'est magique* is based heavily on the High/Scope model (its use is optional in Quebec early childhood programs).

Educator's Role

As might be expected in a process-based curriculum, the role of the educator is one of facilitator and questioner. Asking questions to facilitate children's thinking and problem solving is essential. Questions are usually open-ended, such as, Why do you think that happened? or, How can we find out? The educator encourages children's problem solving in both cognitive and social areas and is responsible for providing open-ended materials for the classroom environment. Many of these materials foster cooperative work. Hohmann and Weikart (1995) describe the educator's role as, "while children interact with materials, people, ideas, and events to construct their own understanding of reality, adults observe and interact with children to discover how each child thinks and reasons. Adults strive to recognize each child's particular interests and abilities, and to offer the child appropriate support and challenges" (p. 20).

Educators in an interactionist program are sometimes described as "partners" with the children, although they are not necessarily equal partners. However, educators may be active participants in the children's activities, play, and conversations. The role of the educator, like that of the children, is typically hands-on.

In the High/Scope model, educators are expected to have training in this model and to receive ongoing training in-service. High/Scope offers summer institutes, conferences, a Web site (see www.highscope.org), videos, and publications including books, a newspaper, and a newsletter.

- Knowledge is actively constructed

- Uses questioning to help children's thinking

- Uses materials that are open-ended and flexible

Curriculum and Program Organization

The current High/Scope curriculum has evolved from previous curricula. The first one was named the Cognitively Oriented Curriculum, and its main premise was that "there cannot be a basic understanding of self and world without the ability to place the self in time and space and to classify and order objects and events" (Weikart, Rogers, Adcock, & McClelland, 1971, p. 6). This curriculum has been revised several times.

The current curriculum is described by its developers as "a curriculum model that is essentially democratic in operation, adaptable to local culture and language, and open to use by thoughtful adults everywhere" (Weikart & Schweinhart, 1993, p. 197). It is still based on Piagetian theory but is not "dauntingly theoretical" (Hyson, 1996, p. 57). The rationale and organization of the High/Scope curriculum are relatively easy to understand and implement.

The High/Scope curriculum is organized around "key experiences" (Hohmann & Weikart, 1995). There are 10 key experiences in the three domains of cognitive development, socio-emotional development, and movement/physical development. The key experiences are:

- Creative representation (e.g., painting, drawing, role playing, modelling with clay or blocks),

- Language and literature (e.g., listening to stories, describing objects and events, writing or dictating stories),

- Initiative and social relations (e.g., making choices, resolving social conflict, self-care),

- Movement (e.g., locomotor, non-locomotor, moving with objects),

- Music (e.g., singing, playing simple musical instruments, moving with music),

■ Uses Piagetian-type
skills, such as
classification and
seriation

- Classification (e.g., describing similarities and differences, sorting, matching, distinguishing shapes),

- Seriation (e.g., patterning, ordering by size, comparing long/short),

- Number (counting, one-to-one correspondence, comparing),

- Space (e.g., fitting objects together, filling/emptying, observing from different spatial perspectives),

- Time (e.g., starting/stopping on signals, remembering events, comparing time intervals).

(Hohmann & Weikart, 1995)

Curriculum guides for specific subjects (i.e., language and literature, mathematics, and science) and the learning environment were developed for the K–3 program. The key experiences are used for planning the daily program, assessing materials, observing the children, and organizing daily routines (Hohmann, 1997).

■ Children's thinking is
different from the
thinking of adults

■ Emphasizes problem-
solving and
communication

■ Needs large blocks of
time for problem-
solving

Although there is no formal timetable required for the High/Scope curriculum, "a consistent daily routine that supports active learning" provides a framework for the day (Hohmann & Weikart, 1995, p. 7). A typical day includes "Plan-Do-Review," small-group times, large-group times, free play, music/movement/physical education, story time, outdoor time, snack/lunch, rest, and transition activities such as cleanup time.

An important part of the daily program is Plan-Do-Review, which is in keeping with the emphasis on children's thinking and problem solving. In the Plan-Do-Review process, each child articulates what he or she wants to do and how he or she proposes to do this (using words, pictures, or symbols); the child then carries out the plan, and finally participates in a debriefing in which each child recalls what he or she did, what went well, and any problems that were encountered. The purpose of this process is to facilitate children's thinking and planning as well as to encourage their reflective thinking. The role of the educator is to "support and guide," but not to direct the children, because the Plan-Do-Review time is meant specifically "for children to carry out *their own* plans" (Hohmann & Buckleiter, 1992, p. 47).

Physical Environment

As might be expected of a Piagetian-based program, the environment is organized in a manner to facilitate children's thinking and problem solving. For example, the materials are organized in logical groupings of clearly delineated interest centres such as blocks, art materials, manipulatives, books and writing materials, and sand/water. Within an area, the materials are grouped in a logical manner, such as blocks arranged on a shelf in order of smallest to largest. In a housekeeping area or a woodworking area, an outline of the object may assist the child in returning it to its proper place. The goal is to enable children to use and return materials independently.

There are no specifically developed materials for children required for this model. The materials are the "general types" of materials found in most early childhood programs. Suggestions for suitable materials (Vogel, 1997) include:

▣ Active learning by interacting with the environment

- Practical, everyday objects (e.g., pots, pans, staplers),

- Natural and found materials (e.g., shells, pine cones, bottle caps),

- Tools (e.g., brooms, saws, sponges),

- Messy materials (e.g., paste, sand, paint, dough),

- Heavy large materials (e.g., hollow blocks, tricycles, balls),

- Easy-to-handle materials (e.g., buttons, pegboards, beads).

Assessment

One of the roles of the High/Scope educators is to observe and record the children's behaviour. This includes making daily anecdotal notes that are used in daily planning sessions. The *High/Scope Child Observation-Record for Ages 2?–6* is organized around the key experiences and assesses initiative, creative representation, language and literacy, social relations, logic and mathematics, and music and movement. The *High/Scope Program Quality Assessment* (1998) is used for rating programs on learning environment, daily routine, adult–child interaction, curriculum planning and assessment, parent involvement and family services, and staff qualifications and development.

▣ Assesses children primarily by observation

High/Scope has carried out longitudinal evaluations of their programs since the Perry Preschool Project. These studies have made a significant contribution to early childhood education and care and are discussed below, after the next program.

Critique

Much of the criticism of interactionist programs in general and High/Scope in particular has come from the debate about the use of Piagetian theory as a basis of curriculum (Evans, 1975). A second concern of some critics has been what they see as a misinterpretation of Piaget. Even within the group of programs typically considered interactionist, developers have been critical of other similar programs because of the differences in the interpretation of Piagetian theory, even though Piaget was not an educational program developer. The developers of High/Scope state that they use more than Piagetian theory as a basis for their program; for example, they also draw on the historical practices of Froebel (Weikart & Schweinhart, 1993). However, while some critics think that the High/Scope curriculum has shifted its theoretical orientation in recent years to a more developmental-maturational approach, others think it still overemphasizes cognitive goals in comparison to socio-emotional ones.

Specific criticisms about the High/Scope curriculum also include the possible restriction of a curriculum organized around 10 key experiences. The degree of flexibility in the program has been questioned. For example, in one study an educator commented that she "saw herself as locked into a script that had been written for her, a schedule that did not allow her to make decisions about what she knew as a teacher she should be doing for her children" (Walsh, Smith, Alexander, & Ellwein, 1993, p. 324). A related concern is the amount of time required for planning, including the daily team meetings. Some critics would like to see more provision for free play outside of the Plan–Do–Review time to provide a more equal balance between the cognitive and socio-emotional areas. The earlier curricula seemed to have had more of a cognitive focus, while the later versions have given more recognition to children's socio-emotional development (Goffin, 1994). Another concern is continuation of the High/Scope curriculum into the primary grades and how it fits into the requirements of elementary school curricula.

The High/Scope model emphasizes children's thinking and problem solving. These skills have been identified as pressing needs for the twenty-first century by educators, business people, politicians, futurists, and others.

The High/Scope program has been modified and adapted for children who have special needs and for Spanish-speaking children, which speaks to its adaptability and flexibility. The support structure available from the High/Scope group is impressive. I have received their catalogue of materials for many years and have seen it grow considerably in size and variety. Most of the materials are suitable for use in non–High/Scope programs. The use of regular materials and an environmental organization pattern that is common to most early childhood programs would reduce costs.

Developmental-Maturationist Programs

A third type of early childhood program based on theory is the developmental-maturationist model. These programs are based on the theories that emphasize the natural development of the young child (e.g., Rousseau, Freud, Erikson, Gesell, Isaacs, 1929/1968). As shown on the continuum in Figure 6.1, these programs are considered child-centred rather than teacher-directed, informal rather than formal, and unstructured rather than structured. Classic examples of these programs are the traditional nursery school (see Chapter 9), including the early Head Start, the British infant school, and the Danish *bornehaven* (Peters, Neisworth, & Yawkey, 1985). I have observed examples of all three of these programs, and have selected for discussion the British infant school because I worked in several nursery and primary schools in England during the 1970s when they were seen as cutting-edge programs. According to Goffin (1994), "the British experience of the 1960s and 1970s remains unique in its successful adaptation of progressive ideas on a large scale" (p. 66). For this reason alone, it is important to know about these programs. In addition, they are excellent examples of the developmental-maturationist approach.

Background

I'll describe my experiences working in programs for children from ages three to six as well as the experiences of others such as Eisner (1974) and Weber (1971),

FOR REFLECTION

The High/Scope approach places a heavy emphasis on problem solving by the children. It relies heavily on educator questioning. A frequent reservation concerns how this approach can be done effectively with children who have English as a second language, or who have limited or no language. Do you agree or disagree with this view? Why?

who spent considerable time observing and writing about these schools. Finally, I'll provide an update on how the English early childhood curriculum and programs have changed recently.

My teaching in England was primarily in (a) reception classes of infant schools (i.e., four-and-a-half- to five-year-olds), (b) half-day nursery classes that were part of a primary school (three- to four-year-olds), (c) a full-day nursery school that was part of a large school complex that included an infant, junior, and middle school (three- to four-year-olds and a class for children who were deaf), and (d) a nursery school that was a separate unit, not connected to a school, that had both full-time and part-time classes (three- to five-year-olds). All of these programs were under the auspices of local educational authorities (i.e., government-funded schools) in the Greater London area.

The informal British infant school received much attention as a result of *Children and Their Primary Schools*, commonly called the Plowden Report (1967). This was a comprehensive national inquiry into primary education (similar to Canadian royal commissions on education but on a national rather than provincial/territorial level). This report commented favourably on the use of informal methodology observed in many infant schools (i.e., schools for children from five to greater than seven years of age; later renamed *primary schools*). It is important to recognize that not all English early childhood programs followed this model, even at the height of the model's popularity. It would likewise be incorrect to overgeneralize my description to include all English schools then or now. For example, at the time it was estimated that about 25 percent of the *primary* schools fit the "true" British infant school model, 40 percent were traditional, and 35 percent somewhere in between (Rogers, 1973). Because much of the curriculum and methodology of the British infant school was based on what is now called *developmentally appropriate practice* in early childhood programs, a much higher percentage of the nursery schools exemplified this model.

Educator's Role

The educator was responsible for planning and implementing almost the entire program. There were very few guidelines available. In the primary grades, there were some commercial materials, such as reading series, but the teacher's guides were much less detailed than North American ones at that time.

The educators I worked with were very different people with very different backgrounds and experiences. Their common beliefs included the need for children to be children and for the children to have opportunities to develop their whole selves. The phrase "the whole child" is particularly meaningful in programs with a developmental-maturationist orientation. The child's total development—cognitive, social, emotional, and physical—was the focus of the curriculum and defined the educators' roles.

The focus on the whole child was also seen in the staffing of these programs. In the nursery programs, every class had an assistant. Typically, these assistants were trained educators holding a Nursery Nurse Examination Board Certificate (NNEB).

■ Sees the educator as a guide and facilitator

Health and nutrition were important parts of the nursery school program. The legacy of the McMillan sisters and their open air nursery school (see Chapter 5) could be seen in the emphasis on children going outside every day—sometimes in weather where this would not be typical in Canada. Most of the programs I worked in served a hot lunch to the children. The women in charge of preparing and serving the meal were referred to by children and adults as "dinner ladies." They were very persuasive in encouraging the children to "try just a bit, dear" of every food so that the child received a nutritious and balanced meal every school day. The children in nursery and infant schools also received free milk for their snack. Children in full-day nursery programs had a nap time after lunch; while some slept soundly for two hours or more, others did not sleep at all (they played quietly by themselves seated on their cots).

Health visitors came approximately monthly to check the children's health, and also visited families in their homes. Sometimes these health checks were general, other times they targeted specific conditions such as lice or skin problems. Specialists, such as speech therapists, were also available from the local educational authority for assessment and therapy.

Curriculum and Program Organization

At the time I was teaching in England, there was no set curriculum, no set sequence, few teachers' guides, and no workbooks. The curriculum was primarily school-based with the head (principal) and the teachers responsible for the curriculum in each school.

The philosophy and theory supporting this model espoused the development of the whole child. As Weber (1971) observed, "it was essential, in the minds of those committed to informal education, that the planning and activity of the school not interrupt the development of these patterns [i.e., of each individual child], but meet, extend, and carry them further" (pp. 132–133). Therefore, there were no mandated times for specific subjects and the curriculum was child-centred and often child-driven. As Rogers (1973) stated, "an idea, a question, an observation—child's or teacher's—acts as a stone thrown into the middle of a quiet pond" (p. 264). A very literal example of this occurred one day when I had taken my reception class to the park to feed the ducks. The children had brought along bread and cake to feed the ducks; this led to a question on the best food to feed ducks, which then resulted in an investigation of what ducks normally eat and this, in turn, expanded into study on birds. Weber (1971) observed "a willingness to go along with the rhythms and interest in a child" in the British infant school (p. 130).

Two key features of the British infant school were the **integrated curriculum** and the **integrated day**. The *integrated curriculum* is the use of a theme or topic into which most of the "subjects" can be accommodated. One aspect of the curriculum in the infant school was the strong use of the arts for children's self-expression and communication. The arts included not only art and music, but also drama and dance. One of the few scheduled activities for

■ Promotes all aspects of development

■ Sees children as explorers

Children's input into curriculum and the use of projects are discussed later in this chapter.

■ Encourages creativity and self-expression

my reception class was the BBC's radio program "Music and Movement," an excellent program devoted to music and expressive movement.

In an *integrated day,* "the work of the day is continuous with each day flowing into the next" (Yardley, 1976, p. 13). My class timetable was very general, with large blocks of time and only a few fixed times such as a radio broadcast, morning break, and lunch time. A typical schedule for the five-year-olds was:

- Group meeting of the children in the classroom to take attendance and discuss the general outline of the day

- Assembly in the hall with the entire school (this included the morning service. Children were excused from attending if their parents objected. One of the few national regulations at that time was religious education)

- Morning activities in the classroom or around the school

- Mid-morning milk break and outdoor play

- Dinner (i.e., hot lunch)

- Classroom activities (continuation of the morning)

- Tidy-up time

- Story, discussion, and dismissal.

The teaching of "subjects" was typically integrated into the theme being studied. The morning and afternoon activities usually included a mix of individual and small-group activities. Occasionally there would be a whole-group activity, such as planting seedlings into the school garden or a field trip out into the community (most of these were walking trips). If the educators had specialty areas, they might trade off classes for a lesson. One school in which I worked designated Friday afternoons as a children's choice time, when they chose among various activities offered by educators and parent volunteers. It was not unusual to have children from ages five to eleven in one group doing drama, an art project, or science experiments. A feature found in some English schools at the time was *family grouping,* multi-age classes where the age range spanned two years or more.

The respect for and accommodation of children's individual differences was very evident for me in the teaching of reading. I was very pleased when a head told me that there was no rush to get the five-year-olds into reading. I found it a very sensible approach compared to the common North American idea that a child who has not learned to read by December in grade 1 is considered a problem. The more relaxed approach of the British infant school gave those children who needed it extra time. For those children who were reading at five or interested in doing so, I worked with them individually or in small groups using both trade and "little books" (i.e., textbooks consisting of one or two stories). The British infant schools encouraged children's drawing, dictating, and writing to share their experiences and learning. Weber (1971) observed that "writing went on all the time . . . . Some of the children seemed to learn reading

▨ Integrates subjects throughout the day

▨ Schedules are flexible

▨ Encourages children's interests

See Chapter 10 for a discussion of multi-age grouping.

▨ Considers development a natural unfolding; pressure is not appropriate by writing, and the writing was valued by the children" (p. 128). Several years later, colleagues and I compared the writing of children in Canada, England, and the United States and found that the English five- to six-year-olds wrote longer and more complex stories than the other children (Ollila, Mayfield, & Williams, 1983). Other forms of communication, such as drawing, painting, drama, and storytelling, were also valued.

■ **Uses common environmental materials**

The mathematics materials were highly manipulative and there were plenty of natural materials such as shells and buttons used for counting, one-to-one correspondence, or sorting activities. The children used these materials individually or in small groups, with occasional whole-group lessons related to the topic of study—for example, graphing children's guesses as to the colour of the flowers of a plant we had been given during our study of plants.

Nature study was a big part of the curriculum. Walks in the schoolyard and local parks were used to observe plants, birds, and insects, and to collect specimens such as leaves, which were then used for classroom projects. Water and sand play also introduced children informally to other science concepts.

■ **Considers play essential**

Play was an integral part of both the nursery and infant school programs. The Plowden Report (1967) stated "Play is the central activity in all nursery schools and in many infant schools" (p. 193). A fixture in nursery and reception classrooms was the Wendy House (i.e., the housekeeping corner). The large blocks of time, open-ended materials, and informal curriculum facilitated play.

Physical Environment

One of the features about the English schools that I most liked was the physical environment. Although the schools I worked in ranged from an older multi-storey brick building built after the First World War, to a nursery school built as a 24-hour-care facility for mothers working in the war plants during the Second World War, to buildings built in the 1960s, I found the environments to be child-centred and child-friendly. There was lots of evidence of the children's work and interests. Children's artwork figured prominently in most schools—from paintings on the walls to sculptures in the corridors to flower arrangements in the entry area. The classroom space extended into the corridors and other areas of the school. It was not unusual to find small groups of children working on a project out in the hall or in the entry area to the school. Many schools had small mini-libraries set up in corridors.

■ **Considers social and affective development important**

■ **Integrates the indoor and outdoor environments**

There was easy access to the outdoors. The boundary between indoor and outdoor space was permeable. Some classrooms had French doors that opened out to a covered area used for water and sand play and woodworking as well as for outdoor play on rainy days. It also served as an extension to the main room and often added much-needed space. All the schools had plants outside the buildings (in pots if not in the ground) and in the corridors and classrooms. In addition, some had gardens where the children could plant things. The nursery schools were typically surrounded by grassy areas with larger play equipment such as swings and climbing frames.

The classrooms were organized around interest or learning centres. In addition to the Wendy House and the sand and water tables, there were arts and crafts, woodworking, block/construction, puzzles/games, small manipulatives, a nature table, and book and music centres. Most of the nursery classrooms had a piano.

Assessment

Observation and anecdotal notes were the major types of child assessment. Individual educators kept their own notes and, usually, samples of the children's work. The infant schools I worked in had a summary page for each child that became part of the school record. Information was shared with parents on an ongoing basis through informal chats when the children arrived or departed. As well, there were periodic formal parent conferences.

■ Uses observation by the classroom educator

The evaluation of the educators and programs was done on an ongoing basis by the heads. Some visited my classroom frequently; others very infrequently. One head required that an outline of lessons for the next week be placed on his desk every Friday noon. The government had inspectors, called Her Majesty's Inspectors, who made infrequent visits to all the government schools and then wrote reports to the local educational authority. I encountered only one HMI during my time there.

Critique

Although I thoroughly enjoyed my time in the British infant and nursery schools, it was not utopia. The strengths of this model as perceived by some, such as its flexibility, adaptability, child-centredness, and open-endedness, are perceived by others as its weaknesses. One difficulty for individuals working in an informal model is knowing what to do, because the curriculum and program are more than usually dependent on the knowledge and experience of the staff. Well-trained, knowledgeable educators who work together well are essential for the success of this type of program. To have a smooth, continual, flowing program requires good communication and attention to detail; of course, this is not always the case. As with the other models profiled in this chapter, the philosophy and organization of this one would not appeal to every educator. For the model to work to its best, individuals need to understand fully its philosophy and underlying principles.

A question often asked is why the British infant school model did not have more impact on education in Canada. I think one reason is that Canadian preschool programs were already basically developmental-maturationist. On the other hand, elementary schools were bound by specific provincial/territorial curriculum guides and regulations that were more academic. These included the use of required or approved materials and set topics for individual grade levels, which made for less autonomy for the educator and the individual school. The English schools I worked in were all part of the public/government education system and there was continuity and communication between the nursery schools and the infant schools, especially in nursery schools housed in the primary school or on the same grounds. This has not usually been the case in Canada.

Update on the British Schools

Over the past decade, the British system has changed dramatically. The 1988 Education Reform Act established a national curriculum for the first time. It was introduced in September 1989, revised in 1995, and scheduled for further revision in 2000. The national curriculum contains three main elements: attainment targets, programs of study, and assessment requirements (e.g., seven-year-olds will be assessed on the core subjects of English, mathematics, and science). According to one leading English early childhood expert, "there is a very real danger that the introduction of the National Curriculum . . . may mean a degree of formality will creep into our infant schools" (Curtis, 1994, p. 5). Many schools are still using themes, integrated curriculum, and integrated days, and "much of the philosophy which permeated the Plowden Report still prevails and the teachers of early childhood education are in the main convinced of the need to have the child as a central focus in the learning process" (Curtis, 1994, p. 13).

In recent years, more children have been able to attend government-funded preschools. The majority of three- and four-year-olds now have preschool experience (Curtis, 1994). The recent trend is more nursery classes in primary schools rather than as freestanding schools. The provision of services for under-fives has become more coordinated with the use of Early Years Development Plans, which are drawn up by local authorities such as education, social services, and health. These are community plans; there is no national approach. The National Childcare Strategy was introduced in 1998, and the government plans to increase free early education for three-year-olds to 66 percent of that group by 2002 (Department for Education and Employment, 1999).

The nursery-school curriculum is still typically play-based. There is a range of early childhood programs available, including High/Scope preschools and Montessori programs in the private sector.

With the national curriculum, a national system of performance-based assessment of children and specific program evaluation was introduced. Program evaluation of English nursery and primary schools was required in the Education Act of 1992 and is outlined in *Guidance on the Inspection of Nursery and Primary Schools* (Office for Standards in Education, 1995). This guide includes sections on inspection requirements, guidance on conducting the inspection, and an inspection schedule. The inspectors' report for under-five programs must include evaluation of "the strengths and weaknesses in attainment, pupils' attitudes, teaching and other provision across the areas of learning" and for ages five and over "pupils' attainment in relation to national expectations or standards" (p. 120).

FOR REFLECTION

The need for a national system of early childhood programs is mentioned frequently by professional organizations and the media. A national system might also mean a national curriculum. What are the advantages and disadvantages to a national early childhood curriculum in Canada?

What Research Says about Early Childhood Curriculum Models

The big question when comparing early childhood programs is always "But which one is best?" This is a very simple question to ask and probably an impossible one to answer conclusively. There has been a lot of research done on this

Playing with blocks can foster young children's cognitive, social, and language development.

question in the past 30 years and there is no 100-percent-definitive, for-all-time answer. The short answer is that the research results over time have been mixed. A more precise question is probably, "Best for whom and in what circumstances?" This section reviews the research on early childhood models that have been part of the Head Start/Follow Through programs. These programs required systematic evaluation and research and have provided a wealth of information. While there were hundreds of studies on the short-term effects of programs (Barnett, 1995), it was also desirable to have good longitudinal studies because not all effects of programs on children and families are immediate. Some effects take years to be seen and others, such as rates of graduation from high school, occur years after the child's participation in an early childhood program. It is therefore important, although difficult and expensive, to follow children for many years.

In reading about the following research studies and their results, it is essential to keep a few caveats in mind. The model programs were set up especially to operationalize certain theories as part of comprehensive research programs. Because these programs were part of experimental programs, they were typically well-funded, well-equipped, and had well-educated staff with excellent child–staff ratios. The children and families in these programs were predominantly from poor areas. In addition, it is not appropriate to generalize these findings to *all* early childhood programs.

Early Head Start Research

The early research on Head Start programs focused on the differences between children enrolled in Head Start programs compared to groups of poor children not attending early childhood programs. These studies tended to focus on IQ scores, in part because of the concern at that time for cognitive development and the relative ease (if not always accuracy) of measuring a child's IQ. The early studies showed that the children attending Head Start did show gains in IQ scores (Datta, 1979). However, later research showed that these cognitive gains did not last through the primary grades (Cicarelli, 1969). This, then, led to the popular perception that Head Start really had no lasting effects. To the contrary, other research showed that the Head Start children did have better social and school adjustment than children without Head Start (e.g., Ryan, 1974). These latter findings, although often receiving less attention than the cognitive results, were more in keeping with the original goals of Head Start (Zigler, Styfco, & Gilman, 1993).

Similar research was done on the British preschools. A study by Osborn and Milbank (1987) looked at long-term educational benefits for children who attended preschool programs. The children who had attended government-funded nursery schools or playgroups had higher mathematics, reading, and language test scores five and ten years after preschool than the children who had no preschool. The researchers reported that "we found that children from all types of social background benefited from attending a preschool facility. However, socially disadvantaged children were found to gain slightly more from their preschool experience than were socially advantaged children" (p. 226).

Comparative Models Research

Because Head Start and Follow Through had Planned Variation programs, in which several models based on specific philosophies and theoretical approaches were developed, there was great interest to see if these programs produced different effects. The Head Start Planned Variation included the Engelmann-Becker model and the High/Scope Cognitively Oriented Curriculum among its 12 models. The Follow Through Planned Variation included Direct Instruction and High/Scope Cognitively Oriented Curriculum among its 13 models. None of the Head Start variation programs was more effective than the regular Head Start program, but they all were more effective than no preschool (Rivlin & Timpane, 1975). The research results for Follow Through's Planned Variation showed that, not surprisingly, the programs with an academic emphasis produced the greatest academic gains as assessed by standardized measures (Kennedy, 1978; Smith, 1975). Children who were younger and more immature did better in the more structured programs, while more competent, mature children did better in the less structured programs. Researchers also found considerable variation between one site of a model and another of the same model (Abt Associates, 1977). However, comparative studies showed that Head Start made a difference, and while no one model was more successful than another, there were differences (Spodek & Brown, 1993).

Longitudinal Research

The early studies showing that cognitive effects seemed to wash out after a few years led to some interesting longitudinal research that has been very informative for early childhood education. One longitudinal study, the Head Start Synthesis Study, looked at more than 200 studies of Head Start programs and concluded that, although children's initial cognitive gains did not last, Head Start children showed improved health, socio-emotional development, nutrition, and immunization rates (Zigler, Styfco, & Gilman, 1993).

An influential longitudinal study by the Consortium for Longitudinal Studies (1978; 1983; Lazar & Darington, 1982) was responsible for much of what we know about the long-term effectiveness of early childhood curriculum models. The consortium was a group of researchers who had looked at effects across different program models (such as Direct Instruction and High/Scope). In 1975, they agreed to try and locate the original participants, gather more information from them, and then "pool" their longitudinal data and see what resulted.

Some of the results reconfirmed the earlier findings that the actual gains in IQ, reading, and mathematics did fade out over the years. However, what was heartening and most significant were the effects that lasted. These lasting effects included that these children, compared to children without these programs, were less likely to have been in special education classes and less likely to have repeated a grade in elementary school; had higher reading and mathematics achievement through most of elementary school; were more likely to have graduated from high school; and had parents who had higher occupational aspirations for them (Consortium, 1983). One of the most quoted conclusions was that "any well-designed, professionally supervised program to stimulate and socialize infants and young children from poor minority families will be efficacious" (p. 462). Although there was no *one* program that was significantly more effective than the others, this did not mean that there were not differences across programs. Subsequent research examined these differences, including longitudinal effects.

The High/Scope Educational Foundation has been doing longitudinal studies of the children in its programs for more than 30 years. In a longitudinal study of the children from the early Perry Preschool Project, it was reported that at age 27 these individuals were significantly more likely to earn more money, own a home and second car, have completed more education, have fewer arrests, and need fewer social services than individuals without a preschool program (Schweinhart, Barnes, & Weikart, 1993). Their analyses showed that females attending the Perry Preschool increased their likelihood of completing high school; this was not the case for males, although it did lessen their commission of delinquent or criminal acts.

The High/Scope Educational Research Foundation has also compared children across different programs. It traced the participants in three types of programs (Direct Instruction, traditional nursery school, and their program) through age 23. Although all three programs resulted in greater academic achievement and school success compared to a control group that had no early childhood program, there were different effects across programs (Schweinhart, Weikart, & Larner, 1986).

The research (Schwienhart & Weikart, 1997) has shown that by age 23, the children in the High/Scope and Nursery School programs were less likely to

FOR REFLECTION

Why would one not be surprised that children from an academic preschool program do well on standardized achievement tests? And children from a Piagetian-based program score well on problem-solving tests? Do these results really tell us anything significant about these programs, or early childhood programs in general?

have required treatment for emotional problems, and more likely to have done volunteer work. Nearly twice as many High/Scope children were planning to graduate from college and three times as many had married than in the other groups. The DISTAR group had a higher rate of juvenile delinquency than the other two programs. This finding and the study's methodology have been criticized by the Direct Instruction developers (Bereiter, 1986; Englemann, 1999). However, Schweinhart and Weikart (1997) concluded, "well-documented, research-proven curriculum models based on child-initiated learning appear to have the best potential for supporting successful child development" (p. 60).

The body of research on the effects of different types of early childhood curriculum models and the programs representing them has increased our understanding of early childhood program design and planning. However, the research has also left many key questions unanswered and raised additional questions. There is still much to investigate. Perhaps the biggest question is, How do we decide what type of program would be most beneficial for individual children? From what we know of child development, theory, practice, and research on program effectiveness, we are aware that different children have different needs and ways of learning. We also know that different curriculum models can affect children differently. The question remains: Which program is best for which child?

Reggio Emilia Approach

The early childhood programs of Reggio Emilia have been called "the best preschools in the world" by the popular press (e.g., *Newsweek*, December, 1991) and academics (e.g., Gardner, 1999, pp. 86–87). What is so interesting about these programs developed in a city in northeastern Italy?

A good, short summary of the Reggio Emilia schools is:

> a collection of schools for young children in which each child's intellectual, emotional, social, and moral potentials are carefully cultivated and guided. The principal educational vehicle involves youngsters in long-term engrossing projects, which are carried out in a beautiful, healthy, love-filled setting. (Gardner, 1998, p. xvi)

A more succinct description of the Reggio Emilia approach is, "a community of inquiry" (Kennedy, 1996, p. 26).

Background

Parent cooperatives in Canada are described in Chapter 9.

The approach to early childhood education and care developed in Reggio Emilia has been the work of a small group of dedicated professionals for the past 50 years. The originator of the Reggio Emilia approach, Loris Malaguzzi, dates the beginning of the enterprise from six days after the end of the Second World War, when some local women decided to build, from the rubble of the war, a school for young children. Thus, the roots of the Reggio Emilia preschool are in the parent cooperative movement.

In the 1950s and 1960s the Italian teachers' movement was active in the reform of education. This, coupled with the increasing number of women in the labour force and the Italian women's movement, led to an increased focus on early childhood education and care. In Italy the municipality is the primary educational authority and, until recently, left-wing political parties supportive of early education have controlled many of the municipalities in northern Italy. The Italian government passed legislation in 1968 establishing a state system of free pre-primary education (*Scuole dell'Infanzia*) for children from three to six. As a result, almost all children three to six years of age now attend early childhood programs (Edwards, Gandini, & Forman, 1998).

Interest in the Reggio Emilia approach outside of Italy grew in the early 1980s, in part from the travelling exhibition "The Hundred Languages of Children." This exhibit, which has visited Canada, documents the Reggio Emilia approach and has inspired many early educators to learn more about it. Many early childhood educators in Canada have implemented the Reggio Emilia approach and described their efforts in journal articles and books (see the Resources section at the end of this chapter). One example is the child-care centre at Loyalist College in Ontario.

Key Principles and Characteristics

The philosophy of the Reggio Emilia approach has been built on the works of Piaget, Vygotsky, Dewey, Erikson, Bronfenbrenner, and other modern theorists. John Dewey's statement that "all thinking is research" (1966, p. 148) could have been said about the Reggio Emilia approach. Some of the key characteristics of the Reggio Emilia approach are:

- Both the physical and social environments are cooperative and pleasant (the amiable environment)

- The child is perceived as an active, capable problem-solver and communicator

- Learning is collaborative

- Small-group-work is fostered

- Children's creativity and creative productions are encouraged

- The children have great input into the program and the curriculum is based on the children's interests

- Projects can last from a few days to several months

- There is an emphasis on observation and recording as a way of learning for both the children and the educators

- There are many ways to document what one has learned

- The relationship of home, school, and community, as well as that of the children, educators, and parents, is interactive and interconnected.

Educator's Role

Perhaps more than most early childhood programs, the educator is the linchpin of the Reggio Emilia approach. The role of the educator has been described as that of partner, nurturer, and guide (Edwards, 1998). In addition to the typical roles of the educator in most early childhood programs, two other essential roles are: (a) participating in political activism in the cause of public early education, and (b) doing research on daily classroom work for curriculum planning and professional development (Edwards, 1998). According to one of the leading exponents of this approach, the teacher's role is "one of continual research and learning process, taking place with the children and embedded in team cooperation" (Gandini, 1997, p. 19).

The educator's role is that of a *provocateur* and a collaborator. Being a provocateur is central to the educator's role. By this is meant, "provoking occasions of discovery through a kind of alert, inspired facilitation and stimulation of children's dialogue, co-action, and co-construction of knowledge" (Edwards, 1993, p. 154). The educators collaborate with the children, other staff, parents, and community to determine the children's interests, knowledge, and what can be investigated. This collaboration results in "a fluid, generative, dynamic curriculum" (Hendrick, 1997, p. 47). The educators "ask questions; discover the children's ideas, hypotheses, and theories; and provide occasions for discovery and learning. In fact, educators consider themselves partners in learning and enjoy discovering with the children" (Gandini, 1993, p. 6). An analogy used by one of the educators in Reggio Emilia is that the children throw the educators the ball, and the educators then toss it back to the children in a way that makes them want to continue the game as well as developing other games (Edwards, 1993).

North American observers have repeatedly commented on the family-like and homey atmosphere of the Reggio Emilia programs (e.g., Katz, 1998). This atmosphere may be due, in part, to the children typically remaining with the same educator for all three years in the program.

An innovative staff position in the Reggio Emilia programs is the *atelierista* (which roughly translates as "studio teacher"). This person, who is trained in the visual arts, works with the children and the other educators to visually represent and communicate their ideas through a variety of media. The atelierista consults several times a day with the educators to be sure everyone's efforts are collaborative and mutually supportive.

The third type of staff position is the *pedagogista*. A team of pedagogical coordinators liaises among educators, parents, community, and municipal administrators. Each pedagogista provides support in three or four schools, including professional development and in-service activities. However, their role is broader and more profound than that. The pedagogista is "the match that keeps the fire of the Reggio approach lit" (Phillips & Bredekamp, 1998, p. 445).

Curriculum and Program Organization

The curriculum in the Reggio Emilia approach is not fixed or determined in advance. The curriculum emerges from the interactions and collaboration of the children and the educators and the creation of projects. Projects are in-depth investigations that may be short-term or that may go on for several months or evolve into still other projects. For example, the children were interested in the birds in the schoolyard, and a project on fountains grew from the children's desire to build an amusement park for birds. Children typically work in small groups of four to six on different aspects of a project.

Another key feature of the Reggio Emilia approach is documentation. Documentation refers to the many different ways in which children can express their thoughts (i.e., the 100 languages of children) including photographs of the children's activities, transcriptions of children's discussions, educators' notes, models produced by the children, drawings, stories, and slides. The atelierista is actively involved in the documentation process. The purposes of documentation are to communicate to the parents and community what children are doing, to provide information about the children for the educators, for staff self-evaluation, to facilitate the exchange of ideas among the educators, to demonstrate to the children that their efforts are valued, and to create an archive of the school's history and a visible record of the children's and educators' joy and fun in learning (Gandini, 1993).

The 13 infant-toddler centres usually have 69 children from 4–36 months of age, divided into four groups by age. There are 11 educators, a cook, and six auxiliary staff (Gandini, 1997). The program operates from 8 a.m. to 4 p.m., although if needed those hours can be extended to 7:30 a.m. and 6:20 p.m. Each of the 19 preschools has 75 children from three to six years, usually with the children divided by age into three classrooms. For each group there are two educators, plus an atelierista, a cook, and five auxiliary staff for each school. The hours are the same as for the infant-toddler centre.

Physical Environment

The physical environment is very important in the Reggio Emilia approach. It has been termed a "third teacher" (Cadwell, 1997, p. 5). The emphasis is on an attractive, beautiful, and stimulating preschool for all. According to Katz (1998), the preschools are more like large homes than schools and are comfortable, pleasant, attractive, nicely furnished with well-organized space and displays of the children's work. The design of the schools also includes the *piazza*, which is a key feature of Italian communities.

A key, innovative feature of the Reggio Emilia preschool's environment is the *atelier* (studio). This is where many of the children come to experiment and develop concrete representations of their ideas. There is a wide variety of materials available. There is a wealth of art, craft, modelling, collage, and constructing materials, as might be expected in a program where children are encouraged to use a variety of media to represent their ideas. Most of the materials are easily accessible and located in the atelier or in a mini–atelier adjacent to each classroom. However, the atelier is more than a well-stocked workshop. Malaguzzi conceived of the atelier as a place of provocation that would stimulate and encourage. He saw it as "most of all a place of research" (1998, p. 74).

Assessment

Assessment of the children's work and ideas is ongoing in the Reggio Emilia approach. Likewise, so is the educators' evaluation of the program and themselves ongoing. In terms of program evaluation, the Reggio Emilia approach "has never been evaluated against its ability to deliver outcomes or meet predetermined criteria" (Dahlberg, Moss, & Pence, 1999). However, formal comparative research on the effectiveness of this approach compared to others would probably not be seen as appropriate, or of much interest, to the Reggio Emilia personnel. It would also be very difficult to do a longitudinal evaluation of this approach, despite its longevity, because it is continually evolving as part of its philosophy.

Critique

Howard Gardner (1998) warns that it is a mistake to romanticize the Reggio Emilia approach even though it seems to work so well. Many of the fundamental principles of Reggio Emilia appeal to many early childhood educators: studying children and attention to the role of child development; the importance of teacher–child relationships; building curricula on the children's experiences and interests; the use of a stimulating and attractive physical environment; inclusion of parents; and continual teacher development (Phillips & Bredekamp, 1998).

Not everyone is uncritical of the Reggio Emilia approach. Phillips and Bredekamp (1998) reported quite different opinions on Reggio Emilia: some think it is an excellent developmentally appropriate early childhood program, while others see it as too teacher-directed and not developmentally appropriate practice.

Another issue raised by programs such as Reggio Emilia is the transferability of programs (discussed in Chapter 13). The Reggio Emilia philosophy envisages an early childhood program developed within a community, its history, culture, social and political institutions, and traditions. Therefore, Reggio Emilia preschools exist in Reggio Emilia. However, the Reggio Emilia approach itself is seen as flexible and open-ended enough that the basic ideas have been adapted in other locations and situations. There have been various Reggio Emilia schools or classes established in Europe (e.g., see Dahlberg, Moss, & Pence, 1999), the United States (e.g., see Cadwell, 1997), and Canada (e.g., see Wien, 1997; Fraser, 2000).

FOR REFLECTION

If you had your choice to work in any of the programs described in this chapter or in Chapter 5, which one would you choose? How does that program compare to the others? Which one would you least want to work in and why?

Issues in Program Development and Planning

As an early childhood educator, you will be planning and implementing programs for young children. There are many decisions that must be made. Some of these are related to curriculum and program organization, including how you'll describe your program's theoretical orientation. A common descriptive phrase I'm sure you've heard others use is "Our program is child-centred."

What Is Child-Centred?

The phrase *child-centred* sounds good, but what does it actually *mean*? "Child-centred" is used in many places and contexts. It is applied (correctly or incorrectly) to programs, types of materials, philosophies, and theories. For example, I recently saw an advertisement that promised if one read the books advertised one could have a child-centred program. Obviously, *child-centred* is used in many different—and sometimes contradictory and confusing—ways.

Child-centred is not a new concept that originated in the discussion of developmentally appropriate practice. Its roots can be traced back to Rousseau, Pestalozzi, Froebel, and Dewey. I recently found a book from 1928 titled *The Child-Centered School: An Appraisal of the New Education* (Rugg & Shumaker, 1928), in which child-centred was both a goal and a method. Child-centredness has also been seen "primarily as a philosophy or point of view" (Regan, 1990 p. 172).

Developing a child-centred program is more than having child-sized furniture. Some common characteristics of child-centred programs are that:

- Each child is seen as an individual with unique developmental patterns
- Individual differences are recognized and accommodated
- Learning is child-initiated and hands-on
- The focus is on the whole child
- Curriculum is determined by the children's interests and needs
- Children make choices about their learning
- Play is encouraged to foster children's development (Darling, 1994; Moyer, Egertson, & Isenberg, 1987; Regan & Weininger, 1988).

A truly child-centred program may seem deceptively simple, but it is not. A program based on individual differences, needs, and choices can be very complex to plan and operate. Because these programs are often so highly individual, cross-program comparisons are not easily or validly done. In a time of increasing accountability, the lack of comparison can be a problem for programs.

Adding to the confusion is use of *child-centred* to imply that if a program is not child-centred, it is therefore anti-child. Of course this is not accurate. As the continuum and questionnaire earlier in this chapter showed, there is a range. The extreme end of child-centred is rarely seen, and is most typically found in a few alternative programs where everything is the choice of the child, including coming to school at all. Most child-centred programs are more moderate.

A major difficulty with *child-centred* is the use of the term by people with very different philosophies and programs. While this use is confusing for educators and students, it is more so for parents trying to select programs for their children.

FOR REFLECTION

Are the Reggio Emilia approach and the Montessori Method child-centred? Why or why not?

What Are Projects, Themes, and Units?

In this chapter, we have seen the use of projects in the British infant school and Reggio Emilia programs. Another set of terms that causes confusion in the field of early childhood education is *projects, themes, and units*. These terms are often used interchangeably. What are these? Where did they come from? Are they different?

Using projects is not a new idea; they have been around since the turn of the century or even earlier. John Dewey was a strong advocate of the use of projects at a time when education was very formal and subject-based. However, Dewey saw education as "a continuing reconstruction of experience" (1959, p. 27), and recommended that children be actively involved in their learning. In his experience-based curriculum, the curriculum could not be planned until the children's needs were known. He criticized Froebel's Gifts as contrived and artificial, not the real experiences children needed. Dewey's view was shared by Patty Smith Hill and Lucy Sprague Mitchell (see Chapter 5).

William Kilpatrick (1918) applied Dewey's ideas to his Project Method, which had children plan, do, and evaluate their own activities. His work influenced generations of educators (Diffily, 1996). Anna Freud used the Project Method in her school in Vienna in the 1920s. Susan Isaacs' (1929/1968) work in England in the 1920s influenced the later British infant school movement in the 1960s and 1970s. In the 1930s, Lucy Sprague Mitchell used the Project Method at Bank Street College of Education in New York City, where the approach has been taught ever since.

A **project** can be defined as "an extended study of a topic usually undertaken by a group of children, sometimes by the whole class, and occasionally by an individual child" (Katz & Chard, 1993, p. 209). An example of a project is, How Are Playgrounds Built? A project is

- An in-depth study

- Based on children's interests

- Linked with children's prior experience

- Meaningful to children's lives

- Selected collaboratively by teachers and children

- Inclusive of the child in exploration, discovery, and active involvement in all stages from selection and planning to evaluation

- Participated in and contributed to by all children

- Encouraging of cooperation and cooperative learning

- Conceptually based

- Able to integrate traditional subject areas

- Of no predetermined length

- Able to be revisited

- Able to evolve into other projects

- Process, not product, emphasized.

Another common organizational structure used in early childhood programs is a theme. A theme is not the same thing as a project. A **theme** is a broader term and "typically does not indicate the direction the work will take" (Katz & Chard, 1993, p. 210). An example of a theme might be Our Neighbourhood. A project explores a theme (e.g., the playground project would be appropriate for the theme of Our Neighbourhood).

A **unit** is typically "a sequence of prespecified lessons on particular topics. . . children rarely influence the topics or subtopics explored, or determine the questions to be answered or the activities undertaken" (Katz & Chard, 1993, p. 210). An example of a unit might be three days spent studying Thanksgiving. It is not unusual for an early childhood program to use themes, projects, and units; there is an appropriate place in the curriculum for each of them.

However, projects, themes, and units have been criticized as actually being teacher-selected and teacher-directed under the guise of child choice. Chambers, Howe, and Petrakas (1997) have cautioned that "thematic units can become teacher-directed curriculum" (p. 253). There is an additional concern if educators select the same topics every year because "everything is ready to use." Other critics have noted that effective use of themes, projects, and units requires educators to be resourceful, well-organized, flexible, and knowledgeable about curriculum design.

FOR REFLECTION

What are some projects and themes you have observed in early childhood programs? Which ones did you think were most effective? How did they compare to the characteristics listed above?

Cost–Benefits of Early Childhood Programs

Another issue facing early childhood programs in times of economic restraint is the cost of programs. Good quality programs for young children are not inexpensive. Politicians and policy-makers are very concerned about cost–benefit (i.e., Is the expenditure of public funds worth the benefits returned?). Thus, the cost–benefit research from the High/Scope Educational Foundation has received a lot of attention from the media and politicians.

Read the following statement by Schweinhart and Weikart (1998) and decide what it says about the cost–benefit of high quality early childhood programs. Some of the findings of the longitudinal High/Scope Perry Preschool Study are "that a high quality preschool cuts participants' lifetime arrest rate in half, significantly improves their educational and subsequent economic success, and provides taxpayers a return equal to 716 percent of their original investment in the program" (p. 57).

What does the above statement *really* say about the cost–benefits of early childhood programs? Does this mean that *any* early childhood program is cost-beneficial? No. What this statement is saying is that "a high quality preschool," meaning the Perry Preschool program, has been shown to be cost-beneficial.

FOR REFLECTION

There has been a lot of media coverage about the importance of the first three years of a child's life. What would your response be if your provincial/territorial government decided that all new funds and resources for early childhood programs would be allocated to infant programs because that would provide the greatest financial return in the long term?

The popular press and some professional publications have misinterpreted and overgeneralized this and similar statements to mean that funding of early childhood programs will save significant amounts of money on services not needed and will guarantee future financial returns. While the potential for cost–benefits for large-scale implementation of early childhood programs has been identified in theory (e.g., Cleveland & Krashinsky, 1998), and we have evidence that individual, relatively small-scale, programs have produced significant savings (e.g., Schweinhart & Weikart, 1998), it is not appropriate to generalize these results to *all* early childhood programs. According to Karoly et al. (1998),

> We know that some targeted early intervention programs have substantial favorable effects on child health and development, educational achievement, and economic well-being. We also know that some of these programs, if targeted to families who will benefit most, have generated savings to the government that exceed the costs of the programs. There is still much that we do not know about these programs, however, and this limits the degree to which these conclusions can be generalized. (p. xx)

Summary of this Chapter

The key themes in this chapter are the:

- Fact that what one believes about how young children develop and learn influences one's program planning, teaching strategies, program organization and structure, selection of materials, management, and so on.

- Fact that child development theories have been a foundation of early childhood programs for the past century. However, their use has been criticized.

- Influence of the following child-development theories on early childhood programs: maturationist, psychodynamic, cognitive-interactionist, and behaviourist theories.

- Curriculum models based on specific child development theories that have been implemented and evaluated extensively as part of Head Start and Follow Through programs.

- Variations across early childhood programs with the same theoretical orientation.

- Longitudinal research that has identified positive long-term effects for high quality early childhood programs. Care is needed to not overgeneralize these findings.

- Fact that although there are many well designed and implemented early childhood programs, no one program or type of program has been conclusively identified as the most effective.

Key Terms

ages and stages model, 217

behaviourism, 219

child-centred, 249

cognitive-interactionist, 220

curriculum model, 226

emotional intelligence, 224

integrated curriculum, 236

integrated day, 236

maturationist or normative theory, 217

project, 250

psychoanalytic theory, 218

psychodynamic theories, 217

psychosocial theory, 218

theme, 251

theory of multiple intelligences, 223

unit, 251

zone of proximal development, 222

Resources

For Further Reading

If you want to know more about models of early childhood programs, try Epstein, A.S., L.J.Schweinhart, & L. McAdoo. 1996. *Models of early childhood education.* Ypsilanti, MI: High/Scope Press. This book discusses the importance of curriculum models and compares six popular curriculum models including Montessori, Direct Instruction, and High/Scope.

For information about High/Scope programs, the most comprehensive source is the manual written for the High/Scope programs: M. Hohmann & D.P. Weikart. 1995. *Educating young children: Active learning practices for preschool and child care programs.* Ypsilanti, MI: High/Scope Press. The Web site for High/Scope and other resources is www.highscope.org.

For more information on the Reggio Emilia approach, try Carolyn Edwards, Lella Gandini & George Forman (Eds). 1998. *The hundred languages of children: The Reggio Emilia approach—Advanced reflections* (2nd ed). Greenwich, CT: Ablex Publishing. This is the authoritative account and description by the people who have developed this approach.

Two books that describe the application of the Reggio Emilia approach to programs in North America are Cadwell, L.B. 1997. *Bringing Reggio Emilia home: An innovative approach to early childhood education.* New York: Teachers College Press; and Hendrick, J. (Ed.). 1997. *First steps toward teaching the Reggio way.* Upper Saddle River, NJ: Merrill.

For shorter descriptions of Canadian experiences with Reggio Emilia, see recent issues of *Canadian Children* (e.g., Spring 1998 and Spring 1999). See also Fraser, S. 2000. *Authentic childhood: Experiencing Reggio Emilia in the classroom.* Toronto: ITP Nelson.

A Web site with information about Reggio Emilia is http://ericps.crc.uiuc.edu/eece.

Two sources for descriptions of Projects and Themes are Katz, L. G. & Chard, S.C. 2000. *Engaging children's minds: The project approach* (2nd ed.). Stamford, CT Ablex Publishing; this is a comprehensive book outlining the project approach, its principles and practices, and stages in planning and implementing projects. See also Sylvia Chard's Web site at www. ualberta.ca/~schard/projects.

Gamberg, R., W. Kwak, M. Hutchings, & J. Altheim. 1988. *Learning it and loving it: Theme studies in the classroom.* Portsmouth, NH: Heinemann and Toronto: OISE Press. Describes project use at Dalhousie University Elementary School.

7

Play: A Perennial Issue

It is important for children to play. Children have a natural mechanism that enables them to make sense of their world—that mechanism is play.
—*Canadian Association for Young Children Position Statement on Play*

Play is among the most frequent activities of children in early childhood programs and one of the most debated. Some people think early childhood curriculum should be based on play, while others do not. Play is seen as both a means to an end and an end in itself. Play is found across ages, programs, cultures, and time. It is valued throughout the world (Woodill, Bernhard, & Prochner, 1992). The right to play is part of the Convention of the Rights of the Child (see Chapter 2). In addition, the International Association for the Child's Right to Play states that:

· Play is essential for the physical and mental health of the child.
· Play is part of education.
· Play is an essential part of family and community life.
· Children need opportunities to play at leisure.

(1989, on-line, www.ncsu.edu/ipa)

Children have been playing for thousands of years. Drawings and murals in ancient Egypt, Greece, and Rome show children playing, and archeologists have found children's toys (Cohen, 1987). Play has been part of early childhood education since its beginning (Almy, 1967). The key people in the history of early childhood education and care (see Chapter 5) all had views on the role, or non-role, of play in early childhood programs. The theories described in Chapter 6 have applications for how play is perceived and applied in early childhood programs today. If play has such a long history, is well-accepted in theory and practice, and is seen as valuable by professional organizations, why do most books on *issues* in early childhood education and care have chapters on play (e.g., Isenberg & Jalongo, 1997; Seefeldt, 1990; Spodek & Saracho, 1991)? In other words, why is there controversy about play in early childhood education and care? And why is it still perceived to be an "issue"? This chapter examines play in a variety of contexts including cultural, historical, theoretical, social, and physical.

Here are some questions to think about while you read this chapter:
- How do *you* define play? Why is this a difficult task?
- How do children perceive play?
- What are the characteristics of play?
- Why is play important in young children's development and in early childhood programs?
- What do theories and research say about play?
- Why is the role of play controversial?
- What are some types of play?
- How can play be fostered in an early childhood program?
- What are the characteristics of appropriate and effective environments for play?

An understanding of play and its role in the early childhood program is an essential part of understanding the goals, curricula, and activities of the different types of early childhood programs in Canada that will be discussed in the next few chapters. All early childhood educators at one time or another have to address the role and purpose of play.

Play: Defining the Undefinable

Although *play* is a small word, it has proved to be an enormously difficult one to define. Take a minute and jot down your definition of *play*. If this task is too broad, focus on defining *children's play*.

Finished? Defining play is not an easy task, is it? Perhaps part of the problem is that for a small word, it represents a very large, complex concept. *The Oxford English Dictionary* takes nine pages to define the various aspects of play—and it doesn't even discuss the implications for early childhood education and care! However, the difficulty of this task has not stopped people from trying to define it. As Shipley (1993) remarked, "there are almost as many definitions of play as there are experts on play" (p. 17). Trying to define play has occupied many hours for philosophers, psychologists, early childhood educators, biologists, anthropologists, sociologists, psychotherapists, and recreation theorists. One reason for the interest in this task by such diverse groups is that play has relevance for all of these fields.

Fein (1985) stated, "the continuing difficulty of play is defining it, an elusiveness that has evoked exasperation, disgust, and a carefree shrug from the more courageous" (p. 45). Part of the difficulty may be that each society and time views play differently. One suggestion to resolve this definitional difficulty is to continually make "new definitions that fit current concepts of play behavior" (Ellis, 1973, p. 22). In other words, is children's play today the same as it was 25, 50, or 100 years ago?

Characteristics of Children's Play

Over many years and after much frustration with trying to define play, researchers have concentrated primarily on identifying the characteristics of play; in other words, what play *looks like* rather than what play *is*. From your attempt to define play, you may have discovered that it was easier to articulate what children playing are doing rather than to define the term. As Johnson, Christie, and Yawkey (1999) concluded, "play is easy to recognize but very hard to define" (p. 15). Research studies have shown that even untrained adult observers can identify children's play when given characteristics (Smith & Vollstedt, 1985). Therefore, for many researchers and writers identification of the characteristics of play is a useful and practical way of "defining" play.

Researchers over the years have examined children's play in both experimental and natural settings and reported the following characteristics:

Play is

- Voluntary, chosen by the child
- Meaningful to children
- Active, with children being actively engaged
- Intrinsically motivating
- Pleasurable and enjoyable for the child
- Non-literal (i.e., involves make-believe/pretense)
- Child-directed
- Natural
- Flexible
- Spontaneous
- Free of rules unless these are agreed upon by the participants, and
- Fun.

(Fromberg, 1990; Hughes, 1995; Johnson, Christie, & Yawkey, 1999; Rogers & Sawyers, 1988; Rubin, Fein, & Vandenberg, 1983; Saracho, 1991; Smith, Takhvar, Gore, & Vollstedt, 1985; Wood & Attfield, 1996)

The characteristics of enjoyability, non–literality, and flexibility are the ones that observers can agree upon as useful and identify consistently in children's play (Smith & Vollstedt, 1985).

What Play Is Not

Another way to examine play is to describe what it is *not*. This approach has resulted in many debates. In general, most researchers and theorists do not consider exploratory behaviour (e.g., a baby playing with her toes), daydreaming, or work to be play. This last one is the most contentious.

Play vs. Work

Which of the following examples do you think are play and which are work:

- A four-year-old washing dishes.

- A fourteen-year-old washing dishes.

- An adult running 10 km on a cold, wet morning.

- An athlete getting prize money for winning a marathon.

- A child making a birthday card for his mother.

- A class of children each making a get-well card for a classmate who is in the hospital.

- An artist spending a 16-hour day making a stained-glass window.

- An advertising executive spending a 16-hour day in the office.

Some of the above examples may be easier than others to classify as, "This is play"/"This is work." In many cases, you can probably think of circumstances when the same example could be play or it could be work. We can all think of examples from our school days when what the teacher may have thought of as a play activity was perceived as work by us, and vice versa. For example, preschool children participating in a dramatic play activity in a housekeeping corner, compared to primary school children role playing a story they have just read so their teacher can assess their comprehension, compared to middle school children recreating a Japanese tea ceremony complete with costumes and props as part of a social studies unit. These three activities share many common features. Are they all play? Are only some play? Are they work? Often an activity can have characteristics of both work and play. When I took physics in high school, experiments in the ripple tank always reminded me of water play in kindergarten—but I'm certain my physics teacher didn't see it that way.

Children's Perceptions of Play and Work

It is important to consider play from the children's perspective, as they are the ones doing the playing. Children as young as three can identify if their activities are play or not (Garza, Briley, & Reifel, 1985; Karrby, 1990). Although adults may sometimes have difficulty distinguishing play and work, young children do not seem to have this problem (Cleave & Brown, 1991; King, 1979). When young children were asked to identify various activities as play or work, they did so with a high level of agreement (Wing, 1995). In one study (King, 1979), the teachers termed more activities play than did the children. To young children, the classic early childhood maxim *Play is the work of the child* is not true, because for them play is not work.

Children's views of play are important. They differentiate play from work along several dimensions:

- Play is voluntary; work is obligatory (e.g., Fein, 1985; Hurst, 1991; Marshall, 1994; Wing, 1995). Play is "can do"; work is "must do."

- Play has positive affective aspects (e.g., Fein, 1985; King, 1982). Play is fun.

- Play is not evaluated; work is (Marshall, 1994; Wing, 1995). Play you can do your way; work someone else will look at and assess.

- Play is child-controlled; work is teacher-controlled (King, 1979; Romero, 1989; Wing, 1995). In other words, who has the power over the activity? (Seefeldt & Galper, 1998).

- Play is more process-oriented; work is more extrinsically goal-oriented (Fein, 1985). Work has to be finished; play can be left. According to Rogers and Sawyers (1988), "adults tend to view play as a means to an end" (p. 9), whereas children focus on the means. And, perhaps, "play can be an end in itself" (Fromberg, 1990, p. 223).

Different types of materials are used for play and work. For example, children in one study listed activities and materials such as painting, housekeeping area, blocks, sand, construction materials (except math materials), caring for the class pet, games, and recess as play (Wing, 1995). Young children's distinction between work and play activity seems to depend on the context of the activity (King, 1979; 1982).

Children's definitions of play change as they develop (King, 1982). Older children distinguish between play and work more finely than younger children. For example, they can give examples of when an activity would be work but could still be fun, such as estimation (Wing, 1995). To children work is not necessarily equated with drudgery (King, 1979), but as they age work no longer has playful features (King, 1982). In other words, a play activity can become work (Polito, 1994). Therefore, it seems that children have a play–work continuum. In 1914, John Dewey identified a play–work continuum of play → amusement → art → work → labor → drudgery (1933, p. 725). Years later, Bergen (1988) suggested a play continuum of free play → guided play → directed play → work disguised as play → work (p. 171). It has been suggested that play activities not be classified as play/not play but placed on a continuum from pure play to non-play (Pellegrini, 1987). This would seem to make sense to children, who distinguish activities such as recess as "real play" (King, 1982).

One implication of play research is how we talk with children about play activities. Wing (1995) states that "it may be time to honestly acknowledge to

FOR REFLECTION

Is calling free play time "work time" accurate? Is it honest?

children that some activities are work rather than attempting to couch required, directed tasks in the language of play" (p. 244).

Numerous times when as a graduate student I was doing formal assessments of children, the instructions to a test required that one explain to the children that "Now we are going to play a game." I always felt uncomfortable about that because I didn't think it was a game, and I always had the feeling that they didn't think so either.

How often have you heard an educator, "You can play after you've finished your work," or "You've worked so hard this morning, run along and play now"? What kind of a message does that send to children about how we as educators think about play? That this statement is heard so frequently in early childhood programs has led some researchers to speculate that this may reflect the North American work ethic (Saracho, 1991). Perhaps we see work as being more valuable or acceptable than play. Goldhaber (1994) poignantly posed the question in a title of an article: "If we call it science, then can we let the children play?"

Another implication of how we conceptualize play is how it is presented in the early childhood curriculum. What message do we give to children and their parents? How does play get translated into curriculum? Might it be that what we think of as play activities or a play-based curriculum is not seen as that by the children or their parents?

FOR REFLECTION

Goldhaber (1994) states "Teachers, parents and administrators are tired, and understandably so, of such overused and potentially meaningless phrases as . . . 'play is the work of the child (p. 27).'" What phrase would you substitute?

Cultural Context of Play

The dilemma of play vs. work and the perception of play as frivolous or less valuable than work reflects North American society's view of children and childhood. The cultural context influences a society's view of play and affects how play is perceived and valued or not valued. Not all cultures necessarily share the belief of Western early childhood education and care that play is important, although many other cultures do (Woodill, Bernhard, & Prochner, 1992). In Canada, it is not unusual or very noteworthy to see a mother or father playing with their child. However, in some other cultures, this would be considered unusual adult behaviour (Rogoff, 1990). Ideas about play and its role in children's development vary across cultures.

Historical Context of Play

From ancient times, people have wondered why children play. The evolution of play and theories about it parallel the evolution of the concept of childhood described in Chapter 2. In past times, children were seen as an important source of labour for families, while during other times they were perceived of as pets and not expected to work. Thus, what society at these two different times thought of play would have reflected the prevailing view of childhood. Also, different countries had different views due to differences in the political or religious contexts. For example, in the seventeenth and eighteenth centuries,

France viewed children's play more tolerantly than did Puritan England, which perceived play as the devil's work (Hughes, 1995).

Rousseau was the first thinker to argue at length the importance of play (Cohen, 1987). The social planners and reformers of the late nineteenth and early twentieth centuries "discovered children's play" and lobbied for urban, community, and school playgrounds (Finkelstein, 1987, pp. 22–23). For example, noted Canadian social reformer J.J. Kelso lobbied for public playgrounds in Toronto in 1889 (Jones & Rutman, 1981).

Theoretical Dimensions of Play

The theoretical dimension is also important to understanding play. People have been developing theories about play for the past 300 years. Play theories provide insights into the role of play, stages of play, and how play affects children's development.

Theories about play are usually divided into classical theories (i.e., prior to 1900) and modern theories (i.e., twentieth-century theories). The classical theories are important to know about because they are the roots of many contemporary theories, and vestiges of them can still be seen in modern views of play. For example, the idea that children run off excess energy in play is from a classical theory of play. And while these classical theories may seem simplistic, they represent major steps in the evolution of play theory that influence what we do in early childhood programs today.

Classical Theories of Play

Four major classical theories of play are:

- Surplus energy

- Relaxation

- Practice

- Recapitulation.

The **surplus energy theory** had its origins with the ancient Greeks and was later developed by Friedrich Schiller, an eighteenth-century philosopher, historian, and poet. He described play in terms of using "idle energy . . . [and] . . . exuberant power . . . in purposeless display" (Schiller, 1954, p. 133). We still hear people today talking about young children "letting off steam" or "running off energy." This theory sees play as something people and animals do after they've met their basic survival needs. And because young children and young animals are dependent on others, they have more energy to play. The surplus energy theory was used as a rationale for the establishment of playgrounds as a means of preventing juvenile delinquency (Sapora & Mitchell, 1961).

Another classical theory was the **relaxation theory**. This theory was rather the opposite of the surplus energy theory. Whereas this latter theory stated that children played to get rid of excess energy, the relaxation theory as promulgated by the nineteenth-century philosopher Lazarus postulated that people needed to play to recoup their energy after labour. Play was seen as part of a restorative process. This theory can still be seen in the idea that children perform best after lunch/nap or first thing in the morning, and better on Mondays than on Fridays.

A third theory was the **practice** or **pre-exercise theory** developed by Karl Groos at the turn of the twentieth century. He postulated that childhood existed so children could play and thereby practice the skills needed for later life; for example, girls played with dolls as preparation for being mothers. He attributed the length of human childhood to the complexity of human adulthood and argued that therefore children needed more time to play (practice) as compared to other organisms. Groos also identified children's evolving play stages, from experimental play to constructive play to games. Groos was a forerunner of contemporary constructivists who view play as important for the development of children's cognitive functioning (Saracho & Spodek, 1995).

The final classical theory presented is the **recapitulation theory** set forth by G. Stanley Hall, an American psychologist frequently referred to as the father of the Child Study Movement (see Chapter 6). According to this theory, the growth of children follows the evolution of human development. Children were thought to go through stages that paralleled the development of humankind: from animal to savage to nomad (e.g., keeping pets) to agricultural (e.g., playing with dolls and playing in sand) to tribal (e.g., group games). An implication of this theory is that play is a combination of heredity and instinct and therefore play is innate in children—children play because they must.

The classical theories have been criticized for being philosophical theories without experimental documentation that explained only relatively small parts of play behaviour. Their significance for us is that they laid the foundations for and influenced the modern theories of play seen in today's early childhood programs.

Modern Theories of Play

In the early years of the twentieth century, new theories of play were developed. These and later theories are called the *modern* or *contemporary* theories of play and include:

- Psychodynamic theories
- Cognitive theories
- Metacommunicative theory
- Arousal modulation or arousal-seeking theory
- Neuropsychological theory.

Psychodynamic Theories

Sigmund Freud saw play as a primarily cathartic activity during which children acted out fears, fantasies, and phobias. The **psychoanalytic theory**, as set forth by Freud, viewed play as wish fulfillment and a way of coping with traumatic events in order to reduce anxiety. For example, a child can use puppets to play out the addition of a younger sibling to the family or a visit to the hospital emergency room. In play, the child could reverse roles (e.g., become the adult) and control the play situation, unlike in real life. Freud stated that "the opposite of play is not what is serious, but what is real" (1959, p. 144).

Erik Erikson modified and expanded Freud's work. He believed that play not only could reduce anxiety but also could strengthen a child's self-esteem (i.e., the ego). He saw play as related to the child's psychosocial development:

- *First stage*—Centres in body functions (autocosmic)
- *Second stage*—Play with objects (microplay)
- *Third stage*—Sharing with others (macroplay).

Psychoanalytic theorists believe that one can gain insight about children from observing their play. This was not a new idea, as Rousseau had advocated studying children's play in the 1700s.

Psychoanalytic theory was the dominant theory about children's play from the 1930s until the mid-1960s (Johnson, Christie, & Yawkey, 1999). Activities such as water play, playdough, and punching bags were thought to help children manage their emotions and aggression. An outgrowth and clinical application of the psychoanalytic theory of play was play therapy.

Play Therapy

Play therapy had its roots in the work of therapists Anna Freud (daughter of Sigmund) and Melanie Klein in the 1920s and 1930s. It is based on the idea that children *play out* their feelings in a way similar to adults, who *talk out* their problems (Axline, 1969). This contrast is considered appropriate as children, especially young children, cannot verbally articulate their feelings the way adults can. Through play, the child plays out feelings, fears, hurt, anger, and failure and "brings them to the surface, gets them out in the open, faces them, learns to control them, or abandons them" (Axline, 1969, p. 16). Play therapy is used with children facing serious illness, family problems, emotional trauma, abuse, or problems with social relationships.

Toys and materials typically found in early childhood programs, such as puppets and playdough, are used to dramatize experiences in play therapy. Play is thought to be useful therapy as it is an accepted, enjoyable activity for children and they can relate easily to play and common toys. Some recommended play therapy materials include playdough, dolls, doll furniture, trucks, cars, building blocks, pounding bench and hammer, toy guns, sand, water, puppets, art materials (e.g., fingerpaints, crayons, chalk, paints), animal figures, and pictures (Axline, 1969; Landreth, 1982). The criteria for choosing suitable play therapy materials are that they be open-ended, representative of the child's life, and easy to manipulate; that they encourage expression of feelings; and that they can be played with by both the child and the therapist (Axline, 1969; Miller, 1984; Trostle, 1984).

There are degrees of structure in the various approaches to play therapy. Some play therapists are more non-directive (e.g., the child selects from a wide variety of toys) and some are more structured (e.g., the child is presented with a set of human figures representing their family).

Play therapy is done by professional therapists, although many materials and activities found in early childhood programs can be considered therapeutic for children—for example, a child might go to the water tank or the easel whenever she's having a "bad day." Although educators' observations of these types of behaviours can provide valuable information about individual children, formal play therapy should be left to play therapists. Harriet Johnson (1936), a leading early childhood educator at the time play therapy became widely used, cautioned about "avoiding the pitfall of amateurish psychology" (p. 31). Her advice is still appropriate today.

Cognitive Theories of Play

See Chapter 6 for more details on Piaget and Vygotsky.

The two names most frequently associated with **cognitive theories of play** are Jean Piaget and Lev Vygotsky. Piaget saw play as used by children to practise and consolidate skills and information that they are acquiring. It is a way for young children to make sense of their world.

Based on his observations of children, Piaget (1945/1962) identified three major stages of play that he matched to cognitive development:

These stages are discussed more fully later in this chapter.

- *Practice Play*—(i.e., repetition of skills already mastered) in the sensorimotor stage.

- *Symbolic Play*—(i.e., the substituting of one object for another as in pretend play) in the preoperational stage.

- *Games with Rules*—(i.e., either formal or informal play with accepted rules such as chess or a made-up game of chase with impromptu rules) in the concrete operational stage.

The influence of this theory can be seen in the inclusion of dramatic-play centres in early childhood programs and acceptance by educators of the idea that play fosters children's cognitive development. Piaget's ideas about the development of play have been criticized for a lack of recognition of the sociocultural dimensions of play.

Vygotsky, also a cognitive theorist, thought that play was important for children's social and emotional, as well as cognitive, development. He placed more emphasis on the role of play in children's development than did Piaget. Indeed, he stated, play "is not the predominant form of activity, but is, in a certain sense, the leading source of development in the preschool years"

(1933/1967, p. 6). According to Vygotsky, children's play occurs in the zone of proximal development (see Chapter 6) and provides the scaffolding or support necessary for children to reach the next level of their development. Adults, initially parents and later teachers, can help provide this support. For example, research shows mother–child play is more sustained and complex than a child's solitary make-believe play (Berk, 1994). Vygotsky also believed that play promotes language acquisition as well as abstract thought. For example, a row of chairs becomes a train when the children are playing railroad.

Metacommunicative Theory

Another modern theory of play is the **metacommunicative theory**, most typically associated with the anthropologist Gregory Bateson (1955; 1956). He believed, as did Piaget and Vygotsky, that play is important for children's development. He thought children establish a play frame or text in their play that helps the players know what they can do and what they cannot do in a particular play situation. For example, if several children were playing pet store and one child who is supposed to be a dog begins to serve a customer, one of the other players is very likely to quickly comment, "You can't do that, you're the *dog*." According to Bateson, children need to develop the idea of what is play and what is not. For example, they need to understand the difference between a pretend argument during play and a real one. Research on children who have problems with play and social relations with their peers relates to the metacommunicative theory in that a common problem of these children seems to be that they do not know how to enter into a play situation (i.e., the play frame). An implication is the use of play intervention to help children learn the behaviours and language that will facilitate their successful entry into play situations with their peers.

> The use of play intervention to help children learn the behaviours and language to facilitate their successful entry into play situations with their peers is discussed in the Issues section later in this chapter.

Arousal Modulation/Arousal Seeking Theory

Another modern theory is the **arousal modulation** or **arousal-seeking theory**. This theory was developed primarily by Berlyne (1960; 1969) and modified by Ellis (1973). It is based on the relationship of play and stimuli and holds that the central nervous system in the human body requires a certain level of stimulation for optimal functioning. If a person is bored, he or she will seek stimulation, and, conversely, if too aroused will try to reduce the stimulation. Play can have the effect of providing stimulation to relieve boredom; for example, a child using a familiar toy in a new way. According to this theory, an optimal degree of novelty in play is important to retain the child's interest and therefore promote learning.

The Neuropsychological Theory

Still another modern theory of play is the **neuropsychological theory** developed by Canadian psychologists Otto Weininger and Daniel Fitzgerald (1988).

According to this theory, pretend or symbolic play helps the integration of the left and right hemispheres of the brain. This building of connections between the two hemispheres facilitates the transfer of information and therefore the development of thinking. See Focus 7.1 for an example of how Weininger applies play to the process of thinking.

Focus 7.1

Play and Thought—Third R Structures

by Otto Weininger, Ph.D

Even though most children have learned to count by the time of school entry, teachers are concerned about how to give greater meaning to the achievement. During the past 30 years mathematicians and teachers of math have addressed this issue by elaborating upon the "concepts" and by broadening the understanding of the structure of the discipline.

Through play the children become agents of their own learning. Here we see "the mathematician, the scientist, the linguist, the dramatist, the artist, the philosopher, the wonderwoman and the superman" as the children interact with the environment. (1) "The process of play in the child is the process of thinking in the adult." This is the approach of "Structures." (1, 4)

"Structures" is a math program for primary grade children which provides materials towards developing math concepts and math sense at the child's individual pace. In it the teacher monitors the child's activities, probes understanding and extends learning challenges. (2)

The role of the teacher is to:

· supply a range of materials in large quantities;

· organize the materials.

· provide the space to build;

· provide large blocks of time to build

· establish routines: eg: storage of materials, labelling of materials, etc.

· observe the activities, extend and question the building;

· add "props" to the building;

· celebrate the structures and the mathematics involved.

The teacher helps the child describe his/her structures by using math terms, and then extends their math thinking by exploring the math functions contained in their structures. For example: when a five year old realized she has 5 more cubes on one tower than another, she added the number of cubes in both towers. A 6 year old counted the bungs she had laid out in a square and announced she now knew what multiplication was all about and with her teacher learned how to write her understanding using the "times" formula. A 5 year old counted the arms on the spiders he constructed and said "multiplication is just like being able to add fast."

The role of the children is to:

·   choose the materials to use in building structures;

·   work alone;

·   work on raised surfaces and/or on raised, clear plexiglass surfaces;

·   build for extended periods of time;

·   consolidate concepts through communication, discussions and questioning by child and teacher;

·   record their construction;

·   deconstruct in an organized manner and put away materials purposefully.

The child constructs towers, pyramids, buildings on table tops and plexiglass platforms. He/she plans, experiments, revises and formulates strategies to develop the constructions. First, each child constructs alone and takes ownership of his/her learning. Later, bridging to another child's structure is made possible by thinking together about how the bridge will occur. (3,5)

By being helped to link math understanding and math function, children make it "their own"—a permanent, integral part of themselves which enables them to think about, talk about, and enjoy math with an understanding of:

·   numeration, as in numbers, functions, multiples, etc.;

·   measurement, as in size, volume, circumference, units of measurement, etc.;

·   problem solving, as in reasoning, language development, exploration, etc.;

·   geometry, as in shape, spatial relations, proportion, sequencing, etc.;

·   data management, as in collecting data, graphing, display data, etc.

References:

1. Weininger, O. (1987) Taylor, M. & Sister Valerie
    The Child as a Scientist and Mathematician. Elementary Science Network 2 (2)

2. Weininger, O. (1991)
    Third -R Structures: The Math Research Program in Primary Grades. Ontario Institute for Studies in Education, University of Toronto, Toronto, Ontario

3. Weininger O. (1979)
    The Cognitive Unconscious: Figurative and operative process in the learning of disturbed children. *Interchange 10* (4) 1-11

4. Weininger O. (1979)
    Play and Education, the Basic Tool for Young Children's Learning Springfield, III. C.C. Thomas

5. Weininger, O. (1974)
    Mathematics through playing, *Orbit 21*, 5(1), 6–7.

As with the classical theories of play, the modern theories also have critics. Some of the most frequent criticisms of the modern theories of play are that they are (a) hierarchical and patriarchal (Gilligan, 1982), (b) sexist and based on male assumptions (Kelly-Byrne, 1989), and (c) not really useful in practice (Monighan-Nourot, Scales, & Van Hoorn, 1987).

Types of Play

The idea of classifying children's play behaviours into categories is not a new one. The rudiments of classification systems can be seen in some of the classical theories of play, which were then modified by later researchers and theorists such as Piaget.

The three most influential categorizations of play stages have been those of Parten, Piaget, and Smilansky. Their developmental categorizations of play have been useful for analyzing children's play activities. Such analysis can provide valuable insights into young children's cognitive and social development through their play. For example, knowing the antecedents of a play incident and the history of the players leads to a more complete and accurate interpretation of a child's play. This in turn means that one is better able to facilitate children's play by adding more or different materials, modifying the physical setting, or using other strategies.

Parten's Stages of Social Play

Mildred Parten identified six types of children's social play in 1932 that have been used by researchers, theorists, and educators ever since. Her work has had long-lasting and important influence on the study of children's play. Parten's (1932) six stages of play are:

Unoccupied behaviour—The child is not playing; for example, wandering around the room. (Many contemporary researchers do not consider this to be a category of play, but rather a non-activity.)

Onlooker—The child watches the other children playing and may talk to the players but does not join the play. All ages of children exhibit this type of play. It is a common approach of young children to new situations—they observe before they join in.

> *Example: Nicole watches four other children building a skyscraper city with Lego. She decides not to join this group and goes off to see what other children are doing in the science centre.*

Solitary Play—The child plays alone and independently; no interaction. Younger children do more solitary play than older children, although all ages do it. Solitary play is sometimes thought of negatively if it is the predominant form of play by a child. However, it is not necessarily negative or an inferior type of play (Almy, Monighan, & Van Hoorn, 1984).

Example: Matthew has been away from the day-care centre for the past week with the flu. This morning he is in a corner of the block area building a garage by himself. A likely explanation for his behaviour is that he is still feeling some of the after-effects of the flu and doesn't have the energy to interact with other children in cooperative play. As Matthew typically participates in cooperative play, the educator is not concerned and makes a note to observe his play behaviour over the next few days.

Parallel Play—The child plays independently or beside other children but plays with similar materials; there's no interaction or sharing of materials. This type of play behaviour has been called "the most common form of young children's social interactions" (Rubin & Coplan, 1998, p. 146) and is particularly common among older toddlers and three-year-olds.

Example: Tamara goes into the block centre and begins to build a tower. A few minutes later Matthew comes and sits at the other end of the block centre and begins to build a house. Two minutes later Nicole arrives and begins to build a kennel for her toy dog. Shortly afterward, Tamara leaves. In parallel play the arrival or departure of a child does not affect the play of the others.

Associative Play—the child plays with other children in a loosely organized way. This type of play usually begins at around ages three or four.

Example: Tamara, Nicole, and Matthew are building roads to their individual block houses. They comment on each other's roads and Nicole suggests Matthew use a curved block for his bridge and hands him the piece.

Cooperative Play—the child plays with other children in an organized way for a particular purpose. The play of one child supports that of another child. (One of the criticisms of Parten's play categories is the difficulty of distinguishing between associative and cooperative play.)

Example: A group of children has built a city of small houses. They then use small human figures to represent the people in the city. Each child takes on the role of one of the figures, including their voice.

Piaget's Stages of Play

Another influential categorization of play was set out by Piaget (1945/1962). His categories grew out of his observations of children's play. He linked these types of play to cognitive stages in children's development. The three stages Piaget identified are:

Practice Play (also called Exercise or Functional Play)—the same movement is repeated over and over. This type of play is related to the sensorimotor stage.

Example: A baby hitting two blocks together for the pleasure of the action, sound, and feel.

The Vanderheyden Family

Street hockey is an example of Games with Rules.

This type of play develops during infancy and comprises 53 percent of the free activity of children between 14 and 30 months of age (Rubin, Fein, & Vandenburg, 1983). Afterwards, practice play declines with age; for example, by ages four and five, it is 33 percent of free activity. However, adults still do practice play, such as jogging or hitting a tennis ball against a wall.

Symbolic Play (also called Pretend, Fantasy, Make-Believe, Dramatic Play)—representation of an object or experience that is not present. This type of play is related to the preoperational stage.

Example: A child pushes a block around the floor making the noises of a race car.

Symbolic play typically begins toward the end of the first year or beginning of the second (Gowen, 1995), and peaks during the preschool and kindergarten years (Bergen, 1988). These years have been called "the golden age of make-believe" (Isenberg & Jalongo, 1997, p. 55). Symbolic play becomes more complex with age, and by age six 20–30 percent of all play is dramatic play (Rubin, Fein, & Vandenburg, 1983). It then decreases through the primary school years (Pellegrini & Galda, 1993).

Games with Rules—this type of play is organized around prearranged rules that can be adjusted with agreement during the play. It is related to the concrete operational stage.

Examples: An infant playing peek-a-boo with an adult, a toddler rolling a ball back and forth to an adult, or older children playing baseball.

This type of play continues into adulthood and includes board games, sports, and paper and pencil games. Some theorists, such as Vygotsky (1966), argue that group play never occurs *without* rules, even if these are not explicitly stated.

Smilansky's Stages of Play

Sarah Smilansky (1968) elaborated on Piaget's stages. Based on her research, she identified four stages of play related to children's cognitive development:

1. *Functional Play*—Ages 0–2

2. *Constructive Play*—The use of materials to make something. For example, children constructing an airport from blocks. This type of play comprises 51 percent of all activities for four- to six-year-olds (Rubin, Fein, & Vandenburg, 1983).

3. *Dramatic Play*—Playing with symbols. Begins at age two and continues into adulthood.

4. *Games with Rules.*

One application of play classification has been the combining of Smilansky's cognitive categories and Parten's social categorization of play by Rubin and his associates (Rubin, Maioni, & Hornung, 1976; Rubin, Watson, & Jambor, 1978) (see Figure 7.1). This is a commonly used classification system for analyzing play, as it provides more depth of information than using either categorization system by itself. You might want to try to write in an example for each box.

Sociodramatic Play

Sociodramatic play is a highly developed and sophisticated form of social play. It involves other people, whereas fantasy play might be only the child herself and

figure 7.1 RUBIN'S PLAY CLASSIFICATION MATRIX

	FUNCTIONAL	CONSTRUCTIVE	DRAMATIC	GAMES WITH RULES
SOLITARY				
PARALLEL				
GROUP PLAY				

Based on the research of Rubin, Maioni, & Hornung (1976).

her doll. Sociodramatic play "occurs when two or more children adopt roles and act out a make-believe situation or story" (Johnson, Christie, & Yawkey, 1999, p. 2). It typically begins around age four.

Six characteristics for sociodramatic play are:

1. Imitative role play

2. Make-believe in regard to objects

3. Make-believe in regard to actions and situations

4. Persistence

5. Interaction

6. Verbal communication.

(Smilansky, 1968)

This type of play is important in the development of children's creativity, thinking processes, language, group cooperation, vocabulary, relationships, perspective taking, sharing, impulse control, literacy behaviours, and social skills (Brewer, 1998; Gowen, 1995; Johnson, Christie, & Yawkey, 1999).

The Importance of Play in Children's Development

So far in this chapter, we have looked at the cultural, historical, and theoretical contexts for play. It is also important to know about the effects of play on young children's development. In Chapter 2, some key areas for children's optimal growth and development identified were health, cognitive stimulation, socio-emotional development, economic security, and safe physical environment. Growth and development in most of these areas can be fostered by play.

Early childhood professionals need to know about and be able to articulate the importance of play. Doing so has become easier due to the dramatic increase in research on play in the past 40 years. One positive effect from the research on play is that "as research increasingly demonstrates the importance of play in children's development, the commitment to encouraging the practice of play grows" (Kagan, 1990, p. 175).

Play for Health

Play can foster children's physical development and health. This is a reciprocal relationship, as healthy children play, which reinforces and further fosters their physical development and health. According to Kaplan-Sanoff, Brewster, Stillwell, & Bergen (1988), "healthy growth and competent motor ability, facilitated through play, make a major contribution to development" (p. 137). Play is considered important for health. Physicians and others exhort us to eat properly, exercise, reduce stress, and adopt a healthy lifestyle. Play is a way for children and adults to achieve some of these aims.

Physical Development

The surplus energy theory of play recognizes that children move a great deal and that this is important for their development. Play promotes children's physical development through its provision of many opportunities for motor activities both indoors and outdoors. Throughout children's development, from the sensorimotor stage to toddling to running to engaging in sports, nearly all children engage in physically active play.

Between the ages of two and seven, there is great growth in children's physical development, particularly in the locomotor skills such as running, skipping, hopping, and swinging (Payne & Rink, 1997). Young children also develop body and spatial awareness through movement activities as well as the many gross motor skills they'll need for later participation in games, sports, dancing, and other activities they can enjoy their entire lives.

Play can also foster the development of fine motor skills through the child's participation in drawing with crayons, writing with pencils, cutting with scissors, and lacing. Children's perceptual motor skills and eye–hand coordination are also fostered through play. Activities that require the child to stack blocks, assemble puzzle pieces, fit road pieces together, cut and paste, manipulate nesting toys, build with interlocking plastic blocks, or string beads facilitate perceptual-motor development and eye–hand coordination.

The old saying "Sound in body, sound in mind" could be applied to play. Because just as play helps foster children's physical development, it also fosters children's cognitive development.

Cognitive Stimulation and Play

The relation of play to young children's cognitive development has long been recognized. Froebel and, later, Montessori designed materials that required children to engage in problem solving (see Chapter 5). As children develop, their play becomes more complex and abstract, reflecting their growing cognitive development. We can see evidence of children's cognitive growth in their approaches to problem solving. For example, an infant will cry if he cannot reach a desired toy, while a three-year-old will crawl up on a chair to reach it.

Play can help develop children's problem-solving abilities (Johnson, Christie, & Yawkey, 1999). An environment in which children are allowed and encouraged to explore and experiment and to try out different options facilitates problem solving. For example, if a group of children are playing together and want to build a road but come up against a large object they cannot move, they'll need to problem-solve: they might explore whether they have enough pieces for their road to go around the obstacle or if they have the appropriate pieces to make a bridge over the object. They may have to try several ways before deciding on the one that works or works best.

Problem solving also encourages children's divergent thinking, which has implications for creativity. According to Isenberg and Jalongo (1997), "creativity can be viewed as an aspect of problem-solving, which has its roots in play" (p. 53).

Creativity and Play

In her review of the research on play and creativity, Pepler (1986) concluded that, "there is considerable support for the effect of play on creativity" (p. 148). Creativity can be fostered by play in many ways. One way is by providing children with materials that are flexible and open-ended and can therefore be used in a variety of ways for a variety of purposes. For example, blocks are an excellent material because they can be used in so many ways by children at a variety of developmental levels. Other useful open-ended materials such as playdough, pieces of fabric and yarn, empty boxes and cardboard tubes, and crayons and paper can also help to foster children's aesthetic appreciation.

Creativity can be seen in young children's invention of play structures, in their use of materials in new ways, and in their problem solving. Creativity can also be seen in children's use of and playing with language. Young children like rhyming words and "funny sounding" words. Language is also an important part of group play. For example, children need to communicate with one another to keep the play going.

Language and Play

Play promotes language and language promotes play. Children begin playing with language when they play with making sounds as babies. If you listen to a baby vocalizing in her crib, you may be surprised at the number of sounds and tones the child makes. These can include speech sounds, humming, blowing bubbles, and other sounds. Word play is seen with somewhat older children in their love of nonsense words, chants, rhymes, songs, fingerplays, jokes, and riddles. Therefore young children benefit from exposure to and enjoyment of appropriate poetry, songs, and fingerplays.

Play is valuable for children's language development because it provides the opportunity and stimulation for using language. Children learn to use language to make their wants known, to participate in conversation, to resolve social situations or problems with other children, and so forth. Through play children learn accepted forms of language such as proper grammar and pragmatics (e.g., taking turns during conversation). According to the eminent educational psychologist Jerome Bruner, "the most complicated grammatical and pragmatic forms of language appear first in play activity" (1983, p. 65). This statement makes sense to those of us who have watched young children play together. The language interactions one hears from children during a 20-minute session in the housekeeping or block centre can encompass many uses of language. For example, children use language to question, answer, negotiate, explain, clarify, justify, correct, and elaborate. The language in this sociodramatic play activity is much richer and more extended and connected than much of the language interaction young children typically have with others, including adults, for much of their day.

Language is stimulated when children have a variety of opportunities to use language for different purposes throughout the day. A variety of themes for the dramatic play centre, in addition to the traditional housekeeping corner, can encourage children to want to play and thereby use language and thus increase their vocabularies and language repertoires. Children who are learning a second language benefit from the situational context of the language and the non-threatening nature and motivation of play.

Emerging Literacy and Play

Play supports and stimulates the process of becoming literate. Some of young children's earliest efforts at reading and writing occur in the context of socio-dramatic play; for example, a child writing/scribbling down someone's order in a restaurant play centre and then giving it to the chef to read and "cook."

The roots of children's literacy can be seen in their dramatic and constructive play (Dyson, 1991). For example, children playing grocery store might demonstrate many of the following literacy tasks:

- Reading labels (i.e., environmental print)

- Writing lists/making signs (drawing and writing)

- Reading and responding to signs (e.g., Open or Closed)

- Making ads (writing and invented spelling)

- Writing the weekly specials on a small chalkboard

- Adding up the bill

- Writing cheques or completing credit or debit card receipts

- Making change and counting money

- Taking dictation from phone orders.

The provision of literacy materials fosters language and literacy (Morrow & Rand, 1991; Neuman & Roskos, 1992). These materials should be included in all centres, not just the book or literacy corner. For example, cookbooks and catalogues can be included in the traditional housekeeping corner, materials for sign making put in the construction area, song charts in the music centre, reference materials on the science table, and so on. Good play environments "rich in literacy, resources, including people, push children to reveal what they know about writing and reading and pull at their literacy development in seemingly beneficial ways" (Roskos & Neuman, 1998, p. 103) (see the photo below).

Margie I. Mayfield

Literacy materials such as this kindergarten writing centre for valentines can foster oral and written language development.

Concept Development and Play

Another area of cognitive development fostered by play is a child's general knowledge and concepts of the world around us. For example, water play helps children understand concepts such as sink and float, conservation of liquid, the effect of gravity on water, fluidity, and surface tension. Young children need an understanding of a concept so they can connect new words with that concept and thus expand their vocabularies.

Emotional Development and Play

Children's play can reflect their emotional states. Children often explore emotions and emotionally significant events in their lives through play, and express their emotions in their play. For example, I have often seen young children who recently have gained a sibling playing out their feelings, anxieties, and sibling rivalry in sociodramatic play. This is not to say that all of a child's play fantasies reflect the reality of that child's life. Children re-enact events, perhaps with a different outcome than reality, learn to cope with their feelings, and come to terms with a traumatic event such as the death of a pet.

Effects of play on young children's emotional development has been a relatively neglected area of research (Rubin, Fein, & Vandenburg, 1983). However, "the few studies done indicate that play supports emotional functioning" (Rogers & Sawyers, 1988, p. 69). Research from play therapy also supports the connection of play and emotional development (Johnson, Christie, & Yawkey, 1999).

Play therapy is described earlier in this chapter.

Research has shown play to have positive effects on key components in healthy socio-emotional development including socialization, social competence, and positive self-concept. For example, in Chapter 2, the importance of attachment was discussed. Play seems to facilitate the development of attachment (Curry & Bergen, 1988). Research has shown maternal play with an infant is correlated with closeness of attachment (Hughes, 1995). Play also encourages children to form attachments and positive relationships with other children (DeWolf & Benedict, 1997).

Social Development and Play

Young children's cognitive and emotional development in play is promoted and enhanced by their social interactions with one another. Children's social play becomes more interactive as they develop. Preschool and kindergarten children typically have more social skills and behaviours such as sharing, turn-taking, and using language to facilitate play than do toddlers.

Socialization

Children are born into a social world. How well they will cope and thrive in this environment depends on their social development. Social development and play reinforce and enhance one another. For example, children who have good social skills are more likely to be seen as good play companions by other children, thus providing more opportunities for further social development. It is during play that children learn and practise key social skills such as sharing, communicating, listening, compromising, negotiating, and cooperating with others. Through social play children can learn, practice, and consolidate social skills (Rubin & Howe, 1986). It is thought that children who do not have good social skills are more at risk for adjustment problems in later life (Kuperschmidt & Coie, 1990; Ladd, 1990; Morrison & Masten, 1991). An early childhood program that provides a good social environment can facilitate children's play and social development.

Social Competence

You can probably remember a child a teacher always chose to be a buddy for a new child who had just moved into the neighbourhood and was beginning in your class. This child likely had excellent social skills and would today be termed "socially competent." These children "exhibit a positive demeanor around or toward others, have accurate social information processing abilities, and display social behaviours that lead them to be well liked by others" (Creasey, Jarvis, & Berk, 1998, p. 118). They are rated as popular by both peers and teachers (Connolly & Doyle, 1984). They are social leaders, cooperative, have social problem-solving strategies, and understand other children's perspectives (Pellegrini, 1987).

Perspective Taking

Another component of social development that can be fostered by play is perspective taking. This is "the ability to see things from other people's points of view. It involves understanding what other people see (visual perspective taking), think (cognitive perspective taking), and feel (affective perspective taking or empathy)" (Johnson, Christie, & Yawkey, 1999, p. 41).

Being able to understand another child's ideas and feelings is important for successful interpersonal relations. You've probably seen a young child comforting another who has been hurt. Even quite young children can show empathetic behaviours towards others. However, this is not a given. Piaget and others demonstrated that it is difficult for young children to see another's point of view or any other viewpoint beyond their own. For example, despite the adult telling the child it is nice to share one's toys, a two-year old who has a toy and wants to keep it does not have a good perspective of the view of another child who wants it. Playing a variety of roles in sociodramatic play encourages children to put themselves into another's shoes (e.g., the baby role, the daddy role, etc.).

Social play has rules that children must learn if they are to be successful in play. These can be simple turn taking in a parent–child peek-a-boo game or older children telling each other knock-knock jokes. Learning the rules of social play also introduces children to the concept of rules in general (Johnson, Christie, & Yawkey, 1999).

Contexts for Play

Children's play occurs in contexts. The contexts influence children's play and children's play influences the contexts. Three important contexts for children's play are social, physical, and temporal; that is, young children need play partners, a space to play in and materials to play with, and time to play.

The Social Context of Play

Children's play is influenced not only by their developmental levels but also with whom they play. When you were a young child, with whom did you play? Play is often interactional, and the social context of the play is therefore important. Given the demographics of today's families (discussed in Chapter 3), there are more children who do not have siblings. In addition, smaller family sizes and safety concerns may limit a child's access to other children as playmates. Some children come into an early childhood program with relatively little experience playing with other children. For many of these children their primary play partner may have been an adult.

The adults in a child's life need to recognize, respond to, and encourage play from infancy. For example, early games with infants such as patty-cake and peek-a-boo help children learn about play and its interactive nature. Research shows that playful children typically have playful mothers (e.g., Damast, Tamis-LeMonda, & Bornstein, 1996; Fiese, 1990).

The Socio-Emotional Environment

Another dimension of the social context of the early childhood program is the socio-emotional environment. This refers to the social climate, atmosphere, or tone of the classroom or centre. In a positive socio-emotional environment for children,

- Interaction with other children and adults is fostered.

- The development of children's social skills is part of the program.

- Independence and self-help skills are encouraged.

- Children's positive self-concepts and self-esteem are fostered.

- Children's individual differences and needs are recognized and accommodated.

- Play is planned for and facilitated.

- The educators establish a positive social-emotional environment (Mayfield, 1992).

The roles of the educator in play are discussed later in this chapter.

The Physical Context of Play

Just as play occurs in a social context, it also occurs in a physical context. This might be a classroom, a playground, or a home. A child interacts with the physical environment during play and the physical environment affects the child's play. Early childhood professionals can facilitate and enhance children's play by establishing a physical environment that promotes children's play and development.

The idea that the physical setting can affect children's learning and play is not a new one. Pestalozzi, Froebel, Montessori, and others wrote about the physical environment and its influence on children's learning (see Chapter 5). In addition, both Froebel and Montessori designed materials to enhance children's play and learning. Early childhood educators can facilitate and enhance children's play by attending to the physical environment—both indoors and outdoors.

The Indoor Environment

The physical arrangement of a classroom or centre can influence both children's and adults' behaviour. You have probably seen classrooms that you thought were attractive and user-friendly. On the other hand, you've likely seen others that were not very welcoming, interesting, or child-friendly. At one time I worked as a program coordinator and part of my job was to assist educators to set up or reorganize their kindergarten and primary classrooms. I learned that although there is no one best way to set up a classroom or centre, there are some key characteristics to consider. An effective indoor physical environment for young children has

- Well-defined areas

- Sufficient space for the number of children

- Developmentally appropriate materials and equipment

- Attractive, safe, and comfortable space

- Flexible and usable space

- Reflection of the program, the curriculum, and the children's interests
- Sufficient, available, and accessible materials.

(Mayfield, 1992)

Well-defined Areas

These areas can help children focus, see relationships among materials, assist in putting materials away properly, and use materials more independently. Furniture, carpeting, and coloured tape are some ways to help visually define areas. In early childhood programs, a frequent organization is the use of *centres* (sometimes called activity, play, or learning centres). Some typical centres are:

- Literacy centre (book, listening, and writing areas),
- Construction and modelling centre (e.g., blocks, Lego, parquetry blocks, playdough, plasticine),
- Dramatic play centre,
- Arts and crafts centre,
- Manipulatives centre (e.g., puzzles, games, pegboards, beads and laces, stacking toys, math materials),
- Music centre (e.g., rhythm instruments, homemade instruments, movement props such as scarves),
- Exploration or discovery centre (e.g., magnifying glasses, prisms, magnets, seeds, thermometer),
- Woodworking centre,
- Sand/water play area,
- Cooking area,
- A quiet area (for a child who needs privacy or a break from the group),
- A large group meeting area, and
- The current theme centre (e.g., a grocery store if doing the community or a train station if doing transportation).

It is important to have a variety of centres available for the children, because children play differently in different areas (Pellegrini, 1985; Rubin, 1977; Pellegrini & Perlmutter, 1989). Some areas, such as a housekeeping corner or construction centre, encourage dramatic or group play; others, such as an art centre, might induce more solitary play or fine motor play; others still, such as a music and movement centre, might encourage more gross motor play. Unfortunately, many programs do not have sufficient space to accommodate all of the centres one would like to have. These programs typically have a few permanent centres such as literacy, construction, dramatic play, discovery/

science, and art/music, and then rotate other centres. One can have well-defined space whether the physical space is large or small.

Sufficient Space

One of the most frequent comments I hear from early childhood professionals about physical space is that they wish they had more. This would indeed be nice, but most of us cannot remodel the space we have and have to make do. The minimum amount of space required for a licensed early childhood program is based on the number of children (i.e., spatial density) and is established by provincial/territorial regulations.

Licensing is discussed in Chapter 12.

There are two types of density to consider: one is physical density, and the other is social density. For example, some research shows that if there are fewer children in an area such as a learning centre, there is likely to be more solitary play and less aggression (Ramsey & Reid, 1988). Less space and more children can result in more group play but also more aggression (Loo & Kennelly, 1979), or crowding might result in fewer interactions (Hartup, 1983). Increased space, especially open space, results in more gross motor activity such as running (Smith & Connolly, 1976; 1980). Of course, the play patterns and responses of individual children vary due to their past experiences, cultural backgrounds, development, and other factors. The effects of spatial and social density on children's play are also influenced by the overall quality of the early childhood program and the expertise of the early childhood professionals (Dempsey & Frost, 1993).

Developmentally Appropriate Materials and Equipment

Child-sized furniture and developmentally appropriate materials help children to function successfully and independently. Novelty is also a factor. For example, adding new items to a centre can add vitality and spark renewed interest in the children. And while children enjoy a certain degree of novelty, it is also important that the materials selected are ones that the children can relate to and include some of their "old favourites" (Howe, Moller, & Chambers, 1994). Novelty can also be fostered by combining two existing centres such as woodworking and art.

References for suggested materials are found at the end of this chapter.

Criteria for selecting play materials are listed in Focus 7.2.

Space That Is Attractive to Children, Safe, and Comfortable for Them and the Adults

Children and early childhood professionals spend much of their days in the early childhood program. It is important that the physical environment be pleasant and interesting for everyone. Children's ideas about attractive and interesting space may not always be the same as ours. For example, young children enjoy bright colours. I once encouraged a group of five-year-olds to choose the colours to paint our kindergarten classroom. After much mixing of paint,

Focus 7.2

Criteria for Selecting Play Materials

Children have used materials in their play since ancient times (Cohen, 1987; Fraser, 1966). Perhaps the professionals who do more selecting of toys than others are toy librarians (toy libraries are described in Chapter 11). The following are the criteria for selecting play materials most frequently given by toy librarians in Canada, England, Sweden, and Australia in a research study I did (Mayfield, 1993):

· Developmentally appropriate

· Durable

· Safe

· Suitable for or adapted for all children

· Open-ended; versatile

· Attractive.

Cost was a concern but it was not one of the top criteria for selection even though toy librarians identified funding as their number 1 problem. No one advocated selecting inferior toys because they were cheaper.

testing, viewing, and discussing sample colour sheets placed on the walls, their final selection was yellow walls with aqua cupboards and bookshelves. I thought it was a bit bright (one parent referred to it as "street-curb yellow"!). However, I was reassured when a grade 1 child looked in at the newly painted classroom and remarked that he wished he could be in this room as it was a much prettier colour than his light blue classroom!

When I was helping educators set up physical environments, one strategy I recommended was to kneel or sit on the floor to be the approximate height of the children and thus see what the environment looked like from their perspective. Most people who do this then lower the artwork on the walls, the clock, and other items so the children can see them clearly. It is essential to remember that the physical space needs to be functional and attractive *for the children*. It is a living-in space, not a decorator's dream space.

Some factors to consider for comfort are good natural and artificial lighting; a comfortable level of heating—especially at the floor level, where the children often play; good ventilation and air circulation; varied and appropriate floor coverings; and cleanliness. In addition, I have always included some non-institutional furniture in all the early childhood settings I've developed. Items such as a rocking chair, floor pillows, plants, and art add a softness and home-like feel.

Flexible and Usable Space

Often, planning an indoor environment means doing the best with the space one has. Sufficient space is important so that essential activities are not excluded from a program because of lack of space. However, well-designed and well-utilized space and flexible arrangements can help; for example, some activities such as music and movement require a large open area, so an environment that can be easily rearranged facilitates the provision of these and other activities.

Reflection of the Program and the Children's Interests and Needs

The physical environment can be used to stimulate and reinforce children's learning. When you enter an early childhood program, you should be able to tell what the current curriculum topics and the children's interests are from what is in the environment. This might include children's drawings and other artwork, realia from a current topic, photos of recent field trips or visitors, dictated stories, the latest recipe in the cooking corner, books on a variety of topics, and songs and fingerplays the children know. The physical environment also reflects the values and philosophy of a program (e.g., non-sexist materials and items from different cultural and ethnic groups).

Sufficient, Available, and Easily Accessible Materials

The availability or lack of play materials influences children's play. There should also be a sufficient amount and number of materials for the children. Although children's social interactions increase when fewer materials are available (e.g., they have to share more), so does their aggression (e.g., there are more disputes over materials). In fact, low availability of play materials contributes more to conflicts over materials and aggression than does lack of space, unless it's very crowded (Smith & Connolly, 1976; Smith & Green, 1975). Availability of sufficient numbers of materials can reduce aggressive behaviour.

Accessibility of materials also influences children's behaviour. For example, if a child knows where to get drawing materials, and if the materials are accessible, the child is more likely to draw and do so independently.

The Outdoor Environment

Indoors is not the only place where young children play. Outdoor play has its own characteristics and advantages. For example, it typically provides the child with more space than indoors, different equipment, different activities, different sights and sounds, exposure to changing weather and seasons, introduction to nature and caring for the environment, and varied terrain, surfaces, and textures (e.g., sand dirt, grass, paving stones, etc.).

The use of outdoor play has long been advocated in early childhood education and care. As described in Chapter 5, the McMillan sisters' nursery school emphasized healthy living outdoors. Even earlier, Froebel promoted outdoor activities as part of his children's garden (kindergarten).

Millie Almy, who has studied children and early childhood programs for 50 years, recently stated, "Outdoor play is so important and so neglected" (Greenburg, 2000, p. 9). Do you agree or disagree with this statement? What are some specific examples to support your response?

The outdoors is rich in play potential and most children enjoy playing outdoors. When asked about their favourite childhood play experiences, 70 percent of adults in one study described an outdoor activity (Henniger, 1994). Many children today do not have free access to a green space. More urban living in apartments or smaller houses may mean no or little back or front yard for play. Concerns about young children's safety lead us to limit their access to community outdoor play areas. Therefore, outdoor play in an early childhood program may be some children's major opportunity for daily outdoor play. Outdoor experiences for children can also occur in local parks, on nature walks, or on field trips.

While it is important that children have a variety of outdoor experiences, this chapter focuses primarily on the outdoor playground, as that is typically where young children will spend most of their outdoor time.

Playgrounds

One physical context for play is the playground. The 1914 *Cyclopedia of Education* defines a playground as "plots of ground set aside for the holding of games, sports, athletic exercises, and amusing activities of various sorts" (Monroe, 1914, p. 728). Playgrounds and their definitions have evolved greatly in the twentieth century.

The history of playgrounds is usually traced back to the outdoor *gymnasia* in Germany in the early nineteenth century and the later "sandgartens." Originally, in the 1880s in Berlin, the sandgarten consisted of piles of sand placed in public parks for children's play. The first one in North America was established in 1886 at the Boston Children's Mission. The outdoor gymnasia and sandgartens combined with the ideas of Froebel resulted in playgrounds for children being introduced in North America at the turn of the century.

Joe Frost has identified three eras in playground development:

- *The Manufactured Apparatus Era*—The early years of the twentieth century saw the commercial manufacture of gymnastic and play apparatus such as swing sets, sandboxes, slides, teeter-totters, climbing frames, and other structures. These were made of steel, iron, and wood and were available through catalogues.

- *The Novelty Era*—The middle of the twentieth century saw innovation in playground design, equipment, and use. Playgrounds became more colourful, better landscaped, and more varied. Architects, landscape designers, artists, recreational specialists, educators, and community groups designed play structures. Play equipment was expanded to include playhouses, complex climbing structures, elaborate slides, and vehicles. Playgrounds were sometimes built around themes such as space travel, nursery rhymes, sea life, trains, and jungles. These playgrounds were sometimes criticized as being unsafe for children, lifeless, static, and more aesthetically pleasing to adults than stimulating for children (Frost, 1992; Hartle & Johnson, 1993).

- *The Modern Era*—Since the 1970s, modular wooden equipment has become more prevalent in children's playgrounds. Much of the metal used in previous eras was replaced with heavy-duty plastics as playground safety became an increasing issue (see below). Some current trends in playground design include designing safer equipment; incorporating softer features such as landscaping, contours, sand, and water; combining different settings and play areas; and designing playgrounds to meet the developmental needs of all children. There has also been a growth in adventure playgrounds.

Today's playgrounds can be classified by their degree of structure and formality. Three types are:

- Traditional
- Creative/Contemporary
- Adventure.

The **traditional playground** is formal, structured, and has steel structures anchored into cement such as swing sets, slides, climbers, and merry-go-rounds. There are no movable materials (e.g., wooden boxes, barrels, boards, or carts) and little provision for dramatic-play structures (e.g., playhouse, truck, or boat). While virtually indestructible and low maintenance, they have been criticized for the lack of materials that can be used in creative ways, hazards of children falling onto steel structures or cement underneath, lack of landscaping, and generally unaesthetically pleasing appearance.

The **creative/contemporary playground** is semi-formal, semi-structured, designed by adults (often architects), incorporated into the landscape, and has modular linked units such as elaborate climbers, bridges, ladders, pulley rides, and platforms made from wood, heavy plastic pipe, cable spools, tires, and timbers. This type of playground is more conducive to children's dramatic play. Movable materials may include sand and water play materials, vehicles, and other similar materials. These playgrounds are sometimes commercial, sometimes community designed and built, and sometimes a combination of the two. An example of this is the Halifax Boat Playground (see Focus 7.3).

Research comparing children's play on traditional and creative playgrounds has shown:

TRADITIONAL PLAYGROUND	CREATIVE PLAYGROUND
MORE PARALLEL PLAY	MORE SOLITARY PLAY
MORE FUNCTIONAL PLAY	MORE ASSOCIATIVE PLAY
MORE GAMES WITH RULES	MORE SOCIAL PLAY
MORE NON-PLAY	MORE DRAMATIC PLAY
MORE ARGUING	MORE COOPERATIVE PLAY
MORE GROSS MOTOR PLAY	MORE GROUP PLAY

(Boyatzis, 1987; Frost, Shin, & Jacobs, 1998; Hayward, Rothenburg, & Beasley, 1974).

Creative playgrounds are designed by adults, usually with little or no input from children, and have been criticized as being nice to look at but not always

Focus 7.3

The Halifax Boat Playground

As its name says: this is a boat, it's a playground for children, *and* it's on the waterfront (but on dry land) in Halifax. When the City of Halifax held public meetings about developing the waterfront area in the late 1980s, concerned citizens, including early childhood professionals, pointed out that if the City wanted families to use the waterfront, there had to be provision for chidren—a playground!

The planning committee called for proposals for a playground and selected a most untypical entry by designer Emanuel Jannasch, who had played among boats during his childhood. His playboat is a cutaway boat with four levels including a hold, wheelhouse, and crow's nest. There is plenty of real equipment to manipulate, such as pulleys, ropes, blocks and tackles, and rope nets. The fittings and details are authentic, including a real captain's wheel, maps, gangway, bowspit, and other features that promote children's dramatic play. This play often involves the parents.

As with typical community playgrounds, problems have included vandalism and the need for ongoing maintenance. Nevertheless, hundreds of families enjoy the Halifax Boat Playground year-round.

Sources: Mac Isaac, 1994: Sue Wolstenholme, personal communications, May 1999.

Halifax Waterfront Development Corporation

functional and sometimes hazardous (Frost, 1992). Often, creative playgrounds are incorrectly termed *adventure playgrounds*. Adventure playgrounds are different from the more common creative playground.

Adventure playgrounds are the most informal, least structured, and least common of the three types of playgrounds. These playgrounds began in Denmark in 1943 when a landscape architect, C. T. Sorensen, designed the first *byggelegepladsen,* or "building playground." He had observed children's pleasure and ingenuity when playing on building sites and designed his playground to replicate some of this play. Denmark has been a leader in playground design in the twentieth century (Eriksen, 1985). For example, it was the first country in 1939 to have laws requiring play areas for children in all public housing projects.

Adventure playgrounds are characterized by their (a) equipment (e.g., loose materials for building such as boards, scraps of building materials, and tools), (b) facilities (e.g., the clubhouse for indoor activities such as arts and crafts, games, and table tennis), and (c) activities (e.g., building houses, climbing structures, gardening, outdoor cooking, and sand and water play).

Perhaps the most important component of a successful adventure playground is the play leader, whose role is to facilitate children's play and safety. The salary for the play leader is often a major obstacle.

Adventure playgrounds have been slower to catch on in North America than they have in Europe due in part to the greater liability issue in North America. Actually, there have been very few injuries on adventure playgrounds and they have excellent safety records (Frost, 1992). These playgrounds have been criticized for being messy, junky looking, and sometimes noisy. A fence or hedge can help to reduce these problems.

In reality, it is probably more useful to think of classifying playgrounds along a continuum from traditional to adventure. This system recognizes the variation across playgrounds and the overlap of characteristics and equipment.

FOR REFLECTION

A climbing structure for young children has been designed to resemble a helicopter. Do you think this encourages young children's imaginative play or limits it? In what ways?

Playground Design

The design and equipping of the outdoor play space requires as much attention and thought as the indoor environment. The first and most important factor is the children and their developmental needs. Other factors to consider in designing outdoor play space are:

Site—The size of the outdoor play area needs to be sufficient for the number of children and a variety of equipment. A first step is to check provincial licensing regulations. The use of the site topography for aesthetic considerations as well as practical ones such as drainage needs to be considered.

Zones—There should be a variety of defined play areas such as sand/water, dramatic play, gross motor activities, natural area (e.g., gardening), open area, manipulative area, seating, and relaxation.

Surfaces—A well-designed outdoor play area needs a variety of surfaces such as hard surfaces for wheeled toys, soft surfaces such as sand or rubber matting under climbing structures, swings, and slides. Appropriate surfacing can reduce accidents and injuries (see Safety, below).

Equipment—Variety and sufficient equipment are necessary so there is enough for the children to do and aggressive behaviour is not fostered (Lambert, 1999). Equipment should be matched to children's physical size, developmental level, interests, and play behaviours. Different types of play equipment can stimulate different types of play (Ledingham, 1998). Oftentimes, outdoor play spaces that have adequate large pieces of equipment are lacking in smaller materials that can be manipulated by the children (Henniger, 1994). One easy way of organizing manipulatives in an outdoor play area is to use plastic crates or totes with lids to transport materials from indoors to outdoors or from a storage shed. These materials might include gardening tools, plastic pipes and connectors for water play, woodworking, blocks, play figures and vehicles, and so on (for details, see Odoy & Foster, 1997).

Positioning—The placement of the materials and equipment can influence how children use the outdoor play space. The equipment should be spread out over the area so there is adequate clearance between pieces of equipment and the children have sufficient room to maneuver around the equipment and each other. Also, there should be one or more quiet areas where children can get away from others but still be observable.

Safety—One of the biggest considerations in designing play areas for young children is safety. According to playground expert Joe Frost, most playgrounds "are poorly equipped and hazardous" (Frost, Shin, & Jacobs, 1998, p. 267). As discussed in Chapter 2, playgrounds are a major place of injury for children. The most frequent injuries by children under five are head and neck injuries (48 percent) followed by upper limb injuries (31 percent) (Health Canada, 1997). Most playground injuries are caused by slides (22 percent), monkey bars (21 percent), and swings (19.5 percent)(Health Canada, 1998 [online]). In particular, falling from equipment is the cause of 83.5 percent of hospital admissions due to playground injuries (Health Canada, 1998 [online]). A fall from even a modest height onto a hard surface can cause serious or fatal injuries to a young child.

Playground safety can be improved by:

- Teaching children how to use playground equipment
- Reviewing safety rules for playgrounds with the children periodically
- Including only materials and equipment appropriate for the size and developmental stages of the children
- Enclosing the play area to keep out animals, reduce vandalism, and prevent children wandering away

- Establishing and keeping clear sight lines to all parts of the playground

- Using child-safe and environmentally friendly landscaping

- Inspecting the equipment and play area every time children use it for items such as glass, cans, needles, and other contaminants

- Doing regular maintenance work on the equipment

- Having a first-aid kit readily available

- Reviewing yearly playground safety standards and making necessary modifications.

Climate—Regional and site climate characteristics can influence playground design. For example, playgrounds in the far North have to consider cold weather, snow, ice, and dark days in mid-winter; playgrounds on the West Coast can provide covered areas to extend use of the outdoor play area during rainy times. Rooftop playgrounds sometimes have special problems with wind. All play areas need to provide places that are out of the prevailing wind and sun.

Addresses of the Canadian Standards Association and playground safety organizations are given at the end of this chapter.

FOR REFLECTION

Recall or observe a neighbourhood playground. What are its good design features? What desirable features are lacking?

Children with Disabilities in the Physical Environment

A good environment for children with disabilities is one that is a good environment for all children (e.g., safety glass in doors). The general characteristics are the same. What is usually needed are modifications and adaptations so that all children can get optimal benefit from their environments. One cannot generalize as to what any child who has special needs will require. There is a wide range and diversity in the individual abilities and needs of children who have the same special need (e.g., there are degrees of visual impairment, from relatively mild to total blindness). The following are some suggestions that may be appropriate to consider when adapting a physical environment for children with disabilities:

- More open spaces and wider entrances

- Clear and obvious pathways

- Surfaces that are not too slippery or too dense (e.g., some carpeting and matting are a problem for wheelchairs)

- Tables, shelves, storage, equipment such as sand/water tables that are at appropriate levels and are accessible (e.g., cut-outs in tables to accommodate a wheelchair)

- Labels or picture cues of a size that can be easily seen or felt (e.g. Braille signs)

- Awareness of noise level and possible use of carpeting or cork on the wall to reduce noise levels

- Adapting materials for easier use (e.g., knobs on puzzle pieces for easier grasping and manipulation)

- The level, direction, and intensity of lighting for children who are visually impaired

- Simple and fixed arrangements of furniture for children who have poor vision.

- Protective helmets for outdoor play for children who have balance difficulties

- Materials that are at an appropriate level and interest for children who are gifted and talented

- Quiet spaces for children who have emotional problems.

In addition to modifying the physical environment, attention needs to be given to the type and quality of play by children with disabilities. Research has shown that "there is considerable evidence that the play of children with disabilities is qualitatively and quantitatively different from the play of children without disabilities" (Linder, 1994, p. 73). Specifically, the play is likely to be less organized, sophisticated, and group oriented.

The Temporal Context of Play

Just as children need a place to play and something to play with, they also need time to play. It takes time for children to do the negotiating, planning, and development required for successful dramatic play. It is also frustrating and discouraging for children if they do not have sufficient time to complete their building project or artwork. The time available and the length of blocks of time influence the duration and the complexity of children's play (Christie & Wardle, 1992).

There is no agreed-upon time that should be devoted to play. Overall, the research has shown that limiting children's play time limits what they can do and the level of their play (Christie, Johnsen, & Peckover, 1988; Christie & Wardle, 1992). Blocks of time of at least 30 minutes or more for play for preschools are supported by research (e.g., Christie & Wardle, 1992; Tegano & Burdette, 1991).

The Roles of the Early Childhood Educator in Play

The roles of the early childhood educator in children's play are multifaceted and multidimensional. As discussed in previous chapters, the roles of the educator are influenced by the philosophy and beliefs of the educator and the curriculum of the program. For example, some educators believe that the only time one should intervene in children's play is if there is danger to the children; other educators may direct children's play. Also, the roles of the educator can change from group to group or child to child.

The most common roles for the early childhood educator in relation to play are:

- *Planner*—It is the responsibility of the professional to plan and provide safe play environments that support the play of children while accommodating their diversity and individuality.

- *Observer*—The role of the educator requires observation and ongoing assessment of the children, their play, and the play setting. This role is more than that of an onlooker. Observation is a process, not a product, and requires instantaneous assessing of what is observed and determining if a response is required. Perhaps the most obvious example is monitoring for children's safety. If the play or the play setting becomes unsafe, appropriate action must be taken immediately.

- *Facilitator*—The early childhood educator facilitates play through the way the physical environment is structured, the length of time that is provided for play, and the materials made available to the children.

- *Resource and supplier*—It is the responsibility of the early childhood educator to see that there are sufficient, accessible, and appropriate materials and equipment available to the children. This may mean purchasing, making, or scrounging materials.

- *Model and collaborator*—The adults in children's lives can be powerful models. If early childhood educators model playfulness and respect for other's play, children will be more likely to do so as well. The role of collaborator is seen when adults join in children's play in order to initiate a play activity, such as playing peek-a-boo with an infant or helping a child with less developed play skills enter a group play situation. In these situations the role of the adult is to assist the child's play by following the child's lead.

  The issue of intervening in children's play is discussed later in this chapter.

- *Mediator and negotiator*—Sometimes, when children's play is in danger of breaking down, the role of the educator may be to mediate the difficulty and perhaps negotiate a solution. For example, if two children are playing parallel in the sandbox and come into conflict when both reach for the same shovel at the same time, the educator may help by pointing out the availability of another shovel or negotiating sharing the tool.

- *Trainer and coach*—Some children need assistance in developing appropriate play skills required for interactive play. For example, a child needs to know how to enter a play situation and how to contribute to the ongoing play in an appropriate way. Some children may need specific training and then coaching in order to develop these skills.

- *Assessor*—Part of the early childhood educator's ongoing role is the monitoring and assessment of children's development. This is true for play as well as for other areas of the curriculum. An example of this role would be determining what types of play individual children engage in, perhaps based on the matrix shown in Figure 7.1.

- *Learner*—The role of learner is an ongoing one to better understand children's play. The early childhood educator needs to keep informed of

Rough and tumble play and super-hero play are discussed later in this chapter.

recent knowledge about children's play. For example, there has recently been a great deal of research and writing about children's rough and tumble play and aggressive play.

- *Advocate*—The early childhood educator is an advocate for children and their rights, including the right to play. Early childhood educators need to be both informed and articulate about children's play. This is not a new suggestion. For example, in 1884 an article in *The Pedagogical Seminary* advised "A clear understanding of the nature of play is of the highest importance to teachers. Play is deserving of better repute than that in which it is sometimes held" (Johnson, 1884, p. 98).

Being an Advocate for Play

Play is not universally accepted as a desirable way for young children to spend their time. Many an early childhood educator has heard a parent say, "I send my child here to learn something, not to play." Play seems to have a long history of criticism. In 1630, Henry Slingsby wrote about his four-year-old son, "I find him duller to learn this year than last, which would discourage one, but I think the cause to be his too much minding play, which takes his mind from his book; therefore they do ill that do foment and cherish that humour in a child" (Pollock, 1987, p. 147). It is, of course, the right of educators and parents to question any part of the early childhood program.

Janet Atkin cautions us about "muddled and distorted thinking about play and its meanings" (1991, p. 30). There is more to defending play than saying it is a good thing and important for children. It is essential for early childhood educators to be able to explain the role of play in children's development and in your program to families, administrators, boards, and funding agencies. There is also need for an advocacy role in the larger community. For example, in community meetings on urban planning an advocate may be needed to promote the inclusion of play spaces for children.

Another aspect of advocacy for play is honouring children's play. One way to demonstrate respect for children's play is by documenting it with photos and displaying these for the children, their families, and visitors. Children's play can also be documented on film or video and then shared with the families of the children. This is also a good opportunity to point out specific play activities and how they can contribute to children's growth and learning.

There are many other ways to explain play to parents and others. For example, a group meeting to explain how children benefit from play can include information on what research has shown about the role of play in children's development, presented in a way that is understandable and interesting to the audience. Another group presentation might be on the characteristics of and guidelines for selecting and using play materials and equipment with children, including examples of play materials that can be made from recyclable materials at no or little cost. Play in the family context can be promoted by sharing prop boxes, play boxes, or play bags with families. These boxes include materials that

Focus 7-4

CAYC Position Statement on Play

Young Children Have the Right to Learn Through Play

The Canadian Association for Young Children exists to provide a Canadian voice on critical issues related to the quality of life of all young children and their families. (CAYC Mission statement). In this regard, CAYC believes that play contributes to the quality of life of young children and, therefore, offers the following position statement on play.

Children learn through play. Through their play, children develop sensory motor control, eye-hand coordination and problem solving skills. Physical, social, intellectual and emotional development are all enhanced through play.

   CAYC believes that:

· play is natural

· play is essential for children

· play is fun, exciting, adventurous, open ended

· play is creative and spontaneous

· play is magical and complex

· play is rewarding and stimulating

· play is non-threatening

· play is non-judgmental

· play is directed by the children

· play is full of choices and decision making opportunities

· play is posing questions and hypothesizing

· play is focussed on the process and not the product.

CAYC believes that it is important for children to play.

Children have a natural mechanism that enables them to make sense of their world—that mechanism is play. For over 100 years, researchers have studied play and have found that play:

· enhances a child's language development (Garvey, 1974).

· encourages creativity and problem solving (Dansky, 1980).

· provides a context through which the child develops representational thought, an essential foundation for reading, mathematics and science (Vygotsky, in J.S. Bruner, A Jolly, & K. Sylva (Eds.)).

· develops higher motivation to learn and develops higher self-esteem (Weininger, 1994).

· is an integral part of a child's being. It is the business of childhood, and it has a unique and vital role in the whole educational process. (Weininger, 1994.)

continued

continued

CAYC believes that children need time to play.

Research has shown that extended blocks of time are needed for children to immerse themselves in play (Tegano and Burdette, 1991). CAYC supports all programs, including the school setting, that provide time for children to play.

CAYC believes that children need space to play.

Space for play enables children to be children. Space affords children the opportunity to explore and change the surroundings, to be in charge and to find out more about people, things and ideas in the environment. Support for play does NOT mean that any behaviour is acceptable in any place at any cost—rather CAYC believes that all children should have the opportunity to be in spaces that are appropriate for them to play.

CAYC believes that children need certain materials for play.

Expensive toys are not necessary, but certain items need to be provided in order to enhance children's play! CAYC understands that a rich play environment does not happen by chance. Early Childhood Education specialists use their knowledge of the play potential of a variety of materials to offer children valuable play opportunities.

CAYC believes that children need adults to support and enable their play.

Adults take on many roles in order to facilitate children's play: stage manager, mediator, planner, communicator, player, observer (Jones and Reynolds, 1992). CAYC appreciates that adults draw upon considerable expertise as they enable, support and extend the play of groups of children in home, preschool, child care, and school settings.

REFERENCES:

Dansky, J.L. 1980. Make believe: A mediator of the relationship between play and creativity. *Child Development*, 51, 576–579.

Garvey, C. 1977. *Play.* Cambridge, MA: Harvard University Press.

Jones. E. & Reynolds. G. 1992. *The Play's the thing: Teacher's roles in children's play.*

Tegano, D.W. & Burdette, M.P. 1991. Length of activity periods and play behaviours of preschool children. *Journal of Research in Childhood Education.* 5(2), 93–99.

Vygotsky, L.S. Play and its role in the mental development of the child. In J.S. Bruner, A. Jolly, & K. Sylva (Eds). *Play: Its role in development and evoluation.*

Weininger. O. 1994.Understanding educational play: An interview with Otto Weininger by Una Villiers, 25(1), 4–6.

Source: CAYC brochure, 1996.

encourage families to play together, such as puzzles, games, art projects, music and dance supplies, puppets, props for playing grocery store, and so forth (see Kalata, 1998). Suggestions for possible activities can also be included.

Another option is to provide print materials that relate the importance of play to specific centres and materials. For example, small charts can be made for each centre that describe what children are learning by playing at each centre. These charts can be hung over the centre or posted in a place out of the children's way. Many of the professional organizations listed at the end of Chapter 4, such as NAEYC, CAYC, and ACEI, have developed statements on play and often have brochures explaining their positions. These can be posted on the family bulletin board or included in newsletters sent home. (See Focus 7.4 for CAYC's Position Statement on Play.)

Families can be invited to observe during play time. For those families that cannot attend, videos or slides can be used. An early childhood educator can use these to discuss with a family what their child could be learning during a particular play activity. This can be an effective strategy in response to the criticism that the children are "just messing about."

FOR REFLECTION

If you were preparing a two-page handout for parents on play, what would you include?

Assessing Play and Play Settings

Play time is an excellent time for assessment because children are involved in natural and sustained activities. One can learn much about children and their development by observing their play. Play showcases what children can do and provides a window to their thinking. Careful observation can also help identify problems of individual children, with the organization of the learning environment, with the materials and their accessibility, and with the amount of space and materials.

Some things that we can find out by observing children's play are:

- Who plays with whom?

- What materials are used?

- Which centres and themes are being used successfully?

- What types of play do children do?

- How are individual children developing and progressing?

- What sociodramatic themes do the children use?

These questions are only a sample of the many questions that can be asked to guide observation of children's play.

The recording of the information from observing children's play can be done informally, with anecdotal notes jotted down at the time and then elaborated upon later if needed. One can also use a play matrix such as the one in Figure 7.1 to record the different types of play. A diagram of the environment can be used to record the centres and play areas used by the children. Other options include a running record giving a continuous description or a check-list of particular aspects of play or play behaviour. Videos, slides, and photographs can also be used to provide a record of children's play. Individual play episodes can be written up for future reference. Sometimes event sampling is used (i.e., a particular type of play or situation such as aggression on the playground is recorded in detail). See Martin (1994) for more on observation and recording strategies.

The play environment can also be assessed. It is important to determine if it is functioning well. For example, individual areas of the classroom and playground need to be examined regularly. Sometimes, a centre or area needs to be modified, changed, or replaced in order to better meet children's changing needs and interests. For example, a housekeeping corner may no longer be attracting children, and by changing it to an office or a grocery store children may again use the area for dramatic play. Much of the evaluation of the physical environment is typically informal assessment, for example answering questions such as, Are the play areas well-defined, accessible, and attractive to the children? For more formal assessment, published rating scales such as the Early Childhood Environment Rating Scale (Harms & Clifford, 1980) have specific items on the physical environment.

> *Evaluation of the environment using published rating scales is discussed in more detail in Chapter 12 as part of assessing the overall quality of an early childhood program.*

Issues in Play

Play can be controversial. It is still debated and some issues are debated more than others are. One of these issues involves rough and tumble, aggressive, and war play. It is an issue every early childhood professional must deal with at some time. And, as with most issues, there is no one easy answer or agreed-upon approach.

Rough and Tumble Play

Rough and tumble play is controversial because of "the belief that children learn antisocial and aggressive behavior in R&T [rough and tumble play] and that what starts off as play fighting usually escalates to real fighting" (Pellegrini & Perlmutter, 1988, p. 14). **Rough and tumble play** is the overlap of gross motor, social, and pretend play and is defined as "playful physical activity" (Howe, Moller, & Chambers, 1994, p. 108). It is characterized by running, jumping, wrestling, chasing and fleeing, play fighting, restraining, laughing, and smiling. Rough and tumble play is playful, non-aggressive, and normal; it is much more common than aggression (Pellegrini, 1989). It is common from preschool into adolescence in many societies and tends to become rougher and more varied with age (Frost, 1992; Humphreys & Smith, 1984). However, rough and tumble play does not usually lead to aggression but to games with rules (Pellegrini & Perlmutter, 1988). Moreover, young children are typically able to distinguish rough and tumble play from aggression (Constabile et al., 1991; Pellegrini, 1989).

A related issue is when or where does rough and tumble play become aggression. Aggression is a concern in today's society where some people, including children, express anger, hurt, and frustration with aggressive acts that injure or kill. A key distinction between rough and tumble play and aggression is that the former is playful, the latter is not. Children who show aggressive behaviour are often rejected by their peers and have difficulty distinguishing rough and tumble play and aggression (Pellegrini, 1988; Pellegrini & Perlmutter, 1988). These children need help with building their prosocial skills through modelling, tutoring, and coaching. Peers can help by being social models, reinforcers, elicitors, and targets (Parke & Slaby, 1983). According to Kostelnik, Whiren, and Stein (1986), aggression is imminent if

- Children stop laughing

- Their voices become strident or complaining

- Facial expressions show fear, anger, or distress

- Talk moves from pretend to real menace (p. 9).

Superhero or War Play

An issue for many early childhood programs is what should be their policy about superhero play. **Superhero play** is defined as "the active, physical play of children pretending to be media characters imbued with extraordinary abilities, including superhuman strength or the ability to transform themselves into superhuman entities. While some view this play as violent and aggressive, it is not so by definition" (Boyd, 1997, p. 23). However, the underlying themes of superhero play are power and control.

Some of the arguments for superhero play are that:

- It provides a potentially rich play experience.

- It facilitates gross motor and sociodramatic play.

- It's part of children's natural play and development.

- It helps children develop peer interaction, planning, perspective taking, negotiating skills, and language development.

- Superheroes are attractive role models (i.e., good, generous, well liked, brave, resourceful, and able to solve all problems).

- Children can work through their anxiety and express their feelings.

- It provides girls with an opportunity to be in a power role.

- It promotes divergent play themes.

    Likewise, some arguments against superhero play are that:

- It glamourizes fighting as a way of solving problems.

FOR REFLECTION

Sweden has banned the production of war toys, Malta has banned their sale, and Spain and Germany do not permit the advertising of war toys. What, if anything, do you think Canada should do about the manufacture, sale, and advertising of war toys? If you were the director of a school-age program (for children from five to nine years of age), what would be your policy on superhero play in your program?

- It desensitizes children to aggression.

- Children re-enact television or video stories rather than using their own imaginations.

- It may frighten other children nearby.

- It sends a message that violence is okay.

- Some children may confuse reality and fantasy.

- This type of play may obsess some children.

- It promotes child consumerism.

Adult Intervention in Children's Play

Another issue in play is adult intervention. Some professionals believe that one should never intervene in children's play unless a child is in danger. This view was especially common prior to 1960. However, the idea that it is appropriate and maybe desirable to intervene in young children's play has been gaining acceptance in the past four decades.

Smilansky's study (1968) showed that children's sociodramatic play could be enriched by training. Subsequent play research from special education programs has also demonstrated that children can be taught effective strategies to facilitate their play with other children. The rationale for play training is that if play is important for young children's development, children with poor play skills are at a disadvantage and can benefit from specific help to improve their play and therefore their development. Overall, research on play training has shown positive effects (Johnson, Christie, & Yawkey, 1999).

Play training is rather a catchall term. It is generally used "to describe a variety of play enrichment strategies employed primarily with preschool-age children" (Trawick-Smith, 1998, p. 118). It is often equated to mean teaching children who are having difficulties with play specific strategies for how to be successful in play situations, usually sociodramatic play. However, the scope of play training and intervention is broader than that.

Some might argue that any adult support of children's play is intervention. Therefore the issue is not so much whether adults do or should intervene in children's play but more the degree of the intervention. Such intervention can range from moving blocks out of a pathway near an exit door to more formal training to help a child develop specific strategies to enter an existing play situation successfully. Most of the play training approaches in the early years are more informal than formal (Trawick-Smith, 1998).

A question for early childhood educators is when and how to intervene. When to intervene may be determined by the individual child's (a) developmental level (e.g., assisting a toddler who is getting frustrated with a too-difficult toy), (b) request (e.g., "We need someone to be the grandma. Will you [the educator] be the grandma?" results in the adult as co-player), or (c) behaviour (e.g, children playing horses with ropes around their necks for reins requires immediate redirection/modification of the play). Some interventions are obvious and necessary for children's safety. Others are desirable to keep a play situation going (e.g., providing alternatives such as "Could you have another bear in your story?"). Sometimes intervention is needed to create or structure a play situation (e.g., retelling a story for the children to act out). Sometimes one needs to serve as an interpreter or coach for a child (e.g., "I think what Mischa is trying to tell you is . . ."). Sometimes the best strategy is to watch and see if intervention is necessary at all. For example, if two children are arguing over who gets to be the "bad guy," watchful waiting may give the children a chance to resolve their problem to their mutual satisfaction through compromise and negotiation without any adult assistance.

Gender Differences in Young Children's Play

A concern of many parents and educators is to prevent gender discrimination. Adults can become concerned when they see young children, despite their best efforts to promote gender-neutral play, preferring to play with same-sex playmates and gender-specific toys.

FOR REFLECTION

Can children's play really be gender-neutral?

Gender differences in young children's play can be seen in their choice of play partners, play materials, and types of play. Children tend to seek out same-sex playmates as early as age two, and this tendency increases with age (Hughes, 1995; Thorne, 1993). When children play with same-sex playmates, the play is more traditionally typed gender play. For example, girls will choose to play with dolls and art materials while boys will choose blocks and wheeled toys (Johnson, Christie, & Yawkey, 1999). This gender preference in materials can be seen between ages two and three or earlier (Hughes, 1995). A gender preference is also seen in outdoor play with girls preferring swings and climbers and boys wheeled toys and construction materials (Frost, 1992). However, generally girls prefer indoor play while boys prefer outdoor play (Henniger, 1985; Thorne, 1993). Boys' outdoor play is likely to be more physical although they also do more dramatic play outdoors than indoors (Frost, 1992). These findings raise questions about the amount of time and types of dramatic play materials for boys in outdoor play environments. Children's individual views of gender appropriateness in play can be influenced by their culture, family, and background experiences.

Idealization of Play

Is play a concept that is really too good to be true? It sometimes seems that play in early childhood education and care is promoted as a cure-all or inoculant in children's early development: If only a young child could, would, should play, then there would be no difficulties with their development. Sadly, this is not the case.

While society may have trivialized play (Kelly-Byrne, 1989), early childhood educators typically have not. Most of us believe that play is important for young children's optimal development and are typically strong advocates for play. A danger is that our support, and often defence, of play may become too simplistic. Play is a very complex subject and to reduce it to a simplistic "Play is good" does not adequately reflect what we know about play. What is needed are early childhood professionals who are knowledgeable, realistic, and articulate about play and its role in young children's development. This means that there are times when one has to state that there is no consensus in the field or the research about a particular question about play. Or that a definitive answer is not possible. To be fair and honest we should present a balanced and realistic view of play, its potential, its effects, and problems.

Summary of this Chapter

The key themes in this chapter are that:

- Play is difficult to define. There is no universally agreed-upon definition.

- Characteristics and types of play can be useful ways of describing play.

- Children and adults seem to have differing views of play.

- Historical, theoretical, cultural, and social contexts influence our ideas about play.

- Stages in and theories about children's play development have been suggested in the play literature.

- Play affects children's development including physical, social, emotional, and cognitive areas.

- The early childhood educator's roles in fostering play include planner, observer, facilitator, resource, model, mediator, coach, assessor, and advocate.

- Both indoor and outdoor play environments are important for fostering children's play.

- The roles and values of play are still debated. Some controversial issues include rough and tumble play, superhero play, adult intervention in children's play, gender differences, and idealization of play.

Key Terms

adventure playground, 286
arousal modulation or arousal-
    seeking theory, 265

cognitive theories of play, 264
creative playground, 285
metacommunicative theory, 265

Resources

For Sharing with Children

A book to share with children is Morris, A., photographs by Ken Heyman. *Play*. 1998. New York: Lothrop, Lee & Shepard Books. One of the series of books by this author with marvellous photos of children playing in more than a dozen countries; very little text.

Also recommended for sharing with children is *National Geographic*, December 1994, Volume 186, No. 6. The lead theme is "animals at play." A series of action photos of animals playing with each other and materials, including a polar bear with a tire near Churchill, Manitoba (Brown, S.L., pp. 2–35). Excellent for discussions with children. Worth the effort to find in a used bookstore or garage sale.

For Further Reading

If you want to know more about play and early childhood, my favourite sources are:

Johnson, J.E., Christie, J.F., & Yawkey, T.D. 1999. *Play and early childhood development* (2nd ed.). New York: Longman. The latest and most comprehensive work on the subject.

Hughes, F.P. 1995. *Children, play, and development* (2nd ed.) Boston: Allyn and Bacon. Excellent overview

Mulligan, V. 1996. *Children's play: An introduction for care providers*. Don Mills, ON: Addison-Wesley Publishers.

Shipley, C.D. 1993. *Empowering children: Play-based curriculum for lifelong learning*. Scarborough: Nelson Canada.

Goleman, H. & E.V. Jacobs. (Eds.) 1994. *Children's play in child-care settings*. Albany, NY: State University of New York Press. Research on play.

For information about play environments indoors:

Vogel, N. 1997. *Getting started: Materials and equipment for active learning preschools.* Ypsilanti, MI: High/Scope Press. Succinct (49 pages); a good beginning.

Bronson, M.B. 1995. *The right stuff for children from birth to 8: Selecting play materials to support development.* Washington, DC: NAEYC. Divided by ages.

Moyer, J. (Ed.) 1995. *Selecting educational equipment and materials for school and the home.* Wheaton, MD: Association for Childhood Education International. 4th revision; detailed; 76 pages.

For information about play environments outdoors:

A somewhat unexpected source of good information about children's play-grounds in Canada is Canada Mortgage and Housing Corporation (a federal government agency). They publish two recently revised (1997) documents on playgrounds: *Play spaces for preschoolers, and Play opportunities for school-age children 6–14 years of age.* Both are available locally from your CMHC office or from

Canadian Housing Information Centre
Canada Mortgage and Housing Corporation
National Office
700 Montreal Road
Ottawa, ON K1A 0P7
www.cmhc-schl.gc.ca

Rivkin, M.S. 1995. *The great outdoors: Restoring children's right to play outside.* Washington, DC: National Association for the Education of Young Children.

Theemes, T. 1999. *Let's go outside! Designing the early childhood playground.* Ypsilanti, MI: High/Scope Press. Good detail, including checklist for maintenance and lists of toxic and nontoxic plants.

For cooperative play and gender issues:

Schlank, C.H. & Metzger, B. 1997. *Together and equal: Fostering cooperative play and promoting gender equity in early childhood programs.* Boston: Allyn & Bacon.

 ## Useful Addresses and Web Sites

In addition to Canada Mortgage and Housing Corporation, listed above, you might try, for details on current Canadian standards for playgrounds:

Canadian Standards Association
178 Rexdale Blvd.
Etobicoke, ON M9W 1R3

Tel: 800-463-6727; 416-747-2620
Fax: 416-747-4292
E-mail: vincicj@csa.ca
Web site: www.csa.ca

For information and workshops about children's playgrounds:

Canadian Parks/Recreation Association
306-1600 James Naismith Drive
Gloucester, ON K1A 5N4
Tel: 613-748-5651
Fax: 613-748-5854
E-mail: cpra@activeliving.ca
Web site: www.activeliving.ca/activeliving/cpra

Health Canada has information on playground injuries/safety and equipment on its Web site at www.hc-sc.gc.ca/hpb/lcdc/brch/.

The International Association for the Child's Right to Play is a non-governmental organization that advocates for children's right to play. It publishes IPA Declaration of the Child's Right to Play (brochure), a magazine, and other publications, and organizes conferences and workshops. Contact: www.ncsu.edu/ipa. The Canadian representative is Valerie Franczek:

Play Resource Centre
Society for Children and Youth of B.C.
3644 Slocan St.
Vancouver, B.C. V5M 3E8
Tel: 604-433-4180
Fax: 604-433-9611

The early childhood professional organizations listed in Resources in Chapter 4 have many good publications about play, including useful brochures to share with families. For example, ACEI's "A Parent's Guide to Playground Safety" by Joe L. Frost & Nita L. Drescher. (n.d.) and NAEYC's "Playgrounds: Safe and Sound" by Janet Brown McCracken (1999).

Part Three

Early Childhood Programs

This dimension focuses on the varied and diverse programs available for young children and their families in Canada today.

Chapter 8 Day Care: Debated and Diverse

Day care is a hot topic. It is the most widely debated type of early childhood program. This chapter describes the development of day care in Canada, the types of day care programs, the effects of day care, and some of the issues surrounding day care.

Chapter 9 Nursery School: Early Childhood Program with a Future?

Nursery school has made important contributions to early childhood education and care in Canada and else-where. This chapter looks at these contributions, the development of nursery school in Canada, the types of programs, children's experiences beginning an early childhood program, and the future of nursery school.

Chapter 10 Kindergarten: Preschool or Primary?

Kindergarten is the most widely accessible early childhood program in Canada. This chapter outlines its development and growth, and the types of kindergartens, as well as the issues of multi-age grouping, retention, curriculum, and continuity. The similarities and differences among kindergarten, nursery school, and day-care programs are also discussed.

chapter 8

Day Care: Debated and Diverse

"I raised my children at home, why can't this generation?"
"I'm a better mother because I work."
"If I don't work, my children don't eat. What am I supposed to do?"
—Comments from mothers

Day care is a hot topic in Canada, and has been for the past 20 years or more. One can scarcely read an article about families with young children in a magazine or newspaper and not find statements about day care. It is also a frequent topic in other media, such as radio talk shows. I sometimes think the shelf with books on day care in my local bookstore grows longer every time I survey it.

Day care is not only a frequent topic of discussion, but also a much-debated issue. In conversations with your family and friends and at social gatherings you have probably heard comments such as the ones above as well as the following:

"Our society doesn't value motherhood. Why doesn't raising a family count?"

"If you want other people to care for your children, you shouldn't have any."

"I need to work for my own self-esteem and satisfaction."

"I loved my job but I think it's important to stay home with my children for their first few years."

"In my profession, a person can't take off three to five years to raise children."

"In my culture, women are expected to stay home and care for the family."

"Caring for children is a joint responsibility of fathers and mothers. Both should be caregivers; both should earn money."

The need for and use of day care has grown in the past 30 years as a result of many of the demographic and societal trends discussed in Chapters 2 and 3. For example, there are now more women with young children in the paid labour force, they are more likely to be working full time, and they are returning to work sooner after the birth of their children. In addition, there are more lone-parent families (usually headed by women), more poor families, and fewer families with relatives who can help with child care.

Two significant societal trends in North America and Europe in the latter half of the twentieth century were the women's movement and the changing nature of work. During this time the status of women in society improved in many respects, although not universally (e.g., women in Canada still earn less than men do, although this gap has decreased). One positive change has been the increasing career options available now that were not possible for my mother's generation. Subsequent generations of women are likely to have more options than you or I have.

On the other hand, Canadians are often ambivalent about working mothers. In a Statistics Canada survey, a majority of respondents thought it was important for women to be in the labour force, yet 59 percent of men and 51 percent of women agreed that a preschool-age child will likely suffer if both parents are employed (Ghalam, 1997). In recent years, there has been increased discussion of the desirability and feasibility of the so-called "supermother," who works full-time at a demanding job, is a great mom and wife, and volunteers in the community. Numerous books (e.g., Crittenden, 1999) and articles (e.g., Chisholm, 1999; Fine, 1999a) have questioned how realistic, achievable, and desirable being a supermother truly is for women with young children.

A second trend that promises to be of even greater import in the future than in the recent past is the changing nature of work. With ever-increasing technology, "going to work" has taken on a wide variety of meanings. For example, some people don't actually "go" anywhere, but work from a home office or telecommute. People are working varied hours and days, many in jobs that did not exist a decade ago. The decline of the manufacturing and resource industries, combined with economic booms and downturns along with the rise of the technological and service sectors, has also changed the face of work in Canada. These trends and other societal and economic trends discussed in previous chapters have resulted in changed dynamics between families and work. According to

McNaughton (1996), "the lessons from past generations do not prepare today's family for their unique experiences" (p. 17).

Two terms that are often used interchangeably are day care and child care. These are not really the same. **Child care** can refer to all types of care for children under legal age including foster care, day care, and care for young offenders. Child care in Canada consists of complex combinations of services and programs that can vary from region to region. It is a more encompassing term than day care. *Day care* typically refers to out-of-home care, by non-relatives, usually for 8 to 12 hours a day for young children in a group setting. The term **day care** is derived from the earlier term **day nursery**. *Day nursery* is the historical term and was defined as "an institution having one primary purpose—namely, the day care of children who remain part of the family unit but who for social or economic reasons cannot receive ordinary parental care" (Whipple, 1929, p. 87).

There are many types of day care, such as group day care, family day care, and school-age care. While day care is usually defined as being from early morning to early evening, primarily for the children of working parents, this is not always the case. For example, many families do not work a nine-to-five, Monday-to-Friday week. For some of these families, "day care" is actually "night care" if their parents work evenings or nights.

Also, day care is not just for families that are working full time. It is needed and used by families working part time and those families with a parent in the home. Some examples of this latter case in my experience have been children placed in a day-care program because a social services agency thought this was a more beneficial environment for the child during the day, in families where the parent was caring for an elderly relative, where a parent was undergoing extended radiation and chemotherapy treatment, or where there was a difficult pregnancy. There are many reasons why day care is needed and used by today's families.

This chapter will describe the variety of day-care programs available in Canada. Never have day-care options been greater than today. This is good news for both families and early childhood educators. There are many career options possible for you as an early childhood educator. (More options are described in Chapters 9, 10, and 11.) In addition, this chapter will examine the development of day care in Canada, the effects of day care, and some of the key issues associated with day care.

Here are some questions to think about while you read this chapter:

· What is it about day care that causes definite and often heated responses? If one mentions kindergarten or nursery school, this does not seem to happen.
· How did day care in Canada develop?
· Why is there a need for day care?
· Why is day care often considered "custodial," while other programs such as kindergarten and nursery school are considered "educational"?
· What are some of the different types of day-care programs?
· What are some roles of the early childhood educator in day-care programs? How do these vary with the type of program?
· What should parents look for when choosing day care? Why might they choose different types of programs?
· Is day care beneficial or harmful for young children?
· Does auspice (i.e., sponsorship) of a program affect program quality?

The Development of Day Care in Canada

As outlined in Chapter 5, the origins of day care in Canada are found in the early day nurseries. The three main groups responsible for the early development of day care in Canada were (a) religious groups, (b) charitable and philanthropic organizations and individuals, and (c) agencies such as social welfare.

Earliest Development

The Grey Nuns in Montreal are credited with establishing the first day-care programs in Canada, in the mid–1850s. This was a time of increasing industrialization and urbanization in Canada that resulted in the need for day care for the children of working mothers. At that time, the only option for care was often an older sibling; if there was no older sibling or another caregiver the alternative was leaving the child alone while the mother worked. The Grey Nuns recognized the problem and established *les salles d'asiles* (shelters). Between 1858 and 1922, 60,271 children attended programs operated by the Grey Nuns (Dumont, in Desjardins, 1989). Similar programs were also established by the Sisters of Providence and Soeurs Franciscaines de Marie. Most of these shelters later became orphanages (Baillargeon, 1989). Also in Montreal, wealthy anglophone women established the Montreal Day Nursery in 1887. Although this was a charitable endeavour, the day nursery also served as an employment agency for domestic help for wealthier families. (The same pattern of development was seen in Toronto.) Religious organizations were also responsible for the establishment of early day nurseries and orphanages in New Brunswick, Prince Edward Island, and Nova Scotia.

James Hughes, who as superintendent of the Toronto public schools was responsible for the first public school kindergarten in Canada (see Chapter 10), was also instrumental in the establishment of early day nurseries in Toronto. Hester How, a principal of a school in Toronto, was concerned that students were unable to come to school because they had to stay home and care for younger siblings. She allowed the children to bring their younger siblings to school and convinced James Hughes to establish the Crèche, which later became the responsibility of a local women's organization (now known as Victoria Day Care Services). Similar efforts by other volunteer groups in other provinces resulted in the establishment of early day nurseries.

Early governmental involvement in day nurseries was seen in the establishment and operation of the City Crèche day nursery at Infants' Hospital Centre in Vancouver. Both charitable groups (i.e., Associated Charities) and local government (i.e., Vancouver City Health Department) funded it. In 1916, the program came under the jurisdiction of the Health Department.

Thus it can be seen that the earliest development of these day nurseries was the result of efforts by charitable, religious, and philanthropic groups. The early day nurseries often provided medical and dental services, counselling, food, clothing, home visits, lectures on child-rearing, and loans of money—many of the services that are now the responsibility of social service agencies. The early decades of the twentieth century saw the rise of social welfare agencies. According to Schulz (1978), "with the 'professionalization' of social work, day care lost the character of an old-fashioned charity and became an institutionalized form of welfare" (p. 148).

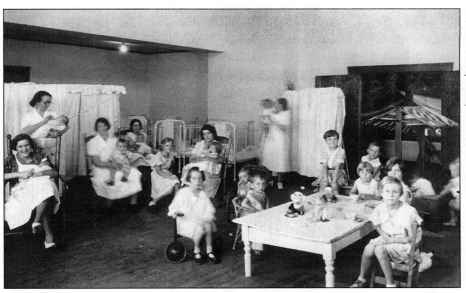

National Archives of Canada/PA147936

Children and staff at the
Ottawa Day Nursery c.1920

A typical day in a day nursery of this time began with the children's arrival, starting from 6:30 a.m. Upon arrival, each child was given a health inspection, a bath, clean clothes, and breakfast. This was followed by outdoor play until about 10 a.m., when the youngest children had a nap and the older children were given milk, followed by indoor play until dinner at noon. The afternoon program was a nap followed by playtime (in or outdoors) until supper, which was between 4 and 5:30 p.m. The children were picked up between 5:30 and 7 p.m. (O'Connor, 1995; Prochner, 1996; Varga, 1997; Whipple, 1929). Most day nurseries were open Monday to Friday, with a few opening on Saturday afternoons. As can be seen from the schedule, there was a heavy emphasis on children's health, nutrition, safety, and hygiene. This focus is understandable as it was still a time of relatively high child, especially infant, mortality. Staff members were called *matrons* and *nurses*. There were no government regulations at this time. For example, the number of children could range from 6 to 8 to more than 100 per day nursery (Varga, 1993).

Day Nurseries and the Second World War

The next significant growth stage in the development of day nurseries in Canada occurred during the Second World War, when there was a need for women to work in the war industries. The Dominion–Provincial Agreement for Wartime Day Nurseries provided a 50-percent federal–provincial cost sharing to fund day-care centres for the children of mothers working in essential industries. However, only Ontario and Quebec established centres under this program. By the end of the Second World War, there were 28 centres in Ontario and six in Quebec (of which only two were francophone, because at that time the Catholic Church condemned day care as government interfering in family life) (Desjardins, 1992).

The first of these day nurseries was No. 1 Wartime Day Nursery in downtown Toronto, which also served as a demonstration centre (Stapleford, 1976). By the end of the Second World War, 28 Ontario day nurseries enrolled 1,200 children from two to five years old; in addition, there were 42 programs for 3,000 school-aged children from ages 6 to 14 (Stapleford, 1976). The wartime day nurseries in Ontario were under the jurisdiction of the Day Nurseries Branch, although municipal governments did the actual supervision. This arrangement established a precedent of municipal and provincial administration of day-care centres that is still found in many provinces.

The staffs were given a training course at the Institute of Child Study at the University of Toronto. Most of the day nurseries had four paid staff members and were open nearly 12 hours a day. In the children's program,

> great stress was laid on outdoor play of a vigorous, active nature, whereas indoors the play was quieter and fostered creative activities on the part of the children. During the routine periods for eating and sleeping, the children were taught to follow good procedures and develop independence. (Stapleford, 1976, p. 3)

Basically, the program of the wartime day nursery was an extended-day version of the Institute of Child Study nursery school.

The wartime day nurseries in Ontario were administered by provincially approved local committees. In 1943, the original provincial advisory committee became the Division of Wartime Day Nurseries and Day Care under the Department of Public Welfare, with Dorothy Millichamp (from the Institute of Child Study) as its director.

When the war ended, the federal–provincial arrangement ceased. The provincial governments planned to close the day nurseries because it was assumed that when the men returned from active service and resumed their jobs, women's services would no longer be needed. However, parents had a different idea and protested. In Ontario, they formed the Day Nursery and Day Care Parents' Association to lobby for retaining the day nurseries. This group held protest marches and lobbied elected officials. Similar protests were held in Quebec by anglophone parents, but these were not successful (Desjardins, 1992). In Ontario, however, these actions resulted in the provincial government drafting the Day Nurseries Act of 1946. The Act was written, in large part, by the staff from the Institute of Child Study and modelled on the program at the Institute's nursery school (this program is described in Chapter 9). Thus, the Act reflected the Institute's perspective. For example, the Act required that a day nursery's timetable "conform to the standards currently accepted by the Institute of Child Study of the University of Toronto" (quoted in Wright, 2000, p. 108). Each revision of the Act included this requirement until 1968 (Richardson, 1989).

The Ontario Day Nurseries Act

This Act was a major force in Canadian legislation on day care. However, it was not the first legislation. Day care regulations had been included in the Welfare

National Archives of Canada/PA112751

A Second World War day nursery in Toronto.

Institutions Licensing Act in British Columbia in 1943 and the Alberta Child Welfare Act in 1944. Again, one can see the child-welfare focus for early day care. Ontario's Day Nurseries Act of 1946 was significant because it changed the focus from child welfare to child care. (Most provincial legislation setting standards for day care was first done in the 1960s.)

The significant features of the Day Nurseries Act were the:

• Establishment of standards and licensing

• Provincial–municipal cost sharing

• Establishment of the Day Nurseries Branch.

According to Elsie Stapleford and Mary Wright (personal communications, December 1999/January 2000), one of the most significant lessons learned from the experience with wartime day nurseries in Canada and Britain was the need to ensure that children experienced good programs. In the Day Nurseries Act not only were standards set out, but also licensing and monitoring compliance through regular inspections were included. Although this is a common approach used today, in 1946 it was considered to be very progressive and innovative. Its immediate effect was somewhat of a mixed blessing, because 16 of the 28 wartime day nurseries in Ontario and all of the school-age programs closed because of the new licensing regulations (Schultz, 1978). However, by 1956, 90 percent of nurseries in Ontario were licensed and this percentage increased to 95 percent by 1966 (Stapleford, 1976).

The Day Nurseries Act also set out provisions for provincial–municipal cost sharing. The province of Ontario contributed 50 percent of the costs of municipally operated centres and 50 percent of a municipality's contribution to other types of centres for children under six years (it did not apply to school-age programs). Thus this cost sharing applied only to specifically designated programs. The number of centres benefiting from this arrangement was 24 out of 164 (15 percent) in 1947 to 46 of 426 (11 percent) in 1967 (Stapleford, 1976).

The establishment of the Day Nurseries Branch was significant because it was the first provincial child care regulatory agency. Elsie Stapleford succeeded Dorothy Millichamp and headed the branch from 1948 to her retirement nearly 30 years later (see Focus 8.1).

Thus, the Ontario Day Nurseries Act of 1946 became the model and standard for day care legislation in not only Ontario but also the rest of Canada. Day care in Canada grew slowly if somewhat erratically until the mid-1960s.

Day Care in the Latter Twentieth Century

The mid-1960s was the beginning of a growth period for day care in Canada. It was also the time that many provinces passed day-care legislation. Another significant impetus for day care was the passing of the Canada Assistance Plan in 1966. According to Howard Clifford, "the first major piece of federal legislation to impact on all provinces and territories was the Canada Assistance Plan

Focus 8.1

Elsie Stapleford: A Profile

Elsie Stapleford was an early graduate of the Institute of Child Study and spent much of her career fostering the development of day care in Ontario. I asked Elsie to tell me about the Day Nurseries Act and the establishment of the Day Nurseries Branch. The wartime day nurseries were based on the program at the Institute of Child Study, as the Institute was very influential in the development of early day-care programs in Ontario and elsewhere. Elsie said, "we showed them [government officials and critics] what a good program the war program was." At the end of the Second World War, when the government wanted to cut out day nurseries, the mothers' lobby was "very important," as was the *Toronto Star*'s campaign to keep the day nurseries: "they got the public aware of it." Therefore, when the Day Nurseries legislation was suggested, "it was not a hard sell." She credits Dr. Blatz and Messrs. Brunelle and Band (minister and deputy minister after the Second World War) with being very supportive of legislation for day nurseries.

In 1992 Elsie Stapleford wrote, "a realization of the remarkable changes that day care has gone through in the past century stimulates innovative thinking on ways to meet the current crisis in child care" (p. 119). I thought of this statement when I asked Elsie what advice she would give to Canadian policy-makers and politicians about day care in the twenty-first century, and she referred me to an article she had written in 1987. In this article, based on a brief

she had presented to the federal government the previous year, she recommended that, "a range of services should be grouped together so that there is as much continuity of care as possible for each child" (p. 16). These services would be housed in the local elementary schools and include:

· Day care (including school-age programs)
· Kindergarten
· Family day home support services
· Playground
· Parent cooperative nursery school
· Counselling services
· Parent education programs
· Family resource centre
· Programs for children with disabilities and their families.

These services would be integrated with existing community services, such as libraries, recreation programs, and health centres. In addition, she recommended a day-care centre in every high school as a laboratory and demonstration facility for students who would observe and assist in programs. This would create "a firm basis for developing a generation of young people better prepared for the responsibilities of parenthood. As citizens, they would be able to make wise decisions as to community support for families and children" (1987, p. 17). Plus, some of these high school students might then choose careers in early childhood education. Elsie Stapleford would be a great role model for them.

Sources: Stapleford, 1987; 1992; interview January 2000

(CAP)" (1992, p. xv). In this legislation, child care came under the general heading of "social welfare." CAP made federal money available to the provinces and territories to assist low-income families. However, it was not meant to be a universal program, therefore it was perceived as a welfare program. It did have the effect of helping to increase the number of day-care programs across Canada.

Day care grew in the 1970s and 1980s. Indicators of its higher profile were two federal reports on child care. The Report of the Task Force on Child Care

FOR REFLECTION

Fein and Clarke-Stewart (1973) wrote, "the history of day care between recurring crises is a history of reformers and kindly people" (p. 13). Is this an accurate statement of the development of day care in Canada?

chaired by Katie Cooke was submitted in 1986 and contained 53 recommendations. The subsequent year, another federal report, *Sharing the Responsibility: Report of the Special Commission on Child Care*, chaired by Shirley Martin, submitted its report, with 39 recommendations. (The reason for two reports so close together was that the Cooke report was commissioned by the Liberal government, and when that government was voted out of office the Conservative government commissioned its own report.) Despite the difference in origins, both of these reports made numerous recommendations applicable to day-care programs, including funding, subsidies, professional education, programs, and special programs for children with disabilities and First Nations communities. Most of the recommendations from these two reports were not enacted by the federal governments that commissioned the reports.

Day-Care Centres

If you ask your friends or family to describe a day-care program, they are likely to describe a centre-based group day care for three- and four-year-old children. Even though this is not the most frequently used type of child care (see Table 8.1), it seems to be the one that most people associate with the term *day care*.

There are many types of group day-care centres, including infant/toddler centres for children under age three, school-age programs, campus day care, work-related child care, cooperative day-care programs, and specialized centres such as those for children with special needs.

Typically, a group day-care centre is located in a building of its own or in another location such as a private home, community centre, church, commercial building, hospital, recreational facility, factory, or at a college or university. Some of these programs are quite small (i.e., fewer than six children), and some are quite large (i.e., 100+ children) when several centres or programs are grouped together, such as in some campus day-care programs.

TABLE 8.1   USE OF DAY-CARE ARRANGEMENTS

Distribution of children aged 0 to 11 years by type of non-parental child-care arrangement, 1994–1995

PRIMARY CARE ARRANGEMENT	%
UNRELATED FAMILY HOME DAY-CARE, UNREGULATED	34.2
CARE BY RELATIVE, IN CHILD'S OR SOMEONE ELSE'S HOME	21.4
REGULATED CHILD-CARE CENTRE	15.7
IN CHILD'S HOME BY NON-RELATIVE, UNREGULATED	14.2
UNRELATED FAMILY HOME DAY-CARE, REGULATED	7.2
BEFORE- OR AFTER-SCHOOL PROGRAM, REGULATED	4.0
SIBLING OR SELF-CARE	2.5
OTHER	0.7*

*Estimate less reliable due to high sampling variability. Source: NLSCY, 1996, p. 25

Just as the location of day-care centres can vary, so can the hours of operation. While most open between 7 and 8 a.m. and close between 5 and 6:30 p.m., some open very early in the morning to accommodate parents whose workday begins at 6 a.m. or earlier. Others stay open late; for example, until 11 p.m. A few are open on weekends. Some others accommodate seasonal demands for care, such as in rural farming communities or near coastal fish processing plants.

The children's program in a day-care centre will vary with the type of program, age of the children, hours of operation, and philosophy of the program. However, in general, children in day care participate daily in:

- Free play, both indoors and outdoors

- Group times (e.g., storytime, singing, sharing time, discussions, etc.)

- Morning and afternoon snack and lunch (these may be provided by the program or brought by the children)

- Nap/rest/quiet time

- Group and/or individual projects (often related to a theme such as planting seeds or gardening when studying spring).

These activities are balanced so that active activities are usually followed by quieter ones (e.g., circle time after morning free play, or snack after outdoor play). Some programs provide activities outside of the centre, such as field trips, swimming lessons, trips to the local library, or play in the local park or recreation centre.

Group day-care centres in Canada are regulated by provincial and territorial legislation. This legislation typically establishes the minimum standards for staff:child ratio, the physical environment including amount of indoor and outdoor space, hours of operation, educator qualifications, the children's program, safety, and other factors. If you would like to check the legislation in your province or territory, Web sites for this information are given in the Resources section at the end of this chapter. Regulations may change frequently and several provinces are currently reviewing their regulations, so early childhood educators need to be aware of sources for the latest information.

Early childhood professional organizations have also set out recommended standards for group day care. (These may or may not be the same as your provincial/territorial ones.) For example, both the Canadian Child Care Federation (CCCF) and the National Association for the Education of Young Children (NAEYC) recommend maximum group sizes and staff:child ratios depending on the size of the group of:

For 3-year-olds	10–14 children	1:5–7
For 4- to 6-year-olds	16–18 children	1:8–9
For 6- to 9-year-olds	20–24 children	1:10–12

Quality and licensing are discussed in Chapter 12.

This means that, according to the above recommendations, for a group of 16 four-year-olds there should be at least two early childhood educators, while for a group of 24 school-age children there should also be at least two early childhood educators. The qualifications required of these educators can vary across provinces/territories.

Although many people think of a group day-care centre when they think of day care, this does not mean that people uncritically accept this form of child care. There are perceived advantages and disadvantages to all types of day care. Some perceived advantages for group day-care centres include:

- Qualified early childhood educators

- Provision of substitute educators when needed

- Group socialization experiences for young children

- More than one adult for the children to relate to

- Variety of equipment and materials

- Equipped outdoor play facility

- Licensed facility that meets at least minimum standards

- Periodic inspections by regulatory agencies.

What other points would you add to the list?

Some common points made against group day-care centres that you may hear are:

- Not every child thrives in a group setting

- Non-traditional work hours are not always covered

- Young children are exposed to more illnesses in groups of children

- Sick children are not permitted

- Young children, especially infants and toddlers, are best cared for at home by their parents

- Taxpayers should not be paying for day-care centres

- Licensing requirements are only a minimum, do not cover all factors influencing quality care, and therefore are not a guarantee of quality and should not be over-relied upon.

What other points would you add to this list? An early childhood educator needs to be aware of and able to respond to both types of arguments.

Cooperative Day Care

Cooperative day-care programs are usually organized and administered by parents. They do not have as long a history in Canada as cooperative nursery schools. One example of cooperative day care is the Ottawa Federation of Parent Day Cares, which is the umbrella organization for several parent co-operative day cares in the Ottawa-Carleton region.

As parents using a day-care centre typically work, it may be impossible for them to participate in the daily program as volunteer staff, which is character-istic of parent cooperative nursery schools. Therefore, parental contributions to a cooperative day care are usually in the areas of policy making, serving on the board of the day care, fundraising, publicity, attending evening meetings, making materials, and participating in weekend activities such as centre maintenance and repair. One type of day-care program that often begins as a cooperative is campus day care.

Cooperative nursery school programs are discussed in Chapter 9.

Campus Day Care

Campus day care provides care for the children of students, faculty, and staff at post-secondary institutions. Children from the community may also enrol if there is space available. Although campus day-care centres are often used for observation and practicum sites, they are not the same as laboratory or demon-stration schools.

Laboratory and demonstration schools are described in Chapter 9.

Students with young children face not only the usual student difficulties of finances, difficult class schedules, demanding courses, lack of study time, and need to work, but also family responsibilities and child-care expenses. Both male and female students with young children experience stress related to family responsibilities, including child care (Rosen & Wilson, 1999). According to a study at Ryerson Polytechnic University in Toronto, the lack of affordable child care was a definite deterrent for students with young children trying to complete their post-secondary education (Rosen & Wilson, 1999).

Some campus day-care programs began when a group of student parents got together to try to organize child care among themselves. In time, these arrangements evolved into centre-based care. Two movements that have helped the development of campus day care are the political activism of students and the women's movement. On many campuses, the women's caucus and the student society have been driving forces in the establishment and expansion of campus day care.

Campus day-care centres are usually located on or near the campus of a post-secondary institution. They range in size from relatively small to those including several centres and accommodating children from infancy through school-age. Focus 8.2 provides a description of one of Canada's larger campus day-care programs.

Campus day-care centres may be administered by a post-secondary institu-tion, student society, parent board, or an outside agency or contractor. Increasingly, campus day care is being recognized and supported by more students, staff, and faculty. For example, at my university, the women's caucus, the faculty association, and several unions have lobbied for expanding the campus

Focus 8.2

Campus Child Care: Camosun College Child-Care Services

by Linda Kusz, Child Care Supervisor

Camosun College has operated child care on two campuses since 1990. Child care is a student service and is part of the Finance and College Services Division. In 1990 the services provided 40 full-time spaces for children aged 18 months to 5 years. In 1995 the Ministry provided funding for a new facility at the Interurban campus and child care expanded its services to 70 full-time spaces for children aged 0 to 6 years. Child care provides spaces for children of students, faculty, staff, and the community. Our goal is to maintain a 75-percent students' children enrollment and 25 percent other.

The centres are open from September 1 to June 30 each year with closure in July and August. The program hours are 8:00 a.m. to 5:00 p.m. Monday to Friday. As the child-care programs are a department of the college, they are closed for all college closures.

There is an Advisory Board made up of parents, staff, student society, and administration. The mandate of the Board is to advise on policy and finances. They are responsible for fundraising events each year as well.

Staff are highly trained to accommodate the expertise needed to plan and implement a cohesive program. There are cyclical stress points each semester (e.g., mid-term exams) that are predictable and require the staff and program to be responsive. There is a real mix of social and economic groups who attend college and their individual needs and issues need to be respected and supported in balance with the program meeting developmentally appropriate practice.

The staff are part of the support staff union CUPE 2081 and wages and benefits make the cost of care higher than market rates in our region. To keep fees affordable for students and allow the department to break even, the College and the student society provide funding each year. The child-care department also applies for wage redress and grants to offset the real cost of care. To assist those students who still struggle to feed their children and pay child-care fees, the College and student society have created a Day Care Bursary Fund and a Trust Fund.

day-care facilities, and the student body approved a referendum on increasing student fees to support campus day care. The administration donated a building for additional infant/toddler spaces and a fundraising campaign raised $44,000 in six months from faculty, staff, campus organizations, and an administrative grant.

The advantages of a campus day-care centre include:

- Enabling women and older students (i.e., those most likely to have young children) to continue or return to college or university.

- Accommodation of the unique needs of students, such as class and exam schedules that are in the evening and on weekends.

- The program's ability to access campus resources such as green space, museums, libraries, and gyms as well as faculty members for parent education activities.

- Subsidization from a post-secondary institution by providing office equipment or supplies, furniture, maintenance, janitorial, or security services.

- Contributions to fund building or renovation costs from post-secondary institutions; some institutions have provided no-interest or low-interest mortgages for these costs.

Some of the disadvantages of campus day care can be:

- Not enough places to meet the need, especially for infant care.

- The capital costs of building centres.

- The institution's concerns about liability issues.

- Location of a day-care centre if there are multiple campuses.

- The need for the director to have good administrative skills, especially if there are several centres.

- The fact that low-income students still have difficulty affording the fees.

- Hours of operation that may not accommodate the schedules of all students.

- The fact that many students need or want care only part time, and it may be difficult to "match" two children to fill one space (this can have both licensing and financial implications for the day-care centre).

- The centre is subject to the vagaries of college and university bureaucracy and decision making.

FOR REFLECTION

Rosen and Wilson (1999) stated, "Generally universities have been slow to respond to work-family issues, and have lagged behind other institutions/corporations in the introduction of supportive family policies for faculty, staff, or students" (p. 350). Is this true at your college or university? What specifically would you like to see changed, if anything?

School-Age Care

Many people assume that once children begin elementary school the "day-care problem" will be resolved. After all, the children are now in school all day. However, the school's day does not usually cover an eight-hour workday. In addition, there are school holidays, summer vacation, and teacher professional development days. Therefore, child care is needed for school-age children as well.

School-age care is defined as centre-based (or home-based) programs for school-age children (i.e., 5–12 years old) to provide care for the hours before school, after school, on school professional days, school holidays, and other times school is not in session. The need for this type of care is most pressing for families with children in the primary grades and children with disabilities. Although not all families need or use this type of care, a Canadian survey found that 67 percent of families with children between six and nine years of age require either full- or part-time day care because of their work schedules (Lero, Goelman, Pence, Brockman, & Nuttal, 1992).

Self-care or "latchkey" children are a concern for parents and educators. This phrase "was coined during World War II to describe a child who is regularly left without adult supervision before or after school" (Strother, 1984, p. 290). The number of latchkey children in Canada is difficult to determine accurately because many children and families will not admit to this practice. One estimate is approximately 14–18 percent of 7- to 13-year-olds are latchkey children (Farrell, 1986). The National Longitudinal Survey of Children and Youth (1996) reported that 2.5 percent of children under age 11 were in sibling or self-care arrangements (see Table 8.1). Parents and educators worry about these children's safety, whereabouts ("hanging out"), substance abuse, accidents, medical emergencies, and unhealthy snacking. Many children will tell you that they find it scary going into or being alone in an empty house. Some children hide and some play the television or audio system very loud for reassurance. On the other hand, some children are not frightened or apprehensive. Some families enroll their children in a multitude of extra lessons, sports, clubs, and other activities to cover these before- and after-school periods. A few parents have told me that one of the major reasons they send their children to private schools is because of the availability of these before- and after-school activities.

Research has indicated that boys are more likely than girls to be latchkey children, and the younger and lower income the latchkey child and the more unsafe the area the more likely were negative effects for the child such as decreased social competence, negative social behaviours, and school behaviour problems (Vandell & Shumow, 1999; Vandell & Su, 1999). However, the effects of self-care are influenced by the age, maturity, and responsibility of the child, the type of neighbourhood, and the child's personality. There is no agreement on at what age children can care for themselves (Vandell & Shumow, 1999). Latchkey children need reassurance and an understanding of emergency procedures they should activate if there is a problem.

Elementary schools are a logical location for before- and after-school programs. As the child spends most of the day in the neighbourhood where the school is located, it is familiar and decreases the number of transitions for a child. (Some family day-care and recreation programs also provide before- and after-school care.) One difficulty faced by many school-age programs is that they are housed in schools or portables on school grounds that are extra space. However, if the school needs that space for classrooms in the future, then the school-age program may be evicted. In addition, the amount of space needed can be problematic. Licensing regulations for space in school-age programs varies from a minimum of 2.5 square metres per child in some Alberta jurisdictions to 4 square metres in the Yukon (Jacobs, Mill, White, & Baillargeon, 1999).

School-age care is not meant to be a continuation of school. Although some children may choose to do their homework, especially if there are adults present who can help them, instruction is not the purpose of school-age care. These programs should provide a variety of activities appropriate for the children enrolled. These activities can include arts and crafts, games and sports, puzzles, reading, work on extended projects, time for play and socializing with friends and peers, and opportunities for solitude and individual pursuits. Few provinces have any specific regulation about the curriculum in school-age programs.

The requirements for staff in school-age programs are established by the provinces and territories. These requirements are generally minimal. Sometimes a minimum age is the only requirement, as young as 16 in Saskatchewan or New Brunswick (Jacobs, Mill, White, & Baillargeon, 1999). In some jurisdictions not even a first aid certificate is required. Other provinces and territories do require education in either child care in general or in this area specifically. The question then arises as to what that education should include. As a result of their research, Jacobs, Mill, White, and Baillargeon (1999) recommended that "regulations regarding the training of staff for school-age programs should not be stipulating ECE diplomas or degrees, but should require programs that address the needs of children in middle childhood as well" (p. 249).

The staff:child ratios vary across Canada; however, 1:15 is the most frequent ratio for licensed school-age programs. The general lack of regulation for school-age care, unlike the more extensive regulation for group day care for younger children, is a concern. For example, according to Jacobs (1995), "the lack of regulations for school-age programs means that even a minimal level of care has not been established. Consequently, there is a wide range in the quality of the after school experiences for young children" (Jacobs, 1995, p. 47).

Some larger programs divide the children by ages; smaller programs usually cannot because there may be only one staff person. However, it has been recommended that, if there are sufficient numbers and the age range is wide (e.g., 5–12 years), the children be divided into three groups: 5–7, 8–10, and 11–13-year-olds (Musson, 1994).

Infant/Toddler Care

Programs for **infant/toddler care** are in great demand in Canada. They are also the programs buffeted by opposing and contradictory views and opinions. For example, because of the increased number of mothers with very young children in the paid labour force, there is a need for infant/toddler programs. However, some people and some cultures in Canadian society believe a mother's place is in the home raising her own children. This view is usually most strongly held for infants and toddlers (i.e., it's okay to go to work when the children are older, but not when they are small). There is also the concern about attachment (see Chapter 2). Parents may wonder if their infant's social and psychological adjustment will suffer and if he or she will really be securely attached to them, or to the early childhood educator.

The recent findings of brain research on the importance of the earliest years (see Chapter 2) have further fuelled this debate on both sides. One side believes that the parents are the most effective people to promote and encourage a

FOR REFLECTION

Some people question the need, desirability, or practicality of regulations regarding curriculum in school-age programs. Some think that this much regulation for curriculum is not necessary, while others think the age range (5–12 years) makes setting standards for curriculum impractical. Still others think that regulations are needed so all children have sufficient, appropriate, and interesting options in the program. Do you agree or disagree with the above points? Why?

FOR REFLECTION

What do you think are the similarities of infant/toddler programs compared to day-care programs for three- to five-year-olds?

child's growth and development. Others think that early childhood professionals can be very important in children's growth and development. Still others say that, although early childhood educators are well educated, they are caring for more than one child at a time and therefore a parent caring for one infant or toddler has more time for the individual child. Also stirred into this debate are many mothers' ambivalent feelings about returning to work after the birth of a child, or the resentment of mothers who would prefer to stay home with their young children but need to work in the paid labour force.

Because of the vulnerability of infants and toddlers, parents may be apprehensive about day care when they read stories in the newspaper about illegal care with several infants being cared for in unhealthy, inappropriate environments by untrained people. Combined with all this is the individual differences of even very young children. As discussed in Chapter 2, two infants can have quite different temperaments and developmental patterns. It's no wonder that many people have questions about infant and toddler day care.

Infancy traditionally has been defined as babyhood or until a child begins to walk, at which stage he or she becomes a *toddler* (i.e., one who toddles). As children walk at different ages and walking may be difficult to define (e.g., first unassisted step, six steps without falling, or some other set of criteria), the age of the child is typically used. A frequent definition of infancy is birth to 18 months, then 19 to 35 months for toddler programs (sometimes infancy is defined as birth to 12, 16, or 24 months).

Although there are many similarities between infant/toddler programs and care for children over three years of age, there are some key differences in emphasis. These differences are outlined in the list below.

- There is a difference in the relative degree of vulnerability of infants and toddlers and their ability to make their needs and wants known.

- Health and safety issues are paramount; information on individual children's sleep, eating, and elimination are recorded throughout the day and then shared with the parents (this is not generally done in programs for children over three unless the children have special needs).

- The younger the child, generally the more physical care the child needs; routines are important learning opportunities.

- There is typically more one-to-one attention with the youngest children (i.e., more individualized care).

- This one-to-one care has implications for the intensity and continuity of the child–educator relationship; stability of an infant's primary care arrangements is more important than for older children.

- Infant and toddler care is more expensive because of the ratios (e.g., in Canada the most common ratios are 1:3 for under 12 months; 1:4 for 12–18 months; and 1:5 for 18–36 months). In 1999, centre-based infant day care was $1,171 a month in Ottawa compared to $450 in Moncton (Pratt, 1999).

- This is a time when developmental delays begin to appear and early childhood educators need to know about early development, especially language and motor development.

- Because of limited social skills, infants especially are more dependent on the relationship with the educator for social interactions.

Overall, there are probably more similarities across levels of day-care programs than differences. For example, all early childhood programs are concerned with children's health and safety and their total development. It is a matter of different weightings or emphases (McMullen, 1999).

How are these similarities and differences translated into a program for infants and toddlers? One obvious characteristic is the small groups with few children per early childhood educator. In addition, children have primary caregivers that remain the same over time. Of course, all educators in a program are familiar with all the children and will assist each other when necessary.

The children's day is organized around children's individual schedules. Infants have different sleep and eating patterns that determine their personal schedules. Likewise, the curriculum is less formal than for older children. However, there is still planning and organization. Routines are an important part of the curriculum, as they are prime times for interaction and learning. For example, an educator talking with a child while diapering and the child looking at herself in the mirror beside the changing table are important routines for social interactions. The educator responds to the child. Often infant and toddler curricula are called *responsive.* As the children get older, there is an increased emphasis on self-help skills, growing autonomy, and independence for toddlers. Toddlers are known for their "do it myself" attitudes and active behaviours. For example, self-feeding efforts can be assisted by serving finger foods, and toddlers' activity needs fostered by opportunities to crawl, run, climb, and explore their physical environments. The toddlers' day includes indoor and outdoor play, small-group times (typically three to five children for five to ten minutes), as well as routines of snack, meals, and nap times.

The educator supports and facilitates children's play by responding to the child's initiative as well as initiating activities such as introducing the sensory activities of finger/foot painting, music-making, rhymes and fingerplays, reading, and experiencing grass, sand, and water during outdoor play. According to Lally (1995), infants and toddlers need freedom to make learning choices and to experience their world, and

> This is done by providing infants and toddlers with close and responsive relationships with caregivers; by designing safe, interesting, and developmentally appropriate environments; by giving infants uninterrupted time to explore; and by interacting with infants in ways that emotionally and intellectually support their discovery and learning.(p. 65)

The Ryerson Multi-Age Early Childhood Education Study examined infants and toddlers including preschool and school-age children in licensed

Multi-age groups with older children are discussed in Chapter 10.

Multi-age groups with older children are discussed in Chapter 10.

FOR REFLECTION

One of the issues with centre-based day care is when is the best time for children to begin. Popular writer on child development Penelope Leach (1994) has written: "While they are babies or young toddlers, even the very best daycare seldom gives them anything they positively need, and being in daycare, all day and every day, often deprives them of what they need from mothers. Daycare only comes into its own as a first choice for children themselves towards the end of the toddler period when it begins to fulfill developmental needs for companionship and education from others" (p. 70). Do you agree with Leach's statement? Why or why not?

day-care centres (Bernard, Pollard, Eggers-Piérola, & Morin, 1999). The researchers reported that there was interest in multi-age programs by families, educators, and policy-makers. Multi-age programs were considered viable especially for children with special needs and for infants and toddlers if some practices and the physical environment were modified. For example, infants should follow their own individual schedules and not the schedule of the older children, and materials should be reviewed for their suitability for a wider range of children. A gradual period of transition from a same-age to a multi-age program including educator preparation and support of families was suggested.

Home-based care is another form of day care used by Canadian families. Some families prefer this type of care; some use it because for them it is what is most available and affordable.

In-Home Day Care

In-home day care may be in a child's own home, in the home of a family member, or in someone else's home. This type of care is the preference for some families, especially those with infants and toddlers and parents who work evenings, nights, or weekends. However, due to availability, cost, or other factors, it may not be possible. Given that very few centre-based programs operate on weekends, evenings, or nights, in-home care is usually the only option for parents of young children working at these times. Three types of in-home care are nannies and au pairs, relative-care, and family day care (regulated or unregulated). In-home care is the type of care experienced by most Canadian children under age 11 (see Table 8.1).

Nannies and Au Pairs

The traditional vision of a Mary Poppins–type nanny may be attractive, but it is not a reality. A **nanny** is a trained early childhood professional caring for one or more children in a child's home. (A male nanny is sometimes called a *manny*.) Although 33 percent of caregivers in a recent Canadian survey called themselves nannies (Goss Gilroy, 1998b), the term technically applies only to those who are trained in early childhood education and care.

A nanny may be live-in or not. There are various work arrangements. For example, some nannies live in the home with the family and are there 24 hours a day, although not on call for 24 hours. They have regular days off, usually on the weekends. Other nannies come to the house five or more times a week for a specified number of hours. Although these are usually the daytime hours, it might be overnight for parents working shifts or on call. Some nannies do only child care; others do light housekeeping or meal preparations or errands such as grocery shopping.

The key characteristic that differentiates nannies from au pairs is professional training. Au pairs are not early-childhood trained and are less costly to employ. The phrase **au pair** means "on par"; in other words, an equal member of the family. It is often a traditional way for young adults to see other countries. Nannies may enter Canada through the federal government's foreign Live-In Caregiver Program visa and may then qualify for landed immigrant status after two years of work. They are not covered by the Canada Labour Code.

Some nannies have early-childhood certificates or degrees and others have completed specially designed nanny courses, usually modelled on the long-established British Nursery Nurse training program. In Canada, nanny training courses are offered by, for example, Canadian Mothercraft in Ottawa and the Canadian Nanny program at Sheridan College in Oakville, Ontario. This training is similar to other early childhood education programs and typically includes child development, child guidance, interpersonal skills, nutrition, health, play, and selecting and using educational materials. It may also include contract writing and negotiating terms of employment.

Care by an early-childhood-trained nanny is the least common form of care (Deiner, 1997). Employing a nanny is an option relatively few families can afford. For example, in Toronto a nanny working more than 24 hours a week costs approximately $22,729 annually, including Canada Pension Plan and Employment Insurance payments; this cost is less in other areas of Canada (Pratt, 1999). (This cost is compared to the national average of $5,500 to $8,200 for in-home care providers in general [Goss Gilroy, 1998b]). In addition, using an agency to find and screen a nanny can cost between $500 and $2,000. The parent-employers are responsible for the supervision of the nanny. Room, board, sick days, use of the family car, paid vacation, health insurance, and other benefits may or may not be included.

Nannies are frequently employed by families with more than one young child at home. The average number of children cared for by in-care providers (including nannies) in Canada is 2.3 children (Goss Gilroy, 1998b). If the nanny is live-in or daily, she or he is an ongoing presence in a child's life and is available if a child is ill. It is an option used by parents who work very irregular hours, travel for business, or work on call. On the other hand, when a nanny is ill there is no replacement easily available, the family assumes the role and problems of employer, there is a need to mesh the family and nanny's values and child-rearing practices, and if the nanny speaks a different language than the family he or she may not be a good role model for young children developing language. In addition, a major drawback can be the lack of or loss of privacy for both live-in nannies and employers (Jennison, 2000).

Relative-Care

Another in-home care option is care by another family member, either in their home or the child's home (see Table 8.1). This has long been a traditional arrangement for families. When you were young, you might have gone to your grandmother's house after school if your parents were not home. Or maybe you spent two or three days a week at your aunt's house and then the other days your cousins joined you at your house. With today's smaller families often not living near relatives, this type of arrangement may no longer be an option for many families. In addition, as discussed in Chapter 3, today's grandparents and other relatives are also likely to be in the labour force or involved in other activities that preclude them from being regular caregivers.

Use of relative-care is most common for families that need infant or toddler care, that work part time, or that are poor (Clarke-Stewart, Gruber, & Fitzgerald, 1994). It is often the preferred option of families, especially for infants and toddlers. In addition, parents using relative care report that they trust a relative with the care of their young children (Kontos, Howes, Shinn, & Galinsky, 1995). This study also reported that while the majority of relative caregivers wanted to help out, not all were enthusiastic about taking care of a young child.

As with nannies and au pairs, it is the parents' responsibility to determine if this is a good arrangement for their children. Not all relatives make good caregivers for young children. In addition, research shows that young children are not necessarily more attached to relatives than to non-related caregivers (Galinsky, Kontos, & Shinn, 1994). An advantage to relative-care may be a shared language and culture.

Family Day Care

A young child cared for in another home is one of the oldest and most frequently used day-care options in Canada (see Table 8.1). Although a relatively low percentage of children are cared for in *regulated* family day care homes, when *unregulated* family day care homes are included this becomes the most prevalent form of day care. Family day care is used most by families with children under age three and those working part time (Kontos, 1992).

Family day care is defined as "care in a home of a non-relative for small groups of children." It is also called *family day homes, home care, family home day care, private home care,* and *community day care homes.* The children may range in age from infancy to school age. These programs may or may not be regulated or licensed. There is no one agreed-upon set of standards for family day care. The requirements for these programs vary from province to province, and indeed the majority of family day cares are not regulated and are not required to be.

Some of the reasons why families may prefer family day care to centre-based care are that:

- It is less expensive.

- It is a home-like setting (often desired for infants and toddlers).

- It can accommodate siblings of different ages (e.g., an infant and a preschooler).

- The multiple ages make it more "family-like" than age-grouped centres.

- Flexible hours may be more possible (e.g., care before 7 a.m. or after 6 p.m., or on weekends).

- The caregiver may have the same background, culture, and language as the family.

- Children may have the same caregiver from infancy through school age.

FOR REFLECTION

What are some of the possible disadvantages of family day care for families and for early childhood educators?

Although one often-mentioned advantage of family day care is that it is typically neighbourhood care close to playmates and school (Dunster, 1994), this claim may not be accurate (Kontos, 1992). For example, one Canadian study found that families using family day care actually drove further (12.3 km) than parents using day-care centres (7.7. km) or nursery schools (6.1 km) (Kivikink & Schell, 1987).

Why else might families prefer a family day-care program?

There are an estimated 170,000 family day caregivers in Canada, which is 51 percent of all early childhood educators (Dunster, 1999). Approximately 95 percent of these arrangements are not licensed or regulated (Goss Gilroy, 1998). Some provinces/territories license the individual caregivers (e.g., British Columbia, Manitoba, Saskatchewan, New Brunswick, Prince Edward Island, the Yukon, and the Northwest Territories). Some other provinces approve or license agencies that supervise family day care homes (e.g., Ontario, Alberta, Quebec, and Nova Scotia).

Likewise, the number and ages of the children permitted in a family day care home varies with the province or territory. For example, a family day care home must be licensed when it has between three and seven children, depending on the province or territory. The maximum number of children permitted in Canada in one family day care with one provider varies with the ages of the children (i.e., the younger the children, the fewer permitted); the maximum is typically eight children. Other standards in provincial or territorial legislation for family day cares can cover the physical environment, safety standards, minimum age of the caregiver, training of the caregiver, health- and criminal-record checks, programs offered, meals/snacks for children, and so on.

The schedule of a family day care home is determined by the ages and needs of the children. For example, a program with younger school-age children will include times for the children to be taken to school in the morning and picked up in the afternoon. If the children are all three- to five-year-olds, their day may resemble that of a day-care centre (e.g., group activities, free play, snack, outdoor play, lunch, rest, and so forth).

The cost of family day care varies with the region of the country. For example, licensed family day care may cost $750 a month in Vancouver and $400 in Saskatchewan (Pratt, 1999). There may be subsidies available for families that qualify to offset the fees. Only Manitoba and the Yukon directly fund family day care homes.

Operating a family day care is the same as operating a small business with the requirements of such an endeavour (e.g., insurance, taxes, and local business licences). The income from a family day care will vary with factors such as the number and ages of the children, the rate charged, whether it is full-time or part-time, whether it is operating at capacity, and what the expenses are. Dunster (1994) states that a family day care can earn from less than $2,000 a year to more than $30,000. A recent survey of Canadian family day-care programs found that reported gross income ranged from $6,400 to $15,600 a year (Goss Gilroy, 1998a, 1998c). This is before expenses have been deducted (business expenses can be written off against income for tax purposes if one is self-employed). The Our Child Care Workforce Study found that 39 percent of responding regulated family day care providers were dissatisfied with their salaries (Beach, Bertrand, & Cleveland, 1998).

At this time, the only provinces and territories that require a formal training program for regulated family day care are the Yukon (60 hours), Prince Edward Island (30 hours), and Quebec (25 hours). Saskatchewan and Manitoba require orientation sessions or courses. In other provinces and territories training is optional, although it is encouraged and often available from agencies such as family day-care support networks (discussed below). In recent years, some colleges have developed courses and certificate programs for family day care (e.g., Home Child Care, offered by St. Lawrence College in Kingston, Ontario, and the Family Day Care certificate program at Vancouver Community College).

Family day care providers have diverse backgrounds, ages, and experience. They are almost all women, married, with children of their own (Goss Gilroy, 1998c). Their average age is late 30s and they have completed at least high school. The majority have five or more years of experience in child care, expect to continue in child care, and would choose to work in child care if they were choosing again (Goss Gilroy, 1998c). These latter findings seem to contradict the dissatisfaction and high turnover rate for family day care providers reported in other studies (e.g., National Association for the Education of Young Children, 1985).

The recent national surveys on in-home care reported "a typical provider working in her own home was living with a partner, was in her late 30s and had children of her own living in the home. In more than half of the cases, at least one of the caregiver's children was under the age of five" (Taylor, 1999, p. 24). In addition, more than three-quarters of family day care providers reported participating in a professional development activity in the past year; the average was 3.7 activities (Goss Gilroy, 1998c).

An issue in family day care is how much regulation is necessary and desirable and the accompanying need for licensing and monitoring. In unregulated or unlicensed family day homes, parents are responsible for monitoring what is happening. However, very young children cannot *tell* a parent what is happening. When I was sitting on a provincial child care licensing board, we frequently had reports of unlicensed family day care homes exceeding the number or age combinations of children legally permitted. This was more frequent than non-compliance by licensed family day cares, in my experience.

Some people in the field have expressed the view that licensing can be a disincentive to operating a family day care. For example, the need to make substantial changes to the home to meet licensing standards may be a financial disincentive to open a licensed facility. A recent survey asked family day care providers why they were licensed or not licensed (Goss Gilroy, 1998a). The group that was licensed said it was because they wanted to obtain support services available only for licensed programs, to increase professionalism, and to receive referrals of families from an agency. Those who chose not to be licensed said it was because they wanted to keep control of their program and that being able to take more children (which they could do if licensed) was not important to them (Goss Gilroy, 1998c).

A family day care does not have to be licensed until the enrollment exceeds a certain number, which varies across provinces. However, it may choose voluntarily to be licensed. Some programs do this in order to participate in family day care support programs or to be eligible for subsidies. (Licensing for a group day-care centre is not optional.)

In the past few years, there has been an increasing trend of more family day care support programs or networks. However, the idea of a family day care agency is not a new one. In the early 1930s, the Vancouver Day Nursery Association established a family day home network (McDonell, 1992). In some provinces these agencies are licensed; in others they operate on contracts from the provincial or municipal government. Registration with an agency is voluntary, but the family day home must meet certain requirements. In return, the family day care provider receives support and services from an agency.

A family day care network, agency, or support service can provide a variety of useful services. These may include workshops, newsletters, resource library (e.g., books, videos, toys, equipment, etc.), referrals of families, a "warm line," on-site visits, advice and assistance, bulk purchasing of supplies, first aid courses, group liability insurance, and other services. One example is the Sackville Family Day Care Association, which was the first licensed family day care agency in Nova Scotia. Since 1980, it has expanded the services it offers to include a resource centre, toy/book/video library, parent education, professional training, referral service, registry kits for new members, and curriculum kits on topics such as colours and sea animals. In addition, it has developed a half-hour television show on the local cable station as well as producing more than 50 videos on topics related to young children, families, and child care.

After a comprehensive review of family day care, Kontos (1992) concluded that what was needed was support, training, and technical assistance. In Canada, local and provincial professional organizations, such as the Child Care Providers Association of Ottawa-Carleton, have provided professional development, peer support, mentoring, professional development, resources, and advocacy. Other services can include a registry of substitute providers, on-site visits by field workers, and recruitment of additional family day homes when necessary.

Professional organizations have also worked to change the public image of family day care from "just babysitting" to a professional service. One way has been to promote professional development. For example, the Western Canada Family Day Care Association developed a 24-hour training program, Starting and Operating a Family Daycare, which has evolved into a one-year certificate program at community colleges. The association has also produced a series of videos and print materials called Good Beginnings . . . Family Day Care (Norman, 1994; Penny, 1996).

In recent years there has been a growing interest in family day care by researchers. There have been several large-scale studies of family day care (e.g., Kontos, Howes, Shinn, & Galinsky, 1995). Overall, the research on the effects of family day care has been mixed (Howes & Norris, 1997). This is not particularly surprising, given the variety of family day care homes and the range of factors that can influence their effects on children, families, and providers.

A frequent focus of family day care research is on the effects of various combinations of numbers and ages of children. For example, one study that examined the effects of adding two school-age children to family day cares (to a maximum of eight children) found that the more children with a wider age range the more difficult it was for the providers, and the more providers shifted their attention from the infants to the older children. However, when the older children were present, there was more fantasy play, arts and crafts activities, and reading (Howes & Norris, 1997). Other research has found that "infants and toddlers appear to be more demanding on caregivers, making it more difficult for them to behave in optimal ways" (Kontos, 1992, p. 22).

Another focus of recent research has been comparing regulated/supervised family day homes with those that are unregulated. For example, a study by Pepper and Stuart (1992) of 240 regulated and unregulated family day care providers in Ontario reported that although both groups treated children with "affection, cheerfulness, and respect" (p. 116), the supervised caregivers used "a more planful and participative approach" (p. 117).

Multiple Care Arrangements

A common pattern of day care for many families is to have more than one arrangement (Vandell & Su, 1999). This is particularly likely if parents work part-time or variable schedules (Folk & Yi, 1994). For example, a single parent who works Thursday through Monday may use a day-care centre or family day care for some days, relatives or neighbours on the weekend, school-age care before and after school for older children, and lessons at the local recreation centre one afternoon a week. Other families try to arrange their work so their children do not need full-time care. These arrangements might include parents working different shifts, one parent working at home, use of flex-time, and telecommuting. In addition, most parents try to have contingency plans for emergencies such as a sick child or unexpected school closure. Some parents use a combination of paid and unpaid maternity and paternity leaves when their children are infants. The use of multiple care arrangements is "a common strategy used by families to manage work and family roles" (Folk & Yi, 1994, p. 678).

Specialized Day Care

Sometimes the usual types of day-care programs do not or cannot meet the needs of families. Specialized day-care programs have been developed to meet these special or unique needs and preferences due to hours of work (e.g., extended hours or rotating shift work), location (e.g., rural or isolated areas), or emergency care (e.g., sick child or regular family day care provider not available). Specialized programs have also been developed for groups such as teen parents and families with children with disabilities.

Work-Related Child Care

I once interviewed hospital-based workers about their child-care needs. This is a group that works many combinations of hours and days; for example, 12-hour rotating shifts, fixed 8-hour shifts, on call, weekends only, weekdays only, regular overtime, and other patterns. The need for child care for these varying patterns of work is one reason why health care organizations and the public sector have been the leaders in the establishment of work-related child-care programs in Canada and the United States (Allis, 1989; Mayfield, 1990). Employees' need for care for their young children has raised a logical question: If parents are going to work, why can't employers provide or assist with day care for the children of their employees? While some employers in Canada are doing this, the practice is not widespread.

Work-related child care can be defined as "the involvement or support of an employer, labour group, or other organization in the provision of a child care facility or the delivery of a service for the children of employees or members" (Mayfield, 1990, p. 2). (It is also referred to as *employer-supported* or *employer-sponsored child care*.) It can include both on-site and off-site programs such as day-care centres or family day care networks, and resource and referral services (see Chapter 11). Family-friendly personnel policies such as flex-time, telecommuting, and maternity/paternity/family leaves are also sometimes included as work-related child care.

Work-related child care is not a new idea. It has its roots in the infant schools Robert Owen established at his textile mills in England (see Chapter 5). Some of the early day nurseries in Canada were organized by wealthy women and charitable organizations to assist in the employment of mothers as domestic servants. The wartime day nursery for the children of parents working in the war industries was also a type of work-related day care. The first "recent" work-related day care in Canada was begun in 1964 at Riverdale Hospital, a rehabilitation and continuing care hospital in Toronto. The hospital had recently expanded and needed additional nursing staff at a time of a nursing shortage. It was hoped that an on-site day-care centre would help recruit the additional staff. The day-care centre was credited with helping to recruit nurses and enabling the facility to then operate at capacity (Mayfield, 1990).

The most frequently cited potential benefits for work-related child care are:

- Recruitment of employees in highly competitive labour markets.

- Retention of experienced employees.

- Reduction of absenteeism and tardiness due to stable and dependable care arrangements.

- Provision of care for hours and days needed.

- Employee peace of mind knowing his or her child is well cared for.

- If a program is on- or near-site, parents may visit their child on breaks or lunch times.

- Increased productivity.

- Improved employee morale.

- Enhanced public relations or corporate image as family-friendly and responsive.

However, some frequently mentioned disadvantages include:

- Cost (may not be cheaper than community-care options for families).

- On-site centres are expensive to build and equip.

- Location may not be convenient if parents have to commute with young children, especially on public transportation.

- May be underutilized if not used by enough employees or if employee demographics change.

- Many families prefer neighbourhood care.

- May not be perceived as an equitable employee benefit by employees without young children.

Overall, in my experience (e.g., Mayfield, 1988) and in the research, the most frequently documented benefit is that the availability, accessibility, and reliability of good-quality day care promotes peace of mind and less worried/ stressed employees who are therefore, in theory, more productive workers. As one hospital administrator asked me: Would you rather have a pharmacist preparing prescriptions and a nurse giving you critical medication who were worried and stressed over their children's care arrangements and therefore distracted, or those who were not?

Often, work-related child care is associated with an on-site day-care centre. Some programs were quite creative in finding or renovating space, such as the Confederation Building Day Care Co-operative for provincial government employees in St. John's, Newfoundland, and La Garderie sur une Patte at Celanese Canada in Drummondville, Quebec, both located in renovated storage buildings. Western Glove Works in Winnipeg included a day-care centre in the design of its new factory.

FOR REFLECTION

A criticism of work-related child care is that when day care is tied to a person's job, it limits job mobility and is exploitive. Some people argue that women can be trapped in low-paying jobs because of the provision of day care. Do you think this is a realistic concern in Canada today? Why or why not?

However, sometimes there is no suitable space available on-site, or it is not appropriate to have young children on-site (e.g., heavy manufacturing, smelters, etc.). One possible solution in this case is an off-site (or near-site) day-care centre. For example, the National Bank of Canada had three headquarter buildings in downtown Montreal in 1980 when it established a near-site day care in its data processing centre (a good choice as it was a security, limited-access building).

A few companies and organizations have joined together as a consortium to establish work-related child-care programs. One of the most comprehensive was the Edmonton Hospital Workers Child Care Society, a consortium of three hospitals, several health care unions, and the Alberta Hospital Association that established an off-site centre, a family day care network, and school-age programs (including summers) beginning in 1982.

Other companies or organizations have found that what was needed was assistance for families in locating available day care and services in the community. This assistance has traditionally been an option for companies where the employees live or work over a scattered area and an on-site centre is not practical. One example of this type of support is a resource and referral service.

Resource and referral services are described in Chapter 11.

Some studies have shown that addressing the needs of families can reduce turnover and absenteeism and increase productivity (e.g., Gordon & Browne, 1993). Work-related child care has grown relatively slowly in Canada over the past 35 years and has not been a major provider of new day-care spaces. Employers are not the sole, or major, answer to the provision of needed day care spaces in Canada.

Shift Work and Extended Hours

Perhaps the group with the most difficulty in arranging care for their children are those families that work shifts or extended hours. Some companies and most health care organizations operate 24 hours a day. In fact, in 40 percent of Canadian couples one partner works some type of shift (Campbell, 1999b). Shift work can have different patterns. For example, some people work permanent shifts (i.e., the same shift every working day, such as the night shift), others work rotating shifts (e.g., the day shift for a month, then the night shift for the next month), and still others work on call, which means they are often called to work on short notice for any shift.

Although some parents with young children work shifts as a way of meeting their day-care needs (Campbell, 1999a), this type of work usually makes it more difficult for families to find care for their children for the hours needed. Parents have told me that night shifts and rotating shifts are the most difficult for finding care. In addition, arranging day care can also be difficult for parents working split days with extended hours. For example, retail workers often work late on Thursday and Friday nights and then on weekends. People in the restaurant and hospitality industry and students also have irregular hours.

Campus day care is discussed earlier in this chapter.

These are times when centre-based care is typically not available. Many of these parents rely on in-family (e.g., one parent works one shift and the other another) or multiple care arrangements, as described previously. A common suggestion for these parents is to use family day care. However, parents working extended hours means extended hours for family day care providers and loss of their family time. In addition, regulated family day cares may be prohibited from operating late or overnight. One promising trend in regulating day-care programs in Canada, especially family day care, has been increasing recognition of the need for accommodating the diverse work patterns of families. However, "government bodies are very concerned about caregiver burnout and often discourage formalized, off-hours or extended hours care" (Clark, 1998, p. 12).

In relatively few situations, centre-based, work-related child care has been the answer. One example is the Downs Children's Centre at Assiniboia Downs Race Track in Winnipeg. This program was developed in 1981 under the sponsorship of the Horsemen's Benevolent and Protective Association. It was designed to accommodate the unique needs of families involved with horse racing. For example, on race days (Friday, Saturday, and Wednesday), day care was needed from 5:30 a.m. to 1:30 p.m. and then from 4 p.m. to midnight. There was no program in the local community for these hours, so the Association developed a program. This is an example of a creative solution to the day-care needs of a specific group. In the future we are likely to see more of this creativity. For example, the food service at Nortel Networks in Brampton, Ontario, provides take-out dinners from the cafeteria for employees. Approximately 10 percent of the employees, especially those with young children, use this service for their families. Meals can be ordered electronically and later delivered to the employee's work location (Campbell, 1999a).

Rural and Isolated Programs

Location can also cause difficulties in providing care for young children. This can be a special problem for the one-quarter of Canadian families not living in urban areas. These parents work and need local day care; however, in small communities, there are not often the resources necessary to develop, support, and operate a day-care facility. For example, there may not be a suitable facility, or a licensed early childhood educator may not reside in the community. In addition, the need in a community may be seasonal, such as in farming communities where the need for flexible and extended-hours day care is greatest during seeding and harvesting. Care may be needed not only for the children of local families but also the children of seasonal workers who move from one area to another. However, not all rural communities are in farming areas.

One example of rural day care for farm workers and those working in seasonal tourist-industry jobs is the Rural Child Care Project in the South Okanagan and Similkameen Valleys in British Columbia. A licensed group day care was established for children from birth to age 12 for a 12-hour day. The project coordinator wrote that, "parents told us that they would never be able to leave their children alone again after they had enjoyed a worry-free picking season for the first time" (Bland, 1997, p. 24).

An example of a day-care program in an isolated community that is also an example of work-related child care is the Nanisivik Day Care Centre in Nunavut. I visited this program when I was doing a study of work-related child care for Labour Canada (Mayfield, 1990). Nanisivik is an isolated mining community at the northern end of Baffin Island, 3,200 km north of Montreal. The Nanisivik program is described in Focus 8.3, which includes my observations as well as current information from a telephone interview with the director and staff. One unique feature of this day care is that when the mining company was unionized a few years ago, the day care staff, as company employees, became union members (except for the director). To my knowledge, they are the only early childhood educators in Canada who are also members of a Steelworkers local union!

Emergency Day Care

For many families, their day-care arrangements, although complex and carefully arranged, work well until there is an emergency. Then they need emergency care. **Emergency child care** is "temporary back-up child care available to parents when regular child care arrangements have been disrupted or when children are mildly ill and must remain at home" (Howe & Swail, 1999, p. 382). Emergency care can be divided into two broad types. One responds to the needs of individual families or programs (e.g., a sick child, parent, or family day care provider). It is also known as *short-term, on-call,* or *back-up day care*. Emergency care can also refer to programs needed as a result of natural or industrial disasters (e.g., floods, earthquakes, evacuation because of chemical spills, or explosions); this is also referred to as disaster care.

Parents with children under age five have the highest absentee rates from work due to family responsibilities: 4.2 days per year for mothers and 1.8 for fathers of preschool-age children (Statistics Canada, 1998e). Sick children are a common reason for a parent taking time from work. As the average young child will "typically have between six and eight respiratory illnesses each year, most of them minor, and one or two digestive illnesses" (Morgan, 1986, p. 167), the potential for absences by parents is likely. The Conference Board of Canada has estimated that absenteeism, in general, costs companies and organizations $1,750 per employee per year (Howe & Swail, 1999).

A sick child is a dilemma for a parent if the child is too ill to attend his or her regular day-care program. If a child is seriously ill, the overwhelming preference of parents is to stay at home to care for their child. However, what about times when the child is in the final stages of recovery from the flu or a bad cold? They are not really ready to return to a day-care centre, but they are not really ill. This is a dilemma for families. Many parents do not have the option of staying at home. For example, if they do not go to work, they do not get paid

Focus 8.3

Nanisivik Day Care Centre, Nanisivik, Nunavut

When I observed this program in 1989, it was the only day-care centre sponsored by a Canadian natural resource company and the only day care funded 100 percent by the company. The site, 750 km above the Arctic Circle, included a zinc and lead mine operating six days a week and a mill operating seven days (the day-care centre was open weekdays only). The mining operation, Canada's first High Arctic mine, began in 1974 and the day-care centre opened in a house in 1976 so family members of mine employees could be employed by the mining company or local community services. The day care moved into the newly built government building in 1979. This building also houses the elementary school, library, store, nursing centre, gym, pool, post office, fire hall, and government offices. The town currently has approximately 250 residents.

Margie I. Mayfield

The day-care centre is licensed by the Nunavut government. There are 5 infants and toddlers, 12 to 15 preschool-age children, and usually 10 children in the school-age program. There is a fenced play area as well as access to the nearby school playground and recreation centre. The dark and cold days of the long winter restrict outdoor play, so the recreation centre with its pool and gym are used.

Small and isolated communities often have difficulty getting qualified early childhood educators. To meet this need, the day-care centre developed its own on-the-job competency-based training program. The early childhood educators also participate in relevant professional development activities such as first aid courses and management seminars provided by the mining company. Because the staff of the day care are all considered employees of the mining company, they receive the same benefits as other employees.

Sources: Wanda Kellogg, day-care supervisor, personal communication, March 2000; Mayfield, 1990; Williams, 1998.

or they are afraid of losing their jobs, or they've used up all their sick days, vacation days, and family days.

Options in backup day care may include the child going to a drop-in daycare centre or specially reserved places in a local group day-care centre, special family day care home, or in-home care by a trained caregiver. One of the few backup day-care programs in Canada is the Short Term Child Care Program of the National Capital Region Emergency Child Care Consortium in Ottawa (see www.stcc.on.ca). This is a non-profit agency serving employees of consortium members (Carleton Board of Education, Nortel, Canadian Union of Postal Workers, Carleton County Law Association, Canada Mortgage and Housing Corporation, and Nepean Hydro). Three options available are in-home care, family day care, and centre-based care (Howe & Swail, 1999). Program evaluation has found high satisfaction levels among the parents using the service, who report lower stress and decreased work–family tension (Howe & Swail, 1999).

Day care is also needed by families after a disaster. Children need to be safe and cared for while parents are taking care of urgent matters. I live in an earthquake zone, and part of the local Emergency Preparedness Program is provision for disaster child care. The program used in this area was developed by the Church of the Brethren and coordinated by the Red Cross and FEMA (the Federal Emergency Management Agency in the United States). There is a 24-hour training course, and volunteers are provided with a "kit of comfort" consisting of a large suitcase with materials and activities for children. While one hopes never to need to use disaster emergency care, it is good to know that it exists and the needs of young children and families are being considered in emergency planning.

In addition to day-care programs developed for special circumstances (e.g., location or extended hours), programs have also been developed for specific groups with specific needs. Two such groups are teen parents and children with disabilities and their families.

Teen Parents

Being a teen parent adds stress to adolescence—a traditionally stressful time. For teen parents who are poor, uneducated, and have limited or no support, parenting can be overwhelming. Day-care programs for the children of teen parents are more than the provision of day care located in a high school. Although a major goal is to enable the teen parents (usually teen mothers) to stay in school and ideally complete their high school education, additional support services are needed. Research shows that access to these support services is important if teen parents are to be successful (Kurtz & Derevensky, 1994).

Comprehensive programs for teen parents often include:

* *Day-care programs for their children that cover the hours of class and study*—The early childhood educators in these programs are important role models as well as sources of support and information.

When the Ontario government decided that teen mothers on welfare would have to return to high school as soon as possible to finish their education and also take parenting courses in order to not remain on welfare for the rest of their lives, agencies that work with teen parents protested that this policy was not fair (Blackwell, 1999). What do you see as the positives and negatives of requiring teen mothers to return to school in order to receive welfare?

- *Social support from their new peer group*—When a teen has a baby, typically her previous friends no longer have much contact with her. Her new peer group becomes other teen mothers.

- *Parenting education*—This component may be offered by an early childhood educator, a parent educator, a social worker, or a public health nurse. Frequent topics are good nutrition, the importance of cognitive stimulation, fostering language development, behaviour-management strategies, child safety, childhood illnesses, and so on.

- *Health services*—Local public health nurses often participate as sources of information, beginning with the importance of prenatal nutrition and delivering healthy babies (see Chapter 2). Later topics may include immunizations, eating problems, illnesses, and typical problems such as diaper rash and teething.

- *Access to needed services*—Social workers can help teen parents access needed services such as vouchers for infant formula, car seats, funds, and other resources.

- *Psychological support*—Counsellors can provide psychological support to help teens understand and adjust to the changes in one's life caused by having and raising a baby.

The day-care program can also serve as an observation site and resource for courses in child development or family life at the high school.

Many teen-parent programs naturally focus on the mother. However, an effort is made to include the father as well. Many teen fathers wish to be involved in their babies' lives, although their involvement typically declines after the birth of the baby (Kurtz & Derevensky, 1994). Research shows that these programs can be effective in promoting teen graduation and child health (Thomson & Caulfield, 1998).

Another special group using day-care programs is families with children with disabilities.

Day Care for Children with Disabilities

If you work in a day-care centre, it is likely that you will work with at least one child with disabilities. The role of quality early childhood programs in the identification and prevention of developmental and other problems in young children has been discussed in previous chapters. In addition, day-care programs play an important role in early childhood special education.

It is estimated that approximately 10 percent of children are disabled (e.g., Deiner, 1993; Norton, 1997). However, it can be difficult to determine a specific diagnosis for young children. Moreover, the younger the child the more difficult diagnosis may be. Many disabilities are not identified until a child is in an early childhood program. This is one reason why you'll see a range of statistics on the percentage of young children with disabilities. For example, it is estimated that while 5 percent of young children have severe handicaps (these are often evident at birth) another approximately 15–20 percent have some special need that requires accommodation by the early childhood program (Canning & Lyon, 1990). You are most likely to see speech/language disabilities, developmental delays, behaviour/emotional problems, and physical handicaps (Wolery, et al., 1993). In recent years there has also been a dramatic increase in the survival rates of infants due to the advances in medical science and technology, which means that more children with special health care needs are in early childhood programs (Norton, 1997). Many of these children have multiple disabilities.

There are various types of day-care programs for children with disabilities. One type is a day-care program that is part of a larger treatment or rehabilitation centre, such as the Alvin Buckwold Child Development Program at Kinsmen's Children's Centre in Saskatoon and the Queen Alexandra Centre for Children's Health in Victoria. In these programs, children with disabilities have daily access to therapists and special-needs educators, if necessary. A day-care program can also be part of an even more comprehensive organization. For example, the *Société pour les enfants handicapés du Québec* (SEHQ) provides services and programs to children with disabilities, their families, educators, and communities in programs including Garderie Papillon, Camp Papillon, Résidence Papillon, Villas Papillon, Transport Papillon, and Ressource Papillon (Patulli, 1994).

The trend in Canada for more than two decades has been increased inclusion of children with disabilities in local community day-care programs. There is no commonly agreed-upon definition for inclusion and it can vary with the age of the child and the type of program (Odom & Diamond, 1998). One definition developed specifically for the early childhood context is "inclusion is a commitment that all children, regardless of their differences, shall receive support and accommodation to ensure their success, and to preserve their right to learn among their peers" (Winter, 1999, p. 7). Children with disabilities benefit from having other children as role models, as young children learn a great deal from one another. For example, a child with disabilities may learn or further develop play behaviours and the skills needed for successful social interactions (see Chapter 7). The inclusion of children with special needs in early childhood programs also helps children recognize, accommodate, and respect the variety among people in our society.

It has been reported in several studies and surveys that most day-care centres in Canada include some children with special needs for at least part of the day (e.g., Doherty, Goelman, LaGrange, Lero, & Tougas, 1999; Irwin, 1997). Some children may attend these programs full time, others may attend a few days a week, and others may attend for a few hours each day. There are many patterns depending on what is best for the individual child. Other factors considered in the selection of an early childhood program for children with disabilities are the nature of the program, the expertise of the educators, the physical environment, and the availability of support. For example, a child in a wheelchair will need a day-care centre that is accessible by ramps. Children with special health needs may require educators or support staff who have special training in areas such as the use of oxygen or a feeding tube.

Another day-care option is home-based programs where a special educator or therapist comes to the child's home to work with the child and family. In a family day home, the professional will also work with and provide support for the family day care educator. Increasingly, families with children with disabilities are using multiple programs that include a day-care centre or family day home.

Finding day care for a child with disabilities can be a challenge. Parents of children with disabilities report that it is not only more difficult to find day care but it is also more difficult to keep it, especially if their child has behavioural problems (Brennan & Freeman, 1999). According to educators, the children requiring the most accommodation in a program are those with challenging behaviours, neurological problems, and autism (Stoiber, Gettinger, & Goetz, 1998). Some of the "barrier factors" for families looking for day care for a child with disabilities can include the limitations of a physical environment; transportation problems; lack of special-needs educators; lack of special equipment; attitudes and beliefs of families, therapists, administrators, and educators; lack of support resources; educator:child ratios; and cost (Buysse, Wesley, & Keyes, 1998; Wolery, et al., 1993).

Another type of program that is used by families with children with disabilities, especially if the disabilities are serious or multiple, is **respite care**. These programs may provide daytime, overnight, weekend, or longer-term care for children with disabilities either in their own home or in another home or location. Respite care provides a break for the parents and other family members. I've asked parents using respite care what they do during this time, and the most frequent response I hear is "Sleep!"

FOR REFLECTION

In Chapter 4, seven key roles of early childhood educators were identified (i.e., nurturer; facilitator, guide, and instructor; model; program and curriculum organizer; observer and evaluator; learner and researcher; and colleague and professional). How do these roles compare and contrast for an early childhood educator working in an infant/toddler program and one working in a school-age program? Do some roles apply more to some types of day care than others? Which roles appeal most and least to you?

Educators' Roles in Day-Care Programs

The early childhood educator in a day-care program has a variety of roles. Which roles are predominant may depend on the type of day care and other factors, such as the ages of the children. For example, an early childhood educator working with infants will likely do more physical care of the child than will an educator working with seven- or eight-year-olds in a school-age program. However, being an early childhood educator also includes tasks other than direct work with children. A characteristic of early childhood educators' work is what is called "multi-tasking" (i.e., doing other things while also caring for children). A recent study examined other tasks educators typically do (Doherty, et al., 1999). Early childhood educators reported that they spent approximately 25 percent of a typical week in planning and preparation, 20 percent with parents of the children, 18 percent in food preparation and cleanup, 14 percent in maintenance/cleaning/repair, and 10 percent supervising practicum students.

Family day care educators also have a variety of roles. This is evident in the description of the day in one family day home: "During the day I have been a playmate, nurse, janitor, cook, dietician, referee, police officer, politician, official nose-blower and resident diaper-changer. I have helped teach the children manners, sharing, co-operation and creativity. We've made snowmen, snow angels, and fudge. We've read our favourite stories" (Hoffard, 1996, p. 14).

Choosing a Day-Care Program

How do parents choose a day-care program for their young children? Many parents find this an intimidating task, and therefore would answer that question, "With great trepidation." I remember one mother who, after inquiring about our vacancies, hours, and fees, asked me, "What else should I be asking you?"

The National Association for the Education of Young Children, in its brochure "Choosing a Good Early Childhood Program—Questions and Answers" (1998b), suggests that parents look for a place where they and their child feel welcome, the children and adults get along well, health and safety are priorities, play and learning are valued, and staff are well trained and dedicated. Another useful piece of information is the one-page resource sheet developed by the Canadian Child Care Federation, which is useful to share with parents looking for child care (see Focus 8.4).

Perhaps the most difficult type of day care for parents not only to locate but also to assess is infant and toddler care. Not only are there fewer spaces, it is often the parents' first experience in choosing child care. The National Association for the Education of Young Children (NAEYC) has published two useful pamphlets on choosing infant and toddler care. Focus 8.5 includes two excerpts from these publications: one on what a parent wants to see in infant care, and one for toddler care. Would you add anything to NAEYC's lists?

A study in Atlantic Canada asked parents the reasons for their choice of a day-care centre (Lyon & Canning, 1996). These parents most frequently gave as their reasons convenience (location, hours, and availability), program characteristics (activities and philosophy), and perception of staff as friendly and competent.

After parents have found a day-care program and enrolled their child, they have feelings of relief combined with doubts. Did I make a good choice? Is my child okay in this program? What is/are the caregiver(s) really like? This is a special problem for parents of the youngest children, who cannot talk about their day, what they did, what they ate, where they went, what the educator did or said, and so forth. Daily information sheets, logs, back-and-forth journals, newsletters, and information bulletin boards are useful ways of communicating with parents. However, sometimes parents want and need to see for themselves.

When I was in charge of early childhood programs, I encouraged parents to drop in whenever they could and to stay as long as they could. Some parents would occasionally stay for 20–40 minutes at the beginning of the day; others would come early at the end of the day. A few would spend a day off observing the

FOR REFLECTION

Parents are quite rightly concerned that their children are being well cared for in an early childhood program. Three day-care centres in Ontario have installed surveillance-type cameras connected to the Internet that enable parents to watch what is happening in the day-care centre and see what their children are doing throughout the day (Stevenson, 1999). As an early childhood educator, would you want to work in one of these centres? Why or why not? If you were a parent, would you want your child in one of these centres? Why or why not?

Focus 8.4

Making a Quality Child Care Choice

Finding and keeping quality child care can be challenging. Where do you start?

What is quality child care?

✓ Child care should support a child's emotional, social, intellectual and physical well-being. Quality child care is not babysitting.

✓ Caregivers are key to quality child care. They should . . .
· understand how child grow and learn
· be affectionate and responsive, open and informative
· provide a stable and stimulating environment
· seek out community resources and support
· be willing to develop common goals.

✓ Quality day care settings have common characteristics . . .
· clean, safe and secure
· a caring, learning environment
· a small number of children with each adult
· space for quiet and active times, indoor and outdoor play
· a balance of interesting activities
· flexible, yet predictable daily routine
· a variety of easily available toys and equipment
· nutritional meals and snacks.

How do you find quality care?

✓ First, identify your needs and priorities.
· Consider your child's age.
· Do you have more than one child requiring care?
· Are you eligible for a government subsidy?
· What fee can you afford?
· Do you prefer centre or home based, regulated or unregulated care?
· What hours?
· In what location—near your child's school, your home, your work?

✓ Provincial and local child offices can offer guidance. Community information services can be invaluable. It is also helpful to talk to neighbours and friends who use child care. Just give yourself plenty of time and find care that suits you and your child.

✓ Once you have a list of caregivers and day care centres, it is time to start telephone interviews. Jot down the questions you want to ask.

✓ Visiting potential centres and family day care homes is the next step.
· Look around.
· Is this a quality child care setting?
· Listen.
· Would you feel good about your child spending time here?

✓ The relationship between you and the caregiver is extremely important.
· It should be one of mutual respect, trust and cooperation.
· The interview is the time to ask plenty of questions.
· Don't forget to discuss hours, fees, discipline, sickness, vacations, the involvement of parents.

✓ Check references before you make a final decision. And write a contract or letter of agreement—it can save unnecessary misunderstandings in the future.

Being an effective child care parent

✓ A parent's responsibility does not end with finding child care.
· The three-way relationship between the parent, caregiver and child requires an ongoing commitment.
· Communication is vital.
· Take the time to hear about your child's day.
· Agree on mutual expectations.
· Voice concerns.
· Express appreciation.
· Live up to the agreement.

Stay aware.
Let's all work towards quality child care!

Canadian Child Care Federation
Resource Sheet, Winter 1996 #34

Focus 8.5

What to Look for in Infant and Toddler Care

What you want to see

Infants:

Group size is limited to no more than eight babies with at least one caregiver for every three children. Each infant is able to form a bond with a primary caregiver, and each caregiver can get to know a few babies very well.

Caregivers show warmth and support to infants throughout the day, making eye contact and talking to them about what is going on.

Alert to babies' cues, adults hold infants or move them to a new place or position, giving them variety in what they are able to look at and do.

Caregivers pay close attention and talk to children during routines such as changing diapers, feeding, and changing clothes.

Caregivers talk, sing, and read to babies, enabling infants to become familiar with language and ultimately to recognize words and sounds.

Babies eat and sleep when they are most comfortable doing so. Caregivers consider infants' individual preferences for food and styles of eating.

Caregivers follow standards for health and safety, including proper handwashing to limit the spread of infectious disease.

Caregivers can see and hear infants at all times.

Parents and caregivers share children's activities and development on a daily basis, building a mutual understanding and trust. Caregivers welcome parents to drop by the home or center.

Toddlers:

Children remain with a primary caregiver over time so they can form a strong relationship with her. The caregiver learns to respond to the toddler's individual temperament, needs, and cues, and builds strong communication with the child's family.

Caregivers praise children for their accomplishments and help them to feel more confident and in control of themselves.

Caregivers, recognizing that toddlers are not yet able to communicate their needs through language, promptly respond to children's cries or other signs of distress.

Caregivers communicate warmth through pats on the back and hugs or holding toddlers in their laps.

Caregivers set good examples for children by treating others with kindness and respect. As children gain in language ability, adults encourage them to resolve differences with words.

Recognizing that frequent testing of limits and saying No! is part of a toddler's healthy development, caregivers minimize their restrictions unless children are in physical or emotional danger. Rather than merely refusing and restraining children, caregivers offer a few options and emphasize what the child is *allowed* to do.

The setting is "inclusive," that is, physical space and activities allow all children to participate. For example, a child with a physical disability eats at the table with other children.

Caregivers frequently read to toddlers, individually on the adult's lap or in groups of two or three. Caregivers sing to toddlers, do finger plays, and act out simple stories as children actively participate.

Sturdy picture books in the child care setting depict people of different ages, racial and cultural groups, family types, and abilities/disabilities.

Everyday tasks such as eating, toileting, and dressing are opportunities for toddlers to learn new skills and better control their own behavior. Caregivers support toddlers' attempts to take care of themselves and provide items that are easy for toddlers to use.

Children have many opportunities for active, large-muscle play both indoors and outdoors. Play equipment is safe and challenging for

continued

continued

toddlers. Their outdoor play space is separate from that of older children.

Adults follow health and safety procedures, including proper handwashing methods and universal precautions. Each area has clearly written procedures for waste disposal.

Caregivers directly supervise toddlers by sight and sound, even when they are sleeping.

Caregivers see parents as the primary source of affection and care for children. Parents are always welcome in the home or center .

Caregivers have training in child development or early education specific to the toddler age group.

They are warm and responsive to children's needs and patient in supporting children as they become more independent.

A maximum group size of 12, with 1 adult for no more than 6 toddlers (preferably fewer) allows for an intimate atmosphere and the high level of supervision that toddlers require.

The staffing schedule allows each toddler to develop a close relationship with a primary caregiver. Toddlers stay in the same group for many months (and from year to year, if possible) to ensure close relationships.

Source: NAEYC, 1997a, 1998d.

program. One excellent situation was in a laboratory nursery school where there was an observation room with one-way glass, so parents could observe the program without being seen by their children. Today there are high-tech alternatives.

Issues in Day Care

This section will focus on three major issues associated with day-care programs in Canada today. The first is auspice, the second affordability, and the third addresses the question, "What are the effects of day care on young children?"

Auspice

Auspice refers to the sponsorship of a program. It addresses the question of who should operate day-care programs. This is an important question because research has shown that auspice is one factor related to the quality of a day-care program. Sometimes auspice is described simply as *profit* or *non-profit centres*. However, there is variety within these terms. For example a *non-profit centre* is typically defined as one that is operated by a board. However, a non-profit day care could be a parent cooperative, or it could be operated by a charitable group or church, a community organization such as the YM/YWCA, a post-secondary institution, or a government agency. Various studies of Canadian day care estimate the percentage of centres that are non-profit at approximately 60 to 70 percent (e.g., Doherty, et al., 1999; Friendly, 1994; Prentice, 2000). The provinces with the highest percentage of non-profit centres are Saskatchewan, Manitoba, Ontario, and Quebec (Doherty et al., 1999; Friendly, 1994). There is also a small number of day-care centres (about three percent) that are operated by municipal governments or school boards (Doherty, et al., 1999).

Terms associated with *for-profit* day care include *commercial, franchise, chains, proprietary,* and *owner-operated.* A for-profit centre may be operated by a corporation, a business partnership, or an individual owner. An example of a corporate-operated day-care chain is KinderCare. A for-profit centre can also be a small day-care centre owned and operated by one person. Three-quarters of day-care programs in 1968 were considered commercial (Childcare Resource and Research Unit, 1997 [on-line]). However, by the end of the twentieth century, only about one-third of day-care centres were for-profit (Doherty, et al., 1999; Prentice, 2000). The provinces with the highest percentage of for-profit day-care programs are Newfoundland and Labrador, Prince Edward Island, Alberta, and New Brunswick (Doherty, et al., 1999). This is due, in great part, to the regulations and funding provisions for day-care programs in these provinces. For example, in most provinces for-profit centres are not eligible for provincial subsidies or operating grants.

One of the difficulties with the definition of for-profit is the grey areas (Friendly, 1994). In the legal sense a for-profit program is incorporated as a profit-making business, whereas a non-profit is not profit making and is governed by a board of directors. However, there are some for-profit centres that have a board and some centres that make a profit that is turned over to the non-profit organization that developed them (Prentice, 2000).

Most of the research on the factors that contribute to the overall quality of an early childhood program include auspice. Auspice seems to be particularly related to salaries and working conditions, staff turnover, staff:child ratios, group size, and programming. For example, if a day-care centre is to make a profit it typically needs to keep down costs. The largest budget item of a day-care centre is salary and benefits. In most non-profit centres this cost is typically around 80 percent, while in some for-profits it is closer to 40 percent (Maynard, 1986). Not unexpectedly, then, for-profit day-care programs tend to pay lower salaries and provide fewer benefits (Doherty, et al., 1999; Prentice, 2000), which in turn can lead to job dissatisfaction and high turnover of staff (see Chapter 4). Also, higher salaries and more benefits attract better-educated professionals who are able to plan and implement quality programs.

Various reviews of the research that looked at auspice in Canada and the United States have concluded that there is sufficient evidence that non-profit day-care centres tend to be higher quality than for-profit centres (e.g., Kaiser & Rasminsky, 1990; Prentice, 2000). The same has been concluded in reviews of research on school-age programs (e.g., Vandell & Su, 1999). However, these reviews of day-care research point out that small for-profit centres vary widely in quality; much more so than the large commercial chains, which by their nature are somewhat standardized. As Prentice (1997) has commented, "although most commercial care critics reserve their harshest criticism for chain, franchised care, the evidence suggests this criticism is misfocused: owner-operated 'Mom and Pop' operations may be the least safe places for children" (p. 44).

The issue of auspice and day care is one where there is often a difference of opinion between day-care advocates and policy-makers. Another of these issues is affordability of day care.

Affordability of Day Care

The issue of affordability for early childhood educators is discussed in Chapter 4.

Affordability of day care is a key issue for families, educators, and programs. According to directors of day-care centres, the most pressing issue is financial stability (Lero, Doherty, Goelman, LaGrange, & Tougas, 1999 [on-line]). Financial resources impact the physical environment of the program, the ability to hire well-qualified staff, the staff:child ratio, and other factors important in quality early childhood programs. The ability of families to afford day care is important for programs if they are to operate at capacity. Most program budgets cannot accommodate a significant percentage of vacancies; a steady and predictable income is essential because most of their budgets are staff salaries and benefits. Day-care programs rely on the fees paid by families. Although there are grants such as operating, startup, emergency (e.g., repair, relocation, etc.), capital costs, maintenance, salary supplement, and grants for children with special needs, these do not cover the total cost of operation. Therefore, parent fees are essential for the operation of day-care centres.

Affordability of day care is also a concern of families with young children. Although all provinces and territories provide fee subsidies for some families, these are not always sufficient or available. In 1998, 31 percent of children in regulated programs were subsidized, down from 36 percent in 1992 (Child Care Resource and Research Unit, 2000 [on-line]). There are criteria that must be met to qualify for subsidies. These typically include low income and other criteria such as parents working (or looking for work), attending an educational institution, or special circumstances (e.g., medical treatment, family emergency, etc.). However, governments are criticized for setting too low an income threshold as the cut-off for receiving fee subsidies (i.e., families that cannot afford day care are still too far above this cut-off to receive subsidies), and for being insufficient so parents must "top up" the subsidy, which many families cannot afford to do. Another criticism is that in provinces that subsidize spaces, there are not enough spaces available where they are needed; for those provinces that subsidize parents, that there is insufficient money in the subsidy budget to adequately cover every family that could apply for subsidy. The resulting dilemma identified by one child-care advocate is that

> As long as child care services are based on a user pay system, the only way to stabilize current services is to increase fees. We know that parents cannot pay more, but we also know that more dollars are needed to hire and keep well trained, committed child care staff. (Cottons, 1999, p. 1)

It is also argued that society has an interest in the affordability of day care because it cannot afford the consequences of *not* providing quality care. For example, according to Galinsky (1990), unsafe physical environments put children at risk, unreliable and fragmented care arrangements stress working families, and insufficient funding results in high turnover and fewer well-qualified early childhood educators.

Two frequently suggested solutions to the affordability issue are free public-funded day care (e.g., day care should be part of the public education system), or changes to the current fee system (e.g., fees based on family income for all families). The province of Quebec has recently addressed the affordability issue by introducing a plan under which day care (including school-age programs) is available to families for five dollars a day. The remainder of the cost of day care is funded by grants from the provincial government to non-profit centres. In 1999, there were 97,000 of these subsidized day-care spaces, with a target of 200,000 spaces by 2005 (Picard, 1999). However, the plan and the government have been criticized for lack of planning, insufficient number of subsidized spaces for families wanting them, and lack of quality control (Clark, 1999). In addition, some early childhood educators claim that the provincial subsidies to the centres do not cover actual operating expenses—in part because the operating grants are based on the provincial regulations that have lower minimal standards than many educators think appropriate. For example, the educator:infant ratio in Quebec is 1:5, rather than the more typical and recommended maximum of 1:3. Therefore a centre with a ratio of 1:3 would receive funding at only a 1:5 rate.

Both auspice and affordability are related to probably the most frequently asked question both by parents looking for day care and by the media reporting on child care: Is day care really good for young children?

Quality care and related policy issues are discussed in Chapter 12.

Research on Day Care

Even though 68 percent of Canadians agreed that "Day care is good for children" in a nationwide *Globe and Mail* survey (Fine, 1999b), parents still ask this question when considering day care. Part of their anxiety may be due to reports they hear and see in the media about a family day care provider shaking a crying baby, or a child wandering away from a day-care centre in the winter. These incidences are rare but tend to reinforce the continuance of the question, "Is day care good for young children?"

Research on various aspects of early childhood education and care is included throughout this book where appropriate. For example, the research on the short and long-term effects of Head Start/Follow Through compensatory programs is presented in Chapters 5 and 6. This section focuses specifically on research on day-care programs and their effects on young children. It is beyond the scope of this book to provide a comprehensive review of the literature and research. The reader is encouraged to follow up on some of the relevant references and resources in this and other chapters. The following sections outline what some of the research has to say about the general question "Is day care good for young children?"

For more on the Child Study Movement, see Chapter 6.

Although day care in Canada can be traced back to the mid-1800s, research on day care is only relatively recent. Most day-care research has only been done in the past two decades, compared to a century of child development research.

Most of the early day care research investigated possible positive and negative effects of day care on young children. This research typically compared children with day-care experience to those without. The studies on the short-term effects of day care found predominantly, although not always, positive effects for:

- Language development

- Level of play

- Social competence

- Cognitive skills

- Following directions and compliance

- Ability to work independently

- Academic achievement

- Transition to kindergarten.

However, not all studies showed positive effects. For example, some reported that children who had attended a day-care program showed more aggressive behaviour. Early day care research also focused on the effects of children attending different types of day-care programs (e.g., family day care compared to day-care centres). Kontos, Howes, Shinn, and Galinsky (1995) concluded that "there is no reason to believe that children are more or less better off in care simply on the basis of the form of care (home versus center). Rather, we now know that there is a wide range of quality in all types of care" (p. 204).

Many of the early studies were criticized for their methods and designs (e.g., Pardeck, Pardeck, & Murphy, 1987). Overall, much of this research was "inconclusive" (Pence & Benner, 2000, p. 145). This led researchers to look more closely at factors that could explain these mixed results. Some of the factors investigated included the type of care, auspice, the environment, the early childhood educators, parent needs and choices, and family variables such as income and education levels of mothers. Thus, the main question for research evolved from Is day care good or bad? to What factors combine in what ways to affect children's development? (Clarke-Stewart, 1987).

The main conclusion from studies investigating factors is that the quality of the program has a critical effect. In other words, high-quality day-care programs tend to produce positive effects; poor-quality programs do not. An example of this is a study by Jacobs, Selig, and White (1992) that looked at children with and without day care experience when they were in grade 1. When the children were compared on day care versus home care, there was no significant difference between the groups. However, when the researchers compared children who had been in high-quality day care, children who had been in low-quality day care, and children in home care, the children from low-quality day care were less independent and had lower language scores than children who had had high-quality day care or home care. The researchers concluded, "it is essential to include a day care quality measure in the research in order to be more precise about the day care experience" (Jacobs, et al., p. 98). This idea was expanded by one of the leading researchers on family day care, who wrote, "an accurate portrayal of how children fare in child care is feasible only if variations in center quality are examined in tandem with family characteristics" (Kontos, 1991, p. 261).

These and other studies reinforced the need for longitudinal studies that looked at a variety of factors and their relationships to one another over an extended period of time. Longitudinal research is desirable because not all effects appear in the short term. These studies also provide useful data for policy-making and identification of good practices (Doherty-Derkowski, 1995). For example, this was seen in the early versus later research on Head Start (see Chapter 6). Longitudinal studies are, however, expensive and difficult to do. Because they monitor subjects for years, it is necessary to periodically locate a number of families and children. In addition, the longer a study continues the more subjects are likely to drop out or be lost. Longitudinal studies of the effects of early childhood programs have also been criticized on design, methodology, and other aspects.

Although longitudinal research exists on the effects of Head Start and related programs such as High/Scope (see Chapter 6), the value of making generalizations to Canadian children, especially those not from backgrounds of poverty, can be debated. In the past few years, results from several longitudinal studies with a broader base have been reported. This information has been very useful and promises to be even more so in the future.

One example is the National Longitudinal Survey of Children and Youth, which began collecting data on almost 23,000 children in Canada from birth to age 13 in 1994 (see Focus 2.1 in Chapter 2 for a description of this survey). One of Statistics Canada's recent announcements from this study was that, "results from analyses of data from the latest release of the National Longitudinal Survey of Children and Youth suggest that children who are enrolled in early childhood programs and day-care centres appear to get a head start in school over youngsters who stay at home with a parent" (*Daily* of October 14, 1999 [on-line]). This survey is looking at a variety of factors impacting child development such as temperament, aggression, and parent practices. Its database is beginning to be used by researchers and should result in some interesting findings in the next few years.

There is a similar longitudinal study in the United States, the National Longitudinal Study of Youth, which has included 12,600 people since 1979. Although previous studies using these data showed mixed results, a recent study found there were no significant long-term differences in academic achievement, behaviour problems, cognitive development, self-esteem, or compliance for 6,000 children at age 12 whose mothers worked outside the home during their first three years, when compared with those whose mothers did not (Harvey, 1999).

Another large U.S. longitudinal study is the National Institute of Child Health and Human Development (NICHD) Study of Early Child Care that has been following 1,300 children since their birth in 1991. This study recently reported no consistent relationship between the number of hours infants and toddlers spend in non-parental care and their cognitive, social, or language development. In addition, it was reported that children in quality programs for more than 10 hours a week do as well on measures of cognitive and language development regardless of the number of hours their mothers worked (NICHD, 1999, www.nichd.nih.gov).

In addition to these comprehensive, large-scale longitudinal studies, individual groups of researchers in Canada have been doing longitudinal research by following up on children from earlier studies, such as the studies by Ellen Jacobs and fellow researchers in Quebec on the effects of day care on children's subsequent development, and the Victoria Day Care Research Project of Alan Pence and Hillel Goelman that compares the effects of different types and quality of care on children's development.

A parent's question, "Is day care good or bad for my young child?" really has two parts. The first part is, "Is day care good or bad?" The short answer would probably be, "It depends." In the words of a leading researcher in this area,

> Essentially, studies, including the one conducted by NICHD, show that parents are first and foremost in children's lives and have the greatest impact on how they develop. Yet, they also show that the quality of child care does matter: Good child care can add value to parental care giving and bad child care can diminish the best parenting. (Galinsky, 1999, p. 16)

The second key part of the parent's question is "for my young child." For example, two parents may each have a three-year-old child. One child might be more comfortable in a family day home with fewer children of a wider age range including an older sibling; the second child may benefit from more social interaction opportunities with a larger peer group possible in a day-care centre. So again, the answer is, "It depends." Researchers are investigating these individualized effects because "as we learn more about the effects of child care in general, we must pay more attention to its influence on different [individual] children" (Morrison, 1998, p. 458).

Summary of this Chapter

The key themes of this chapter are that:

- The early establishment of day nurseries in Canada was done mostly by religious and charitable groups and philanthropic individuals. Their primary purpose was to care for the young children of working mothers.

- Health, safety, and hygiene were strong aspects of early day nurseries.

- Today's day-care programs vary in type, organization, and philosophy. They include infant/toddler programs, school-age programs, family day care homes, cooperative day-care centres, and in-home care by relatives or nannies.

- Day-care programs have been developed to meet special needs of families with young children, such as work-related child care, extended-hours care, parenting teens, and children with disabilities.

- Some families use multiple care arrangements.

- Each type of day care has advantages and disadvantages and may be more appropriate and preferred by some families rather than others.

- The early childhood educator has a variety of roles in a day-care program. These can vary with the type of program and the needs of the children.

- Affordability of day care is an issue for families, educators, and society.

- Auspice is a controversial issue, and relates to indicators of quality programs such as staff turnover, ratios, and programming.

- Research on day care shows that quality of day-care programs has a critical effect, with high-quality day-care programs tending to result in positive effects. However, more research needs to be done on the effects of the interaction of variables for individual children.

Key Terms

affordability, 348

au pair, 327

auspice, 346

campus day care, 319

child care, 309

cooperative day care, 318

day care, 309

day nursery, 309

emergency child care, 337

family day care, 328

infant/toddler care, 323

nanny, 326

respite care, 342

school-age care, 321

work-related child care, 333

Resources

If you wish to know more about some of the topics in this chapter, here are a few suggested publications, organizations, and Web sites:

For Sharing with Children

Rogers, F. 1985. *Going to day care*. New York: G.P. Putnam's Sons. One of the Mr. Rogers' First Experiences series books; illustrated with colour photographs; relatively little text.

Kelley, T. 1990. *Day-care teddy bear.* New York: Random House. Anna and her teddy bear go to day care for the first time.

Spinelli, E., illustrated by Melissa Iwai. 2000. *Night shift daddy.* New York: Hyperion Books for Children.

If you'd like to know more about the history of day care in Canada, try:

Varga, D. 1997. *Constructing the child: A history of Canadian day care.* Toronto: James Lorimer & Company.

Also see the suggestions in the Resources section in Chapter 5.

For a recent survey of day care in Canada that includes detailed descriptions of day care in each province/territory written by early childhood people from that province/territory, see:

Canadian National Child Care Study. 1992. *Canadian child care in context: Perspectives from the provinces and territories.* Allan Pence (coordinating editor). Ottawa: Statistics Canada/Health and Welfare Canada. Background papers for each province/territory are available from the Canadian Child Care Federation (see Chapter 4 for address).

For day care from a child's perspective, see:

Galinsky, E. 1999. *Ask the children: What America's children really think about working parents.* New York: William Morrow & Company. For the parents' perspective, Modigliani, K. 1996. *Parents speak about child care.* New York: Families and Work Institute.

For more information about infant and toddler care, see:

Shimoni, R., Baxter, J., & Kugelmass, J. 1992. *Every child is special: Quality group care for infants and toddlers.* Don Mills, ON: Addison-Wesley Publishers.

Deiner, P.L. 1997. *Infants and toddlers: Development and program planning.* Fort Worth, TX: Harcourt Brace College Publishers.

Lally, J.R., Griffin, A., Fenichal, E., Segal, M., Szanton, E., & Weissbourd, B. 1995. *Caring for infants and toddlers in groups.* Arlington, VA: ZERO TO THREE/The National Center.

For school-age programs, see:

Musson, S. 1999. *School-age care: Theory and practice* (2nd edition). Don Mills, ON: Addison-Wesley Longman.

For emergency child care, see:

Farish, J.M. 1995. *When disaster strikes: Helping young children cope.* Washington, D.C.: NAEYC [brochure].

For more information on family day care, see:

Dunster, L. 1994. *Home child care: A caregiver's guide; Supporting family day care providers;* and *Caregiver to caregiver.* A series of practical handbooks on beginning and operating family day homes. Available from Child Care

Providers Association, 2085 Alton Street, Ottawa, ON K1G 1X3; Telephone 613-731-1991.

Kontos, S. 1992. *Family day care: Out of the shadows and into the limelight.* Washington, DC: National Association for the Education of Young Children. An excellent overview of the issues, by one of the leading researchers on family day care.

Family Day Care Association of Manitoba. 1994. *Family day care: An aboriginal perspective.* Winnipeg: Author. A useful resource for early childhood educators working with Aboriginal families in a variety of programs.

For programs for children with special needs, see:

Baxter, J. & Read, M. 1999. *Children first: Working with young children in inclusive group settings in Canada.* Toronto: Harcourt Brace Canada.

Kaiser, B. & Rasminsky, J.S. 1999. *Meeting the challenge: Effective strategies for challenging behaviours in early childhood environments.* Ottawa: Canadian Child Care Federation.

 ## Useful Web Sites

Many of the Web sites suggested in Chapters 2 through 4 are relevant for information on day care (e.g., Canadian Child Care Federation, Child Care Advocacy Association of Canada, Child & Family Canada, National Association for the Education of Young Children, etc.).

Some other sites are

SpecialLink, the National Centre for Child Care Inclusion
P.O. Box 775
Sydney, NS B1P 6G9
Telephone: 902-562-1662
Fax: 902-539-9117
E-mail: speclink@atcon.com
Web site: highlander.cbnet.ns.ca/~speclink

Canadian Mothercraft Society
32 Heath Street West
Toronto, ON M4V 1T3
Telephone: 416-920-3515
Fax: 416-920-5983
Web site: www.tvo.org/GRTL/resources/can-mothercraft-soc.htm

Childcare Resource and Research Unit
Web site: www.childcarecanada.org
Centre for Urban and Community Studies
University of Toronto
455 Spadina Avenue, Room 305
Toronto, ON M5S 2G8

Telephone: 416-978-6895
Fax: 416-971-2139
E-mail: cmu@chass.utoronto.ca
Their Childcare Information Reference Collection is very useful and user-friendly.

Families and Work Institute
330 Seventh Avenue, 14th Floor
New York, NY 10001
Telephone: 212-465-2044
Fax: 212-465-8637
Web site: www.familiesandwork.org

ZERO TO THREE/The National Center
2000 14th Street N, Suite 380
Arlington, VA 22201-2500
Telephone: 800-899-4301 or 202-638-1144
Web site: www.zerotothree.org

Working Mother
Web site: www.workingmother.com
Links to several sites such as the International Nanny Association, ZERO TO
THREE, and so on.

National Child Care Information Center
243 Church Street NW, 2nd floor
Vienna, VA 22180
Telephone: 800-616-2242
Fax: 800-716-2242
Web site: nccic.org

For the most up-to-date information about day care in a province or territory:

Alberta–Alberta Children's Services, www.gov.ab.ca/CS
British Columbia–Ministry for Children and Families, www.mcf.gov.bc.ca
Manitoba–Manitoba Family Services, www.gov.mb.ca/fs
New Brunswick–Family and Community Social Services, www.gov.nb.ca/hcs-ssc
Newfoundland and Labrador–Department of Health and Community Services, www.gov.nf.ca/health
Northwest Territories–Department of Education, Culture, & Employment, Early Childhood and School Services, www.gov.nt.ca/ECE
Nova Scotia: Department of Community Services, www.gov.ns.ca/coms
Nunavut: www.gov.nu.ca
Ontario–Ministry of Community and Social Services, www.gov.on.ca/CCS
Prince Edward Island–Department of Health and Social Services, Child, Family and Community Services, www.gov.pe/cfacs-info/index.asp
Quebec: Ministère de la Famille et de l'Enfance, www.famille-enfance.gouv.qc.ca
Saskatchewan–Saskatchewan Social Services, Programs and Services, www.gov.sk.ca/govt/socserv
Yukon: Health and Social Services, www.gov.yk.ca

Nursery School:
Early Childhood Program with a Future?

*Nursery school has been a very positive experience for both my daughter
and me. We have both learned so much. It's been great!*

—Comment of the father of a four-year-old in a cooperative nursery school, March 2000

Nursery school has evolved with the times. From its beginnings as the Open
Air Nursery School of the McMillan sisters in England it has evolved in
Canada from a laboratory and demonstration school to the half-day
programs we know today. The current question is, How will nursery schools evolve
in the future? As more provinces include four-year-olds in junior kindergarten
programs and more families need full-time child care, what will be the role of
nursery school?

Most people associate the term **nursery school** with a neighbourhood half-day
program, often in the local church hall or community centre. This common
perception does not truly reflect the variety of nursery school programs both
historically and currently. For example, although nursery school is typically a half-
day program, it may be a five-day-, three-day-, or two-day-a-week program. It is
usually attended by three- and four-year-olds; however, the age for nursery school
attendance in Canada ranges from two to six years depending on the individual
provincial/territorial regulations.

In addition, nursery schools are located in a variety of settings such as
churches, schools, houses, remodelled garages, storefronts, portables, community
centres, colleges, universities, recreation centres, and specially adapted buses and
vans. I have also visited a correspondence program for families living in isolated
areas of Australia.

There is debate about what these half-day programs should be called. The most frequent term in Canadian provincial/territorial legislation is *nursery school* (Friendly, 1994). However, programs are also designated as *preschools, part-day programs,* and *day-care centres.* In addition, a term used by some people is *playschool.* The use of this variety of names can be confusing for early childhood educators, but it is especially confusing for parents trying to choose an early childhood program for their child. It must be very confusing until one realizes that all of these terms could refer to the same type of program.

The term *nursery school* was originated by Rachel and Margaret McMillan for their Open Air Nursery School, begun in London in 1911 (see Chapter 5). The focus of their program was not *nursing* or *nutrition,* but rather *nurturance.* By "nurturance," the McMillans meant fostering the development of the whole child. An early publication on nursery school states that, "nursery school education nurtures the many phases of child development taking place during the early years" (Davis & Hansen, 1932, p. 5). This is an accurate description of the general purpose of nursery school.

The use of *school* in *nursery school* was supposedly to distinguish these programs from the day nurseries of that time (Omwake, 1971). The implication was that the focus of the nursery school was *education,* while that of the day nurseries was *care.* Some of my early childhood colleagues dislike the use of *nursery* in *nursery school* because it implies "a baby program" (e.g., as in nurseries for newborns in hospitals). Some of them prefer the term *preschool.*

I personally have reservations about the term *preschool,* and prefer *early childhood programs.* Preschool as a descriptor implies *pre*-school. Therefore, does this mean it is a pre-junior kindergarten or a preparation for elementary school? A program for three- and four-year-olds should be a program that is appropriate for three- and four-year-olds, and not a *pre*-anything. For these reasons, I think *preschool* is not the most descriptive or accurate term, and is often misleading as well.

Although *preschool,* as a term, might be used more accurately to refer to all programs from infant programs up to kindergarten, an even more encompassing term that better reflects the realities of our field is **early childhood programs**. Early childhood programs include children from birth to age nine. There is more to early childhood education and care than programs for three- and four-year-old children. In order to avoid misunderstanding in this text, the term *nursery school* is used to refer to half-day programs typically for three- and four-year-old children. [The reader is encouraged to use whichever of the above terms they are most comfortable or familiar with.] These programs are usually "independent" programs and may be operated privately or operated under the auspices of organizations. They are not junior kindergartens (described in Chapter 10) or day cares (see Chapter 8).

You may know relatively few children who attend a nursery school. And indeed, the enrollment numbers overall are less than for kindergarten and day-care programs. Therefore, you may be wondering, why devote a separate chapter to nursery school? There are several reasons for this. Perhaps the most obvious one is "because it's there," and it has been since the early days of early childhood programs in Canada. Second, it is another career option for early childhood educators. Third, nursery school in Canada has experienced an interesting evolution that illustrates some of the forces of change that affect early childhood programs. And finally, educated early childhood professionals need to be knowledgeable about *all* types of early childhood programs—not just one or two of current personal interest.

Here are some questions to think about while you read this chapter:

· How did nursery schools in Canada develop? What were the sources and forces in the development of nursery schools in Canada?

· What lasting effects did laboratory nursery schools have on early childhood education and care in Canada?

· What types of nursery schools are found in Canada?

· Who uses nursery school programs and why?

· What are some characteristics of quality nursery school programs?

· How do parent cooperative nursery schools differ from traditional nursery schools?

· How can educators and families foster young children's transitions from home to an early childhood program?

· With the increased need for full-day child care, what does the future hold for half-day nursery school programs?

This chapter will examine nursery schools from their historical development in Canada to the types of nursery schools today, characteristics of good nursery schools, and finally some of the current issues associated with nursery schools.

Early Nursery Schools in Canada

The origins of the first nursery school, established by the McMillan sisters in England, are described in Chapter 5. The first nursery schools in Canada had rather different origins and owe much to the Child Study Movement (described in Chapter 6). The Child Study Movement, popular in the late nineteenth and early twentieth centuries, promoted the detailed observation and assessment of children, especially young children. It was natural that these researchers would create programs where groups of children could be studied. These programs were the laboratory nursery schools established in North America in the 1920s and 1930s during these "golden years of scientific child study" (Prochner, 1998, p. 33).

The laboratory nursery schools were very well known, and many still exist today. The first two nursery schools in Canada were laboratory nursery schools: St. George's School for Child Study at the University of Toronto (now the Institute of Child Study), and the Day Nursery and Child Laboratory at McGill University in Montreal (it operated from 1927–1930 only). These programs had a dual focus: research on children's development, and professional education. The provision of programs for young children tends to be mentioned third, if at all, in the descriptions of and by the early laboratory nursery schools. It is interesting that the Web site for the Institute of Child Study states that its current goals are research and professional education (www.oise.utoronto.ca/ICS/).

The origins of the early nursery schools were multidisciplinary. If one reflects on the backgrounds of many of the early nursery school pioneers discussed in Chapter 5, one can see this multidisciplinary nature of nursery school's beginnings. For example,

- Rachel McMillan—Public health
- Margaret McMillan—Education
- Abigail Eliot—Social work
- Harriet Johnson—Nursing
- Caroline Pratt—Education
- Lucy Sprague Mitchell—Philanthropy
- Patty Smith Hill—Education

The nursery school was becoming established at a time when several significant trends found applicability in the nursery school. In addition to the Child Study Movement, other forces that shaped the nursery school and helped distinguish it from the kindergarten and day care programs of the time were the mental hygiene movement and Freudian psychology combined with the support of philanthropic organizations and individuals. For example, the mental hygiene movement (later called *mental health* and now frequently included in *wellness*) studied topics such as the early origins of delinquency. Also, the preventive medicine movement was beginning to promote the idea of disease prevention and the importance of nutrition for young children as prevention of future problems. These orientations can be seen in the morning health inspections that were a common beginning to the day in early nursery schools, including St. George's School for Child Study. Developmental psychologists such as Arnold Gesell (who worked at the laboratory nursery school at Yale University) were interested in the scientific study of children's social, intellectual, and emotional development.

Emotional development was also an area of particular interest for psychoanalysts. The early years of the nursery school were a time of prominence for psychoanalytic theory (see Chapter 6). Freudian and neo-Freudian theories were popular and influenced the nursery school into the 1960s. The emphasis on children's healthy emotional and social development and research on children's personality development and the causes of children's behaviour reflects this influence. The work of Susan Isaacs was especially influential in nursery school development. In fact, some of her books are still in print (e.g., *Social Development in Young Children*), and others are available in libraries.

The First Nursery Schools in Canada

The earliest known nursery schools in Canada were the laboratory nursery schools at the University of Toronto and McGill University in Montreal. These nursery schools were funded by a matching grant from the Laura Spelman Rockefeller Memorial, which funded many university-based nursery schools in Canada and the United States. The matching funds were from the Lady Byng of Vimy Fund and the Metropolitan Life Insurance Company (Richardson, 1989). The Rockefeller grant stipulated three objectives to be met: (a) study of preschool children, (b) parent education, and (c) "the establishment of standards for child directed services in public agencies" (Richardson, 1989, p. 117). The St. George's School for Child Study met all three objectives and, in the process, permanently influenced early childhood education and care in Canada.

The Nursery School at the University of Toronto

The program developed at St. George's School for Child Study became the most widely known nursery school program in Canada. In addition and more importantly, its program served as the primary model for later nursery schools throughout Canada.

St. George's School for Child Study opened in 1926 under the direction of Dr. William Blatz, a physician and psychologist. It enrolled children from two to five years of age. Because the program was supported by fees, the children enrolled in the nursery school were from middle- and upper-income backgrounds. And because its hours were from about 8:45 a.m. to 3 p.m., it was not used by working families needing full-day care. This nursery school was divided into two divisions: the Nursery School Division and the Parent Education Division (Wright, 2000). The children's program will be described first.

The Nursery School Program

Health was a big part of the nursery school program. At this time, there was public concern for the health risks of young children in groups. When the Institute nursery school first opened there were only six children. This low enrollment was attributed to the perceived health risk of group care (Varga, 1997). By the 1930s this fear had subsided and the enrollment was at 30 with a wait-list. In fact, as was common with other later nursery school programs and day nursery programs, the St. George's program began each day with a health inspection of every child by public health nurses before the child was permitted into the school (the parent waited until the child was pronounced healthy).

The emphasis on "the orderly and predictable division of the child's day" can be seen in the daily schedule of activities with its emphasis on health, nutrition, and play (Strong-Boag, 1982, p. 171). Following the morning health inspection, the child was encouraged to use the toilet and drink a glass of water before going to the outdoor playground for free play. After cleanup and toileting, the child had half a glass of juice at 10:30, followed by indoor playtime. Cleanup was followed by circle time and a quiet time before lunch at noon. After lunch, toileting was followed by nap; then toileting, dressing, and snack (glass of milk). The parents picked up their children between 2:45 and 3 p.m. You can see the emphasis on health, nutrition, elimination routines, rest, and play.

The children were divided into groups by ages: 2 to 3-1/2, 3-1/2 to 5, or by yearly ages when there were more children. This reflects the Child Study Movement's orientation of ages and stages and the assumed similarity within each individual age group. For example, play materials were classified and divided by their appropriateness for each chronological age. This organization of children by narrow age range would later be adopted by day nursery programs as well (Varga, 1997). The curriculum was based on maturationist child development theory (see Chapter 6) and mental hygiene principles (Varga, 2000).

The nursery school served as an observation site for researchers. Many early photos of the Institute of Child Study nursery school show adults with clipboards (almost always women) standing or seated discreetly in the background observing the children's activities and taking notes. A characteristic of the early laboratory nursery schools, which is still found in these programs today, is the observation room with one-way mirrors. Researchers, parents, or practicum students can sit at a window and watch and hear the children, but the children cannot see through the window and so are oblivious to the observers.

The Parent Education Program

One of the strengths of this and other nursery school programs was parent education and participation. According to Beatty (1995), "the universal theme of the nursery school movement was that all parents, rich and poor, could become better parents through the application of scientific educational principles and

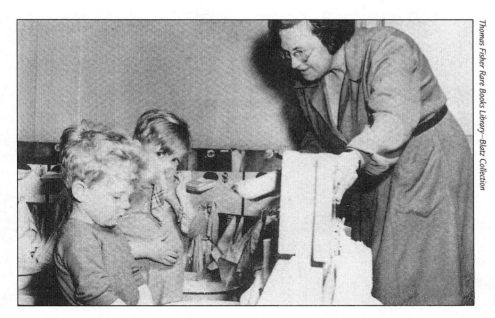

Educator and children at St. George's School for Child Study in the early years.

the enrollment of their young children in nursery school" (p. 136). In fact, parent education had been part of the nursery school since the McMillan sisters' Open Air Nursery School in England. At St. George's School, parent education was an important part of the overall program, as it was in later nursery schools in Canada.

The parent education program consisted of specific courses such as:

• Habit Training—Preschool age

• Management of Child—Preschool age

• Thinking and Acting—School age

• Adolescence

• Family Relationship.

(Whipple, 1929, p. 289)

In addition, the parents were expected to participate in child study research by doing observations of their children at home. They were required to keep notes on their children's behaviours using "Home Records for Parents." The Home Records included:

• The Daily Record, which had spaces for noting the time of arising, dressing, breakfast, play, supper, evening activities, bed, sleep, and tasks such as piano practice.

• The Weekly Meal Chart, for indicating what the child ate, wouldn't eat, behaviour at mealtimes, and with whom the child ate.

• The Weekly Sleep Chart, for recording the times for naps and bedtime as well as behaviour, physical location, previous activities, and quality of sleep.

- The Elimination Record, for noting bladder and bowel control.

- The Play Activities Form, for noting time, type, location, and playmates.

- The Emotional Disturbance Chart, for recording details of emotional behaviour such as tantrums, sulking, or fears (Blatz & Bott, 1928).

The parents who enrolled in this program did not represent a cross-section of Toronto society at that time; they were, according to the school's records, well-educated and from upper-middle-class and upper-class backgrounds (Strong-Boag, 1982).

The lasting significance of the early programs at the Institute of Child Study lies in the contributions to the child development research of the time, its parent education program, and the setting of standards for early childhood programs. Blatz and his colleagues and students such as Dorothy Millichamp, Elsie Stapleford, and Mary Wright developed the standards for licensing day nurseries in the original Ontario Day Nurseries Act (see Chapter 8). Their influence continued for many years.

In child study and research, Blatz initiated a longitudinal study of children that continued until they were 24 years old (Wright, 1999). Another research project for Dr. Blatz was observing and studying the Dionne quintuplets of Quebec. This was highly prominent research and helped to establish the place of the Institute of Child Study at the University of Toronto (Wright, 1999).

In parent education, Blatz and his colleagues were high-profile; they presented frequently to parent groups and at conferences as well as doing parent education programs at the nursery school. Blatz also published some popular and influential books, such as *Understanding the Young Child* (1944), *The Management of Young Children* (Blatz & Bott, 1930), and *Parents and the Pre-school Child* (Blatz & Bott, 1928); the latter was awarded *Parents' Magazine*'s medal for the best parent book of 1928. A book written for educators was *Nursery Education: Theory and Practice* (Blatz, Millichamp, & Fletcher, 1935).

The Nursery School at McGill University

The nursery school at McGill University in Montreal was relatively short-lived and operated only from 1927 to 1930. The program was for 20 children from 2-1/2 to 5 years of age, from 9 a.m. to 3 p.m. five days a week (Strong-Boag, 1982). It had a similar emphasis on health to the St. George's School program. For example, the children played outdoors half the morning, weather permitting. There were two teachers from England: one was Frobel-educated and the other Montessori-educated. The director was Katherine Banham-Bridges, a psychologist who did research on the social and emotional development of infants.

The Rockefeller funding was withdrawn in 1930 because of the lack of use of the nursery school for research and teaching. However, the parents raised funds to continue it as a private school, St. George's Nursery School of Montreal (Wright, 2000).

Types of Nursery Schools

Nursery schools can be classified into four major types:

- Laboratory or demonstration nursery schools

- Traditional and modern nursery schools

- Parent cooperative nursery schools

- Playgroups.

Laboratory or Demonstration Nursery Schools

A **laboratory** or **demonstration nursery school** is one that is affiliated with a university, college, or institute for the purposes of research, professional education, and provision of early childhood programs. Traditionally, laboratory nursery schools have been affiliated with departments of psychology (e.g., University of Waterloo), education (University of British Columbia, University of Calgary), or home economics/family studies (University of Manitoba, Ryerson Polytechnic University). These three disciplines are ones that support early childhood education and care. The affiliation with a university is often beneficial for the nursery schools, as the university may help with finances and provide a building and utilities and services such as janitorial or accounting. They are most typically preschools but may include elementary school (e.g., Institute of Child Study at the University of Toronto).

The first nursery school, the McMillan sisters' Open Air Nursery School, could be considered a demonstration school and certainly it was used for the training of early childhood educators and as a practicum site (and continues to be so used today). In North America the early kindergartens of Matilde Kriege

The original Head Start program is also usually considered a traditional nursery school program; it is discussed in Chapter 5.

Montessori programs, which can be nursery schools as well as kindergarten through elementary school programs, are discussed in Chapter 5

Campus child care, which is not the same as a laboratory school, is discussed in Chapter 8.

A parent cooperative nursery school (discussed on page 369).

in Boston in 1868 and Maria Kraus-Boelte in New York in 1872 were demonstration and teacher education centres (Williams, 1992). The early nursery schools of Abigail Eliot in Boston, Patty Smith Hill at Columbia Teachers College in New York, and Harriet Johnson at the Bureau for Educational Experiments (later Bank Street College of Education) included professional education. These could be considered demonstration schools in the strictest sense of the definition. Later on they added research and became what we now term *laboratory schools*. Laboratory schools today maintain the traditional multiple purposes of the original programs in the 1920s and 1930s.

The research function of the laboratory schools has been important since the 1920s. Much of the early research was normative research on young children (i.e., what young children did at certain ages, their characteristics, etc.), because relatively little scientific study of young children had been done up to that time. An example of this important research was Mary Salter Ainsworth's research on attachment of children (see Chapter 2); she began her research career as a doctoral student of William Blatz. The influential play research of Parten (discussed in Chapter 7) was done at the Institute of Child Development laboratory nursery school at the University of Minnesota. This and much of the research done in laboratory nursery schools was and still is multidisciplinary. For example, in the Yearbook of the National Society for the Study of Education, it was reported that university researchers from "psychology, anatomy, physiology, dentistry, psychiatry, education, household sciences, pediatrics, and the school of public health nursing" used the Institute of Child Study as a site for their research studies (Whipple, 1929, p. 289). The Institute's current Web site also includes social work, sociology, family law, and other academic fields (www.oise.utoronto.ca/ICS/). Thus, laboratory nursery schools have had a long history of contribution to what we know about young children and how they develop.

An example of a laboratory nursery school today is the current Institute of Child Study. It is part of the Department of Human Development and Applied Psychology of the Ontario Institute for Studies in Education of the University of Toronto. Like its earlier version, its mandate is still child development research and professional education. It offers graduate degree programs in human development, including early childhood education and child psychology. The laboratory school now has an enrollment of approximately 200 children from 3 to 12 years of age and a staff of more than 30. The nursery school operates from 8:45 to 11:45 a.m., with a staff including a teacher, assistant teacher, and three student teachers. Their stated roles include role model, mentor, constructor of the environment, curriculum planner, researcher, observer, assessor, and colleague.

In addition to the nursery laboratory school, there are junior and senior kindergartens, grades 1 to 6, and an after-school-care program. There is also an Infant Centre program for children from 3 to 24 months of age and their parents. Each family attends the program one morning a week. Its purposes are typical of a laboratory school: observation of the children by students, infant

FOR REFLECTION

The stated philosophy of the current Institute of Child Study's nursery school is that "Children learn easily and best in an environment which: captures their imagination, deals with their interests, challenges their intellect, develops their skills, and allows them to see the results of their labours in positive, satisfying ways and offers them the emotional and psychological security to make learning possible" (www.oise.utoronto.ca/ICS/ labschool.html#Philosophy). How is this statement similar to the goals of the original St. George's School for Child Study?

education program for the children, and parent education. A parent library is available.

Recent social and economic trends have impacted laboratory nursery schools. For example, more of them are open longer hours and summers to accommodate working families, as well as including a wider age range of children (e.g., infant/toddlers to school-age children). A concern for many laboratory nursery schools in recent years has been funding. The reduction of funding is a main reason for the closure or reduction of programs (e.g., the Child Study Centre at the University of British Columbia). Limitation of funding has also led to amalgamation or partnerships with other programs or groups such as campus day care and local school boards. (For a description of this process, see Stuart, Brophy, Lero, Callahan, & de Voy, 1998, on the development of the University of Guelph Child Care and Learning Centre.)

Traditional and Modern Nursery Schools

The label **traditional nursery school** refers to the early versions of the nursery schools found in many Canadian communities. From the following description of "What Nursery School Is Like," published in a booklet for parents in 1948, what do you think the goals of the traditional nursery school were?

> It [the nursery school] is a place where young children learn how to get along with others of the same age, a place designed especially to allow children to be as noisy, as active, as creative as they wish. The play and activities are according to a plan based upon the needs of young children in their growth and development. The teacher's role is that of a guide in seeing that these needs are fulfilled. (New York Committee on Mental Health, 1948, p. 1)

Traditional nursery schools were typically characterized by their emphasis on health, broadly defined. A 1927 publication stated that "The health-care and health-education of the children are conspicuous features of the activity of well-equipped nursery schools" (Forest, 1927, p. 301). The Freudian influence can be seen in the attention to children's social and emotional development.

In the traditional nursery school, "the basic underlying belief is the importance of interpersonal connections children make with themselves, each other and adults" (Gordon & Browne, 1993, p. 39). This belief is reflected in the title of possibly the most influential textbook on nursery school, Katherine Read's *The Nursery School: A Human Relationships Laboratory,* originally published in 1950 and now in its ninth edition (1993).

In addition to children's social and emotional development, the traditional nursery school sought to foster children's creativity and to encourage their imaginations. To facilitate this, nursery schools provided unstructured materials such as sand, water, art supplies, and blocks (Williams, 1992). Some, such as the nursery school of Harriet Johnson (see Chapter 5), put out very few materials for the children so they would be required to interact with each other cooperatively and use their imaginations in their play. Music and rhythmic activities were also part of the curriculum.

The daily schedule of the traditional nursery school as described by Read is very similar to that of the St. George's School for Child Study described earlier, although there is more flexibility for children's choice of individual activities. There was variation among traditional nursery school programs (Davis & Hansen, 1932). For example, the early nursery schools did not all have the same length of day. Some were half-day programs, some were full-day programs, and still others had diverse hours.

One area of general agreement was that the traditional nursery school did not include formal instruction. As Grace Owen stated emphatically in her 1920 textbook on nursery school, "no mention has been made of instruction in the Nursery school, because in any formal sense it has no place. No reading, no writing, no number lessons should on any account be required—no object lessons as commonly known should be allowed" (p. 25). Even in the earliest days of the nursery school, nursery educators were quite clear that nursery school was not the same as kindergarten. However, many of the activities in the traditional nursery school were similar to the progressive kindergarten (Forest, 1927).

Overall, from their earliest days, nursery school programs were designed to foster the development of the whole child. However, in the earliest programs, the emphasis on the children's social and emotional development seemed to be somewhat stronger than physical or cognitive development. There was a great emphasis placed on stimulating children's creativity and imaginations.

The Nursery School Today

The nursery school of today typically has a broader program than the traditional nursery school. There is now less emphasis on health and nutrition. This is due, in great part, to improved child health care, reduction or elimination of many childhood diseases, and parents' greater awareness and knowledge. This is not to say that these topics are not important or no longer part of the program and its curriculum. Although the formal morning health inspection is no longer practised, early childhood educators still informally assess children's health and well-being on first greeting them in the morning (e.g., does the child look well-rested, is the child and his or her clothes clean, does the child look ill or upset?). There are differences, but these are more a matter of emphasis. Likewise, the cognitive emphasis is greater in today's nursery school than in the traditional nursery school, which placed greater emphasis on fostering children's emotional development. There is also typically a greater variety of materials available for the children. The traditional nursery school was often limited to unstructured materials such as sand, water, paints, and blocks (Williams, 1992). However, overall, the differences are between the two types of nursery schools are primarily in emphasis.

This similarity of orientation of the early and current nursery school programs can be attributed to its comprehensive focus from the beginning. The early kindergartens had an educational focus and the day nurseries a social welfare one, whereas the nursery school movement was multidisciplinary from its beginnings (Osborn, 1991). The multidisciplinary origin and program of the nursery school from its earliest days has influenced other early childhood programs. In this area, the nursery school has been a leader and deserves significant credit for the multidisciplinary curricula of today's early childhood programs. This orientation has also been credited as one of the reasons why, unlike kindergarten, nursery school has not experienced such dramatic conflicts over content. As Spodek and Saracho (1994) commented, "the original eclectic approach to nursery education was broad enough to encompass modification and diversity without serious conflict" (p. 41). The nursery school seems to have a history of adapting and adopting new ideas without radical change.

If you were to review the brochures and handbooks of dozens of nursery schools today, you would very likely note key words reappearing in their descriptions of goals and objectives, such as:

- Self-esteem

- Creativity

- Socialization

- Social skills

- Cognitive stimulation/enrichment,

- And, most frequently, play.

Indeed, oftentimes individual nursery schools have play in their titles: Playhouse, Playschool, or Playcentre.

The most common schedule for nursery schools in Canada is the half-day program for three- and four-year-olds. One configuration is Monday–Wednesday–Friday mornings or afternoons for the older children, and Tuesday–Thursday mornings or afternoons for the younger children. Some nursery schools operate five days a week.

Parent Cooperative Nursery Schools

The first nursery school in North America was a cooperative nursery school, and since that time this type of program has played a significant role in the development of early childhood education as well as parent participation. In Chapter 1, a **parent cooperative nursery school** was defined as a type of nursery school that is operated by a parent board elected by all the parents. It is commonly referred to as a *co-op*. Typically, an early childhood educator is assisted by several parents. The parents have organizational, administrative, and service roles. The program may take place daily or two to three mornings or

FOR REFLECTION

You are the owner and operator of a nursery school named the Happy Children Play School. One day, a prospective parent comes to visit and asks you: "This is called a play school. So what do they do—only play, or learn, like in a real school?" What would you reply to this parent?

afternoons a week, although it may be either a half-day or full-day program. There are cooperative day-care programs (see Chapter 8), as well as the more widely known nursery schools. However, "co-operation came to day care rather later than to preschools and has not yet developed to nearly the same extent" (McCready, 1992, p. 4). Therefore, this section will focus on the cooperative nursery school. Canada, the United States, Britain, and New Zealand are leaders in preschool cooperative programs. (co-ops are called *playcentres* in New Zealand and *playgroups* in Britain.)

A common characteristic of nursery schools since their beginnings has been inclusion of the home. Early on, parents were recognized as important for the optimal development of young children, and parent education was included as part of the early nursery school's responsibilities. The parent cooperative nursery schools extended parent participation to another level. A parent cooperative nursery school is typically established and administered by parents for the provision of quality early childhood experience for their young children. It is unique in terms of its parent education function and organization, and the role of the early childhood educator.

The first parent cooperative nursery school in North America was begun at the University of Chicago by 12 faculty wives who were active in the Red Cross volunteer efforts during the First World War. They wanted "social education for their children, parent education for themselves, and a little free time for Red Cross work" (Taylor, 1967, p. 294). The program actually began as an outdoor playgroup in 1915, which in winter moved into the women's gymnasium at the University of Chicago. It became a co-op in 1916 with the hiring of a professional early childhood educator. As described in Chapter 8, many college and university day-care programs in Canada were also established by student and faculty parents.

Cooperative nursery schools were often part of the larger cooperative movement in Canada. This was a grassroots movement that developed without philanthropy or public monies. Canada, especially in the Prairie and Maritime provinces, has a long history of cooperative movements. For example, the Hudson Nursery School in Newfoundland is part of the Newfoundland and Labrador Federation of Cooperatives (Glassman, 1992). Saskatchewan used the model of parent cooperative boards in its early requirements for early childhood programs (Nykyforuk, 1992).

Women were active in the general cooperative movements, and especially in the cooperative nursery school movement. Although cooperative nursery schools include the entire family, women have been the primary initiators, organizers, and managers of cooperative early childhood programs in Canada as well as other countries (Muir, 1990). The establishment of cooperative early childhood programs is another example of the significance of women in the development of early childhood education and care. Focus 9.1 describes one influential woman in the development of cooperative nursery schools.

According to Stevenson (1991), Canadian cooperative nursery schools began in the 1930s; the first was probably the Manor Road Nursery School in

Focus 9.1

Katharine Whiteside Taylor

Katharine Whiteside Taylor (1897–1989) is the name probably most associated with the development of cooperative nursery schools in North America. She came from an educational background. Her mother was the first principal of a Pestalozzi-Froebel normal school in North America, a suffragette, and a friend of Patty Smith Hill. Katharine Whiteside Taylor began one of the early cooperative nursery schools, located in Berkeley, California, in 1927. She received her doctorate in 1937 and was a tireless advocate for and promoter of cooperative nursery schools throughout North America and abroad under UNESCO auspices. Her book, *Parents and Children Learn Together*, is considered a classic on how to establish and operate a cooperative preschool. In the preface to this book, Taylor (1967) states, "Parent cooperative nursery schools have come of age; they have been thoroughly established as one important type of education for young children *and* their parents." The Katharine Whiteside Taylor Centre for Cooperative Education was established in Baie d'Urfe, Quebec, in 1969. It was the centre for the Parent Cooperative Preschools International for many years and included a day-care centre, two cooperative nursery schools, library, gymnasium, and craft area, and served as a practicum site with an observation room and lounge looking down into three classrooms. Dorothy Hewes summed up Katharine Whiteside Taylor's efforts by saying, "she was a charismatic leader endowed with the ability to inspire personal loyalty" (1998, p. 79).

Toronto, established in 1935, which became a parent cooperative in 1937. Cooperative preschools were also begun on the West Coast and the Prairies in the early 1940s. For example, Gertrude Elsie McGill began the first cooperative nursery school in western Canada in her back garden in Victoria in 1944. The Children's Garden Library was originally a summer program for three- to eight-year-olds three mornings a week. McGill was motivated by her concern with the "trashy reading to which little children are often exposed . . . . Perhaps I could entice them into reading better than the funnies" (quoted in Johnson-Dean, 1984). She was assisted with donations from 14 Canadian book publishers. In addition to good literature, the program included games, songs, crafts, and outdoor activities for 75 children in the first year. The next year there were 196 children. The program was written up in numerous magazines and was filmed not only by the National Film Board of Canada but MGM, Fox, and Paramount Studios for newsreels that were shown in movie theatres.

Gertrude McGill later met Katharine Whiteside Taylor (see Focus 9.1) at a conference in Seattle, and was convinced of the merits of involving mothers in her program. She then expanded the program to include not only mother volunteer helpers but also a Mothers' Study Group with lectures by experts in child care and psychology. More than 100 mothers participated in these courses between 1944 and 1946 (Siska, 1984).

Gertrude Elsie McGill travelled extensively throughout British Columbia promoting cooperative nursery schools. In 1949, 50 parents from Victoria formed the Vancouver Cooperative Play Group Association (now the Vancouver Island Cooperative Preschool Association), which offered non-credit courses for both educators and parents through Victoria College (now the University of Victoria). Some of the parents and educators participating in cooperative nursery schools in Victoria in recent years attended Gertrude McGill's program when they were children.

The Victoria cooperative preschool was followed in 1945 by a cooperative playgroup in Saskatoon at the Community Apartments, a housing development on a former military base for the families of veterans. The cooperative nursery school grew rapidly in Canada during the 1950s and 1960s. This was due, at least in part, to the post-war baby boom coupled with a growing interest in early childhood education. The movement plateaued during the 1970s as more and more women joined the paid labour force and needed full-time child care (Hewes, 1998).

A cooperative early childhood program has a unique organization in that the parents own it and are responsible for its administration and management, including the hiring of an early childhood educator. A parent board is elected by all the parents, and policies are democratically determined by the group. The role of the early childhood educator in a cooperative early childhood program is also unique. He or she is the person in charge of the children's program but is technically an employee of the parents as represented by the board. (The implications of this arrangement are discussed later in this chapter.)

The cooperative nursery school program has two major components catering to two different groups of learners—the children and their parents. While parent participation and education have been important for and included in many nursery schools since their beginning at the turn of the twentieth century, these are required components of the cooperative nursery school. The parents' roles in a co-op include educator, learner, and advocate in their children's education—now, and in the future.

The parent education component typically consists of two major aspects: orientation training and ongoing parent education. The orientation sessions usually occur before the beginning of the school year and explain the nature of a cooperative nursery school, its policies and rules, the responsibilities of the parents, characteristics of young children, the roles and duties of the parent volunteer, strategies to use (and not use) when working with young children in groups, and relevant licensing regulations. In addition, some programs provide families with a handbook containing the above and other useful information.

The ongoing parent education component typically consists of monthly evening sessions on topics of interest and importance to the parents. The board usually determines this set of topics after consultation with the other parents. In my experience, recent popular topics for these parent education sessions have

FOR REFLECTION

How would you ensure that the privacy and confidentiality of children and families be maintained when using parent volunteers in your parent cooperative nursery school? What would you do if you found out someone had discussed another family's problem with their child outside the school?

included children's literacy development, television and media, streetproofing children, allergies, identifying learning problems, sibling rivalry, teaching environmental awareness at home and in the community, child guidance strategies, child abuse, choosing good books for young children, self-esteem, stress in parents and children, death, the importance of play, and promoting oral language.

Parent duties as part of a cooperative early childhood program usually include serving as a volunteer parent, typically once or twice a month. By using parent volunteers, a nursery school can keep the tuition cost down (salaries and benefits is the largest part of an early childhood program's operating budget). Although the parents are taught the basics during the orientation sessions, quite a bit of their learning is on-the-job. The duties of the parent volunteer may include providing and serving the snack, setting up and putting away playground equipment, supervising learning centres and playground activities, participating in circle time (usually led by the early childhood educator), cleaning up, and generally assisting the early childhood educator.

Outwardly, the program of the typical cooperative nursery school looks much like other early childhood programs. As in other early childhood programs, the curriculum for the children may "run the gamut of preschool theories and practices" (Goodlad, Klein, & Novotney, 1973, p. 71). However, the most obvious difference is the role of the parents. Focus 9.2 describes a day in a cooperative nursery school that I observed as part of a research study (Mayfield, 1990). This program was in two large rooms in a church hall with a grassy play area located between the hall and the church. The program had 55 families and operated three mornings a week (9:30–11:45) for four-year-olds, two mornings a week for three-year-olds, and three afternoons a week for a mixed class of three- and four-year-olds (1–3:15). Provincial licensing regulations in British Columbia required that there be one qualified early childhood educator and two parents for a maximum of 20 children enrolled in the morning class I observed. This description focuses on the roles and activities of the parent volunteers.

Each parent cooperative establishes its own rules and procedures. Some programs require that all parents participate as volunteers working directly with the children. Other programs will permit substitution of other tasks for direct participation. These tasks might include fundraising; publicity (doing the newsletter, brochures, posters, and organizing recruiting for the next year); accounting; developing a computing program to handle applications, registrations, and payment of tuition; maintenance and repair of facilities and equipment; and so forth. Some programs also require one or more group workdays or evenings when the parents fix equipment, paint, and do general maintenance. Still other programs permit family substitutes, to enable parents working full-time to enrol their children. For example, I have observed programs where the substitute was a grandparent, a teenage sibling, or the family nanny.

What do parents think of the cooperative nursery school? Some parent comments from formal interviews and informal conversations with parents, including a group I spoke to recently about children's emerging literacy, typically include:

FOR REFLECTION

Some parent co-ops permit other family members such as grandparents or nannies to replace parents on volunteer days; other programs insist a parent must be the volunteer. What are the pros and cons of each of these policies?

Parents' Roles in a Cooperative Nursery School

The duty parents for the day and their children arrived by 9 a.m. The first parent put on the coffee and began to get the main activity room organized for the morning session. This included taking down the chairs, filling the water tank with warm water, putting out playdough and art materials, and checking the bathroom for cleanliness and supplies. The second parent was busy putting out the outdoor play equipment including trikes, balls, sandbox equipment, and other materials as well as checking the swings, slide, climber, and grounds for safety hazards.

This program began with most of the children playing outside. The early childhood educator and one parent were outside supervising the play and talking with parents and children as they arrived around 9:30. The other parent was inside for the children who chose to play there. At about 10:20, all the children were inside for free play in the main room. On this day, in addition to the usual centres (e.g., art, library, dramatic play, etc.), one duty parent was doing Chinese cooking with the children, as it was close to the lunar New Year. She was assisted by her son, who did most of the explaining about the Chinese food they ate at home. The other duty parent was assisting those children who were making dragon kites for the dragon dance they were learning. Both parents kept an eye on the children near them but did not intervene unless there was a problem. The early childhood educator circulated among the groups of children.

At about 11 a.m., the parents prepared the snack they had brought (part of the responsibilities for the day's duty parents was to provide the snack). The children put away materials and equipment and then washed their hands and found a place at one of several round tables. The son and daughter of the duty parents poured the juice and passed the tray with the fruit. All of the adults ate with the children.

After snack, the early childhood educator read the children a story while one duty parent cleaned up from snack and the other tidied the room and sorted children's drawings, paintings, and other items to be placed in their cubbies to go home. After discussion about the story and a Chinese song taught to the children by one of the duty parents, the children went into the other room, which had a large open space, and did their dragon dance with the kites. This was so popular that the children asked to repeat it three times. One duty parent was responsible for the tape player and the other assisted the early childhood educator, who was helping the children keep their dragons from getting tangled up.

At 11:45 a.m., the early childhood educator and one duty parent helped the children get ready to leave. The second duty parent began sweeping the floors and cleaning the bathrooms for the afternoon session. In addition, there were special tasks assigned for each day of the week. For example, on Tuesdays, in addition to the usual daily tasks, the duty parents cleaned the pet area and watered the plants, and the Wednesday parents scrubbed all the tables and chairs. There was a short debriefing of the duty parents with the early childhood educator at the end of every session. The duty parents left about noon.

- I understand a child's developmental stages better now.

- I learned a lot about my child!

- It's given me lots of parenting tools.

- It's been good to meet and be with adults.

- I made lots of new friends and so did my son.

- I realize how important early education is.

- I now realize I can do lots of things I never knew I could do.

- I know I'm not alone.

- I know what is going on in my child's program.

- The best way to spend my time is in the co-op with my kids.

In a related part of a research study, I found that many of the parent volunteers in the early grades of an elementary school had been parents in a parent cooperative nursery school and wanted to continue their participation in their children's education (Mayfield, 1990). It is not unusual for parents from cooperative nursery schools to also continue their own education to become early childhood educators or elementary school teachers. Other families commented on how it was a positive experience for them, as they were new to the community and made friendships with other adults that have lasted for years.

A common question about parents volunteering in their child's preschool program is, How do children behave when Mommy or Daddy is the parent volunteer? According to the parents I interviewed, this was not usually a problem. While some children were clingy, more demanding, and less interactive when their parent was there, the most common reactions of the children seemed to be excitement and pride in their parent (e.g., "That's my Mom in the art centre"). On the other hand, a few children almost ignored their parent and had very little interaction with them. Both the parents and educator reported that only rarely was a child jealous of the attention given to other children by their parent.

Cooperative nursery schools are not an option for all families. Working parents may require additional care beyond a half-day program. However, some of these parents arrange for their children to attend a family day care before or after nursery school. The requirement for parent volunteering in the program can be a problem for single-parent families and working parents. However, I have been impressed at the ingenuity of families in arranging their work schedules in order to participate in their young children's programs. For example, one family volunteer was the child's grandfather, who was very popular with all the children; two parents who were both nurses worked different shifts; a father who worked at home was his family's volunteer; a mother who was a real estate agent volunteered on a morning that was traditionally slow for showing houses; and a symphony musician had practices in the afternoon and arranged giving private lessons around her volunteer days.

When I asked parents what they thought the obstacles were to participating in a parent cooperative nursery school, they suggested:

- Lack of time

- Lack of knowledge about cooperatives

- Lack of interest

- Not being comfortable with a group of young children

- Having family responsibilities at home (e.g., new baby or ill parent).

True to their cooperative-movement roots, cooperative nursery schools in Canada are organized into local and regional councils. This not only facilitates mutual professional activities but also enables many of them to sponsor yearly or bi-yearly conferences for educators and parents. These councils provide advice and assistance to individual program boards. This is important because a program's parent board is likely to change every year, and sometimes there may not be much or any carryover of its membership from one year to the next. There is also an international organization: Parent Co-operative Preschools International (see the Resources section at the end of this chapter for contact information). As stated in its brochure, its purposes are to promote the parent cooperative movement, standards for programs, interchange of information among programs, and legislation for children and families, and to cooperate with other early childhood and family organizations. Canadian educators and parents have been leaders in this professional organization, and some of its conferences over the years have been held in Montreal, Hamilton, Toronto, London, Vancouver, and Victoria (Stevenson, 1990).

Another type of nursery school program that is somewhat similar to the parent cooperative nursery school is the playgroup.

Playgroups

The following is a good definition of a **playgroup**: "four or five children who meet regularly at each other's homes to play, with each mother supervising the whole group in turn, make up a playgroup. A playgroup is *not* a babysitting arrangement. It is a small organization that is planned and prepared, with equipment supplied for the children's play and activities introduced by the mothers in charge" (Winn & Porcher, 1967, p. 3). Playgroups are also sometimes referred to as *playschools*. (Requirements for licensing group early childhood programs vary across provinces and territories and can affect the number of children in and organization of a playgroup.)

The key distinguishing feature of a playgroup is that it is an informal program organized, developed, and implemented by parents for their children; in other words, a grassroots effort. It may meet only one morning or afternoon a week, or more frequently. Unlike in cooperative nursery schools, no early childhood educator is hired: the parents, usually mothers, run the playgroup. Many of the early cooperative nursery schools began this way (Hewes, 1998). For example, the first nursery school in North America, at the University of Chicago, was originally a playgroup. Britain, Australia, and New Zealand are known for their playgroup movements (Lloyd, Melhuish, Moss, & Owen, 1989).

A playgroup is similar to other good programs for young children. There are a variety of materials and activities such as crafts, playdough, water, sand, art materials, manipulatives, books, construction materials, and dramatic play materials. There is typically a group time with songs, fingerplays, and stories, as well as snacks and sometimes lunch depending on the length of the playgroup session.

The advantages of a playgroup are that it provides opportunities for:

- An initial group experience for young children in a familiar neighbourhood setting

- Children to meet and play with other children in their neighbourhoods

- Children to learn to relate to other adults outside their families

- Separating children from their families in a less stressful local and familiar environment

- Adjusting to a limited number, and

- Having fun!

The playgroup is a relatively inexpensive option for parents who want some free time. It is local, convenient, and reflects the neighbourhood's culture and language. In addition, it can take advantage of individual parents' particular expertise, such as music, crafts, or nature study. As well, parents experience the general benefits of parent participation, such as learning more about their own children and child development in general.

Other benefits of parent participation are discussed in Chapter 3.

Obviously, the initiation and continuation of a playgroup depends on parents being ready and able to participate and to find replacements for families that drop out or move on to other programs. Often a playgroup exists for a relatively short time. However, some playgroups have operated for many years while others have developed into nursery schools or day-care programs. For example, an informal playgroup at the YM-YWCA in St. John's in 1969 evolved into a more formal early childhood program and subsequently expanded to include toddler and after-school programs (Glassman, 1992).

What Is a Good Nursery School?

Although there are different types of nursery schools, it is important that all are quality early childhood programs. What one wants to see in a good nursery school program for three- and four-year-olds is, of course, similar to other good early childhood programs for young children. For example, characteristics of

A comprehensive discussion of quality in early childhood programs is included in Chapter 12.

good infant and toddler programs are described in Chapter 8, and kindergarten programs are discussed in Chapter 10. Focus 9.3 is the National Association for the Education of Young Children's suggested list of what one should see in an early childhood program for three- and four-year-olds.

Focus 9.3

What to Look for in an Early Childhood Program
What you want to see

Teachers provide meaningful classroom activities that challenge children to move forward. At the same time, children are able to successfully complete many of the tasks encountered so that they gain self-confidence, feel proud of their accomplishments, and learn to love learning.

Teachers plan a curriculum that engages the children. The classroom has been arranged to give children easy access to toys and other materials. Children have the space to interact with their peers and adults.

Teachers maintain a safe, healthy environment and carefully supervise the children.

Teachers take adequate safety precautions so that children can take age-appropriate risks. For instance, 3- and 4-year-olds can help bake cookies and, with a grownup's assistance, use pot holders to take the baking sheets out of the oven.

Teachers plan a balanced schedule in which children don't feel rushed or fatigued.

Teachers nurture the 3- and 4-year-old's developing language and communication skills by encouraging conversation. They talk to the children, listen to their responses, and they provide opportunities for children to talk with one another.

Teachers help children get the most out of every learning situation. They ask the child questions about what she is doing, offer suggestions about other things to do, and add new challenges as the child is ready for them.

Teachers set clear limits about acceptable social behavior. At the same time, they know that 3- to 4-year-olds get easily frustrated and are not always able to express their feelings verbally.

Adults read to the children every day—individually, in small groups, and sometimes even as a whole class. Teachers help the children talk about what they have heard and help them relate the stories to activities in the classroom or at home.

Teachers make parents part of the community of learners. Parents are welcomed into the classroom, and teachers consult with them about their child's needs and progress.

Source: NAEYC, 1997a

Participants in Nursery Schools

The participants in nursery school have shifted throughout its evolution. The original participants targeted by the McMillan sisters' Open Air Nursery School were poor families. However, the first nursery schools in Canada were the laboratory schools that enrolled children from middle- and upper-income families that could afford to pay the fees and were willing and able to participate in parent education programs and help researchers by collecting data on their children in their homes.

In the 1940s and 1950s, non-working mothers were expected to be full-time homemakers and mothers. It would not have been considered appropriate for these women to place their children in full-day early childhood programs. The half-day nursery schools or neighbourhood playgroups were thought of as complementing the home and providing opportunities for young children to develop social skills and prepare for elementary school. More recently, there has been another shift.

The late 1960s saw the rise of compensatory programs such as Head Start that began as nursery school programs. In Canada, the Brunswick-Cornwallis Preschool program in Halifax, the Moncton Head Start program, and the St. John's Head Start program were examples of this type of nursery school (Gamble, 1992; Glassman, 1992; Irwin & Canning, 1992). However, it is probably accurate to say that the majority of families using nursery school programs since the 1960s have been middle-income families (in recent years subsidies have become available to assist families that cannot afford the fees; bursaries have been available at some nursery schools for many years to assist low-income families). Today there seems to be a trend to more nursery school programs being established for a wider range of children, including the Aboriginal Head Start program described in Chapter 11.

A common misconception about the participants in nursery schools is that participation is possible only for families with a parent at home and that it is not an option for working families. This is not accurate. Although the half-day program cannot by itself cover full-day, five-days-a-week care, these programs are used by many working families. As was noted in the description of cooperative nursery schools, some families have flexibility in their work schedules that thereby provides them with more options for child-care arrangements. For example, possible combinations can be family day care and nursery school, relative-care and nursery school, and parents doing shift or part-time work and nursery school.

Roles of Nursery School Educators

Professional education was an important component of the early laboratory nursery schools. The original training targeted both educators and future mothers. For example, many of the early nursery schools in Canada and the United States were affiliated with schools of home economics, and one of their stated purposes was "to train future mothers and to enhance the study of family life" (Osborn, 1991, p. 125). This was different from the professional education for kindergarten and elementary teachers at that time. The education for future mothers and nursery educators included how to be skilled observers and apply child development principles. This role as trained observer in the background making notes on children is reflected in the early ideas about the role of the educator in nursery school. For example, according to Blatz and Bott (1928), "while the teachers in a nursery school remain in the background and interfere with the activities of the children as little as possible, there are occasions when it is necessary to interfere to protect the weak against the strong, and to secure a fair sharing of toys" (p. 174). Now compare that statement with a recent one: "the teacher's role in the nursery school is to create an environment that facilitates learning. Teachers also support social and emotional development by encouraging children to verbalize their feelings" (Feeney, Christensen, & Moravcik, 1991, p. 40). What aspects are the same? How has the perception of the nursery educator changed?

As mentioned earlier, the role of the early childhood educator in the parent cooperative nursery school has unique features. The parent/educator partnership is "the foundation of the cooperative preschool's operation" (Stevenson, 1990, p. 226). For example, you need to be in agreement with the basic philosophy of cooperative programs. You must also like and be able to work with both child and adult learners. This is different from other types of early childhood programs because the parents are also technically the employers, and therefore you will be supervising your employers. These parents are not early childhood professionals, and parent volunteers change on a daily basis. In addition, there is often considerable yearly turnover as children go on to other early childhood programs such as kindergarten. While part of your responsibility is the planning of the curriculum, both the parents and educator are jointly responsible for its implementation on a daily basis. In addition, the educator also advises the board as it sets policies, determines budgets, and makes other decisions that affect the operation of the program.

One inaccurate and inappropriate perception that sometimes is heard or read is that because nursery school is only a half-day program, and maybe not even every day, professional education is not necessary. Others will tell you that in nursery school "all they do is play" and "you don't need to be a teacher to do that." This is not true. As discussed in Chapter 4, professional education is necessary for working with groups of young children and their families no matter the length of the program or its frequency.

FOR REFLECTION

If you were going to be interviewed for the position of early childhood educator in a parent cooperative nursery school, what questions would you ask that you wouldn't ask in a typical early childhood interview?

Issues for Nursery Schools

Two issues for nursery schools are (a) helping some children adjust to what is perhaps their first out-of-home early childhood program, and (b) the need for the nursery school to adapt to changing social and demographic trends.

The Transition from Home to Early Childhood Program

For some two- or three-year-olds, their first group experience without their parents may be a nursery school or neighbourhood playgroup. Some parents think a half-day program one to three times a week is a good experience without being too demanding for their children who have until then been at home. However, many of these children have probably experienced drop-in programs, such as kindergym at the local recreation centre or storytime at the library. Generally, the parent is present or nearby for these programs.

Whether a child is beginning a group experience at age three in a parent cooperative nursery school or as an infant in a day-care centre, the home-to-preschool **transition** is important. Some children make this transition easily, others have some difficulty initially, and a few have a serious adjustment problem that persists for weeks. Unfortunately, there is no 100-percent-accurate way of predicting which children will adjust quickly and which will have difficulty. And sometimes a child that had no difficulty adjusting to one program may have difficulty with the next one. This section focuses on children's *initial* adjustment to an early childhood program.

Why do some children have problems? There are several different factors that can contribute to the ease of children's transitions. One factor can be children's previous experiences or lack of experiences separating from their parents. When I was working in nursery schools, I would occasionally have a child enrolled in a program who had never been away from his or her parent—not even to a babysitter. On the other hand, some of the children had had lots of experiences, such as a childminding group while their parent was at a fitness class or another activity.

Another factor is the individual child's temperament. As discussed in Chapter 2, children have different temperaments. For example, some children are more daring and others are more timid. Also related to this factor is the relationship of the child and the parent. It matters if the child has a secure or insecure attachment to their parents. An insecure child may interpret being enrolled in an early childhood program as the parent trying to "get rid of them" or not wanting them around. Children who are securely attached are more able to cope with the sense of loss or abandonment that some children feel when beginning an early childhood program.

Still another factor is timing. There are times when, even for the best-adjusted child, it is not a good time to begin a new early childhood program; for example, if a child has been seriously ill, if there has been a recent death in the family, or if there is a new baby in the family. In the latter circumstance, it is easy for a young child to misinterpret enrollment in an early childhood program at that time as being displaced by the baby.

There are four potential areas for difficulty for young children making their initial transition into an early childhood program, whether this is a day care, nursery school, or kindergarten program. These areas can be referred to as the four Ps: *place, people, program,* and *previous experience.*

The transitions from daycare or nursery school to kindergarten, and kindergarten to grade 1, are discussed in Chapter 10.

Place

Many early childhood programs are located in buildings that are much larger than the child's home and do not resemble a setting the child knows well. Many children are frightened of big buildings. This is not surprising, as many big buildings, such as hospitals or clinics, may be associated with less-than-enjoyable experiences for the child. Also, most children seem to sense that it is easier to get lost and harder to find one's parents in a bigger building. For a child attending a nursery school located in the church basement where they attend Sunday school, or a community centre where they've gone for a Mom and Tot program, this fear may not exist or be lessened. For some children, the contents of an early childhood program can seem overwhelming on first encounter. Most children have not had the exposure to such a great number and variety of materials and equipment prior to an early childhood program.

People

Young children vary in their experience with other adults outside their families. For example, some children have had many babysitters, others only grandparents or an older sibling. With today's smaller family size, many young children have not had to share their parents' attention with another child. For some children, one of the most difficult aspects of the transition from home to an early childhood program is being just one of several children sharing the attention and time of an early childhood educator. Many children find it is an adjustment to have to share not only materials but also the adults. Other children may experience what is commonly called "stranger anxiety"; that is, they have had relatively little experience with adults outside their immediate families or have had unfortunate experiences with strangers and are therefore excessively fearful. For other children, a nursery school or day care will be the first place they have been without a family member. These children may find a photograph of themselves with their family hung on their cubby—or by the changing table, for younger children—to be reassuring. Another option is to make key-chain-type photos for the children to wear as bracelets or necklaces for the first few days or weeks (Simons, 2000).

Program

The length of a new early childhood program can also be a factor in children's adjustment. For example, a child who has been fine once a week in a neighbourhood playgroup may find a daily half-day nursery school or day-care program to be too long initially. These are the children who often seem fine at the beginning of the day but become upset and tearful later in the session. Yet another program factor that can cause difficulties is the need to learn routines and rules that are new and perhaps different from those at home. Transition times, such as cleanup or washing up for snack, are often times when children will miss their parents and begin to cry. This may be due to their insecurity in not knowing what is expected of them. For example, What is the procedure for cleanup time here? At home, it may be tossing all the toys into a toybox. But there is no toybox here and they do not know what to do. This is why it is important to teach young children the routines and rules from the first day. Many early childhood educators will tell you that during the first few weeks of a program they spend a lot of time working on routines such as cleanup, moving from indoors to outdoors, playground rules and behaviour, snack time transitions, lunch and nap procedures, circle time, and so forth. Educators need to be aware that children need to be taught what is meant by things like "circle time." These terms may be part of our professional vocabularies as early childhood educators, but are not part of the average two- or three-year-old's vocabulary.

The organization of the daily program can be a source of security or insecurity for young children. Perhaps you remember your early experiences in elementary school, where you felt quite secure in that you knew that after recess came circle time. And then one day, the teacher said you were going to the gym or library or for swimming lessons for the first time. All of a sudden you may have felt very apprehensive and insecure, because you did not know what this meant or what you were expected to do or not do.

Still another program factor is the philosophy of the program and the "problem of match." This refers to the idea that some programs are better suited to some children than others. In Chapters 5 and 6, several programs with varied orientations are discussed. These programs have quite different philosophies, pedagogy, procedures, and contents. It is therefore logical that they are not equally appropriate or appealing to every child. For example, a child who likes a lot of structure in his or her life would probably feel more comfortable in a program that was quite structured, while a child who disliked structure would probably not like that program. It is important for educators to help parents understand what their program is like and what this means for young children.

Previous Experience

If a young child's previous experience with an out-of-the-home program has not been successful, the child quite naturally will not be eager to try another one; however, if the previous experiences have been positive, the child is more likely to be willing to attempt a new program. This also applies to short-term interruptions in the child's attendance, such as an extended holiday or illness. It may take the child a few days to get back into the routines and procedures; however, this adjustment will usually be shorter than the initial one.

Parents' Adjustment

Just as young children have to adjust to their initial experience in an early childhood program, so must their parents and family adjust. Research has shown that parents often have mixed feelings about their children beginning an early childhood program for the first time (e.g., Balaban, 1985). For some parents this can be an emotional time because it marks a transition in their lives, too (McClelland, 1995). Both mothers and fathers recognize that a child beginning an early childhood program signifies a milestone in the child's life. Parents often ask themselves many questions at this time, such as:

• Did I select a good program for my child?

• How can I help my child adjust, especially if I can't stay with him or her for the first few days?

• Will my child like this program?

• Will the early childhood educators like my child and vice versa?

• Will the educator understand my child and recognize his or her unique strengths and needs?

• Will the educators think I'm a good parent—even if my child misbehaves?

These are all questions that parents have told me they have asked themselves when their children began an early childhood program.

This can also be a stressful time for some parents. Often, a mother or father who has been staying home with the child up to this point is asked by their friends and relatives, "What are you going to do now that your child is in day care or nursery school?" The expectation is that the parent will be going out to work or school. Many of these parents have told me that this transition for their children put pressure on them to decide what they should be doing. It is an emotional time as well, with the parents thinking about their child getting older and growing up. Some parents are concerned that their child will like the teacher better than them. Although early childhood educators may think this is an unreasonable fear, parents have very occasionally been known to be jealous of their children's relationships with early childhood educators.

For some parents, their own experiences with early childhood programs or in the primary grades were not pleasant ones and they are concerned that their child will have a similar experience. This, in turn, makes them more apprehensive and often their child then senses this.

In some families it is not the child beginning the program or the parents who have difficulty, but a younger sibling who is too young to attend the early childhood program. Most experienced early childhood educators can tell you stories of a younger sibling who is led out the door in tears by a parent explaining that their turn will come next year or the year after. It is hard for a younger child to see their sibling stay in a place that looks so attractive and fun when they are not allowed to stay. Thus it is clear that the initial transition into an early childhood program can be a transition for the entire family.

What can early childhood educators do to facilitate these initial transitions into early childhood programs for young children and their families? Obviously, the specifics will depend on the age of the child and the type of program, as well as specifics relevant to the factors discussed above. However, some general guidelines are to:

- Acknowledge
- Plan
- Provide options.

Acknowledge

The first step is to recognize and acknowledge that some children and families will have more difficulty with this transition than will others and that not all children and families will react in the same way. It also needs to be acknowledged that some may have difficulties for a longer time than others may. Still another difficulty to consider is the delayed separation reaction. This is the child who seems to adjust easily to the early childhood program, only to become tearful or distressed days or weeks after the program has begun. This is not unusual. How one deals with these difficulties should include a variety of options, some of which, through planning, are implemented before children even begin an early childhood program.

Plan

Planning on how children's and families' transitions can be facilitated may greatly reduce later problems. One typical thing educators can do is to plan pre-visits of the children and their families. There can be several visits if there is time. The initial visit is usually the parent or parents by themselves when they are looking at program options that meet the families' needs and wishes. At this time, the parents need information about the program (e.g., a description of the program, the fees, the hours, etc.). What the parents are trying to do is assess if your program would be appropriate for their child and if it meets the family's needs in terms of hours of care, location, availability, and cost. Printed information materials can be helpful for parents at this stage (these should be translated into the languages spoken in the community, if possible). On a subsequent visit, the parent may bring the child (depending on the child's age) to see what the child thinks of the program. For some families, especially single parents who are working, these visits may not be possible as they cannot take time off work, even though they would like to do so.

Once the family has decided to enrol the child, other meetings may occur. For example, some early childhood educators do home visits before the child begins the program in order to become acquainted with the child in the child's home. Other educators make or maintain contact with families beginning the program in the near future through letters and/or telephone calls. Some programs have scheduled orientations for parents and children either on an individual or group basis.

Another key part of the planning process is to think about the first day. What will be your policy about parents staying with their child for the first day, week, or longer? What will you do about the child who needs someone to stay but the parent can't or won't? If your program is a nursery school or kindergarten you may have all or most of the new children beginning at the same time, whereas a day-care centre may have children beginning throughout the year (although September is always a popular time to begin). It is important that both the children and their families feel a warm welcome upon their arrival. Sometimes it takes a bit of logistical planning to be sure there is a staff member at the door to greet all of the new arrivals. Many programs have available activities and materials that the child is likely to be familiar with, such as playdough, crayons, books, and Lego. One important precaution to consider is security of the children. It is not unusual for a young child to decide after an hour or two that they would really like to go home and to leave—or try to leave. The child does not yet know the routines and has not realized that the program has a beginning time and an ending time determined by others.

Provide Options

The provision of options recognizes and accommodates children's and families' individual needs and differences. Some children feel comforted if they have a readily available photo of their family or know they can telephone a parent any time during the first few days. I have seen children in Asia being taken to school the first day with their backpack on their back and a cellphone clutched in their hand. Some children may find an entire day or session too much at the beginning and may benefit from a more gradual entry. For some parents, it is not possible to stay with the young child. In these cases, another family member or a buddy from the neighbourhood that the child knows can help. I've had grandparents or teenage siblings in my programs helping a child with the initial transition. Some families have used a family friend or neighbour that the child knows and trusts. Another option is an adult volunteer who speaks the child's language. It can be very frightening to be in a new place without your family *and* no one understands what you are saying.

With children who have taken a long time to make the initial adjustment, I have used their parents as volunteers in the classroom. Thus, although the parent is present, they are not focused on their own child the entire time and the child becomes accustomed to sharing their parent with other children. For one child, I had his mother do short errands such as to the corner mailbox or to the nearby store to buy something I had "forgotten" for snack so the child could experience short but gradually lengthening separations.

The Future of Nursery School

A major issue—perhaps the most significant—faced by nursery schools in Canada today is their future. Some have speculated that the need for full-day child care combined with a trend of increasing junior kindergartens in the public schools will result in the demise of the half-day nursery school program. In addition, there are now more early childhood program options available for families wanting only part-time programs. For example, there are recreational programs such as kindergym, library-based programs such as children's story-time, craft classes, toy library programs, family resource centres, and other drop-in programs that also provide early childhood experiences for young children.

In a survey done for cooperative nursery schools in Ontario, McReynolds noted that difficulties included turnover of parents yearly, following the school calendar, and the need for recruitment every summer (Hewes, 1998). Many nursery schools are examining possible options. Some options implemented include coordinating their half-day programs with local family day-care programs, providing *both* half-day and full-day centre-based programs, and integrating half-day programs with programs designed for children with special needs. In the future, there may be an increasing number of coooperative day-care programs as well as nursery schools attached to other programs, such as on-campus co-op housing.

It is interesting that the early nursery schools had more diverse schedules that provided part-time and full-time options (Beatty, 1995). One trend for the future might be nursery schools returning to this more varied scheduling. However, this is not to say that there is no future for the half-day nursery school as we know it today. The half-day program meets the needs of many families—both working and non-working.

As mentioned earlier in this chapter, many families have by choice or necessity become quite creative at arranging their work schedules and other commitments to accommodate their children's care. Some families with two parents working outside the home are still able to use a nursery school, and do so because they think it is the best option for their children and themselves. Just as nursery schools have historically shown themselves to be adaptable, so have families.

Some people have speculated that if programs for four-year-olds in the public school system become more widely available, nursery schools may need to focus more on programs for two- and three-year-olds. Others have speculated that nursery schools could become part of the public school systems. Early childhood educators, such as Patty Smith Hill in the early twentieth century, discussed the nursery school as part of the public school system. Before public school kindergartens became common, nursery schools enrolled many five-year-olds. When kindergarten became part of the school system, nursery schools focussed on three- and four-year-olds. In addition, there could be more integration of nursery schools with other early childhood programs, such as family day homes and family resource centres. The relationships among nursery school, day care, and kindergarten are likely to continue to shift and blend in the future.

Nursery School's Contributions to Early Childhood Education

Nursery school has made many contributions to early childhood education and care in Canada. For example, the earliest nursery schools in Canada became a model for subsequent early childhood programs, including day care programs. These programs had a strong child development focus that is still dominant in early childhood programs today (see Chapter 6).

The contributions of nursery school were recognized early in its existence. For example, the 1929 yearbook of the National Society for the Study of Education stated that nursery schools "show soundness of purpose, execution, and achievement that have set new standards in educational value for preschool children" (Whipple, 1929, p. 234). One area of contribution that improved overall standards was professional education.

The early and continued professionalization of early childhood educators was a significant contribution of the nursery school. From the early days of the Canadian nursery school at the Institute of Child Study in Toronto, professional education has been seen as important. The early pioneers in nursery education in Canada did much to increase the professional image of the nursery school educator and to promote and enable professional education programs. This was the beginning of the tradition of professional early childhood education at universities and colleges.

Many of these early graduates were then instrumental in the establishment and operation of both nursery-school and day-care programs. Many leaders in our field in the past 75 years have been part of nursery schools. These people have also been responsible for the establishment or continuation of early childhood professional organizations. In fact, the largest early childhood professional organization in North America, the National Association for the Education of Young Children, was at one time named the National Association for Nursery Education.

Parent cooperative preschools and their local, regional, and international organizations have provided education for many parents in Canada in the past 50 years. These groups have promoted parent education and parent participation so that today these are commonly accepted practices in early childhood programs. Overall, parent involvement in nursery school has traditionally been stronger than in kindergarten or day-care programs. Indeed, many nursery school programs in Canada have originated with parents.

Nursery schools in Canada appeared later than day-care programs and kindergartens. The day nursery programs at that time were considered to be primarily "custodial," while the kindergartens were seen as "educational." The early nursery schools also emphasized young children's social and emotional development, creativity, and imaginations. This broadening of early childhood program goals and curriculum contributed to the shift from the relatively narrow focuses of early day nurseries and kindergartens to a more comprehensive focus on the "whole child" that is reflected in the stated philosophies of most early childhood programs today.

Summary of this Chapter

The key themes of this chapter are that:

- The early development of nursery school in Canada was strongly influenced by the Child Study Movement, the mental hygiene movement, psychoanalytic theories, and philanthropic organizations and individuals.

- Professional education and parent education have traditionally been strong aspects of nursery schools in Canada.

- Nursery schools vary in type, organization, and philosophy. They include laboratory/demonstration nursery schools, parent cooperative preschools, and playgroups.

- Nursery schools are used by a variety of families—both working and non-working.

- Some children and families have difficulties making the home–school transition. Early childhood educators can do much to facilitate this transition.

- Nursery schools have made significant contributions to early childhood education and care in Canada, especially in the areas of professional education and broadening the focus of early childhood programs, in general, to emphasize the whole child.

- The future of nursery school in Canada is being questioned. However, nursery schools have adapted in the past and can continue to do so in the future.

Key Terms

early childhood programs, 358
laboratory or demonstration
    nursery school, 365
nursery school, 357

parent cooperative nursery
    school, 369
playgroup, 376
traditional nursery school, 367
transition, 381

Resources

If you wish to know more about some of the topics in this chapter, here are a few suggested publications, organizations, and Web sites:

For Sharing with Children

For the youngest children, two board books are Roth, H. 1986. *Nursery school.* London: Putnam Publishing; and McQuade, J. 1999. *At preschool with teddy bear.* New York: Dial Books for Young Readers.

A story with photographs is Kuklin, S. 1990. *Going to my nursery school.* New York: Bradbury Press. The last part of the book is a section for parents on what to look for in a nursery school.

Boelts, M., illustrated by Kathy Parkinson. 1996. *Little bunny's preschool countdown.* Morton Grove, IL: Albert Whitman and Company. Little Bunny's anxiety about starting school in September is fuelled by stories from his cousin Maxine.

For books with series or popular media characters, there are:

Worth, B., illustrated by David Prebenna. 1997. *I can go to preschool.* New York: Golden Books. (A Muppet Babies book.)

Metzger, S., illustrated by Hans Wilhelm. 1996. *Dinofours: It's time for school.* New York: Scholastic Books.

Bernthal, M., photographs by Dennis Full. 1994. *Baby Bop goes to school.* Allen, TX: The Lyons Group. (A Barney book.)

For the younger child who wants to go to school with a sibling: Lindgren, A., illustrated by Ilon Wikland. 1987. *I want to go to school too.* Stockholm: R & S Books.

For Further Reading

For more information about parent cooperative nursery schools, try Hewes, D. 1998. *"It's the camaraderie": A history of parent coooperative preschools.* Davis, CA: Center for Cooperatives, University of California. An excellent look at the preschool cooperative movement, including Canada, past and present.

Driscoll, A. 1995. *Cases in early childhood education: Stories of programs and practices.* Boston: Allyn & Bacon. Includes a chapter on a cooperative nursery school and the Kamehameha travelling preschools in Hawaii.

Taylor, K. W. 1967. *Parents and children learn together.* New York: Teachers College Press. A classic, available in college and university libraries.

For information on the history of laboratory nursery schools in Canada, see Brophy, K. 2000. "A history of laboratory schools." In L. Prochner & N. Howe (Eds.), *Early childhood care and education in Canada* (pp. 115–132). Vancouver: UBC Press. Also see Wright, M. J. "Toronto's Institute of Child Study and the teachings of W.E. Blatz" (pp. 98–114).

For selecting a nursery school:

Anbar, A. 1999. *How to choose a nursery school: A parent's guide to preschool education* (2nd ed.). Palo Alto, CA: Pacific Books, Publishers.

For more information on home–school transition:

Balaban, Nancy. 1985. *Starting school: From separation to independence—A guide for early childhood teachers.* New York: Teachers College Press.

Separation:

Jervis, K., photographs by Jean Reiss Berlfein. 1984. *Strategies for helping two- to four-year-olds.* National Association for the Education of Young Children. Also from NAEYC is a brochure by Janet Brown McCracken.1986. *So many goodbyes: Ways to ease the transition between home and groups for young children.* (The address for NAEYC is in Chapter 4.) Both of these would be good additions to an early childhood program's parent library.

Organizations:

In addition to the early childhood organizations listed at the end of Chapter 4, there are provincial and regional parent cooperative preschool organizations.

The Parent Cooperative Preschools International's Canadian office is

PCPI Canadian Office
3767 Northwood Drive
Niagara Falls, ON L2H 2Y5
Telephone: 1-800-636-6222
E-mail: pcpi@ncba.org
Web site: www.iupui.edu/~millg

10

Kindergarten: Preschool or Primary?

Okay, I know how to do all the art stuff, play games, and sing.
When do I learn to read in kindergarten?
—Five-year-old child to mother at end of second week of kindergarten

Kindergarten is an early childhood education and care success story. Within a hundred years of its modest beginning in Germany in the mid-1800s it developed to be part of the public-funded education systems in many countries, including Canada. Today kindergarten is an accepted part of public and private schools. It is the most widely available and widely attended early childhood program in Canada. However, *what* kindergarten should be is still debated. It seems that everyone, including the child quoted above, has ideas of what kindergarten should be.

In Chapter 1, a basic definition of *kindergarten* was provided: "A program for children the year before beginning grade 1 (also called **senior kindergarten** in some provinces). Kindergarten may have half-day, full-day, or alternating-day schedules. **Junior kindergartens** are programs for four-year-old children. Public school junior kindergartens are available in very few provinces."

Despite its success, kindergarten traditionally has had a bit of an identity crisis. Its roots and early development are closely related to those of preschools, while its current placement in Canada typically puts it with the primary grades in the elementary schools (i.e., K–3). The subtitle of this chapter reflects kindergarten's position between nursery school and day care and the primary grades. Although it is most frequently thought of as part of public school systems, it can be a separate, private program or part of a day-care program.

Here are some questions to think about while you read this chapter:

· What do you remember about your own childhood kindergarten experience?

· How did kindergarten become so accepted in Canada?

· What types of kindergartens are there?

· Should three- and four-year-olds be in kindergarten?

· What does the widely used phrase "readiness to learn" mean for kindergartens?

· What are the characteristics of a good kindergarten program?

· How can educators and families facilitate children's transitions into kindergarten and from kindergarten into grade 1?

· What is the place of reading and writing instruction in the kindergarten curriculum?

· How is kindergarten similar to and different from nursery school and day-care programs? Is there continuity across these programs?

The first part of this chapter will describe what kindergarten in Canada is like and its historical development. The second part will discuss some issues associated with kindergarten today.

Development and Growth of Kindergarten

Whether the reasons for the successful development and growth of kindergarten are as straightforward as kindergarten being the right program in the right place at the right time or the result of a complex interaction of circumstances, events, and people can be debated. However, one can agree that, "the kindergarten, originally established by Friedrich Froebel, has had the longest [continuous] history and greatest impact on the field of early childhood education" (Spodek, 1991, p. 4). Froebel's kindergarten was brought to many countries by teachers he had trained, missionaries, philanthropists, charities, and interested individuals.

Although the first Canadian kindergarten was private, public-school kindergartens followed shortly, due initially to the efforts of Ada and James Hughes in Toronto (see Chapter 5 for details). Indeed, Ontario was the early leader in the establishment of kindergartens in Canada.

Kindergarten grew in the Toronto system, and by 1890 there were 24 kindergartens enrolling 1,554 children (Dixon, 1994). By 1902 there were 120 kindergartens in Ontario with 247 teachers and more than 11,000 five-year-olds (Stamp, 1982). Kindergartens were also spreading in other Ontario cities and elsewhere (see Table 10.1). By 1891, Hughes was claiming that "the desirability of making the kindergarten the foundation of a thorough educational system is

TABLE 10.1

Early Kindergartens in Canada

1877	SAINT JOHN, NEW BRUNSWICK (PRIVATE KINDERGARTEN)
1878	TORONTO, ONTARIO (PRIVATE)
1882	BERLIN (NOW KITCHENER), ONTARIO (PRIVATE)
1883	TORONTO, ONTARIO (PUBLIC-SCHOOL KINDERGARTEN)
1884	HAMILTON, ONTARIO (PUBLIC)
1887	LONDON, ONTARIO (PUBLIC)
1892	MONTREAL, QUEBEC (PUBLIC)
1895	OTTAWA, ONTARIO (PUBLIC)
1900	REGINA, SASKATCHEWAN (PUBLIC)

no longer a debatable question" (quoted in Corbett, 1989). Hughes was enthusiastic although premature with his assessment.

Ontario was not the only province to have early kindergartens. Kindergartens spread relatively quickly, although not geographically or in great numbers, to other provinces. As early as 1888, kindergarten was being discussed at teacher conferences, such as one in the Maritime provinces, and at the Dominion Education Association Conference in 1894, where papers on kindergarten were presented by a Nova Scotia kindergarten teacher and kindergarten inspectors from Ontario (Logan & Logan, 1974).

Early Kindergartens

The earliest kindergartens in Canada were strongly Froebelian in philosophy (Dixon, 1994). However, these were not clones. For example, kindergartens in Ontario "reflected varying degrees of Froebelianism" (Corbett, 1989, p. 51). This variation can also be seen in the description of the Froebelian kindergarten described in Focus 10.1 when compared to the ones described in Chapter 5.

Patty Smith Hill, a leading early childhood educator in the early twentieth century (see Chapter 5), identified four stages of development of kindergarten in a 1916 speech (Forest, 1935). The first stage, according to Hill, was the naïve stage, which was the transference of Froebel's kindergarten to North America. This transference was characterized by great commitment and conviction. Corbett (1989) concurs that the introduction and early years of Froebel kindergartens in Ontario were marked by enthusiasm. In the second stage, "kindergartners as a whole formed an exclusive, self-satisfied, rather intolerant group" (Hill, quoted in Forest, 1935, p. 16). They believed that the Froebel method as outlined by Froebel himself was *the* way to teach kindergarten. They were highly critical of other approaches, such as Montessori.

The third stage was one of disagreement between traditional and progressive kindergarten factions (described in the next section). Then, according to Hill, the fourth stage was the coming of age of kindergarten, which recognized the need

Recollections of a Froebel Kindergarten

Edna Aedy attended a Froebel kindergarten in the public schools of Fort William in 1921–22, when she was four years old. Her recollections of the Gifts and Occupations from an interview are provided here.

Yarn balls—We played a guessing game where a child held a ball behind his or her back and we guessed the colour.

Gifts—The Gifts came in wooden boxes with tops. When working with the Gifts, we each had one in front of us. We sat with our hands behind our backs until the teacher rang a bell. We took the box, and when she rang the bell again we emptied it.

I remember building with the blocks. There was one Gift that had four wooden shapes. Each had a small hook to hang it on a small wooden bar attached across the top of the box.

The most difficult Gift was the soaked peas and toothpick-like sticks. The peas kept splitting. I remember making people with a pea for the head, toothpicks for the body, arms, and legs, and a tissue paper circle for the skirt.

I also remember the metal rings and the wooden sticks. The wooden tablets were beautiful—like slices of dark and light woods.

Occupations—I can remember the difficulty of doing the weaving tasks. Some were done with woodlike slats (bamboo or grass); others were done with coloured paper.

For the perforating, the teacher drew the outline on cardboard pieces, the assistant poked the holes, and we sewed around the edges. For paper folding, we did three-dimensional folded houses. One end was cut off to make the sofa.

The teacher pasted finished paper weaving and paper folding into our exercise books. These books were entered in competitions at the local fall fair.

There were two teachers for more than 25 children. The classroom was very large and light. There was one long table about two feet wide

and then small individual tables pushed together to make a long table. Two children sat on one side of each small table. The tables were arranged in a u-shape with a table in the middle for the teacher and materials. The tabletops were scored into one-inch squares and the blocks placed on those squares to make patterns as dictated by the teacher but they made drawing difficult.

We played with blocks and there was a sand table in the room, but I don't remember using it. There was no paint, snack, outdoor play, or rest time. I wanted to learn to read but reading wasn't taught in this Froebel kindergarten.

A typical day—I went in the afternoons only. I hung my coat in the cloakroom and then took a chair down from the tabletop and sat down. The opening exercises began with march music. We carried our chairs on our heads to the large black circle painted on the floor and sat down. Next there was a Bible story, prayer, and a song (e.g., "Jesus Loves Me"), followed by more singing (e.g., "Here's a Ball for Baby"). Then came the work period with the Gifts and Occupations. Later there was circle time and games. During circle time there were more songs, fingerplays directed by the teacher, and storytelling. I remember a lot of singing games (e.g., "Farmer in the Dell" and "I Wrote a Letter to My Love and Then I Dropped It"). There was an assistant teacher who played the piano. We did skipping games on the circle. The afternoon finished with a goodbye song.

There were special occasions; for example, the Halloween party and the Christmas concert for parents where Santa Claus came.

I did a Department of Education summer course given by Claire Senior Burke, a Froebel teacher, in Toronto in the summer of 1941. I wanted to teach kindergarten but there were no normal school courses offered because of the war. I tried teaching using Froebel's methods but found they didn't work well for me, so I adapted them by trial and error.

for the continual growth and evolution of the kindergarten. Today's kindergarten could be considered to be still in Hill's fourth stage, as it has been changing and evolving throughout the twentieth century and into the twenty-first century.

In addition to its development as part of public school systems, kindergarten, like day nurseries, could be considered part of the social reform movement in the early twentieth century (see Chapter 5). One type of early kindergarten that was part of this movement in Canada and the United States was the charity kindergarten organized by charitable and philanthropic groups. For example, the Free Kindergarten Association in Winnipeg operated kindergartens in Winnipeg from the end of the nineteenth century until kindergartens were introduced into the Winnipeg public schools after the Second World War (Larry Prochner, personal communication, February 2000). A charity kindergarten was established in Calgary around the Second World War, until it too was incorporated into the public school system. According to Prochner, one of the social conditions that spurred the creation was the presence of large numbers of immigrants or newcomers to a city. For example, churches established charity kindergartens for the children of Japanese and Chinese immigrants in British Columbia (Prochner, 2000) (see the photo below).

See Chapter 5 for a description of Susan Blow's kindergarten.

Kindergarten, from its North American beginnings, focused on helping the family in the community. Froebel himself had suggested that kindergartners (i.e., kindergarten teachers) visit children's homes, and in the early kindergartens this was done. These early kindergartens were half-day programs for the children in the morning with home visits by the kindergartners in the afternoon and occasional mothers' meetings in the evenings. The home visits and mothers' meetings were considered by the kindergartners to be important and integral components of their programs. According to one historian of early kindergartens, "at such meetings, kindergartners explained the purpose and activities of the kindergarten and lectured on practical subjects, or held informal

B.C. Archives

An early kindergarten for immigrant children in British Columbia.

discussions" (Ross, 1976, p. 43). Common topics included nutrition, child health, hygiene, housekeeping (e.g., the importance of ventilation), and discipline, as well as issues raised by the mothers (Ross, 1976). The home visiting component often became a social welfare task (Hill, 1942/1992). Kindergartners provided assistance to families in finding employment, obtaining necessary medical or dental care, or other needed services.

Another model linked the early kindergartens to the primary grades. For example, in 1894 in London, Ontario, kindergartners who taught kindergarten in the mornings assisted in the primary grades in the afternoons. Some were principals' assistants (Corbett, 1989).

Early kindergartner education programs were also primary teacher education programs. In 1885, kindergarten teacher educators joined the faculty of the Toronto Normal School and the Normal School in Ottawa for the purpose of providing courses on kindergarten. The next year, the Ontario Ministry of Education urged communities to establish public-school kindergartens. Then, in 1887, the Ministry began exams for kindergarten teaching diplomas. These were "the first formal early childhood education credentials awarded in Canada" (Dixon, 1994, p. 7). Following the 1913 recommendations of Ontario kindergartners, the Department of Education authorized the Toronto Normal School to organize a kindergarten-primary education program, which was also offered in the summers (Corbett, 1989). The Normal College in Nova Scotia began kindergarten courses in 1891 (Logan & Logan, 1974).

Criticism and Controversy

As indicated in Hill's stages of kindergarten's development, critics and reformers of the Froebelian approach were part of the fourth stage of its development. Criticism and controversy were certainly not new to the kindergarten movement. For example, Froebel's original kindergarten had been banned in Germany (see Chapter 5).

In Canada, early critics questioned whether taxpayers' money should be used for kindergartens in the public schools and whether kindergarten was indeed a "serious education" (Dixon, 1994, p. 7). Other frequently voiced objections were the encroachment of kindergarten on the family's role (i.e., young children were the responsibility of the family); the difficulty in getting enough qualified kindergarten teachers; and the opinions that children were too young to go to school at age five, that large groups were unhealthy for young children, that the school should not be responsible for the social welfare of children, and that the kindergarten was an unnecessary frill (Goodykoontz, Davis, & Gabbard, 1948; Shapiro, 1983). It is interesting that many of these arguments are the same ones heard today in discussions of four-year-olds in kindergartens or day care as part of the public school system. However, the most serious early challenge for kindergarten was an internal one—the clash between the traditional Froebel group and the reform group (Hill's third stage, in which she was a major player, as was Ada Marean Hughes of Toronto).

The debate had arisen as a result of the combination of various forces such as the scientific approach of the Child Study Movement typified by the research of Hall and Gesell (see Chapter 6); the waning of the philosophies of Rousseau, Pestalozzi, and Froebel (see Chapter 5); and the increasing acceptance of progressive education as set forth by John Dewey (see Chapter 6). In addition, kindergarten teachers were questioning the general applicability of a method developed in the previous century in Europe. This was especially an issue for those working with poor or immigrant groups who felt they needed to adapt Froebel's curriculum and ideas to meet the specific needs of the children in their kindergartens. This debate over basing a program primarily on a theoretical approach (e.g., Froebel) without recognizing the social and cultural contexts of the time and the diverse needs of young children would be revisited in the later twentieth century in the Developmentally Appropriate Practice guidelines issued by the National Association for the Education of Young Children (NAEYC) (see Chapter 12).

The International Kindergarten Union (IKU) was founded in 1892. Ada Hughes was a charter member and became president in 1906 (Corbett, 1989). In 1903, the IKU established a committee to examine all sides of the debate between the traditionalists who believed that kindergarten should be how Froebel outlined it, and the reformists who felt that the Froebelian kindergarten needed to be adapted and modified for North America and the new century. The committee's original task was to find a way to reconcile the different positions. Eventually, the Committee of 19, as it was called, decided in 1909 that reconciliation was not possible. Therefore, it published three separate reports in 1913: the traditionalists, the progressives, and a compromise group. Ada Hughes and Susan Blow (chair and author, respectively) were members of the traditionalists group, while Patty Smith Hill wrote the progressives' report. By the 1920s, the progressive kindergarten was the dominant kindergarten philosophy (Cuban, 1992).

While some of the progressive teachers were replacing Froebel's approach with new ideas such as blocks, housekeeping corners, woodworking, and paints, progressive kindergartens did keep many aspects of the Froebelian approach (e.g., circle time, fingerplays, and singing games). However, these progressive kindergartens were more child-oriented, and the curriculum was less structured, used the children's own experiences, and included more time spent on music, drama, and art. Although many of the Gifts remained, their use was not as structured or formalized. Most of the Occupations gradually disappeared. Eventually, the progressive kindergarten was quite similar to what is today termed the traditional nursery school (see Chapter 9) and the original model for Head Start (see Chapter 5).

Kindergarten in Public and Private Schools

Kindergarten's relationship to the public school system has been described as "initially a curiosity added on to the elementary school in the closing decades of the nineteenth century" (Cuban, 1992, p. 167). The progression of kindergarten from an add-on to the recognized and accepted beginning of public education was a significant achievement. Today, elementary education is usually described as K-6 or K-8, and while the end point may vary, the beginning is kindergarten.

The development of kindergarten in Canada was uneven to say the least. A few provinces were leaders in the provision of kindergarten from the earliest days. For example, Ontario approved kindergartens in 1885. Approved means that school boards were allowed to have kindergartens, but the province was not obligated to provide the funds. Still, Ontario was very progressive in this regard and ahead of other provinces. Early kindergartens were found predominantly in urban areas.

Although public-school kindergartens did spread in Canada, the public systems could not meet the demand and not all public-school systems included kindergarten in the first two-thirds of the century. Eventually, private and not public school kindergartens became dominant in Canada (Logan & Logan, 1974).

Some historians of kindergarten believe that this prevalence of private kindergartens delayed the adoption of kindergarten by the public schools (e.g., Logan & Logan, 1974; Ross, 1976). Many of the children attending private kindergartens were from middle- and upper-income homes that could afford the tuition fees. This inequity of access to kindergarten was also a concern for some of the early Froebelists in North America. For example, Susan Blow wrote, "had the Froebelian movement developed only upon these [private] lines the kindergarten must have remained forever the privilege of the wealthy few, and the occasional gift of charity to the abject poor" (1900/1969, p. 5). Similar statements have been expressed in recent times in the debates over affordability of quality day-care programs (see Chapter 8).

Most of the public-school kindergartens in Canada have been established since the Second World War. Until the 1970s it was not uncommon for children to begin school with grade 1, although a few provinces had significant kindergarten enrollments, such as Ontario with 75-percent kindergarten attendance at that time (Eden, 1991). Since then, the provision of kindergarten has become mandatory in every province except Prince Edward Island. (While it is mandatory for a province to provide and fund public-school kindergartens, it is not compulsory in most provinces for kindergarten-aged children to attend kindergarten.)

Not all that long ago early childhood educators and parents were lobbying most provincial/territorial governments to provide publicly funded kindergarten—a position somewhat analogous to day care today. However, nearly all children today attend kindergarten, even where not required; the usual figure suggested is 97–98 percent (e.g., Woodill, Bernhard, & Prochner, 1992). Kindergarten has been a success story for not only early childhood education but education as a whole in Canada.

Types of Kindergartens

A kindergarten may be on a half-day, full-day, or alternating-day schedule. The early public-school kindergartens were typically mornings only, to enable the kindergartner to do home visits and to assist families in the afternoons. Later, because of the increased enrollment and financial constraints, a kindergarten became both a morning and afternoon session taught by the same teacher. Traditionally and historically, Canadian kindergartens have been half-day programs throughout most of the twentieth century. Today, however, a variety of patterns exist, including full-day kindergartens and alternating-day kindergartens (these latter kindergartens are also full-day, but only every other day) as well as half-day programs. In addition, some provinces have senior and junior kindergartens (i.e., for five- and four-year-olds, respectively) or combined senior/junior kindergartens. Each of these types of kindergartens will be described and discussed in the following sections.

Half-Day Kindergarten

A half-day kindergarten, either morning or afternoon, for five-year-olds has been the traditional kindergarten in Canada. The half-day model became accepted as the norm after the Second World War, when rising school enrollments, costs, and shortage of space in schools made half-day programs (mornings and afternoons) more economical and logistically possible than full days or mornings only.

The difficulty with half-day programs for many families today is that they need child care beyond the 2-1/2- to 3 hour-a-day attendance in a typical half-day kindergarten session. For some children, this has meant another early childhood program or programs to cover the time before school, the other half of the day, and until their parents pick them up.

Perhaps the most frequently suggested disadvantage of the half-day program for the teacher is the need to get to know 40 or more children and their families. Interacting with two sets of 20 to 25 active five-year-olds every school day can be tiring. In addition, having two sets of children means twice the number of parent conferences and reports to write compared to a grade 1 teacher. Many kindergarten educators also comment on the difficulty of "getting everything in" during a 2-1/2- to 3-hour time block.

Although the half-day program has been the traditional kindergarten model in Canada, other types are also found, including the full-day kindergarten.

Full-Day Kindergarten

The original kindergartens of Friedrich Froebel in Europe and Marguerite Schurz in the United States were full-day programs, as were some of the early Canadian kindergartens. In more recent times, full-day kindergartens have been first made available to specific groups, such as children with special needs, as done by the Toronto Board of Education; Aboriginal groups, as done by British Columbia; or rural areas, as done by Manitoba.

The rationale for full-day kindergartens typically includes the following points:

• Better coverage for working families than half-day kindergarten.

• Fewer transitions for the children.

• Children previously in day care are accustomed to a full-day early childhood program.

• School districts/boards save on transportation (some estimate by 50 percent [Ulrey, Alexander, Bender, & Gillis, 1982]) by not having to run special buses at mid-day for the kindergarten children.

• The full day provides educators with more time to observe, diagnose, and accommodate children's special needs.

• There is more time to provide individual assistance to children who need it.

• There is time to provide a hot lunch and nutritious snacks.

• Larger blocks of time allow for more flexibility of scheduling and permit longer projects; longer play periods, including outdoor play; and activities such as field trips, library, gym, and swimming lessons.

• The curriculum can be broadened because of the extra time (Olsen & Zigler, 1989).

• It is easier for educators to get to know and communicate with fewer children and families.

However, full-day kindergarten is not without its critics. The most frequently cited disadvantages of full-day kindergartens are:

• Cost, as more educators are required than are needed for half-day programs.

• The potential difficulty of finding additional well-qualified early childhood educators who also meet provincial requirements for teacher certification.

• The need for after-school and possibly before-school care for the children of working families, because full-day is not really a full day, but rather a school day (typically 6 to 6-1/2 hours).

• Full-day kindergarten may seem more like grade 1 than half-day kindergarten because of its length.

• There is more time available and therefore increased opportunity to add more formal instruction.

The key issue isn't really the length of the day but what is done during the day, the quality of the program, if it is developmentally appropriate, the qualifications and experience of the educators, and other factors related to quality. A quality kindergarten for five-year-olds is a quality program, whether it is a half-day program or a full-day program. As Fromberg (1995) has stated: "The full-

FOR REFLECTION

The Ontario Early Primary Education Project concluded that, "For some children, extended or full-day kindergarten may be particularly advantageous. These are children who may not experience an environment in which reading books, solving problems, playing with numbers, and interacting with adults is encouraged. Lacking the enriched experiences which all children require for learning and development, these children are often at a serious disadvantage in later schooling" (Ontario Ministry of Education, 1985, p. 38). What does such a statement imply about the purpose and philosophy of full-day kindergarten?

day kindergarten is not a stepping-stone to first grade. It is not a traditional first grade begun one year earlier, nor is it an extended nursery school. Ideally, it is a unique time with its own distinctive knowledge bases and practices that adjust to children's diverse personal cultures" (p. 243).

Alternate-Day Kindergarten

The major rationale for full-day alternate-day kindergartens is usually travel and transportation. This type of kindergarten is most frequently found in rural areas. The idea is that a child has to make the long bus trip to school and then home only once every two days and not every day. In some rural districts, the bus ride to school can be more than an hour each way and requires a young child to be waiting for the bus in the dark morning and returning home in the dark, especially in the winter. However, school districts can save money and fuel by running the buses in the morning and late afternoon only and not doing mid-day runs for relatively few kindergarten children. Parents often prefer the alternate-day full-day schedule because the kindergarten child can then go to and return from school with an older sibling or neighbourhood child.

The disadvantages of the full-day alternate-day kindergarten schedule include a long day with bus trips before and after school. For children not being bused, there can still be a need for day care before and after school, as the typical school day is 6 to 6-1/2 hours. Also, finding care on the alternate days when the child is not in school can be difficult. Not all parents favour the full-day alternate-day kindergarten schedule (Ulrey, et al., 1982). In addition, some teachers feel that the every-other-day gap between the kindergarten sessions is not the best configuration for optimum continuity for learning by young children.

What Does the Research Say about Kindergarten Schedules?

As there is very little Canadian research on this topic (Eden, 1991), much of the following research cited is from other countries. In general, the research shows favourable results for full-day kindergarten over half-day (Ontario Royal Commission on Learning, 1994). For example, children in full-day programs tend to have higher test scores and less retention in grades through the primary grades (Cryan, Sheehan, Wiechel, & Bandy-Hedden, 1992; Karweit, 1994; Peck, McCaig, & Sapp, 1988). Children in full-day kindergartens also showed better social skills and general behaviour (Chmelynski, 1998; Cryan, et al., 1992). The effects of full-day kindergarten are seen more strongly for disadvantaged children; the results for higher-socio-economic children are more mixed and less conclusive (Karweit, 1993; Olsen & Zigler, 1989). Instructional differences between full-day and half-day kindergartens reported include more use of learning centres and individual work and less group time in full-day programs (Elicker & Mathur, 1997). In addition, parents and teachers—especially those experienced with full-day kindergarten—tend to like full-day programs (Corter & Park, 1993; Johnson & Mathien, 1998). Unfortunately, there is little research on the long-term effects of half-day versus full-day kindergartens (Karweit, 1994; Olsen & Zigler, 1989). One of the few studies was done in Toronto and followed full-day kindergarten children through grade 4 (Bates, Deeth, Wright, & Vernon, 1986). It found there was a lower failure rate for these children versus a comparison group.

After reviewing the literature on the effects of full-day, alternate-day programs and half-day kindergarten programs, Peck, McCaig, and Sapp (1988) concluded, "most of the studies on full-day alternate programs found that this arrangement was at least as effective as half-day every-day kindergarten attendance" (p. 64). There is generally no significant difference in effects between half-day-every-day programs and full-day alternating-day programs (Gullo & Clements, 1984).

In considering the research findings on the length of the kindergarten day it is essential to keep in mind that there are many factors that influence effectiveness in early childhood programs (these factors are discussed in Chapter 12). This is a complex topic to research. Even only two kindergartens can be difficult to compare because factors such as curriculum, teacher quality, group size, and background of the children can all affect outcomes of research studies. It is a mistake to overgeneralize the research to assume that longer is always better. A longer but poor-quality program is not better for children than an excellent shorter program. For example, as Naron (1981) points out, if the longer program has an inappropriate curriculum or schedule, little positive change can be expected. The key is how the time is used, not the amount of the time.

Junior Kindergarten

Four-year-olds in kindergarten is not a new idea. In fact, the original Froebel kindergarten included three- to seven-year-olds. In Canada, many of the early kindergartens were multi-aged. For example, in British Columbia the first legislation authorizing kindergarten in the public schools in 1922 stipulated ages four to six (it was changed to five in 1958). In addition, many individual examples exist of younger children starting school early. My father began school at age four in a rural school because his older sister would not go to school alone, so my grandmother asked the teacher if my father could go as well. Junior kindergartens were typically first made available for children at risk or with special needs, which was a common theme of both the late nineteenth and early twentieth centuries and of the 1960s/1970s period that saw the greatest growth of kindergartens (Bloch, Seward, & Seidlinger, 1989).

Ontario, which has been a leader in junior kindergartens in Canada, is a good example of this development. Ottawa kindergartens enrolled three- and four-year-olds in 1943–44 (Corbett, 1989). The first junior kindergartens in Toronto schools were in 1947. These programs were described as being similar to half-day nursery schools (Corbett, 1989). They typically began with a brief health inspection on the children's arrival, followed by free play. The daily schedule also included outdoor play, singing, movement activities, stories, snack, and rest. In 1950, the Hope Commission report recommended that school boards establish junior kindergarten, but recognized that the cost was a limiting factor (Corbett, 1989). As with the establishment of the early kindergartens at the turn of the twentieth century, the junior kindergartens were perceived as compensatory education and first targeted "children of low income, immigrant, inner-city and multi-problem families" (Ontario Ministry of Education, 1985, p. 37).

Although provision of junior kindergarten was optional for school boards in Ontario until 1992, by 1986 approximately half of all four-year-olds attended a junior kindergarten (Biemiller, Regan, & Lero, 1992). These authors noted that the provincial government announcement in 1989 that by 1992 junior kindergartens would be provided by all school boards "appears to have been primarily a political decision—there have been no studies to support (or refute) this decision in terms of criteria including the quality of education or care" (p. 149). Early researchers of junior kindergartens commented on the many possible factors that could account for effects. Provincial documents at the time cited the research from Head Start as part of the rationale for junior kindergartens (Ontario Ministry of Education, 1985). If there was no compelling specific research on junior kindergartens, then what is the rationale for their inclusion in the public school system?

The rationale for placing programs for four-year-olds in a public school system is strongly based on the long history of the public school and its provision of universal education. If early childhood programs for four-year-olds are available only if the family can pay the fees or qualifies for subsidies, then there is not equal or universal access for all children. Another rationale frequently given for the placement of these programs in schools is that elementary schools are typically neighbourhood schools and are thus readily accessible by families. Their neighbourhood placement can also enhance the continuity of home to school. For example, the children attending a kindergarten may be ones a child already knows from the neighbourhood. In addition, attendance in a junior kindergarten in a local school may make subsequent transitions to senior kindergarten and grade 1 in that school easier.

The inclusion of junior kindergartens as part of the public school system has also raised some concerns. Many of today's concerns, such as whether four-year-olds should be in public school, were raised about five-year-olds when kindergarten was first introduced in the early 1900s and later (Shapiro, 1983).

A basic concern is whether programs for four-year-olds would be damaged by their inclusion in the public school system. According to Zimilies (1986), "there is a danger that universal preschool education, when conducted under the auspices of the public schools, will alter the character of early education .... they will become incorporated into a body of educational thinking and programming that is primarily concerned with academic instruction" (p. 11). A few people even advocate children not beginning school until age eight or ten (e.g., Moore & Moore, 1979).

Another concern is whether inclusion of another "lower" grade in the public education system might push young children into ever-earlier academic-type

FOR REFLECTION

According to Clifford, Early, and Hills (1999), "schools constitute a major new force in the early childhood field, a force whose presence has both positive and negative implications for the field" (p.50). What do you see as these positives and negatives?

programs. The argument is that if kindergarten is good for five-year-olds, then junior kindergarten will be even better (i.e., the "more-and-earlier-is-always-better" idea).

Still another concern voiced by critics is that if four-year-olds are included in the public education system, can inclusion of three-year-olds be far behind? The Ontario Royal Commission on Learning in 1994 recommended that "Early Childhood Education (ECE) be provided by all school boards to all children from 3 to 5 years of age whose parents/guardians choose to enrol them" (p. 19). It recommended full-day kindergartens for the three-year-olds. It is interesting that, in the case of Ontario, the 1887 Ontario Education Act had designated kindergartens as being for three- to five-year-olds (Corter, 1995). In France, two-year-olds are currently part of the public education system (McMahan, 1992).

Other concerns about junior kindergarten relate to the institutional design, appearance, and functioning of the typical elementary school. Would most elementary schools have the space, and the type of space, necessary for a developmentally appropriate program for four-year-olds? Most older elementary schools were not designed with five-year-olds in mind, much less four-year-olds. Kindergarten classrooms, especially in more recent elementary schools, tend to have less space than a day-care centre would have for the same number of children, due to provincial/territorial licensing requirements for early childhood programs. School districts would need to be willing and able to also cover the additional costs for purchasing appropriate materials and equipment for four-year-olds.

There are concerns about multiple transitions for four-year-olds in half-day junior kindergartens as opposed to full-day or at-home care. Therefore, is the daily routine of a half-day junior kindergarten program with transitions from home to a school-age program to kindergarten to the school-age program to home an improvement in the lives of four-year-olds? (An advantage for many families is that public-school kindergarten, even half-day, is free and day care is not, unless the family qualifies for subsidy.)

A very common concern is the educator qualifications for teaching junior kindergarten. A perennial issue with kindergartens in the public schools is the professional education and experience of the educators. It is not unusual for people teaching kindergarten to lack specific education in early childhood. The concern is that if there are already people teaching kindergarten without appropriate qualifications in early childhood education, will the same be true for junior kindergartens now or in the future?

A final concern is the use of limited educational funds for junior kindergartens. The issue here is not whether junior kindergartens are worthwhile, but rather, whether limited resources would be best allocated to making half-day kindergartens full-day, or providing school-age programs or other possible options. This issue came to the fore recently when some provinces reduced or threatened to reduce funding for kindergartens.

↓
The role of formal instruction/ academics is discussed later in this chapter.

↓
The issue of educator qualifications is discussed more fully later in this chapter.

FOR REFLECTION

If you were a school board member and your school district had sufficient resources for either beginning junior kindergartens or increasing the current half-day senior kindergartens to full-day programs, which would you choose and why?

Sometimes senior and junior kindergartens are combined for philosophical or enrollment reasons. Focus 10.2 describes a day in a junior/senior kindergarten.

Multi-Age Groups

As described in Chapter 5, Froebel's kindergarten included children from ages three to seven, and Montessori's children's houses were also multi-age. The early kindergartens in North America were also mixed-ages, with children sometimes from two or three to five or six years of age together (Bloch, Seward, & Seidlinger, 1989). Today, kindergarten for multiple ages is a common model in other countries.

Focus 10.2

A Day in a Junior/Senior Kindergarten

by Karen Letsche-Biemiller, Toronto

I teach Junior Kindergarten/Senior Kindergarten in downtown Toronto. My class is made up of mainly non–English-speaking children. The school runs on a ten-day cycle. Every day begins by me meeting my 26 children at the door. I take them straight to their cubbies (which are outside the classroom) so they can hang up their coats, backpacks, and borrow book bags. For some children locating the cubby with their name on it can be difficult—a teachable moment for me to talk with them about what the letters are in their name. After hanging up their coats the children come into the room, and their first task is to locate their name cards and then wait in line to "sign in" (a large piece of newsprint is posted on an easel with two markers). After signing in the children go to the book area of the classroom and sit quietly looking at books for a short period of time. Once everyone has signed in and had an opportunity to look at books we sing a quick song or poem that involves some body movement and then we settle in for our "opening time." During this large group time we talk about the month—what is the name of the month and also the letters that spell the month. We sing a song about the days of the week, count to find the date, and so on. We also clap our hands, pat our shoulders, and stomp our feet (one-to-one correspondence) using the date (i.e., it is the twentieth of November so we

would clap 20 times). I also write a letter to the children on big chart paper; we read it together and then we look for letters (both upper- and lower-case) that may appear more than once in the letter. We also look for simple words that they may recognize or that may be in the letter more than once. I also use this time on the carpet to teach the children the weekly poems that I have chosen and/or any group lesson that I want to do (e.g., making a group chart about signs of winter, graphs about what kind of face our pumpkin should have, shape games, etc.). From here the children have activity time, which for the most part is free choice for the children (I do not limit the number of children who can be at any given centre; rather, as many as can get along and work cooperatively can be at a centre). There are some children and/or some days when I may direct the children to certain activities. During activity time, I work with small groups of children on their response journals (a book where the children draw a picture and then, with support, the children attempt to write a word or simple words/sentences to go with their pictures). I also work with small groups of children on math and literacy concepts (counting, shapes, estimating, letter identification, matching letter games, etc.). We always end the day with a large group story time, and if time permits we have outdoor play and sharing (also known as show and tell). On any given day the children may also have gym, library, or music.

Multi-age classes have been part of the primary grades in Canadian public schools, such as the K–3 primary-only schools or the traditional one-room schoolhouse. Sometimes these patterns evolved because of low enrollment and sometimes as philosophical decisions. It is common in elementary schools to have what are called *split grades* because there are insufficient numbers to make two complete classes. For example, there may be a sufficient number of children for three classes but only enough for one grade 1 and one kindergarten, so the remaining children become a K–1 class.

Multi-age or **mixed-age grouping** has been defined as "placing children who are at least a year apart in age into the same classroom groups" (Katz, Evangelou, & Hartman, 1990, p. 1). It is also known as *vertical grouping, heterogeneous grouping,* or *family grouping*.

See Chapter 6 for a description of family grouping in the British schools.

Rationale for Mixed Ages

One rationale for this pattern is that it reflects the society in which the children live and have their experiences. Society comprises different ages and these people interact with each other daily. If there is more than one child in a family, children are accustomed to dealing with children of different ages. However, with today's smaller families, many children have not had experience living with a sibling. For these children, daily interaction with children of differing ages can be beneficial.

Children can learn from more advanced peers. For example, Vygotsky's zone of proximal development and the use of scaffolding in young children's learning are described in Chapter 6. Multi-age groups can provide a "coach" or more advanced peer to challenge and assist in a young child's learning.

Children learn from each other, especially social skills and prosocial behaviours. For example, in a mixed-age group, older children can be models for the younger children. For older children with poorer social skills, there may be the opportunity to further refine their skills and develop new ones while playing with younger children, and thus be able to have leadership roles that would be unlikely in interactions with their more socially competent agemates.

A multi-age playgroup also reflects children's typical choice of a playgroup in natural settings (Ellis, Rogoff, & Cromer, 1981). Mixed-age playgroups of two- to five-year-olds also use more cooperative and complex play patterns (Howes & Farver, 1987). Of course, in any group of children who are the same age, there will be a range of abilities, competencies, and interests. Also, if the group is large enough, there will be children the same age as well as older and/or younger children.

On the other hand, there are concerns about multi-age grouping in kindergarten and early primary grades. For example, parents may object when their children are the oldest because they fear that their children do not have the older role models and may not be challenged sufficiently in play and learning with younger children (Theilheimer, 1993). From a pedagogical perspective, the educator needs to be knowledgeable about several levels and developmental stages beyond what one would expect to find in a single-age group. In addition, because there is more range in a multi-age group, a variety of equipment and materials is required, and this has financial implications.

Looping

A multi-age combination of children with an age difference of three or more years suggests that the children and the educator could stay together for more than one year. This arrangement is called **looping** (also called *multi-year grouping* or *persistence grouping*). In looping, "children stay with the same teacher for two or three years" (Kuball, 1999, p. 76). For example, in a kindergarten situation, one teacher of a junior kindergarten would stay with the same group of children for senior kindergarten, and perhaps grade 1 or longer. Although this practice is common in day-care and nursery school programs, it is not typical of kindergarten in Canada.

An advantage of looping is that both the children and the educator come to know each other very well. It can provide security and stability for the children. This is particularly important for children who have moved a lot, or who have experienced family changes, as it can help reduce their stress (Chapman, 1999). The reduced number of transitions between different educators at each grade level can also lessen child anxiety. The children know that come September they will have a teacher and classmates they know and who know them and they will already know the routines and how to function in the classroom. For the teacher, it means less time spent teaching routines and getting to know and assess a group of children. Many teachers who loop report that a family-like atmosphere develops in the classroom (Bellis, 1999). This can encourage some children to feel more comfortable and secure and thus participate more in class (Burke, 1996). However, the downside of the family-like atmosphere is the possible problem of inter-personal conflicts and negative sibling-like behaviours (Bellis, 1999). Unfortunately, there is a shortage of research on looping and its effects, especially longitudinal effects (Chapman, 1999).

From parents' point of view, they get to know their child's educator very well and vice versa. A potential negative is that if the parents or child do not like the educator, three years together may not be wise. Most schools that use looping have procedures for rearranging combinations that do not work.

How Are Kindergartens Different from Nursery School and Day Care?

Early childhood programs and the educators' roles in these programs typically are much more similar than different. For example, in a study of the personal philosophies of nursery school, day care, kindergarten, and grade 1 educators, Dickinson (1989) found that differences were as likely to occur within each of the four groups as across the groups. Therefore, this section will focus on only three areas of difference:

- Their roots and development
- Class size/ratios
- Educator qualifications.

Focus 10.3

Early Childhood Services in Alberta

An innovative arrangement for kindergarten in Canada was the original Early Childhood Services model in Alberta. There were kindergartens in some public schools in Calgary as early as 1941. However, the big push for publicly funded kindergartens in Alberta was in the mid and late 1960s. (Alberta was one of the last provinces to adopt publicly funded kindergartens.) A government task force in the early 1970s examined the issue and recommended the Early Childhood Services (ECS) model. This model was originally intended to be a comprehensive system integrating education, health, social, recreational, and other programs for children from birth to eight and their families. The original model was intended to provide a wide variety of programs and delivery options from which families could choose.

ECS began with children ages 4-1/2 to 5-1/2, with children with special needs or children living in rural areas getting priority. ECS programs were operated by public school districts as well as private operators throughout Alberta. As ECS did not ever expand to provide comprehensive services for the age range of birth to eight, the term Early Childhood Services or ECS has become synonymous with kindergarten (and is often referred to as kindergarten by parents and others in Alberta). Currently, ECS funding is available for children with severe disabilities or hearing impairment from age 2-1/2, with mild or moderate disabilites from age 3-1/2, and other children from age 4-1/2.

In 1994, the provincial government cut ECS funding by 50 percent as part of its overall cuts to education, health, and social programs. ECS programs responded to these cuts in a variety of ways. For example, some programs reduced their hours from 400 to 200 hours, others charged substantial user fees, others did vigorous fundraising, others reduced the level of certified teaching staff by using paraprofessionals and parent volunteers, others reduced the length of the school year, others used a combination of these measures, and some closed. The programs in the smaller communities and rural areas were especially hard-hit by the cutbacks.

The cutbacks in Alberta put the provision of publicly funded kindergarten at risk. This came as a shock to many parents, early childhood professionals, and other educators in Alberta and elsewhere who had taken for granted that kindergarten would always be available. Many educators credit the reinstatement of funding for ECS largely to the efforts of parent and professional groups who lobbied the government for return of the funding. One particularly outspoken group was parents who had been the earliest participants in ECS programs and now had children of their own. In 1996, most, but not all, of the funding was reinstated. However, by then many well-qualified early childhood professionals had moved from ECS programs to the greater security of teaching assignments in the primary grades. Some programs did not reopen. Perhaps more importantly, the stability and permanence of kindergarten has been undermined in the minds of both educators and the public. Kindergarten seems vulnerable and is not, perhaps, as universally accepted and well-respected as many of us in early childhood education and care assume. (The cutbacks to junior kindergartens in Ontario is another illustrative example.)

Sources: Alberta Education, 1997 (on-line); Brown, Turner, LaGrange, Massing, & Sherwood, (1996); Ethel King-Shaw, personal communication, December 1999; LaGrange, Turner, & Sharp (1995).

Roots and Development

As described in Chapter 5, the kindergarten evolved from Friedrich Froebel's original German kindergarten as it was transported, modified, and adapted to North America. The nursery school has its roots in the early nursery schools in England and later North America (see Chapter 9). The direct ancestor of day-care programs in Canada is the day nurseries that were begun in the mid-1800s to assist working mothers who had young children (see Chapter 8). As Granucci (1990) states, "along the way, paths might have crossed and mingled, but each movement remained distinct" (p. 7). Although early childhood programs have become more similar in the last half of the twentieth century, their early roots and development have had lasting effects. Some believe that "the lack of a common history is one of the causes of disunity among child care and nursery school, kindergarten, and elementary school" (Granucci, p. 7).

Continuity and children's transitions among programs are discussed later in this chapter.

Class Size and Ratios

In the early days of kindergarten in Canada, classes of 50 to 60 children were not uncommon (Corbett, 1989). Today, the numbers are considerably fewer. However, the number of children and educators in typical kindergarten class-rooms would usually be in violation of provincial/territorial licensing regulations for nursery schools and day-care centres. The typical kindergarten has between 20 and 25 children, with one teacher and perhaps a part-time aide. Kindergarten teachers report that their idea of an ideal class size is between 14 and 16 children; for administrators it is 15 to 18, and for parents it is 14 (Mayfield, Dey, Gleadow, Liedtke, & Probst, 1981; Pelletier, Power, & Park, 1993). A widely accepted group size for four- and five-year-olds is 15 to 18, with an adult-to-child ratio of 1:8 or 9 (e.g., NAEYC, 1998). For example, a group of 20 four-year-olds in day care would require two or three early childhood educators. But if they were in a public school kindergarten only one kindergarten educator would be required, because day-care regulations are more rigorous in this area than are most school district rules.

The National Association for the Education of Young Children has recently launched a campaign to reduce class sizes in kindergartens and primary grades. Their key reasons for reducing class size are:

1. Teachers get to know students better and can give them the one-to-one attention they need.
2. Children have more opportunities to engage in active learning.
3. Students' performance increases in small classes.
4. Professionals can handle their additional job responsibilities, including involving parents, more effectively. (NAEYC, 1999b, [on-line])

NAEYC's recommendation for kindergartens is 1 educator for 10 to 12 children with a maximum group size of 24; for programs for four- and five-year-olds, it's 1 educator for 8 to 10 children with a maximum group size of 20

(NAEYC, 1998). Class size for four- and five-year-olds in publicly funded schools is an issue in countries outside North America as well. For example, in Britain the average class size for four- to five-year-olds in the publicly funded schools is 26.8, which is larger than in the secondary schools (Blatchford & Martin, 1998).

Another area related to regulation that can result in significant differences between nursery school/day care and kindergarten is space requirements. Traditionally, it has been accepted that young children need more space than older children do. However, most public-school kindergartens that I have observed do not have as much space as would be required if they were licensed day-care facilities. For example, NAEYC (1998) recommends a minimum of 35 square feet per child indoors and 75 outdoors. Provincial/territorial regulations set the minimum amount of space required for day-care programs.

These differences in class size and physical space between nursery school/day care and kindergarten have implications not only for the program, but also for the children's transitions between programs (transitions are discussed later in this chapter). A final area of difference is that of the qualifications of kindergarten educators. It has long been recognized that "teachers of young children must be well grounded in child development and education for specific ages of the children they teach" (Mitchell & Modigliani, 1989, p. 58).

Educator Qualifications

Although the qualification of the educators is recognized as a key determinant of quality for early childhood programs, the question of what these qualifications should be is probably more contentious for kindergarten than other early childhood programs. Kindergarten's position between preschool and grade 1, and its having characteristics of each, has not been more evident in any area than in who should teach kindergarten in the public schools.

In one Canadian study, kindergarten teachers and consultants reported that it is primarily the teacher who distinguishes ordinary kindergartens from the extraordinary ones (Pelletier, Power, & Park, 1993). These respondents also indicated that child development knowledge and specialized primary education were the most worthwhile training for a kindergarten teacher and that the combination of a professional teacher's certificate and an early childhood education diploma was the preferred credential.

In public schools, the kindergarten teacher is typically required to have a teaching certificate that has been issued by the province or territory. This certificate usually requires the completion of a bachelor's degree. However, this does not necessarily mean that the educator has specific early childhood education courses or experience. For example, in British Columbia a teaching certificate does not specify a particular grade level so one can, in theory, teach any grade if hired by a school district. Although the need for specific kindergarten/early childhood education has been identified by kindergarten teachers and administrators as important, as well as recommended by a

FOR REFLECTION

What roles or activities do educators in nursery school/day care have that are the same as and different than they would be in kindergarten?

See Chapter 4 for more on the question of who should teach kindergarten in the public schools.

provincial assessment team (Mayfield, et al., 1981), one can still teach kindergarten in British Columbia with no formal early childhood education training. (British Columbia is not the only province in this situation.) If one wishes to start a kindergarten in one's home or as part of a day-care program in British Columbia, one must have an early childhood educator's certificate, but this certificate is not recognized for teaching kindergarten in the public school system. It is a source of frustration and discouragement for many people with early childhood education certificates when they see people with less early childhood training teaching kindergarten in the public schools.

Early childhood educators, school and district administrators, parents, and early childhood professional organizations all agree that special training in early childhood education is important for assignment to kindergarten (e.g., Mayfield, et al., 1981; NAEYC, 1998; Pelletier, Power, & Park, 1993). Whether this professional education must be in a four-year degree program is debatable. A recent study of a pilot project by the Ottawa Board of Education, in which early childhood educators with diplomas from colleges were hired to teach junior kindergarten, found that there was no difference in the social, literacy, or numeracy development of the children in classes of educators with diplomas or degrees (Coplan, Wichmann, Lagace-Seguin, Rachlis, & McVey, 1999). Similar results were found in a previous study in the United States (Howes, Phillips, & Whitebrook, 1992). However, Johnson and Mathien (1999) reported that among parents participating in focus groups in Alberta, Quebec, Ontario, and New Brunswick, "there was strong opposition to the idea of replacing qualified kindergarten teachers with college-trained early childhood educators, even on a two-for-one basis" (p. 378).

Kindergarten has been seen by some in the early childhood profession as the bridge between nursery school/day care and elementary school. By having access to this bridge, early childhood educators might increase their professional image in the eyes of the public and other professionals, and also possibly their salaries. Early childhood educators already work in some elementary schools in day-care centres or school-age programs. However, these programs are typically under the jurisdiction or regulations of the agencies responsible for day care rather than those responsible for public-school education.

A difficulty faced by many kindergarten teachers in the elementary school is isolation (Marxen, Irvine, Carlson, Billman, & Sherman, 1997). This isolation is both physical and curricular. When I taught kindergarten in an elementary school, the kindergarten had different starting and ending times than the rest of the school to accommodate two half-day sessions of equal time. Therefore, my lunchtime barely overlapped with other staff, and I didn't see those who typically came to the staff room in the last half of the lunch hour at all. As I was the only kindergarten teacher (with half-day programs there is one kindergarten teacher for every two grade 1 teachers), I had no recess break to share with other staff. Outdoor times for the kindergartens were scheduled when the play area would be available to only the kindergarten children so they did not have to compete with the older, bigger children for use of the somewhat limited equipment. Often, when schools are crowded and portables

Career ladders and lattices are discussed in Chapter 4.

are used, the kindergarten is moved to a portable (or sometimes placed at the end of a corridor). Such arrangements may have been what led two kindergarten teachers in Ontario to comment: "I feel so isolated being a Kindergarten teacher." "I agree. I could die in my room and no one would know" (Pelletier, Power, & Park, 1993, p. 104). Some kindergarten teachers may feel even more disconnected from their colleagues because they teach in one school in the morning and another in the afternoon. Collegial interaction, interchange, and support are necessary components of being a professional.

Another misconception about kindergarten is that its teachers have an easier job than other teachers in the elementary school because it is a half day and one can "simply repeat" what was done in the morning session. While half-day kindergartens may facilitate two people job-sharing, they are certainly not to be seen as a "good placement for older teachers who are tailing off" as one personnel officer for a school district told me! Having taught kindergarten, I can attest that kindergarten is not the placement for anyone who is "tailing off." Half-day kindergartens have sometimes been a way for younger educators to get a part-time position in a school district in order to begin their careers or accommodate family responsibilities.

While it is widely recognized that the educator is a key ingredient in a quality kindergarten program, research has identified other factors as well.

Characteristics of Quality Kindergarten Programs

There is no one model kindergarten program that is the best for all situations. However, there are general characteristics that are common across quality early childhood programs. This section will examine program quality, specifically in the context of kindergarten programs. Focus 10.4 discusses what to look for in a quality kindergarten program.

An informative research study commissioned by the Ontario Ministry of Education examined what makes exemplary kindergarten programs effective (Corter & Park, 1993). This study gathered information from kindergarten educators and consultants in Ontario, British Columbia, and Quebec, as well as from case studies of kindergartens in Ontario.

The practitioners surveyed in this research study identified the following as some of the characteristics of an ideal kindergarten program:

General characteristics common to quality early childhood programs are discussed in detail in Chapter 12.

- 14–15 children in junior kindergarten; 16–18 children in kindergarten,

- Half-day program for both junior and senior kindergartens,

- Play has a central role in the curriculum,

- A variety of instructional activities are used and children choose from a variety of activities,

- A variety of materials and equipment are available, especially blocks, sand, water table, books, art materials, manipulatives, clay/dough, and a computer,

Focus 10.4 is a list of nine items from the brochure "A Good Kindergarten for Your Child" published by NAEYC (1997b). Is there anything you would add to that list? Is there anything you would delete? Why?

Focus 10.4

What to Look for in a Kindergarten Program

What you want to see

Children may enroll in kindergarten if they are age-eligible; the curriculum and teaching strategies are attuned to 5- and 6-year-olds, and teachers know how to adapt activities to the range of developmental levels in the group.

Reasonable class size—no more than 25 children with two adults (or 15–18 with one adult)—makes it possible for kindergartners to learn as they learn best (through actively exploring materials, doing hands-on activities, working and playing together).

Taking into account the range of children's developmental capabilities, teachers design the curriculum so each child learns what she is ready for and moves at her own optimal pace.

For extended periods of the day, children can choose from a variety of available activities. The teacher also regularly changes the materials and activities to provide the children with challenges and fresh interest.

The classroom and school display children's work, which is clearly valued.

Teachers engage the children in conversation, both individually and as a whole group. Children are encouraged to describe what they're doing and communicate their ideas.

Teachers give each child the support he needs to pursue his ideas and acquire new skills.

Teachers value parents' input and have frequent dialogue with them about what's going on in the classroom and about their child's progress.

Teachers have taken college-level courses that specifically prepared them to teach kindergarten children. The school encourages collaboration among teachers and ongoing professional development.

Source: NAEYC, 1997b

- Personable, experienced, and well-educated teachers with specialized early childhood education,

- A supportive administration (Corter, 1993).

The first-ranked goal was developing children's feelings of self-worth; academic preparation was least important. It was concluded that "the goals and means of kindergarten education are complex and . . . need to be adjusted to the social context as well as the unique characteristics of individual children" (Corter, 1993, p. 133).

Issues in Kindergarten

Some key issues related to the quality of kindergarten programs that need to be examined in more depth are:

- Continuity and transitions with nursery school and grade 1

- The nature of kindergarten curriculum

- Reading and writing in kindergarten

- Readiness to learn

- Retention and transition.

Continuity and Transitions with Nursery School and Grade 1

"But they've been to _____; they shouldn't have any trouble making the transition to the next program." You can fill in the blank with either *nursery school, day care,* or *kindergarten* to complete this sentence, frequently heard by early childhood educators. Ideally, we'd like this to be the case. Young children do not seem to have a problem going from grade 2 to grade 3, so why should they have a problem going between nursery school/day care and kindergarten, or between kindergarten and grade 1?

Unfortunately some children *do* have a problem with these transitions. Research studies have shown that it can be an issue (e.g., Pianta & Kraft-Sayre, 1999). One study found that more than 90 percent of teachers and principals said some children found the transitions into kindergarten and into grade 1 difficult. Seventeen percent of the parents said their child had had trouble with the transition into kindergarten, while 28 percent of parents reported a difficult transition from kindergarten to grade 1 (Mayfield, 1983). Other studies suggest that between 13 and 15 percent of children have difficulty with transitions (Woodhead, 1989). Thus, parents, educators, and administrators agree that this can be a difficult time for some children. Even young children agree it can be difficult (Yeom, 1998). It can be difficult whether or not a child has previously attended another early childhood program, although it is more likely to be easier (Ladd & Price, 1987; Pianta & Kraft-Sayre, 1999; Sokal & Madak, 1999), especially if that program was a high-quality program (Howes, 1990). However, it is still a major change in their young lives (Maxwell & Eller, 1994).

The difficulties associated with making transitions between programs are not new. For example, both the 1908 and 1929 yearbooks of the National Society for the Study of Education focused on this topic. And school superintendents were giving speeches about it one hundred years ago (Wortham, 1992). Nor is this solely a Canadian issue. A UNESCO survey of 67 countries found that most of the countries referred to the problem of continuity between preschool programs and compulsory education (Mialaret, 1976). Countries such as Germany, Britain, and Australia have addressed this issue (Cleave, Jowett, & Bate, 1989; Horn, 1992; Stubbs, 1988). Likewise, so has Canada. As Eden (1991) has stated, if the issue persists it is not for lack of trying: "For all the fine things done, the need for continuity and consistency remains an unattainable goal" (p. 6). Whether this goal is attainable or not, early childhood educators consider the need for continuity between nursery school and day-care programs and kindergarten and grade 1 as one of great importance (e.g., Barbour & Seefeldt, 1993; Honig, 1986; Ladd & Price, 1987; Woodhead, 1979).

Continuity is the way and degree to which one program relates to and builds on another for the benefit of the children. There are multiple components to continuity, including environmental, organizational, philosophical, curricular, and developmental continuity. **Discontinuity**, on the other hand, results when there is a mismatch. Unfortunately, "nowhere is this discontinuity more striking than in the educational settings available during the early years of life" (Caldwell, 1991, p. 69).

Nursery school, day-care programs, and elementary-school kindergartens are typically housed in different locations, administered and funded by different government agencies, and implemented by educators trained at different training institutions for different lengths of time to meet differing qualifications and who may, on top of this, have different educational philosophies and use different curricula. Therefore, it is hardly surprising that the potential for discontinuity between programs for young children exists and that it is a concern to early childhood educators.

Environmental Continuity

Perhaps there is no more obvious and easily observed aspect of continuity/discontinuity than the physical environments of different types of early childhood programs, especially kindergarten and grade 1 classrooms.

Focus 10.5

Day Care, Kindergarten, and Grade 1

Can you identify which of these photographs is a kindergarten, a day-care centre, and a grade 1 classroom? How could you tell?

It was probably relatively easy to identify the grade 1 classroom, whereas it may not have been possible for you to tell the day-care centre from the kindergarten. Although some grade 1 classrooms may look the same or very similar to kindergartens, this is not usually the case in Canada.

Organizational Continuity

The transition from a nursery school or day-care program to a public school kindergarten can involve a different length of day, transitions to and from out-of-school programs, fewer educators (typically one teacher per kindergarten or grade 1), being part of a larger student body, and perhaps having to master the procedures and rules for taking a bus to school. All of these are possible sources of discontinuity for young children.

Philosophical Continuity

Another area of possible discontinuity between nursery school and day care and kindergarten and grade 1 can be the differing philosophies at these levels. Van der Eyken (1982) noted that "it has often been pointed out that the transition from preschool to primary education reflects a movement from childhood to pupildom, from a 'child-centred' philosophy to a 'school-oriented' philosophy" (p. 63). Although this discontinuity can be seen in the differing philosophies of early childhood educators, perhaps this difference is manifest most clearly in the differing curricula.

Curricular Continuity

It has been pointed out that although early childhood educators spend a lot of effort facilitating children's actual transitions from one program to another, the importance of curricular continuity is "largely overlooked" (Chazan, Laing, & Harper, 1987, p. 181). Discontinuity of curriculum can be due to either *overlap*, where the children are doing the same things in two different programs such as nursery school and kindergarten, or *underlap*, where there is too great a leap between the curricula of kindergarten and grade 1. The overlap of redundant experiences can lead children to complain that they're bored and there is nothing new to do (Sigel, 1987). It leads parents to question what, if anything, their child is learning. For example, parents can have different ideas and expectations about the kindergarten curriculum than the educators (Graue, 1993; McClelland, 1995). This is often seen related to the topic of teaching reading in early childhood kindergarten programs. Parents need and want a clear explanation and understanding about each early childhood program their children attend.

Parents' and educators' differing ideas and expectations about the kindergarten curriculum are discussed later in this chapter.

Ideally, a common, continuous curriculum from preschool through the primary grades would be desirable; this would be difficult to accomplish, but there have been some attempts. When Patty Smith Hill and others called for a unified curriculum from preschool through grade 3 more than 50 years ago, there was little support. Recently, other initiatives have received more support. For example, the National Association for the Education of Young Children's Developmentally Appropriate Practice (discussed in Chapter 12) and the original philosophy and goals of Alberta's Early Childhood Services (see Focus 10.3) are two initiatives that, in theory, can promote continuity among early childhood programs.

Developmental Continuity

Developmental continuity reflects the idea that just as children's development is continuous so should be their learning. It recognizes that each child develops differently, and accommodates these differences. According to Barbour and Seefeldt (1993), this means, "basing curriculum and education decisions on each child's social, emotional, physical, and intellectual development [and] adjusting teaching and schooling so all children experience success and demonstrate progress in academic achievement appropriate to their individual learning styles" (p. 11).

Developmental continuity includes beginning where each child is, and not where the curriculum, textbooks, or other children are. If educators', parents', and administrators' expectations of children are grounded on beginning where children are and continuing in a developmentally continuous way, many children might have an easier experience making the transition into kindergarten and then into grade 1. As Hymes has stated, the idea is "not to housebreak them for becoming 5 or 6" (1987, p. 51).

What Can Educators Do to Promote Continuity?

It is highly desirable that we, as early childhood educators, work to create continuity for young children among all our programs. More coherent, stronger, and cohesive continuity between nursery school or day care and kindergarten and between kindergarten and grade 1 could be "a key step in ensuring early school success for young children and their families" (Meier & Schafran, 1999, p. 40). One important step is increasing our knowledge and understanding about other programs and our communication with other early childhood educators. Some ways in which this can be accomplished include:

- Mutual exchange visits to each other's programs.

- Joint planning for children's transitions between programs.

- Exchanging visits with the children.

- Shared activities such as group picnics, puppet shows, service projects (e.g., singing at the local seniors' centre), and outings such as renting the local skating rink or swimming pool, or holding fun fairs by preschool, kindergarten, and grade 1 programs.

- Inviting other early childhood educators in the community to attend and plan joint workshops, presentations, and conferences on topics of mutual interest or concern (e.g., play, child abuse, language and literacy development, or children with disabilities). These meetings could also include families.

- Arranging for credit or non-credit courses to be given in the local community.

- Observations or practica experiences in a variety of early childhood programs.

- Sharing ideas, materials, and resources (e.g., a toy lending library, as described in Chapter 11).

- "Make and take" sessions.

- Working together for community-based advocacy.

- Sharing information about children.

In some of the research I've done, I've found that nursery school/day care and kindergarten educators agree there is a need to establish closer contacts and are willing to do so. The difficulty seems to be the actual logistics and procedures (Mayfield, et al., 1981; Mayfield, 1983; Mayfield, 1988).

Another aspect of continuity is the transitions made by the children. Morrison (1998) defines a **transition** as "a passage from one learning setting, grade, program or experience to another" (p. 245). Caldwell (1991) has noted that while parents and professionals used to worry more about the transition from kindergarten to grade 1, now the focus of their concern is the transition from nursery school or day care to kindergarten.

Ways to assist children making the transition from home to an early childhood program are suggested in Chapter 9. Some ideas that are typically used to facilitate children's transition from nursery school or day care to kindergarten include:

- Visits by the child and parents to the kindergarten before beginning the program. These can be individual family visits or larger group visits.

- Joint planning for transitions by families and schools.

- Open houses for families to come to see the school and the classroom, and to meet the kindergarten teacher before September.

- Making printed information available in multiple languages, if necessary.

- Letters or telephone calls from the kindergarten teacher to the child during the summer. Suggestions for summer activities and good books to read could be given to families.

- Home visits by the kindergarten teacher to meet the family and to explain the program.

- Organizing family activity nights, such as literacy fairs at the elementary school, to include all young children and families in the local community.

- Finding a "bus buddy" for the kindergarten child who does not have a sibling or neighbour to assist with the first few weeks of learning the ins and outs of school busing.

- Educators permitting parents or another family member to stay with an anxious child for the first day or so or until the child feels comfortable in the kindergarten. (For many working parents, this will not be an option.)

What Should Be the Nature of the Kindergarten Curriculum?

Perhaps nowhere does the debate over kindergarten's position between preschool and primary school come to the fore as much as in discussions about what should be the nature of the kindergarten curriculum. Should it be the child-oriented, individual developmental approach of most nursery school and day-care programs, or the academic-oriented, subject and skills approach of the grade 1 curriculum—or should it be something in between, if that is even possible. From the continuum of programs and theories ranging from the child-centred/informal to the teacher-initiated/didactic approaches outlined in Chapter 6, it's obvious that there can be a range of approaches based on philosophy and beliefs. For example, an academically oriented kindergarten would be characterized by drill and practice on isolated skills, heavy use of worksheets, workbooks, teacher-directed whole-group lessons, and relatively short free-choice play periods (Peck, McCaig, & Sapp, 1988).

It is with this issue that the legacy of early childhood education and care's differing roots is evident. Spodek (1988) identified the different emphases as play for preschool, socialization to school for kindergarten, and skill-based learning for grade 1. The elementary school has traditionally been more academically oriented than nursery school or day-care programs. Indeed, research has shown that teachers tend to become more academically oriented with increasing grade levels (Vartuli, 1999). However, academic and child-centred educators can be found at all levels (Stipek, Daniels, Galluzzo, & Milburn, 1992). Indeed, conceptualization of early childhood curriculum or programs as either cognitive development or socialization creates a false dichotomy and is counterproductive.

What do parents and early childhood professionals think the kindergarten curriculum should be? Numerous studies over the years have investigated this issue. Typically, these studies ask people what they consider to be most important in a kindergarten curriculum. In a study of the opinions of kindergarten and day-care parents and kindergarten and day-care educators in Alberta, New Brunswick, Ontario, and Quebec, Johnson and Mathien (1998) reported that all these groups rated social goals as the priority. An earlier British Columbia study of preschool and kindergarten parents; preschool, kindergarten, and grade 1 teachers; and school and district administrators found that although all groups rated children's social development as important, kindergarten and grade 1 parents wanted more of an academic program than did the educators or administrators (Mayfield, et al., 1981).

To further complicate the discussion, historically there have been periods that emphasize academics (Cuban, 1992; Cuffaro, 1991). These are often referred to as "back to the basics" periods. However, many early childhood educators have noted a generally increasing trend in recent years of kindergartens becoming more academic (e.g., Doherty, 1996; Hatch & Freeman, 1988). There has been growing concern about the "pushing down" of the grade 1 curriculum to kindergarten and even to nursery school and day-care programs. According to the NAEYC (1995), "children entering kindergarten are now typically expected to be ready for what previously constituted the first grade curriculum. As a result, more children are struggling and failing" [on-line].

Where has this pressure for increasing academics in the kindergarten come from? Some sources can be:

- Provincial curriculum guides or school-district guidelines that over time have "moved down" some of the grade 1 content into the kindergarten curriculum.

- Materials that school districts purchase for use in the kindergartens; for example, if a school district has purchased a particular reading series and it has a workbook for kindergarten, the expectation by the district administration will likely be that this workbook will be used in the kindergarten.

- Primary teachers can pressure teachers in earlier grade levels. Patty Smith Hill in 1900 termed this phenomenon "the tyranny of the primary teacher" (p. 48). When I taught grade 1, I often wished the kindergarten teacher had "done more" with the children and, at the same time, the grade 2 teacher would pointedly remark that she hoped I was "doing more" than the last grade 1 teacher. Then when I taught kindergarten, I better understood why the teacher had not and could not have "done more." The same pattern was present when I later taught four-year-olds.

- Administrators can also be a source of pressure. In my experience, relatively few elementary school principals and district administrators had early childhood training or experience. Many did not understand what kindergarten was, or what five-year-olds were like, or what constituted an appropriate curriculum for kindergarten.

- Parents can also be a source of pressure. They naturally want the best for their children and recognize the importance of education in today's world. The idea of children getting an earlier start so they can learn more sooner because there is so much more to know is a common idea, and on the surface not illogical. However, expecting young children to learn more and more at earlier ages can result in stress, anxiety, negative feelings toward school and learning, and loss of self-esteem.

The hurried child syndrome is discussed in Chapter 2.

A great deal has been written in the early childhood literature about the effects of primary curriculum on kindergarten curriculum. In fairness, it should be recognized that although kindergarten has certainly been affected by a "push down" effect from the primary grades, it has over time affected the curriculum in the primary grades. For example, the morning sharing/circle time; songs/singing games/fingerplays; child-sized tables and chairs rather than bolted-down desks; manipulatives used for instruction (e.g., math); and mothers' meetings that evolved into parent associations have all been "gifts" from the kindergarten (Cuban, 1992; Ross, 1976; Vandewalker, 1908). However, many

More than 30 years ago, James Hymes wrote: "More and more kindergartens are like bad first grades; first grades are not becoming like good kindergartens" (1968, pp. 11–12). Do you think that statement is still applicable? If yes, what do you think would need to be changed to help "bad first grades" become more like "good kindergartens"?

kindergarten educators would agree with fellow kindergarten teacher Anne Martin's statement:

> Kindergarten used to mean brightly colored paintings, music, clay, block building, bursting curiosity, and intensive exploration. Now the kindergarten's exuberance is being muted, its color drained and its spirit flattened, leaving us with stacks of paperwork and teacher manuals. No longer even designated "preschool," kindergarten is becoming an adjunct to first grade, with workbooks replacing art materials and formal instruction replacing activities that follow the children's interests. (1985, p. 318)

One area of the kindergarten curriculum that is subject to more heated debate than other areas is literacy, especially reading. This debate has been a long-term one in both kindergarten and the primary grades. For example, Patty Smith Hill wrote in 1926 that, "the first grade curriculum has been 'reading driven' for centuries, and failures continue" (p. 15). The concern of many early childhood professionals is that kindergarten, nursery school, and day-care programs are also becoming literacy-driven.

Reading and Writing in the Kindergarten

The research and literature on children's literacy development is clear on the importance of the early childhood years (i.e., 0–8) for the development of young children's literacy. It is the time of laying the foundation. For example, children who have been read to from the time they are babies will often have had thousands of hours of experience with books and stories before they ever begin formal reading instruction. Likewise, and unfortunately, some children have not had the opportunity to benefit from exposure to reading and books. Kindergarten and grade 1 teachers will tell you it's obvious which children have been read to regularly since they were very young.

Reading is not something that is solely taught in school, nor does reading instruction begin in kindergarten or grade 1. Young children try to make sense of their environment, and when print is part of that environment they try to make sense of that as well. For example, many if not most three-year-olds recognize the sign for McDonald's. Most four- and five-year-olds know what the print on a stop sign means, even if they can't write the individual letters S-T-O-P.

Young children's reading development occurs on a continuum. The descriptive term for this literacy development of young children is **emerging literacy**. Emerging literacy is "the natural, gradual development of a young child's listening, speaking, reading, and writing abilities" (Ollila & Mayfield, 1992, p. 1). Literacy is more than reading.

A recent joint statement by the International Reading Association and the National Association for the Education of Young Children (2000) identified five phases in children's reading development:

Phase 1: Awareness and Exploration (Preschool)
Children are becoming aware of print and developing their language and listening.

Phase 2: Experimental Reading and Writing (Kindergarten)
Children are learning about the basic print concepts such as left-to-right and top-to-bottom nature of print.

Phase 3: Early Reading and Writing (Grade 1)
Children are reading simple stories and writing about meaningful topics.

Phase 4: Transitional Reading and Writing (Grade 2)
Children are reading and writing more fluently.

Phase 5: Independent and Productive Reading and Writing (Grade 3)
Children are continually expanding and refining their reading and writing knowledge.

The grade levels for the above phases are goals; they are not what every child must, will, or should accomplish in that grade. From what we know of children's literacy development, it is unrealistic to assume that every child will be an independent reader by grade 3. Likewise, I have had a few children in my kindergarten classes who have been reading at a grade 4 or 6 level. This developmental range has implications for the early childhood educator. One implication is the need to be aware of the possible range and to assess carefully individual children's literacy development. Another implication is the need to provide for a variety of activities and materials to accommodate this range of literacy development. According to the International Reading Association and the National Association for the Education of Young Children (2000), "not all children typically come to kindergarten with similar levels of knowledge about printed language. Estimating where each child is developmentally and building on that base, a key feature of good teaching, is particularly important for the kindergarten teacher" (p. 9).

Even though this chapter focuses on kindergarten, fostering children's literacy is a responsibility of all early childhood programs. It is a mistake to believe that "the schools can do it all" when it comes to young children's literacy development. Babies are not too young to enjoy and benefit from hearing rhymes, songs, and stories. Bredekamp (1997) warns of misinterpreting developmentally appropriate practice for literacy and from a fear of pushing children, educators not providing what they need. She quotes the example of

> One kindergarten teacher actually boasted that she was so developmentally appropriate that you wouldn't see an alphabet on her wall! Given the current knowledge of emerging literacy and children's own interest in and desire to use symbols at kindergarten age, such a misinterpretation of developmentally appropriate practice is alarming. (p. 38)

How Early Childhood Educators Can Foster Literacy

There are many, many activities in a developmentally appropriate early childhood program that can help foster young children's emerging literacy. Many are appropriate for a range of children (e.g., three- to five-year-olds). These activities are functional, meaningful for the children, part of a rich literacy environment, and initiated by either children or educators. The following are a few typical activities that illustrate these characteristics:

- *Functional*—Young children need to see that the purpose of print is to communicate meaning. This can be conveyed by putting their names on their cubbies, having a sign-in sheet, using their names on the class job chart, and putting brief captions or labels on pictures and posters displayed in the classroom.

- *Meaningful for the children*—Children need to see writing and reading being used for specific purposes. For example, the group can dictate thank-you notes after their field trips, refer to recipes/charts when cooking, have a song and fingerplay book to which new pieces are added for them to take home and share with their families, make signs such as "Please do not touch" when they want to save a particular art or construction project to continue working on later, and keep a personal journal with their thoughts expressed by pictures, print, or dictation.

- *A rich literacy environment*—Children of all literacy levels need to have access to a variety of literacy materials, such as different types of paper and writing instruments, a variety of types and levels of books, flannel board and felt pieces for telling and retelling stories, magnetic alphabet letters, materials to make greeting cards and booklets, and other materials.

- *Child-initiated literacy activities*—These activities include independently looking at books, writing messages or making cards for family members or other children, sharing their reading or writing with others, and talking about books or favourite authors. These types of activities not only foster literacy development but also facilitate oral language development.

- *Educator-initiated activities*—These activities emphasize language as the foundation of reading and writing, such as reading and discussing books with individuals, small groups, or the whole group; storytelling; taking dictation from individuals, small groups, or the whole group; making lists; writing instructions (e.g., the care of the class hamster in both pictures and print); using big books to demonstrate print concepts (e.g., left to right); and bookmaking with the children (e.g., a picture book about their family).

Families also play an important role in young children's literacy development. In my experience and research I have found that families are more than willing to help foster young children's literacy but they may not be certain what they can or should be doing or how to do it. Focus 10.6 is an example of some of the suggestions I share with some families in workshops. The list can be

Focus 10.6

Example of Handout on Literacy for Families

10 Ideas for Helping Your Child with Literacy

1. Talk *with* your child.
2. Read with your child.
3. Let your child see you read and write.
4. Provide new experiences for your child.
5. Use the public library *with* your child.
6. Encourage your child to help around the house.
7. Encourage your child to draw/dictate messages and stories.
8. Praise your child's literacy efforts.
9. Monitor television viewing.
10. Encourage family games and activities.

adapted and modified for specific groups. Some families also appreciate more detailed information on *how* to do some of these activities. It is one thing to suggest reading with children; but what if no one in that family was read to as a child or doesn't have much confidence in his/her own reading ability? They may not be certain what to do. You can model how to read a book to a young child and answer frequently asked parent questions, such as what types of questions should I ask my child while reading, what are the characteristics of good books for young children, how often should I read with my child and for how long at one time, and who should read to the child (it's a good idea to encourage fathers, older brothers, grandfathers, and other male family members to read so young children, especially boys, do not develop the idea that reading is a feminine activity only).

By thinking of children's literacy development as a continuum, the early childhood professional recognizes that all children are capable of some literacy-related learning and activities and can benefit from some assistance, whether it is listening to stories, writing signs for the classroom, or being helped to decode words in a picture book. Reading is no longer thought of as a point, as in you can read or you can't read. Every child is somewhere on the reading continuum. Therefore, reading readiness is no longer thought of as a specific age or a specific set of skills.

Readiness to Learn

A popular theme in both the Canadian and U.S. media is that children should be "ready to learn" by the time they begin kindergarten. According to Walsh (1992), "school is now seen as beginning in kindergarten rather than in first grade. Kindergarten is no longer the year to get ready" (p. 90).

FOR REFLECTION

What would your response be if a group of parents came to you and said that although their children were very happy in your kindergarten, they think the children need more of a challenge—and would you please send home reading worksheets for the children every day? How would you respond?

"Ready to learn" has been used to mean both readiness for learning and readiness for school. These two ideas are not the same. Most early childhood educators would probably argue that young children have been learning since birth, so the idea that children need to be made "ready to learn" before they can begin kindergarten is not accurate. NAEYC's Position Statement on School Readiness states emphatically that "every child, except in the most severe instances of abuse, neglect, or disability, enters school ready to learn school content" (1995, on-line). They do not need to be made "ready to learn." The issue seems to be more "ready for school" than "ready to learn." The larger question is really, Readiness for *what*?

Readiness is a controversial term and a complex and multidimensional concept. It usually is thought of as "some combination of cognitive, psychomotor, and social-emotional development that should be present in balance and congruent with the child's chronological age" (Graue, 1992, p. 62). However, in typical usage, readiness is often not or poorly defined and is open to various interpretations (Kagan, 1990). For example, does readiness mean the child should be ready for kindergarten, or the kindergarten should be ready for the child?

Children are not the same developmentally; two five-year-olds can be very different. Also, from your experience you have probably noted the differences within each five-year-old. For example, a child may have excellent language skills but poor fine motor skills. Or a child may have excellent gross motor skills and poor social skills. There is not only a range of "readiness" for young children in general but also for each individual child. Every child is "ready." It is the task of the early childhood educator to discover for what each child is ready and how they can most benefit from the early childhood program, whether that program is a toddler program, a kindergarten, or a school-age program.

An area of debate surrounds the question of whose responsibility it is to get the child ready to learn. Sometimes, it sounds as if it is the child's responsibility to appear at the door of the kindergarten in September ready to learn. Other groups say the primary responsibility rests with the families, who are the child's "first teachers." The families—while they may admit that they could do more (Harris & Lindauer, 1988)—may say they do not know what to do, how to do it, or have the time to do it. Others say it is the responsibility of the nursery school or day-care program. Others will tell you it is the responsibility of the government to ensure an educated citizenry. Others will say it is everyone's responsibility.

Is Retention an Answer?

The concept of readiness implies that some children may not be "ready" for kindergarten or grade 1. The question is, then, should something be done to help the children who are not ready, and what should be done? One traditional answer in kindergarten and primary grades has been to consider retention. **Retention** means that a child repeats or does not enter the next year of programming with his or her peers. The underlying rationale here is that if the child had an additional year to "mature" or "catch up," he or she could then cope better with the increasing demands of the next level.

There are two aspects to retention: *holding out* and *holding back*. **Holding out** means that the child is not enrolled in a program for which he or she is eligible. For example, a child may be eligible because of chronological age to begin kindergarten in September; however, the parents choose to not enrol the child that year but to wait one or more years. (How long one can wait depends on the age of compulsory education in a province/territory.) The child may attend a nursery school or day-care program instead of going to kindergarten, or may remain at home.

Some parents hold out their children from kindergarten for an extra year because they do not want their child to be the youngest, as they feel this would place their child at a disadvantage. This is generally not considered to be a good practice. There will always be a child who is the youngest in any group of children. It is important to remember that chronological age is a number, and not a developmental level. However, "the use of developmental age as the criterion for kindergarten entrance is questionable in that we don't have reliable and valid assessment tasks to guide decision making" (Charlesworth, 1989, p. 10).

Research has shown that although some of the youngest children do have a bit more difficulty academically in kindergarten (Peck, McCraig, & Sapp, 1988), "the small disadvantage of youngness eventually disappears, usually by about third grade" (Shepard & Smith, 1986, p. 79). On the other hand, holding out a child from kindergarten who is old enough to attend so they'll be among the oldest does not guarantee success.

Holding back means that although the child has begun kindergarten, he or she is not coping well and will repeat the level again or be placed in a special grade or class. In kindergarten, the options may be for the child to repeat kindergarten the next year (perhaps with a different teacher) or to be placed in a transition class. A K–1 transition class is meant to provide a program that is not as academically difficult as grade 1 but is still different from the kindergarten program the child experienced the previous year.

FOR REFLECTION

When you were in kindergarten and grade 1, were you one of the oldest or one of the youngest children? What effect, if any, do you remember this having on your elementary school experience?

What Does the Research Say about Retention?

Research shows that boys are more likely to be held out or retained than girls (e.g., Bellisimo, Sacks, & Mergendoller, 1995). Overall, research on the K–1 option has shown no difference between the children who are placed in a K–1 program and those who went into grade 1 instead, even though they were eligible for a K–1 placement (Gredler, 1984; Karweit, 1992). Although parents and educators believe that repeating kindergarten is effective, research shows there is no difference between those children and comparable children who attended grade 1 instead of the K–1 program, except that the K–1 children had slightly more negative attitudes about themselves and school (Meisels, 1991; Shepard & Smith, 1986). One potential negative effect of retention is that children will be stigmatized or labelled by retention, as in "You flunked kindergarten." In addition, being one year older than others in a grade level has been shown to increase a child's risk of dropping out by 40 to 50 percent (Meisels, 1991).

In summary, both the practices of holding out and holding back are considered to be ineffective. Some educators and researchers go further and have called these practices "both indefensible and an outrage" and have advocated their abolition (Siegel & Hanson, 1991, p. 17).

Summary of this Chapter

Despite kindergarten's success story, its future in Canada is not necessarily secure. Funding cuts to kindergartens in the 1990s were particularly upsetting to the early childhood community in Canada as it was assumed, perhaps naïvely, that kindergarten is an established and accepted part of the public education system.

Do you have an answer to the question posed at the beginning of this chapter as to kindergarten being preschool or primary? Is it part of both? Is it part of neither?

The key themes in this chapter are that:

- Public-school kindergartens began relatively early in Ontario. Other provinces soon followed, although development was uneven and usually in urban areas.

- Kindergartens faced early criticism and a significant split occurred in the early twentieth century that still influences today's kindergarten.

- Kindergarten can be on a half-day, full-day, or alternate-day schedule. Some provinces have both junior and senior kindergartens and multi-age programs.

- The quality of kindergarten programs is more influential than the length of the kindergarten day.

- The characteristics of a good kindergarten program are basically the same as those for nursery schools and day-care programs.

- Some differences among nursery schools, day cares, and kindergartens are their origins and development, class size and educator-to-child ratios, and required educator qualifications. There are more similarities than differences.

- Some children have difficulty with the transitions into kindergarten and from kindergarten to grade 1. Educators, schools, and families can help these children.

- There are many potential areas of discontinuity between preschool and kindergarten programs as well as between kindergarten and grade 1.

- Children's literacy development occurs throughout their early years; it does not begin with formal instruction.

- Kindergarten activities, including literacy activities, should be appropriate and meaningful for the children.
- Retention and holding out eligible children from kindergarten are not effective practices.

Key Terms

continuity, 416

discontinuity, 416

emerging literacy, 422

holding back, 427

holding out, 427

junior kindergarten, 392

looping, 408

multi-age or mixed-age groups, 407

readiness, 426

retention, 426

senior kindergarten, 392

transition, 419

Resources

If you wish to know more about some of the topics in this chapter, here are a few suggested publications and Web sites.

For Sharing with Children

The following are some children's books about starting kindergarten or going to grade 1:

M. Cohen, illustrated by L. Hoban. 1967. *Will I have a friend?* New York: Macmillan Publishing. A classic book that addresses the common child fear of not knowing anyone in kindergarten.

E. Herman, illustrated by R.J. Flanigan. 1992. *My first day at school.* New York: McClanahan Book Company.

P. Baehr, illustrated by R.W. Alley. *School isn't fair.* 1992. New York: Aladdin Books. A bad day in the kindergarten.

Some books for children that have photographs for illustrations:

E.B. Senisi. 1994. *Kindergarten kids.* New York: Scholastic.

S. Berger and P. Chanko. 1999. *School.* New York: Scholastic. The people one encounters in a school.

C. Solomon. 1989. *Moving up from kindergarten to first grade.* New York: Crown Publishers.

J. Howe, photos by B. Imershein. 1986. *When you go to kindergarten.* New York: Alfred A. Knopf. A book for parents to share with their children.

H. Hains. 1992. *My new school.* New York: Dorling Kindersley. Combines photos and drawings.

Davis, L. 1996. *P.B. Bear's school day.* Toronto: Stoddart. Photos and rebus text.

Series characters with which the children may already be familiar include:

P. Bourgeois and B. Clark. 1995. *Franklin goes to school.* Toronto: Kids Can Press. (Franklin the turtle.)

N. Bridwell. 1999. *Clifford's first school day.* New York: Scholastic. (Clifford the big red dog.)

K. Zoehfeld, illustrated by R. Cuddy. 1997. *Pooh's first day of school.* New York: Disney.

J. Langreuter and V. Sobat. 1997. *Little Bear goes to kindergarten.* Brookfield, CT: The Millbrook Press.

S. and J. Berenstain. 1978. *The Berenstain Bears go to school.* New York: Random House.

For Further Reading

For more information about starting kindergarten:

Hannigan, I. 1998. *Off to school: A parent's-eye view of the kindergarten year.* Washington, DC: National Association for the Education of Young Children. A series of diary-type entries and letters of a mother to her kindergarten son during the kindergarten year.

Waterland, L. 1995. *The bridge to school: Entering a new world.* York, ME: Stenhouse Publishers. Children's transitions from preschool to kindergarten from a principal's perspective.

Golant, S.K. & Golant, M. 1999. *Kindergarten isn't what it used to be* (3rd ed.). Los Angeles: Lowell House. Discusses parents' concerns about their children beginning elementary school.

Walmsley, S. & Walmsley, B.B. 1996. *Kindergarten: Ready or not? A parent's guide.* Portsmouth, NH: Heinnemann.

Many school districts also prepare their own brochures, handbooks, or other materials with information for families and children beginning kindergarten.

For more information about emerging literacy:

The most definitive statement on emerging reading and writing by the largest early childhood and literacy groups in North America (NAEYC and the International Reading Association). Neuman, S.B., Copple, C. & Bredekamp, S. 2000. *Learning to read and write: Developmentally appropriate practices for young children.* Washington, DC: National Association for the Education of Young Children. One of those references that should be on every early childhood educator's bookshelf as well as in a program's parent library.

Burns, M.S., Griffin, P., & Snow, C.E. (Eds.) 1999. *Starting out right: A guide to promoting children's reading success.* Washington, DC: National Academy Press. Information, recommendations, and activities for parents and early childhood educators, prepared by the Committee on the Prevention of Reading Difficulties in Young Children for the National Research Council (www.nap.edu).

Ready to go: What parents should know about school readiness [brochure] 1999a. Washington, DC: National Association for the Education of Young Children. US$0.50 a copy. Presents general ideas on providing a solid background for children's development from pregnancy to kindergarten. Also has list of resources. Another NAEYC brochure and also available from the International Reading Association is *Raising a reader, raising a writer: How parents can help.* 1998.

For more information about issues in kindergarten:

Goffin, S.G. & Stegelin, D.A. (Eds.) 1992. *Changing kindergartens: Four success stories.* Washington, DC: National Association for the Education of Young Children. Chapters on current policy and practice, the teacher as change agent, developmentally appropriate practice, the role of parents, and an administrator's education about kindergarten.

Barbour, N.H. & Seefeldt, C. 1993. *Developmental continuity across preschool and primary grades.* Wheaton, MD: Association for Childhood Education International.

For more information about full-day kindergartens:

The classic and most cited book on this topic is Fromberg, D. P. 1995. *The full-day kindergarten: Planning and practicing a dynamic themes curriculum* (2nd ed.) New York: Teachers College Press.

For more information about multi-age grouping:

A short, readable argument for mixed-age grouping is L. Katz, D. Evangelou, & A. Hartman. 1990. *The case for mixed-age grouping in early education.* Washington, DC: National Association for the Education of Young Children.

A recent brochure is S.J. Stone. (n.d.). *The multiage classroom: A guide for parents.* Wheaton, MD: Association for Childhood Education International.

For review of Canadian regulations and issues on multi-age groupings in day-care centres, see:

Bernhard, J., Pollard, J., Chud, G., Vukelich, G., & Pacini-Ketchabaw, V. 2000. The regulation of multi-age groupings in Canadian centre-based child care settings: An analysis of provincial and territorial policies, legislation, and regulations. *Canadian Journal of Early Childhood Education 8(3)*, 7–22.

Useful Addresses and Web Sites

The International Reading Association
800 Barksdale Road
Newark, DE 19714
Tel: 302-731-1600
Fax: 302-731-1057
Web site: www.reading.org

An excellent resource for inexpensive, quality materials on children's emerging literacy and parent participation in children's literacy development.
For NAEYC and AECI addresses and information, see Resources in Chapter 4.

11

Family Support Programs: Community-based Programs for Families with Young Children

*I don't know how I could raise my kids and keep my sanity without the
programs for families in this community.*

—Mother of three, ages two, five, and eight

All families need support; but not all the time, not at the same time, and maybe not very much. However, raising young children is a complex and complicated endeavour, and most parents appreciate having support available. In the past, many parents received support from their extended family members. From the discussion of Canadian families in Chapter 3, you saw that Canadian families of today are relatively small and most do not have many relatives living in the same community. Family support programs recognize and respond to the needs of today's families in a variety of ways, and these programs are used by a variety of families. They are not developed solely for families having problems, but for *all* families. Family support programs are preventive, are proactive, promote family strengths, and foster family wellness.

Chapters 8, 9, and 10 look mostly at centre-based programs having a primary focus on young children. This chapter examines community-based programs that focus on families with young children.

Here are some questions to think about while you read this chapter:

· What are family support programs?

· How are families supported by community-based programs?

· What are some types of family support programs?

· How did family support programs develop?

· Who participates in family support programs?

· What are some career options for early childhood educators in family support programs?

· What are some characteristics of effective family support programs?

· How can family support programs be monitored and evaluated?

Scope of Community-Based Family Support Programs

The most striking characteristic of family support programs is their variety and diversity. These programs are typically community-based and often locally developed. In this way, they are better able to meet local needs and concerns. This also explains, in large part, why they are so varied and diverse.

Family Support Programs

Family support programs are basically designed to complement and perhaps enhance a family's existing strengths. They can also help prevent potential family problems as well as help remediate existing problems. The category "family support programs" is a broad one that encompasses a variety of programs, sponsors, participants, goals, educator roles, approaches, and locations. For example, the following can all be considered family support programs:

- Family resource centres
- Toy libraries
- Parent education/support
- Family literacy programs
- Recreation programs (e.g., children's museums)
- Intergenerational programs
- Home visiting programs
- Information and resource services
- Counselling and peer support groups
- Respite/emergency care
- Telephone warm-line (i.e., non-crisis telephone information service)
- Clothing or toy exchange
- Adult education and job training
- Babysitting or child-minding cooperatives
- Nutritional or financial counselling, and
- Programs developed for specific groups, such as incarcerated parents, teen parents, recent immigrants, or Aboriginal families.

There are even more programs that could be listed as family support programs. In this chapter, the first eight programs on the above list will be described, as they illustrate the diversity and variety of family support programs. Programs developed for Aboriginal families and incarcerated parents and their children will also be described as examples of family support programs developed to meet specific needs.

All of the above programs provide support and resources for families with young children. This support can be formal or informal. For example, a parent education program such as Nobody's Perfect or a family literacy program are formal support programs, whereas parents getting together for coffee and discussing children and family life after their weekly Mom and Tot swim at the local recreation centre is an example of informal support. Some family support programs, such as family resource centres, provide both formal and informal support for families with young children.

Community-based Programs

Family support programs are typically **community-based**. This means that they are located in the communities they serve, are designed or modified for local communities, and are administered locally. Because the locus of community-based programs is in the local community, these programs, including family support programs, are well positioned to address local concerns and culture, and incorporate community input in designing and implementing programs.

Family support programs are readily accessible for families with young children. The fact that they are community-based increases the likelihood that families can and will use these programs. I have visited family support programs in a variety of locations including schools, churches, seniors' residences, public libraries, community centres, women's centres, storefronts, recreation centres, social services offices, clinics, apartment buildings, and a prison.

Another dimension is a sense of community that community-based programs typically foster. Many participants develop lasting friendships with other families. These relationships can serve as informal support for families as well as foster a sense of belonging among the participants and the larger community.

Family support programs have also become a catalyst for coordination with other community-based programs and agencies, which can result in organized community action aimed at meeting identified community needs on a broader scale. According to Kagan (1997), "ideally, family support programs are also embedded in, and contribute to, communities" (p. 285). Recognition of the importance and desirability of a sense of community and support has also motivated some individuals to initiate programs. For example, when I was visiting a family resource centre in Toronto, one mother of two young children told me that the first thing she does when she moves into a new community is find the local family resource centre. Once, when her new community did not have a family resource centre, she organized a group to start one!

Sponsorship of Family Support Programs

Diversity is also seen in the sponsorship of family support programs. Some sponsors of family support programs in Canada include:

FOR REFLECTION

"It takes a village to raise a child" is a frequently heard phrase. What arguments can be made for and against that statement as applied to community-based family support programs?

- Community organizations

- Service organizations (e.g., Kiwanis)

- Parent organizations

- Charitable and philanthropic organizations

- School districts

- Women's groups

- Aboriginal groups

- Recreation organizations (e.g., YM/YWCA)

- Public libraries

- Health and mental health organizations.

Another sponsor is sometimes federal or provincial government agencies; for example, Aboriginal Head Start and the Military Family Support Program of the Department of National Defence. Although these are federally or provincially originated programs, they are typically modified and adapted to meet the needs and backgrounds of local participants and communities.

Characteristics of Family Support Programs

Although community-based family support programs vary in specific program content, they generally share common characteristics that include:

- A holistic emphasis on family strengths and wellness (i.e., a non–deficit orientation)

- An ecological perspective that views children and families in the context of the community

- A recognition and accommodation of the diversity of families and communities

- A prevention focus

- A multidisciplinary approach

- A grassroots orientation that is highly responsive to and accommodating of local culture, values, and needs

- An openness to change to meet evolving needs

- Staff with varied backgrounds and education

- Voluntary participation

- Accessibility for participants and "user-friendly" facilities

- Multiple funding sources, and

- Development frequently in response to unmet community needs or gaps in services (Mayfield, 1993a).

Rationale for Family Support Programs

Theoretical rationale for family support programs is derived from family theories and child development as well as from research on early childhood programs and parent education. The two theories most frequently mentioned in the early childhood literature as rationale for family support programs are **family systems theory** and **ecological theory**.

Family systems theory sees the family as a "system" or "organized whole," wherein one individual influences every other one and changes in, or by, one individual affect the other members of the family. These relationships are complex and interdependent (Hyson, 1996). For example, if one member of the family becomes seriously ill, this impacts not only that individual but all the other family members as well. Within the general family system, there are parent–child, sibling, and marital subsystems operating. Family systems theory has been particularly influential in early intervention and therapy programs.

The theory most used as rationale for family support programs is *ecological theory*. This theory emerged from developmental theory (Bretherton, 1993). This may be why it is conceptually attractive and perceived as relevant and applicable to early childhood programs, especially those with a strong family or community emphasis.

The person most associated with ecological theory as it applies to early childhood education and care is Urie Bronfenbrenner (e.g., 1979, 1987, 1989). Briefly, Bronfenbrenner postulated that human development occurs within contexts. This is an expansion beyond family systems theory to include other systems and their interactions. He identified four increasingly broad or more encompassing levels:

- *The microsystem*—For example, the family and the early childhood program

- *The exosystem*—The contexts of the microsystems (e.g., the neighbourhood, the workplace, and the local government)

- *The macrosystem*—For example, the culture, political system, societal values, and other belief systems

- *The mesosystem*—That is, the concept that all of these systems interact with and influence each other.

According to Bretherton (1993), "what is original about Bronfenbrenner's framework is not the basic idea that individuals develop in a familial and societal context, but rather its emphasis on studying interrelationships among systems" (p. 286).

The implication of family systems theory and ecological theory is that children cannot be separated from the context of their families and communities. In addition, the community is seen as integral to family life (Weissbourd & Patrick, 1988). A key premise of community-based family support programs is that the community, as a whole, has a responsibility to support families raising children. Therefore, knowledge and consideration of context is essential in the development and operation of family support programs.

The recognition of the importance of the early years for children's optimal development and the crucial role of the family in this development also provides rationale for family support programs. Research also supports the need for informal and formal support for families and the efficacy of these programs. For example, program evaluations of individual family support programs have shown beneficial effects for a diversity of families, including parents who stay at home, employed parents, teen parents, immigrant families, low-income families, families living in rural areas, families living in inner-city areas, and families with children with disabilities (Mayfield, 1993a).

See Chapters 2 and 3 for information on early-years development and roles of families.

Development of Family Support Programs

The historical development of family support programs has parallels with the history of early childhood programs focusing on young children. As discussed in Chapter 5, ancient philosophers such as Plato recommended active parental participation in their children's early years. Major thinkers and proponents of early childhood education and care, such as Comenius, Pestalozzi, and Froebel, recognized the role and importance of the family. Comenius' *School of Infancy* and Pestalozzi's *How Gertrude Teaches Her Children* might be considered early parent education guides (see Chapter 5).

The impetus for modern family support programs has come primarily from the fields of early childhood education and care, health, and social work. In addition to the efforts of early childhood programs throughout the twentieth century that have fostered parent participation and education, early public health clinics and nurses in Canada provided support and education for families through home visits, weighing stations, milk distribution, prenatal care, and well-baby clinics (Kyle & Kellerman, 1998).

The increase in immigration and urbanization in the late nineteenth and early twentieth centuries in Canada and the related stresses on families led religious, charitable, and voluntary organizations to help support these families. These efforts were largely replaced in the early twentieth century by the rise of settlement houses and social work. An early Canadian example is the University Settlement House in Toronto organized by J.J. Kelso and others to serve immigrant families. (It is still in operation.) According to Halpern (1988), these early settlement workers "provided practical assistance with child care, housing, legal and other problems. And they worked to restore a sense of community and mutual support in the rapidly growing slums of the larger cities" (p. 286).

Another force in the development of family support programs was the mental hygiene and mental health movements (see Chapter 9), which evolved into the self-help movement of the 1960s and 1970s and then into today's wellness movement. Parent education was also part of programs for young children, especially the cooperative nursery school movement (see Chapter 9) and the social and educational initiatives of the 1960s such as Head Start (see Chapter 5).

Women have also been instrumental in the development of family support programs in Canada. They often identified community needs, organized informal and formal programs, and worked as volunteers, staff, and advocates both as individuals and in organizations such as the Women's Institutes and the *Cercle des Fermières* (Kyle & Kellerman, 1998). Most of the family support programs that I have visited in Canada were initiated by women, usually from the local communities.

The growth of family support programs in Canada is readily apparent when one considers that 50 years ago community support for families was generally limited. In many communities the family physician, public health nurse, social worker, and clergy were typically the only options available outside family and friends.

In the mid-1980s, two federal reports both recommended more family support programs (Cooke, 1986; Martin, 1987). The public profile of family support programs was further heightened later on through the efforts of public- and private-sector groups during the International Year of the Family in 1994. The evolution of family support programs has moved from a remediation to a prevention to a promotion of wellness approach in less than 100 years. The goal of family support programs today is the promotion of family wellness and the recognition of family strengths. There are a variety of ways to accomplish this goal.

Types of Family Support Programs

The descriptions of the following types of family support programs illustrate the variety, scope, and diversity of family support programs in Canada today. According to the Canadian Association of Family Resource Programs (personal communication, May 2000), their database contains approximately 2,000 listings, with family resource centres the largest single category.

Family Resource Centres

A very visible family support program in many Canadian communities is the **family resource centre.** (Some other names for this are *neighbourhood house, resource centre, family place, parent–child resource centre, family centre, maisonnette des parents,* and *carrefour familial.*) Canada is known internationally for its family resource centres (Bjorck-Akesson, Brodin, Hellberg, Lindberg, & Sinker, 1990). These centres are typically facilities that offer programs in informal neighbourhood settings to all families in the community. Because the overall goal of these centres is to respond to local needs, the programs offered by family resource centres vary from community to community. Some of the more frequent program components are:

- Drop-in

- Parent support groups

Margie I. Mayfield

The West Side Family Place in Vancouver is a family resource centre.

- Clothing and toy exchanges

- Workshops and courses

- Community and child-care information

- Child care, playgroups, and programs for young children

- Special events for families

- Counselling services

- Babysitting or child-minding cooperatives

- Parent libraries

- Family and community bulletin boards

- Advocacy and community development (Mayfield, 1993a).

One example of a family resource centre serving all families in a community is the West Side Family Place in Vancouver. One of the oldest family resource centres in Canada, it was begun in 1973 through the efforts of two young mothers concerned about the isolation of parents with young children. It began as a drop-in centre. As is typical with family resource centres, the programs evolved and expanded over time to include workshops, courses, and a yearly conference, as well as support groups for nannies, au pairs, home-based caregivers, new parents, single parents, parents in crisis, parents with children with disabilities, and unemployed parents.

The orientation of family resource centres is to *both* adults and children. In my experience, the most frequent users of family resource centres are parents with young children who use the centres for play and socialization opportunities for their children and social interaction with other adults for themselves.

Although most family resource centres in Canada are designed for the general community, some have been developed for special groups such as teen parents (e.g., Terra Child and Family Support Centre in Edmonton), families with children with special needs (e.g., Daybreak Parent–Child Centre in St. John's), or Aboriginal families (e.g., Awasheshuk Resource Centre in Hornepayne, Ontario). One example of a family resource centre developed for specific groups is the Mobile Family Resource Program located in East York and east Toronto (Cox, Devlin, & Addetia, 1998). Its target groups are isolated home caregivers and families with young children who cannot access existing programs because of poverty, language, lack of transportation, weather, or other reasons. This resource centre is actually a van that travels to different locations in the community. During each half-day session, information and referrals are provided along with clothing, emergency food, and information about child development, health, safety, parenting, and local resources. Toy libraries have also been leaders in using vans and buses (also called *playbuses*) to deliver mobile family support programs.

Toy Libraries

One of my favourite types of family support programs is the toy library (*ludothèque* in French). For several years I did research on toy libraries in Canada, England, Sweden, and Australia (e.g., Mayfield, 1988, 1993b). I saw a variety of excellent programs that support a variety of families while promoting the value and practice of play. **Toy libraries** are resource centres for parents and children that provide developmentally appropriate play materials (e.g., toys, games, books, media, etc.), as well as activities and information related to play, learning, and child development. According to Head and Barton (1987), toy libraries

> can meet the needs of families in a low key way that is acceptable to
> parents regardless of their social and economic circumstances, cultural
> and ethnic backgrounds. They can provide an informal meeting place
> where parents can make friends and find support. (p. 109)

Although the first toy library was established in Los Angeles in 1935, it was not until the mid-1960s that they began in Europe and then came to Canada. They are now found worldwide.

Sweden and England were early leaders in the establishment of toy libraries. In Sweden, toy libraries (called *lekoteks*) originated in 1963 to serve children with special needs and their families, including siblings. The primary focus of Swedish *lekoteks* remains children with special needs. Toy libraries in England began in the late 1960s and developed in a wide variety of community settings. Although the first one in England was for children with disabilities, rapid growth of more general community-oriented toy libraries followed. The English toy libraries had a more diverse clientele than the Swedish ones. These two major models of toy libraries are often referred to as the *Swedish model* and the *English model* or the *special needs* and *community models*, respectively. Both models are found in Canada, although the community-oriented toy library model is predominant. The toy libraries for children with special needs have specially modified, adapted, and designed play materials. Many of these toy libraries are connected with therapy and rehabilitation programs.

In Canada, toy libraries began to be established in 1972. The first ones were TOTS, established in Winnipeg for children with disabilities, and a community-oriented toy library in Toronto established by Joanna von Levetzow to serve a large multi-ethnic community. Subsequent toy libraries in Canada have been established by varied individuals and organizations, such as early childhood educators, community or charitable groups, public librarians, therapists, elementary teachers, and parents of children with special needs (Mayfield, 1988). Often, these have been grassroots efforts in local communities. They are all found in a variety of locations including family resource centres, clinics, and treatment centres, public libraries, recreation centres, public schools, shopping malls, government buildings, storefronts, community centres, and prisons.

The most frequently given goals for toy libraries in Canada, as well as in some other countries, are:

- Provision of toys and play materials to children without toys, including adapted toys for children with special needs

- Promotion of play and children's development

- Parent education about play and play materials

- Provision of a family-focused program not otherwise available in the community

- Provision of social opportunities for families

- Prevention or remediation (Mayfield, 1988; 1993b).

Participants in toy libraries in Canada are most frequently families with children under six years of age. In addition to parents, home-based caregivers and grandparents also participate in libraries. Several toy library directors I've spoken with have reported that many adults, especially mothers, use the toy library for their own socialization needs. Some families use the toy library regularly and others only occasionally.

Toy libraries may be open as little as one hour a week or several hours a day for four or more days a week. Community toy libraries tend to be open longer hours than special-needs toy libraries. Most operate on a drop-in basis and they look rather like drop-in centres, with lots of shelving and other storage for play materials. Adults and children come and go frequently. Some stay for an hour or more, some less than 30 minutes. Materials are labelled and displayed attractively on shelves, hangers, poles, or in containers of various descriptions (see the following photo). Parents (usually mothers) help children select possible toys, books, or other materials to borrow, often trying them out in the toy library before making the final choices. There are also print and audio materials for families, as well as a bulletin board and library on topics related to toys and play.

Margie I. Mayfield

Toy libraries display and loan a variety of play materials.

Some programs have periodic group stories or songs or activity times. When the parent or caregiver and child have selected the materials they wish to borrow they sign these out, like a public library. Some toy libraries charge for borrowing each item, others have a yearly membership fee, and some do both. Some special-needs toy libraries will deliver and pick up play materials for special-needs families.

The most frequently available toys in the toy libraries I visited in my research studies were the "classic" toys, such as puzzles, stacking and nesting toys, blocks, pull toys, simple board games, telephones, rattle toys, farm animal sets, and small cars (Mayfield, 1993b). The most popular toys also tended to be the "classics" (e.g., puzzles and construction sets) as well as the current high visibility/popular toys, especially those being advertised in the media. Examples of appropriate toys for children of various ages are found in the Canadian Toy Testing Council's annual *Toy Report* (see Resources in Chapter 2).

I have asked toy library professionals about the benefits of toy libraries for children. The most frequently mentioned benefits were increased socialization, improved play and social skills, and increased access to and experience with a variety of play materials. For adults, reported benefits of participation in toy libraries included (a) increased knowledge about play and how to facilitate it, (b) more knowledge about toy selection and child development, (c) improved parenting skills, and (d) adult socialization opportunities outside of the home thereby reducing the parent's social isolation (Mayfield, 1993b). Research in other countries has reported similar benefits (e.g., Head & Barton, 1987; Bjorck-Akesson, Brodin, Hellberg, Lindberg, & Sinker, 1991).

The major issues facing toy libraries are similar to those facing many other family support programs: lack of funding; under-utilization, often due to insufficient publicity; lack of sufficient space; and difficulty in finding qualified staff. These issues are seen in toy libraries in Canada and other countries I have visited (Mayfield, 1988; 1993b).

Criteria for selection of play materials are discussed in Chapter 7.

FOR REFLECTION

If you were the director of a toy library for three- to six-year-olds, what five toys or play materials would you consider essential to have? Why would you choose these?

Parent Education/Support

Many a new parent has commented, "I'm not sure what to do. I thought I would but people aren't born knowing how to be parents, and having a baby didn't automatically teach me this." Numerous surveys of parents have shown that they are often unsure of how young children develop and what they can do to facilitate this development (e.g., Invest in Kids, 1999 [on-line]).

Although the education of parents has long been a theme in early childhood education and care, historically it is only relatively recently that formal parent education programs have been readily available. Such help has long been advocated and some programs were developed. For example, the early twentieth century saw the rise of the Child Study Movement (see Chapter 9). The program at the Institute of Child Study nursery school at the University of Toronto had a strong parent-education component from its beginning (see Chapter 9). Moreover, the National Society for the Study of Education's yearbook in 1929 noted that "parenthood . . . is at present one of the most recent concerns of education" (Whipple, 1929, p. 433). However, these efforts in North America were not necessarily widespread. In 1948, Caroline Pratt (see Chapter 5) commented, "We have not educated parents. If they have been educated they have done the educating themselves. Or they have been educated as we have, by the children" (p. 188). Some would agree that this statement is still applicable today. Early childhood programs (e.g., Head Start and parent cooperative nursery schools) and early childhood special education programs have had a long history of parent participation and education.

Parent education programs were developed to try to make learning to be a parent less of "a trial-and-error process with countless frustrations" (Wandersman, 1987, p. 207). For many parents, their initial experience with a formal parent education program is a prenatal course. Some of them continue with a child development course, while others rely on informal support.

There is no single model for parent education. In fact, there is a wide variety of both formal and informal options possible. For most parents, the informal options are probably used most frequently. For example, parents who want to know how to stop their child from biting a sibling will likely first consult friends or relatives. Impromptu discussions with other parents are another frequently used option. If these suggestions are not effective or acceptable, the next step for many parents is the family physician, a nurse at a well-baby clinic, or an early childhood educator. Many of the questions parents ask early childhood educators are about child development or parenting topics.

Some formal parent-education programs are developed for specific groups such as teen parents, fathers only, stepparents, or recent immigrants. In general, these programs have some similar components, including child development, parent–child relationships, decision-making and parent roles, and group processes especially for networking informal support groups (Gullo, Bersani, & Conlin, 1987). Formal parent education options include courses such as STEP (Systematic Training for Effective Parenting) or Nobody's Perfect. This latter program was developed in the 1980s by a coalition of health groups in Atlantic Canada, piloted, revised for national use, and is currently used widely across Canada in partnership with provincial and territorial governments and voluntary organizations. Nobody's Perfect focuses on children from birth to age five and provides parents with five booklets about children's behaviour, health, development, parenting, and safety. It is usually a six-to-eight-week program, with group meetings once a week. Nobody's Perfect includes a training program for facilitators and resource materials in English, French (the program is called *Y'a personne de parfait* in French), Spanish, Chinese, Vietnamese, and Punjabi. The program is coordinated by the Canadian Association of Family Resource Programs, the Canadian Institute of Child Health, and provincial and territorial coordinators. (For more information, see Resources at the end of this chapter.)

While many families prefer a more structured approach to parent education, others do not. For example, some families are unable to commit to weekly attendance or may avoid a program they perceive as "too much like school." In addition, although parent surveys consistently show high levels of interest by parents in taking these courses, attracting and retaining parents can be difficult (Wandersman, 1987). Parent education can also be one component of a more comprehensive family support program, such as a family resource centre.

Despite the current prevalence and popularity of parent education programs, there are criticisms. For example, some people see these programs as an intrusion or interference in family life. Others are critical of structured programs that do not evolve from and focus on the specific cultural and social contexts of the participating families. Still others think the term *parent education* implies a deficit approach rather than a family-strengths orientation.

A recent trend in parent education, in part because of criticisms such as the above, has been a clearer emphasis on parent *support* rather than parent *education*. The latter is perceived as a need to educate parents because there is a deficit of information or skill, whereas a **parent support** orientation recognizes that the provision of information, no matter how relevant or valuable, may be insufficient without consideration of the social context of families and importance of social support (Powell, 1989). The concept of parent support also recognizes that families have strengths and that most families are doing a good job. For these parents, parent education and support may provide additional knowledge, support, or reassurance that they are doing a good job. In addition, for some parents it can be "a powerful preventive tool . . . . [For example] It directly combats many of the factors which can lead to escalating violence against children: isolation, stress, unrealistically high expectations, and a lack of knowledge about non-damaging discipline methods" (Bennett, 1989, p. 102).

Family Literacy

Another type of family support program is a **family literacy** program, which promotes literacy for children and their families. The statement of Purcell-Gates (1993) that "family literacy, as a term, today refers to the many and varied projects

---

FOR REFLECTION

Why do you think retaining parents in parent education courses can be difficult? What are some possible strategies to retain more parents?

See Chapter 2 for discussion of the effects of culture on child-rearing practices.

being proposed or currently operating that are designed to enhance literacy within the home" (p. 670) is an appropriate one. Moreover, many professionals "have become increasingly convinced of the promise of family literacy programs in promoting successful learning experiences for children and their families" (Morrow, 1995, p. 8).

Family literacy programs, like other family support programs, are diverse, with diverse clientele, diverse activities, diverse materials, and diverse objectives. Diversity is seen also in the literacy activities that occur regularly in the family context. Families typically engage in a variety of literacy activities during daily life (e.g., shopping, paying bills, reading directions on packages, and driving). These can and often are incorporated into family literacy programs. It is not accurate to assume that a family does not use or model literacy activities because the adult members are low-income, teens, seniors, or recent immigrants. An important implication of this is that "family literacy projects are best viewed as augmenting what is already there rather than as filling a vacuum" (Harrison, 1995, p. 227). Enhancing family strengths is a key principle of family literacy, as it is for family support programs in general.

Two additional key principles of family literacy are (a) that literacy begins at birth and therefore the early years are important for children's literacy development, and (b) that families are concerned about and are important in the literacy development of their children. Some family literacy programs begin with babies and their families. For example, the Books for Babies program in Cardston, Alberta, provides incentives and encouragement for parents to read to their children from birth (Peterson & Palmer, 1998). This program is a joint endeavour of several community groups. Parent–child packets containing three children's picture board books (suitable for children from birth to age two); a Blackfoot-language colouring book (given to all families); brochures on ideas for sharing books with children; and information sheets on television viewing,

Family literacy can be an inter-generational experience: this photo shows a grandfather reading to his grandson.

adult literacy programs, use of the public library, and parents' role as teachers of their children are included in a canvas book bag. The book bags are given to parents of newborns in the municipal hospital by volunteers who show a video and explain the project and the importance of reading to children from the earliest age. The program also developed a Books for Babies newsletter and a Books for Babies section in the local public library. Variations on book bag programs include Writer's Suitcase (Welken, 1993; Wrobleski, 1990), which contains writing materials for the children to take home, and book boxes containing children's books that are located in areas used frequently by families, such as Laundromats and clinics (Morrow, Tracey, & Maxwell, 1995).

A family literacy program for young children and their families that began on a small scale in Toronto and subsequently has been replicated in other communities across Canada is the Parent–Child Mother Goose Program. It was originally developed by storyteller Joan Bodger and social worker Barry Dickson and was funded by the Toronto Children's Aid Society as a pilot project. The Parent–Child Mother Goose Program evolved from this pilot in 1986, with funding from Metro Toronto Community and Social Services, under the leadership of storytellers Celia Lottridge and Katherine Grier. The aim of this program is to promote young children's oral language and literacy development and to strengthen parent–child relationships through rhymes, songs, and stories (Lottridge, 1998). The program initially targeted parents who were low-income, socially isolated, recent immigrants, or lacked positive role models for parenting; it is now intended for a wide variety of families. The program has also been offered in a variety of community settings such as church halls, recreation centres, homeless shelters, and health centres.

The basic program is organized for a group of parents and their young children and two group leaders. The participants sit on the floor in a circle and learn new rhymes, songs, and stories; they also repeat old favourites. Ways these rhymes can be used in daily family life are discussed. At the end of the ten-week series of sessions, the parents receive a folder with printed versions of the rhymes and songs. Variations of the Parent–Child Mother Goose Program have been developed for ESL groups, parents with children under two years of age, parents with children between two and four years, and parents with three- and four-year-olds about to begin an early childhood program. The latter program emphasizes use of a school library. There is also a training program for group leaders. The Rhymes that Bind program in Alberta is based on this program (Sykes, Wolfe, Gendreau, & Workman, 1998).

Family literacy programs are flexible, to accommodate a wide variety of family and community factors. For example, these programs are intergenerational and all family members are possible participants. An example of this intergenerational participation is the Parenting and Family Literacy Centres in Toronto, where participants range from teen parents to grandparents.

Under the direction of Mary Gordon, in 1981 the Toronto Board of Education established Parenting Centres for parents and caregivers of children up to age four in inner-city areas to promote children's future academic success.

By 1998, there were 34 Parenting and Family Literacy centres serving more than 7,000 culturally and linguistically diverse families, and 11,000 children yearly (Gordon, 1998). The centres are all located in public schools.

The centres are drop-in family resource centres with hours of operation that are determined primarily by the participants. Most are open mornings Monday to Thursday and some afternoons (Fridays are for staff meetings and professional development). Typical centre activities include play, gym, snack, story reading, and various informal activities. Every session has a circle time with music and story reading. Parents and children learn rhymes, chants, songs, and fingerplays. Learning materials were developed in 1997 to foster family literacy and numeracy development. Parents attend sessions to learn how to use these materials with their children. Role-playing is a primary teaching and learning strategy. There are also multilingual book lending libraries, toy lending libraries, parenting courses, and family literacy evenings.

An example of a community-based, outreach type of family literacy program is provided by the Hants Shore Community Health Centre along the Bay of Fundy in Nova Scotia. The Health Centre's philosophy is that it is more than a treatment centre and should also promote the total well-being of the families in the community (Helliwell, 1998). The Learning Together Program at the Hants Shore Community Heath Centre uses provincially developed family literacy materials in a series of workshops for parents that include parent discussions, activities, videos, bookmaking, and sharing of literacy strategies. Home visits subsequent to the workshops, as well as other efforts in conjunction with Nobody's Perfect and Moms and Tots weekly meetings and special activities, promote family literacy in the community.

According to the National Center for Family Literacy, program evaluations have shown that family literacy programs can improve the parenting and literacy skills of adults, increase children's language and literacy skills, improve parent–child relationships, and enhance parents' backgrounds related to employment and further education (Brizius & Foster, 1993). These programs can also build a sense of community, reduce social isolation, improve adults' language and literacy skills, and provide parents with peer support (Thomas, 1998).

Family literacy programs in Canada have also been developed for and with specific groups such as Aboriginal families in the Families in Motion program in the Fraser Valley of British Columbia (Bate, 1998), and immigrant women in Book Bridges in Winnipeg (Zakaluk, 1998). Families with diverse backgrounds can benefit from family literacy programs. One adult population that often has low literacy skills is incarcerated individuals.

Prison Programs

One of the most unique locations for a family support program I have ever visited was the Preschool in Prison Project at the Fort Saskatchewan Correctional Centre in Alberta. This program was begun in 1982 by OMEP Canada (see Chapter 4), an early childhood professional organization, to address the needs of a very specific group of families.

Parents who are in prison still want to see their children and families; however, these visits can be very traumatic for children. Prisons are not child or family-friendly places by definition. In addition, young children may be tired and hungry after a lengthy trip to the prison which, combined with the security concerns that often prohibit them from bringing along their favourite toys, can make the experience even more stressful for them. Also, visiting areas have traditionally been designed for security concerns, not children's or families' needs (e.g., there are no changing areas or available water). Once at a prison, families are responsible for constantly monitoring and supervising children while visiting with the incarcerated family member. This creates additional stress on the family and family ties. The dilemma for families then becomes leave the children home or don't come as frequently or at all. This, in turn, further stresses family ties that the visiting programs are intended to sustain.

Many incarcerated parents had difficult childhoods and lacked positive parenting models. The original Preschool in Prison program included not only a children's program during visiting hours, but also a six-week parenting course (Living with Children) for inmates, and an early childhood educator to co-ordinate this program. The children's program provided inmates in the parenting course with opportunities to observe children's play and behaviour as well as the early childhood educator as a model for them.

A current version of this program is described in Focus 11.1 by Joyce Waddell-Townsend, who was largely responsible for the establishment of Children Visiting Prisons in Kingston, Ontario, in 1993.

Recreational Programs

You are probably aware of recreational programs for young children and their families in your community such as Mom and Tot Drop-In, Kindergym, or Baby Swim. Recreation programs for families with young children are sponsored by local government (e.g., parks and recreation departments), the YM/YWCA, and various sports organizations. These programs help support families by providing positive physical activity that can promote fitness, reduce stress, and provide opportunities for family activities.

One interesting example of a recreation program that may not be available in your community is a children's museum. Children's museums are fun programs that provide a recreational and educational experience for both children and their families. Over the past 60 years, "support for children's museums has flourished around the world" (Cohen, 1989, p. 21), including Canada. Children's museums are community-based, and "the grassroots way in which most participatory and children's museums are launched underscores their essential reason for being—to serve children and families" (Cleaver, 1992, p. 10).

The basic philosophy of children's museums is congruent with that of most early childhood programs. Children's museum exhibits are designed to be interactive and hands-on. They are applications of the concept of learning through

Children Visiting Prisons

by Joyce Waddell-Townsend, Kingston, Ontario

Suppose you were taking your three-year-old child to visit his/her father after a separation of some weeks and the visit was going to take place in a very public area where you would be watched constantly over a three- to six-hour period. Suppose also that there would be hardly any toys, or crayons, or books available to amuse your child and you were not allowed to bring any with you. How long do you think your pleasant reunion would remain pleasant before your child started running around, whining for coins for the vending machine, bugging other adults, and generally making you look like a bad parent? Does this sound like a positive experience for you, your husband, or child? Have you guessed that we might be describing a prison visiting room?

The focus of Children Visiting Prisons, Kingston (an associate member of OMEP Canada) is to improve this situation as much as possible. The goal is to enhance the visiting experience for children and their families by encouraging the provision of suitable toys, books, and writing materials in prison visiting rooms, by consulting about how to store and display toys (on shelves rather than in toy boxes), by providing a volunteer to tidy and cleans toys on a regular basis, and by offering craft and story times as volunteers are available.

Most parents are very grateful for this support. Most guards are too, but some, like the one who said, "I don't know why children should have fun in prison. I don't even know why they should visit in prison at all," still need to be convinced of the value of play materials that encourage healthy family interactions.

After all, fathers and mothers are very important to their children, and play is the child's most basic means of communication. Through play children can relax and enjoy their time "behind bars" as they build ties with their parents, for the present and for the future. They are also helping to build a foundation for a more solid family life when the inmate returns to society.

But the needs of children should be addressed for their own sake too. The children have not committed any crimes, but those who have a parent in prison suffer the loss of that parent at a critical time in their lives. Some of the problems that may develop include feeling unwanted and unloved, feeling guilty for the parent's incarceration, becoming withdrawn and isolated, or becoming aggressive and acting out. These children may have school performance problems; they may be rejected by relatives, peers, or society in general. In fact, research cited in *Putting Families First* (Kagan & Weissbourd, 1994) indicates that children of prisoners are five to six times more likely to become incarcerated than their peers. They are a population at risk who deserve more of society's support.

play and interacting with one's environment. As Cleaver (1992) points out, the first children's museums in North America began during the time when Dewey's and Montessori's theories were popular (see Chapters 5 and 6). (The first children's museum in North America, the Brooklyn Children's Museum, opened in 1899.) Children's museums then expanded rapidly during the 1960s, when Piagetian theory was becoming predominant. They are popular with people of all ages because of their hands-on, please-touch, get-involved approach. How many times have you been in a traditional museum and really wanted to touch an exhibit marked Do Not Touch, or were frustrated because you couldn't get a closer view of an object in a glass case?

The interactive nature of children's museums also encourages children's attention. They'll spend 5 to 10 *minutes* at one exhibit, compared to the 10 to 30 *seconds* adults typically spend at a traditional museum exhibit if they are interested in it (Cleaver, 1992).

There are several models of children's museums in Canada:

- *Separate museum for children*—For example, Manitoba Children's Museum in Winnipeg (see Focus 11.2)

- *Museum in a museum*—For example, at the Canadian Museum of Civilization in Hull, Quebec

- *Children's room/Discovery room*—For example, at the Royal Ontario Museum in Toronto

- *Wing of another museum*—For example, at the Vancouver Maritime Museum, and

- *Interactive discovery type of exhibits designed especially for children as part of the regular museum displays*—For example, at the Saskatchewan Science Centre in Regina.

According to Susan Riddell, communications officer at the Manitoba Children's Museum, the biggest issues for children's museums today are:

- Providing safe, secure environments in which children can explore

- Keeping exhibits interesting and up to date, and

- Funding (personal communication, April 2000).

One of the most unique recreational programs for young children and their families is Legoland. I recently visited the original Legoland, established in 1968 in Billund, Denmark. It is a family-friendly place designed for family members of all ages. As the name implies, this amusement park is based on Lego. Most of the exhibits are made from plastic Lego blocks—sometimes more than one million blocks per model. The models are all to scale, and include well-known structures with moving parts from many countries (Copenhagen airport, Amsterdam canals, Scandinavian villages, Mount Rushmore, the Acropolis, Abu Simbel,

Copenhagen harbour, the Statue of Liberty, Brussels Town Hall, and castles on the Rhine River) as well as jungle animals, a space shuttle, and amusement rides.

Focus 11.2

The Manitoba Children's Museum

The Manitoba Children's Museum opened in 1986 and in its first year had more than 65,000 visitors. The museum expanded space and then in 1994 moved to its present location in the Forks in the oldest (1899) surviving train repair facility in Manitoba. The stated mandate of the museum was

> to enhance the cultural, educational, social, recreational and economic resources in the community, to provide a "hands-on" museum designed for children between the ages of 2 to 13 years, to teach children more about themselves and the world around them within an interactive learning environment and to foster a better understanding of our cultures: past, present and future. [on-line, www.childrensmuseum.com]

The original three galleries were The Grain Elevator and Train (my favourite), The Making Sense Gallery, and The Big Top. These have now been expanded to the following six galleries:

1. *All Aboard Gallery*—A 1952 diesel train engine and 1910 coach

2. *Tree and Me Gallery*—Including a popular 17-foot oak tree that can be climbed, and an underwater beaver dam

3. *Our TV Gallery*—A state-of-the-art television studio where children can produce shows as well as record their comments for possible replay on a local television station

4. *Live Wire Gallery*—Advanced technology

5. *Winnipeg Jets Goals for Kids Gallery*—Including a reproduction of the Jets locker room

6. *WonderWorks*—The infrastructure gallery where children can design cities, and build roads, bridges, and other infrastructure.

The museum exhibits are hands-on. For example, children can climb on the train and go into the beaver dam.

I asked Susan Riddell, the museum's communications officer, where they get their ideas for exhibits. She replied that they use a variety of sources such as lists of available travelling exhibits, professional publications, their own ideas, regular updating of current exhibits, such as the computing exhibits, as well as serendipitous sources (e.g., they were given a fairy-tale gallery when the local Eaton's department store closed, and this is now used for literacy activities and exhibits).

The Manitoba Children's Museum is well used and was visited by 1.3 million people from 1994 to 1999. It is open daily, with longer hours in the summer. In addition, the museum offers special drop-in activities on weekends, holidays, and school breaks, including Imagination Station. The museum has School Break and Summer Day Camps for children over age six. Special programs for younger children are offered on Preschool Mondays (e.g., spring, dinosaurs, music, using your hands, and circus). Special workshops are offered for school-age children (e.g., ventriloquism, birdhouse building, and hot air balloons). Recent special events have included a celebrity storytelling series, a haunted museum, night-light club (children wear their pajamas and bring a pillow for bedtime stories with juice and cookies), ice cream for breakfast, and earth day. In addition, the museum offers birthday and other party activities for families on a rental basis. This provision of a variety of activities and services is a current trend in children's museums in Canada and other countries.

The museum is a not-for-profit organization with a volunteer board of directors.

Sources: Susan Riddell, communications officer at the Manitoba Children's Museum, interview April 2000; The Manitoba Children's Museum [on-line, www.childrensmuseum.com]

Margie I. Mayfield

One of several towns made of Lego bricks and Legoland in Denmark.

Play is discussed in Chapter 7.

There is also a western town called Legoredo, a traffic school with electric cars and traffic wardens, a pirate ship, a castle, a safari ride (with Lego animals), a gold mine, a circus, and an observation tower. There are large play areas with thousands of Duplo and Lego blocks of various types for children (and adults) to use to build their own models, as well as a computer design centre for older children (also used by the adults with the children!). The park reflects the stated Lego philosophy that "children should be able to use play to develop and to learn about the wide world as they go through the various stages of growing up" (Legoland A/S, 1997, n.p.).

Legoland attracts a wide variety of visitors, especially families. When I was there I noticed many three-generation families as well as combinations of single parent and child, groups of children with teachers, and grandparents with grandchildren. I talked with three Asian businessmen who had detoured from Copenhagen to see Legoland so they could tell their children and grandchildren about the park. Legoland has expanded to now include parks in England and the United States.

Intergenerational Programs

Because family support programs include parents and children they are, by definition, **intergenerational**. Examples of parent–child family support programs have already been described in this chapter. Therefore, this section describes programs that are intergenerational between young children and seniors. Chapter 3 discusses the "greying" of Canadian society, in which more people will live longer and older adults will make up a growing percentage of the population. They will become an even more highly visible part of local communities and therefore more likely to be part of family support programs. Intergenerational programs can provide, in many ways, "the extended family and neighbourhood support systems that were the social norm in most American and Canadian communities before the Second World War" (Shipman, 1999, p. 22).

Intergenerational programs should be reciprocal and mutually beneficial and supportive for both young children and adults. The potential benefits for young children are that children can:

- Develop an accurate view of seniors (not the common view by many children that seniors are sick, infirm, physically unattractive, and smell funny) and intergenerational programs can counteract age stereotyping and bias

- Learn about aging over the human life span

- Develop an understanding of and respect for older adults

- See themselves and seniors as participants in the local community

- Learn from the knowledge and expertise of older adults

- Nurture another age group.

In addition, a caring senior is another source of nurturing and a listener for a child.

The potential benefits of intergenerational programs for seniors include:

- Opportunity to share information and culture with a younger generation

- Involvement in a nurturing, meaningful community activity

- Becoming more knowledgeable about young children today, their experiences, interests, and challenges

- Reduction of social isolation for some older adults

- Satisfaction of being a nurturer, mentor, and friend for a young child.

In addition, the participation of multiple generations in programs provides a more accurate reflection of today's society as well as helping to create a family atmosphere in programs. Shipman (1999) posed the interesting question about what could be the possible effects on programs if just five percent of today's three million seniors would volunteer in a program for young children.

Seniors can be involved in programs in a variety of ways. The two most frequent ways are (a) seniors as volunteers (and, less frequently, as paid staff) and (b) young children and seniors regularly visiting or communicating with each other. Seniors and young children sharing a facility such as a day-care centre in a seniors' residence or with an adult day-care program is an excellent opportunity for intergenerational activities. Examples of a day-care facility within a seniors' residence are the Seven Oaks Child Day Care Centre in Winnipeg and the Sherbrooke Community Centre in Saskatoon (Schmidt & Roe, 1999).

An example of children visiting seniors is the Baycrest Centre for Geriatric Care in Toronto, which has had a long relationship with the Esther Exton Childcare Centre operated by George Brown College (Swartz, 1999). British

Columbia's South Delta Family Child Care Association has an ongoing program with the community Kinsmen Extended Care Program (Jamieson, 1999). Once a month the children visit the seniors for up to an hour and a half. The children come with games, puzzles, books, and activities to do with the seniors. A popular joint activity is dress-up. The visits conclude with a snack and a singalong. One program that I observed, at Bethany Care Centre in Calgary, had a daily exercise time for the children in the on-site day care centre and seniors together that emphasized flexibility as a major fitness goal for both groups.

An example of ongoing child–senior communication is happening in an elementary school in my community. The seniors are e-mail pen pals for school-age children. This is an excellent way for seniors who are not able to physically come to school, or who do not wish to, to participate in an intergenerational school-based program.

Seniors are frequently volunteers, and sometimes paid staff, in early childhood programs. Many Aboriginal programs include older members of the community as one way to continue and promote culture, traditions, and language. Over the years, I have been fortunate to observe many excellent Aboriginal volunteers working with parents and young children in family support programs in Canada and Hawaii. I have been especially impressed with their storytelling and the responses of both children and parents to these seniors.

As with any volunteer program, attention to the preliminary steps such as recruitment, screening potential volunteers, providing orientation, as well as supervision is as essential as it is for other staff members. Not every adult, senior or non-senior, is suited or suitable to work with young children and families. And just because a volunteer is not paid does not mean that screening, interviewing, and in-service are unnecessary.

Likewise, young children need to be oriented to being with seniors. Some ideas include discussion of what the children already know about the elderly, sharing intergenerational literature with children (see Resources at the end of this chapter), and responding to their questions about seniors (e.g., Why do they have wrinkles?) and items such as wheelchairs and hearing aids.

There are organizations in British Columbia, New Brunswick, Nova Scotia, Ontario, and other provinces that arrange surrogate grandparents for young families. One of the oldest of these is the Volunteer Grandparents Society of British Columbia. However, in some other families, it is the grandparents who are raising their grandchildren in place of the parents due to death, drugs, divorce, desertion, imprisonment, and other reasons (Smith, Dannison, & Vach-Hasse, 1998).

FOR REFLECTION

If you were the director of a family support program or a day-care centre and you wanted to include seniors in your program, what would you include in the orientation for these volunteers?

Home Visiting Programs

Home visiting programs are community-based programs supporting families and young children, especially those with disabilities. They are found in North America and most European countries, and have been in some countries for many years (Roberts, Wasik, Casto, & Ramey, 1991).

The history of home-visiting programs in Canada stretches back to the nineteenth century, with efforts to assist families in the urban slums during the early days of urbanization and industrialization. These home visitors were frequently volunteers from religious or charitable organizations who provided "a mixture of support, scrutiny, and advice" (Halpern, 1988, p. 285).

You are probably familiar with home visiting by public health nurses. However, family support and early childhood programs, especially those for children with special needs and their families, also often include home visits. A contemporary example of this is the infant development or home-based early intervention programs found in communities across Canada. These programs provide therapy for children with disabilities and education and support for their families. Some of these programs are almost solely home-based, others combine home-based and centre-based locations.

A growing home-visiting type of program in Canada and elsewhere is the Healthy Start–type program (usually modelled on Hawaii's Healthy Start program). These programs promote the healthy growth and development of children, usually from birth, and their parents. They "focus on improving parenting skills to promote healthy child development. In addition, most seek to prevent child abuse and neglect" (Gomby, Culross, & Behrman, 1999, p. 7). One Canadian example is Babies Best Start in Scarborough, Ontario. This preventive program recruits, trains, and supervises parents from the community who do home visits to families of similar cultural and linguistic background. Parents are also encouraged to attend a local Nobody's Perfect program led by a home visitor, the Parent–Child Mother Goose Program, and other programs offered in the community (personal communication, Babies Best Start staff, June 2000).

Aboriginal Programs

Programs developed for Aboriginal children and families typically have very strong roots in the community and are also developed to meet local community needs in the context of Aboriginal culture, values, and traditions. Aboriginal communities are diverse; for example, solely in terms of location, they range from reserves to cities to isolated and northern communities. In addition, there can be great variation among reserves even within the same province. In 1996, there were more than 272,000 Aboriginal children (i.e., First Nations, non-status, Metis, and Inuit peoples) nine years of age and younger in Canada (Childcare Resource and Research Unit, 2000 [on-line]).

A federal report on the health of Canadians reported that although there have been "impressive improvements in education levels and equally impressive reductions in infant mortality rates and substance abuse," Aboriginal people are still at higher risk for health problems related to poverty, poor housing, and unemployment than the general Canadian population (Health Canada, 1999, [on-line]).

Over the past 30 years, various federal task forces and Royal Commissions have identified the need for more programs for young children and families in

Aboriginal communities. For example, "the RCAP [Royal Commission on Aboriginal Peoples] child care report recommended the establishment of a Canada-wide aboriginal child care system, controlled by aboriginal peoples and funded on a long-term basis" (Colbert, 1999, p. 360). One of the ways some of these problems are being addressed is through early childhood and family support programs.

One recent significant initiative has been Aboriginal Head Start. This program, modelled on Head Start in the United States (see Chapter 5), was begun in 1995 out of Health Canada. It was originally developed for urban and northern communities but expanded its mandate to include reserves in 1998.

Aboriginal Head Start has a dual focus on developing both young children to age six and their families and promoting local participation, development, and control. All Aboriginal Head Start programs must have six components: Aboriginal culture and language, health, education, nutrition, social support programs, and family involvement. However, each program is developed to meet the needs and culture of the local community. For example, the Aboriginal Head Start program at the Waabinong Centre in Sault Ste. Marie has Ojibwe lessons for children and parents and a visiting elders program (Dunning, 2000). The Tungasuvvingat (i.e., Welcoming Place) Head Start program in Ottawa uses the Inuktitut language in activities throughout the day (Reynolds, 1998). The Inuktitut syllabics are used for the children's names and labelling objects and in games, on the calendar, and hung on the wall. Traditional Inuit materials such as *ulus* (i.e., knives), seeds, and clothing are included in various learning centres. Inuit music, games, and books are also included.

Aboriginal Head Start programs are locally controlled and designed. According to the program's guidelines, the development of Aboriginal Head Start programs "must meet child, family, and community needs. Aboriginal Head Start projects therefore need to establish relationships with related community programs while recognizing that communities can also shape their projects to meet families' social and economic goals" (National Aboriginal Head Start Committee, 1996, p. 6).

Aboriginal communities are concerned about providing professional education for those working in local programs for families and children. The need for culturally appropriate and community-based post-secondary training programs for delivery in often-isolated areas has resulted in the development of Aboriginal professional education programs in a variety of fields. One example is the professional education program developed in partnership by the Meadow Lake Tribal Council and nine communities in northern Saskatchewan with the School of Child and Youth Care at the University of Victoria. The resulting generative curriculum, based on co-constructed principles, was appropriate for the communities' contexts and met legislated licensing and accreditation requirements (Dahlberg, Moss, & Pence, 1999). The curriculum included weekly opportunities for elders to speak to the class on a variety of topics (often in Cree or Dene). This curriculum model has also been used by other Aboriginal communities.

The Union of Ontario Indians initiated an early childhood educator diploma program, the Binoojiinyag Kinoomaadwin Native Early Childhood Education Program, in development with Cambrian College in Sudbury (Anishinabek Early Childhood Education Program, 1994). In addition to the typical early childhood courses, this program included understanding and appreciating the Aboriginal family, community, language, and culture, as well as Aboriginal curriculum content and links with community resources. In Atlantic Canada, the MicMac Maliseet Child Care Council's Native Early Childhood Training Program was developed in close consultation with First Nations communities. The two-year program included courses in communication, growth and development, educational methods, curriculum, health, safety, and nutrition, and a practicum each year (Ryerse, 1995). These are all examples of the local or regional development of professional education programs to meet the needs of professionals working with Aboriginal children and families.

Information and Resource Services

Another type of family support program is the **information and resource service** or **agency** (also called *information and referral, resource and referral, information and counselling,* or *advisory service*). Families need up-to-date information and other resources in order to make choices and decisions affecting their children and themselves. An information and resource service disseminates information via print, telephone, media, personal interviews, workshops, seminars, displays, and other means. It is usually community-based and provides information about services and programs related to families and young children available in that community. A major topic is helping families find out about, locate, and select programs for their young children and themselves. Frequently asked questions include how to find good day care, what to look for, the types and availability of child care options in the community, and how to access subsidized fees or spaces. Because of possible liability issues, it is typical for information and resource services to match a family's wishes and needs to some early childhood programs with existing openings but to leave the final selection to the family.

A strength of these services is that they can add information to their databases as the need for that information is identified. Some information and resource services that began by providing information only on child care have gradually broadened their resources to include a wide range of programs and services in the community that are useful to families with young children. For example, some information and resource services have added recruitment of family day home providers to their mandate as well as workshops and courses. Another example is a telephone help line (also called warm lines, to distinguish them from crisis hotlines). These can provide families with information, assistance, or referrals to more appropriate resources.

One challenge faced by information and resource services is keeping their databases up to date and well organized. Most of the services are computerized, which greatly increases their capacity but also increases the cost (e.g., hardware, specially designed software, and staff training).

Roles of Professionals in Family Support Programs

How are the roles of professionals in early childhood programs such as a centre-based program for three- and four-year-old children different from those in a family support program such as a family resource centre?

The roles of professionals in family support programs are similar to those in day care, nursery school, or kindergarten programs. For example, the nurturing role is shared by professionals in all these programs; however, in a family support program, the nurturer role is extended more towards all members of a family than in a day care or kindergarten program where the nurturance is directed most of the time at the young child.

In a day-care program with several staff, the director or lead educator is responsible for organizing and coordinating the staff. In a family support program, the role of coordinator may also include coordination with other professionals and agencies in the community to a greater extent than in a day-care centre. In addition, the coordinator is more likely to make, and therefore follow up on, referrals to other programs or agencies.

In both centre-based early childhood programs and family support programs the professionals are advocates for children and families, facilitators, guides, instructors (e.g. parent education), colleagues, observers, evaluators, program organizers, and other roles as discussed in Chapter 4. The following description of the characteristics of effective family support workers by Stott and Musick (1994) could apply equally well to many professionals working with children and families, whether in a day-care centre, kindergarten, or family support program:

> Commitment to dialogue with participants and the ability to establish relationships with children and families; a capacity for empathy and warmth; concern, compassion, sensitivity, and respect for the varied values and ways of diverse families and cultures; and flexibility and receptivity.(p. 191)

The old conception of family support professionals as good-willed experts dispensing knowledge and advice has evolved into a collaborative approach that perceives families and professionals as partners in a reciprocal relationship. This approach recognizes and builds on the strengths of the families and the professionals. Also, part of being a collaborator rather than the all-knowing expert is to know when and how to call upon other professionals or resources in the community.

This collaborative approach, wherein both families and professionals relate reciprocally, is often referred to as **empowerment**. The empowering of families in family support programs and special education programs has resulted in a significant shift in the role of the professionals working in these programs. This shift to a more collaborative and facilitative approach is characteristic of community-based programs and the ecological theory that emphasizes the relationships among individuals, groups, and organizations within a community.

Just as family support programs are flexible and diverse, so too are the staffing arrangements and the backgrounds and professional education of the people working in these programs (Kellerman & MacAulay, 1998). For example, a common staffing pattern for a family resource centre is to have one staff person with an early childhood education and care background and another with a counselling or social work background. Other common background areas are nursing, education, psychology, human services, family studies, or women's studies.

There is no agreed-upon standard for professional education for family support program staff. One of the few post-secondary programs for family support professionals in Canada is the Family Supports Certificate with specializations in Family Life Education or Family Resources Programs at Ryerson Polytechnic University in Toronto (available on campus and through distance education).

Issues for Family Support Programs

Family support programs have been increasing in number across North America in the past 20 years and are likely to continue to do so. They not only can fill a gap in programs and services available in communities but also can serve to link existing programs. Because of their multidisciplinary nature, they are not seen as solely early childhood or health or social service programs, but typically as combinations. In addition, their often-grassroots development has permitted and encouraged diversity across family support programs. This has, in turn, led to some confusion by policy-makers, funding agencies, and the general public as to what *is* a family support program. This issue is discussed in the following section along with issues related to needs assessment and evaluation of family support programs.

Typically, family support programs do more formal evaluation than centre-based early childhood programs (e.g., day care, kindergarten, or nursery school). This is due, in great part, to the requirements of funding agencies for documentation and evaluation. It is usual for funding sources to require this documentation and evaluation in order to verify that (a) there is a need for a specific family support program, and (b) the program has been effective. The end purpose of evaluation is to improve a program. Evaluation and its results can and should be applicable and practical.

Defining Quality Family Support Programs

Because formal family support programs are relatively recent and are so diverse, it is difficult to develop a short definition that is both accurate and inclusive. This is especially a problem when trying to explain family support programs to groups such as policy-makers, politicians, funding agencies, and sometimes other professionals and families. The term **family support program** can be applied to many programs.

A second part of this issue is the question of what is meant by a *quality* family support program. An answer to this question is important in the development and evaluation of these programs. There has been much more discussion about quality in centre-based and home-based early childhood programs than for family support programs. Family support programs are not the same, so the same standards for quality are not applicable to all. However, a few standards do apply, such as the importance of appropriately well-educated, committed staff, and some of the roles are similar.

Because of the diversity of family support programs and their relatively short history, a suggestion is to begin with a description of the characteristics of effective/successful family support programs. The following list of characteristics is based on my research and observations of scores of family support programs. Effective family support programs and their staffs:

- Have knowledge of local families and community

- Have respect for and responsiveness to families and community

- Build on family strengths

- Systematically identify needs and concerns

- Collaborate with families and coordinate with other community programs and services

- Are user-friendly

- Have adequate funding (initial and ongoing)

- Are in an accessible and acceptable location

- Have effective publicity and recruitment programs

- Include a variety of activities and strategies

- Undertake program monitoring and evaluation, including regular feedback from families.

(Mayfield, 1993a, 1995)

Assessing Family and Community Needs

For a community-based program to be successful it must meet community needs and do so on a continuing basis. In order to respond effectively to local needs, the developers of family support programs need to know what these needs are. As discussed previously, the role of "all-knowing expert" is not appropriate for family support programs today. It is inappropriate and presumptuous for professionals to decide what local families or communities should have without systematically assessing what is needed and wanted. This is usually done by a needs assessment.

The purpose of a **needs assessment** is to systematically investigate what are the needs and determine the extent to which they are or are not being met in the community and what people in the community want and would use (Mayfield, 1993a). Useful sources of information can include demographic information about the community and its inhabitants, identification of what programs and services currently exist in the community, other professionals in the community, and potential participants in a program.

A needs assessment is usually done as part of the planning or initial stages of a program. According to Epstein, Larner, and Halpern (1995), "well-designed programs engage in a needs assessment of their population, using existing research where available and supplementing it with their own local investigation when feasible" (p. 15). For example, in one community, professionals became concerned about the social isolation of single teen mothers and their infants. They were aware of the research about the negative effects such social isolation can have on teen mothers and their children. A needs assessment determined that there were very few options in the community for these teen parents. Another needs assessment of the teen mothers found that the teens would use a drop-in centre if it were designed for teens and was readily accessible by public transportation. A needs assessment need not be limited to parents and children. A family resource centre in Vancouver broadened its programs when the staff identified and then investigated the needs of recent immigrant in-home caregivers with limited English proficiency.

A needs assessment can use a variety of methods to gather information. Many needs assessments use more than one method. These methods can include questionnaires, telephone interviews, focus groups, public meetings, discussions with other professionals in the community, and a survey of existing community programs and services. In preparing questions for an interview or a written questionnaire, the language and literacy backgrounds of potential respondents need to be considered. A pilot, where the questions are tried out, is a good idea to determine if the questions are really clear and will get the type of information needed.

A common pattern in the development of family support programs is that they begin small in response to an identified need for which existing community options are lacking. They then expand as other needs become apparent. This is why two family support programs in two neighbouring communities may offer quite different programs. The types of programs offered depend on the identified needs. However, assessing needs does not stop there. It is an ongoing process throughout the life of the family support program.

Program Evaluation

Program evaluation is part of the ongoing cycle of program development, evaluation, review, determination of changes for improvement, implementation of those changes—and the cycle continues.

An essential source of evaluative information is the participants in the family support program. Families are especially important sources of information.

How families use and perceive a family support program is a critical part of the monitoring and evaluation process. There should be regular opportunities for family input, feedback, and suggestions for how a program can be improved. Families can also help in determining goals and future directions. Also, families who feel they have a voice and can participate in the evaluation and improvement of the family support program are more likely to continue to participate, be more supportive of the program and staff, and be advocates for the program in the community. In addition, the results of an evaluation can provide a baseline for future comparisons (e.g., the number of families using which programs, how satisfied they say they are with these, and how this changes over time).

Another source of information for needs assessments is other professionals and programs in the community. Initially, information from these groups can help identify gaps in community programs and services as well as help determine what is needed. Later on, they can provide feedback as to how well the family support program is meeting those needs and how it could be improved.

Program evaluation must be ongoing. An initial needs assessment, no matter how accurate and well-done, is not sufficient for a total program evaluation. Although initial evaluation (e.g., needs assessment) can help to determine if a program is needed and feasible and what it should be like, program evaluation continues as part of program documentation and accountability. Whereas all early childhood programs are accountable, in some sense, to their participants, sponsors, licensing agencies, or other bodies, family support programs are often required to do evaluations and provide the results to their funding sources as part of the terms of their funding grants. Anecdotal information or testimonials, by themselves, are usually no longer considered sufficient. The information from program evaluation is not only useful for improving the program and meeting the terms of the funding grant, but also in subsequent grant applications to demonstrate the effectiveness of the program, the satisfaction of the participants with the program, and its ability to meet identified family and community needs.

Program evaluation is often divided into three types or stages: *initial* (discussed above), *formative*, and *summative*. Formative evaluation, as the name implies, is done as the program is ongoing. Its primary purpose is to provide feedback to determine if the program is "on track" or whether some fine-tuning needs to be done. It is an in-progress evaluation. For example, some underlying questions are: How is the program doing so far? Is it meeting identified needs and how well? How satisfied are the participants (both families and professionals)? And most importantly, how can the family support program be improved? Possible methods for gathering information for formative evaluation are varied and include written questionnaires, tallies of participation, anecdotal comments, structured focus groups, telephone logs, observation journals, individual interviews, and community meetings.

Summative evaluation has a different overall purpose than formative evaluation; it is more of a conclusive statement. Its major purpose is to answer the question, How well did the program do? This is a question that funding agencies and researchers like to have answered. Many family support programs see formative evaluation as more immediately useful. However, summative evaluation can give a program additional credibility and enhance future funding or expansion efforts.

Program evaluation can sometimes seem to be just one more demand on an already busy program, stretched staff, and limited budget. In addition, the scope, methods, and procedures of program evaluation can seem daunting. Numerous publications that can assist with program evaluation are available, including some with clear step-by-step procedures (see some suggestions in Resources at the end of this chapter).

Useful though program evaluation can be for family support programs and other groups, there is a moral or ethical issue about to what extent, if any, the establishment or continuation of a family support program "should depend not only upon evaluation results, but upon a belief in society's commitment to supporting and strengthening families" (Weissbourd, 1991, p. 82). However, a reality in the past few years in Canada and many other countries has been that too many good and effective programs are pursuing a limited amount of funding, so the results of program evaluations as an "objective" measure have become more prominent in decision-making about the future of individual family support programs.

Summary of this Chapter

Family support is not a new concept. It has existed since the days of community quilting bees, church gatherings, and community events such as barn raisings (Kagan, Powell, Weissbourd, & Zigler, 1987). Informal family support still exists today and is used by most families at various times. Many families, at some time or another, need or want more support than their informal networks of family and friends can provide. For more formal support and assistance, family support programs in the local community can meet this need. This is the primary role and strength of family support programs. This is also why such programs have been increasing in number. They are now found in communities in all parts of Canada and are likely to continue to be so in the foreseeable future.

The key themes in this chapter are:

* The need for some support by all families at some time

* The community-based, grassroots development of family support programs

* The difficulty in defining family support programs

* The building on family strengths from an ecological, not a deficit, perspective

* The variety and diversity of family support programs even within one type

* The role of the professional as collaborator, coordinator, and facilitator rather than all-knowing expert

* The characteristics of family support programs

* The need for and uses of initial, formative, and summative program evaluation.

Key Terms

community-based support, 434
ecological theory, 436
empowerment, 458
family literacy program, 444
family resource centre, 438
family support program, 460
family systems theory, 436
home visiting program, 454

information and resource service, 457
intergenerational support, 452
needs assessment, 461
parent support program, 444
program evaluation, 461
toy libraries, 440

Resources

Also see Resources in Chapter 3 for details about materials and organizations concerned with families, such as the Vanier Institute of the Family.

For Sharing with Children

Some books about families, from an intergenerational perspective, to share with young children are:

Bunting, E., illustrated by Donald Carrick. 1989. *The Wednesday surprise.* New York: Clarion. A young girl teaches her grandmother to read—one of my favourites.

Crews, D. 1991. *Bigmama's.* New York: Trumpet. The author's reminiscences about visiting his grandmother during the summers.

Dorros, A., illustrated by Elisa Kleven. *Abuela.* A young Latina girl's adventures with her grandmother (i.e., *abuela*).

Flournoy, V., illustrated by Jerry Pinkey. 1985. *The patchwork quilt.* New York: Dial Books for Young Readers. Grandmother lives with Tonya and her family.

Gilman, P. 1992. *Something from nothing.* New York: Scholastic. A classic folk tale about how his grandfather preserves Joseph's beloved blanket by making it into ever-smaller items as it wears out. Illustrations show a parallel story about a mouse family.

Zolotow, C. 1972. *William's doll.* New York: HarperCollins. Grandmother supports William's wish to have a doll. A modern classic.

Ainslie, J. & Meyer, M., illustrated by L. Cheng. 1992. *Daddy is in jail; Why are there jails?; Daddy is home from jail.* Originally published by the John Howard Society of Alberta; out of print and may be photocopied. Recommended by Joyce Waddell-Townsend.

For Further Reading

An excellent source for publications and information on family support programs is the Canadian Association of Family Resource Programs (FRP Canada)

707-331 Cooper Street
Ottawa, ON K2P 0G5
Telephone: 613-237-7667
Fax: 613-237-8515
E-mail: info@frp.ca
Web Site: www.frp.ca (includes information on provincial organizations)

Some of their recent publications are:

Chen, P. & MacAulay, J. 1999. *Improving facilities: Innovative approaches for community programs.* Ottawa: Canadian Association of Family Resource Programs. A practical guide to establishing community-based programs.

Ellis, D. 1998. *Finding our way: A participatory evaluation method for family resource programs.* Ottawa: Canadian Association of Family Resource Programs. Useful, step-by-step guide.

Kyle, I. & Kellerman, M. 1998. *Case studies of Canadian family resource programs: Supporting families, children and communities.* Ottawa: Canadian Association of Family Resource Programs. Information on family resource programs and 15 case studies.

Canadian Association of Toy Libraries and Parent Resource Centres—TLRC Canada. 1990. *Caring about families: The "how to" manual for developing Canadian family resource programs.* Ottawa: Canadian Association of Family Resource Programs. An excellent comprehensive resource. There are also publications on toy libraries, play, and working with families. In addition, this organization has a database of family resource programs in Canada, a newsletter with supplements, an informative Web site, an information and referral service, and sponsors workshops and an annual conference.

Other useful publications include:

Dorion-Coupal, K. 1996. *A toy library for you/Une ludothèque pour toi.* Montreal: CIDE-OMEP. A three-volume set on establishing toy libraries in general and in a project in Latin America.

Epstein, A.S., Larner, M. & Halpern, R. 1995. *A guide to developing community-based family support programs.* Ypsilanti, MI: High/Scope Press. A general resource on establishing family support programs.

For a more detailed technical resource on needs assessments, try B.R. Witkin. 1984. *Assessing needs in educational and social programs.* San Francisco: Jossey-Bass.

Thomas, A. (Ed.) 1998. *Family literacy in Canada: Profiles of effective practice.* Welland, ON: éditions Soleil publishing. Excellent source of information about a variety of family support programs across Canada with a family literacy focus.

Children visiting prisons: A good practice guide. Available from Scottish Forum on Prisons and Families, c/o Save the Children Scotland, Haymarket House, 8 Clifton Terrace, Edinburgh EH12 5DR. Telephone: 0131527-8200; Fax 01310527-8201. (Recommended by Joyce Waddell-Townsend.)

Shimoni, R. & Baxter, J. 1996. *Working with families: Perspectives for early childhood professionals.* Don Mills, ON: Addison-Wesley Publishers. General reference on working with families; suitable for a variety of programs.

Washington, V., Johnson, V., & McCracken, J.B. 1995. *Grassroots success! Preparing schools and families for each other.* Washington, D.C.: National Association for the Education of Young Children. Useful information on establishing programs for families, including transition into kindergarten. Examples from 20 programs funded by WK Kellogg Foundation.

 ## Organizations and Useful Web Sites

Intergenerational sources:

United Generations Ontario
1185 Eglinton Ave. E., 6th floor
Toronto, ON M3C 3C8
Telephone: 416-426-7115
Fax: 416-426-7388
E-mail: lynda@intergenugo.org
Web Site: www.integenugo.org

Parent Education/Support:

Nobody's Perfect
Nobody's Perfect Canada National Office
c/o Canadian Association of Family Resource programs
707-331 Cooper Street
Ottawa, ON K2P 0G5
Telephone: 613-237-7667, ext. 222
Fax: 613-237-8515
E-mail: np-yapp@frp.ca or macaulay@frp.ca
Web Site: www.frp.ca/NobodysPerfect.asp (has links to provincial and territorial coordinators).

Dads Can (a non-profit organization promoting healthy fathering)
St. Mary's Hospital
Box 30
21 Grosvenor Street
London, ON N6A 1Y6
Telephone: 1-800-DADS CAN; or 519-646-6095
E-mail: info@dadscan.org
Web Site: www.dadscan.org

Babies Best Start
1641 Pharmacy Avenue
Scarborough, ON M1R 2L2
Telephone: 416-447-2885
Fax: 416-510-1425

The Parent-Child Mother Goose Program
720 Bathurst Street, Suite 402
Toronto, ON M5S 2R4
Telephone: 416-588-5234
Fax: 416-588-1355
E-mail: mgoose@web.net

National Adult Literacy Database (NALD) (national clearing house for family literacy; lots of links to other organizations and programs)
NALD Inc.
Scovil House
703 Brunswick Street
Fredericton, NB E3B 1H8
Telephone: 1-800-720-NALD, 506-457-6900
Fax: 506-457-6910
E-mail: info@nald.ca
Web Site: www.nald.ca

Aboriginal Head Start
Child and Youth Division
Health Promotion and Programs Branch
Finance Building, PL 0202C
Tunney's Pasture
Ottawa, ON K1A 1B5
Telephone: 613-952-9769

Manitoba Children's Museum
109 Pacific Avenue
Winnipeg, MB
Telephone: 204-924-4000 (Info line is 204-956-KIDS)
Web Site: www.childrensmuseum.com

Canadian Children's Museum
Canadian Museum of Civilization
PO Box 3100, Station B
Hull, QC J8X 4H2
Telephone: 819-776-8294
Fax: 819-776-8300
E-mail: lynn.mcmaster@civilization.ca
Web site: www.civilization.ca

The Association of Youth Museums (professional organization for children's museums)
Web site: www.aym.org

A book reference on children's museums in the United Sates and Canada is

Cleaver, J. 1992. *Doing children's museums.* Charlotte, VT: Williamson Publishing. A guide to 265 children's museums, plus information about children's museums in general.

Legoland
DK-7190 Billund
Denmark
Telephone: 0045 75 33 13 33
Fax: 0045 75 35 31 79
Web Site: www.lego.com

12

Quality Early Childhood Programs

Quality Programs Matter—They Matter a Lot!
—Handmade poster seen on a bulletin board at a community college

Central questions in early childhood education and care are, What is a quality early childhood program? and How can we have quality early childhood programs? These pivotal questions have been the focus of innumerable articles, books, conference presentations, workshops, and research studies for the past 25 years or more.

Quality programs is a theme that has run through most of the chapters in this book. The chapters on types of programs each have a section on characteristics of quality for that type of program (e.g., day-care centres, kindergarten, nursery schools, and family support programs). Chapter 5 examines what a good program for young children was considered to be from a historical perspective. Chapter 6 does the same from a theoretical perspective and discusses the perennial question of What model is best? Chapters 4 and 7 examine two of the factors that many people consider essential to examine when looking at quality early childhood programs: the educators in an early childhood program and the role of play. Many of the issues discussed in the preceding chapters are related to quality of early childhood programs, such as auspice, ratios, educators' qualifications, and working conditions.

This chapter first looks at what is meant by *quality,* and discusses the factors generally recognized by the early childhood field as indicative of high-quality early childhood programs. Then, some policy issues related to these topics are examined. This chapter should assist you in pulling together much of what you have learned and thought about as you've read this book.

Here are some questions to think about as you read this chapter:

- What is quality?
- What factors contribute to quality in early childhood programs?
- Who should be responsible for early childhood programs?
- What is the relationship of regulation to quality and the role of provincial/territorial licensing?
- Should all early childhood educators be required to have a certificate?
- Should there be national guidelines or standards for early childhood programs?
- Is accreditation viable and needed?
- How could and should the various types of programs (e.g., centre-based day care, kindergarten, family day homes, nursery schools, family support programs, etc.) be integrated with each other?

What Is Quality?

Quality, as in "quality programs," is used throughout the early childhood education and care literature as a shorthand expression for high-quality programs. It is common sense that good quality programs are preferable to poor quality programs, and that no one would want poor quality programs for young children.

Quality is desirable—most would say essential—in early childhood education and care because

- The early years are important for children's growth and development

- Young children are especially vulnerable

- Early childhood programs have the potential for affecting children positively and negatively

- There are now a significant number of young children in early childhood programs.

In addition, we as professionals are aware that there is a range of quality programs available (i.e., not every program currently in existence is a high-quality one).

Quality early childhood programs are a concern not only for early childhood professionals and families but also for governments and society as a whole. A national survey in 1998 found that 89 percent of the respondents agreed that high-quality early childhood education and care is an important factor for Canada's future social and economic well-being (Child care issues, 1999). While it is relatively easy to get general agreement on the desirability of quality early childhood programs, what constitutes high quality and how to achieve it is not as readily agreed.

FOR REFLECTION

How do you think a parent, educator, licensing officer, principal of an elementary school, student educator, parent of a child with special needs, and a child would define a "quality early childhood program"? What might be common points in their definitions? What might be different?

Defining Quality

The above activity raises the question, Whose definition of quality should be used? There is no one agreed-upon definition. Indeed, some will argue that there never will be or can be one definition. In a sense, each definition of quality is individually based.

What is a quality early childhood program is very difficult to explain. This is understandable. Although the concept of quality seems obvious (as in "I know it when I see it"), quality is deceptively difficult to define. According to Hunter and Pence (1995), it "is a complex concept comprised of children's experiences, the involvement of parents, staff and community, and supported by government funding and policies. It cannot be summarized in a word, a sentence, or even a paragraph" (p. 30).

Perhaps this difficulty in definition and the complexity of the concept are more understandable with the use of an analogy. The following analogy is used to clarify a difficult concept by relating it to a concrete example (i.e., chocolate chip cookies). It is not meant to make light of the concept of quality or to disparage our profession.

Consider the chocolate chip cookie. How would you define a *high-quality* chocolate chip cookie? These cookies are readily available in a variety of forms across Canada. Most people in Canada have probably eaten, or at least seen, one. Will your definition be the same as your friend's? For example, for me, one characteristic of a high-quality chocolate chip cookie is that it is crunchy (like my mother's recipe). Probably 50 percent of you are now thinking "No way. A high-quality chocolate chip cookie should be chewy." This is an example of individual experience influencing a definition of what is quality. The same idea can apply to defining high-quality early childhood programs.

Whose Definition?

Another influence on defining quality is one's individual or personal value base. For example, I may think that the number and quality of the chips in a chocolate chip cookie are the key indicators of quality. Other individuals may place more value on texture, sweetness, size, shape, or general appearance. With early childhood programs, we may agree that the physical environment of a program influences program quality; however, we may not agree on its relative overall importance, especially vis-à-vis other factors. For example, list what you think are the three most important factors in a quality early childhood program. Now look at the list of individuals in the For Reflection box on the previous page. Do you think each of them would have the same three top factors on their list?

The question of whose definition also implies whose definition it is *not*. Not every participant in an early childhood program or every member of society has a voice in discussions and decisions about high-quality early childhood education programs. Going back to defining high-quality chocolate chip cookies: Who should have input on this discussion? Should it be people who regularly eat chocolate chip cookies, those who eat them occasionally, those who hate them, or all of the above? By excluding a particular group, do we limit or narrow the opinion and pool of information about chocolate chip cookies? A similar question can be posed about defining quality early childhood programs. In Canada, a legal definition of an early childhood program (which implies a certain level of quality) has typically been developed by provincial/territorial governments for regulatory purposes. There may or may not have been consultation with and input from various stakeholders in developing this definition. One group that was likely excluded, despite their ready experience and their being the participants in these programs, is young children.

Children are rarely involved in discussions of what is quality early childhood education and care. Yet, as we saw in Chapter 4, when they are asked about what is a good educator they have valid ideas and opinions. In fact, some of these ideas and opinions are the same as those found in early childhood literature and research (e.g., likes and relates well to children); others are quite individual or unique to that age group. For example, I have often heard children comment that good teachers wear pretty beads or coloured shoes or funny ties; I have not seen this mentioned in the research or in licensing regulations. If young children can discuss good educators in a meaningful way, why should we assume they could not also discuss good programs? In some places, children *are* being included in these discussions. For example, Denmark has begun to specifically include input from children into discussions about government policies or regulations that directly affect their lives and well being. A question to consider is at what age and how children can be included in such decision-making. For example, many elementary schools in Canada have included children and children's voices in decision-making that affects them, including children under age nine.

See Chapter 4 for more on children's ideas about what is a good educator.

Contexts in Defining Quality

In addition to being individually based, definitions of quality early childhood programs are also historically, culturally, and values-based. What textbooks and professional journal articles today consider factors in high-quality early childhood programs is not necessarily the same as it was 100 years ago. In Chapter 5, a review of the history and development of early childhood education and care shows changing views over time. For example, in the nineteenth century, "quality was associated with saving children's lives within a context of charity-based social welfare" (Prochner, 1996, p. 5). I doubt if this view of quality is prevalent in Canada today. Just as current recipes for chocolate chip cookies that include ingredients such as carob chips or butterscotch pieces did not exist in the 1930s, when the original chocolate chip recipe was first published in North America, so too have early childhood programs and the search for quality evolved.

The definition of a high-quality chocolate chip cookie can also vary across cultures. Indeed, many people do not have cookies, much less chocolate chip cookies, as part of their culture. Others who do have a cookie-type food may see chocolate chip cookies as some kind of exotic North American version. Likewise, the definition of a quality early childhood program is also culturally influenced. Some of the factors that we in Canada take for granted as being essential for high-quality programs may not be considered to be so in other cultures. Chapter 2 discusses the differences in child-rearing practices across cultures. Differences can also be seen in what educators in other countries or cultures think about quality early childhood programs. For example, some educators in Asia consider our accepted ideas about group size or physical space to be "different." In early childhood programs I have observed in Hong Kong, there is typically considerably less space per child than in Canadian programs. This is considered to be reasonable and appropriate by Hong Kong early educators because space is at a premium in Hong Kong, and homes, shops, restaurants, and streets are all more crowded than in most areas of North America.

If "quality" is so difficult to define, one wonders why we pursue trying to clarify and pin down this concept. However, just as this task has fascinated researchers for decades, it has frustrated the people who most need to determine what it means, such as early childhood educators, licensing officials or inspectors, accreditation teams in elementary schools, program developers, and, of course, families who are selecting early childhood programs. The approach taken by most researchers has been to try to identify specific factors that are part of the larger concept of quality.

Factors in Quality Early Childhood Programs

Some researchers have wondered whether it is really possible to identify key factors in high-quality early childhood programs (e.g., Phillips, 1987). However, research on this topic has become increasingly more sophisticated, more precise, and therefore more informative about specific factors related to high-quality early childhood programs. Some researchers think there is now sufficient research to identify several key factors in quality early childhood programs. The factors that are most consistently identified in research studies as being factors in high-quality early childhood programs are

- Children to educator ratios

- Group size

- Stability of educator–children relationships

- Educator qualifications

- Health and safety

- Physical environment

- Administrative environment.

(e.g., Doherty-Derkowski, 1995; Friendly, 1994)

FOR REFLECTION

You are chatting with someone at a social gathering or on a bus and they discover you are an early childhood educator. This person then asks you, "What should I look for that tells me an early childhood program for my child is a high-quality program?" How would you complete the sentence: You know it's a high quality program if

_____

The factors most often considered indicators of quality in early childhood programs are sometimes divided into three categories:

- Structural factors

- Dynamic factors

- Contextual factors.

(e.g., Doherty-Derkowski, 1995; Phillips & Howes, 1987)

A fourth category sometimes suggested is interactive effects between the early childhood program and the family. Each of these four factors is discussed separately below.

Structural Factors of Quality

Structural factors are concrete and relatively easy to assess objectively and accurately (this is also the reason they are typically components in provincial/territorial licensing regulations). These include health and safety features, ratios, group size, and educator qualifications. In addition, structural factors have been the focus of many research studies; because of this, we know a fair amount about these factors and their effects in specific settings.

Health and Safety Factor

Perhaps the most obvious, and one of the oldest, identified factors in quality early childhood programs is health and safety. For example, the McMillan sisters' Open Air Nursery School in the early twentieth century had a dual focus on health and early education (see Chapter 9), and many of the early Canadian day-care-centre programs were based on a custodial model of keeping children clean, fed, and physically safe while their parents worked.

The health and safety factor is evident in early childhood programs today in the inclusion of nap/rest times, snacks and meals, and curricular topics such as nutrition and personal safety. Health and safety has long been an important part of governmental regulations for early childhood programs (e.g., the requirements for a specific number of fire exits, first aid kits and training, etc.). Centre-based programs are subject to periodic fire and public health inspections.

Children to Educator Ratio

Another factor affecting quality in early childhood programs is the ratio of children to educators. The attention of an adult is valuable in fostering young children's development. If there are too many children for each adult, the children do not get sufficient attention because the children have less access to the adult, less time with the adult, and fewer one-to-one opportunities with the adult. Adult attention can facilitate language development, encourages social interaction and engagement in play, and help reduce aggressive behaviour.

BC Archives/I25293

A good educator to children ratio is an important factor in high quality programs.

Young children are less likely to receive appropriate care and attention the larger the number of children to educator (Howes, Phillips, & Whitebrook, 1992). The adult in this case has less time for each child, and is therefore less responsive and likely more harried and stressed. There is a tendency for the educator to be less individually responsive and to use more group activities and routines (Russell, 1990). There are also safety concerns with an increased number of children per educator. A review of research studies from other countries reported generally similar results (Doherty-Derkowski, 1995).

Not only does the number of children make a difference, but also their ages and unique needs. For example, because family day care typically has a range of ages there is a wider range of developmental needs. The addition of children of different ages can change the dynamics of the family day home. For example, in a study by Howes and Norris (1997) when two school-aged children were added to family day homes, the caregivers had a more difficult time attending to the younger children.

The National Statement on Quality Child Care (1991) of the Canadian Child Care Federation sets *maximum* educator to children ratios at:

- 1 to 3 for under 24 months

- 1 to 6 for 2-year-olds

- 1 to 7 for 3-year-olds

- 1 to 9 for 4- and 5-year-olds

- 1 to 12 for 6- to 9-year-olds.

It is important to keep in mind that these are maximum numbers, not recommended ones. A factor related to the educator to children ratio is the total group size.

Group Size

Group size is the total number of children in a group (e.g., one class). The total number of children in a group can affect the quality of an early childhood program and is typically considered in conjunction with educator:child ratios. For example, there could be a 1:4 ratio in two programs, but if one program has 3 educators and 12 children, there will likely be different dynamics and interaction patterns than the second program with 9 educators and 36 children—even though both have the same 1:4 ratio.

Research by Ruopp, Travers, Glantz, and Coelen (1979) showed that even though two groups had ratios of 1:6 or 1:7, the group of three- to five-year-olds in a maximum size of 12 to 14 children with 2 adults fared more positively socially and behaviourally than one of 24 to 28 children with 4 adults. For preschoolers, class size was a more influential factor in quality than ratio. In addition, research has found that smaller overall group size has had positive effects for infants and toddlers and family day-care programs.

Small groups for young children are more likely to foster cooperation, independence, positive social behaviours, more focused and active involvement, and less crying. Educators in this situation tend to be more responsive (including more language interaction), less restrictive and controlling, and provide for more individualization. (It is important to recognize that not all studies show the same results and some may even show contradictory results. This is one reason why similar studies—or even the same study, called a *replication*—are done repeatedly.)

The National Statement on Quality Child Care (CCCF, 1992) has recommended the following as *maximum* group sizes:

- 0–12 months—maximum of 6 children

- 12–24 months—maximum of 8 children

The Slide Farm/Al Harvey

A small group permits more individual child participation.

- 2-year-olds—maximum of 12 children

- 3-year-olds—maximum of 14 children

- 4- to 6-year-olds—maximum of 18 children

- 6- to 9-year-olds—maximum of 24 children.

The current trend of many school districts of trying to reduce the class size of kindergartens to below 20 is congruent with the above recommendations.

Professional Education and Development

Perhaps the factor related to quality that most people in early childhood education and care as well as the general public will agree with most readily is that professional education can positively affect the quality of early childhood programs. A 1998 national poll reported that 81 percent of those surveyed agreed that the single most important factor in determining quality early childhood programs is the staff (Child care issues, 1999). Professional education includes both pre-service and ongoing, in-service education.

According to the National Statement on Quality Child Care, educators should "have experience and formal post secondary accredited early childhood education and care. Their training minimally includes the study of child development and developmentally appropriate practice for the early years and includes supervised practicum experiences to ensure transfer of knowledge" (Canadian Child Care Federation, 1991, p. 3). Specialization in early childhood education and care is more effective than simply obtaining more years of non-specialized education.

The content of professional education including ethics as well as the need for continuing in-service professional education are discussed in Chapter 4.

It is not surprising to professionals in this field that research shows that programs "employing staff with specific training in early childhood education at a post-secondary level generally provide better quality child care than those that don't" (Friendly, 1994, p. 220). Research has also shown that professional education has positive effects on the quality of family day care (e.g., Kontos, Howes, Shinn, & Galinsky, 1995).

See Chapter 8 for more about the positive effects of professional education on the quality of family day care.

The specialized professional educational levels of early childhood educators in Canada have been increasing. For example, according to figures from the Childcare Resource and Research Unit at the University of Toronto (2000 [online]), the percentage of staff in Canadian day-care centres with one-, two-, or three-year post-diploma training in early childhood care and education (ECCE) increased from 55 percent in 1991 to 71 percent in 1998; staff with an ECCE-related B.A. or higher education increased from 7 percent to 11 percent.

The structural factors discussed in this section, such as ratios, group size, and professional education, are the ones that are most likely to be prescribed in licensing regulations. However, several researchers have questioned whether structural factors are truly valid measures of overall quality (e.g., Elfer & Wedge, 1996; Scarr, Eisenberg, & Deater-Deckard, 1994; Tietze, Cryer, Bairrão, Palacios, & Wetzel, 1996). While recognizing that structural factors may be necessary,

Licensing is discussed under Issues later in this chapter.

their function is primarily to support and facilitate positive and constructive interactions between educators and young children, and this may be a better, truer indicator of quality in early childhood programs.

Dynamic Factors of Quality

Dynamic process factors of quality relate to "the actual experiences of adults and children in early childhood programs" (File & Kontos, 1993, p. 3). Dynamic factors include the educator and child relationship and the work environment. These dynamic factors are important, as research suggests that these factors are more influential on child outcomes than structural factors (Howes & Smith, 1995).

Educator–Child Relationship

One of the most important factors for quality, and one of the most difficult to assess and measure, is the interaction among the participants in early childhood programs. Young children in an early childhood program may interact daily with many people: educators, other staff, volunteers, and other children. Adults play a particularly important role in fostering young children's sense of security and well being. File and Kontos (1993) reported that, "research consistently shows that children are more likely to flourish in programs where caregivers are sensitive, responsive, and verbally stimulating in their interactions with them" (p. 3).

Some educator behaviours that promote constructive interactions and positive experiences for young children include:

*   Encouraging children's exploration of their environments and participation in activities

The interactions of children and educators are factors in the quality of a program.

- Conversing with children frequently

- Facilitating child-to-child as well as child-to-adult interactions including social play

- Using questions to stimulate children's thought and language

- Being responsive to children (e.g., listening attentively, answering their questions, responding promptly, etc.)

- Responding non-verbally as well as verbally to children (e.g., smiling, holding, touching, etc.)

- Reading to children, playing interactive games (e.g., peekaboo with infants), and singing with children.

Work Environment

Another factor that influences the dynamics of an early childhood program is the work environment for the adults in the program. As discussed in Chapter 4, good wages and working conditions contribute positively to job satisfaction, staff morale, and reduced turnover. All of these factors are, in turn, related to high-quality early childhood programs. For example, reduced turnover helps to create stability and continuity of caregivers for the children (see below), while positive morale influences how people do their work, the cooperation of the adults in the program, and the general level of team feeling.

Another widely recognized factor in quality early childhood programs is the consistency and continuity of the same early childhood educators. Young children, especially infants, need to feel secure and safe if they are to develop optimally. They can't do this if their primary caregivers in the family and early childhood programs change continually.

Contextual Factors of Quality

Contextual factors are the setting in which an early childhood program operates. These factors include the type of program (see Chapters 8, 9, 10, and 11), the location and physical environment of the program, its auspice, and government regulations.

Location and Physical Environment

Unless one is establishing a new early childhood program or relocating, the location is usually already determined. The location might be a home in a suburban area, a church hall, an elementary school, a community centre, a workplace, or any of another dozen possible places. Accessibility, convenience, and cost are variables that influence the choice and effects of a location. For example, a program needs to be convenient for the participants, as most families are not willing to commute long distances on public transportation or by car.

Margie I. Mayfield

Materials need to be easily accessible and attractively displayed.

The effects of materials on children's play are discussed in Chapter 7.

See Chapter 6 for descriptions of the physical environments of different curriculum models.

Sometimes a location needs to be changed for external reasons, for example, the building was sold, the lease to the early childhood program was not renewed, there was a fire—or in one case I know of, the soil around the building was found to be contaminated by lead.

The physical environment of an early childhood program, be it a day-care centre, family day home, or a kindergarten, is an important context and includes both the indoor and outdoor environments. Appropriate and sufficient equipment and materials are also part of the physical environment.

In addition to being clean, healthy, safe, child-friendly, and attractive, a physical environment can facilitate the program. Whereas an excellent physical environment cannot make up for other factors, such as an uncaring, inattentive staff, it can have a positive effect on the overall quality of an early childhood program.

Although there are published rating scales (see below) and checklists that have items for assessing the physical environment, most early childhood educators develop their own questions. Some general questions that I have found useful in evaluating the overall physical environment of an early childhood program are:

- Is the physical environment (both indoors and outdoors) safe, attractive, clean, and organized?

- Does the physical environment reflect and foster the philosophy and curriculum of the program?

- Is the children's work displayed?

- Is the physical environment arranged with well-defined and accessible areas?

- Are all areas of the indoor and outdoor environments easily visible for supervision?

- Is there adequate space for the materials, equipment, activities, and people?

- Are the traffic patterns efficient and obvious for the children?

- Does each child have his or her own individual storage space?

- Is there a quiet space where children can have some solitude?

- Is the physical environment comfortable (e.g., heating, light, ventilation, noise level, etc.)?

One can also gain a lot of evaluative information about the physical environment by observing what areas children use and do not use and what sorts of activities occur in the different areas.

Formal, published rating systems for the physical environment in early childhood programs include *Planning Environments for Young Children: Physical Space* by Kritchevsky and Prescott (1983) and the *Early Childhood Physical Environment Rating Scale* developed by Gary Moore (see Moore, 1997).

An example of an interaction of two factors related to quality in the physical environment is **density**, which involves (a) the amount and organization of space, and (b) the number of children in that space. Obviously, there are too many children for a space when they can no longer move around safely and comfortably and the crowdedness negatively affects the program. This is why most government regulations in Canada and the United States, especially for centre-based programs, stipulate the minimum amount of space required per child and how this is to be calculated (e.g., closets or hallways cannot be included in the space calculation). The NAEYC Information Service (1989) recommends 3.7 to 4.65 square metres per child for centre-based programs, with 3.25 square metres as the minimum.

It is important to keep in mind that the amount of space one needs before not feeling crowded is partially culturally determined. For example, when I was doing some work in Thailand, early childhood educators commented that they would like larger rooms (I agreed as I thought they were rather crowded for the number of children). However, the educators wanted to be able to have more learning centres; they did not think there was insufficient space for the number of children. They also placed more importance on group learning, group cooperation, and group activities than is typical in most early childhood programs in Canada. This is an example of Bronfenbrenner's ecological theory and the implication that programs occur in the larger context of cultures and societies.

Auspice

Auspice is discussed in Chapter 8.

Research has demonstrated significant differences in the quality of programs related to auspice (e.g., sponsorship). Early childhood programs in Canada can be operated by non-profit organizations (e.g., parent cooperative nursery schools), by for-profit organizations (e.g., franchised day-care centres), or by governments (e.g., public-school kindergartens). As discussed in Chapter 8, auspice is most frequently an issue for centre-based day-care programs and in discussions of for-profit versus non-profit day-care programs.

For several years I was a member of a provincial child-care licensing board. One issue faced by licensing boards is for-profit versus non-profit centres. Some people argue that as long as a day-care centre continues to meet licensing requirements, it doesn't matter what its auspice is. Others argue that as the budgets of day-care centres are typically "lean," the only way to make a profit is to cut corners. Some others argue that making a profit is okay as long as the money goes back into the program as increased salaries or better facilities. Still others argue that morally it is not appropriate to make money from the care of young children. What is your position on this issue? With which of the above positions do you agree?

Views on the efficacy and desirability of government regulation are discussed later in this chapter.

After reviewing Canadian research studies, Doherty-Derkowski (1995) concluded that non-profit programs tended to be rated higher on quality than for-profit programs and were more likely to have better educated staff, better ratios, and higher job satisfaction. However, some research has found differences related to quality within single types of auspice.

Auspice and wages are often related. Non-profit, especially unionized, centres typically pay the highest wages in Canada. This, in turn, may contribute to job satisfaction, and higher job satisfaction is related to lower turnover rates. Kindergarten teachers typically have higher wages than do educators in day-care programs.

Government Regulation

Another contextual factor is government regulation. Although not all early childhood programs in Canada are subject to regulation, it is provincial/territorial regulations that determine which are excluded (e.g., a family day home with fewer than four children). The purpose of government regulation is to establish and then enforce minimum standards. These standards, in and of themselves, do not guarantee a high-quality program; they are the minimum level that is acceptable in that jurisdiction. However, research does show that government regulation positively influences the quality of early childhood programs. For example, regulations would prevent a person from caring for 12 infants in her home. Indeed, research studies have shown that regulated family day homes are more likely to be rated as higher quality than unregulated homes (e.g., Kontos, Howes, Shinn, & Galinsky, 1995; Pence & Goelman, 1991; Pepper & Stuart, 1992).

Regulation is one way of enforcing ratios, staff qualifications, group size, safety, health, and other factors known to be positively related to quality in early childhood programs. However, not everyone in early childhood education and care agrees on the efficacy and desirability of government regulation.

Interactive Factors of Quality

Another set of factors that are related to quality early childhood programs is called **interactive** or **joint factors** or **effects**. These are the effects that the family and home can have on the early childhood program and vice versa. As discussed in Chapters 2 and 3, the family and home have powerful, long-lasting effects on young children's growth and development. It is well accepted that there is a relationship between programs and families that is interactive, and each influences the other. It is a logical progression, knowing what we know about the variation across individual children, individual families, and individual programs. To assume that these influential variables do not interact is not logical. The study of the complex interactions and joint influences of these effects with the effects of early childhood programs is relatively recent. To date, most of this type of research has been done in early childhood special education, especially early intervention. Another source of this type of research has been from family support programs (see Chapter 11). Examination of interactive effects is of growing interest to and importance for research, and we should learn more about this area in the future.

The research, in general, has been somewhat inconclusive as to the relative effects of family variables versus program variables (Phillips & Howes, 1987). However, given the complexity of these relationships and the number of potential variables, and the difficulty in measuring many of these, this is not surprising. An early childhood program may have both direct and indirect effects on children and families. According to Williams (1998), "the results across a number of studies clearly suggest that children cared for in day care are influenced by both the family and the day care setting." (p. 40). However, some research has shown that a poor quality early childhood program can have negative effects on a young child even if that child is from a "good" two-parent, middle-income home (Howes, 1990; Vandell, Henderson, & Wilson, 1988). We have learned the importance of looking at the interactive effects of variables rather than only one or two (e.g., family income and children's developmental levels). As Doherty-Derkowski (1995) states, "everything matters" (p. 109). The task for future research is to continue to expand examination of the interactive effects between early childhood programs and families.

An important implication of interactive effects in early childhood programs is that improving one factor may not necessarily improve the quality of the early childhood program. For example, improving salaries in a program may not improve the overall quality if there is still a large number of children per educator. Possible interactive effects need to be considered as well.

Global Assessments

Another way of considering quality in early childhood programs is **global assessment**. This term refers to evaluating multiple factors in one measure and using a resulting composite or total score as a summary indicator of quality. Use of a comprehensive rating scale is one example of a global assessment.

Although other global assessment instruments have been developed, usually for use in research, the one most widely used in North America is the *Early Childhood Environment Rating Scale* developed by Thelma Harms and Richard M. Clifford in 1980 and revised in 1998 (often referred to as the ECERS). The ECERS is widely used as it is considered reliable, valid, and user-friendly (e.g., Martin, 1994).

The ECERS has 37 items in seven subscales: Personal Care Routines, Furnishings and Display for Children, Language-Reasoning Experiences, Fine and Gross Motor Activities, Creative Activities, Social Development, and Adult Needs. Items are rated on a scale of 1 (inadequate) to 7 (excellent). Some sample items are free play, using language, gross motor equipment, schedule, space to be alone, cultural awareness, and provision for parents. The ratings for each item are recorded on a score sheet for each subscale, then totalled for each subscale and again for an overall total score.

Variations of the ECERS have been used in other countries; for example, an expanded version was developed for early childhood programs in Scotland: the *Pre-Five Environment Rating Scale* (Vernon & Smith, 1994).

Additional rating scales in the ECERS series have been developed for specific types of early childhood programs:

- *Family Day Care Rating Scale* (FDCRS) (Harms & Clifford, 1989), with similar scales to ECERS

- *Infant/Toddler Environment Rating Scale* (ITERS) (Harms, Cryer, & Clifford, 1990)

- *School-Age Care Environment Rating Scale* (SACERS) (Harms, Jacobs, & White, 1995).

The use of global assessment has been questioned in terms of how these instruments define quality (i.e., Whose definition?) and the quantification of quality.

Policy and Early Childhood Programs

Policy is important to any discussion of quality early childhood programs because, "a formal statement of policy is valuable in providing a basic framework for operational decisions; in defining a broad vision from which all else should flow; in providing general guidance and a sense of direction to staff at all levels; and as providing a key element in a local authority's message to users of services" (McQuail & Pugh, 1995, p. 43). Policy addresses key issues such as who is responsible for early childhood programs, what types of programs should be provided, and how these programs should be delivered. This section examines the responsibility for early childhood and family programs and related policies, including the role of the federal government, the role of the provincial/territorial governments, and the role of the private sector.

A policy question that follows from What is a quality early childhood program? is, How do we get these—or, Who is responsible for providing quality early childhood programs? Of course, a broader underlying question is, Who is responsible for children and families? These questions have been debated since the days of the ancient philosophers (see Chapter 5).

Should early childhood education and care be a public or a family responsibility? A response to this question encompasses several aspects. For example, the moral aspect looks at the importance of young children and families for society and the importance of the early years. Some argue that we, as members of society, need to provide these programs because it is the right thing to do, especially as we have a moral obligation to young children.

A legalistic, constitutional response to this question is that it is the family's responsibility. Early documents such as the British North America Act did not mention children. Today, one legal requirement in early childhood education and care is that children must attend school (or its equivalent) at a certain age (this varies across provinces). It is the responsibility of the provincial/territorial governments to provide public schools, and it is the responsibility of families to enroll their children or show they have made equivalent provisions (e.g., home schooling). On the other hand, another legal-type argument is that children have rights and because they are citizens they should be entitled to education and care from birth. Therefore, this argument sees early childhood education and care as a public responsibility.

There is also an economic response. Some believe that the family is responsible for any cost of education and care for young children before they begin public education. Others believe that the provinces and territories should be responsible for early childhood programs, as they are already responsible for other education programs. And still others think that the federal government should be responsible, to ensure equitable, universal coverage. Historically, the federal government has taken varying degrees of financial responsibility for early childhood programs. For example, in the recent past the Canadian government has cost-shared with the provinces through the Canada Assistance Plan (CAP). They are still responsible for special programs such as Aboriginal Head Start (see Chapter 11).

There is also a political response. As Grubb (1989) noted, "children do not vote, so their political cause has always been weak. For children under 6, public support has always vied with the idea that parents should be wholly responsible" (p. 358).

The Role of the Federal Government

Early childhood education and care occurs in the context of a country and a society. As Kagan (1994) has stated, "each nation's choices in allocating responsibility for children and families have deep roots in specific cultural values and norms that have developed over time" (p. 4).

In Canada, the federal government constitutionally and legally does not have direct jurisdiction over education, health, or social welfare in Canada. These are the responsibilities of the provinces and territories (Friendly, 2000). Federal government involvement and interest in young children and families has waxed and waned historically. In Canada's early days, government social services were non-existent, so these were provided by families, churches, and charitable organizations.

The federal governments in some countries (e.g., Scandinavian countries) have a long record of supporting young children and families. In Canada, the federal government was most active in social programs from the 1940s through the 1980s (Friendly & Oloman, 2000). This time period saw the establishment of universal programs such as public education to the post-secondary level, health care, unemployment insurance, and pensions. Also at this time, the federal government was involved with the funding of early childhood programs through the federal-provincial cost-sharing program Canada Assistance Plan (CAP). However, the need for early childhood programs, especially day care, as a result of demographic trends such as the increasing numbers of mothers in the paid labour force put early childhood programs on the federal policy agenda in the early 1980s (Friendly, 1992). According to Friendly and Oloman (2000), as the greatest need for child care programs did not occur until the end of this growth period, it "failed to 'catch the wave' of social policy programs for development" (p. 71). Indeed, in Canada, it seems as though children and families go in and out of policy fashion. In the 1990s, early childhood education and care slipped from the top of the national agenda (Friendly & Oloman, 2000). This was also a difficult time for family and early childhood programs in western Europe and Australia and New Zealand (Kamerman & Kahn, 1997).

Family and early childhood programs also slipped from being a priority in some provinces. A provincial example was the growth of family resource centres in Ontario and then the closing of many of these centres in the 1990s due to provincial cutbacks in funding.

A National Policy for Children and Families

A criticism of policies and programs for young children and families in Canada is that they are fragmented, a piecemeal patchwork of local, provincial/territorial, and federal efforts that are not coordinated and are sometimes even contradictory. Friendly (1998) has stated, "although the need for early childhood care and education in Canada has never been greater, this country has no unified vision for the provision of these services" (p. 6). As Lero (2000) and others have pointed out, this situation is not unique to Canada.

One approach to dealing with this fragmentation that has been suggested over the past two or more decades is a national policy. A national policy for children and families is common in European countries, especially those in the European Union. Early childhood educators have long discussed and advocated national policies for children and families in those countries without national policies, such as Canada (see below), the United States (e.g., Kagan, Klugman, & Zigler, 1983), and the United Kingdom (e.g., Pugh, 1996).

A recent attempt at an embryonic national policy in Canada is the proposed National Children's Agenda. In May 1999, the federal, provincial, and territorial governments issued a National Children's Agenda. This document, widely distributed across Canada, "proposes a common vision for children . . . . suggests goals . . . and offers directions" (1999, preface). It identifies six areas for "cooperative efforts" (p. 11):

1. Supporting parents and strengthening families

2. Enhancing early childhood development

3. Improving economic security for families

4. Providing early and continuous learning experiences

5. Fostering adolescent development

6. Creating supportive, safe, and violence-free communities.

FOR REFLECTION

The National Children's Agenda does not identify specific programs that should or would be included. It asks for feedback and dialogue. What programs for young children and their families do you think are essential to include in a national policy?

Criticisms of the National Children's Agenda have included that it is presented by a federal government that has previously cut billions of dollars from family and child programs, that it is another example of political rhetoric, and that what it says has been heard before. There is a low expectation by the Canadian public that there will actually be effective implementation of such a policy (Mitchell, 2000). Despite reservations such as these, Insight Canada research polls in 1993 and 1996 reported that two-thirds of Canadians do support a national child-care program (Friendly, 1997).

Professional organizations and advocacy groups in the late 1980s identified three principles that should be included in a national policy on early childhood programs:

- Universal access (i.e., that programs would be available to all children and families regardless of circumstances or need, a common policy in European countries)

- Comprehensiveness (i.e., a range of program options would be provided)

- High-quality programs.

(Friendly, 1994)

In 1994, early childhood organizations met and identified the principles of:

- Shared values (e.g., children are important and every child and family has a right to early childhood programs)

- Availability and accessibility (see Chapter 8)

- Affordability (see Chapter 8)

- Quality

- Accountability.

(Highlights of National Forum, [on-line])

In response to the National Children's Agenda, Battle and Torjman of the Caledon Institute (2000) identified comprehensiveness, universality, accessibility, quality, and accountability as the key principles for a national policy. They also recommended that desirable practices identified in the literature be included: these are service integration (i.e., components fitting together in a coherent system), mixed delivery (i.e., by federal, provincial/territorial, and municipal governments and the private sector and voluntary sector), and community base (i.e., locally determined, implemented, and administered programs and services).

Role of the Provincial/Territorial Governments

Because the areas most relevant to early childhood programs (i.e., education, health, and social services) are provincial/territorial responsibilities in Canada, the pattern of development and current provision of programs and services for young children and their families varies across the 13 jurisdictions. For example, kindergarten is part of the public school system in all provinces except Prince Edward Island, attendance is optional in all these jurisdictions except New Brunswick, and it is typically a half-day program for five-year-olds but four-year-old kindergartens are available in some school districts in Ontario and Quebec, with full-day programs in New Brunswick. The variations across jurisdictions for day-care and family support programs are even greater, with differences in legislation, regulation, monitoring, funding, procedures, and staff qualifications. The recent cutbacks by the federal government in its transfer of funding and responsibility to the provinces/territories (a process referred to as *devolution*) has increased the differences across the provinces/territories in the areas of family and child policy and provision of programs.

The province that currently has the most comprehensive and cohesive family policy is Quebec. In 1997, the provincial government created a family policy that includes:

- Family allowances for low-income families

- Creation of 73,000 new child-care spaces within five years

- $5/day day-care fees (see Chapter 8)

- Tax credits for children

- Insurance for prescription drugs for children

- Housing subsidies for low-income families

- Extended parental insurance (to replace income during maternity and paternity leaves)

- Creation of a Ministry of Family and Children's Services

- Early Childhood Centres/Centres de la petite enfance (CPEs) to provide both centre- and family-based day-care programs. Each CPE is autonomous, community-based and not-for-profit, with a board of directors that is two-thirds parents. Two-thirds of the staff must have three-year college certificates in early childhood education, and family day-care providers must complete a 45-hour course. Wages are to be increased approximately 35 percent over three years. Eventually, each CPE will also provide flexible, extended day care and other family services.

Quebec's family policy has been criticized primarily on organizational and financial grounds. For example, the large expenditure of funds spent implementing this policy has meant more limited funds for other programs. Some educators and parents are concerned about a narrower range of programs (e.g., there has been a reduction in the number of drop-in programs in order to convert those spaces to full-time care). There is not currently a sufficient number of $5/day spaces for all the families on wait-lists, and the wait-lists are very long in some areas. Day-care and family-care educators are more stressed and burnout is more common due to changes. Low-income families previously paid less than the current $5/day fee for day care (Major-Hamza, 2000; Rose, 1999).

Role of the Private Sector

Another player in the provision of family and child policy is the private sector. Many working families receive additional family health benefits, maternity/paternity leave, family responsibility days, and other child and family benefits as part of their employment (often on a cost-shared basis between employer and employees).

Family-friendly workplaces are frequently identified in popular-press magazines (e.g., *Working Mother* and *Report on Business* magazines' annual lists of the top family-friendly companies). This information is used both by people looking for employment and by employers trying to recruit employees. Some family-friendly policies include flex-time, job-sharing, maternity and paternity leaves (paid and/or unpaid), telecommuting, parenting courses, workshops on family or child-related topics, part-time work, and counselling or stress management strategies to help balance work–family stress. However, these family-friendly policies are not universal across Canadian employers. Although some companies and organizations have instituted these provisions for philosophical or company-policy reasons, most have been done for practical reasons such as union agreements or recruitment (Mayfield, 1990). Many of these provisions have been introduced to assist in the recruitment of highly skilled professionals in times of economic growth, especially in areas that are highly competitive. For example, in the past some hospitals in Canada established on-site day-care centres in order to help recruit nurses. Many high-technology firms currently offer a variety of benefits from which employees can select. The flexible-benefits approach has also been suggested as a way of avoiding backlash from employees who do not have young children or families and therefore may not perceive any direct benefits from family-friendly provisions.

FOR REFLECTION

Some countries permit parents to have long maternity/paternity leaves (e.g., up to three years in France), often with partial pay (e.g., 90 percent for the first 12 months in Sweden), and a guarantee of a job upon return. If Canada had as good a system of maternity and paternity leaves (provided by either the public or private sector), there would not be a need for centre-based infant day care. Do you agree or disagree with this statement? Why?

A brief definition of developmentally appropriate practice is given in Chapter 1.

Issues for Program Quality and Policy

This section discusses three issues related to quality and policy: the role of developmentally appropriate practice; possible models for providing integrated services for young children and families; and the relationship of registration, licensing, credentials, and accreditation to quality early childhood programs.

Developmentally Appropriate Practice

The concept of developmentally appropriate practice, especially as outlined by the National Association for the Education of Young Children (NAEYC), has become "a rallying cry" in early childhood education and care in North America (Davis & Goffin, 1994, p. 3). The statement *Developmentally Appropriate Practice in Early Childhood Programs Serving Children from Birth Through Age 8* has been called "the most influential document guiding the field of early childhood education today" (Hart, Burts, & Charlesworth, 1997, p. 1) and "the dominant perspective of educational programs" (Varga, 2000, p. 89). It is a major force in contemporary early childhood programs in North America. For many people in the field of early childhood education and care, the statement has come to mean what is desirable and the standard by which early childhood programs should be judged. According to Vander Wilt and Monroe (1998), "it is a way of thinking about and working with children" (p. 17).

From the earliest NAEYC publications on developmentally appropriate practice, the claim has been made of the relationship of developmentally appropriate practice to the quality of early childhood programs. For example, while recognizing that many factors affect the quality of an early childhood program, it is asserted that, "a major determinant of program quality is the extent to which knowledge of child development is applied in program practices—the degree to which the program is *developmentally appropriate*" (Bredekamp, 1986, pp. 1–2). Bredekamp (1997) later wrote, "the position statement on developmentally appropriate practice is a political document about what NAEYC and its members believe constitutes quality care and education for young children" (p. 39).

History of Developmentally Appropriate Practice

The origins of developmentally appropriate practice are not new, and did not originate in the 1980s. Although the origins of the term have not been documented or traced (Bredekamp, 1991; Osborn, 1991), its roots go back to the first half of the twentieth century or earlier (Perry & Duru, 2000). These roots include the works and ideas of John Dewey (see Chapter 6), Patty Smith Hill (see Chapter 5), Maria Montessori (see Chapter 5), Carolyn Pratt (see Chapter 5), Katharine Whiteside Taylor (see Chapter 9), and the work of the early pioneers in Head Start in the United States. The dominance of child development was seen early on in the Child Study Movement in Canada (see Chapter 9) and in early childhood education textbooks since the 1920s and 1930s. Children's individual growth patterns were written about by early theorists such as Rousseau, Pestalozzi, and Froebel (see Chapter 5).

The idea for NAEYC's statement on developmentally appropriate practice originated at a conference on kindergarten curriculum where NAEYC and NAECS/SDE (National Association of Early Childhood Specialists in State Departments of Education [USA]) identified the need for curriculum guidelines for kindergarten (Bredekamp & Rosegrant, 1992). Two motivating factors were the concern over the increasing academic orientation of kindergartens (a particular concern at that time, as kindergartens for four-year-olds were becoming more common) and NAEYC's efforts to develop an accreditation system for early childhood programs. The original attempt at a statement by the accreditation group "looked too much like a developmental checklist and was rejected by the original Steering Committee of the accreditation project" (Bredekamp, 1991, p. 200). The task was next given to the Commission on Appropriate Education for 4- and 5-Year-Olds established by NAEYC in 1984.

This committee of 29 members was very reminiscent of the Committee of 19 of the International Kindergarten Union in the early 1900s, whose task it was to develop standards and curriculum guidelines for kindergarten. Their report consisted of three parts: the liberal/progressive view, the traditional view, and a compromise position (see Chapter 10). Likewise, the NAEYC committee was unable to reach consensus and submitted a main report with minority reports. This committee had also divided into three major groups: the child development group; the curriculum group concerned that the statement was about *how* to teach without providing guidance on *what* to teach (i.e., content); and the special education/behaviourist group, which supported a more direct instruction orientation.

The Governing Board of NAEYC did not approve the report and had its staff develop a series of "position statements" over the next three years. This development process included "review and comment from hundreds of early childhood professionals and thorough debate by the entire NAEYC Governing Board" (Bredekamp, 1991, p. 201), as well as distribution of more than 175,000 copies of the book and about one million copies of a brochure. NAEYC published its position statements on developmentally appropriate practice in 1986, an expanded edition in 1987, and a revised edition in 1997.

Definition of Developmentally Appropriate Practice

The early definition of **developmentally appropriate practice** included two dimensions:

FOR REFLECTION

1. *Age appropriateness*—"There are universal, predictable sequences of growth and change that occur in children during the first 9 years of life," and

2. *Individual appropriateness*—"Each child is a unique person with an individual pattern and timing of growth, as well as individual personality, learning style, and family background."

(Bredekamp, 1986, p. 2)

Do you think placing children in groups or classes by chronological age is age appropriate, individually appropriate, or developmentally appropriate?

Bredekamp (1991) later wrote that the original intent was to focus on the developmental appropriateness of programs and not other types of program appropriateness, such as educational, ethical, or financial appropriateness.

A major component of NAEYC's statement on developmentally appropriate practice has been the use of paired exemplars of appropriate and inappropriate practice. For example:

*   *Appropriate*—"Children work individually or in small, informal groups most of the time."

*   *Inappropriate*—"Large group, teacher-directed instruction is used most of the time" (Bredekamp, 1986, p. 50).

From the earliest editions, developmentally appropriate practice as presented by the NAEYC publications has been a target of debate and criticism. Subsequent editions of the statement have considered and often responded to these concerns. For example, according to Bredekamp (1997), one of the earliest issues was whether to keep the appropriate/inappropriate exemplars, which had been criticized for "apparently dichotomizing the complexity of practice, making it look as if there is one right way and one wrong way to practice" (p. 35). Some critics thought this approach oversimplified educator decision-making into an either-or situation. NAEYC's response was to continue this format, but individual items have been revised, deleted, or added.

The definition of developmentally appropriate practice (DAP) has also evolved, in part due to criticism of the narrowness of the initial definition and the need to recognize cultural and social contexts. In the 1997 edition, developmentally appropriate practice is defined as:

> The outcome of a process of teacher decisionmaking that draws on at least three critical, interrelated bodies of knowledge: (1) what teachers know about how children develop and learn; (2) what teachers know about individual children in their group; and (3) knowledge of the social and cultural context in which those children live and learn. (Bredekamp & Copple, 1997, p. vii)

Criticisms of Developmentally Appropriate Practice

Criticisms of NAEYC's statement on developmentally appropriate practice can be divided into four broad categories: (a) its development, (b) its theoretical base, (c) its content (or lack of), and (d) its use.

The criticisms about the development of NAEYC's statement on developmentally appropriate practice concern the process used. Some critics questioned how representative the committee and the NAEYC Board were at the time of its development (i.e., most of the players were child developmentalists), others questioned how much real input from the profession was sought and received. Still other critics had concerns about the dichotomous, either/or, good/bad quality of the exemplar statements (e.g., Fowell & Lawton, 1992).

Another criticism related to development and subsequent dissemination is the claim by NAEYC that DAP represents a consensus of the profession: "This book represents the early childhood profession's consensus definition of developmentally appropriate practice" (Bredekamp, 1987, p. iv). Walsh (1991) and others have questioned this assertion. Early childhood educators do not necessarily agree on what is developmentally appropriate practice.

A greater concern has been the theoretical base of developmentally appropriate practice. The most frequent criticism has been the heavy reliance on child development, specifically Piagetian theory, for justification, and the relative exclusion of other theoretical bases, such as the behaviourist. Especially in the earliest editions, some of the inappropriate exemplars were common practices in early childhood special education programs (e.g., the use of extrinsic rewards, such as tokens or stickers, was considered inappropriate practice). Others questioned the labelling of structured learning as inappropriate, as they believed that many children with special needs benefit from more structured, teacher-directed learning (e.g., Fowell & Lawton, 1992; Wortham, 1995). In an analysis of NAEYC's Developmentally Appropriate Practice and the Division for Early Childhood of the Council for Exceptional Children's statement of *DEC Recommended Practices* (1993), Wolery and Bredekamp (1994) recognized that although there were similarities in the content of the two documents, there were also differences due to different assumptions, theoretical support, disciplinary values, and the nature of the children. They concluded that, "children with and without disabilities may require some similar and some different practices" (p. 335).

While it is overwhelmingly accepted that child development has a role in early childhood programs and has had for many years, some critics think there is too much emphasis on a maturationist approach and a lack of recognition of culture and knowledge (e.g., Spodek & Brown, 1993). That is, the development of curriculum and programs needs to consider what it is society wants for its children and wants them to be, as well as what knowledge is needed now and in the future. Others, such as Kessler (1991), thought that philosophical and political contexts of curriculum had been neglected. Others questioned the basic assumption that children develop along the same pattern regardless of circumstances and backgrounds (e.g., Göncü & Fitzgerald, 1994).

Although proponents have asserted that DAP is for use with all children (e.g., Bredekamp & Rosegrant, 1992; Charlesworth, 1998), others have questioned this (e.g., Lubeck, 1994). The appropriateness and suitability of trying to develop "universal" guidelines when today's North American society is characterized by cultural diversity and plurality has also been questioned (e.g., Williams, 1994). Jipson (1991) and others have pointed out that cultural differences (see Chapters 2 and 3) such as child-rearing and learning/teaching styles make a universal approach unrealistic. Others argue that to really understand children, one must analyze social, political, and economic parameters as well as theoretical perspectives (e.g., Beyer & Bloch, 1996).

Another area of criticism was about the content; that is, what was included or not included in developmentally appropriate practice. In addition to not identifying what things it is important for children to know, the lack of guidance on the selection of particular practices in specific circumstances has also been criticized (e.g., Johnson & Johnson, 1994).

A third area of criticism has been the use of the statement on developmentally appropriate practice. One concern is the dominance of the concept of developmentally appropriate practice in early childhood education and care today. For example, Powell (1994) writes that, "a critical question facing the field of early childhood programs is the extent to which the dominant professional culture will control decisions about the appropriateness of programs providing early education and care" (p. 166). Spodek (1991) has termed developmentally appropriate practice "the New Orthodoxy" (p. 12).

NAEYC is currently the largest early childhood professional organization in North America and as such has significant influence and the means for getting out its message to its members and the public. The dominance of DAP has implications for it being used as the basis for evaluating early childhood programs. DAP has been criticized as too narrow and inadequate by itself to be the basis of program evaluation (e.g., Spodek & Saracho, 1994). However, others do not agree with this view (e.g., Kostelnik, 1992).

Although NAEYC's latest statement on developmentally appropriate practice states, as did previous ones, that the document is intended for "use by teachers, administrators, curriculum developers, parents, policymakers, and others involved with programs serving young children" (Bredekamp & Copple, 1997, p. vi), some have questioned how much of a catchword *developmentally appropriate practice* and DAP have become and how much true understanding there is, especially on the part of parents and the general public (e.g., Powell, 1994). In a review of the research on developmentally appropriate practice, Dunn and Kontos (1997) reported that the research "suggests that few early childhood classrooms exemplify developmentally appropriate practice" at both the preschool and primary levels (p. 4). They also concluded that, "teachers' beliefs are more consistent with developmentally appropriate practices than their behaviours" (p. 7). As Elkind (1989) observed, "developmental appropriateness has been honored more in word than in deed" (p. 113).

A danger related to any type of global statement such as NAEYC's Developmentally Appropriate Practice is *mis*interpretations by others. The proponents of DAP have identified several frequent misinterpretations of the NAEYC statement (Bredekamp & Rosegrant, 1992; Kostelnik, 1992; Raines, 1997) including:

- Developmentally appropriate practice is a set curriculum.

- The early childhood program is child-directed.

- Developmentally appropriate practice does not apply to all children.

- Developmentally appropriate practice can be implemented in only one way.

- DAP classrooms have no or very little structure.

- Educators do not formally teach the children.

- Skills are not taught.

For the 1997 revision, NAEYC conducted hearings and meetings, solicited written input from members, and reviewed the current research, theory, and critiques of the previous statement of DAP (Bredekamp & Copple, 1997). This process resulted in the 1997 revision, which addressed many of the issues raised from previous versions such as the role of culture and the importance of individual appropriateness. However, as Bredekamp (1997) notes, debate over DAP will no doubt continue in the future.

Integration of Programs for Young Children and Families: A Solution for Fragmentation?

Early childhood programs and services for young children and families in Canada are often perceived as fragmented, both conceptually and organizationally. In fact, the current Canadian situation is frequently described as patchwork, chaotic, or incoherent. The integration of programs and services is an oft-suggested solution, or partial solution, for this fragmentation. For example, according to a report by the National Council of Welfare in 1999, "very strong integration of child care with education, health care and other provincially delivered family services makes good sense" (quoted in Johnson & Mathien, 1999, p. 370).

Integration of programs and services for young children and families means a holistic approach with comprehensive programs and services available locally, for example, "one-stop centers where the educational, physical, psychological, and social requirements of students and their families are addressed in a rational, holistic fashion" (Dryfoos, 1996, p. 18). Part of the rationale for integration of programs and services is that coordination and collaboration are desirable for the avoidance of discontinuity, overlap, and gaps in available programs and services, as well as unnecessary competition for limited resources. Integration has the potential to increase accessibility of programs and services for families and affordability of programs by reducing duplication and improving efficiency. In theory, it could also help to improve the quality of these programs and services.

The current fragmentation in early childhood education and care is often traced to the different historical origins of early childhood programs (e.g., kindergarten, nursery school, and day care) as well as other programs such as family support programs. In an article in 1924, Arnold Gesell (see Chapter 6) advised that the coordination of the various agencies concerned with the growth and development of young children "should be hastened" (p. 18).

Others attribute fragmentation to incoherent governmental jurisdictions, including differing funding sources and regulations. There is a perceived lack of collaboration and continuity among provincial/territorial, local, and private agencies and programs. According to Goffin (1983), "current programs are not organized to deal with children and families in a coordinated, holistic way. The fragmentation of services and the resulting problems of coordination and conflict can be especially burdensome for families with multiple needs" (p. 286).

David Weikart (1989) has referred to "the virtues and problems of fragmentation [of programs and services for young children]" (p. 23). The early childhood literature typically discusses the problems of fragmentation, but what might be some of the virtues of fragmentation?

Continuity and Co-Location

There are various possible levels of program integration. A basic level is to increase the coordination and continuity between early childhood programs and between other programs and home. The coordination is initiated by the individual early childhood educators in the programs or by parents for their own children.

In addition to educators and families facilitating continuity for children and programs, continuity and program integration can also be promoted by physical proximity of programs. For example, in many school districts, declining enrollments in elementary schools left vacant classrooms or portables. Districts then used or rented this space for junior kindergartens, school-age programs, family resource centres, day-care centres, toy libraries, nursery schools, or other child/family-related community programs. The underlying idea is that by being located in the same building, staff and participants from programs will interact with each other, become more knowledgeable about the other programs, and thus be more willing to collaborate.

Facilitating the transition of young children between home and their first early childhood program is discussed in Chapter 9; the transitions from a preschool program to kindergarten and kindergarten to grade 1 are discussed in Chapter 10.

Ontario has many school-based day-care programs. Typically, a day-care centre in a school is licensed by the Ministry of Community and Social Services and operated under the regulations of the Ontario Day Nurseries Act. In contrast, kindergarten and kindergarten teachers operate under the Ministry of Education and the Education Act. Ontario is not the only province with this dichotomy. On the other hand, Spain recently included policies and programs for early childhood in a comprehensive Education Act.

Early childhood programs are good places to begin service integration because of their traditions and history of family and community involvement. This is especially true for early childhood special education programs, because of the family-centred philosophy and integration of medical, therapy, social services, and care and education personnel on multidisciplinary teams coordinating work with young children with special needs and their families. These teams are usually multidisciplinary, and often multi-agency.

School/Neighbourhood-Based Models

Another model for integrated programs is the school-based or family resource centre-based option. This is a community-based model (see Chapter 11). A rationale for this model is that it is easier for families to access community-based programs and services; thus, locating programs and services in a central, easily accessible location in a neighbourhood or community would facilitate their use. Two possibilities often suggested are a local school or a family resource centre.

Schools are often suggested because there is one located in every community of any size in Canada. Their locations are known by their respective communities, even by the families that do not have school-age children. Schools also have much of the needed infrastructure. On the other hand, a family resource centre is also community-based, and while not so common and perhaps not so high-profile as the local school, is usually known to people in the community. In addition, family resource programs have "traditions that are characterized by their comprehensiveness and their tacit integration of services" (Kagan, 1993, p. 61). Public schools, on the other hand, are sometimes criticized for not having these features. However, schools have traditionally provided many "integrated" services. When I was a child in public school, my schools had hot lunches and morning milk (nutrition); school nurses and clinics; vision, hearing, and dental checkups and immunizations (health); speech therapy (special education); social workers and counselling (psychological services); monthly meetings for parents (parent support); and playgrounds for after-school and weekend use by the community (recreation). I also remember Friday activity nights in the local high school when all students could use school facilities at no cost (my favourite activity was roller-skating in the halls).

Full-Service-School Model

The full-service school model is becoming more popular in North America. According to one expert, "demands for more comprehensive, collaborative, unfragmented programs located in schools are coming from a wide spectrum of organizations and individuals" (Dryfoos, 1994, p. 6). I have visited several examples, and the specific programs and services vary based on community need, local interest, and funding availability.

Schools are community buildings and as such could be operated for longer periods than just weekdays 9 a.m. to 3 p.m., September through June. After-hours programs that I have seen in schools include adult education, tutoring for children, recreational activities, clubs, sports, community events, music lessons, choir, crafts, parent education course and support groups, drug prevention programs, counselling for children and families, personal development courses, job training, literacy programs, and mental health services.

In addition to providing programs after school, in the evenings, and on weekends, which are convenient times for families, each school seems to have its own unique reasons for its particular success. The personnel in one school I recently visited in Baltimore credited much of the success of their programs to the fact that almost all of them involve food (e.g., evening parent education courses are accompanied by pizza). Another school's personnel recommended providing programs for all ages in the community, as one member of a family will often encourage another to come along, especially if two programs of interest are offered on the same evening. I met one mother who was working on her GED because her daughter wanted to play basketball in the evening and her son was in the computer club. As she said, "I'd have to bring them and pick them up so I figured I might as well stay and do something useful for me." Another program provided a popular activity for children of participants in an adult literacy class. One young boy recruited his grandmother for the literacy class just so he could attend the activity program.

Well-known examples of full-service schools are the School of the 21st Century developed by Edward Zigler, who was instrumental in the establishment of Head Start, and the School Development Program developed by James Comer, a physician and public health expert. These models combined recently to form the Comer/Zigler Initiative (referred to as Co/Zi). This model is a comprehensive school-based program for children from birth to age 12 that includes early childhood and family support programs. When a wide variety of programs are located in a school, "the school is no longer seen as a building delivering formal schooling during limited hours. Instead, the school becomes a place where formal schooling, child care, and the coordination of other services occur together from early morning until evening during 12 months of the year" (Finn-Stevenson & Stern, 1997, pp. 53-54). Some components of the Co/Zi model are:

- Day care for children aged 3 to 5 years

- School-age programs for 5- to 12-year-olds

- Home visiting for families with children under 3

- Support for local family day homes

- Family support programs

- Information and resource service

- Health and nutrition programs

- Family literacy programs

- On-site prenatal services

- Intergenerational programs

- Professional development for all professionals

- Parent involvement

- School planning and management team

- Mental health team (focus on prevention).

(Finn-Stevenson, Desimone, & Chung, 1998; Zigler, Finn-Stevenson, & Marsland, 1995)

Family resource centres, day-care programs, or other community programs can also be locations of a full-service model.

Hub/Satellite Model

Integrated services are not always based in a centre, or even in one location. In rural areas with large distances and no public transportation, a single centre location is not practical. In these situations, a hub or satellite model may be appropriate. One example of this model is Haldimand–Norfolk R.E.A.C.H. (Resources, Education, and Counselling Help), located on the north shore of Lake Erie (see Focus 12.1).

Although integrated services may seem like a logical and viable approach to addressing the issue of fragmentation of programs and services for young children and their families, it is not without obstacles or disadvantages. Dryfoos (1999) has recommended that, "all have to sit down together and figure out who should do what, and to devise ways to work together and be flexible" (p. 127). This latter part is particularly important, because as Mann (1996) has commented, "collaboration is more than redrawing organizational charts" (p. 11). Some potential obstacles are:

- Redefining roles and responsibilities

- Sharing of ownership and power

- Sharing of space

- Differences in program philosophies

- Lack of staff understanding of or commitment to an integrated services model

- Attitudinal barriers by staff

Focus 12.1

A Rural Satellite Model

Haldimand-Norfolk R.E.A.C.H. is a non-profit, multiservice umbrella agency that provides both direct services and support to families as well as referrals to other programs. With one telephone call to the R.E.A.C.H. helpline, families can access all community programs and services.

Early childhood and family programs include:

· Parent help line
· Counselling (e.g., employee assistance program)
· Day care (for children 18 months to 12 years old)
· Family day care support
· Early intervention programs (e.g., an infant development program and a support program for early childhood programs)
· Toy libraries
· Respite service
· Family support
· Workplace wellness services
· Drop-in centres
· Parenting courses
· Playgroups
· Volunteer programs

R.E.A.C.H. has formed partnerships with existing programs, services, and community organizations. For example, the toy libraries, drop-in centres, and playgroups are available in several communities and are housed in churches, public libraries, the Mennonite Help Centre, and other locations.

Source: Chatterson & Kelleher, 1998; Karin Marks and H-N R.E.A.C.H. staff, personal communication, May 2000.

- Protection of "turf" (i.e., self-interest)

- Amount of time to establish and operationalize this model

- Stability of the partnerships

- Regulatory barriers (e.g., combining programs under the jurisdiction and funding of different ministries).

Zetlin (1995) has identified five characteristics of successful integrated services models: (a) long-term commitment, (b) participation by families and educators, (c) participation by public- and private-sector organizations and agencies, (d) integration of health, human services, and education, and (e) strong administrative commitment.

Registration, Licensing, Credentialing, and Accreditation

Many in the field of early childhood education and care believe that program quality can be enhanced by *registration, licensing, credentialing* (also called *certificating*), and *accreditation*. Others believe that these things by definition set only minimum standards and therefore cannot significantly raise the quality in early childhood programs, much less guarantee high quality.

Registration, licensing, credentialing, and accreditation can exist independently or in combination. For example, a family day-care home may be registered or it may be licensed. The family day-care provider may not have any formal early childhood credentials or may have an early childhood certificate.

Although regulation and supervision of early childhood programs can and does vary across Canada, a common goal is protecting children. This concern for protection has been present from the early days of licensing early childhood programs. For example, there is still an emphasis on health and safety (e.g., fire exits, clean facilities, disease prevention, first-aid kits, safety hazards, child abuse, and injury) in provincial and territorial regulations.

Not everyone is in favour of regulation. Some consider it an intrusion in their lives, others think that parents should be responsible for their children and therefore should also be responsible for selecting good programs, and some think that the marketplace should be the regulator (i.e., good programs will be used by families and poor ones will not and will therefore disappear). Still others think that regulations by definition reflect white, middle-class values and unfairly disadvantage some ethnic and cultural groups and practices. Others think that regulation is not particularly effective given the horror stories one reads in the newspapers and therefore it isn't worth the cost and time it takes. Other concerns focus on who sets the standards, how standards are determined, how standards are assessed, and how standards are enforced.

Another issue that policy-makers and legislators have to wrestle with is who and which programs should be regulated, and to what degree. For example, most regulations requiring licensing for family day care set a minimum number of children below which a day care home does not have to be licensed.

Registration

Registration typically applies to family day care. A family day-care provider voluntarily presents documentation that they, their facility, and their program meet a predetermined set of standards. (The standards for registration are typically less stringent than for licensing.)

The motivation for many family day-care providers to pursue registration is to receive support services (e.g., a registering agency may provide professional development activities, loan of materials, advice and information, access to group purchasing of supplies, financial advice, and group insurance rates for liability/business insurance), and to be eligible for financial subsidies and referrals from an agency. Registered family day-care homes are typically subject to inspection. Parents are often reassured when a family day home is registered and

FOR REFLECTION

In their position statement Licensing and Public Regulation of Early Childhood Programs, *NAEYC (1998a) states, "Any program providing care and education to children from two or more unrelated families should be regulated; there should be no exemptions from this principle" (p. 46). Do you agree or disagree with this statement? Why?*

inspected as opposed to unregulated. Caregivers themselves feel, and are perceived by parents as, more professional and less that "I'm just a babysitter."

Licensing

Licensing is more extensive and rigorous than registration. It most frequently applies to group day-care programs. A licensing system includes:

- Set minimum legislated requirements or standards

- Monitoring of programs for continued compliance

- Enforcement of requirements and penalties for non-compliance.

Standards set for licensing are higher than for registration (e.g., more education is required for staff) and the standards typically include more areas (e.g., programming, daily schedule, evaluation, etc.). However, licensing standards still represent a minimum acceptable level. Licensing standards vary across provinces and territories, especially in the areas of educator qualifications, educator-to-children ratios, and maximum group size (Jacobs, Mill, White, & Baillargeon, 1999).

Provincial/territorial governments are frequently criticized for setting their licensing standards too low. According to Friendly (1994), none of the provincial/territorial standards for day care meet the recommendations of experts and professional organizations for high-quality programs. Research on quality early childhood programs has found that higher-quality early childhood programs are more likely if the minimum standards set are higher rather than lower (see Friendly, 1994).

Establishing regulations and licensing procedures is a political process and therefore is subject to all the pressures, lobbying, negotiating, and compromising for which the political process is known. Some current political pressures on legislators and policy-makers are to provide more spaces, to control costs, and to keep constituents happy. A common pressure point is to lower the standards. For example, because the biggest budget item for an early childhood program is salaries, if the educator-to-children ratio is changed so that more children (i.e., more fees) can be admitted to a program with no additional staff hired, the program will be better off financially. On the other hand, if the standards are changed so that the maximum number of children allowable in a family day care will be reduced by one child, this will reduce a caregiver's income and he or she is likely to complain and perhaps lobby provincial/territorial legislator. However, it is important to note that many programs exceed registration or licensing standards and support high standards.

Initial licensing procedures are more comprehensive and take longer than registration. They may also require approval from other agencies, such as municipal fire inspection and zoning authorities.

Monitoring is essential for accountability. Families and the public need to be assured that once a program is given a licence, it must continue to meet or exceed licensing standards. Some factors that influence the overall effectiveness of monitoring can be

- The agency responsible for monitoring

- The frequency of inspections

- Unannounced rather than pre-scheduled visits

- The background and education of the inspectors and their total caseloads

- Whether the monitoring includes support and professional development.

(Corsini, Wisendale, & Caruso, 1988)

For example, an hour-long visit by an inspector once a year is not adequate to thoroughly understand or assess a program. Any visit, by inspectors or parents, is only one snapshot. One cannot be certain whether this is a typical day, especially if the visit was scheduled in advance.

Another type of quality control is parents being able to drop in unannounced whenever they wish. My policy was that parents could come whenever they wished, and if we were not at the centre or in the classroom (e.g., on a walk, at the park, on a field trip, etc.), there would be a note on the door and parents were welcome to join us wherever we were.

Stated explicitly in licensing legislation is that just as licences can be granted they also can be removed for cause. Enforcement and penalties for non-compliance are important components of a licensing system if the system and the inspections are to be seen as credible by educators, families, and the community. However, the removal of a licence is often a long and expensive process subject to appeals at numerous stages.

Licensing is also usually time-limited. The licence is valid for a specific period of time and can be renewed subject to satisfactory periodic inspections by licensing officers and no proven complaints against the program or staff.

Credentialing

Credentialing (or certification) can be thought of as licensing educators, not programs. It has a long history in public schools for teachers as well as in other professions such as medicine, engineering, social work, and some trades.

Credentialing is another frequently suggested policy to improve program quality (e.g., Grubb, 1991). Requirements for credentialing typically include education, experience, and personal attributes.

As with licences granted to programs, a certificate or credential is typically renewable and can be withdrawn for cause. Renewal usually requires continued work in the profession and/or completion of some type of professional development.

Issues include the trend of increasing credentialing requirements by provincial/territorial governments while cutting funding of post-secondary institutions that are expected to provide formal education in early childhood education and care. Another issue that is raised by many individuals trying to get a credential is the lack of provision for previous experience and the difficulty of getting equivalency for education done in other provinces or countries.

FOR REFLECTION

Should everyone who works with young children be required to have a credential? What are some possible arguments against or limitations of credentialing? Should there be differential certification for educators who want to work with children with special needs? Some people will say no, because "all children are the same." Others, such as the Division of Early Childhood of the Council for Exceptional Children, say there should be differential certification (McCollum, McLean, McCartan, & Kaiser, 1989).

Accreditation

Accreditation is also a type of quality control. The term *accreditation* is familiar from its use in post-secondary institutions, hospitals, and public and private schools. It is also applicable for early childhood programs. Accreditation builds on existing regulations and licensing. However, it goes beyond what is required for licensing. Accreditation sets higher standards than does licensing and therefore can help identify early childhood programs that are significantly above the basic requirements of licensing. It does this by focusing on the way a program actually functions (Brennan, 1998). It assesses many of the more subtle areas of a program that licensing does not.

Unlike licensing, accreditation is owned and administered by a profession. An early childhood program seeks accreditation and, if successful, receives a "seal of approval" from a recognized professional body. This, in turn, conveys "images of professionalism and educational achievement" (Stoney, 1996, p. 116). It is a type of external accountability and helps to improve not only the image of the accredited program, but also the image of the profession. In addition, it helps parents in selecting programs.

There are usually three major steps in the accreditation process:

1. Self-study by the program.

2. Validation by an external peer evaluator.

3. An accreditation decision by a professional body.

The self-study component is often seen as the most valuable by programs. It is a formative evaluation where the staff members of a program carefully examine their own program (i.e., self evaluation) using guidelines or criteria provided by the accrediting body. According to a position statement on accreditation by the NAEYC (1999), "accreditation can be a very powerful program-improvement tool because it provides a process by which professionals and families can evaluate programs in relation to professional standards and identify areas needing improvement" (p. 37).

The staff members decide what aspects of the program meet the guidelines and what aspects need to be improved before formal accreditation can be sought. Once the improvements have been made and the staff members are satisfied with the state of the program, a report is prepared documenting why and how the program meets the accreditation criteria. This report is submitted to the accrediting body.

In a survey of accredited early childhood programs, directors of programs reported that they initially sought accreditation as validation that their program was a good program as well as to increase the visibility and marketability of the program (Herr, Johnson, & Zimmerman, 1993). The directors reported that the **self-study** component was especially beneficial and the areas most typically improved as a result of the self-study were curriculum, administration (e.g., development of written policies and program handbooks), and health and safety (especially in the outdoor environment).

The next stage in accreditation is **validation**. The accrediting body reviews the report, and if everything is in order an external validator is assigned. A trained validator, who is an early childhood educator and has likely been a director of a program, does an on-site evaluation visit to verify the accuracy and completeness of the submitted materials. A trained validator can also be a source of advice and suggestions for program improvement.

The validator then makes a report to the accrediting body including a recommendation about granting or not granting accreditation. If the recommendation is to *not* grant accreditation, this report will include specifics about what areas of the program need to be improved.

The next step is the decision of the accrediting body to either grant or withhold accreditation. Accreditation is usually granted for a specific period, at the end of which the program applies for reaccreditation. There are usually provisions for appealing negative decisions. Accreditation is meant to be an ongoing process of continual improvement and renewal.

The world's largest accreditation system for early childhood programs in centres and schools was developed by the National Association for the Education of Young Children (1998b). It was begun in 1981 and after four years of development an extensive set of guidelines was published. These guidelines were revised in 1998 and published as *Accreditation Criteria and Procedures of the National Association of Young Children* (1998b). The criteria are divided into ten areas:

- Interaction among Teachers and Children

- Curriculum

- Relationships among Teachers and Families

- Staff Qualifications and Professional Development

- Administration

- Staffing

- Physical Environment

- Health and Safety

- Nutrition and Food Services

- Evaluation.

For each area specific items are listed. For example:

- Physical Environment: "Private areas are available indoors and outdoors for children to have solitude" (p. 51).

- Interactions among Teachers and Children: "The sound of the environment is primarily marked by pleasant conversation, spontaneous laughter, and exclamations of excitement rather than harsh, stressful noise or enforced quiet" (p. 20).

- Curriculum: "The program has written curriculum plans based on knowledge of child development and learning, and assessment of individual needs and interests. The learning environment and activities for children reflect the program's philosophy and goals" (pp. 22–23).

In the NAEYC accreditation system, an early childhood program completes the self-study component using the *Guide to Accreditation by the National Academy of Early Childhood Programs* (NAEYC, 1991) and submits the results on the three-part Program Description rating scale (i.e., Center Profile, Results of Classroom Observation, and Results of Administrator Report).

Validators in the NAEYC system are approved and trained by NAEYC and are early childhood professionals living not more than 160 km from the program. A validation visit takes between one and two days and may include one to three validators, depending on the total size of the program. The final decision is made by a commission of three early childhood professionals. Accreditation is valid for three years and the program must submit annual reports.

According to Kagan and Neuman (1997), "research indicates that accreditation—a voluntary process of self-assessment—significantly raises program quality" (p. 55). Other research studies have found that accredited early childhood programs scored higher on global measures of quality than non-accredited programs (e.g., Bloom, 1996; Bredekamp & Willer, 1996; Cryer & Phillipsen, 1997; Whitebook, 1996).

A limitation of accreditation for promoting quality is that not everyone participates. Only approximately five percent of any profession will pursue voluntary accreditation (Bredekamp, 1999). Some of the reasons why programs do not or cannot undertake accreditation are

- Lack of time

- Program deficiencies and cost to remediate these deficiencies

- Level of staff does not meet accreditation criteria

- High staff turnover

- Staff resistance (e.g., anxiety, feeling threatened)

- Lack of staff agreement on goals and program direction

- Ineffective director of the early childhood program.

(Bredekamp, 1999; Harris, Morgan, & Sprague, 1996)

One central issue in the accreditation of early childhood programs is how the criteria were developed and how culturally appropriate they are. This is the same concern as for licensing. Also, as the NAEYC criteria are closely tied to the association's statement on developmentally appropriate practice, many of the concerns about DAP apply to the accreditation criteria as well. For example, as Cunningham (1996) observes, "the question of the cultural appropriateness of the whole accreditation system, and specifically developmentally appropriate practice, has been raised in many communities" (p. 81).

Another interesting issue has surfaced in Australia that raises the question of how voluntary accreditation really is or should be. The government of Australia has linked government subsidies (i.e., funding) to accreditation (Bredekamp, 1999; Brennan, 1998). There is concern among educators that the government has turned accreditation into a de facto higher second level of licensing, but has a professional body do the "higher licensing" work of the government.

Thus, while accreditation can be a component in improving the quality of early childhood programs, it is not the total answer. Barnett (1996) predicts that, "accreditation will be most successful if it is developed in the context of a comprehensive strategy for increasing awareness of the importance of quality, shaping professional development, increasing public funding for ECE, and increasing government support for accreditation" (p. 161). Quality is a combination of many factors. It is an important, complex, and much-discussed and debated concept. However, as the poster quoted at the beginning of the chapter stated, quality does matter—a lot.

Summary of this Chapter

The key themes in this chapter are that:

- High-quality early childhood programs and how to provide these is a central concern in contemporary early childhood education and care.

- A universally accepted definition of quality does not, and probably cannot, exist. A definition of quality is influenced by individuals' views and experiences, as well as cultural, theoretical, and historical contexts.

- Some generally accepted factors found in high-quality early childhood programs include ratios, group size, children–educator relationships, educators' qualifications, health and safety, working and physical environments, and interaction between families and programs.

- Responsibility for and policies about children and families in Canada are often seen as fragmented and patchwork. There are overlapping, gapping, and contradictory roles and policies. The federal government has recently proposed a National Children's Agenda.

- Developmentally appropriate practice, as set forth by NAEYC, is very influential in the field of early childhood education and care. However, DAP has been criticized for its definition, content, theoretical base, and use. Early childhood educators need to be knowledgeable about the content, possible applications, and criticisms of DAP.

- The integration of early childhood programs and other programs and services for young children and their families has been suggested as one way of reducing fragmentation. Some possible options include more attention and consideration by programs to promoting continuity between programs; co-locating programs on the same site; and implementing neighbourhood, full-service-school, or hub/satellite models.

- Registration, licensing, credentialing, and accreditation can all positively influence the quality of early childhood programs. However, all have their specific strengths and limitations.

Key Terms

accreditation, 503

contextual factors, 479

credentialing, 502

density, 481

developmentally appropriate practice, 491

dynamic process factors, 478

global assessment, 483

group size, 476

interactive factors, 482

licensing, 501

registration, 500

self-study, 503

structural factors, 474

validation, 504

Resources

For more information on quality and policy, you could try:

Doherty-Derkowski, G. 1995. *Quality matters: Excellence in early childhood programs*. Don Mills, ON: Addison-Wesley Publishers. Comprehensive overview; good review of the research.

Phillips, D. A. (Ed.). 1987. *Quality child care: What does research tell us?* Washington, DC: National Association for the Education of Young Children. Examines this question carefully but doesn't give a definitive answer.

Wien, C.A. 1995. *Developmentally appropriate practice in 'real life': Stories of teacher practical knowledge*. New York: Teachers College Press. The application of DAP.

Hart, C.H., Burts, D.C., & Charlesworth, R. 1997. *Integrated curriculum and developmentally appropriate practice*. Albany: State University on New York Press. DAP applied to specific curriculum areas.

Friendly, M. 1994. *Child care policy in Canada: Putting the pieces together.* Don Mills, ON: Addison-Wesley Publishers. Aptly titled book; a good reference.

Canadian Child Care Federation. 1991. *National statement on quality child care.* Ottawa: Author. Should be required reading for all early childhood educators in Canada. (See Resources in Chapter 4 for address.)

 ## Some Useful Organizations and their Web Sites

For a wealth of readily accessible information, and an especially useful source for statistics and policy-related information:

Childcare Resource and Research Unit
Centre for Urban and Community Studies
University of Toronto
455 Spadina Avenue, Room 305
Toronto, ON M5S 2G8
Telephone: 416-978-6895
Fax: 416-971-2139
E-mail: crru@chass.utoronto.ca
Web site: www.childcarecanada.org

Halidimand-Norfolk R.E.A.C.H.
101 Nanticoke Creek Parkway
PO Box 5054
Townsend, ON N0A 1S0
Telephone: 519-587-2441 or 905-772-3418
Fax: 519-587-4798
E-mail: hnreach@nornet.on.ca
Web site: www.hnreach.on.ca

The National Association for the Education of Young Children (see Resources in Chapter 4) has materials on developmentally appropriate practice and NAEYC's accreditation materials. Also brochures and other publications on DAP. Current position statements by NAEYC on a variety of topics are available on their Web site, www.naeyc.org. Their catalogue of publications is on-line.

13

Current Issues and Future Directions in Early Childhood Education and Care

As for the future, your task is not to foresee, but to enable it.
—*Antoine de Saint Exupéry,* The Wisdom of the Sands *(translated by Stuart Gilbert)*

It seems appropriate to end a book finished in the first year of a new millennium with a look at future directions. As a new century stretches ahead of us, it is a natural time for reexamination, reflection, and hopefully renewed energy and inspiration. It is particularly appropriate in a book for early childhood educators. We are made aware of the responsibility to and for the next generation every day we work with young children and their families. What better place to begin looking at future directions than from early childhood education and care? The theme of the National Association for the Education of Young Children's 1999 Week of the Child could be the theme for this final chapter—Early Childhood: Where Our Future Begins.

The purpose of this chapter is to review and synthesize some of the themes from previous chapters and to discuss some possible future directions for early childhood education and care. However, it is not possible to predict the future. There are too many variables, contexts, and unforeseeable changes and events that will influence what happens in early childhood education and care in the next five years, much less the next 50 years. In addition, trends tend to interact with and influence each other. For example, the need for infant care combined with the recent research on infant development (see Chapter 2) in turn leads to more awareness and attention to the needs of infants, including care issues. Nevertheless, reflecting on where we are now can help us identify ideas, wishes, and possible actions for future directions. A useful perspective is to look back, while looking around, while looking forward. Some say that early childhood education and care is at a crossroads in Canada (e.g., Howe, 2000). It may be that early childhood education and care is always at a crossroads, if we can only read the signs.

Here are some questions to think about as you read this chapter:

- How is the past a prologue to early childhood education and care today, and how is today a prologue to the future?
- What do you think are the most significant and urgent issues facing Canadian children, families, and early childhood educators today?
- Which of these issues are likely to continue into the future?
- What can we learn from early childhood education and care in other countries?
- What do you think early childhood education and care will be like 20 years from now?
- What would you like to see early childhood education and care be 20 years from now?

The Present into the Future

Many themes from the previous chapters have important implications for future directions in early childhood education and care in Canada. These themes bridge the present and the future and sometimes the past as well. For example, two themes introduced in Chapters 2 and 3 are change and diversity. Change is one theme that bridges the past to the present and the present to the future. Two themes found in Chapters 8 through 12 are quality and the need for a variety of programs for young children and their families. Another theme that runs through many chapters is the importance of and the many varied roles of early childhood educators. While Chapter 1 presents an overview of early childhood education and care today, Chapters 5, 6, and 7 examine the theme of development and change in early childhood education and care from ancient times to the present. These chapters also have the theme of what early childhood education and care should be, its purpose, the theories that support it, and how these are translated into practice. Several omnibus themes throughout the previous dozen chapters are diversity, continuity, flexibility, and variety.

All of the above themes have implications for future directions in early childhood education and care. These themes and some of the issues associated with them will be examined in this chapter. In addition, this chapter has an international early childhood focus. Early childhood education and care has a long international history (e.g., the spread of kindergarten described in Chapters 5 and 10). One of the most significant characteristics of today's society is an increasingly global perspective. In early childhood education and care this means that we have more knowledge about and easier access to information about early childhood programs and issues throughout the world, as well as more communication with other early childhood educators through electronic media. There is much we can share and much we can learn from others, both in Canada and internationally. My life, both professionally and personally, has been greatly enriched by the many early childhood educators I have met and the early childhood programs I have seen in many countries. (As an aside, this chapter was written in Canada, Indonesia, and Singapore.)

Most of the international examples in this chapter are from my own observation and experience. Thus, it is necessary for you to keep in mind that these are my impressions and are therefore of limited generalizability. In addition, there is variation within countries as well as across countries. Canada is an example of this: An early childhood educator from another country visiting Toronto can see many early childhood programs and meet many early childhood educators. While some of the information and observations from these programs may be applicable to other programs in Toronto, Ontario, and Canada, the educator cannot generalize that early childhood education and care in the rest of Canada is the same as it is in Toronto.

Change

If one wished to try to predict the future for early childhood education, perhaps the only safe prediction would be this: There will be changes. Early childhood education and care has changed over time (see Chapter 5), as have concepts about children and childhood (Chapter 2), the demographics of families (Chapter 3), and the issues confronting Canadian society. For example, think of the changes you've seen in the development and use of technology just in your lifetime.

One of the reasons there has been so much emphasis placed on demographics in recent years—besides the fact that it is interesting to learn more about ourselves—is that it is prediction with a fair amount of certainty. For example, it is known how many people there are at each age in Canada. Therefore, predicting that the current large cohort of baby boomers will make up a large and influential group of seniors in the early twenty-first century is not much of a speculation.

The implications of demographic trends in Canada, as discussed in Chapters 2 and 3, are not necessarily the same internationally. For example, a Canadian response to the current low birth rate was Quebec's past use of additional baby bonuses to try to increase the number of children (unsuccessfully). Japan's response to its historically low birth rate has been for the government and employers to launch initiatives including baby bonuses, flexible working hours, family leave, more early childhood programs, increased family allowance, and extended hours for early childhood programs (Sims, 2000). On the other hand, many other countries are concerned about high birth rates (e.g., parts of Asia and Africa). China's draconian one-child policy has not been successful either (Pomfret, 2000).

One successful effort to reverse a trend that is affecting children negatively has been the international effort to increase immunization of children in all

Media and technology in early childhood education and care are discussed later in this chapter.

FOR REFLECTION

What demographic trends discussed so far in this book do you think are the most significant for early childhood education and care today? Why?

parts of the world. Due to the concerted and coordinated efforts of individual countries, governments, and non-government and private organizations, millions of children have been immunized against six major childhood diseases that can be fatal (i.e., measles, tetanus, whooping cough, diphtheria, tuberculosis, and polio). Deaths "have been slashed by 3 million a year, and at least 750,000 fewer children are left blind, paralysed or mentally disabled"; this has been hailed as "the greatest public health success story in history" (Henderson, 1998, p. 13). However, the effort is not completed; malaria and AIDS are still major killers of young children. For example, 3.8 million children have died of AIDS, 480,000 in 1999 alone. In addition, 13.2 million have been orphaned by AIDS and 1.3 million are living with HIV/AIDS (Masland, 2000). By 2010, estimates of the number of children who will have been orphaned by AIDS range from 40 to 100 million (Picard, 2000). This epidemic has been particularly bad in sub-Saharan Africa and is gaining in parts of Asia.

Continuity

Continuity is a theme in many areas of early childhood education and care: continuity for children from home to an early childhood program and from one early childhood program to another (Chapters 9 and 10), for early childhood educators (Chapter 4), for programs (Chapter 11), for curriculum (Chapter 6), and for program policy and regulation (Chapter 12). Continuity for children (a) between home and early childhood programs and (b) between early childhood programs is examined from a focus on young children in Chapters 9 and 10. The issue of professional continuity, including career ladders and coordinated professional educational opportunities, is discussed in Chapter 4. Therefore this section will focus on curricular, program, and system-wide continuity.

Kagan (1991) has identified three distinct, although interactive, aspects of continuity: philosophical, pedagogical, and structural. **Philosophical continuity** refers to the values and beliefs of the participants in early childhood programs. Given the diversity of Canadian society and the variety of early childhood programs, it is not realistic to expect a common philosophy. Indeed, early childhood education and care has historically been enriched by the intersection and interaction of various disciplines, theories, and philosophies (see Chapters 5 and 6). However, differences in basic beliefs and practices can make continuity difficult. For example, a child from a home where children are supposed to be seen and not heard may have a difficult time making the transition to an early childhood program that has a strong emphasis on oral language and active verbal participation in group activities.

Pedagogical continuity builds on philosophy. As seen in Chapter 6, the theoretical base of a model determines, in great part, what the curriculum is and what the program looks like. More needs to be done to match individual children with curriculum and instructional strategies that are most appropriate for them, rather than expecting all young children to accommodate themselves to the same curriculum and instructional strategies. For example, continuity is likely to be an issue for a young child who goes from an unstructured, discovery-oriented kindergarten into a highly structured grade 1.

Structural continuity includes aspects such as regulations, auspice, funding, bureaucracy, and policy (Kagan, 1991). This is the property of continuity that is currently much discussed and debated. If you read analyses of policy for early childhood education and care in Canada today, you'll frequently see descriptors such as "fragmented," "disorganized," "incoherent," "tangled," and "patchwork" (see Chapter 12). Canada is not the only country in this situation.

In a comparison of programs in Canada, the United Kingdom, the United States, and Australia, Lero (2000) concluded there was "a lack of systemic planning and policy development and a lack of funding and political will that has resulted in uncoordinated programs of variable quality" (p. 445). Lack of coordination and communication results in structural discontinuity in many other countries as well. For example, Evans has commented that in many countries "it is not uncommon for parallel programmes to be developed in one community, each addressing a particular need of the child without reference to other needs that may or may not be met" (1997, [on-line]).

Key questions in the discussion on continuity are, How are early childhood programs and services linked together with one another and with other related programs? and, Who should be responsible—the federal government, provincial/territorial government, local government, or other agencies? An early childhood program in Canada may have involvement with several of these. For example, an early childhood program on a First Nations reserve may receive funding from the federal government, be licensed by the provincial government, and receive subsidies through a local government agency.

I have usually found that the main concern of early childhood educators is not necessarily what group is responsible, or even if there are multiple administrative groups, as long as it is a seamless system that works efficiently with a minimum of bureaucratic hassle and red tape. An international example of a system involving multiple layers that is integrated and promotes continuity is Denmark (see Focus 13.1).

It is interesting that while many people in Canada are calling for a national policy for young children and families, as well as more control and regulation by the federal government in order to create a system that is more coherent and operates more smoothly, some early childhood educators in other countries with centrally administered systems are calling for more regional or local control. For example, many early childhood educators that I have talked with from the People's Republic of China have expressed the view that because their country is so large and diverse, it has not been possible to efficiently and effectively set policies and practices that are appropriate for all early childhood programs in all parts of the country. They would prefer more regional or local control. Moreover, Cochran (1993) has cautioned that centralization and concentration of decision-making in a central bureaucracy "is very likely to lead to dense bureaucracy and institutional rigidity" (p. 638).

FOR REFLECTION

According to Cochran (1993) in his analysis of policies and practices from 29 countries, there was "general support" for national regulations for factors such as ratios, group size, and educator qualifications (the structural factors of quality discussed in Chapter 12), but also "growing sentiment" for local decision-making with parental input for program content (p. 638). Do you think this statement could be made for Canada?

Early Childhood Education and Care in Denmark

Denmark's comprehensive and integrated approach to early childhood education and care is often given as an example of what Canada or other countries should emulate. Children and families have long been a priority of Danish (and Scandinavian) society. Denmark has a very high level of provision for quality early childhood programs (Kamerman, 1994; Polakow, 1997). It is also an example of a fully integrated system of programs and services for children from birth to 18 and their families (Moss, 1996). Danish laws and policies on children and families have evolved over the past 25 years; there has been no specific national child and family policy set forth.

Briefly, the Danish system includes generous maternity and paternity leaves, a shorter work week for parents of young children, full-time early childhood programs for children from birth to school-age, extensive school-age programs, child allowances (extra in special cases), home-visiting nurses, recreation programs, supervised and supported family day homes, cooperative programs, summer/holiday programs, adventure playgrounds, environmental centres ("forest kindergartens"), and other programs. Most of these programs are located in neighbourhoods in order to emphasize the link between home and programs as well as for the convenience of families (Jensen, 1994).

The Danish system is considered a decentralized one as relatively little decision-making rests at the federal levels and most is at the local, and especially program, levels (i.e., a bottom-up approach). There are very few rules and regulations (i.e., structural factors) established by the central governments (Jensen, 1994; Lowe, 2000). The Ministry of Social Welfare sets only a few broad curricular guidelines and then educators and parents can develop programs to fit their needs and wishes (Penn, 1999). There is

A Danish school-age centre

Margie I. Mayfield

also no national curriculum in the elementary schools, only general guidelines that are interpreted by local schools. This is a major reason for the variety of curriculum and programs found in Danish early childhood programs (e.g., Reggio-Emilia, Montessori, Waldorf, environmental emphasis, etc.). In day-care centres, a parent committee is responsible for the program and policies as well as the quality of the program. Primary school begins at age six and is under the jurisdiction of the Ministry of Education.

One of the reasons generally cited for why this decentralized model works well in Denmark is the quality of the professional education for early childhood educators (Jensen, 1994; Langsted & Sommer, 1993). Basic training at a college is now 3.5 years. In addition, there is a strong tradition of ongoing in-service and professional development (Birkvad, 1997).

I visited early childhood programs and talked with early childhood educators in Hungary and the Czech Republic after the collapse of their highly centralized Communist governments. These educators told me that they really had mixed feelings about the change to a less centralized system: on the one hand, they liked being able to make more decisions for their own programs, especially in program and curriculum content; on the other hand, they found this frightening and difficult, as none of their professional education had prepared them for these tasks (Mayfield, 1997; 1998).

Clarity

The theme of **clarity** can be seen in the purposes of a program, roles of early childhood educators, or one's personal vision of early childhood education and care. This concept refers to how clearly one knows what one is doing, why, and how everyone fits into the larger context. Caldwell (1989) states that "those concerned with early childhood programs should be aware of the way in which theory, knowledge, and social relevance are melded in the past and present" (p. xi). I would also add, "and be able to articulate this to families, community members, policy-makers, politicians, and others."

The multiple and varied roles of the early childhood educator are discussed in Chapter 4 as well as the chapters on specific types of programs (see Chapters 8–11). It is essential for early childhood educators to have and convey clarity about their roles and the roles of others in specific programs and to recognize that these roles can change from program to program.

A clarity issue applicable to many early childhood programs is mission clutter. The term **mission clutter**, originally used by business and the military, means "doing too many tasks and playing too many roles to be effective" (DeCicco & Allison, 1999, p. 274). Mission clutter is a particular danger for early childhood programs, with their multidisciplinary orientation, ecological focus, and commitment to the development of the whole child. An example of mission clutter is the statement of goals or purposes written out by many early childhood programs. While writing down and sharing these goals with families and others is a recognized practice in early childhood education and care, one needs to examine these goals and purposes and, specifically, their number and scope. I've seen lists that go on for several pages and could not all be accomplished in 10 years, much less one. For a profession that has traditionally been grounded in developmental theory, it is ironic that there is sometimes a tendency to try to "do it all now." We are so committed to the importance of the early years that we sometimes forget that a child has many more years for development after these early years. We don't need to try to do or teach everything before age nine.

Diversity and Variety

Another theme in early childhood education and care is diversity and variety. Our field has been characterized by diversity for a long time (see Chapters 8–11). This diversity and variety can be seen in participants, program types and organization, curriculum, sponsors, and other aspects.

The diversity of today's families is discussed in Chapters 2 and 3. This diversity owes much to immigration. Canada is becoming more dependent on immigration to maintain its current population level. In fact, Statistics Canada projections are that by 2030, "immigration will be Canada's only source of population growth" (Chui, 1996, p. 5). Therefore, the multicultural, multi-ethnic, multiracial nature of Canadian society will increase.

Diversity of participants in early childhood programs in many other countries has also increased due to immigration or large refugee movements. For example, when I was visiting early childhood programs in Sweden, I noticed many more children from other countries than I had a few years previously. The early childhood educators confirmed my impressions. An example of how these children are being accommodated by the Swedish system is the Turkish teacher I met while I was there who arrived at one centre to work with four Turkish children who had recently arrived in Sweden. She said her task was to help the children further develop their first language of Turkish. Large movements of people, such as those fleeing the warfare in parts of Africa, can change the demographics of host countries and influence programs for young children and their families.

Another aspect of the diversity of participants is age. Participants in early childhood programs can range in age from babies a few weeks old to seniors in their nineties. The inclusion of a wide range of ages reflects the current composition of Canadian society. The diversity of participants in Canadian early childhood programs is illustrated in the examples of programs given in previous chapters.

The theme of diversity is also seen in the variety of early childhood programs. There are more types of early childhood programs today than at any time

A related topic, hurried children, is discussed in Chapter 2.

The implications of immigration and diversity for early childhood programs are discussed in previous chapters.

FOR REFLECTION

Does diversity get too much attention and emphasis in early childhood education and care? Should the central focus be on improving the lives of all children and families, rather than diversity (Washington & Andrews, 1999)?

in the past in Canada. This proliferation of programs has meant not only more options, but improved potential for a better "match" between the needs and wishes of families and programs. However, some have argued that the growth of variety and diversity can lead to a lack of coordination and integration of programs and services for young children and their families.

Early childhood programs reflect their own country's historical, cultural, social, political, and economic contexts. Early childhood programs and educators exist and function in multiple contexts simultaneously. These contexts contribute to diversity across countries and variety in early childhood programs. For example, even programs that are based on the same model, such as Montessori, will still be somewhat different from one country to another or from one time to another. Historical context helps explain why kindergarten is a program for five-year-olds in Canada and the United States (with, sometimes, junior kindergartens for four-year-olds), while in other countries kindergarten refers to full-day programs for children from ages three to six (e.g., China).

Economic context can have a powerful effect on early childhood programs. For example, in Venezuela development and expansion of early childhood programs has depended heavily on the country's oil revenues. I have been to Venezuela in times of economic boom and corresponding expansion of programs for young children and families, as well as less economically prosperous times with reduction in government funding for early childhood programs.

The political context, especially the prevailing ideology, is reflected in early childhood programs. For example, some countries value diversity more than others; there is more conformity in totalitarian systems than in democracies. In addition, political changes can also affect early childhood programs. In Canada in recent years, a pattern has been for political parties to propose programs to meet the needs of young children and families as part of its election campaign, only to put these promises on hold after being elected. In other countries, political changes have had dramatic effects on early childhood programs (e.g., the collapse of Communist governments in Eastern Europe and of apartheid in South Africa).

It is necessary to investigate a country's historical, social, political, economic, political, and cultural contexts in order to understand why a practice that would not be permitted in one country may be seen as acceptable, and even desirable, in another country. For example, China has many boarding kindergartens where children from ages three to six spend typically 24 hours a day, five-and-a-half or six days a week.

This model originated during the Communist Revolution in the 1940s. I once met the woman who had been responsible for kindergartens when the Communist army was based in the mountains near Xian. I met her many years later, when she was director of a boarding kindergarten in Xian (it recently celebrated its fiftieth anniversary and is no longer a boarding kindergarten). There was a great increase in the number of boarding kindergartens during the Cultural Revolution (1966–1976) to provide care for the children of soldiers in the People's Liberation Army, party leaders, and parents from urban areas who had been assigned to work in the countryside (Tobin, Wu, & Davidson, 1989).

Various reasons are given by Chinese educators today for the use of a boarding school model for very young children, including parents living or studying abroad, parents' work schedules, or, according to one director I interviewed, "because they [the parents] are so busy with their work, they don't have time to be at home with their children" (Mayfield, 1994, p. 28). However, the popularity of boarding kindergartens seems to be declining in recent years, due, in part, to increased recognition by educators and parents that, "'young children need more love and attention of their mothers between the ages of three and six and therefore, a day program is better' according to one kindergarten director" (p. 29).

Today, there is variety in the sponsors and auspices of early childhood programs in Canada. Whereas the early programs were sponsored primarily by charities and philanthropic organizations and individuals, today's sponsors are more diverse. These include the public sector, charitable organizations, First Nations bands, employers, individuals, non-profit societies, franchises, and others. On the other hand, in Communist countries, the sponsor of early childhood programs was historically the state or a state-controlled organization such as workers' groups. In Eastern Europe, the variety of sponsors and auspices has increased since the collapse of the Communist governments, resulting in more variety of programs and program philosophies.

While there seems to be much diversity and variety, at least on the surface, some educators speculate whether this is really so. For example, Dahlberg, Moss, and Pence (1999) question that, although there seems to be more diversity in *discussions* about early childhood education, this may not actually be the reality. They attribute this to the current pervasiveness and dominance of North American (English-language) curricular and program concepts such as developmentally appropriate practice, cost-effectiveness, and regulation standards.

Flexibility and Adaptability

One of the strengths of many types of early childhood programs is their flexibility and adaptability. This can be seen particularly clearly in the grassroots-initiated family support programs described in Chapter 11. Early childhood programs need to be adaptable and modifiable, as there is no "one size fits all" model program or curriculum.

A countervailing tendency of early childhood educators to variety seems to be the eternal quest for The One Way or The Best Program (or curriculum, instructional strategy, or materials). As Jalongo (1999) observes, "the assumption is that there is one, right answer and that it is our job as educators to perpetually seek it" (p. 12). While it is important to be open to new ideas, it is essential to be reflective and not to succumb to faddism or the lure of a bandwagon or a deceptively simple solution.

While flexibility has long been a key feature of family support programs, there is now a trend toward more flexibility in other types of programs as well; for example, day-care centres open for extended hours and on weekends, work-

Margie I. Mayfield

A dormitory for four-year-olds in a Chinese boarding Kindergarten

related programs for families, and including four-year-olds in public-school junior kindergartens.

Equity

Another theme in the latter half of the twentieth century has been the provision of and availability of early childhood programs for all children. However, this is not a twentieth-century idea; several of the early theorists in early childhood education and care believed in universal access to early education, often for religious reasons (see Chapter 5). An equity success story for early childhood education has been kindergarten. Public kindergarten is available in all but one province, and attendance in Canada is almost universal. The same cannot be said for other early childhood programs, such as centre-based day care.

Equity means equal access to early childhood programs for all young children and their families regardless of their background, origins, income level, gender, location, special needs, religion, or culture. In Canada, the law prohibits discrimination on most of these grounds. However, many educators would argue that the availability of programs for young children is not equitable. For example, there are parts of Canada where there are relatively few programs available despite identified need (e.g., rural and isolated areas). The availability of early childhood programs is also not equitable across countries. For example, in some European countries almost all three- and four-year-olds attend an early childhood program, while in other countries such programs are available only to a privileged few. Sometimes the way to get access to programs is to develop them, as was the case for the Mäori Te Köhanga Reo centres ("language nests") in New Zealand (see Focus 13.2).

Another issue is equal access. One dimension of equal access in Canada and other countries is the affordability of early childhood programs. A space in a program may be available, but a family may not be able to access it because they

---

Focus 13.2

Māori Te Kōhanga Reo in New Zealand

Māori children were seriously underrepresented in early childhood programs in New Zealand in 1982 when the first Te Kōhanga Reo centres were opened by the Department of Māori Affairs for the purpose of preserving the Māori language and culture (Smith, 1992). These centres have proved very popular and have improved access to early childhood programs for Māori children (birth to age five) and families: a 296-percent increase in enrollment in 10 years (Meade, 2000). There are more than 700 licensed Kōhanga Reo centres with more than 13,000 children (Government of New Zealand, 1998, [on-line]).

A Kōhanga Reo is a full- or half-day centre-based early childhood program based on the principle that Māori children need to be immersed in the Māori language, values, and culture from birth. Te Kōhanga Reo was originated as part of the Māori response to concern over the continuing survival of their language, which is seen as key to the continuation of their culture. The programs are administered by Te Kōhanga Reo National Trust, but each program is developed to meet local community needs and wishes. The relatively unstructured curriculum uses songs, games, storytelling, conversations, and movement activities including traditional dances. However, instruction in language is more structured and there is less free play than in other New Zealand early childhood programs (Smith, 1992). Educators (*kaiako*) in the Kōhanga Reo programs must be fluent Māori speakers and knowledgeable about Māori culture and traditions. Many of the *kaiako* are volunteers and elders (*kaumatua*).

The Kōhanga Reo model has been adapted for Pacific island language nests for children from the Pacific islands such as Samoa and the Cook Islands. In addition, Māori groups have established Kura Kaupapa Māori (i.e., Māori-philosophy elementary schools) to continue the philosophy and practices of Te Kōhanga Reo and to make the Māori language and culture central to curriculum, instruction, assessment, and administration (Corson, 1998). Like the Kōhanga Reo programs, these are open to non-Māoris.

---

cannot afford it. While families with limited incomes can usually obtain subsidies, and higher-income families can usually afford to pay the fees, it is often lower-income families (the "working poor"), who have too much income to qualify for subsidies but not enough to pay the fees, who are not able to access early childhood programs of their choice.

Equity is also an issue for early childhood educators working in day-care programs when they compare their salaries to early childhood educators working in public-school kindergartens. Many of these educators have similar educational backgrounds and experiences and perform similar tasks, yet their salaries are not similar. This has been an ongoing issue in our profession for a relatively long time with relatively little progress (see Chapter 4).

Another aspect of equity is a non-deficit focus. This is clearly seen in the family support programs described in Chapter 11 that target all families, not just low-income families or families in crisis or families with children with disabilities. Most federal and provincial/territorial family and child policies still reflect a deficit or crisis management orientation (i.e., programs are available only for families or children "with a problem," such as disabilities, low income, child abuse, etc.). This is a major difference of approach between Canada and countries such as Sweden, Germany, and Denmark, which make programs available to all families. A characteristic of these countries is the universality or near-universality of public-funded early childhood programs for all three- and four-year-olds. Part of the philosophy of Reggio Emilia (see Chapter 6) is that their early childhood programs are accessible and designed for all children in the community. Canada seems to be going in an opposite direction. As Lero (2000) has noted, "while current high-quality early childhood programs that already serve vulnerable children are experiencing funding cuts, there is increased interest in developing separate initiatives to provide primary prevention and intervention programs for children at risk" (p. 449).

Equity is also related to the decision of who provides programs. Is society responsible for all children, or only for some children? If it is only some children, then who is responsible for the rest? If those responsible are their families, what happens when a family cannot or does not provide? Kamerman (1991) has noted that, unlike North America, provision of programs for young children in European countries is viewed "as a public responsibility . . . and as an entitlement" (p. 194).

An equity issue for many countries is equitable access to early childhood programs for young children with disabilities. Although North America has been including children with special needs in early childhood programs for more than 20 years, this is a new idea in many countries. For example, toy libraries in Argentina have been trying to foster a non-clinical, non-medical approach to young children with disabilities and have included them in the programs offered by toy libraries in non-hospital settings.

When I visit early childhood programs in many countries and talk with other early educators, the issue of including special-needs children in regular programs is often raised, especially the question of how this is done. Canada and the United States are seen as leaders in this area, an area many countries have only recently begun to address.

FOR REFLECTION

What are the advantages and disadvantages of targeting early childhood programs for special groups compared to all children and families?

Quality and Quantity

This issue flows from the dilemma raised in the previous section: Should early childhood programs be equally available and accessible for all children and families? This question is especially problematic for many of the so-called "developing" countries with limited resources. The question of whether quantity should be emphasized more than quality is a real and pressing one.

(No one is saying that either is not important or desirable.) I have been told by educators from developing countries that philosophical discussions on quality are a luxury of Western industrialized countries that developing countries are not able to indulge in. For some countries, in other words, quantity is more heavily weighted than quality in the early stages of developing an early childhood education and care system. There is a tendency for quality to become the focus as the quantity of early childhood programs increases. However, world economic downturns can adversely affect both the quantity and the quality of early childhood programs. Thus, a concern of many early childhood programs is sustainability. Both quality and quantity depend on adequate and dependable resources.

In Western industrialized countries, the emphasis on quality, including how to define it, achieve it, and measure it (see Chapter 12), is part of what has been termed "the age of quality" (Dahlberg, Moss, & Pence, 1999, p. 4). Quality is not a simple concept. This age of quality has included debate over the appropriateness, utility, and desirability of guidelines or standards such as developmentally appropriate practice. A recent international symposium organized by the World Organization for Early Childhood Education (OMEP) and the Association for Childhood Education International (ACEI) (1999) attempted to "develop a set of basic international guidelines for programs serving the world's children under the age of formal school attendance" (p. 2). This type of activity extends the discussion and debate about what is quality and how it is defined and operationalized across countries as well as within individual countries.

Issues for the Future

The issues discussed in the following section are really present issues that extend into the future. These issues are technology, media, postmodernism, professional education, transferability and transportability of programs, and the need for information and research in early childhood education and care.

Technology

If one asked 100 people what is going to be an important trend for the twenty-first century, most of them would likely mention technology. The growth in the development and use of technology globally has been phenomenal. One can communicate today in a variety of ways that were not possible just a decade or two ago. For example, I am writing this section in Singapore and communicating with an editor in Toronto by fax and courier, an editor in Waterloo by telephone and fax, and my university by e-mail and fax. You've probably noticed that some of the references used in this book are from the Internet (i.e., the "on-line" references). Also, the Resource sections at the end of each chapter have suggestions for useful Web sites for further information. Technology is here to stay in our lives, but the question is, In what ways? A major question for

FOR REFLECTION

Do you think it is possible and practical to develop international guidelines for early childhood programs? What could be some uses for these guidelines? What are some difficulties associated with the development and use of such guidelines?

Lloyd Ollila

At what age should a child be introduced to computers?

parents and educators concerns what role technology should play in the lives of young children. Perhaps the part of technology currently most prominent for parents and educators of young children is the computer.

Statistics Canada has reported that 36 percent of Canadian households have at least one person using computers regularly (Dickinson & Ellison, 1999) in addition to the growing use of computer technology in schools. More than nine of every ten children in elementary, intermediate, and secondary schools in Canada have access to the Internet for educational purposes (Statistics Canada, 1999c). However, Statistics Canada has also cautioned that this does not mean maximal use of computers exists. Frequent obstacles are lack of computers and computer training for educators. There has been a push for further increasing student access to computers. For example, both the British Columbia and Ontario governments have stated that they want every school-age child to have access to a computer. In Singapore, the goal is a computer for every two children and 30 percent of the curriculum delivered via computers by 2002 (Cordingley, 2000). Computers and computer use are and will continue to be a growing educational reality.

The first question about computers that I am asked during talks to parent groups about young children's literacy development is, At what age should children start using a computer? The general consensus seems to be that computer use is not recommended for children under age three (Haugland, 1999). This is not because children under three cannot manipulate a keyboard or push command keys (see the photo above), but because of young children's need to learn through hands-on manipulation and experimentation. As Haugland has noted, "computers are not a good choice for the developmental skills these children are learning to master: crawling, walking, babbling, talking, toilet training and making friends, to name just a few" (p. 26). Also, not all young children are interested in learning about computers.

Another related question of parents and educators is, Will young children be at a disadvantage if they do not use computers? Computers are not essential to young children's development. Peers and adults to interact with and a rich environment to explore are essential. Computers may be part of this environment or they may not. A key point to keep in mind is that the real issue is how computers are used, rather than if they are used.

Selecting Computers

In selecting a computer for an early childhood program, it is important to determine how it will be used, by whom, and for what purposes. The software that will likely be used can also help determine what is needed (e.g., amount of memory). However, new software is published every day. The next step is to check with the local suppliers and see what they recommend. It is difficult to give specific suggestions because individual circumstances vary—plus there are such rapid advancements in this field that advice can be out of date almost as soon as it is given. Some general thoughts are that the computer should have as much memory as the purchaser can afford, as software is requiring more and more memory, and that it be upgradeable. A CD-ROM drive is useful as it enables more software options, and compact discs hold more information than diskettes. Young children like colour monitors and printers. In addition to initial costs, one needs to consider upkeep (e.g., printer cartridges), operating costs, and insurance. Repair and service are also items to think about, as computers in early childhood programs can get hard wear.

Consideration also needs to be given to where the computer will be used. In early childhood programs, computers are most typically set up as another learning or activity centre. This centre needs to be located near electrical and telephone connections (if the Internet is to be used by modem), away from noisy activity areas such as block play, and so the monitor and the children's activity can be seen easily for supervision by educators or volunteers. In addition, the physical security of the computer equipment needs to be planned for (e.g., prevention of theft and damage).

Selecting Software

There is a booming market in software developed for young children. Unfortunately, the quality of software varies greatly. And quality is more important than quantity, for both early childhood programs and children's homes. Research has shown that the software selected affects how often children use a computer and the benefits they derive from this use (Haugland & Shade, 1994.). You may ask other early childhood educators, parents, and children for their recommendations as well as read reviews and check Web sites.

Three areas for consideration in selecting software are:

- Child features (e.g., the software is child-friendly, interesting to children, usable, interactive, and educationally appropriate and worthwhile)

- Teacher features (e.g., teacher-friendly, usable, flexible, appropriate for the curriculum, reinforces values promoted by the program, and affordable)

- Technical features (e.g., aesthetically pleasing, technically appropriate for the hardware, and appropriate in speed and ease of installation) (Haugland & Shade, 1994).

For more specifics on evaluating software, see Focus 13.3.

The software selected has a major effect on how children benefit or do not benefit from using computers. Some possible benefits reported in the research include improved social skills, such as sharing and cooperation if used with other children; problem-solving; cognitive skills, such as seeing relationships; fine motor skills; eye–hand coordination; language development; and feelings of self-confidence and self-concept (see Wright & Shade, 1994). However, it is important to recognize that inappropriate software, hardware, and instructional practices can result in negative experiences for children. The NAEYC position statement on *Technology and Young Children—Ages Three through Eight* (1996b) states that:

> Although now there is considerable research that points to the positive effects of technology on children's learning and development . . . , the research indicates that, in practice, computers supplement and do not replace highly valued early childhood activities and materials, such as art, blocks, sand, water, books, exploration with writing materials, and dramatic play. (p. 11)

Some of the issues around computers in early childhood programs include:

- *Gender equity*—Use of computers by boys and girls is similar until about grade 4, when boys become the predominant users (Haugland, 2000). Two large international studies by IEA found that girls are less likely to say they enjoy computers, are less knowledgeable, and engage in fewer computer activities than boys. However, the gender of their educators did not make a difference in children's computer use (Brusselmans-Dehair & Henry, 1997). It was concluded that "the concern of many educational practition-ers over the gender inequity that computer use causes, or helps to preserve, is well-founded" (p. 17).

- *Accessibility*—Children from low-income homes or attending programs with limited budgets have less access to computers (Haugland, 2000; NAEYC, 1996). Therefore, it is important for educators to provide oppor-tunities and encouragement for *all* children to experience computers and not just those who are interested and proficient because they have com-puters at home. However, many young children's interest in computers waxes and wanes, especially after the initial novelty wears off; others are more steady users.

IEA and its research in early child-hood education and care are dis-cussed later in this chapter.

Focus 13.3

Checklist for Evaluating Software for Young Children

Child Features

Active Learning Emphasized ❑
Age Appropriate Concepts ❑
Child Controlled Interaction ❑
Child is Agent of Change ❑
Children Can Stop Anytime ❑
Children Set the Pace ❑
Child Uses Independently ❑
Concrete Representations ❑
Concrete Reps. Function ❑
Creativity (Divergent Thinking) ❑
Discovery Learning ❑
Engages Student Interest ❑
Experimentation Is Possible ❑
Intrinsically Motivating ❑
Logical Learning Sequence ❑
Low Entry, High Ceiling ❑
Not Skill Drilling ❑
Makes Learning Fun ❑
Models World Accurately ❑
Open-Ended ❑
Operate From Picture Menu ❑
Process Highlighter ❑
Process not Product Oriented ❑
Simple & Precise Directions ❑
Speech Used When Helpful ❑
Teaches Powerful Ideas ❑
Verbal Instructions & Help ❑

Teacher Features

Can be Customized ❑
Childproof ❑
Curriculum Congruence ❑
Delivers on Ad Promises ❑
High Educational Value ❑
High Value per Dollar ❑
Mixed Gender/Role Equity ❑
Mult. Languages Available ❑
Represents Differing Ability ❑
Represents Differing Ages ❑
Represents Alt. Family Styles ❑
Represents People of Color ❑
Supplemental to Curriculum ❑
Understandable Users Manual ❑
Universal Focus (all children) ❑

Name of the Program: _____

Publisher: _____

Special Skills or Scaffolding Required by Children: _____

Content Appropriate for Integration into My Curriculum: _____

Age Range Indicated on Box: _____ Child-Tested (yes/no): _____

This Program is Appropriate for My Students (yes/no): _____

This Program Contains Valuable Educational Concepts (yes/no): ____

This Program Contains Powerful Ideas and Concepts (yes/no): _____

Technical Features

Animation Other than Reward ❑
Aesthetically Pleasing ❑
Available on Mac & IBM ❑
Corresponding Sound Effects ❑
Corresponding Music ❑
Designed with Children in Mind ❑
Digitized Human Speech Used ❑
Easy Installation on Hard Drive ❑
Fast Installation and Set Up ❑
Max Use of Computer's Power ❑
No Gratuitous Music & Sounds ❑
Realistic Sound Effects/Music ❑
Realistic, High-Res Graphics ❑
Runs Quickly—Min. Waiting ❑
Speech is Clear and Distinct ❑

Notes:

The above checklist has been developed from the overviews of the various software evaluation methods reviewed in this chapter. No effort has been made to compute a score based upon this checklist. Rather it is intended that as a teacher fills out the checklist, s/he will come to a general decision about the appropriateness of the program. This form may be duplicated for personal and classroom use.

Source: Haugland & Shade, 1994, p. 74

- *Inappropriate Web sites and Internet content*—Supervision of children's use of computers is important; in addition, screening programs such as Net Nanny (www.netnanny.com), Kid Desk: Internet Safe, and Cyber Patrol (www.cyberpatrol.com) can be installed. Even though children prefer to explore and experiment with software programs (Griffiths, 1999), some formal instruction and ongoing support and supervision are essential. Children need to be taught that if anything scares, upsets, or makes them uncomfortable, they should close the program or Web site and tell an adult. Parents can be provided with a list of Web sites and software used in the early childhood program. Workshops can also be offered on choosing and using these at home.

- *Deception*—Software programs such as the Three CyberPigs series developed by Media Awareness Network (see Resources) can help children (ages 6–9) understand the manipulation effects of advertising on the Web and how to ensure privacy and safety in Internet use. Internet advertising targets children, parents, and educators. Computer and video games is a US$10-billion industry (Tapscott, 1998).

- *Pressure to have a computer*—Quite a few parents and educators have told me that they feel pressured to get a computer so their children will not be disadvantaged. They need to be reassured that this is not necessary.

- *Inappropriate use*—Computers are not intrinsically good or bad for young children; it depends on *how* they are used. One aspect of use—or misuse—is the amount of time a child spends at a computer. It is not only what the child is doing, but also what the child is *not* doing, such as playing with peers. (This is not to say that children cannot or do not interact with others, both children and adults, when using computers.) Overuse of computers can result in physical injury. For example, one Toronto clinic that specializes in the treatment of repetitive strain injuries (such as carpal tunnel damage caused by excessive computer use) has reported beginning to see children as young as eight with these problems (Armstrong, 2000). In conclusion, as Haugland (2000) has stated, "when used effectively, computers make an excellent learning tool" (p. 12).

Media

An older medium that has issues for parents and educators is television; its younger cousins are videos and video games. Many educators and parents have a love-hate relationship with television—although children usually love it. Indeed, by age three, most children are regular users of TV (Signorielli, 1991). Television has both negative and positive potentials: "television is an incredibly powerful tool that has yet to realize its potential for good, and it sometimes demonstrates an awesome capacity to do harm" (Washington & Andrews, 1999, p. 90). (Note that *media* includes both print media, such as magazines and books, and electronic media, such as TV, movies, and video games. The focus of this section is on television because it is the most debated and generally the most available and accessible in children's homes.)

The television set has become almost a member of the family. Young children may spend more time each day with the television than with other family members. A common figure in the literature is that young children watch television an average of four hours a day (Signorielli, 1991). Some children also spend additional time watching videos or playing video games. Therefore, "many young children spend far more time watching the TV screen than they spend in school, engaged in play or interacting with others" (Levin & Carlsson-Paige, 1994, p. 38)—in other words, in every other activity except sleeping. A typical recommendation for young children is no more than one to two hours of television viewing per day (e.g., NAEYC, 1996). This should also include time spent at a computer.

It is important to keep in mind that many of the statistics on children's television viewing are averages across ages. Children's viewing and comprehension of television is different at different ages. For example, infants are not typically interested in TV except for short periods when attracted by sound and light, while preschool-age children, although still attracted by the sensory stimulation, try to make sense of what they are seeing (Josephson, 1995). The early years are important because "the viewing patterns children establish as toddlers will influence their viewing habits throughout their lives" (Josephson, p. 5).

Although television can be a beneficial tool, excessive and inappropriate viewing can negatively affect children's physical fitness (inactivity and consumption of snack foods), language development, sense of personal efficacy, perceptions of others (i.e., stereotypes of boys, girls, gender roles, racial groups, and ages), sensitivity and empathy for others, and use of imagination and creativity. It can increase children's consumerism and aggressive behaviour, and can encourage anti-social behaviour. This last potential effect is of growing concern to parents, educators, and communities.

A large, longitudinal study of violence on TV found that perpetrators went unpunished and negative consequences of violence were not often portrayed. Public broadcasting channels had the least amount of violence in their programs, while cable channels had the most (National Television Violence Study, 1996). Children's programs, especially cartoons, tended to portray violence in a humorous context and were least likely to show the long-term negative consequences of violence. According to Josephson (1995), it is the attractive production features rather than the violence that makes these programs appealing to preschool-age children. However, this is also the developmental stage when "they are unlikely to be able to put the violence in context since they are likely to miss any subtlety conveyed mitigating information concerning motivation and consequences" (pp. 5–6). If you haven't watched children's television programs lately, you might want to view or videotape some of the Saturday morning or weekday afternoon children's television shows.

Some good suggestions on television viewing for families from a resource sheet of the Canadian Child Care Federation (1997) and a brochure from the International Reading Association (1998) are to:

- Watch and discuss TV with your children

- Engage in and encourage reading related to TV topics

- Control children's viewing, and explain why

- Set limits for viewing time

- Make a family TV viewing plan

- Avoid violent newscasts

- Pre-record programs for viewing later

- Use TV for purposeful viewing and to encourage family conversations

- Help children distinguish between fantasy and reality on TV.

Basically, what CCCF and IRA are suggesting with the above ideas is for families to engage in critical viewing. This is something we need to teach young children and reinforce for older children. Television is not necessarily a benign box sitting in the family room, but it can be made to work for young children. Moreover, parents and educators can also be advocates for improved programming for children. Two general goals are, "to promote programming that serves the diverse needs of children for education, entertainment, aesthetic appreciation and knowledge about the world, and to protect children from content and advertising practices that exploit their special vulnerability" (Huston, Watkins, & Kunkel, 1989, p. 427).

FOR REFLECTION

"More and more being a good parent means resisting the popular and media culture that society has allowed to be created for children" (Levin, 1998, p. 160). Do you agree or disagree?

Postmodernity

A growing trend at the end of the twentieth century in early childhood education and care, as well as in other disciplines, has been the critical examination of basic ideas, theories, and practices of our field. This has been called **deconstruction.** According to Lubeck (1996), "the practice of deconstructing thus provides a way to interrogate how and what we know; to question the very constructs, categories, and theories we use; and to open these conceptions to new possibilities" (p. 149). Its goal is to identify biases, contradictions, and inconsistencies (Cannella & Bailey, 1999).

Deconstruction is often paired with **reconceptualization**. One view is that to criticize and challenge concepts and beliefs without offering an alternative is not productive, hence the idea of reconceptualization. For example, reconstructionists emphasize the consideration of historical, feminist, political, class, racial, gender, and cultural factors and perspectives in planning curriculum (Charlesworth, Hart, Burts, & DeWolf, 1993).

Neither critical examination nor reformulation of ideas, theories, and practices is new to the twentieth century. There have been times of fundamental reexamination and change periodically throughout the history of early childhood education and care (see Chapter 5). The current period is often referred to as **postmodernism** or *postmodernity*. However, not everyone recognizes or accepts this view.

This current looking inward and reflection may be seen as an indicator of the maturity of the early childhood education and care profession. It is also indicative that there are important issues that need to be seriously and deeply examined, from multiple perspectives and in multiple ways.

Postmodernists in early childhood education and care question whether many of the current key assumptions and ideas in the field, such as developmentally appropriate practice (DAP) (see Chapter 12) and the role of child development reflect the values and beliefs of the dominant groups in early childhood education and care. For example, the conception and uses of DAP are criticized as being based on dominant North American research, values, and practices; in other words, they are not necessarily reflective of and therefore appropriate or useful in other cultural, social, or political contexts. Dahlberg, Moss, and Pence (1999) have commented that "too much discussion of early childhood occurs in a social, political, economic and philosophical vacuum, as if young children exist apart from the world, as if concepts like quality and child development are ahistorical and free of value and context" (p. 10).

There is a belief that concepts such as quality or standards cannot be universal absolutes and that these need to be examined more critically. For example, Cannella (1997), in her discussion of the role of child development, writes, "we have not questioned development as a socially constructed notion, embedded within a particular historical context and emerging from a distinctive political and cultural atmosphere, and based on a specific set of values" (p. 45). The implication is that to do so would severely limit its generalizability, applicability, and utility.

One aspect of deconstruction and reconceptualization in early childhood education and care that I find interesting is the ongoing discussion about what is early childhood education and care. For me, this seems like a good opportunity to address some of the perceptions that still seem to separate early childhood education and care into *education* and *care* (see Chapter 1). One possible result could be a new, more accurate descriptive term for our field.

A term often used to refer to early childhood programs in the context of international development efforts is "early child development programs," and a recent Canadian report uses the term "early childhood development centres." What do you think of this term as a replacement for "early childhood education and care"?

Professional Education and Opportunities

One area of early childhood education and care that is becoming of growing interest to postmodernist thinkers and others is early childhood teacher education in other countries. In Canada, early childhood educators typically receive their pre-service professional education at a post-secondary institution on a part-time or full-time basis. This is then followed by in-service educational opportunities while working (e.g., conferences, workshops, institutes, etc.). This is also the prevailing pattern in Europe. However, it is not the model for all countries. Many countries rely on in-service and on-the-job training by peers as the major, or only, professional education option.

A worldwide concern in early childhood education and care is professional education of educators and others working with young children and families. As Saracho (1992) has written, "the improvement of early childhood education and the preparation of its practitioners is an international phenomenon" (p. 228). It is widely recognized internationally that there is a need for continual professional education throughout an educator's career. However, ideas vary on how preservice and in-service can and should be done. There are a growing number of options including distance education by satellite or print materials, interactive Web sites for sharing ideas and gaining information, modular programs and courses, audio and video packages, and so on.

Staffing in early childhood programs varies. For example, many countries use paraprofessionals and volunteers in their early childhood programs. A question is, How can these groups receive training in early childhood education and care? One interesting early childhood training model that has been effective in both developed and developing countries is more experienced and knowledgeable individuals training others while receiving more training themselves. This has been done successfully in the HIPPY program in Israel, Turkey, Chile, the United States, South Africa, the Netherlands, Australia, and elsewhere, as well as in other early childhood programs.

HIPPY (Home Instructional Program for Preschool Youngsters) is a home-based program for three- to six-year-olds where paraprofessional aides visit the home to work with the mother, who then uses provided materials to work with her own children. It was begun by Avima Lombard of the Hebrew University in Israel in 1969, and is now funded by the Ministry of Education as one of its designated programs for "disadvantaged" families. HIPPY was originally developed to assist recent immigrant families to Israel (especially those from North Africa) to strengthen their young children's language, sensory and perceptual skills, and problem-solving abilities "by enhancing the home literacy environment, the quality of parent-child verbal interaction, and parents' ability to help their children learn" (Baker, Piotrkouski, & Brooks-Gunn, 1999, p. 117). In Israel, HIPPY has expanded to include approximately 6,000 families a year in approximately 80 urban and rural locations (Young, 1997).

In this program, each paraprofessional home visitor (often a former program participant) visits approximately 12 to 18 mothers and children at their homes twice a month. They provide a package of activity materials and books, which the paraprofessional explains and demonstrates to each mother through role-playing. The paraprofessional and the mother take turns playing the role of mother and child using the new materials. The mother is then expected to use the new activities with her child for approximately ten to twenty minutes a day over the next two weeks until the next home visit. HIPPY mothers in a local

FOR REFLECTION

The content of professional education is a perennial issue. Given the ever-expanding body of knowledge relevant to early childhood education and care, some advocate longer professional education programs. However, others claim that more is not necessarily better or perhaps possible (when funding is not increasing), and still others question if we can really know what will be needed for the future. For example, Peter Moss (1999) poses the question, "How can we prepare ourselves to undertake early childhood work in the 21st century, given that we can have no idea of the political, social, cultural, economic, or environmental conditions that will develop?" (p. 19). How would you answer Moss's question?

community have group meetings organized by their local paraprofessional aide and the local coordinator every two weeks or so. At these meetings, the mothers share their experiences, learn new skills or activities, and discuss topics such as child development, health, hygiene, and other family-related topics.

The paraprofessional home visitors are, in turn, provided with in-service instruction by a local coordinator. These training sessions follow the same general pattern as the mother–paraprofessional sessions. The local coordinators are, in turn, provided with in-service by a regional coordinator. The regional coordinators meet monthly with the national coordinator (see Lombard, 1994 for more details).

I observed this program in several areas of Israel in the early 1980s and was impressed with the efficiency and effectiveness of this training model. The mothers I spoke with commented that they liked having paraprofessionals and local coordinators from their own community, especially if they had previously been participants themselves. The paraprofessionals agreed that their roots in the local community usually made their jobs easier. This training model has also been part of HIPPY in other countries.

Eldering and Vedder (1999), who have been involved with HIPPY in the Netherlands, caution that "before transferring an intervention program to another country, the societal context of the new country has to be explored in order to ascertain the program's transferability and to identify the most relevant groups to be targeted for intervention" (p. 259). This raises the issue of transferability and transportability of early childhood programs.

Transferability and Transportability

Transferability or **transportability** refers to taking programs, practices, or policies from one country (or geographical area) and introducing them, with little or no change, into another country (or area). The Montessori approach (see Chapter 5) is a historical example of this; the British infant school model (see Chapter 6) is a more recent example, and HIPPY (see above) and Reggio-Emilia are contemporary ones.

Just because a program developed in one place has been successful in that location does not necessarily mean it will be successful in another location. Although early childhood education and care is appropriate across all countries, individual programs need to be examined for possible needed modifications or adaptations based on the social, cultural, political, historical, and economic contexts of the new location. This principle applies whether an early childhood program is transported from one province to another or from one country to another. There are no "one size fits all" early childhood programs.

Although it is important for early childhood educators to know about and learn more about early childhood programs from all parts of the world, we must avoid the temptation to transfer and adopt programs without due consideration for the new contexts. I saw an excellent example of this recently in Taiwan when I was visiting a kindergarten (four- to six-year-olds). The director of the

Taiwanese early childhood program.

program was explaining their approach. Partway through her explanation, she stopped and said that, although their project approach might sound and look like that of Reggio Emilia, "ours is for Taiwan, it is not from Italy." Although the educators in this kindergarten were familiar with the Reggio Emilia approach, they had developed their own approach to meet their specific needs identified in the context of Taiwanese society today and the children and families in their programs.

Likewise, Howe (2000) has raised the question of transferability in relation to the province of Quebec's recent decision to adopt the High/Scope model (see Chapter 6). This model was developed for a program in Ypsilanti, Michigan, and although it has been effective there, Howe notes that, "it seems rather naïve to expect it to have the same value for the children of Quebec without considering the characteristics of the local milieu" (p. 311).

Need for Information and Research

Many individuals and groups developing, or thinking about developing, early childhood programs lament the lack of or the difficulty in getting information about other programs. This is one of the reasons why I have included so many examples of programs (and references) in this book. Knowing about other programs in Canada and other countries is part of being an educated professional. Unfortunately, it is not always easy to get this information.

This knowledge is particularly important and valuable for program developers because it saves us from reinventing the wheel. Reinventing the wheel is not always necessary and what is needed is better dissemination and access to information about early childhood programs and practices. This access and dissemination is becoming easier through increasing use of electronic media for accessing and sharing information as well as discussing it across international

FOR REFLECTION

One of the evaluation tasks of the IEA Preprimary Project asked parents and educators to answer questions about what they thought was important for four-year-olds. How would you rank the following eight areas in order from the most important (1) to the least important (8)?

· *Language skills*
· *Motor/physical skills*
· *Pre-academic skills (e.g., basic concepts in math, reading, etc.)*
· *Self-assessment skills (e.g., self-confidence, pride in accomplishments, etc.)*
· *Self-expression skills (e.g., art, music, dance, and play)*
· *Social skills with adults*
· *Social skills with peers*
· *Self-sufficiency skills (e.g., independence, self-care, etc.) (Weikart, 1999).*

(For the results from the IEA Preprimary Project, see Focus 13.4.)

boundaries. There are also more print materials available, such as journals and publications by professional organizations (see Chapter 4 for a listing). For example, useful early childhood research-oriented journals in North America include the *Canadian Journal of Research in Early Childhood Education, Early Childhood Research Quarterly* (from NAEYC), and the *Journal of Research in Childhood Education* (from ACEI), among others.

Research can produce information and insights that are useful for both policy and practice. Early childhood has had a history of this mutual relationship between research and practice. For example, the Child Study Movement and the Institute of Child Study had considerable influence on the early development of programs for young children in Canada. In an 1896 book on kindergarten, the authors commented on this relationship: "There is apparently no end to the modifications and improvements necessary in the kindergarten in order to make our work keep pace with our growing ideals and our growing knowledge both of the child's nature and the world's needs" (Wiggin & Smith, p. 200). A similar statement could probably be made today about early childhood education and care in general. A current example of this interplay between research and practice is the recent research on infant brain development that has affected how we think about and plan programs for infants.

Research in early childhood education and care has evolved in the past 50 years. There is now more emphasis on and a broadening of both the scope of research and the methods used. There is also a more holistic approach to determining the questions to be investigated in research. Researchers are now less hesitant to attempt large, complex topics, such as quality in early childhood programs or the interaction effects of children, families, educators, and early childhood programs. In addition, a broader range of variables is being investigated (often the ones that are difficult to measure). More attention is also being paid to the contexts in which the research occurs, and the multiple perspectives of participants and researchers. There is also a growing body of research related to policy and its effects. However, postmodernist critics question the ability and utility of research, in both theory and practice, to provide answers and especially "truths" (Cannella & Bailey, 1999).

There has always been a need for longitudinal studies in early childhood education. The research studies related to Head Start and Follow Through described in Chapter 6 illustrate how the effectiveness of early childhood programs needs to be evaluated over both the short and long term. A current longitudinal research project in Canada that will be interesting to watch develop is the National Longitudinal Survey of Children and Youth being done by Statistics Canada and Human Resources Development Canada (see Chapters 2 and 3).

Another type of research that is rarely done because of its cost and complexity is large-scale, cross-national comparative studies. One recent example of this type of research is the IEA Preprimary Project described in Focus 13.4.

Focus 13.4

The IEA Preprimary Project

The International Association for the Evaluation of Educational Achievement (IEA) is a non-profit organization of research groups in more than 50 countries based in the Netherlands that organizes large-scale, cross-national assessments. It has been doing these comparative international studies of academic areas such as science, math, and written composition since 1959. If you've ever seen a headline in a newspaper or magazine about "Children in _____ score higher in _____ than children in Canada," the article is likely about the results of the latest IEA study.

From 1987–1997, IEA sponsored a study of children and the early childhood settings experienced by young children a year before they enter the formal school system. As this year varies from country to country, IEA selected four-year-olds as the focus of the study. Seventeen countries have participated. Canada was involved in the preliminary planning stages, but Canadian researchers were unable to obtain the necessary funding to participate in the study. The study had three phases: (a) identification of the types of early childhood programs and services used by young children and their families, (b) on-site observations in early childhood programs, assessment of children, and interviews and surveys of a sample of early childhood professionals and parents in each country, and (c) follow-up on the children's development at age seven. Data collection for all three phases is complete and results from the second phase have been published.

The focus of phase two was on children's development, including which areas of development parents and educators considered to be most important (Montané, 1999). (These are the areas you ranked in the For Reflection box.) Of the 15 countries participating in this phase,* the top three areas for educators were:

1. Social skills with peers (14 of 15; the exception not ranking this as important was Thailand)
2. Language skills (12 of 15; except Thailand, Greece, and Italy)
3. Self-sufficiency skills (12 of 15; except Nigeria, Poland, and Slovenia)

The least important areas for educators were:

8. Social skills with adults (11 of 15 ranked this as not important; exceptions were Finland, Poland, and Romania)
7. Self-assessment skills (11 of 15; except Belgium, Greece, Ireland, and the United States)
6. Pre-academic skills (10 of 15; except Nigeria, Thailand, Indonesia, Romania, and Spain).

For parents, the most important areas were:

1. Language skills (11 of 14**)
2. Self-sufficiency skills (10 of 14)
3. Social skills with peers (9 of 14)

The least important areas were:

8. Self-expression skills (12 of 14)
7. Self-assessment skills (10 of 14)
6. Motor/physical skills (7 of 14)

There was high agreement (i.e., statistically significant) between educators' and parents' rankings in Finland, Romania, Poland, Nigeria, Belgium, Italy, the United States, and Thailand (Karwowska-Struczyk, 1999).

* Belgium, China, Finland, Greece, Hong Kong, Indonesia, Ireland, Italy, Nigeria, Poland, Romania, Slovenia, Spain, Thailand, and the United States

** Parents in China were not participants in the survey

Research methodology in early childhood education and care has also shifted and broadened in the past two decades. There is proportionately less experimental research, but there is a wider variety of types of research. For example, today research studies utilize a range of methods, from large surveys and longitudinal research, to those that focus in depth on one child, to action research studies with educators collaborating with researchers in field-based research. There are dozens of research methodologies that are applicable to early childhood education and care (see Goodwin & Goodwin, 1996).

Summary of this Chapter

Although it is not possible to predict the future, we as early childhood professionals must still prepare for it; as de Saint Exupéry said in the quotation at the beginning of this chapter, to enable it. And for whom is the future more worth enabling than young children? I hope this book has helped you with this task—now and in the future.

The key themes of this chapter are that:

- Although there are too many variables and factors for us to predict the future, we can be aware of and knowledgeable about present trends that might extend into the future.

- Early childhood education and care has had a long history of international development.

- There is a need to provide for continuity for children, programs, and policies.

- The diversity and variety of early childhood programs continues to increase. Social, cultural, historical, economic, and political contexts contribute to this diversity.

- Current issues for early childhood programs include equity, clarity, quality, quantity, transferability, and the role of media and technology.

- There is a current trend of critical reexamination and possible reformulation of many of the basic assumptions, theories, and practices in early childhood education and care.

- There is a need for increased and more effective and efficient dissemination of information and research in early childhood education and care.

Key Terms

clarity, 515
continuity, 512
deconstruction, 529
equity, 519
mission clutter, 515
pedagogical continuity, 512

philosophical continuity, 512
postmodernism, 530
reconceptualization, 529
structural continuity, 513
transferability, 532
transportability, 532

Resources

For Sharing with Children

Scholastic publishes a series of small books about other countries such as D. Moreton & S. Berger. 1999. *A Day in Japan.* New York: Scholastic. Colour photos of a child's day, including school, in Japan.

The *Picture a Country* series uses photographs to illustrate life in Germany, India, France, Jamaica, China, Egypt, Spain, and Japan. For example, H. Pluckrose. 1998. *Japan.* New York: Franklin Watts.

Postcards from ... is another series including Australia, Brazil, Canada, China, France, Germany, Great Britain, Japan, Mexico, Russia, South Africa, and Spain. For example, H. Arnold. 1996. *Spain.* Austin, TX: Raintree Steck-Vaughn Publishers.

An example of a book on one topic with examples from many countries is *Homes around the world*, edited by B. Kalman. 1994. New York: Crabtree Publishing Company.

Also see the books about children around the world listed in Resources in Chapter 2.

For Further Reading

For information about early childhood programs and other countries, try:

Young, M.E. 1997. *Early child development: Investing in the future.* Washington, DC: The World Bank. Discusses the planning and delivery of early childhood programs in other countries, especially developing countries.

Cochran, M. (Ed.). 1993. *International handbook of child care policies and programs.* Westport, CT: Greenwood Press. Chapters on 29 countries including Canada, Denmark, Sweden, Israel, and Italy.

Woodill, G.A., Berhard, J., & Prochner, L. (Eds.). 1992. *International handbook of early childhood education.* New York: Garland Publishing. Chapters on preschool, primary, and special education in 43 countries, including many smaller countries.

Olmstead, P.P. & Weikart, D.P. (Eds.). 1995. *The IEA Preprimary Study: Early childhood care and education in 11 countries.* Oxford: Pergamon Press. This was published in North America as P.P. Olmstead & D.P. Weikart (Eds.). 1994. *Families speak: Early childhood care and education in 11 countries.* Also from the IEA Preprimary Study (published by High/Scope Press in Ypsilanti, MI): Olmstead and Weikart (Eds.). 1989. *How nations serve young children: Profiles of child care and education in 14 countries*; D.P. Weikart (Ed.). 1999. *What should young children learn? Teacher and parent views in 15 countries.*

The IEA Web site is www.iea.nl. This site has a link to High/Scope (see Resources in Chapter 6) for more information on the IEA Preprimary Project.

Address: IEA Secretariat
Herengracht 487
NL1017 BT Amsterdam
The Netherlands
Tel: 31-20625-3625
Fax: 31-20420-7136
E-mail: department@iea.nl

For research methods and their uses in early childhood education and care:

Goodwin, W.L., & Goodwin, L.D. 1996. *Understanding quantitative and qualitative research in early childhood education.* New York: Teachers College Press.

A general reference:

Isenberg, J.P. & Jalongo, M.R. 1997. *Major trends and issues in early childhood education: Challenges, controversies, and insights.* New York: Teachers College Press. Includes chapters on diversity, families, DAP, technology, play, and international early childhood education.

For media and technology:

Levin, D. 1998. *Remote control childhood? Combating the hazards of media culture.* Washington, DC: National Association for the Education of Young Children.

Wright, J.L. & Shade, D.D. (Eds.). 1994. *Young children: Active learners in a technological age.* Washington, DC: National Association for the Education of Young Children.

Steinberg, S.R. & Kinchloe, J.L. (Eds.). 1997. *Kinderculture.* Boulder, CO: Westview Press.

McDonnell, K. 1994. *Kid culture: Children and adults and popular culture.* Toronto: Second Story Press.

 ## Useful Web Sites and Addresses

UNICEF: United Nations Children's Fund, www.unicef.org (includes the latest *Progress of Nations*). Also see entry in Chapter 2.

The World Bank (funds many early childhood programs in developing countries and publishes information on early child development. Good links to additional Web sites):

1818 H. Street NW
Washington, D.C., 20433
Tel: 202-477-1234
Web site: www.worldbank.org/children

Future of Children (an on-line and hard-copy journal that has articles on international early childhood programs and issues; for example, one by S.S. Boocock on research support for early childhood programs "Early childhood programs in the nations: Goals and outcomes." Winter, 1995, vol. 5, no. 3. www.futureofchildren.org.

Early Childhood Care and Development (an interagency organization with interests in international early childhood education and care): www.ecdgroup.com.

The site has links to participating groups. The co-director is:

Louise Zimanyi
Ryerson Polytechnic University
School of Early Childhood Education
350 Victoria St.
Toronto, ON M5B 2K3
Tel: 416-979-5000
Fax: 416-979-5239
E-mail: info@ecdgroup.com

For early childhood programs in New Zealand, the Government of New Zealand's Ministry of Education publishes on-line updates at www.min.edu.govt.nz/curriculum/updates.

For descriptions of HIPPY in the United States and elsewhere, including research and references, contact:

HIPPY USA
220 East 23rd St., Suite 300
New York, NY 10010
Tel: 212-532-7730
Fax 212-532-7899
Web site: www.c3pg.com/hippyusa.htm

For media and technology:

Media Awareness Network (a Canadian organization)
E-mail: info@media-awareness.ca
Telephone: 1-800-896-3342 and 613-224-7721
Web site: www.schoolnet.ca/medianet

Children's House in Cyberspace, childhouse.uio.no, is an umbrella site for many organizations interested in young children and children's rights.

Two other groups concerned about media violence and children are the National PTA, at www.pta.org, and the Family and Community Critical Viewing Project at www.widmeyer.com/tv/viewing/tips.htm.

Also see the professional organizations listed in Chapter 4, as many of them have brochures and other publications about media and technology.

References

Abt Associates. (1977). *Education as experimentation: A planned variation model.* Cambridge, MA: Author.

Adams, M. (1997). *Sex in the snow: Canadian social values at the end of the millennium.* Toronto: Penguin Books.

Ade, W. (1982). Professionalization and its implications for the field of early childhood education. Young Children, 37 (3), 25–32.

Ainslie, J., & Meyer, M. (1992a). *Daddy is home from jail.* Edmonton: John Howard Society.

Ainslie, J., & Meyer, M. (1992b). *Daddy is in jail.* Edmonton: John Howard Society.

Ainslie, J., & Meyer, M. (1992c). *Why are there jails?* Edmonton: John Howard Society.

Ainsworth, M.D.S., Biehar, M.C., Waters, E., & Wall, S. (Eds.). (1978). *Patterns of attachment: A psychological study of the strange situation.* Hillsdale, NJ: Lawrence Erlbaum.

Alberta Education. (1997). *Early Childhood Services* [On-line]. Available: http://ednet.edc.gov.ab.ca/educationguide/pol-plan/pol-regs/113htm

Allard, H., & Marshall, J. (1977). *Miss Nelson is missing!* New York: Scholastic.

Allen, A.T. (1982). Spiritual motherhood: German feminists and the kindergarten movement, 1848–1911. *History of Education Quarterly, 22,* 319–339.

Allen, A.T. (1988). "Let us live with our children": Kindergarten movements in Germany and the United States, 1840–1914. *History of Education Quarterly, 28* (1), 23–48.

Allis, J.M. (1989). *Child care programs for health care organizations.* Ann Arbor, MI: Health Administration Press Perspectives.

Almy, M. (1967). Spontaneous play: An avenue for intellectual development. *Young Children, 22* (5), 265–277.

Almy, M., Monighan, P., Scales, B., & Van Hoorn, J. (1984). Recent research on play: The teacher's perspective. In L.G. Katz (Ed.), *Current topics in early childhood education: Vol. 5* (pp. 1–25). Norwood, NJ: Ablex Publishing.

Alston, P. (1998). Hardship in the midst of plenty. In *The progress of nations* (pp. 29–31). New York: United Nations Children's Fund.

Ames, L.B., & Ilg, F.L. (1976). *Your four-year-old: Wild and wonderful.* New York: Delacorte Press.

Anbar, A. (1999). *How to choose a nursery school: A parent's guide to preschool education* (2nd ed.). Palo Alto, CA: Pacific Books, Publishers.

Anderson, L.F. (1931). *Pestalozzi.* New York: AMS Press.

Andrews, J., & Sweeny, J. (1986). *Multiculturalizing parent involvement: Vol. 1, No.3.* (Catalogue No. Ci96–34/1986E). Ottawa: Department of the Secretary of State of Canada.

Anishinabek Early Childhood Education Program. (1994). Anishinabek Early Childhood Education Program. *Focus, 3* (3), 21–25.

Archard, D. (1993). *Children: Rights and childhood.* London: Routledge.

Ariès, P. (1962). *Centuries of childhood: A social history of family life* (R. Baldick, Trans.). New York: Vintage Books.

Aristotle (1962a). The principles of education. In E. Barker (Trans.), *The politics of Aristotle, Vol. VII,* ivi, 1335 (pp. 314—320). New York: Oxford University Press.

Aristotle (1962b). The training of youth: A general scheme of training. In E. Barker (Trans.), *The politics of Aristotle, Vol. VII,* ii, 1337 (pp. 332–337). New York: Oxford University Press.

Armstrong, A. (2000, April, 14). Suffer the children: Programmed for failure. *The Globe and Mail,* p. A15.

Arnold, H. (1996). *Spain.* Austin: TX: Raintree Steck-Vaughn publishers.

Arnold, T. (1999, January 13). Study finds dramatic rise in childhood asthma cases. *National Post,* pp. A1, A2.

Ashworth, M. (1993). *Children of the Canadian mosaic: A brief history to 1950.* Toronto: OISE Press.

Association of Teacher Educators. (1985). *Developing career ladders in teaching,* Reston, VA: Author.

Atkin, J. (1991). Thinking about play. In N. Hall & L. Abbott (Eds.), *Play in the primary curriculum* (pp. 29–37). London: Hodder & Stoughton.

Axline, V.M. (1969). *Play therapy.* New York: Ballantine Books.

Baehr, P. (1992). *School isn't fair.* New York: Aladdin Books.

Baker, A.J.L., Piotrkowski, C.S., & Brooks-Gunn, J. (1998). The effects of the Home Instruction Program for Preschool Youngsters (HIPPY) on children's school performance at the end of the program and one year later. *Early Childhood Research Quarterly, 13,* 571–588.

Baker, M. (1993). Family trends and family policies. *Transition, 23* (4), 7–9.

Balaban, N. (1985). *Starting school: From separation to independence - A guide for early childhood teachers.* New York: Teachers College Press.

Ball, J., & Pence, A.R. (1999). Beyond developmentally appropriate practice: Developing community and culturally appropriate practice. *Young Children, 54* (2), 46–50.

Barbour, N.H., & Seefeldt, C. (1993). *Developmental continuity across preschool and primary grades.* Wheaton, MD: Association for Childhood Education International.

Barnett, W.S. (1995). Long-term effects of early childhood programs on cognitive and school outcomes. *The Future of Children, 5* (3), 25–50. [On-line]. Available: http://www.futureofchildren.org/lto/02_lto.htm

Barnett, W.S. (1996). Creating a market for quality through NAEYC accreditation. In S. Bredekamp & B.A. Willer (Eds.), *NAEYC accreditation: A decade of learning and the years ahead* (pp. 149–162). Washington, DC: National Association for the Education of Young Children.

Bate, B. (1998). Families In Motion Chilliwack, British Columbia. In A. Thomas (Ed.)., *Family literacy in Canada: Profiles of effective practices* (pp. 55–69). Welland, ON: éditions Soleil publishing.

Bates, J., Deeth, M., Wright, E., & Vernon, J. (1986). *Kindergarten programs: Comparison and follow-up of full- and half day programs.* Toronto: Ministry of Education.

Bateson, G. (1955). A theory of play and fantasy. *Psychiatric Research Reports, 2*, 39–51.

Bateson, G. (1956). The message "this is play". In B. Schaller (Ed.), *Group processes* (pp. 145–151). New York: Josiah Macy.

Battle, K., & S. Torjman. (2000). *Ottawa should help build a national early childhood development system*. Ottawa: Caledon Institute of Social Policy. [On-line]. Available: http://wwwcaledoninst.org/9415990x.htm

Baxter, J., & Read, M. (1999). *Children first: Working with young children in inclusive group settings in Canada*. Toronto: Harcourt Brace Canada.

Baxter, S. (1993). *A child is not a toy: Voices of children in poverty*. Vancouver: New Star Books.

Beach, B.A. (1992). Teaching, nurturing, and gender across three generations of rural early childhood teachers. *Early Childhood Research Quarterly, 7*, 463–480.

Beach, J., Bertrand, J., & Cleveland, G. (1998). *Our child care workforce: From recognition to remuneration: A human resource study in child care in Canada: More than a labour of love: Main report*. Ottawa: Child Care Human Resources Steering Committee.

Beatty, B. (1995). *Preschool education in America: The culture of young children from the colonial era to the present*. New Haven, CT: Yale University Press.

Belfry, J. (1996). Canadian children face activity and fitness crisis. *Interaction, 10* (3), 25-26.

Bellis, M. (1999). Look before you loop. *Young Children, 54* (3), 70–83.

Bellisimo, Y., Sacks, C.H., & Mergendoller, J.R. (1995). Changes over time in kindergarten holding out: Parents and school contexts. *Early Childhood Research Quarterly, 10*, 205–222.

Belsky, J. (1988). The "effects" of infant day care reconsidered. *Early Childhood Research Quarterly, 3*, 235–272.

Belsky, J., & Rovine, M.J. (1988). Nonmaternal care in the first year of life and the security of infant-parent attachment. *Child Development, 59*, 157–167.

Bennett, H. (1989). Parent education programs: Growing healthy children. In F. Fearnley (Ed.), *Strengthening families, cherishing children* (pp. 100–102). Ottawa: TLRC Canada.

Bereiter, C. (1986). Does direct instruction cause delinquency? *Early Childhood Research Quarterly, 1*, 289–292.

Bereiter, C. (1999). How sound is High/Scope research? *Educational Leadership, 56* (6), 83–84.

Bereiter, C., & Engelmann, S. (1966). *Teaching disadvantaged children in preschool*. Englewood Cliffs, NJ: Prentice-Hall.

Berenstain, S., & Berenstain, J. (1978). *The Berenstain bears go to school*. New York: Random House.

Berenstain, S., & Berenstain, J. (1992). *The Berenstain bears and too much pressure*. New York: Random House.

Bergen, D. (1988). Using a schema for play and learning. In D. Bergen (Ed.), *Play as a medium for learning and development: A handbook of theory and practice* (pp. 169–180). Portsmouth, NH: Heinemann.

Berger, E.H. (1991). Parent involvement: Yesterday and today. *Elementary School Journal, 91* (3), 209–219.

Berger, E.H. (1996). Communication: The key to parent involvement. *Early Childhood Education Journal, 23*, 179–183.

Berger, S., & Chanko, P. (1999). *School*. New York: Scholastic.

Berk, L.E. (1994). Vygotsky's theory: The importance of make-believe play. *Young Children, 50* (1), 30–39.

Berk, L.E., & Winsler, A. (1995). *Scaffolding children's learning: Vygotsky and early childhood education*. Washington, DC: National Association for the Education of Young Children.

Berliner, D.C. (1994). Developmental stages in the lives of early childhood educators. In S.G. Goffin & D.E. Day (Eds.), *New perspectives in early childhood teacher education: Bringing the practitioners into the debate* (pp. 120–123). New York: Teachers College Press.

Berlyne, D. (1960). *Conflict, arousal and curiosity*. New York: McGraw-Hill.

Berlyne, D.E. (1969). Laughter, humor, and play. In G. Lindzey & E. Aronson (Eds.), *Handbook of social psychology: Vol. 3. The individual in a social context* (2nd ed., pp.795–852). Reading, MA: Addison-Wesley.

Bernhard, J., Pollard, J., Chud, G., Vukelich, G., & Pacini-Ketchabaw, V. (2000). The regulation of multi-age groupings in Canadian centre-based child care settings: An analysis of provincial and territorial policies, legislation and regulations. *Canadian Journal of Research in Early Childhood Education, 8* (3), 7–22.

Bernhard, J.K., Lefebvre, M.L., Chud, G., & Lange, R. (1995). *Paths to equity: Cultural, linguistic and racial diversity in Canadian early childhood education*. New York: York Lanes Press.

Bernhard, J.K. (1995). Child development, cultural diversity, and the professional training of early childhood educators. *Canadian Journal of Education, 20* (4), 415–436.

Bernhard, J.K., Pollard, J., Eggers-Piérola, C., & Morin, A. (1999). *Infants and toddlers in Canadian multi-age, childcare settings: Age, ability and linguistic inclusion*. Toronto: Human Resources Development Canada, Child Care Visions and Ryerson Polytechnic University.

Bernthal, M. (1994). *Baby Bop goes to school*. Allen, TX: The Allen Group.

Better Beginnings, Better Futures Project. (2000). *What is better beginnings, better futures?* [On-line]. Available: http://www.opc.on.ca/bbbf

Beyer, L.E., & Bloch, M. (1996). Theory: An analysis (part I). In S. Reifel (Series Ed.) & J.A. Chafel & S. Reifel (Vol. Eds.), *Advances in early education and day care: Vol. 8. Theory and practice in early childhood teaching* (pp.3–39). Greenwich, CT: JAI Press.

Bhavnagri, N.P., & Gonzalez-Mena, J. (1997). The cultural context of infant caregiving. *Childhood Education, 7* (1), 2–8.

Bibby, R.W., & Posterski, D.C. (1992). *Teen trends: A nation in motion*. Toronto: Stoddart.

Biemiller, A., Regan, E.M., & Lero, D. (1992). Early childhood education in Canada. In G.A. Woodill, J. Bernhard, & L. Prochner (Eds.), *International handbook of early childhood education* (pp. 147–154). New York: Garland.

Birkvad, B. (1997). Teacher professional development in Denmark. *Phi Delta Kappa, 78*, 611–614.

Bisson, J. (1997). *Celebrate! An anti-bias guide to enjoying holidays*. St. Paul, MN: Redleaf Press.

Björck-Åkesson, E., Brodin, J., Hellberg, G., Lindberg, M., & Sinker, M. (1990). *Play is for all!: Toy libraries in an international perspective*. Rockneby, Sweden: WRP International.

Blackwell, T. (1999, March 6). Teen welfare moms forced back to class. *National Post*, p. A9.

Bland, J. (1997). The Rural Child Care Project. *Interaction, 11* (3), 23–12.

Blatchford, P., & Martin, C. (1998). The effects of class size on classroom processes: "It's a bit like a treadmill - working hard and getting nowhere fast!" *British Journal of Educational Studies, 46* (2), 118–137.

Blatz, W.E. (1944). *Understanding the young child.* Toronto: Clarke Irwin.

Blatz, W.E., & Bott, H.M. (1928). *Parents and the pre-school child.* Toronto: J.M. Dent.

Blatz, W.E., & Bott, H.M. (1930). *The management of young children.* New York: William Morrow.

Blatz, W.E., Millichamp, D.A., & Fletcher, M. (1935). *Nursery education in theory and practice,* New York: Morrow.

Blitzer, S. (1991). "They are only children, what do they know?" A look at current ideologies of childhood. *Sociological Studies of Child Development* (Vol. 4, pp. 11–25). Greenwich, CT: JAI Press.

Bloch, M.N., Seward, D., & Seidlinger, P. (1989). What history tells us about public schools for 4-year-olds. *Theory into Practice, 28* (1), 11–18.

Bloom, B. (1964). *Stability and change in human characteristics.* New York: Wiley.

Bloom, P.J. (1996). The quality of work life in early childhood programs: Does accreditation make a difference? In S. Bredekamp & B.A. Willer (Eds.), *NAEYC accreditation: A decade of learning and the years ahead* (pp. 13–24). Washington, DC: National Association for the Education of Young Children.

Bloom, P.J. (1997). *A great place to work: Improving conditions for staff in young children's programs* (Rev. ed.). Washington, DC: National Association for the Education of Young Children.

Blow, S. (1969). Kindergarten education. In N.M. Butler (Ed.), *Education in the United States* (Vol. 1, pp. 4–44). New York: Johnson Reprint Corporation. (Original work published 1900)

Blow, S.E. (1903). *The songs and music of Friedrich Froebel's mother play.* New York: D. Appleton. (Original work published 1895)

Blow, S.E. (1910). *Symbolic education: A commentary on Froebel's "Mother Play".* New York: D. Appleton. (Original work published 1894)

Bodrova, E., & Leong, D.J. (1996). *Tools of the mind: The Vygotskian approach to early childhood education.* Engelwood Cliffs, NJ: Prentice-Hall.

Boelts, M. (1996). *Little Bunny's preschool countdown.* Morton Grove, IL Albert Whitman.

Bornstein, M.H. (Ed.). (1991). *Cultural approaches to parenting.* Hillsdale, NJ: Lawrence Erlbaum.

Bouchard, C. (1996). A world of adults worthy of children. In the *National Forum on Family Security: Family security in insecure times* (Vol. II, pp. 177–196). Ottawa: Canadian Council on Social Development.

Bourgeois, P., & Clark, B. (1995). *Franklin goes to school.* Toronto: Kids Can Press.

Bowlby, J. (1982). Attachment. In C. Yorke (Ed.), *The International Psycho-analytical Library. Attachment and loss: Vol. 1* (2nd ed.). London: The Hogarth Press and The Institute of Psycho-Analysis.

Bowman, B. (1990). Issues in the recruitment, selection, and retention of early childhood teachers. In B. Spodek & O.N. Saracho (Eds.), *Yearbook in early childhood education: Vol. 1. Early childhood teacher preparation* (pp.153–175). New York: Teachers College Press.

Boyatzis, C.J. (1987). The effects of traditional playground equipment on preschool children's dyadic play interaction. In G.A. Fine (Ed.), *Meaningful play, playful meaning* (pp. 101–110). Champaign, IL: Human Kinetics Publishers.

Boyd, B.F. (1999). Should gay and lesbian issues be discussed in elementary school? *Childhood Education, 76* (1), 40–41.

Boyd, B.J. (1997). Teacher response to superhero play: To ban or not to ban? *Childhood Education, 74* (1), 23–28.

Boyden, J. (1993). *Families: Celebration and hope in a world of change.* London: Gaia Books/UNESCO Publishing.

Boyer, E.L. (1991). *Ready to learn: A mandate for the nation.* Princeton, NJ: The Carnegie Foundation for the Advancement of Teaching.

Boyer, E.L. (1993). Ready to learn: A mandate for the nation. *Young Children, 48* (3), 54–57.

Bradburn, E. (1989), *Portrait of a pioneer.* London: Routledge.

Bradburn, E. (1990). *Childhood, culture and class in Britain: Margaret McMillan, 1860–1931.* London: Virago.

Bradburn, E. (1995). Margaret McMillan (1860–1931). *International Journal of Early Childhood, 27* (2), 69–73.

Braun, S.J., & Edwards, E.P. (1972). *History and theory of early childhood education.* Worthington, OH: Charles A. Jones Publishing.

Bredekamp, S. (1987). *Developmentally appropriate practice in early childhood programs serving children from birth through age 8: Expanded edition.* Washington, DC: National Association for the Education of Young Children.

Bredekamp, S. (1991). Redeveloping early childhood education: A response to Kessler. *Early Childhood Research Quarterly, 6,* 199–209.

Bredekamp, S. (1992). Composing a profession. *Young Children, 47* (2), 52–54.

Bredekamp, S. (1995). What do early childhood professionals need to know and be able to do? *Young Children, 55* (2), 67–69.

Bredekamp, S. (1997). NAEYC issues revised position statement on developmentally appropriate practice in early childhood programs. *Young Children, 52* (2), 34–40.

Bredekamp, S. (1999). When new solutions create new problems: Lessons learned from NAEYC accreditation. *Young Children, 54* (1), 58–63.

Bredekamp, S. (Ed.). (1986). *Developmentally appropriate practice.* Washington, DC: National Association for the Education of Young Children.

Bredekamp, S. (Ed.). (1987). *Developmentally appropriate practice in early childhood programs serving children from birth through age 8* (Expanded ed.). Washington, DC: National Association for the Education of Young Children.

Bredekamp, S., & Copple, C. (Eds.). (1997). *Developmentally appropriate practice in early childhood programs* (Rev. ed.). Washington, DC: National Association for the Education of Young Children.

Bredekamp, S., & Rosegrant, T. (Eds.). (1992). *Reaching potentials: Appropriate curriculum and assessment for young children* (Vol. 1). Washington, DC: National Association for the Education of Young Children.

Bredekamp, S., & Willer, B. (1992). Of ladders and lattices, cores and cones: Conceptualizing an early childhood professional development system. *Young Children, 47* (3), 47–50.

Bredekamp, S., & Willer, B. (1993). Professionalizing the field of early childhood education: Pros and cons. *Young Children, 48* (2), 82–84.

Bredekamp, S., & Willer, B.A. (Eds.). (1996). *NAEYC accreditation: A decade of learning and the years ahead.* Washington, DC: National Association for the Education of Young Children.

Brennan, E., & Freeman, L. (1999). Inclusive child care. *Focal Point, 13* (1), 1, 8–9.

Bretherton, I. (1993). Theoretical contributions from developmental psychology. In P.G. Boss, W.J. Doherty, R. LaRossa, W.R. Shumann,

& S.K. Steinmetz (Eds.), *Sourcebook of family theories and methods: A contextual approach* (pp. 275–297). New York: Plenum Press.

Brewer, J. (1998). *Introduction to early childhood education: Preschool through primary grades* (3rd ed.). Boston: Allyn and Bacon.

Bridwell, N. (1999). *Clifford's first school day.* New York: Scholastic.

Briggs, B.A., & Walters, C.M. (1985). Single-father families: Implications for early childhood educators. *Young Children, 40* (3), 23–27.

Brizius, J.A., & Foster, S.A. (1993). *Generation to generation: Realizing the promise of family literacy.* Ypsilanti, MI: High/Scope Press.

Bromer, J. (1999). Cultural variations in child care: Values and actions. *Young Children, 54* (6), 72–78.

Bronfenbrenner (1974). *Is early intervention effective? A report on longitudinal evaluations of preschool programs.* Washington, DC: U.S. Department of Health, Education, & Welfare.

Bronfenbrenner, U. (1979). *The ecology of human development: Experiments by nature and design.* Cambridge, MA: Harvard University Press.

Bronfenbrenner, U. (1987). Forward/Family support: The quiet revolution. In S.L. Kagan, D.R. Powell, B. Weissbourd, & E.F. Zigler (Eds.), *America's family support programs: Perspectives and prospects* (pp. xi–xvii). New Haven, CT: Yale University Press.

Bronfenbrenner, U. (1989). Ecological systems theory. In R. Vasta (Ed.), *Annals of child development* (vol. 6, pp. 187–249). Cambridge, MA: Harvard University Press.

Bronfenbrenner, U. (1992). Ecological systems theory. In R. Vasta (Ed.), *Six theories of child development: Revised formulations and current issues* (pp.187–249). London: Jessica Kingsley Publishers.

Bronson, M.B. (1995). *The right stuff for children from birth to 8: Selecting materials to support development.* Washington, DC: National Association for the Education of Young Children.

Brooks, R.B. (1994). Children at risk: Fostering resilience and hope. *American Journal of Orthopsychiatry, 64,* 545–553.

Brophy, K. (2000). A history of laboratory schools. In L. Prochner & N. Howe (Eds.), *Early childhood care and education in Canada* (pp. 115–132). Vancouver: UBC Press.

Brosterman, N. (1997). *Inventing kindergarten.* New York: Harry N. Abrams Publishers.

Brown, B. (1985). Head Start: How researched changed public policy. *Young Children, 40* (5), 9–13.

Brown, S., Turner, L.E., LaGrange, A., Massing, C., & Sherwood, F. (1996). The effects of change on ECS in Alberta: A report of preliminary findings of phase one of the Alberta Kindergarten Study. *Early Childhood Education, 29*(1), 52-55.

Brown, S.L. (1994, December). Animals at play. *National Geographic, 186,* 2–35.

Bruce, T. (1984). A Froebelian looks at Montessori's work. *Early Child Development and Care, 14,* 75–84.

Bruder, M.B. (1997). Children who are homeless: A growing challenge for early care and education. In S. Reifel (Series Ed.) & C.J. Dunst & M. Wolery (Vol. Eds.), *Advances in early education and day care: Family policy and practice in early child care: Vol. 9* (pp. 223–246). Greenwich, CT: JAI Press.

Bruer, J.T. (1998). Brain science, brain fiction. *Educational Leadership, 56* (3), 14–18.

Bruer, J.T. (1999). *The myth of the first three years.* New York: The Free Press.

Bruner, J. (1983). Play, thought, and language. *Peabody Journal of Education, 60* (3), 60–69.

Brusslemans-Dehairs, C., & Henry, G.F. (1997). Part I: Evidence from the studies carried out by the International Association for the Evaluation of Educational Achievement (IEA), 1964–92. In C. Brusselmans-Dehairs, G.F. Henry, M. Beller, & N. Gafni, *Gender differences in learning achievement: Evidence from cross-national surveys* (pp. 9–40). Paris: United Nations Educational, Scientific and Cultural Organization.

Bueckert, D. (1999, January 13). Experts link homes, asthma. *Victoria Times Colonist,* p. C6.

Bunting, E. (1989). *The Wednesday surprise.* New York: Clarion.

Burke, D.L. (1996). Multi-year teacher/student relationships are a long-overdue arrangement. *Phi Delta Kappan, 77,* 360–361.

Burns, M.S., Griffin, P., & Snow, C.E. (Eds.). (1999). *Starting out right: A guide to promoting children's reading success.* Washington, DC: National Academy Press.

Buysse, V., Wesley, P.W., & Keyes, L. (1998). Implementing early childhood inclusion: Barrier and support factors. *Early Childhood Research Quarterly, 13* (1), 169–184.

Cadwell, L.B. (1997). *Bringing Reggio Emilia home: An innovative approach to early childhood education.* New York: Teachers College Press.

Caldwell, B.M. (1989). Foreword: Prologue to the past. In E.D. Cahan, *Past caring: A history of U.S. preschool care and education for the poor, 1820–1965* (pp. vii-xi). New York: National Center for Children in Poverty.

Caldwell, B.M. (1991). Continuity in the early years: Transitions between grades and systems. In S.L. Kagan (Ed.), *The care and education of America's young children: Obstacles and opportunities* (pp. 69–90). Chicago: University of Chicago Press.

Cameron, C.A., & Lee, K. (1997). Bridging the gap between home and school with voice-mail technology. *Journal of Educational Research 90,* 182–190.

Campaign 2000. (1997). *Child poverty in Canada: Report card 1997* [Brochure]. Toronto: Family Service Association.

Campaign 2000. (1998). *Child poverty in Canada: Report card 1998* [Brochure]. Toronto: Family Service Association.

Campbell, C. (1999a). Dinner's ready - Before leaving work. [The Vanier Institute of the Family] *Families and Health, 6,* 7).

Campbell, C. (1999b). More parents on shifts passing in the night. [The Vanier Institute of the Family] *Families and Health, 6,* 1, 3.

Canada Mortgage and Housing Corporation. (1997a). *Play opportunities for school-age children 6–14 years of age* (Rev. ed.) Ottawa: Author.

Canada Mortgage and Housing Corporation. (1997b). *Play spaces for preschoolers* (Rev. ed.). Ottawa: Author.

Canadian Association for Young Children. (1996). *Play: Young children have the right to learn through play* [Brochure]. Ottawa: Author.

Canadian Association of Toy Libraries and Parent Resource Centres - TLRC Canada. (1990). *Caring about families: The "how to" manual for developing Canadian family resource programs.* Ottawa: Canadian Association of Family Resource Programs.

Canadian Child Care Federation. (1991). *National statement on quality child care.* Ottawa: Author.

Canadian Child Care Federation. (1994). National guidelines for training in early childhood care and education, draft document, May, 1994. *Interaction, 8* (2),6–9.

Canadian Child Care Federation. (1995). *Towards excellence in ECCE training programs: A self-assessment guide.* Ottawa: Author.

Canadian Child Care Federation. (1996, Winter). Making a quality child care choice. *Resource Sheet 34.* Ottawa: Author

Canadian Child Care Federation. (1997). Managing the television at home. *Resource Sheet # 39.* Ottawa: Author.

Canadian Child Care Federation. (1999). Research Update: Child care issues and the child care workforce: A survey of Canadian public opinion. *Interaction, 12* (4), 31–32.

Canadian Child Care Federation. (2000). *Tools for practitioners in child care settings: Standards of practice, code of ethics, guide to self-reflection.* Ottawa: Author.

Canadian Child Day Care Federation and Canadian Day Care Advocacy Association. (1991). *Caring for a living: A study on wages and working conditions in Canadian child care: Final report.* Ottawa: Author.

Canadian Child Day Care Federation. (1985). *The child's rights in a preschool setting* [Resource sheet 3]. Ottawa: Author.

Canadian Commission for the International Year of the Child. (1979). *For Canada's children.* Ottawa: Author.

Canadian Council on Children and Youth. (1978). *Admittance restricted: The child as citizen in Canada.* Ottawa: Author.

Canadian Council on Social Development. (1996). *The progress of Canada's children 1996.* Ottawa: Author.

Canadian Council on Social Development. (1997). *The progress of Canada's children 1997.* Ottawa: Author.

Canadian Council on Social Development. (1998). *The progress of Canada's children, 1998: Focus on youth.* Ottawa: Author.

Canadian Fitness and Lifestyle Research Institute. (1998). *1995 physical activity monitor* [On-line]. Available: http://www.cflri.ca/cflri/surveys/95survey/95survey.html

Canadian Institute of Child Health. (1994). *The health of Canada's children: A CICH profile* (2nd ed.). Ottawa: Author.

Canadian National Child Care Study. (1992). *Canadian child care in context: Perspectives from the provinces and territories* (A. Pence, Coordinating Ed.). Ottawa: Statistics Canada/Health and Welfare Canada.

Canadian Paediatric Society. (1992). *Well beings: A guide to promote the physical health, safety and emotional well-being of children in child care centres and family day care homes.* Ottawa: Author.

Canadian Toy Testing Council. (1999). *Toy Report: Canada's year-round guide to toys 1999.* Ottawa: Author.

Cannella, G.S. (1997). *Deconstructing early childhood education: Social justice and revolution.* New York: Peter Lang.

Cannella, G.S., & Bailey, C. (1999). Postmodern research in early childhood education. In S. Reifel (Ed.), *Advances in early education and day care: Foundations, adult dynamics, teacher education and play* (Vol. 10, pp. 3–39). London: JAI Press.

Canning, P.M., & Lyon, M.E. (1990). Young children with special needs. In I.M. Doxey (Ed.), *Child care and education: Canadian dimensions* (pp.254–268). Scarborough, ON: Nelson Canada.

Cartwright, S. (1999). What makes good early childhood teachers? *Young Children, 54* (4), 4-7.

Caruso, J.J. (2000). Cooperating teacher and student teacher phases of development. *Young Children, 55* (1), 75–81.

Case, R. (1985). *Intellectual development: Birth to adulthood.* Orlando, FL: Academic Press.

Case, R. (1991). *The mind's staircase: Exploring the conceptual underpinnings of children's thought and knowledge.* Hillsdale, NJ: Lawrence Erlbaum.

Cattermole, J., & Robinson, N. (1985). Effective home/school communication- from the parent's perspective. *Phi Delta Kappan 67* (1), 48–50.

Chambers, B., Howe, N., & Petrakos, H. (1997). The role of curriculum preparation in facilitating children's dramatic play and content knowledge. *Canadian Journal of Research in Early Childhood Education, 6* (3), 251-261.

Chamot, A.U. (1988). Bilingualism in education and bilingual education: The state of the art in the United States. *Journal of Multilingual and Multicultural Development, 9* (1–2), 11–35.

Chapman, J. (1999). A looping journey. *Young Children, 54* (3), 80–83.

Charlesworth, R. (1983). *Understanding child development: For adults who work with young children.* New York: Delmar Publishers.

Charlesworth, R. (1989). "Behind" before they start? Deciding how to deal with the risk of kindergarten "failure". *Young Children, 44* (3), 5–13.

Charlesworth, R. (1998). Developmentally appropriate practice is for everyone. *Childhood Education, 74,* 274–282.

Charlesworth, R., Hart, C.H., Burts, D.C., & DeWolf, M. (1993). The LSU studies: Building a research base for developmentally appropriate practice. In S. Reifel (Ed.), *Advances in early education and day care: Perspectives on developmentally appropriate practice* (Vol. 5, pp. 3–27). London: JAI Press.

Chatterson, S., & Kelleher, L. (1998, June). *Rural satellites: A new travelling model.* Paper presented at the Canadian Association of Family Resource Programs Biennial National Conference, Montréal.

Chattin-McNichols, J. (1992). *The Montessori controversy.* Albany, NY: Delmar Publishers.

Chavkin, N.F, & Williams, D.L. (1989). Low-income parent's attitudes toward parent involvement in education. *Journal of Sociology and Social Welfare, 16* (3), 17–28.

Chazan, M., Laing, A., & Harper, G. (1987). *Teaching five to eight year-olds.* Oxford: Basil Blackwell.

Che-Alford, J. Allan, C., & Butlin, G. (1994). *Focus on Canada: Families in Canada* (Catalogue No. 96–307E). Ottawa: Statistics Canada and Prentice Hall.

Che-Alford, J., & Hamm, B. (1999). Under one roof: Three generations living together (Catalogue No. 11–008–XPE). *Canadian Social Trends, 53,* 6–9.

Chen, C, & Uttal, D.H. (1988). Cultural values, parents' beliefs, and children's achievement in the United States and China. *Human Development, 31,* 351–358.

Chen, P., & MacAulay, J. (1999). *Improving facilities: Innovative approaches for community programs.* Ottawa: Canadian Association of Family Resource Programs.

Cherney, E. (1999, February 10). Quebec rights commission calls for ban on spanking. *National Post,* pp. A1, A2.

Child Care Issues. (1999). Research update: Child care issues and the child care workforce: A survey of Canadian public opinion. *Interaction, 12* (4), 31–32.

Childcare Resource and Research Unit. (1997). *Public policy context of child care: the issue of auspice* [On-line]. Available: http://www.childcare-canada.org/resources/CRRUpubs/factsheets/sheet3.html

Childcare Resource and Research Unit. (2000a). *Aboriginal child care* [On-line]. Available: http://www.childcarecanada.org/pt98/abor/abor.html

Childcare Resource and Research Unit. (2000b). *Statistics summary: Canadian early childhood care and education in the 1990s: 3 financing child care* [On-line]. Available: http://www.childcarecanada.org/resources/CRRUpubs/factsheets/statsum3.html

Childcare Resource and Research Unit. (2000c). *Statistics summary: Canadian early childhood care and education in the 1990s (revised): Human resources* [On-line]. Available: http://www.childcarecanada.org/resources/CRRUpubs/factsheets.statsum4.html

Childhood Accident Prevention. (1987, July). Childhood accident prevention concept in Sweden. *Swedish Press*, p. 4.

Children's Defense Fund. (1989). *Call for action*. Washington, DC: Author.

Chisholm, P. (1997, February 24). Growing up poor. *Maclean's*, 42–45.

Chisholm, P. (1999, March 1). The mother load. *Maclean's*, 112, 46–50.

Chmelynski, C. (1998). All-day kindergarten on the rise. *The Education Digest, 64* (1), 32–34.

Christie, J.F., & Wardle, F. (1992). How much time is needed for play? *Young Children, 47* (3), 28–32.

Christie, J.F., Johnsen, E.P., & Peckover, R.B. (1988). The effects of play period duration on children's play patterns. *Journal of Research in Childhood Education, 3*, 123–131.

Chud, G. & Fahlman, R. (1995). *Honouring diversity with child care and early education: An instructor's guide*. Victoria: Ministry of Skills, Training and Labour and the Centre for Curriculum and Professional Development.

Chui, T. (1996). Canada's population: Charting into the 21st century (Catalogue No. 11–008–XPE) . *Canadian Social Trends,42*, 3–7.

Cicarelli, V. (1969). *The impact of Head Start: An evaluation of the effects of Head Start on children's cognitive and affective development*. Athens, OH: Westinghouse Learning Corporation, Ohio University.

Clark, A. (Ed.). (1981). *Culture and children*. Philadelphia: F.A. Davis.

Clark, C. (1999, December 10). Auditor slams PQ's program as ill-planned. *National Post*, p. A6.

Clark, D. (1998). Off-hours care in Canada. *Interaction, 11* (4), 12–13.

Clark, K. (1996) *First Nations families*. Victoria: Greater Victoria School District, First Nations Education Division.

Clark, R.M. (1983). *Family life and school achievement: Why poor black children succeed or fail*. Chicago: University of Chicago Press.

Clarke-Stewart, K.A. (1987). In search of consistencies in child care research. In D.A. Phillips (Ed.), *Quality in child care: What does the research tell us?* (pp. 105–125). Washington, DC: National Association for the Education of Young Children.

Clarke-Stewart, K.A. (1988). Evolving issues in early childhood education: A personal perspective. *Early Childhood Research Quarterly, 3*, 139–149.

Clarke-Stewart, K.A., Gruber, C.P.,& Fitzgerald, L.M. (1994). *Children at home and in day care*. Hillsdale, NJ: Lawrence Erlbaum.

Clay, J.W. (1990). Working with lesbian and gay parents and their children. *Young Children, 45* (3), 31–35.

Cleave, S., & Brown, S. (1991). *Early to school: Four year olds in infant classes*. Slough, UK: NFER/Nelson.

Cleave, S., Jowett, S., & Bate, M. (1989). *...And so to school: A study of continuity from preschool to infant school*. Windsor, Berks: NFER-Nelson.

Cleaver, J. (1992). *Doing children's museums: A guide to 265 hands-on museums*. Charlotte, VT: Williamson Publishing.

Cleveland, G., & Krashinsky, M. (1998). *The benefits and costs of good child care: The economic rationale for public investment in young children: A policy study*. Toronto: Childcare Resource Unit, Centre for Urban and Community Studies.

Cleverley, J., & Phillips, D.C. (1986). *Visions of childhood: Influential models from Locke to Spock* (Rev. ed.). New York: Teachers College Press.

Clifford, H. (1992). A national perspective and forward: Canadian child care in context: Perspectives from the provinces and territories. In A.R. Pence (Coordinating Ed.), *Canadian National Child Study: Canadian child care in context: Perspectives from the provinces and territories* (pp. xiii-xvii). Ottawa: Statistics Canada/Health and Welfare Canada.

Clifford, R.M., Early, D.M., & Hills, T.W. (1999). Almost a million children in school before kindergarten: Who is responsible for early childhood services? *Young Children, 54* (5), 48–51.

Cochran, M. (1993b). Public child care, culture, and society: Crosscutting themes. In M. Cochran (Ed.), *International handbook of child care policies and programs* (pp. 627–658). Westport, CT: Greenwood Press.

Cochran, M. (Ed.). (1993a). *International handbook of child care policies and programs*. Westport, CT: Greenwood Press.

Cohen, D. (1987). *The development of play*. London: Croom Helm.

Cohen, M. (1967). *Will I have a friend?* New York: Macmillan.

Cohen, S. (1989). Fostering shared learning among children. *Young Children, 44* (4), 20–24.

Colbert, J.A. (1999). Child care and the family-work balance: An international perspective on needs and responses in aboriginal communities. *Canadian Journal of Research in Early Childhood Education, 7*, 357–367.

Cole, M. (1953). *Robert Owen of New Lanark*. London: Batchworth Press.

Coleman, M. (1997). Families and schools: In search of common ground. *Young Children, 52* (5), 14–21.

Coleman, M., & Churchill, S. (1997). Challenges to family involvement. *Childhood Education, 73*, 144–148.

Coles, R. (1990). *The spiritual life of children*. Boston: Houghton Mifflin.

Coles, R. (1997). *The moral intelligence of children*. New York: Random House.

Collins, W.A., Maccoby, E.E., Steinberg, L., Hetherington, E.M., & Bornstein, M.H. (2000). Contemporary research on parenting: The case for nature and nurture. *American Psychologist, 55*, 218–232.

Comenius, J.A. (1896). *School of infancy: An essay of the education of youth during the first six years* (W.S. Monroe, Ed.). Boston: D.C. Heath Publishers. (Original work published 1628)

Comenius, J.A. (1967). *The great didactic of John Amos Comenius* (M.W. Keatinge, Ed. and Trans.). New York: Russell & Russell. (Original work published 1657)

Comenius, J.A. (968). *Orbis pictus*. London: Oxford University Press. (Original work published in 1657)

Connolly, J., & Doyle, A. (1984). Relation of social fantasy play to social competence in preschoolers. *Developmental Psychology, 20*, 797–806.

Consortium for Longitudinal Studies. (1978). *Lasting effects after preschool*. (DHEW Publication No. OHDS 79–30178). Washington, DC: US Government Printing Office.

Consortium for Longitudinal Studies. (1983). *As the twig is bent: Lasting effects of preschool programs.* Hillsdale, NJ: Erlbaum.

Consortium on Diversity in Education. (1997). *Celebrating the mosaic: A handbook and guide to resources for multicultural education* (2ⁿᵈ ed.). Vancouver: Author.

Constabile, A., Smith, P.K., Matheson, L., Aston, J., Hunter, T., Boulton, M. (1991). Cross-national comparison of how children distinguish serious and playful fighting. *Developmental Psychology, 27,* 881–887.

Cooke, K. (1986). *Report of the Task Force on Child Care.* Ottawa: Minister of Supply and Services.

Coontz, S. (1995). The American Family and the nostalgia trap [Special report]. *Phi Delta Kappan, 76,* K1–K20.

Coplan. R.J., Wichmann, C., Lagace-Sequin, D.G., Rachlis, L.M., & McVey, M.K. (1999). The "degree" of instructor education and child outcomes in junior kindergarten: A comparison of certificated teachers and early childhood educators. *Journal of Research in Childhood Education, 14* (1), 78–90.

Corak, M. (1998). *Labour markets, social institutions, and the future of Canada's children* (Catalogue No. 89–553–XPB). Ottawa: Statistics Canada.

Corbett, B. (1990). A Froebelian perspective on early childhood education. In I.M. Doxey (Ed.), *Child care and education: Canadian dimensions* (pp. 98–108). Scarborough, ON: Nelson Canada.

Corbett, B.E. (1989). *A century of kindergarten in Ontario, 1887–1987.* Mississauga, ON: The Froebel Foundation.

Cordingley, P. (2000, May 12). Wired for life. *Asiaweek, 26,* 36–42.

Cornell, C. (1998, May). "Give me a break!" *Today's Parent, 15,* 50–54.

Corsini, D.A., Wisensale, S., & Caruso, G.A. (1988). Family day care: System issues and regulatory models. *Young Children, 43* (6), 17–23.

Corson, D. (1998). *Changing education for diversity.* Buckingham, England: Open University Press.

Corter, C. (1993). Exemplary kindergarten programs: Conclusions from the study. In C. Corter & N.W. Park (Eds.), *What makes exemplary kindergarten programs effective?* (pp. 128–135). Toronto: Ontario Ministry of Education and Training.

Corter, C., & Park, N.W. (Eds.). (1993). *What makes exemplary kindergarten programs effective?* Toronto: Ontario Ministry of Education and Training.

Corter, C.M. (1995). Is early childhood education an engine or caboose? *Orbit, 26* (2), 12–14.

Costantino, M. (1998). *The life and works of Frank Lloyd Wright.* London: PRC Publishing.

Cottons, D. (1999, Winter/Spring). Child care funding: Is anybody listening? The time to act is now: A message from the president. *BC Association of Child Care Services,* 1, 3.

Coulter, R.P., & McNay, M. (1993). Exploring men's experiences as elementary school teachers. *Canadian Journal of Education, 18,* 398–413.

Cox, M., Devlin, D., & Addetia, S. (1998, September). The mobile family resource program: A community collaboration. Paper presented at the Canadian Association of Family Resource Programs Conference, Montreal.

Creasey, G.L., Jarvis, P.A., & Berk, L.E. (1998). Play and social competence. In B. Spodek & O.N. Saracho (Eds.), *Multiple perspectives on play in early childhood education* (pp. 116–143). Albany, NY: State University of New York Press.

Crews, D. (1991). *Bigmama's.* New York: Trumpet.

Crittenden, D. (1999). *What our mothers didn't tell us: Why happiness eludes the modern woman.* New York: Touchstone.

Cryan, J.R., Sheehan, R., Wiechel, J., & Bandy-Hedden, I.G. (1992). Success outcomes of full-day kindergarten: More positive behavior and increased achievement in the years after. *Early Childhood Research Quarterly, 7,* 187–203.

Cryer, D., & Phillipsen, L. (1997). Quality details: A close-up look at child program strengths and weaknesses. *Young Children, 52* (5), 51–61.

Cuban, L. (1992). Why some reforms last: The case of the kindergarten. *American Journal of Education, 100,* 166–194.

Cuffaro, H.K. (1991). A view of materials as the texts of the early childhood curriculum. In B. Spodek & O.N. Saracho (Eds.), *Yearbook in early childhood education: Vol. 2. Issues in early childhood curriculum* (pp. 64–83). New York: Teachers College Press.

Cunningham, G. (1996). The challenge of responding to individual and cultural differences and meeting the needs of all communities. In S. Bredekamp & B.A. Willer (Eds.), *NAEYC Accreditation: A decade of learning and the years ahead* (pp. 79–82). Washington, DC: National Association for the Education of Young Children.

Curry, N., & Bergen, D. (1988). The relationship of play to emotional, social. and gender/sex role development. In D. Bergen (Ed.), *Play as a medium for learning and development: A handbook of theory and practice* (pp. 107–132). Portsmouth, NH: Heinemann.

Curtis, A. (1994). *Early childhood education explained: A review of provision in England and Wales.* London: OMEP (UK) Publications.

Dahlberg, G., Moss, P., & Pence, A. (1999). *Beyond quality in early childhood education and care: Postmodern perspectives.* London: Falmer Press.

Damast, A., Tamis-LeMonda, S., & Bornstein, M. (1996). Mother-child play: Sequential interactions and the relation between maternal beliefs and behaviors. *Child Development, 67,* 1752–1766.

Darling, J. (1994). *Child-centred education and its critics.* London: Paul Chapman Publishing.

Datta, L. (1979). Another spring and other hopes: Some findings from national evaluations of Project Head Start. In E. Zigler & J. Valentine (Eds.), *Project Head Start: A legacy of the war on poverty* (pp. 405–432). New York: Free Press.

Dauber, S.L., & Epstein, J.L. (1993). Parents' attitudes and practices of involvement in inner-city elementary and middle schools. In N.F. Chavkin (Ed.), *Families and schools in a pluralistic society* (pp. 53–71). Albany, NY: State University of New York Press.

Davis, L. (1996). *P.B. Bear's school day.* Toronto: Stoddart.

Davis, M.D., & Goffin, S.G. (1994). Program improvement in early childhood education: Facilitating the change process. *Journal of Early Childhood Teacher Education, 15,* 3–7.

Davis, M.D., & Hansen, R. (1932). *Nursery schools: Their development and current practices in the United States,* Washington, DC: U.S. Government Printing Office.

De Guimps, R. (1909). *Pestalozzi: His life and work.* New York: D. Appleton.

De Saint-Exupéry, A. (1950). *The wisdom of the sands* (S. Gilbert, Trans.). New York: Harcourt, Brace & World.

DeCicco, E.K., & Allison, J. (1999). Ockham's razor applied: It's mission clutter. *Childhood Education, 75* (5), 273–275.

Declaration of the Rights of the Child. (1959). New York: United Nations.

Deiner, P.L. (1993). Family day care and children with disabilities. In D.L. Peters & A.R. Pence (Eds.), *Family day care: Current research for informed public policy* (pp. 129–145). Toronto: Canadian Scholars' Press.

Deiner, P.L. (1997). *Infants and toddlers: Development and program planning.* Forth Worth, TX: Harcourt Brace College Publishers.

Delpit, L.D. (1990). Language diversity and learning. In S. Hynds & D.L. Rubin (Eds.), *Perspectives on talk and learning*)pp. 247–266). Urbana, IL: National Council of Teachers of English.

Demos, E.V. (1989). Resiliency in infancy. In T.F. Dugan & R. Coles (Eds.), *The child in our times: Studies in the development of resiliency* (pp. 3–22). New York: Brunner/Mazel Publishers.

Dempsey, J.D., & Frost, J.L. (1993). Play environment in early childhood education. In B. Spodek (Ed.), *Handbook of research on the education of young children* (pp. 306–321). New York: Macmillan.

Dence, T. (1911). *Reminiscences of a septuagenarian.* London: Sir Joseph Causton & Sons.

Department for Education and Employment. (1999). *UK early years development and childcare plan.* London: Author.

Department of Indian Affairs and Northern Development. (2000). *National Aboriginal Day* [Brochure, On-line]. Available: http://www.inac.gc.ca/june21/pamp_e.pdf

Derman-Sparks, L., & the A.B.C. Task Force. (1989). *Anti-bias curriculum: Tools for empowering young children.* Washington, DC: National Association for the Education of Young Children.

Desjardins, G. (1989). *Faire garder ses enfants au Québec: Toute une histoire...* Québec: Gouvernement du Québec.

Desjardins, G. (1992). An historical overview of child care in Quebec. In (A. Pence, Coordinating Ed.), *Canadian child care in context: Perspectives from the provinces and territories* (pp. 31–46). Ottawa: Statistics Canada/Health and Welfare Canada.

Dewey, J. (1914). Play. In P. Monroe (Ed.), *A cyclopedia of education: Vol. 4* (pp. 725–727). New York: Macmillan.

Dewey, J.D. (1959). *Dewey on education: Selections.* New York: Bureau of Publications.

Dewey, J.D. (1966). *Democracy and education: An introduction to the philosophy of education.* New York: The Free Press. (Original work published 1916)

Dewolf, M., & Benedict, J. (1997). Social development and behavior in the integrated curriculum. In C.H. Hart, D.C. Burts, & R. Charlesworth (Eds.), *Integrated curriculum and developmentally appropriate practice: Birth to age eight* (pp.257–284). New York: State University of New York Press.

Dickinson, P. (1987). *The many faces of ECE: Similarities and differences in various educators of young children.* Unpublished doctoral dissertation, University of Toronto.

Dickinson, P. (1989). Educators of young children: similar or different? *Canadian Journal of Research in Early Childhood Education, 3,* 3–14.

Dickinson, P., & Ellison, J. (1999). Plugged into the Internet (Statistics Canada Catalogue No. 11–008). *Canadian Social Trends, 55,* 7–10.

Diffily, D. (1996). The project approach: A museum exhibit created by kindergartners. *Young children, 51* (2), 72–75.

Division for Early Childhood, Council for Exceptional Children. (1993). *DEC recommended practices: Indicators of quality in programs for infants and young children with special needs and their families.* Reston, VA: Author.

Dixon, G. (1994). The first years of kindergarten in Canada. *Canadian Children, 19* (2), 6–9.

Doherty, G. (1996). School for three-and four-year olds: What does the research tell us? *Canadian Journal of Research in Early Childhood Education, 5,* 135–142.

Doherty, G., Goelman, H., LaGrange, A., Lero, D.S., & Tougas, J. (1999). *You bet I care!* [On-line]. Available: http://www.cfc-efc.ca/docs/00001269.htm

Doherty, G., Lero, D., Goelman, H., Tougas, J., & LaGrange, A. (1999). Wages and long-term income security in child care centres. *Interactions, 13* (3), 32–35.

Doherty-Derkowski. G. (1995). *Quality matters: Excellence in early childhood programs.* Don Mills, ON: Addison-Wesley Publishers.

Dooley, N. (1991). *Everybody cooks rice.* Minneapolis: Carolrhoda Books.

Donaldson, M. (1978). *Children's minds.* New York: W.W. Norton.

Dorion-Coupal, K. (1996). *A toy library for you/Une ludotheque pour toi.* Montreal: CIDE-OMEP.

Dorros, A. (1991). *Abuela.* New York: Trumpet.

Downs, R.B. (1975). *Heinrich Pestalozzi: Father of modern pedagogy.* Boston: Twayne Publishers.

Downs, R.B. (1978). *Friedrich Froebel.* Boston: Twayne Publishers.

Driscoll, A. (1995). *Cases in early childhood education: Stories of programs and practices.* Boston: Allyn and Bacon.

Dryfoos, J.G. (1994). *Full-service schools: A revolution in health and social services for children, youth, and families.* San Franciso: Jossey-Bass Publishers.

Dryfoos, J.G. (1996). Full-service schools. *Educational Leadership, 53* (7), 18–23.

Dryfoos, J.G. (1999). The role of the school in children's out-of-school time. *The Future of Children, 9* (2), 117–134. [On-line]. Available: http://www.futureofchildren.org/wso/wso_10.pdf

Duff, R.E., Brown, M.H., & Van Scoy, I.J. (1995). Reflection and self-evaluation: Keys to professional development. *Young Children, 50* (4), 81–88.

Duffy, A. (1999, July, 15). Newcomers to Canada hit 10–year low. *National Post,* p. A2.

Dumas, J. (1997). Marriage and divorce in Canada: What the statistics can and cannot tell us. *Transition, 27* (4), 9–11.

Duncan, G.J., Brooks-Gunn, J., & Klebanov, P.K. (1994). Economic deprivation and early childhood development. *Child Development, 65,* 296–318.

Dunn, L., & Kontos, S. (1997). What have we really learned about developmentally appropriate practice. *Young Children, 52* (5), 4–13.

Dunning, P. (2000). Aboriginal Head Start. *Education Canada, 39* (4), 38–39.

mide. Ottawa: Child Care Providers Association.

Dunster, L. (1999). Caring 'cross Canada. *Interaction, 13* (2), 36–38.

Dupuis, D. (1998). What influences people's plans to have children? (Catalogue No. 11–008–XPE). *Canadian Social Trends, 48,* 2–5.

Dyson, A.H. (1991). The roots of literacy development: Play, pictures, and peers. In B. Scales, M. Almy, A. Nicolopoulou, & S. Ervin-Tripp (Eds.), *Play and the social context of development in early care and education* (pp. 98–116). New York: Teachers College Press.

Eccles, J.S., & Harold, R.D. (1993). Parent-school involvement during the early adolescent years. *Teachers College Record, 94,* 568–587.

Eden, S. (1991). Early education: A Canadian perspective. *Canadian Children, 16* (1), 1–10.

Edmonds, B.C., & Fernekes, W.R. (1996). *Children's rights: A reference handbook.* Santa Barbara, CA: ABC-CLIO.

Edwards, C. (1993). Partner, nurturer, and guide: The roles of the Reggio teacher in action. In C. Edwards, L. Gandini, & G. Forman (Eds.), *The hundred languages of children: The Reggio Emilia approach to early childhood education* (pp. 151–169). Norwood, NJ: Ablex Publishing.

Edwards, C. (1998). Partner, nurturer, and guide: The role of the teacher. In C. Edwards, L. Gandini, & G. Forman (Eds.), *The hundred languages of children: The Reggio Emilia approach - Advanced reflections* (2nd ed., pp. 179–198). Greenwich, CT: Ablex Publishing.

Edwards, C., Gandini, L., & Forman, G. (1998b). Introduction: Background and starting points. In C. Edwards, L. Gandini, & G. Forman (Eds.), *The hundred languages of children: The Reggio Emilia approach - Advanced reflections* (2nd ed., pp. 5–25). Greenwich, CT: Ablex Publishing.

Edwards, C., Gandini, L., & Forman, G. (Eds.). (1998a). *The hundred languages of children: The Reggio Emilia approach - Advanced reflections* (2nd ed.). Greenwich, CT: Ablex Publishing.

Eichler, M., & Bullen, M. (1986). *Families in Canada: An introduction.* Toronto: The Ontario Institute for Studies in Education.

Eisner, E.W. (1974). *English primary schools: Some observations and assessments.* Washington, DC: National Association for the Education of Young Children.

Eldering, L., & Vedder, P. (1999). The Dutch experience with the Home Intervention Program for Preschool Youngsters (HIPPY). In L. Eldering & P.P.M. Leseman (Eds.), *Effective early education: Cross-cultural perspectives* (pp. 259–285). New York: Falmer Press.

Elfer, P., & Wedge, D. (1996). Defining, measuring and supporting quality. In G. Pugh (Ed.), *Contemporary issues in the early years: Working collaboratively for children* (2nd ed., pp. 51–67). London: Paul Chapman Publishing and the National Children's Bureau.

Elicker, J., & Mathur, S. (1997). What do they do all day? Comprehensive evaluation of a full-day kindergarten. *Early Childhood Research Quarterly, 12,* 459–480.

Eliot, L. (1999). *What's going on in there? How the brain and mind develop in the first five years of life.* New York: Bantam Books.

Elkind, D. (1981). *The hurried child: Growing up too fast too soon.* Reading, MA: Addison-Wesley Publishing.

Elkind, D. (1987). *Miseducation: Preschoolers at risk.* New York: Alfred A. Knopf.

Elkind, D. (1989). Developmentally appropriate practice: Philosophical and practical implications. *Phi Delta Kappan, 71,* 113–117.

Elkind, D. (1993). *Images of the young child: Collected essays on development and education.* Washington, DC: National Association for the Education of Young Children.

Ellis, D. (1998). *Finding our way: A participatory evaluation method for family resource programs.* Ottawa: Canadian Association of Family Resource Programs.

Ellis, M.J. (1973). *Why people play.* Englewood Cliffs, NJ: Prentice-Hall.

Ellis, S., Rogoff, B., & Cromer, C.C. (1981). Age segregation in children's social interactions. *Developmental Psychology, 17,* 399–407.

Ellsworth, J., & Ames, L.J. (1998). Introduction. In J. Ellsworth & L.J. Ames (Eds.), *Critical perspectives on Project Head Start: Revisioning the hope and challenge* (pp.vii-xvii). Albany, NY: State University of New York Press.

Emblen, V. (1998). Providers and families: Do they have the same views of early childhood programs? Some questions raised by working on early childhood education in the Lao People's Democratic Republic. *International Journal of Early Childhood, 30* (2), 31–37.

Emlen, S.T. (1995). An evolutionary theory of the family. *Proceedings of the National Academy Science, 92,* 8092–8099.

Engelmann, S. (1999). A response: How sound is High/Scope research? *Educational Leadership, 56* (6), 83–84.

Engelmann, S., & Osborn, J. (1976a). *Teacher's guide: Distar Language I: An instructional system* (2nd ed.). Chicago: Science Research Associates.

Engelmann, S., & Osborn, J. (1976b). *Teacher presentation book B: Distar Language I: An instructional system* (2nd ed.). Chicago: Science Research Associates.

Epstein, A.S., Larner, M., & Halpern, R. (1995). *A guide to developing community-based family support programs.* Ypsilanti, MI: High/Scope Press.

Epstein, A.S., Schweinhart, L.J., & McAdoo, L. (1996). *Models of early childhood education.* Ypsilanti, MI: High/Scope Press.

Epstein, J.L. (1990). School and family connections: Theory, research, and implications for integrating sociologies of education and family. *Marriage and Family Review, 15* (1–2), 99–126.

Epstein, J.L. (1991a). Effects on student achievement of teachers' practices of parent involvement. In B.A. Hutson (Series Ed.) & S.B. Silvern (Vol. Ed.), *Advances in reading/language research: Vol. 5. Literacy through family, community, and school interaction* (pp. 261–276). Greenwich, CT: JAI Press.

Epstein, J.L. (1991b). Paths to partnership: What we can learn from federal, state, district, and school initiatives. *Phi Delta Kappan, 72,* 344–349.

Epstein, J.L. (1995). School/family/community partnerships: Caring for the children we share. *Phi Delta Kappan, 76,* 701–712.

Epstein, J.L. (1996). Parents' reactions to teacher practices of parent involvement. *The Elementary School Journal, 86* (3), 277–294.

Epstein, J.L., & Dauber, S.L. (1991). School programs and teacher practices of parent involvement in inner-city elementary and middle schools. *The Elementary School Journal, 91,* 289–305.

Eriksen, A. (1985) *Playground design: Outdoor environments for learning and development.* New York: Van Nostrand Reinhold.

Erikson, E.H. (1950). *Childhood and society.* New York: W.W. Norton.

Erikson, E.H. (1963). *Childhood and society* (2nd ed.). New York: W.W. Norton.

Evans, E.D. (1975). *Contemporary influences in early childhood education* (2nd ed.). New York: Holt, Rinehart and Winston.

Evans, J.L. (1997, February). *Breaking down the barriers: Creating integrated early childhood programs.* Paper presented at the Conference on the Holistic/Integrative Concept in Early Childhood Education and Development, Larnaca, Cyprus. [On-line], Available: http://www.ecdgroup.com/archive/integrat.html#Integrated Programming

Family Day Care Association of Manitoba (1994). *Family day care - An Aboriginal perspective.* Winnipeg: Author.

Family Services Canada. (1998). *National Family Week* [Promotional kit]. Ottawa: Health Canada.

Farish, J.M. (1995). *When disaster strikes: Helping young children cope* [Brochure}. Washington, DC: National Association for the Education of Young Children.

Farrell, M. (1986). Latchkey children: A growing phenomenon. *Journal of the Canadian Association for Young Children, 10* (1–2), 133–144.

Fast, J.E., & Frederick, J.A. (1996). Working arrangements and time stress (Catalogue No. 11–008–XPE). *Canadian Social Trends, 43,* 14–19.

Feeney, S., & Freeman, N.K. (1999). *Ethics and the early childhood educator: Using the NAEYC code.* Washington, DC: National Association for the Education of Young Children.

Feeney, S., Christensen, D., & Moravcik, E. (1991). *Who am I in the lives of children? An introduction to teaching young children* (4th ed.). New York: Merrill.

Fein, G.G. (1985). Learning to play: Surfaces of thinking and feeling. Children's views of play. In J.L. Frost & S. Sunderlin (Eds.)., *When children play: Proceeding of the International Conference on Play and Play Environments* (pp. 45–53). Wheaton, MD: Association for Childhood Education International.

Fein, G.G., & Clarke-Stewart, A. (1973). *Day care in context.* New York: John Wiley.

Fiese, B. (1990). Playful relationships: A contextual analysis of mother-toddler interactions and symbolic play. *Child Development, 61,* 1648–1656.

File, N., & Kontos, S. (1993). The relationship of program quality to children's play in integrated early intervention settings. *Topics in Early Childhood Special Education, 13* (1), 1–18.

Fine, S. (1999a, September 13). The new stay-at-home moms. *The Globe and Mail,* pp. A1, A6–A7.

Fine, S. (1999b, October, 15). Stay-home toddlers lag in school. *The Globe and Mail,* pp. A1, A2.

Fine, S. (1999c, October, 1). When parents break up. *The Globe and Mail,* p. A21.

Finkelstein, B. (1987). Historical perspectives on children's play on school. In N.R. King & J.H. Block (Eds.), *School play* (pp. 17–37). New York: Teachers College Press.

Finn-Stevenson, M., & Stern, B.M. (1997). Integrating early-childhood and family-support services with a school improvement process: The Comer-Zigler initiative. *The Elementary School Journal, 98,* 51–66.

Finn-Stevenson, M., Desimone, L., & Chung, A.M. (1998). Linking child care and support services with the school: Pilot evaluation of the School of the 21st Century. *Children and Youth Services Review, 20* (3), 177–205.

Fitch, S., & Labrosse, D. (1997). *If you could wear my sneakers!* Toronto: Doubleday Canada.

Flournoy, V. (1985). *The patchwork quilt.* New York: Dial Books.

Folk, K.F., & Yi, Y. (1994). Piecing together child care with multiple arrangements: Crazy quilt or preferred pattern for employed parents of preschool children? *Journal of Marriage and Family, 56,* 669–680.

Foot, D.K. (with Stoffman, D.). (1998). *Boom, bust, and echo 2000: Profiting from the demographic shift in the new millennium.* Toronto: Macfarlane Walter & Ross.

Forest, I. (1927). *Preschool education: A historical and critical study.* New York: Macmillan.

Forest, I. (1935). *The school for the child from two to eight.* Boston: Ginn and Company.

Fowell, N., & Lawton, J. (1992). An alternative view of appropriate practice in early childhood education. *Early Childhood Research Quarterly, 7,* 53–74.

Fowler, W. (1983). *Potentials of childhood: Volume I. A historical view of early experience.* Lexington, MA: D.C. Health.

Fraser, A. (1966). *A history of toys.* London: Weidenfeld & Nicolson.

Fraser, S. (2000). *Authentic childhood: Experiencing Reggio Emilia in the classroom.* Toronto: ITP Nelson.

Frederick, J.A., & Hamel, J. (1998). Canadian attitudes to divorce (Catalogue No. 11–008–XPE). *Canadian Social Trends, 48,* 6–11.

Freud, A. (1968). Answering teachers' questions. In *The writings of Anna Freud: Indications for child analysis and other papers - 1945–1956* (Vol. IV, pp. 560–568). New York: International Universities Press. (Original work published 1952)

Freud, S. (1959). Beyond the pleasure principle. In J. Strachey (Ed.), *The standard edition of the complete psychological works of Sigmund Freud* (pp. 60–63). London: The Institute of Psychoanalysis.

Frieman, B.B. (1998). What early childhood educators need to know about divorced fathers. *Early Childhood Education Journal, 25,* 239–241.

Friendly, M. (1992). Moving towards quality child care: Reflections on child care policy in Canada. *Canadian Journal of Research in Early Childhood Education, 3,* 123–132.

Friendly, M. (1994). *Child care policy in Canada: Putting the pieces together.* Don Mills, ON: Addison-Wesley Publishers.

Friendly, M. (1997). What is the public interest in child care? *Policy Options, 18* (1), (pp. 3–6).

Friendly, M. (1998). Canadian child care: Can we make order out of chaos? *Perception, 22* (2), 6–7.

Friendly, M. (2000). Child care as a social policy issue. In L. Prochner & N. Howe (Eds.), *Early childhood care and education in Canada* (pp. 252–272). Vancouver: UBC Press.

Friendly, M., & Oloman, M. (2000). Early childhood education on the Canadian policy landscape. In J. Hayden (Ed.), *Landscapes in early childhood education: Cross-national perspectives on empowerment - A guide for the new millennium* (pp. 69–81). New York: Peter Lang.

Froebel, F. (1887). *The education of man.* New York: D. Appleton (Original work published 1826)

Froebel, F. (1908). *Autobiography of Friedrich Froebel* (E. Michaelis & H.K Moore, Trans.). London: Swan Sonnenschein.

Fromberg, D.P. (1990). Play issues in early childhood education. In C. Seefeldt, *Continuing issues in early childhood education* (pp. 223–243). Columbus, OH: Merrill.

Fromberg, D.P. (1995a). *The full-day kindergarten: Planning and practicing a dynamic themes curriculum* (2nd ed.). New York: Teachers College Press.

Fromberg, D.P. (1995b). The simplicity of complexity: Professionalism in early childhood teacher education. *Journal of Early Childhood Teacher Education, 16* (3), 7–10.

Frost, J.L. (1992). *Play and playscapes.* Albany, NY: Delmar Publishers.

Frost, J.L., & Drescher, N.L. (nd). *A parent's guide to playground safety* [Brochure]. Olney, MD: Association for Childhood Education International.

Frost, J.L., Shin, D., & Jacobs, P.J. (1998). Physical environments and children's play. In B. Spodek & O.N. Saracho (Eds.), *Multiple perspectives on play in early childhood education* (pp. 255–294). Albany, NY: State University of New York Press.

Fueyo, V. (1999). Understanding direct instruction and instructional design. In C.H. Wolfgang & M.E. Wolfgang (Eds.), *School for young children: Developmentally appropriate practices* (2nd ed., pp. 114–143). Boston: Allyn and Bacon.

Fuller, P. (1979). Uncovering childhood. In M. Hoyles (Ed.), *Changing childhood* (pp. 71–108). London: Writers and Readers Publishing Cooperative.

Galinsky, E. (1990). The costs of not providing quality early childhood programs. In B. Willer (Ed.), *Reaching the full cost of quality in early childhood programs* (pp. 27–40). Washington, DC: National Association for the Education of Young Children.

Galinsky, E. (1999). *Ask the children: What America's children really think about working parents.* New York: William Morrow.

Galinsky, E., Howes, C., Kontos, S., & Shinn, M. (1994). The study of children in family child care and relative care - Key findings and policy recommendations. *Young Children, 50* (1), 58–61.

Gamberg, R., Kwak, W., Hutchings, M., & Altheim, J. (1988). *Learning and loving it: Theme studies in the classroom.* Portsmouth, NH: Heinemann.

Gamble, J. (1992). An historical overview of child care in New Brunswick. In A.R. Pence (Ed.), *Canadian child care in context: Perspectives from the provinces and territories* (Vol.II, pp. 131–144). Ottawa: Statistics Canada and Health and Welfare Canada.

Gandini, L. (1993). Fundamentals of the Reggio Emilia approach to early childhood education. *Young Children, 49* (1), 4–17.

Gandini, L. (1997). Foundations of the Reggio Emilia approach. In J. Hendrick (Ed.), *First steps toward teaching the Reggio way* (pp. 14–25). Upper Saddle River, NJ: Merrill/Prentice Hall.

Garbarino, J.A. (1995). *Raising children in a socially toxic environment.* San Franciso: Jossey-Bass Publishers.

Gardner, H. (1989). Learning - Chinese style. *Psychology Today, 23* (12), 54–56.

Gardner, H. (1993). *Multiple intelligences: The theory in practice.* New York: Basic Books.

Gardner, H. (1998). Foreword: Complementary perspectives on Reggio Emilia. In C. Edwards, L. Gandini, & G. Forman (Eds.), *The hundred languages of children: The Reggio Emilia approach - Advanced reflections* (2nd ed., pp. xv-xvii). Greenwich, CT: Ablex Publishing.

Gardner, H. (1999). *The disciplined mind: What all students should understand.* New York: Simon & Schuster.

Gardner, H., & Kritchevsky, M. (1993). The emergence and nurturance of multiple intelligences in early childhood: The Project Spectrum approach. In H. Gardner, *Multiples intelligence: The theory in practice* (pp. 86–111). New York: Basic Books.

Gargiulo, R.M. (1990). Child abuse and neglect: An overview. In R.L. Goldman & R.M. Gargiulo (Eds.), *Children at risk: An interdisciplinary approach to child abuse and neglect* (pp. 1–36). Austin, TX: Pro-Ed.

Garmezy, N. (1991). Resiliency and vulnerability to adverse developmental outcomes associated with poverty. *American Behavioral Scientist, 34,* 416–430.

Garmezy, N. (1993). Children in poverty: Resilience despite risk. *Psychiatry, 56,* 127–136.

Garza, M., Briley, S., & Reifel, S. (1985). Children's views of play. In J.L. Frost & S. Sunderlin (Eds.)., *When children play: Proceeding of the International Conference on Play and Play Environments* (pp. 31–37). Wheaton, MD: Association for Childhood Education International.

Gesell, A. (1924). The significance of the nursery school. *Childhood Education, 1,* 11–20.

Gesell, A. (1946). Introduction: How this book is built and how it may be used. In A. Gesell & F.L. Ilg, *The child from five to ten* (pp. 1–6). New York: Harper & Brothers Publishing.

Gestwicki, C. (1997). *The essentials of early education.* New York: Delmar Publishers.

Ghalam, N.Z. (1997). Attitudes toward women, work and family. *Canadian Social Trends, 46* (Catalogue No. 11–008–XPE), 13–17.

Gilligan, C. (1982). *In a different voice: Psychological theory and women's development.* Cambridge, MA: Harvard University Press.

Gilman, P. (1992). *Something for nothing.* New York: Scholastic.

Glassman, M. (1992). An historical overview of child care in Newfoundland. In A.R. Pence (Ed.), *Canadian child care in context: Perspectives from the provinces and territories* (Vol.II, pp. 347–362). Ottawa: Statistics Canada and Health and Welfare Canada.

Goffin, S.G. (1983). A framework for conceptualizing children's services. *American Journal of Orthopsychiatry, 53,* 282–290.

Goffin, S.G. (1994). *Curriculum models and early childhood education: Appraising the relationship.* New York: Merrill.

Goffin, S.G. (1996). Child development knowledge and early childhood teacher preparation: Assessing the relationship - A special collection. *Early Childhood Research Quarterly, 11,* 117–133.

Goffin, S.G., & Lombardi, J. (1988). *Speaking out: Early childhood advocacy.* Washington, DC: National Association for the Education of Young Children.

Goffin, S.G., & Stegelin, D.A. (Eds.). (1992). *Changing kindergartens: Four success stories.* Washington, DC: National Association for the Education of Young Children.

Golant, S.K., & Golant, M. (1999). *Kindergarten isn't what is used to be* (3rd ed.). Los Angeles: Lowell House.

Goldhaber, J. (1994). If we call it science, then can we let the children play? *Childhood Education, 71* (1), 24–27.

Goleman, D. (1995). *Emotional intelligence.* New York: Bantam books.

Gomby, D.S., Culross, P.L., & Behrman, R.E. (1999). Home visiting: Recent program evaluations-analysis and recommendations. *The Future of Children, 9* (1), 4–17. [On-line]. Available: http://www.futureofchildren.org/hv2/hv2_01.pdf

Göncü, A., & Fitzgerald, L.M. (1994). The early childhood curriculum: Notes on the transformations of a field. *Journal of Curriculum Studies, 26,* 447–452.

Gonzalez-Mena, J. (1993). *Multicultural issues in child care.* Mountain View, CA: Mayfield Publishing Company.

Good, H.G. (1960). *A history of western education* (2nd ed.). New York: Macmillan.

Goodlad, J.I., Klein, M.F., & Novotney, J.M. (1973). *Early schooling in the United States.* New York: McGraw-Hill.

Goodman, Y.M. (1989). Roots of the whole-language movement. *The Elementary School Journal, 90,* 114–127.

Goodwin, W.L., & Goodwin, L.D. (1996). *Understanding quantitative and qualitative research in early childhood education.* New York: Teachers College Press.

Goodykoontz, B., Davis, M.D., & Gabbard, H.F. (1948). Recent history and present status of education for young children. In N.B. Nelson (Ed.), *The forty-sixth yearbook of the National Society for the Study of Education: Early childhood Education* (pp. 44–69). Chicago: University of Chicago Press.

Gopnik, A., Meltzoff, A.N., & Kuhl, P.K. (1999). *The scientist in the crib: Minds, brains, and how children learn.* New York: William Morrow and Company.

Gordon, A., & Browne, K.W. (Eds.). (1993). *Beginnings & beyond: Foundations in early childhood education* (3rd ed.). New York: Delmar.

Gordon, I.J., & Breivogel, W.F. (1976). *Building effective home-school relationships.* Boston: Allyn & Bacon.

Gordon, M. (1998). Parenting and family literacy centres of the Toronto District School Board. In A. Thomas (Ed.), *Family literacy in Canada: Profiles of effective practices* (pp. 139–151). Welland, ON: éditions Soleil publishing.

Gordon, P. (1994). Robert Owen (1771–1858). *Prospects, 24* (1), 279–296.

Goss Gilroy Inc. (1998a). *Providing home child care for a living: A survey of providers working in the regulated sector.* Ottawa: Canadian Child Care Federation.

Goss Gilroy Inc. (1998b). *Providing home child care for a living: A survey of providers working in the unregulated sector in the child's home.* Ottawa: Canadian Child Care Federation.

Goss Gilroy Inc. (1998c). *Providing home child care for a living: A survey of providers working in the unregulated sector in their own home.* Ottawa: Canadian Child Care Federation.

Government of New Zealand. (1998). *Update 27: Kōhanga Reo* [On-line]. Available: www.minedu.govt.nz/Curriculum/updates/update27/index27.htm

Gowen, J.W. (1995), The early development of symbolic play. *Young Children, 50* (3), 75–84.

Graeme, J., & Fahlman, R. (1990). *Hand-in-hand: Multicultural experiences for young children.* Don Mills, ON: Addison-Wesley.

Granucci, P.L. (1990). Kindergarten teachers: Working through our identity crisis. *Young Children, 45* (3), 6–11.

Graue, M.E. (1992). Meanings of readiness and the kindergarten experience. In S.A. Kessler & B.B. Swadener (Eds.), *Reconceptualizing the early childhood curriculum: Beginning the dialogue* (pp. 62–90). New York: Teachers College Press.

Graue, M.E. (1993). Expectations and ideas coming to school. *Early Childhood Research Quarterly, 8,* 53–75.

Gredler, G.R. (1984). Transition classes: A viable alternative for the at-risk child? *Psychology in the Schools, 21,* 463–470.

Greenberg, P. (1987). Lucy Sprague Mitchell: A major missing link between early childhood education in the 1980s and progressive education in the 1890s-1930s. *Young Children, 42* (5), 70–84.

Greenberg, P. (2000). What wisdom should we take with us as we enter the new century? An interview with Millie Almy. *Young Children, 55* (1), 6–10.

Greenwood, G.E., & Hickman, C.W. (1991). Research and practice in parent involvement: Implications for teacher education. *Elementary School Journal, 91* (3), 279–288.

Griffiths, C. (1999). Making the most of computers. *Interaction, 12* (4), 8–9.

Grindstaff, C.F. (1995). Canadian fertility 1951 to 1993 (Catalogue No. 11-008E). *Canadian Social Trends, 39,* 12–16.

Grover, M.B. (1999, September 6). Daddy stress. *Forbes, 164,* 202–208.

Grubb, W.N. (1989). Young children face the state: Issues and options for early childhood programs. *American Journal of Education, 97,* 358–397.

Grubb, W.N. (1991). Policy issues surrounding quality and content in early care and education. In B. Scales, M. Almy, A. Nicolopoulou, & S. Ervin-Tripp (Eds.), *Play and the social context of development in early care and education* (pp. 32–49). New York: Teachers College Press.

Guild, P. (1994). The culture/learning/style connection. *Educational Leadership, 51* (8), 16–21.

Gullo, D.F., & Clements, D.H. (1984). The effects of kindergarten schedule on achievement, classroom behavior, and attendance. *Journal of Educational Research, 78* (1), 51–56.

Gullo, D.F., Bersani, C.U., & Conlin, S. (1989). Parent-infant-toddler program: Building family support networks. *Early Child Development and Care, 29,* 273–287.

Gutek, G.L. (1968). *Pestalozzi and education.* New York: Random House.

Gutek, G.L. (1997). *Historical and philosophical foundations of education: A biographical introduction* (2nd ed.). Upper Saddle River, NJ: Prentice-Hall.

Guy, K.A. (Ed.). (1997). *Our promise to children.* Ottawa: Canadian Institute of Child Health.

Hains, H. (1992). *My new school.* New York: Dorling Kindersley.

Hall, N.S., & Rhomberg, V. (1995). *The affective curriculum: Teaching the anti-bias approach to young children.* Toronto: Nelson Canada.

Halpern, R. (1987). Major social and demographic trends affecting young families: Implications for early childhood care and education: What national trends affect low-income young families? Should society help? How? *Young Children, 42* (6), 34–40.

Halpern, R. (1988). Parent support and education for low-income families: Historical and current perspectives. *Children and Youth Services Review, 10,* 283–303.

Hamburg, D.A. (1995). A developmental strategy to prevent lifelong damage. *Report of the president: Annual report of the Carnegie Corporation of New York.* New York: Carnegie Corporation of New York.

Han, E.P. (1995). Reflection is essential in teacher education. *Childhood Education, 71,* 228–230.

Hannigan, I. (1998). *Off to school: A parent's-eye view of the kindergarten year.* Washington, DC: National Association for the Education of Young Children.

Harms, T. & Clifford, R.M. (1998). *Early Childhood Environment Rating Scale (ECERS).* New York: Teachers College Press.

Harms, T., & Clifford, R.M. (1989). *Family Day Care Rating Scale (FDCRS)*. New York: Teachers College Press.

Harms, T., Jacobs, E.V., & White, D.R. (1995). *School-Age Care Environment Rating Scale (SACERS)*. New York: Teachers College Press.

Harms. T., Cryer, D., & Clifford, R.M. (1990). *Infant/Toddler Environment Rating Scale (ITERS)*. New York: Teachers College Press.

Harris, K., & Lindauer, S.L. (1988). Parental and teacher priorities for kindergarten preparation. *Child Study Journal, 18* (2), 61–73.

Harris, L., Morgan, G., & Sprague, P. (1996). Facilitated accreditation project. In S. Bredekamp & B.A. Willer (Eds.), *NAEYC Accreditation: A decade of learning and the years ahead* (pp. 83–96). Washington, DC: National Association for the Education of Young Children.

Harrison, A.O., Wilson, M.N, Pine, C.J., Chan, S.Q., & Buriel, R. (1990). Family ecologies of ethnic minority children. *Child Development, 61,* 347–362.

Harrison, C. (1995). Family literacy practices in the United Kingdom - An international perspective. In D.K. Dickinson (Ed.), *Bridges to literacy: Children, families, and school* (pp. 150–174). Oxford: Blackwell.

Harrison, J.F.C. (1968a). Introduction. In J.F.C. Harrison (Ed.), *Utopianism and education: Robert Owen and the Owenites* (pp. 1–40). New York: Teachers College Press.

Harrison, J.F.C. (Ed.). (1968b). *Utopianism and education: Robert Owen and the Owenites.* New York: Teachers College Press.

Hart, C.H., Burts, D.C., & Charlesworth, R. (Eds.). (1997). *Integrated curriculum and developmentally appropriate practice: Birth to age eight.* New York: State University of New York Press.

Hartle, L., & Johnson, J.E. (1993). Historical and contemporary influences of outdoor play environments. In C.H. Hart (Ed.), *Children on playgrounds: Research perspectives and applications* (pp. 14–42). Albany, NY: State University of New York Press.

Hartup, W.W. (1983). Peer relations. In P. Mussen (Series Ed.) & E.M. Hetherington (Vol. Ed.), *Handbook of child psychology: Vol.4. Socialization, personality, and social development* (4th ed., pp. 103–196). New York: Wiley.

Harvey, E. (1999). Short-term and long-term effects of early parental employment on children of the National Longitudinal Survey of Youth. *Developmental Psychology, 35,* 445–459.

Hashima, P.Y., & Amato, P.R. (1994). Poverty, social support, and parental behavior. *Child Development, 65,* 394–403.

Hatch, J.A., & Freeman, E.B. (1988). Kindergarten philosophies and practices: Perspectives of teachers, principals, and supervisors. *Early Childhood Research Quarterly, 3* (2), 151–166.

Hatch, V., Hegstad, P., Heimgartner, N., Izumi, W., Konrad, K., & Miller, B. (1992). *Human rights for children: Curriculum for teaching human rights to children ages 3–12.* Alameda, CA: Hunter House.

Haugland, S.W. (1999). What role should technology play in young children's learning? *Young Children, 54* (6), 26–31.

Haugland, S.W. (2000). Early childhood classrooms in the 21st century: Using computers to maximize learning. *Young Children, 55,* (1), 12–18.

Haugland, S.W., & Shade, D.D. (1994). Software evaluation for young children. In J.L. Wright & D.D. Shade (Eds.), *Young children: Active learners in a technological age* (pp. 63–76). Washington, DC: National Association for the Education of Young Children.

Hausherr, R. (1997). *Celebrating families.* New York: Scholastic Press.

Hayward, D., Rothenburg, M. & Beasley, R. (1974). Children's play and urban playground environments: A comparison of traditional, contemporary, and adventure playground types. *Environment and Behavior, 6,* 131–168.

Head Start Bureau. (1998). *Head Start 1998 fact sheet* [On-line]. Available: http://www2.acf.dhhs.gov/programs/ hsb/research/98_hsfs.htm

Head Start Bureau. (1999). *Head Start fact sheet* [On-line]. Available: http://www.acf.dhhs.gov/programs/opa/facts/headst.htm

Head Start. (1982). *Project Head Start.* [Brochure]. Washington, DC: Administration for Children, Youth and Families and Department of Health and Human Services.

Head, J., & Barton, P. (1987). *Toy libraries in the community.* London: Eltan.

Health Canada. (1996). *The development of national goals for vaccine-preventable diseases of infants and children.* [On-line]. Available: http:// www.hc-sc.gc.ca/hpb/ lcdc/ publicat/ ccdr/97vol23/imm_sup/ Imm_c_e.html

Health Canada. (1997a). *Celebrate National Child Day, November 20 1997* (Catalogue No. H34–334/1997E) [Activity guide]. Ottawa: Author.

Health Canada. (1997b). *For the safety of Canadian children and youth: From injury data to preventive measures.* Ottawa: Author.

Health Canada. (1998). *Playground equipment* [On-line]. Available: http://www.hc-sc.gc.ca/hpb/lcdc/brch/injury/plygrnde.html

Health Canada. (1999a). *Backgrounder: Improving the health of Canada's aboriginal people* [On-line]. Available: http://www.hc-sc.gc.ca/hppb/phdd/ report/toward/eng/back/impro.html

Health Canada. (1999b). *Childhood and youth division* [On-line]. Available: http://www.hc-sc.gc.ca/childhood-youth

Helliwell, P. (1998). Learning together at the Hants Shore Health Centre. In A. Thomas (Ed.), *Family literacy in Canada: Profiles of effective practices* (pp. 107–115). Welland, ON: éditions Soleil publishing.

Henderson, A.T. (1988). Parents are a school's best friend. *Phi Delta Kappan, 70,* 148–153.

Henderson, R.H. (1998). Immunization: Going the extra mile. In *The progress of nations: 1998* (pp. 13–19). New York: United Nations Children Fund.

Hendrick, J. (1997). Reggio Emilia and American schools: Telling them apart and putting them together - Can we do it? In J. Hendrick (Ed.), *First steps toward teaching the Reggio way* (pp. 41–53). Upper Saddle River, NJ: Merrill/Prentice Hall.

Henniger, M.L. (1985). Preschool children's play behaviors in an indoor and outdoor environment. In J.L. Frost & S. Sunderlin (Eds.), *When children play: Proceedings of the International Conference on Play and Play Environments* (pp. 145–150). Wheaton, MD: Association for Childhood Education International.

Henniger, M.L. (1994). Planning for outdoor play. *Young Children, 49* (4), 10–15.

Herman, E. (1992). *My first day at school.* New York: McClanahan Book Company.

Herr, J., Johnson, R.D., & Zimmerman, K. (1993). Benefits of accreditation: A study of directors' perceptions. *Young Children, 48* (4), 32–35.

Hevey, D., & Curtis, A. (1996). Training to work in the early years. In G.

Pugh (Ed.), *Contemporary issues in the early years: Working collaboratively for children* (2nd ed., pp. 211–231). London: Paul Chapman Publishing and National Children's Bureau.

Hewes, D.W. (1996). *NAEYC's first half century 1926–1976.* Washington, DC: National Association for the Education of Young Children.

Hewes. D.W. (1998). *"It's the camaraderie": A history of parent cooperative preschools.* Davis, CA: Center for Cooperatives, University of California.

High Scope Educational Research Foundation. (2000). *High/Scope Child Observation Record (COR).* Ypsilanti, MI: High/Scope Press.

High/Scope Educational Research Foundation. (1998). *High/Scope Program Quality Assessment: PQA - preschool version: Administration manual.* Ypsilanti, MI: High/Scope Press.

Highlights of National Forum. (n.d.). *Highlights of National Forum on guiding principles for quality child care in Canada* [On-line]. Available: http://www.home.istar.ca/~cccns/principles.html

Hill, P.S. (1900, November). The future of kindergarten. *Teachers College Record, 10,* 48–54.

Hill, P.S. (1928). The home and the school as centers of child life. *Progressive Education, 5,* 211–216.

Hill, P.S. (1987). The function of kindergarten [Reprint of 1926 article]. *Young Children, 42* (5), 12–19.

Hill, P.S. (1992). *Kindergarten.* Olney, MD: Association for Childhood Education International (Original work published 1942)

Hillman, C.B. (1988). *Teaching four-year-olds: A personal journey.* Bloomington, IN: Phi Delta Kappa Educational Foundation.

Hoffard, C. (1996). A day in the life of a home child care provider. *Interaction, 10,* (2), 13–14.

Hohmann, C., & Buckleiter, W. (1992). *High/Scope K–3 curriculum series: Learning environment.* Ypsilanti, MI: High/Scope Press.

Hohmann, M. (1997). *A study guide to educating young children: Exercises for adult learners.* Ypsilanti, MI: High/Scope Press.

Hohmann, M., & Weikart, D.P. (1995). *Educating young children: Active learning practices for preschool and child care programs.* Ypsilanti, MI: High/Scope Press.

Holst, C.B. (1999). Buying more can give children less. *Young Children, 54* (5), 19–23.

Honig, A.S. (1986). Emerging issues in early childhood education, Part 2. *Day Care and Early Education, 13* (4), 22–27.

Honig, A.S. (1993). Mental health for babies: What do theory and research teach us? *Young Children, 48* (3), 69–76.

Hoover-Dempsey, K.B., & Sandler, H.M. (1997). Why do parents become involved in their children's education? *Review of Educational Research, 67,* 3–42.

Horn, H.A. (1992). Primary education in Germany. In G.A. Woodill, J., Bernhard, & L. Prochner (Eds.), *International handbook of early childhood education* (pp. 223–226). New York: Garland Publishing.

Horton, J., & Zimmer, J. (1990). *Media violence and children* [Brochure]. Washington, DC: National Association for the Education of Young Children.

Howe, J. (1986). *When you go to kindergarten.* New York: Alfred A. Knopf.

Howe, N. (1994). Reflections on early childhood education training: A tribute to Mary J. Wright. *Canadian Children, 19* (2), 16–19.

Howe, N. (2000). Early childhood care and education in Canada: An overview and future directions. In L. Prochner & N. Howe (Eds.), *Early childhood care and education in Canada* (pp. 293–314). Vancouver: UBC Press.

Howe, N., Jacobs, E., & Fiorentino, L.M. (2000). The curriculum. In L. Prochner & N. Howe (Eds.), *Early childhood care and education in Canada* (pp. 208–235). Vancouver: UBC Press.

Howe, N., Moller, L., & Chambers, B. (1994). Dramatic play in day care: What happens when doctors, cooks, bakers, pirates and pharmacists invade the classroom? In H. Goelman & E.V. Jacobs (Eds.), *Children's play in child care settings* (pp. 102–118). Albany, NY: State University of New York.

Howe, S., & Swail, H. (1999). The emergency child care research project: Action research to strengthen community-based child care and work/life initiatives. *Canadian Journal of Research in Early Childhood Education, 7,* 381–388.

Howes, C. (1990). Can the age of entry into child care and the quality of child care predict adjustment in kindergarten? *Developmental Psychology, 26,* 292–303.

Howes, C., & Farver, S.A. (1987). Social pretend play in two-year-olds: Effects of age of partner. *Early Childhood Research Quarterly, 2,* 305–314.

Howes, C., & Norris, D.J. (1997). Adding two school age children: Does it change the quality in family day care? *Early Childhood Research Quarterly, 12,* 327–342.

Howes, C., & Smith, E.W. (1995). Relations among child care quality, teacher behavior, children's play activities, emotional security, and cognitive activity in child care. *Early Childhood Research Quarterly, 10,* 381–404.

Howes, C., Hamilton, C.E., & Matheson, C.C. (1994). Children's relationships with peers: Differential association with aspects of the teacher-child relationship. *Child Development, 65,* 253–263.

Howes, C., Phillips, D.A., & Whitebrook, M. (1992). Thresholds of quality: Implications for the social development of children in centre-based care. *Child Development, 63,* 449–460.

Hoyle, M., & Evans, P. (1989). *The politics of childhood.* London: Journeyman.

Huberman, M. (1989). The professional life cycle of teachers. *Teachers College Record, 91* (1), 31–57.

Hughes, F.P. (1995). *Children, play, and development* (2nd ed.). Boston: Allyn and Bacon.

Hummel, C. (1994). Plato (428–348 B.C.). *Prospects, 24,* 329–342.

Humphreys, A.P., & Smith, P.K. (1984). Rough-and-tumble in preschool and playground. In P.K. Smith (Ed.), *Play in animals and humans* (pp. 241–266). Oxford: Basil Blackwell.

Humphryes, J. (1998). The developmental appropriateness of high-quality Montessori programs. *Young Children, 53* (4), 4–16.

Hunt, J.M. (1961). *Intelligence and experience.* New York: Ronald Press.

Hunter, T., & Pence, A. (1995). Supporting quality in early childhood programs. *Interaction, 9,* 30–34.

Hurst, V. (1991). *Planning for early learning: Education in the first five years.* London: Paul Chapman.

Huston, A., Watkins, B., & Kunkel, D. (1989). Public policy and children's television. *American Psychologist, 44,* 424–433.

Huston, A.C. (1991). Antecedents, consequences, and possible solutions for poverty among children. In A.C. Huston (Ed.), *Children in poverty: Child development and public policy* (pp. 282–315). Cambridge, MA: Cambridge University Press.

Hymes, J.L. (1968). *Teaching the child under six.* Columbus,OH: Charles E. Merrill.

Hymes, J.L. (1975). *Early childhood education: An introduction to the profession* (2nd ed.). Washington, DC: National Association for the Education of Young Children.

Hymes, J.L. (1987). Public school for 4–year-olds. *Young Children, 42* (2), 51–52.

Hyson, M.C. (1994). *The emotional development of young children: Building an emotion-centred curriculum.* New York: Teachers College Press.

Hyson, M.C. (1996). Theory: An analysis (Part 2). In S. Reifel (Series Ed.) & J.A. Chafel & S. Reifel (Vol. Eds.), *Advances in early education and day care: Vol. 8. Theory and practice in early childhood teaching* (pp.41–89). Greenwich, CT: JAI Press.

Institute of Child Study. (n.d.). *The Institute of Child Study* [On-line]. Available: http://www.oise.utoronto.ca/ICS

International Association for the Child's Right to Play. (1989). *IPA declaration of the child's right to play* [On-line]. Available: http://www.ncsu.edu/ipa

International Reading Association and the National Association for the Education of Young Children. (2000). *Learning to read and write: Developmentally appropriate practices for young children.* Newark, DE: International Reading Association.

International Reading Association. (1998). *Making the most of television: Tips for parents of young viewers* [Brochure]. Newark, DE: Author.

Invest in Kids. (1999a). *A national survey of parents of children under six.* [On-line]. Available: http://www.cfc-efc.ca/aeceo/articles/IIKsurvey.htm

Invest in Kids. (1999b) *The parent poll: A national survey of parents of children under six.* [On-line]. Available: http://www.investinkids.ca/eng/parents_exec_poll.htm

Irwin, S., & Canning, P. (1992). An historical overview of child care in Nova Scotia. In A.R. Pence (Ed.), *Canadian child care in context: Perspectives from the provinces and territories* (Vol.II, pp. 269–288). Ottawa: Statistics Canada and Health and Welfare Canada.

Irwin, S.H. (1997). Special needs inclusion: Including all children. *Interaction, 10* (4), 15–18.

Isaacs, S. (1968). *The nursery years: The mind of the child from birth to six years.* New York: Schocken (Original work published 1929)

Isenberg, J.P., & Brown, D.L. (1997). Development issues affecting children. In J.P. Isenberg & M.R. Jalongo (Eds.), *Major trends and issues in early childhood education: Challenges, controversies, and insights* (pp. 29–42). New York: Teachers College Press.

Isenberg, J.P., & Jalongo, M.R. (1997a). *Creative expression and play in early childhood* (2nd ed.). Upper Saddle River, NJ: Prentice-Hall.

Isenberg, J.P., & Jalongo, M.R. (1997b). Development issues affecting children. In J.P. Isenberg & M.R. Jalongo (Eds.), *Major trends and issues in early childhood education: Challenges, controversies, and insights* (pp. 29–42). New York: Teachers College Press.

Isenberg, J.P., & Jalongo, M.R. (Eds.). (1997c). *Major trends and issues in early childhood education: Challenges, controversies, and insights.* New York: Teachers College Press.

Jacobs, E.V. (1994). Introduction. In H. Goelman & E.V. Jacobs (Eds.), *Children's play in child care settings* (pp. 1–19). Albany, NY: State University of New York.

Jacobs, E.V. (1995). School-age child care: Quality and regulations. *Canadian Children, 20* (2), 46–47.

Jacobs, E.V., Mill, D., White, D.R., & Baillargeon, M. (1999). Regulatory systems for school-age care in Canada: Are the regulations appropriate? *Canadian Journal of Research in Early Childhood Education, 7,* 245–270.

Jacobs, E.V., Selig, G., White, D.R. (1992). Classroom behaviour in grade one: Does the quality of preschool day care experience make a difference? *Canadian Journal of Research in Early Childhood Education, 2,* 89–100.

Jalongo, M.R. (1999). Introduction. In M.R. Jalongo (Ed.), *Resisting the pendulum swing: Informed perspectives on education controversies* (pp. 7–16). Olney, MD: Association for Childhood Education International.

Jamieson, S. (1999). Seniors and children share special time. *Interaction, 13* (2), 31.

Jenkins, E.J., & Bell, C.C. (1997). Exposure and response to community violence among children and adolescents. In J.D. Osofsky (Ed.), *Children in a violent society* (pp. 9–31). New York: The Guilford Press.

Jennison, K. (2000, March 22). The ex-nannies club. *National Post,* p. B1.

Jensen, C. (1994), Fragments for a discussion about quality. In P. Moss & A.R. Pence (Eds.), *Valuing quality in early childhood services: New approaches to defining quality* (pp. 142–156). New York: Teachers College Press.

Jervis, K. (Ed.). (1984). *Separation: Strategies for helping two-to-four-year-olds.* Washington, DC: National Association for the Education of Young Children.

Jewett, J. (1997). Childhood stress. *Childhood Education, 73,* 172–173.

Jipson, J. (1991). Developmentally appropriate practice: Culture, curriculum, connections. *Early Education and Development, 2,* 120–136.

Johnson, G.E. (1894). Education by plays and games. *The Pedagogical Seminary, 3* (1), 97–133.

Johnson, H.M. (1936). *School begins at two: A book for teachers and parents* (B. Biber, Ed.). New York: Republic.

Johnson, J.E., & Johnson, K.M. (1994). The applicability of developmentally appropriate practice for children with diverse abilities. *Journal of Early Intervention, 18,* 343–346.

Johnson, J.E., Christie, J.F., & Yawkey, T.D. (1999). *Play and early childhood development* (2nd ed.). New York: Longman.

Johnson, L.C., & Mathien, J. (1998). *Early childhood services for kindergarten-age children in four Canadian provinces: Scope, nature and models for the future.* Ottawa: The Caledon Institute of Social Policy.

Johnson, L.C., & Mathien, J. (1999). Early childhood services for kindergarten-age children in four Canadian provinces: Scope, nature and models for the future. *Canadian Journal of Research in Early Childhood Education, 7,* 369–380.

Johnson-Dean, C. (1984, October 21). 40 years of co-op preschools. *Victoria Times-Colonist, The Islander,* pp.6–7.

Jones, A., & Rutman, L. (1981). *In the children's aid: J.J. Kelso and child welfare in Ontario.* Toronto: University of Toronto Press.

Jones, E. (1993). Introduction: Growing teachers. In E. Jones (Ed.),

Growing teachers: Partnerships in staff development (pp.xii–xxiii). Washington, DC: National Association for the Education of Young Children.

Jorde-Bloom, P. (1988a). *A great place to work: Improving conditions for staff in young children's programs.* Washington, DC: National Association for the Education of Young Children.

Jorde-Bloom, P. (1988b). Teachers need "TLC" too. *Young Children, 43* (6), 4–8.

Josephson, W.L. (1995). *Television violence: A review of the effects on children of different ages.* Ottawa: Canadian Heritage.

Kagan, J. (1994). *Galen's prophecy: Temperament in human nature.* New York: Basic Books.

Kagan, J. (1998). *Three seductive ideas.* Cambridge, MA: Harvard University Press.

Kagan S.L. (1999a). A⁵: Redefining 21st-century early care and education. *Young Children, 54* (6), 2–3.

Kagan, S.L. (1990b). Children's play: The journey from theory to practice. In E. Klugman & S. Smilansky (Eds.), *Children's play and learning: Perspectives and policy implications* (pp. 173–187). New York: Teachers College Press.

Kagan, S.L. (1990c, December). Readiness 2000: Rethinking rhetoric and responsibility. *Phi Delta Kappan,* 272–279.

Kagan, S.L. (1991a). Moving from here to there: Rethinking continuity and transitions in early care and education. In B. Spodek & O.N. Saracho (Eds.). *Yearbook in early childhood education: Vol. 2. Issues in early childhood curriculum* (pp. 132–151). New York: Teachers College Press.

Kagan, S.L. (1991b). *United we stand: Collaboration for child care and early education services.* New York: Teachers College Press.

Kagan, S.L. (1993). *Integrating services for children and families: Understanding the past to shape the future.* New Haven, CT: Yale University Press.

Kagan, S.L. (1994). Families and children: Who is responsible? *Childhood Education, 41,* 4–8.

Kagan, S.L. (1997). Support systems for children, youths, families, and schools in inner-city situations. *Education and Urban Society, 29,* 277–295.

Kagan, S.L. (1999b). The more things change, the more they stay the same: Fact or fiction? *Young Children, 54* (1), 2, 65.

Kagan, S.L., & Weissbourd, B. (Eds.). (1994). *Putting families first: America's family support movement and the challenge of change.* San Francisco: Jossey-Bass.

Kagan, S.L., Klugman, E., & Zigler, E.F. (1983). Shaping child and family policies: Criteria and strategies for a new decade. In E.F. Zigler, S.L. Kagan, & E. Klugman (Eds.), *Children, families, and government: Perspectives on American social policy* (pp. 415–438). Cambridge, MA: Cambridge University Press.

Kagan, S.L., Powell, D.R., Weissbourd, B., & Zigler, E.F. (Eds.). (1987). *America's family support programs: Perspectives and prospects.* New Haven, CT: Yale University Press.

Kagan. S.L., & Neumann, M.J. (1997). Highlights of the Quality 2000 initiative: Not by chance. *Young Children, 52* (6), 54–62.

Kaiser, B., & Rasminsky, J.S. (1990). What matters in daycare centres? The implcations of auspice and location. *Canadian Children, 15* (2), 21–29.

Kaiser, B., & Rasminsky, J.S. (1999a). *Meeting the challenge: Effective strategies for*

challenging behaviours in early childhood environments. Ottawa: Canadian Child Care Federation.

Kaiser, B., & Rasminsky, J.S. (1999b). *Partners in Quality.* Ottawa: Canadian Child Care Federation.

Kalata, D.E.T. (1998). Parents, let's play. *Young Children, 53* (5), 40–41.

Kalman, B. (Ed.). (1994). *Homes around the world.* New York: Crabtree Publishing.

Kamerman, S.B. (1991). Child care policies and programs: An international overview. *Journal of Social Issues, 47,* 179–196.

Kamerman, S.B. (1994). Childcare policies and programs: International overview. In T. Husén & T.N. Postlethwaite (Eds.), *International Encyclopedia of Education: Vol. 2* (2nd ed., pp.693–701). New York: Pergamon.

Kamerman, S.B., & Kahn, A.J. (1997). Investing in children: Government expenditure for children and their families in Western industrialized countries. In G.A. Cornia & S. Danziger (Eds.), *Child poverty and deprivation in the industrialized countries, 1945–1995* (pp. 91–121). Oxford: Clarendon Press.

Kaplan-Sanoff, M., Brewster, A., Stillwell, J., & Bergen, D. (1988). The relationship of play to physical/motor development and to children with special needs. In D. Bergen (Ed.), *Play as a medium for learning and development: A handbook of theory and practice* (pp. 137–162). Portsmouth, NH: Heinemann.

Karen, R. (1990, February). Becoming attached. *The Atlantic, 265,* 35–70.

Karen, R. (1994). *Becoming attached: Unfolding the mystery of the infant-mother bond and its impact on later life.* New York: Warner Books.

Karoly, L.A., Greenwood, P.W., Everingham, S.S., Houbé, J., Kilburn, M.R., Rydell, C.P., Sanders, M., & Chiesa, J. (1998). *Investing in our children: What we know and don't know about the costs and benefits of early childhood interventions.* Washington, DC: Rand.

Karrby, G. (1990). Children's conceptions of their own play. *Early Child Development and Care, 58,* 81–85.

Karweit, N. (1992). The kindergarten experience. *Educational Leadership, 49* (6), 82–86.

Karweit, N. (1993). Effective preschool and kindergarten programs for students at risk. In B. Spodek (Ed.), *Handbook of research on the education of young children* (pp. 385–411). New York: Macmillan Publishing.

Karweit, N.L. (1994). Issues in kindergarten organization and curriculum. In R.E. Slavin, N.L. Karweit, & B.A. Wasik (Eds.), *Preventing early school failure: Research, policy, and practice* (pp. 78–101). Boston: Allyn and Bacon.

Karwowska-Struczyk, M. (1999). Congruence between teachers' and parents' expectations. In D.P. Weikart (Ed.), *What should young children learn? Teacher and parent views in 15 countries* (pp. 109–123). Ypsilanti, MI: High/Scope Press.

Katz, L.G. (1977). *Talks with teachers: Reflections on early childhood education.* Washington, DC: National Association for the Education of Young Children.

Katz, L.G. (1980). Mothering and teaching-some significant distinctions. In L.G. Katz (Ed.), *Current topics in early childhood education.* (Vol. III, pp. 47–63). Norwood, NJ: Ablex Publishing.

Katz, L.G. (1987). The nature of professions: Where is early childhood education? In L.G. Katz (Ed.), *Current topics in early childhood education* (Vol. VII, pp. 1–16). Norwood, NJ: Ablex Publishing.

Katz, L.G. (1988). Where is early childhood education as a profession? In B. Spodek, O.N. Saracho, & D.L. Peters (Eds.), *Professionalism and the early childhood practitioner* (pp. 75–83). New York: Teachers College Press.

Katz, L.G. (1996). Child development knowledge and teacher preparation: Confronting assumptions. *Early Childhood Research Quarterly, 11*, 135–146.

Katz, L.G. (1998). What can we learn from Reggio Emilia? In C. Edwards, L. Gandini, & G. Forman (Eds.), *The hundred languages of children: The Reggio Emilia approach - Advanced reflections* (2nd ed., pp. 27–45). Greenwich, CT: Ablex Publishing.

Katz, L.G., & Chard, S.C. (1993). The project approach. In J.L. Roopnarine & J.E. Johnson (Eds.), *Approaches to early childhood education* (2nd ed., pp. 209–222). New York: Merrill.

Katz, L.G., & Chard, S.C. (2000). *Engaging children's minds: The project approach* (2nd ed.). Stamford, CT: Ablex Publishing.

Katz, L.G., & McClellan, D.E. (1997). *Fostering children's social competence: the teacher's role.* Washington, DC: National Association for the Education of Young Children.

Katz, L.G., Evangelou, D., & Hartman, J.A. (1990). *The case for mixed-age grouping in early education,* Washington, DC: National Association for the Education of Young Children.

Keating, D.P., & Mustard, J.F. (1996). The National Longitudinal Survey of Children and Youth: An essential element for building a learning society in Canada. In the *National Longitudinal Survey of Children and Youth: Growing up in Canada* (pp. 7–13). (Catalogue No. 89–550–MPE, no.1). Ottawa: Statistics Canada and Human Resources Development Canada.

Kellerman, M. (1996). *Reflecting our communities: A handbook on ethnocultural diversity in family resource programs.* Ottawa: Health Canada.

Kellerman, M., & MacAulay, J. (1998). *Training and professional development in the family resource field.* Ottawa: Canadian Association of Family Resource Programs.

Kellerman, S. (1998). *All in the family: A cultural history of family life.* Toronto: Penguin Books.

Kelley, T. (1990). *Day-care teddy bear.* New York: Random House.

Kelly-Byrne, D. (1989). *A child's play life.* New York: Teachers College Press.

Kendrick, A.S., Kaufmann, R., & Messenger, K.P. (Eds.). (1988). *Healthy young children: A manual for programs.* Washington, DC: National Association for the Education of Young Children.

Kennedy, D.K. (1996). After Reggio Emilia: May the conversation begin! *Young Children, 51* (5), 24–27.

Kennedy, M.M. (1978). Findings from the Follow Through Planned Variation Study. *Educational Researcher, 7* (6), 3–11.

Kerns, K.A., Cole, A., & Andrews, P.B. (1998). Attachment security, parent peer management practices, and peer relationships in preschoolers. *Merrill-Palmer Quarterly, 44* (4), 504–522.

Kessen, W. (1979). The American child and other cultural inventions. *American Psychologist, 34*, 815–820.

Kessler, S.A. (1991). Alternative perspectives on early childhood education. *Early Childhood Research Quarterly, 6*, 183–197.

Khaki, A. (1994). *The Rights of the Child.* Vancouver, BC: Committee for Racial Justice.

Kilbride, K.M. (Ed.). (1997a). *Include me too! Human diversity in early childhood.* Toronto: Harcourt & Brace.

Kilbride, K.M. (1997b). *Multicultural early childhood education.* Toronto: Ryerson Polytechnic Institute.

Kilpatrick, W.H. (1914). *The Montessori system examined.* Boston: Houghton Mifflin.

Kilpatrick, W.H. (1918). The project method. *Teachers College Record, 19,* 319–335.

Kincheloe, J.L. (1997). Home alone and "bad to the bone": The advent of a postmodern child. In S.R. Steinberg & J.L. Kincheloe (Eds.), *Kinderculture: the corporate construction of childhood* (pp. 31–52). Boulder, CO: Westview Press.

Kindersley, B., & Kindersley, A. (1995). *Children just like me.* Bolton, ON: Fenn Publishing.

King, N.R. (1979). Play: the kindergarteners' perspective. *The Elementary School Journal, 80* (2), 81–87.

King, N.R. (1982). Work and play in the classroom. *Social Education, 46,* 110–113.

Kivikink, R., & Schell, B. (1987). Demographic, satisfaction, and commitment profiles of day care users, nursery school users, and babysitter users in a medium-sized Canadian city. *Child and Youth Care Quarterly, 16,* 116–132.

Klein, E.L. (1988). How is a teacher different from a mother? Young children's perceptions of the social roles of significant adults. *Theory into Practice, 27* (1), 36–43.

Klotz, H. (1999, October 17). Chinese will soon be spoken more than French outside Quebec. *National Post,* p. A1.

Kontos, S. (1991). Child care quality, family background, and children's development. *Early Childhood Research Quarterly, 16,* 249–262.

Kontos, S. (1992). *Family day care: Out of the shadows and into the limelight.* Washington, DC: National Association for the Education of Young Children.

Kontos, S., Howes, C., Shinn, M., & Galinsky, E. (1995). *Quality in family child care and relative care.* New York: Teachers College Press.

Koralek, D.G., Colker, L.J., & Dodge, D.T. (1998). *The what, why, and how of high-quality early childhood education: A guide of on-site supervision* (Rev. ed.). Washington, DC: National Association for the Education of Young Children.

Korbin, J.E. (Ed.). (1981). *Child abuse and neglect: Cross-cultural perspectives.* Berkeley, CA: University of California Press.

Kostelnik, M.J. (1992). Myths associated with developmentally appropriate programs. *Young Children, 47,* 17–23.

Kostelnik, M.J., Whiren, A.P., & Stein, L.C. (1986). Living with He-Man: Managing superhero fantasy play. *Young Children, 41* (4), 3–9.

Kramer, R. (1988). *Maria Montessori: A biography.* Reading, MA: Addison-Wesley.

Kritchevsky, S., & Prescott, E. (with Walling, L.). (1983). *Planning environments for young children: Physical space.* Washington, DC: National Association for the Education of Young Children.

Kuball, Y. (1999). A case for developmental continuity in a bilingual K-2 setting. *Young Children, 54* (3), 74–79.

Kuklin, S. (1990). *Going to my preschool.* New York: Bradbury Press.

Kuperschmidt, J., & Coie, J. (1990). Preadolescent peer status, aggression, and school adjustment as predictors of externalizing problems in adolescence. *Child Development, 61,* 1350–1362.

Kurtz, L., & Derevensky, J.L. (1994). Adolescent motherhood: An application of the stress and coping model to child-rearing attitudes and practices. *Canadian Journal of Community Mental Health, 13* (I), 5–25.

Kyle, I., & Kellerman, M. (1998). *Case studies of Canadian family resource programs: Supporting families, children and communities.* Ottawa: Canadian Association of Family Resource Programs.

Kysela, G.M., McDonald, L., Drummond, J., & Alexander, J. (1996). The child and family resiliency research program. *The Alberta Journal of Educational Research, 42*, 406–409.

La Novara, P. (1993). *A portrait of families in Canada* (Catalogue No. 89–523E). Ottawa: Statistics Canada.

Labi, N. (1998, November 23). Burning out at nine? *Time, 152,* 44.

Ladd, G. (1990). Having friends, keeping friends, making friends, and being liked by peers in the classroom: Predictions of children's early school adjustment? *Child Development, 61*, 1081–1100.

Ladd, G.W., & Price, J.M. (1987). Predicting children's social and school adjustment following the transition from preschool to kindergarten. *Child Development, 58,* 1168–1189.

LaGrange, A., Turner, L.E., & Sharp, A. (1995). Teachers' perspectives on changes to ECS funding. *Early Childhood Education, 28*(I), 48-51.

Lally, J.R. (1995). The impact of child care policies and practices on infant/toddler identity formation. *Young Children, 51* (I), 58–67.

Lally, J.R., Griffin, A., Fenichal, E., Segal, M., Szanton, E., & Weissbourd, B. (1995). *Caring for infants and toddlers in groups.* Arlington, VA: ZERO TO THREE/The National Center.

Lambert, E.B. (1999). Do school playgrounds trigger playground bullying? *Canadian Children, 24* (I), 25–31.

Landers, C. (1990, October). Enhancing early child development: Alternative programme strategies. A briefing note presented to the Workshop on Early Child development, UNICEF, Cairo [On-line]. Available: http://www.ecdgroup.com/archive/cairo.htm

Landreth, G.L. (1982). *Play therapy: Dynamics of the process of counseling with children.* Springfield, IL: Charles C. Thomas Publisher.

Langreuter, J., & Sobat, V. (1997). *Little Bear goes to kindergarten.* Brookfield, CT: The Millbrook Press.

Langsted, O., & Sommer, D. (1993). Denmark. In M. Cochran (Ed.), *International handbook of child care policies and programs* (pp. 143–165). Westport, CT: Greenwood Press.

Lansdown, G. (1996). Respecting the right of children to be heard. In G. Pugh (Ed.), *Contemporary issues in the early years: Working collaboratively for children* (2nd ed., pp. 68–82). London: Paul Chapman Publishing and National Children's Bureau.

Lanser, S., & McDonnell, L. (1991). Creating quality curriculum yet not buying out the store. *Young Children, 47* (I), 4–9.

Laroche, M. (1998). In and out of low income (Catalogue No. 11–008–XPE). *Canadian Social Trends, 50,* 20–24.

Latham, A.S. (1998). Teacher satisfaction. *Educational Leadership, 55* (5), 82–92.

Lazar, I., & Darlington, R. (1982). Lasting effects of early education: A report from the Consortium for Longitudinal Studies. *Monographs of the Society for Research in Child Development, 47* (2–3, Serial No. 195). Chicago: Society for Research in Child Development.

Leach, P. (1994). *Children first: What society must do - And is not doing - for children today.* New York: Vintage Books.

Lechky, O. (1994). Epidemic of childhood obesity may cause major public health problems doctor warns. *Canadian Medical Association Journal, 150* (I), 78–81.

Ledingham, J.E. (1998). How playgrounds affect children's behavior. *Canadian Journal of Research in Early Childhood Education, 6,* 353–356.

Legoland A/S. (1997). *Legoland: Legoland park - A happy adventure.* Aalborg, Denmark: Nordyllands.

Lero, D.S. (2000). Early childhood education: An empowering force for the twenty-first century? In J. Hayden (Ed.), *Landscapes in early childhood education: Cross-national perspectives on empowerment - A guide for the new millennium* (pp. 445–457). New York: Peter Lang.

Lero, D.S., Doherty, G., Goelman, H., LaGrange, A., & Tougas, J. (1999). *The most pressing issues facing child care centres* [On-line]. Available: http://www.cfc-efc.ca/docs/00000122.htm

Lero, D.S., Goelman, H., Pence, A.R., Brockman, L.M., & Nuttall, S. (1992). *Canadian National Child Care Study: Parental work patterns and child care needs.* Ottawa: Statistics Canada/Health and Welfare Canada.

Levin, D.E. (1998). *Remote control childhood? Combating the hazards of media culture.* Washington, DC: National Association for the Education of Young Children.

Levin, D.E., & Carlsson-Paige, N. (1994). Developmentally appropriate television: Putting children first. *Young Children, 49* (5), 38–44.

Levin, I, & Trost, J. (1992). Understanding the concept of family. *Family Relations, 41,* 348–351.

LeVine, R.A., Miller, P.M., & West, M.M. (Eds.). (1988). *Parental behavior in diverse societies.* San Francisco: Jossey-Bass.

Liddell, C., & Krueger, P. (1989). Activity and social behavior in a crowded South African township nursery: A follow-up study on the effects of crowding at home. *Merrill-Palmer Quarterly, 35,* 209–226.

Liebschner, J. (1992). *A child's work: Freedom and play in Froebel's educational theory and practice.* Cambridge: The Lutterworth Press.

Lightfoot, S.L. (1978). *Worlds apart: Relationships between families and schools.* New York: Basic Books.

Lin C.C., & Fu, V.R. (1990). A comparison of child-rearing practices among Chinese, immigrant Chinese, and Caucasian-American parents. *Child Development, 61,* 429–433.

Lindbergh, A.M. (1935). *North to the Orient.* San Diego, CA: Harcourt Brace.

Linder, T. (1994). The role of play in early childhood special education. In P.L. Safford (Ed.), *Early childhood special education: Vol. 5* (pp. 72–95). New York: Teachers College Press.

Lindgren, A. (1987). *I want to go to school too.* Stockholm: R & S Books.

Little Soldier, L. (1989). Cooperative learning and the native American student. *Phi Delta Kappan, 71,* 161–163.

Lloyd, E., Melhuish, E., Moss, P., & Owen, C. (1989). A review of research on playgroups. *Early Child Development and Care, 43,* 77–99.

Lochhead, C., & Shillington, R. (1996). *A statistical profile of urban poverty.* Ottawa: Centre for International Statistics and the Canadian Council on Social Development.

Logan, L.M., & Logan, V.G. (1974). *Educating young children.* Toronto: McGraw-Hill Ryerson.

Lombard, A.D. (1994). *Success begins at home: The past, present and future of the Home Instruction Program for Preschool Youngsters* (2nd ed.). Guilford, CT: Dushkin Publishing.

Loo, C., & Kennelly, D. (1979). Social density: Its effects on behaviors and perceptions of preschoolers. *Environmental Psychology and Non-Verbal Behavior, 3* (3), 131–146.

Lottridge, C. (1998). The Parent-Child Mother Goose program. In A. Thomas (Ed.), *Family literacy in Canada: Profiles of effective practices* (pp. 119–126). Welland, ON: éditions Soleil publishing.

Louv, R. (1990). *Childhood's future.* New York: Doubleday.

Lowe, E. (2000). Quality child care, Danish style. *Interaction, 13* (4), 19–20.

Lubeck, S. (1994). The politics of developmentally appropriate practice: Exploring issues of culture, class, and curriculum. In B.L. Mallory & R.S. New (Eds.), *Diversity and developmentally appropriate practices: Challenges for early childhood education* (pp. 17–43). New York: Teachers College Press

Lubeck, S. (1996). Deconstructing "child development knowledge" and "teacher preparation". *Early Childhood Research Quarterly, 11,* 147–167.

Lundy, C. (1997). *An introduction to the Convention on the Rights of the Child.* Sparta, ON: Full Circle Press.

Lyon, M., & Canning, P. (1996). The Atlantic day care study: Summary report for parents. *Interaction, 10* (2), 33–36.

MacIsaac, M. (1994, June). Playgrounds that work: How a Halifax playground sets the example. *Today's Parent, 11* (4), 55–58.

Major-Hamza, S. (2000). Five dollars a day: The flip side of Quebec's family policy. *Interaction, 14* (2), 5–6.

Malaguzzi, L. (1998). History, ideas, and basic philosophy: An interview with Lella Gandini (L. Gandini, Trans.). In C. Edwards, L. Gandini, & G. Forman (Eds.), *The hundred languages of children - The Reggio Emilia approach - Advanced reflections* (2nd ed., pp. 49–96). Greewich, CT: Ablex Publishing.

Mann, B. (1996, Summer). The benefits and pitfalls of collaboration. *Play and Parenting Connections,* 11.

Mansbridge, A. (1932). *Margaret McMillan: Prophet and pioneer: Her life and work.* London: J.M. Dent and Sons.

Marans, S., & Adelman, A. (1997). Experiencing violence in a developmental context. In J.D. Osofsky (Ed.), *Children in a violent society* (pp. 202–222). New York: The Guildford Press.

Marcil-Gratton, N. (1999). Growing up with mom and dad? Canadian children experience shifting family structure. *Transition, 29* (1), 4–7.

Marsden, L.R. (1996). Children, women and our economy: Building reconciliation for the 21st century. In the *National Forum on Family Security: Family security in insecure times* (Vol. II, pp. 277–235). Ottawa: Canadian Council on Social Development.

Marshall, H.H. (1994). Children's understanding of academic tasks: Work, play, or learning. *Journal of Research in Childhood Education, 9* (1), 35–46.

Marshall, J. (1999, July 21). The great burden some children bear. *National Post, I,* B1.

Marshall, K. (1998a). Balancing work and family (Catalogue No. 71–535–MPB, no.8). *Work Arrangements in the 1990s: Analytic Report No. 8.* Ottawa: Statistics Canada.

Marshall, K. (1998b). Stay-at-home dads (Catalogue No. 75–001–XPE). *Perspectives, 10* (1), 9–15.

Martin, A. (1985). Back to kindergarten basics. *Harvard Educational Review, 55* (3), 318–320.

Martin, R.P. (1994). Child temperament and common problems in schooling: Hypotheses about causal connections. *Journal of School Psychology, 32* (2), 119–134.

Martin, S. (1987). *Sharing the responsibility: Report of the Special Committee on Child Care.* Ottawa: Queen's Printer.

Martin, S. (1994). *Take a look: Observation and portfolio assessment in early childhood.* Don Mills, ON: Addison-Wesley.

Marxen, C., Irvine, G., Carlson, H., Billman, J., & Sherman, J. (1997). Empowerment effect through involvement in a statewide research study on kindergarten education. *Journal of Early Childhood Teacher Education, 18* (3), 35–42.

Masland, T. (2000, July 17). Breaking the silence. *Newsweek,* 30–32.

Matthews, G.B. (1994). *The philosophy of childhood.* Cambridge, MA: Harvard University Press.

Maxwell, K.L., & Eller, S.K. (1994). Children's transition to kindergarten. *Young Children, 49* (6), 56–63.

Mayer, F. (1973). *A history of educational thought* (3rd ed.). Columbus, OH: Charles E. Merrill Publishing.

Mayfield, M.I. (1983). Orientation to school and transitions of children between primary grades. *The Alberta Journal of Educational Research, 29* (4), 272–284.

Mayfield, M.I. (1988a). Employer-supported child care: Three research studies, issues and recommendations. *Canadian Journal of Research in Early Childhood Education, 2,* 149–158.

Mayfield, M.I. (1988b). Toy libraries in Canada: A research study. *Canadian Children, 13* (2), 1–18.

Mayfield, M.I. (1990a). Parent involvement in early childhood programs. In I.M. Doxey (Ed.), *Child care and education: Canadian dimensions* (pp. 240–253). Scarborough, ON: Nelson Canada.

Mayfield, M.I. (1990b, June). *The roles and perceptions of parents participating in three early childhood programs.* Paper presented at the XVIII Canadian Society for the Study of Education Annual Conference, Victoria, B.C.

Mayfield, M.I. (1990c). *Work-related child care in Canada.* Ottawa: Women's Bureau, Labour Canada.

Mayfield, M.I. (1992). The classroom environment: A living-in and learning-in space. In L.O. Ollila & M.I. Mayfield (Eds.), *Emerging literacy: Preschool, kindergarten, and primary grades* (pp. 166–195). Needham Heights, MA: Allyn and Bacon.

Mayfield, M.I. (1993a). Family support programs: Neighbourhood programs helping families. *International Journal of Early Childhood, 25,* 45–50.

Mayfield, M.I. (1993b). Toy libraries: Promoting play, toys, and family support internationally. *Early Child Development and Care, 87,* 1–13.

Mayfield, M.I. (1994). Changes in China's boarding kindergartens. *Canadian Children, 19* (2), 28–31.

Mayfield, M.I. (1995, August). Family support programs in Canada. Paper presented at the 21st World Congress of the Organisation Mondiale de l'Education Prescolaire (OMEP), Yokohama, Japan.

Mayfield, M.I. (1997). Early childhood education in Hungary: Changes and challenges. *Early Childhood Education in British Columbia, 12* (2), 5–7.

Mayfield, M.I. (1998). Kindergarten in the Czech Republic: Tradition and transition. *Canadian Children, 23* (2), 22–27.

Mayfield, M.I., Dey, J.D., Gleadow, N.E., Liedtke, W., & Probst, A. (1981). *Kindergarten needs assessment: General report.* Victoria: Ministry of Education. (ERIC Documentation Reproduction Service No. Ed 219 139)

Maynard, F. (1986). *The child care in crisis: The thinking parent's guide to day care.* New York: Penguin Books.

McBride, B.A., & Rane, T.R. (1997). Father/male involvement in early childhood programs: Issues and challenges. *Early Childhood Education Journal, 25* (1), 11–15.

McCabe, A., & Beltrame, J. (1998, December 5). UN report slams Canada for its stand on poverty. *National Post,* p.A1.

McCann, W. (1999, January 15). Face of homelessness changes in Toronto toward young, families. *Times-Colonist,* p. A8.

McClelland, J. (1995). Sending children to kindergarten: A phenomeno-logical study of mothers' experiences. *Family Relations, 44,* 177–183.

McCollum, J., McLean, M., McCartan, K., & Kaiser, C. (1989). Recommendations for certification of early childhood special educators. *Journal of Early Intervention, 13,* 195–211.

McCracken, J. (1999). *Playgrounds: Safe and sound* [Brochure]. Washington, DC: National Association for the Education of Young Children.

McCracken, J.B. (1986). *So many goodbyes: Ways to ease the transition between home and groups for young children* [Brochure]. Washington, DC: National Association for the Education of Young Children.

McCready, K.J. (1992). *The role of co-operatives in childcare.* Ottawa: Co-operatives Secretariat.

McDonell, L. (1992). An historical view of child care in British Columbia. In (A. Pence, Coordinating Ed.), *Canadian child care in context: Perspectives from the provinces and territories* (pp. 19–42). Ottawa: Statistics Canada/Health and Welfare Canada.

McDonnell, K. (1994). *Kid culture: Children and adults and popular culture.* Toronto: Second Story Press.

McGillicuddy-DeLisi, A.V., & Subramanian, S. (1996). How do children develop knowledge? Beliefs of Tanzanian and American mothers. In S. Harkness & C.M. Super (Eds.), *Parents' cultural belief systems: Their origins, expressions, and consequences* (pp. 143–168). New York: Guilford Press.

McKie, C. (1993). Population aging: Baby boomers into the 21st century. (Catalogue No. 11–008E). *Canadian Social Trends, 29,* 2–5.

McMahan, I.D. (1992). Public preschool from the age of two: The Ecole Maternelle in Fance. *Young Children, 47* (5), 22–28.

McMillan, M. (1901). *Early childhood.* London: Swan Sonnenschein and Company.

McMillan, M. (1919). *The nursery school.* London: J.M. Dent and Sons.

McMullen, M.B. (1999). Achieving best practices in infant and toddler care and education. *Young Children, 54* (4), 69–76.

McNaughton, M. (1996). The stats story. *Family, 3* (4), 17–19.

McQuade, J. (1999). *At preschool with teddy bear.* New York: Dial Books for Young Readers.

McQuail, S., & Pugh, S. (1995). *Effective organisation of early childhood services.* London: National Children's Bureau Enterprises.

Meade, A. (2000). The early childhood landscape in New Zealand. In J. Hayden (Ed.), *Landscapes in early childhood education: Cross-national per-spectives on empowerment - a guide for the new millennium* (pp. 83–93).

New York: Peter Lang.

Meier, D., & Schafran, A. (1999). Strengthening the preschool-to-kinder-garten transition: A community collaborates. *Young Children, 54* (3), 40–46.

Meisels, S.J. (1991). Four myths about America's kindergartens. *Focus on Early childhood, 4* (1), 1, 3.

Meston, J. (1993). *Child abuse and neglect prevention programs.* Ottawa: Vanier Institute of the Family.

Metzger, S. (1996). *Dinofours: It's time for school!* New York: Scholastic Books.

Mialaret, G. (1976). *World survey of pre-school education.* Paris: UNESCO.

Millar, W.J., & Wadhera, S. (1997). A perspective on Canadian teenage births, 1992–94: Older men and younger women? *Canadian Journal of Public Health, 88,* 333–336.

Miller, P.H. (1993). *Theories of developmental psychology* (3rd ed.). New York; W.H. Freeman.

Miller, T.J. (1984). Therapist-child relations in play therapy. In T.D. Yawkey & A.D. Pellegrini (Eds.), *Child's play and play therapy* (pp. 85–103). Lancaster, PA: Technomic Publishing.

Mirabelli, A., & Glossop, R. (1997). Of wings and roots: Canada's fami-lies: An update. *Transition, 27* (3), 5–10.

Mitchell, A. (2000, January 21). The children's budget: Faith and disbe-lief. *The Globe and Mail,* p.A16.

Mitchell, A., & Modigliani, K. (1989). Young children in public schools? The "only ifs" reconsidered. *Young Children, 4* (6), 56–61.

Modigliani, K. (1996). *Parents speak about child care.* New York: Families and Work Institute.

Monighan-Nourot, P., Scales, B., & Van Hoorn, J. (with Almy, M.). (1987). *Looking at children's play: A bridge between theory and practice.* New York: Teachers College Press.

Monroe, P. (Ed.). (1914). Playgrounds. In P. Monroe (Ed.)., *A cyclopedia of education* (pp. 728–730). New York: Macmillan.

Montané, M. (1999). The expectations questionnaire's eight skill cate-gories - How do teachers and parents rank them? In D.P. Weikart (Ed.), *What should young children learn? Teacher and parent views in 15 countries* (pp. 79–107). Ypsilanti, MI: High/Scope Press.

Montessori, M. (1912). *The Montessori Method* (A.E. George, Trans.). New York: Frederick A. Stokes.

Montessori, M. (1914). *Dr. Montessori's own handbook.* New York: Frederick A. Stokes.

Montessori, M. (1917). *The advanced Montessori method: Vol. 2. The Montessori elementary materials* (A. Livingston, Trans.). Cambridge, MA: Robert Bentley.

Montessori, M. (1964). *The Montessori Method* (A.E. George, Trans.). New York: Schocken Books (Original work published 1912)

Montessori, M. (1966). *The secret of childhood* (M.J. Costello, Trans.). Notre Dame, IN: Fides Publishers.

Montessori, M. (1974). *Childhood education* (A.M. Joosten, Trans.). Chicago: Henry Regnery.

Montessori, M. (1976). *From childhood to adolescence: Including "Erdkinder" and the functions of the university* (A.M. Joosten, Trans.). New York: Schocken Books.

Montessori, M. (1995). *The absorbent mind* (C.A. Claremont, Trans.). New York: Owl Books. (Original work published 1967)

Moore, G.T. (1997). New scales for assessing the quality of the physical environment of child care centers. *Interaction, 11* (3), 34–36.

Moore, R.S., & Moore, D.N. (with Willey, T.J., Moore, D.R., & Kordenbrock, D.K.). (1979). *School can wait.* Provo, UT: Brigham Young University Press.

Moreton, D., & Berger, S. (1999). *A day in Japan.* New York: Scholastic.

Morgan, G.G. (1986). Supplemental care for young children. In M.W. Yogman & T.B. Brazelton (Eds.), *Support of families* (pp. 156–172). Cambridge, MA: Harvard University Press.

Morris, A. (1998). *Play.* New York: Lothrop, Lee & Shepard Books.

Morrison, G.S. (1998). *Early childhood education today* (7th ed.). Upper Saddle River, NJ: Prentice-Hall.

Morrison, R., & Masten, A.S. (1991). Peer reputation in middle childhood as a predictor or adaptation in adolescence: A seven-year follow up. *Child Development, 62,* 991–1007.

Morrow, L.M. (1995). Family literacy: New perspectives, new practices. In L.M. Morrow (Ed.), *Family literacy: Connections in schools and communities* (pp. 5–10). Newark, DE: International Reading Association.

Morrow, L.M., Tracey, D.H., & Maxwell, C.M. (Eds.). (1995). *A survey of family literacy in the United States.* Newark, DE: International Reading Association.

Morrow, L.M., & Rand, M. (1991). Preparing the classroom environment to promote literacy during play. In J.F. Christie (Ed.), *Play and early literacy development* (pp. 141–165). New York: State University of New York Press.

Morrow, V. (1995). Invisible children? Toward a reconceptualization of childhood dependency and responsibility. *Sociological Studies of Children, 7,* 207–230.

Morss, J.R. (1996). *Growing critical: Alternatives of developmental psychology.* New York: Routledge.

Morton, A.L. (1962). *The life and ideas of Robert Owen.* London: Lawrence & Wishart.

Moss, P. (1996). Perspectives from Europe. In G. Pugh (Ed.), *Contemporary issues in the early years: Working collaboratively for children* (2nd ed.). London: Paul Chapman and National Children's Bureau.

Moss, P. (1999). International standards or one of many possibilities? In *Early childhood education and care in the 21st century: Global guidelines and papers from an international symposium hosted by the World Organization for Early Childhood Education (Organisation Mondiale pour L'Éducation Préscolaire) and the Association for Childhood Education International.* Olney, MD: Association for Childhood Education International and World Organization for Early Childhood Education (Organisation Mondiale pour L'Éducation Préscolaire).

Moyer, J. (Ed.). (1995). *Selecting educational equipment and materials for school and the home* (4th ed.). Wheaton, MD: Association for Childhood Education International.

Moyer, J., Egertson, H., & Isenberg, J. (1987). The child-centered kindergarten. *Childhood Education, 63,* 235–243.

Muir, E.S. (1990). Parent's talk in parent cooperative groups: Old words, new meanings. *Journal of the Canadian Association of Young Children, 15* (2), 13–20.

Mulligan, V. (1996). *Children's play: An introduction for care providers.* Don Mills, ON: Addison-Wesley.

Multiculturalism and Citizenship Canada. (1990). *The Canadian Multiculturalism Act: A guide for Canadians.* Ottawa: Author.

Musson, S. (1994). *School-age care: Theory and practice.* Don Mills, ON: Addison-Wesley.

Musson, S. (1999). *School-age care: Theory and practice* (2nd ed.). Don Mills, ON: Addison-Wesley.

Naron, N.K. (1981). The need for full-day kindergarten. *Educational Leadership, 38* (1), 306–309.

National Aboriginal Head Start Committee. (1996). *Aboriginal Head Start: Principles and guidelines.* Ottawa: Author.

National Association for the Education of Young Children and International Reading Association. (1998). *Raising a reader, raising a writer: How parents can help* [Brochure]. Washington, DC: National Association for the Education of Young Children.

National Association for the Education of Young Children Information Service. (1989). *Facility design for early childhood programs: An NAEYC resource guide.* Washington, DC: Author.

National Association for the Education of Young Children. (1985). In whose hands? A demographic fact sheet on child care providers. Washington, DC: Author.

National Association for the Education of Young Children. (1991a). *Guide to accreditation by the National Academy of Early Childhood Programs* (Rev. ed.). Washington, DC: Author.

National Association for the Education of Young Children. (1991b). NAEYC to launch new professional development initiative. *Young Children, 46* (6), 37–39.

National Association for the Education of Young Children. (1994). NAEYC position statement: A conceptual framework for early childhood professional development. *Young Children, 49* (3), 68–77.

National Association for the Education of Young Children. (1995). *NAEYC position statement on school readiness* [On-line]. Available: http://www.naeyc.org/about/position/psredy98.htm

National Association for the Education of Young Children. (1996a). *Guidelines for preparation of early childhood professionals.* Washington, DC: Author.

National Association for the Education of Young Children. (1996b). NAEYC position statement: Responding to linguistic and cultural diversity - recommendations for effective early childhood education. *Young Children, 51* (2), 4–12.

National Association for the Education of Young Children. (1996c). NAEYC position statement: Technology and young children - ages three through eight. *Young Children, 51* (6), 11–16.

National Association for the Education of Young Children (1997a). *A caring place for your toddler* [Brochure]. Washington, DC: Author.

National Association for the Education of Young Children. (1997b). *A good kindergarten for your child* [Brochure]. Washington, DC: Author.

National Association for the Education of Young Children. (1997c). *A good preschool for your child* [Brochure]. Washington, DC: Author.

National Association for the Education of Young Children. (1998a). *Accreditation criteria and procedures of the National Academy of Early Childhood Programs.* Washington, DC: Author.

National Association for the Education of Young Children. (1998b). *Choosing a good early childhood program: Questions and answers* [Brochure]. Washington, DC: Author.

National Association for the Education of Young Children. (1998c). NAEYC position statement on licensing and public regulation of early childhood programs. *Young Children, 53* (1), 43–50.

National Association for the Education of Young Children (1998d). *A caring place for your infant* [Brochure]. Washington, DC: Author.

National Association for the Education of Young Children. (1999a). NAEYC position statement on developing and implementing effective public policies to promote early childhood and school-age care program accreditation. *Young Children, 54* (4), 36–40.

National Association for the Education of Young Children. (1999b). *Ready to go: What parents should know about school readiness* [Brochure]. Washington, DC: National Association for the Education of Young Children.

National Association for the Education of Young Children. (1999c). *Reducing class size: A goal for children's champions* [On-line]. Available: http://www.naeyc.org/public_affairs/champions/classize2.htm

National Children's Agenda - Developing a shared vision. (1999, May). Ottawa: The Federal-Provincial-Territorial Council on Social Policy Renewal.

National Crime Prevention Council. (1997). *Preventing crime by investing in families: Promoting positive outcomes in children six to twelve years old.* Ottawa: Author.

National Institutes of Health. (1999, November 7). *Only small link found between hours in child care and mother-child interaction* [On-line]. Available: http://www.nichd.nih.gov/new/releases/timeinchildcare.htm

National Longitudinal Survey of Children and Youth. (1996). *Growing up in Canada* (Catalogue No. 89–550–MPE, no.1). Ottawa: Statistics Canada. (See also Ross, D.P., Scott, K., & Kelly, M.A. (1996). Overview: children in Canada in the 1990s. In *National Longitudinal Survey of Children and Youth: Growing up in Canada* (pp. 15–45). (Catalogue No. 89–550–MPE, no. 1). Ottawa: Statistics Canada and Human Resources Development Canada.)

National Television Violence Study. (1996). The National Television Violence Study: Key findings and recommendations. *Young Children, 51* (3), 54–55.

Nault, F. (1997). Infant mortality and low birthweight, 1975 to 1995 (Catalogue No. 82–003–XPB). *Health Reports, 9* (3), 39–45.

Nett, E.M. (1979). *Canadian families past and present.* Scarborough, ON: Butterworths.

Neuman, S., & Roskos, K. (1992). Literacy objects as cultural tools: Effects on children's literacy behaviors during play. *Reading Research Quarterly, 27,* 203–223.

Neuman, S.B., Copple, C., & Bredekamp, S. (2000). *Learning to read and write: Developmentally appropriate practices for young children.* Washington, DC: National Association for the Education of Young Children.

New York Committee on Mental Health. (1948). *What nursery school is like: A pamphlet for parents.* New York: New York Committee on Mental Health of the State Charities Aid Association.

New, R.S., & Mallory, B.L. (1996). The paradox of diversity in early care and education. In E.J. Erwin (Ed.), *Putting children first: Visions for a brighter future for young children and their families* (pp. 143–166). Baltimore: Paul H. Brookes.

Newberger, J.J. (1997). New brain development research - A wonderful window of opportunity to build public support for early childhood education! *Young Children, 52* (4), 4–9.

Noddings, N. (1990). Feminist critiques in the professions. In C.B. Cazden (Ed.), *Review of research in education* (Vol. 16, pp. 393–424). Washington, DC: American Educational Research Association.

Noddings, N. (1998). *Philosophy of education.* Boulder, CO: Westview Press.

Norman, K. (1994). Good beginnings: Family day care. *Focus, 5,* 25–29.

Normand, C.L., Zoccolillo, M., Tremblay, R.E, McIntyre, L., Boulerice, B., McDuff, P., Pérusse, & Barr, D.G. (1996). In the beginning: Looking for the roots of babies' difficult temperament. In *National Longitudinal Survey of Children and Youth: Growing up in Canada* (pp. 57–68). (Catalogue No. 89–550–MPE, no. 1). Ottawa: Statistics Canada and Human Resources Development Canada.

Norton, T. (1997). Special health care for child care settings: Minimize the risks. *Interaction, 10* (4), 19–20.

Novick, R. (1998). The comfort corner: Fostering resiliency and emotional intelligence. *Childhood Education, 74,* 200–204.

Nykyforunk, J. (1992). An historical overview of child care in Saskatchewan. In A.R. Pence (Ed.), *Canadian child care in context: Perspectives from the provinces and territories* (Vol.II, pp. 213–230). Ottawa: Statistics Canada and Health and Welfare Canada.

O'Connor, S.M. (1995). Mothering in public: The division of organized child care in the kindergarten and day nursery, St. Louis, 1886–1920. *Early Childhood Research Quarterly, 10,* 63–80.

Oberhuemer, P. (1995). Forum for the debate on early childhood issues in Germany. [Special Congress Ed.]. *International Journal of Early Childhood, 26–28.*

Odom, S.L., & Diamond, K.E. (1998). Inclusion of young children with special needs early childhood education: The research base. *Early Childhood Research Quarterly, 13,* 3–25.

Odoy, H.A.D., & Foster, S.H. (1997). Creating play crates for the outdoor classroom. *Young Children, 52* (6), 12–16.

Office for Standards in Education. (1995). *Guidance on the inspection of nursery and primary schools.* London: Her Majesty's Stationary Office.

Okagaki, L. & Diamond, K.E. (2000). Responding to cultural and linguistic differences in the beliefs and practices of families with young children. *Young Children, 55*(4), 74-80.

Ollila, L., Mayfield, M., & Williams, B.M. (1983). A study of the creative writing of grade 1 level children in England, United States and Canada. *Prime Areas, 25* (3), 39–43.

Ollila, L.O., & Mayfield, M.I. (Eds.). (1992). *Emerging literacy: Preschool, kindergarten, and primary grades.* Needham Heights, MA: Allyn and Bacon.

Olmstead, P.P. (1991). Parent involvement in elementary education: Findings and suggestions from the Follow Through Program. *Elementary School Journal, 91* (3), 221–231.

Olmsted, P.P., & Weikart, D.P. (Eds.). (1989). *How nations serve young children: Profiles of child care and education in 14 countries.* Ypsilanti, MI: High/Scope Press.

Olmsted, P.P., & Weikart, D.P. (Eds.). (1994). *Families speak: Early childhood care and education in 11 countries.* Ypsilanti, MI: High/Scope Press.

Olmsted, P.P., & Weikart, D.P. (Eds.). (1995). *The IEA preprimary study: Early childhood care and education in 11 countries.* Oxford: Pergamon Press.

Olsen, D., & Zigler, E. (1989). An assessment of the all-day kindergarten movement. *Early Childhood Research Quarterly, 4,* 167–186.

Olson, L. (1983). *Costs of children.* Lexington, MA: Lexington Books.

Omwake, E. (1971). Preschool promtorical perspective. *Interchange, 2,* 27–40.

Ontario Ministry of Education. (1985). *Report of the Early Primary Education Project.* Toronto: Author.

Ontario Royal Commission on Learning. (1994). *For the love of learning: Vol. II: Learning: Our vision for schools.* Toronto: Queen's Printer.

Oppenheim, J. (1987). *Buy me! buy me! The Bank Street guide to choosing toys for children.* New York: Pantheon Books.

Osborn, A.F. (1990). Resilient children: A longitudinal study of high achieving socially disadvantaged children. *Early Childhood Development and Care, 62,* 23–47.

Osborn, A.F., & Milbank, J.E. (1987). *The effects of early education: A report from the Child Health and Education Study.* Oxford: Clarendon Press.

Osborn, D.K. (1991). *Early childhood education in historical perspective* (3rd ed.). Athens, GA: Daye Press.

Osofsky, J.D. (Ed.). (1997). *Children in a violent society.* New York: The Guildford Press.

Ott, D.J., Zeichner, K.M., & Price, G.G. (1990). Research horizons and the quest for a knowledge base in early childhood teacher education. In B. Spodek & O.N. Saracho (Eds.), *Yearbook in early childhood education: Vol. 1. Early childhood teacher preparation* (pp. 118–137). New York: Teachers College Press.

Owen, G. (1920). *Nursery school education.* New York: E.P. Dutton.

Owen, R. (1970). *A new view of society and report to the County of Lanark.* London: Pelican Books. (Original work published 1813)

Owens, A.M. (1998, December 30). Skin cancer rates decline after almost 20 years. *National Post,* p. A8.

Paley, V.G. (1979). *White teacher* [Reissued 2000]. Cambridge, MA: Harvard University Press.

Paley, V.G. (1984). *Boys and girls: Superheroes in the doll corner.* Chicago: University of Chicago Press.

Paley, V.G. (1992). *You can't say you can't play.* Cambridge, MA: Harvard University Press.

Paley, V.G. (1995). *Kwanzaa and me: A teacher's story.* Cambridge, MA: Harvard University Press.

Paley, V.G. (1999). *The kindness of children.* Cambridge, MA: Harvard University Press.

Pardeck, J.T., Pardeck, J.A., & Murphy, J.W. (1987). The effects of day care: A critical analysis. *Early Childhood Development and Care, 27,* 419–435.

Parke, R.D., & Slaby, R.G. (1983). The development of aggression. In P.H. Mussen (Series Ed.), & E.M. Hetherington (Vol. Ed.), *Handbook of child psychology: Vol. 4. Socialization, personality, and social development* (4th ed., pp. 547–641). New York: John Wiley.

Parten, M.B. (1932). Social participation among pre-school children. *Journal of Abnormal Social Psychology, 27,* 243–269.

Patulli, G. (1994). Ressource Papillon. *Focus, 5,* 17–20.

Payne, V.G., & Rink, J.E. (1997). Physical education in the developmentally integrated curriculum. In C.H. Hart, D.C. Burts, R. Charlesworth (Eds.), *Integrated curriculum and developmentally appropriate practice: Birth to age eight* (pp.145–170). New York: State University of New York Press.

Peabody, E., & Mann, E. (1877). *Guide to kindergarten and intermediate class*

(Rev. ed.). New York: Steiger. (Original work published 1863)

Peck, J.T., McCaig, G., & Sapp, M.E. (1988). *Kindergarten policies: What is best for children?* Washinton, DC: National Association for the Education of Young Children.

Pellegrini, A.D. (1985). Social-cognitive aspects of children's play: the effects of age, gender, and activity centers. *Journal of Applied Developmental Psychology, 6,* 129–140.

Pellegrini, A.D. (1987). *Applied child study: A developmental approach.* Hillsdale, NJ: Lawrence Erlbaum.

Pellegrini, A.D. (1988). Elementary-school children's rough-and-tumble play and social competence. *Developmental Psychology, 24,* 802–806.

Pellegrini, A.D. (1989). Elementary school children's rough-and-tumble play. *Early Childhood Research Quarterly, 4,* 245–260.

Pellegrini, A.D., & Galda, L. (1993). Ten years after: A reexamination of symbolic play and literacy research. *Reading Research Quarterly, 28* (2), 163–175.

Pellegrini, A.D., & Perlmutter, J.C. (1988). Rough-and-tumble play on the elementary school playground. *Young Children, 43* (2), 14–17.

Pellegrini, A.D., & Perlmutter, J.C. (1989). Classroom contextual effects on children's play. *Developmental Psychology, 25* (2), 289–296.

Pellegrini, N. (1991). *Families are different.* New York: Holiday House.

Pelletier, J., Power, R., & Park, N. (1993). Research on excellence. In C. Corter & N.W. Park (eds.), *What makes exemplary kindergarten programs effective?* (pp. 101–127). Toronto: Ontario Ministry of Education and Training.

Pence, A.R. (1990). The child-care profession in Canada. In I.M. Doxey (Ed.), *Child care and education: Canadian dimensions* (pp. 87–97). Scarborough, ON: Nelson Canada.

Pence, A.R., & Benner, A. (2000). Child care research in Canada, 1965–99. In L. Prochner & N. Howe (Eds.), *Early childhood care and education in Canada* (pp. 133–160). Vancouver: UBC Press.

Pence, A.R., & Goelman, H. (1991). The relationship of regulation, training and motivation to quality in family daycare. *Child and Youth Care Forum, 20,* 83–101.

Penn, H. (1999). Ideas from Europe about good practice in early years service. *Interaction, 13* (3), 21–22.

Penny, K. (1996). The Western Canada Family Daycare Association. *Interaction, 9* (4), 9.

Pepler, D. (1986). Play and creativity. In G. Fein & M. Rivkin (Eds.), *The young child at play: Reviews of research, Vol. 4* (pp. 143–153). Washington, DC: National Association for the Education of Young Children.

Pepper, S., & Stuart, B. (1992). Quality of family day care in licensed and unlicensed homes. *Canadian Journal of Research in Early Childhood Education, 3,* 109–118.

Perry, B. (1997). Incubated in terror: Neurodevelopmental factors in the "cycle of violence". In J.D. Osofsky (Ed.), *Children in a violent society* (pp. 124–149). New York: The Guildford Press.

Perry, G., & Duru, M.S. (Eds.). (2000). *Resources for developmentally appropriate practice: Recommendations from the profession.* Washington, DC: National Association for the Education of Young Children.

Pestalozzi, H. (1800). *Leonard and Gertrude.* Bath: S. Hazard. (Original work published 1781)

Pestalozzi, H. (1900). *How Gertrude teaches her children* (L.E. Holland, & F.C.

Turner, Trans.). London: Swan Sonnenschein and Company. (Original work published 1801)

Peters, D.L., Neisworth, J.T., & Yawkey, T.D. (1985). *Early childhood education: From theory to practice*. Monterey, CA: Brooks/Cole.

Peterson, M., & Palmer, S. (1998). Books for babies. In A. Thomas (Ed.), *Family literacy in Canada: Profiles of effective practices* (pp. 27–32). Welland, ON: éditions Soleil publishing.

Petzold, M. (1994, July). *The psychological definition of the family*. Paper presented at the Second International Congress of the Family, Padua, Italy.

Phillips, C.E. (1957). *The development of education in Canada*. Toronto: W.J. Gage.

Phillips, D.A. (Ed.). (1987). *Quality in child care: What does research tell us?* Washington, DC: National Association for the Education of Young Children.

Phillips, D.A., & Bredekamp, S. (1998). Reconsidering early childhood education in the Unites States: Reflections from our encounters with Reggio Emilia. In C. Edwards, L. Gandini, & G. Forman (Eds.), *The hundred languages of children: The Reggio Emilia approach - Advanced reflections* (2nd ed., pp. 439–454). Greenwich, CT: Ablex Publishing.

Phillips, D.A., & Howes, C. (1987). Indicators of quality in child care: Review of research. In D.A. Phillips (Ed.), *Quality in child care: What does research tell us?* (pp. 1–20). Washington, DC: National Association for the Education of Young Children.

Piaget, J. (1957). Introduction. In *John Amos Comenius: 1592–1670* (pp. 11–31). Paris: United Nations Educational, Scientific and Cultural Organization.

Piaget, J. (1962). *Play, dreams and imitation in childhood* (C. Gattegno, & F.M. Hodgson, Trans.). New York: W.W. Norton. (Original work published 1951?)

Piaget, J. (1970). *Science of education and the psychology of the child* (D. Coleman, Trans.). New York: Orion Press.

Pianta, R.C., & Kraft-Sayre, M. (1999). Parent's observations about their children's transitions to kindergarten. *Young Children, 54* (3), 47–52.

Picard, A. (1999, September 14). Quebec a working parent's paradise. *The Globe and Mail*, pp., A1, A8.

Picard, A. (2000, July 14). AIDS epidemic creates generation of orphans. *The Globe and Mail*, p. A9.

Pines, A., & Aronson, E. (1988). *Career burnout: Causes and cures*. New York: The Free Press.

Pipher, M. (1996). *The shelter of each other: Rebuilding our families*. New York: G.P Putnam's Sons.

Plowden Report. (1967). *Children and their primary schools: A report of the Central Advisory Council for Education (England): Volume 1: The report*. London: Her Majesty's Stationery Office.

Pluckrose, H. (1998). *Japan*. New York: Franklin Watts.

Poest, C.A., Williams, J.R., Witt, D.D., & Atwood, M.E. (1990). Challenge me to move: Large muscle development in young children. *Young Children, 45* (5), 4–10.

Polakow, V. (1989). Deconstructing development. *Journal of Education, 171*, 75–87.

Polakow, V.(1997). Who cares for the children? Denmark's unique public child-care model. *Phi Delta Kappan, 78*, 604–610.

Polito, T. (1994). How play and work are organized in a kindergarten classroom. *Journal of Research in Childhood Education, 9*, 47–57.

Pollitt, E. (1994). Poverty and child development: Relevance of research in developing countries to the United States. *Child Development, 65*, 283–295.

Pollock, L.A. (1983). *Forgotten children: Parent-child relations from 1500 to 1900*. London: Cambridge University Press.

Pollock, L. (1987). *A lasting relationship: Parents and children over three centuries*. London: Fourth Estate.

Pomfret, J. (2000, May 7). Babies are winning in population 'war'. *Sunday Hong Kong Standard*, p.9.

Popov, L.K. (1997). *The family virtues guide: Simple ways to bring out the best in children and ourselves*. New York: Plume/Penguin.

Powell, D.R. (1989). *Families and early childhood programs*. Washington, DC: National Association for the Education of Young Children.

Powell, D.R. (1994a). Head Start and research: Notes on a special issue [Special issue]. *Early Childhood Research Quarterly, 9*, 241–242.

Powell, D.R. (1994b). Parents, pluralism, and the NAEYC statement on developmentally appropriate practice. In B.L. Mallory & R.S. New (Eds.), *Diversity and developmentally appropriate practices: Challenges for early childhood education* (pp. 166–182). New York: Teachers College Press.

Powell, D.R. (1998). Reweaving parents into the fabric of early childhood programs. *Young Children, 53* (5), 60–67.

Pratt, C. (1948). *I learn from children: An adventure in progressive education*. New York: Simon and Schuster.

Pratt, C. (1970). *I learn from children*. New York: Cornerstone Library (Original work published 1948)

Pratt, L. (1999, October 23). Nanny or mommy? *Financial Post*, p. C5.

Prentice, S. (1997). The deficiencies of commercial day care. *Policy Options: Child Care, 18* (1), 42–45.

Prentice, S. (2000). The business of child care: The issue of auspice. In L. Prochner & N. Howe (Eds.), *Early childhood care and education in Canada* (pp. 273–289). Vancouver: UBC Press.

Prior, M. (1992). Childhood temperament. *Journal of Child Psychology and Psychiatry, 33* (1), 249–279.

Prochner, L. (1994). A brief history of daycare in Canada: The early years. *Canadian Children, 19* (2), 10–15.

Prochner, L. (1995). A commentary on the marginal place of history in the field of early childhood care and education. *Canadian Journal of Research in Early Childhood Education, 4*, 54–55.

Prochner, L. (1996). Quality of care in historical perspective. *Early Childhood Research Quarterly, 11*, 5–17.

Prochner, L. (1998). Missing pieces: A review of history chapters in introductory early childhood education textbooks. *Journal of Early Childhood Teacher Education, 19*, 31–42.

Prochner, L. (2000). A history of early education and child care in Canada, 1820–1966. In L. Prochner & N. Howe (Eds.), *Early childhood care and education in Canada* (pp. 11–65). Vancouver: UBC Press.

Prochner, L. & Howe, N. (Eds.). (2000). *Early childhood care and education in Canada*. Vancouver: UBC Press.

Puckett, M., Marshall, C.S., & Davis, R. (1999). Examining the emergence of brain development research: The promises and the perils.

Childhood Education, 76, 8–12.

Pugh, G. (Ed.). (1996). *Contemporary issues in the early years: Working collaboratively for children* (2nd ed.). London: Paul Chapman Publishing and the National Children's Bureau.

Pugh, G., De'Ath, E., & Smith, C. (1994). *Confident parents, confident children: Policy and practice in parent education and support.* London: National Children's Bureau.

Purcell-Gates, V. (1993). Issues for family literacy research: Voices from the trenches. *Language Arts, 70,* 670–677.

Raeside, A. (1998, December 26). Cartoon. *Victoria Times-Colonist,* p.A15.

Raikes, H. (1996). A secure base for babies: Applying attachment concepts to the infant care setting. *Young Children, 51* (5), 59–67.

Raines, S.C. (1997). Developmental appropriateness: Curriculum revisited and challenged. In J.P. Isenberg & M.R. Jalongo (Eds.), *Major trends and issues in early childhood education: Challenges, controversies, and insights* (pp. 75–89). New York: Teachers College Press.

Ramsey, P., & Reid, R. (1988). Designing play environments for preschool and kindergarten children. In D. Bergen (Ed.), *Play as a medium for learning and development: A handbook of theory and practice* (pp. 213–239). Portsmouth, NH: Heinemann.

Ransbury, M.K. (1982). Friedrich Froebel 1782-1982: A reexamination of Froebel's principles of childhood learning. *Childhood Education, 59*(2), 104-106.

Rasmussen, M. (1961). Over the editor's desk. *Childhood Education, 7,* 352–353.

Raver, C.C., & Zigler, E.F. (1991). Three steps forward, two steps back: Head Start and the measurement of social competence. *Young Children, 46* (4), 3–8.

Read, K.H. (1950). *The nursery school: A human relationships laboratory.* Philadelphia: W.B. Saunders.

Read, K.H. (1955). *The nursery school: A human relationships laboratory* (2nd ed.). Philadelphia: W.B. Saunders.

Read, K.H., Gardner, P., & Mahler, B.C. (1993). *Early childhood programs: Human relationships and learning* (9th ed.). New York: Holt Rinehart & Winston.

Regan, E., & Weininger, O. (1988). Toward defining and defending child centred curriculum and practice. *International Journal of Early Childhood, 20* (2), 1–10.

Regan, E.M. (1990). Child-centred programming. In I. Doxey (Ed.). *Child care and education: Canadian dimensions* (pp. 171–177). Scarborough, ON: Nelson Canada.

Renken, B., Egeland, B., Marvinney, D., Mangelsdorf, S., & Sroufe, A. (1989).Early childhood antecedents of aggression and passive-withdrawal in early elementary school. *Journal of Personality, 57,* 257–281.

Reyer, J. (1989). Friedrich Fröbel, the profession of kindergarten teacher and the bourgeois women's movement. *Western European Education, 21* (2), 29–44.

Reynolds, G. (1998). Welcoming place: An urban community of Inuit families. *Canadian Children, 23* (1), 5–11.

Richardson, T.R. (1989). *The century of the child: The mental hygiene movement and social policy in the United States and Canada.* New York: State University of New York Press.

Richman, A.L., LeVine, R.A., New, R.S., Howrigan, G.A., Welles-

Nystrom, B., & LeVine, S.E. (1988). Maternal behavior to infants in five cultures. In R.A. LeVine, P.M. Miller, & M.M. West (Eds.), *Parental behavior in diverse societies* (pp. 81–97). San Francisco: Jossey-Bass.

Rivkin, M.S. (1995). *The great outdoors: Restoring children's right to play outside.* Washington, DC: National Association for the Education of Young Children.

Rivlin, A.M., & Timpane, P.M. (Eds.). (1975). *Planned variation in education; Should we give up or try harder?* Washington, DC: Brookings Institution.

Roberts, R.N., Wasik, B.H., Casto, G., & Ramey, C.T. (1991). Family support in the home: Programs, policy, and social change. *American Psychologist, 46,* 131–137.

Robinson, B.E. (1988). Vanishing breed: Men in child care programs. *Young Children, 43* (6), 54–58.

Rodd, J. (1996). Children, culture and education. *Childhood Education, 72,* 325–329.

Rodgers, K. (1994). Wife assault: The findings of a national survey (Catalogue No. 85–002). *Juristat Service Bulletin, 19* (9), 1–21.

Rogers, C.S., & Sawyers, J.K. (1988). *Play in the lives of children.* Washington, DC: National Association for the Education of Young Children.

Rogers, F. (1985). *Going to day care.* New York: G.P. Putnam's Sons.

Rogers, V.R. (1973). English and American primary schools. In B. Spodek (Ed.), *Early childhood education* (pp.263–274). Englewood Cliffs, NJ: Prentice-Hall.

Rogoff, B. (1990). *Apprenticeship in thinking: Cognitive development in social context.* Oxford: Oxford University Press.

Röhrs, H. (1994). Maria Montessori (1870–1952). *Prospects, 24* (1), 169–183.

Romero, M. (1989). Work and play in the nursery school. *Educational Policy, 3,* 401–419.

Rose, R. (1999). Quebec's family policy: The good, the bad and the ugly. *Interaction, 13* (1), 9–11.

Rosen, R., & Wilson, S. (1999). Work, study, family: Undergraduates with dependent care responsibilities. *Canadian Journal of Research in Early Childhood Education, 7,* 349–356.

Rosenfeld, A., & Wise, N. (2000). *Hyper-parenting: Are you hurting your child by trying too hard?* New York: St. Martin's Press.

Roskos, K., & Neuman, S.B. (1998). Play as an opportunity for literacy. In B. Spodek & O.N. Saracho (Eds.), *Multiple perspectives on play in early childhood education* (pp. 100–115). Albany, NY: State University of New York Press.

Ross, E.D. (1976). *The kindergarten crusade: The establishment of preschool education in the United States.* Athens, OH: Ohio University Press.

Roth, H. (1986). *Nursery school.* London: Putnam Publishing.

Rousseau, J.J. (1968). *La nouvelle Héloïse/Julie, or the new Eloise. Letters of two lovers, inhabitants of a small town at the foot of the Alps.* (J.H. McDowell, Trans.). University Park, PA: the Pennsylvania State University Press. (Original work published 1761)

Rousseau, J.J. (1993). *Émile* (B. Foxley, Trans.). London: J.M. Dent (Original work published 1762)

Rubin, K.H. (1977). The social and cognitive value of preschool toys and activities. *Canadian Journal of Behaviour and Science, 9,* 383–385.

Rubin, K.H., & Coplan, R.J. (1998). Social and nonsocial play in childhood: An individual differences perspective. In B. Spodek & O.N. Saracho (Eds.), *Multiple perspectives on play in early childhood education* (pp. 144–170). Albany, NY: State University of New York Press.

Rubin, K.H., & Howe, N. (1986). Social play and perspective-taking. In G. Fein & M. Rivkin (Eds.), *The young child at play: Reviews of research, Vol. 4* (pp. 113–125). Washington, DC: National Association for the Education of Young Children.

Rubin, K.H., Fein, G.G., & Vandenberg, B. (1983). Play. In P.H. Mussen (Series Ed.), & E.M. Hetherington (Vol. Ed.), *Handbook of child psychology: Vol. 4. Socialization, personality, and social development* (4th ed., pp. 693–774). New York: John Wiley.

Rubin, K.H., Maioni, T.L., & Hornung, M. (1976). Free play behaviors in middle- and lower-class preschoolers: Parten and Piaget revisited. *Child Development, 47,* 414–419.

Rubin, K.H., Watson, K.S., & Jambor, T.W. (1978). Free-play behaviors in preschool and kindergarten children. *Child Development, 49,* 534–536.

Rugg, H., & Shumaker, A. (1928). *The child-centered school: An appraisal of the new education.* Yonkers-on-Hudson, NY: World book.

Ruopp, R., Travers, J., Glantz, F., & Coelen, C. (1979). *Children at the center.* Cambridge, MA: Abt Associates.

Rusk, R.R. (1933). *A history of infant education.* London: University of London Press.

Russell, A. (1990). The effects of child-staff ratios on staff and child behavior in preschools: An experimental study. *Journal of Research in Childhood Education, 4* (2), 77–89.

Rutter, M. (1985). Resilience in the face of adversity: Protective factors and resistance to psychiatric disorder. *British Journal of Psychiatry, 147,* 598–611.

Ryan, S. (1974). *A report on longitudinal evaluations of preschool programs: Volume 1: Longitudinal evaluation* (DHEW Publication No. OHD 74–27) Washington, DC: Department of Health, Education and Welfare.

Ryan, T.J. (1972). *Poverty and the child: A Canadian study.* Toronto: McGraw-Hill Ryerson.

Ryerse, C. (1990). *Thursday's child: Child poverty in Canada: A review of the effects of poverty on children.* Ottawa: National Youth in Care Network.

Ryerse, C. (1995). Clams for the next generation: The Micmac Maliseet Child Care Council early childhood training project. *Focus, September Supplement,* 2–6.

Sager, E.W. (1998, March). *The national sample of the 1901 census of Canada: A new source for the study of the working class.* Paper presented to the Social Science History Conference, Amsterdam. [On-line]. Available: http://castle.uvic.ca/hrd/cfp

Sailor, D. (1998, August). *Homeless preschool children in Head Start programs.* Paper presented at 22nd World Congress of the Organisation Mondiale de l'Education prescolaire (OMEP), Copenhagen.

Salend, S.J., & Taylor, L. (1993). Working with families: A cross-cultural perspective. *Remedial and Special Education, 14* (5), 25–32.

Sapora, A.V., & Mitchell, E.D. (1961). *The theory of play and recreation.* New York: The Ronald Press.

Saracho, O.N. (1991). The role of play in the early childhood curriculum. In B. Spodek & O.N. Saracho (Eds.), *Yearbook in early childhood education: Vol. 2. Issues in early childhood curriculum* (pp. 86–105). New York: Teachers College Press.

Saracho, O.N. (1992). The future of teacher education in the changing world. In R. Evans & O.N. Saracho (Eds.), *Teacher preparation in early childhood education* (pp. 225–229). Yverdon, Switzerland: Gordon and Breach Science Publishers.

Saracho, O.N., & Spodek, B. (1991). Curriculum alternatives for the future. In B.Spodek & O.N. Saracho (Eds.), *Issues in early childhood curriculum* (pp. 230–234). New York: Teachers College Press.

Saracho, O.N., & Spodek, B. (1995). Children's play and early childhood education: Insights from history and theory. *Journal of Education, 177* (3), 129–148.

Scarcella, R. (1990). *Teaching language minority students in multicultural classrooms.* Englewood Cliffs, NJ: Prentice Hall.

Scarr, S., Eisenberg, M, & Deater-Deckard, K. (1994). Measurement of quality in child care centers. *Early Childhood Research Quarterly, 9,* 131–151.

Schiller, F. (1954). *On the aesthetic education of man* (R. Snell, Trans). London: Routledge & Kegan Paul.

Schlank, C.H., & Metzger, B. (1997). *Together is equal: Fostering cooperative play and promoting gender equity in early childhood programs.* Boston: Allyn and Bacon.

Schlein, L. (1995, May 28). UN criticizes Canada about children's rights. *Times-Colonist, p.A3.*

Schmidt, K., & Roe, P. (1999). It takes a village: Oak trees and acorns together. *Interaction, 13* (2), 28–30.

Schön, D.A. (1983). *The reflective practitioner: How professionals think in action.* New York: Basic Books.

Schulz, P.V. (1978). Day care in Canada: 1850–1962. In Ross, K.G. (Ed.), *Good daycare: fighting for it, getting it, keeping it* (pp. 137–158). Toronto: Women's Educational Press.

Schweinhart, L.J., & Epstein, A.S. (1996). Adopting a curriculum model: Is it really worth the effort? *High/Scope Resource, 15* (1), 4–7.

Schweinhart, L.J., & Weikart, D.P. (1998). Why curriculum matters in early childhood education. *Educational Leadership, 55* (6), 57–60.

Schweinhart, L.J., Barnes, H.V., & Weikart, D.P. (1993). *Significant benefits: The High/Scope Perry Preschool study through age 27.* Ypsilanti, MI: High/Scope Press.

Schweinhart, L.J., Weikart, D.P., & Larner, M.B. (1986). Consequences of three preschool curriculum models through age 15. *Early Childhood Research Quarterly, 1,* 15–45.

Seefeldt, C. (1990). *Continuing issues in early childhood education.* Columbus, OH: Merrill.

Seefeldt, C., & Galper, A. (1998). *Continuing issues in early childhood education* (2nd ed.). Upper Saddle River, NJ: Prentice-Hall

Seifert, K.L. (1988a). The culture of early education and the preparation of male teachers. *Early Child Development and Care, 38,* 69–80.

Seifert, K.L. (1988b). Men in early childhood education. In B. Spodek, O.N. Saracho, & D.L. Peters (Eds.), *Professionalism and the early childhood practitioner* (pp. 105–116). New York: Teachers College Press.

Seifert, K.L. (1993). Cognitive development and early childhood education. In B. Spodek (Ed.), *Handbook of research on the education of young children* (pp. 9–23). New York: Macmillan.

Seifert, K.L. & Handzuik, D. (1993). Informal theories of the child among early childhood educators. *Canadian Children, 18* (2), 21–25.

Seiter, E. (1993). *Sold separately: children and parents in consumer culture.* New

Brunswick, NJ: Rutgers University Press.

Senisi, E.B. (1994). *Kindergarten kids.* New York: Scholastic.

Shanker, A. (1996). Quality assurance: What must be done to strengthen the teaching profession. *Phi Delta Kappan, 78,* 220–224.

Shapiro, M.S. (1983). *Child's garden: The kindergarten movement from Froebel to Dewey.* University Park, PA: Pennsylvania State University Press.

Shepard, L. A., & Smith, M.L. (1986). Synthesis of research on school readiness and kindergarten retention. *Educational Leadership, 44* (3), 78–86.

Shimoni, R. (1991). Professionalization and parent involvement in early childhood education: Complementary or conflicting strategies? *International Journal of Early Childhood, 23* (2), 11–19.

Shimoni, R., & Baxter, J. (1996). *Working with families: Perspectives for early childhood professionals.* Don Mills, ON: Addison-Wesley Publishers.

Shimoni, R., Baxter, J., & Kugelmass, J. (1992). *Every child is special: Quality group care for infants and toddlers.* Don Mills, ON: Addison-Wesley.

Shipley, C.D. (1993). *Empowering children: Play-based curriculum for lifelong learning.* Scarborough, ON: Nelson Canada.

Shipman, M. (1999). An intergenerational approach to child care: A challenge during the International Year of Older Persons. *Interaction, 13* (2), 22–25.

Shore, R. (1997). *Rethinking the brain: New insights into early development.* New York: Families and Work Institute.

Siegel, D.F., & Hanson, R.A. (1991). Kindergarten educational policies: Separating myth from reality. *Early Education and Development, 2* (1), 5–31.

Sigel, I.E. (1987). Early childhood education: Developmental enhancement or developmental acceleration? In S.L. Kagan & E.F. Zigler (Eds.), *Early schooling: The national debate* (pp. 129–150). New Haven, CT: Yale University Press.

Signorielli, N. (1991). *A sourcebook on children and television.* New York: Greenwood Press.

Silin, J.G. (1985). Authority as knowledge: A problem of professionalization. *Young Children, 40* (3), 41–45.

Silin, J.G. (1987). The early childhood educator's knowledge base: A reconsideration. In L.G. Katz (Ed.), *Current topics in early childhood education* (Vol. VII, pp. 17–31). Norwood, NJ: Ablex Publishing.

Silin, J.G. (1988). On becoming knowledgeable professionals. In B. Spodek, O.N. Saracho, & D.L. Peters (Eds.), *Professionalism and the early childhood practitioner* (pp. 117–136). New York: Teachers College Press.

Silva-Wayne, S. (1995). Contributions to resilience in children and youth: What successful child welfare graduates say. In J. Hudson & B. Galaway (Eds.), *Child welfare in Canada: Research and policy implications* (pp. 308–323). Toronto: Thompson Educational Publishing.

Simons, B. (2000). A more tender separation. *Young Children, 55* (1), 30–31.

Sims, C. (2000, May 30). Japanese company offers baby bounty. *National Post,* p. A13.

Sipes, D.S.B. (1993). Cultural values and American-Indian families. In N.F. Chavkin (Ed.), *Families and schools in a pluralistic society* (pp. 157–173). Albany, NY: State University of New York Press.

Siska, H.S. (1984, September/October). It's our 35th: A look at our co-op roots (pp. 8–10). *Cover All: Vancouver Island Cooperative Preschool Association.* Victoria, BC: Vancouver Island Cooperative Preschool Association.

Slaby, R.G., Roedell, W.C., Arezzo, D., & Hendrix, K. (1995). *Early violence prevention: Tools for teachers of young children.* Washington, DC: National Association for the Education of Young Children.

Sluss, D.J., & Thompson, E.H. (1998). In search of the zone of proximal development: A sociocultural view of the stages of teaching as experienced by novice and experienced early childhood teachers. *Journal of Early Childhood Teacher Education, 19,* 193–201.

Smilansky, S. (1968). *The effects of sociodramatic play on disadvantaged preschool children.* New York: John Wiley & Sons.

Smith, A.B. (1992). Early childhood education in New Zealand: The winds of change. In G.A. Woodill, J. Bernhard, & L. Prochner (Eds.), *International handbook of early childhood education* (pp. 383–398). New York: Garland Publishing.

Smith, A.B., Dannison, L.L., & Vach-Hasse, T. (1998). When "grandma" is "mom": What today's teachers need to know. *Childhood Education, 75* (1), 12–16.

Smith, M.S. (1975). Evaluation findings in Head Start planned variation. In A. Rivlin & P.M. Timapane (Eds.), *Planned variation in education: Should we give up or try harder?* (pp. 101–112). Washington, DC: Brookings Institution.

Smith, P.K., & Connolly, K.J. (1976). Social and aggressive behavior in preschool children as a function of crowding. *Social Science Information, 16,* 601–620.

Smith, P.K., & Connolly, K.J. (1980). *The ecology of preschool behavior.* Cambridge: Cambridge University Press.

Smith, P.K., & Green, M. (1975). Aggressive behavior in English nurseries and play groups: Sex differences and responses of adults. *Child Development, 46,* 211–214.

Smith, P.K., & Vollstedt, R. (1985). On defining play: an empirical study of the relationship between play and various play criteria. *Child Development, 56,* 1042–1050.

Smith, P.K., Takhvar, M., Gore, N., & Vollstedt, R. (1985). Play in young children: Problems of definition, categorisation and measurement. *Early Child Development and Care, 19,* 25–41.

Smith, S., & Zaslow, M. (1995). Rationale and policy context for two-generation interventions. In I.E. Sigel (Series Ed.) & S. Smith (Vol. Ed.), *Advances in applied developmental psychology: Vol. 9. Two generation programs for families in poverty: A new intervention strategy* (pp. 1–35). Norwood, NJ: Ablex Publishing.

Snyder, A. (1972). *Dauntless women in childhood education: 1856–1931.* Washington, DC: Association for Childhood Education International.

Soëtard, M. (1994). Johann Heinrich Pestalozzi (1746–1827). *Prospects, 24* (1), 297–310.

Sokal, L., & Madak, P.R. (1999). The more, the better? Effects of early peer experiences on children's adjustment to kindergarten. *Canadian Journal of Research in Early Childhood Education, 8* (1), 9–18.

Soloman, C. (1989), *Moving up from kindergarten to first grade.* New York: Crown Publishers.

Spinelli, E. (2000). *Night shift daddy.* New York: Hyperion Books for Children.

Spodek, B. (1985). Early childhood education's past as prologue: Roots of contemporary concerns. *Young Children, 40* (5), 3–7.

Spodek, B. (1988). Implicit theories of early childhood teachers: Foundations for professional behavior. In B. Spodek, O.N.

Saracho, & D.L. Peters (Eds.), *Professionalism and the early childhood practitioner* (pp. 161–172). New York: Teachers College Press.

Spodek, B. (1990). Forward. In J.A. Schickedanz, M.E. York, I.S. Stewart, & D.A. White (Eds.), *Strategies for teaching young children* (3rd ed., pp. ix-x). Englewood Cliffs, NJ: Prentice Hall. k, B. (1991). Early childhood curriculum and cultural definitions of knowledge. In B. Spodek & O.N. Saracho (Eds.), *Yearbook in early childhood education: Vol.2. Issues in early childhood curriculum* (pp. 1–20). New York: Teachers College Press.

Spodek, B., & Brown, P.C. (1993). Curriculum alternatives in early childhood education: A historical perspective. In B. Spodek (Ed.), *Handbook of research on the education of young children* (pp. 91–104). New York: Macmillan.

Spodek, B., & Saracho, O.N. (1988). Professionalism in early childhood education. In B. Spodek & O.N. Saracho, & D.L. Peters (Eds.), *Professionalism and the early childhood practitioner* (pp. 59–74). New York: Teachers College Press.

Spodek, B., & Saracho, O.N. (Eds.). (1991). *Yearbook in early childhood education: Vol.2. Issues in early childhood curriculum.* New York: Teachers College Press.

Spodek, B., & Saracho, O.N. (1994). *Right from the start: Teaching children ages three to eight.* Boston: Allyn and Bacon.

Spodek, B., Saracho, O.N., & Peters, D.L. (Eds.). (1988a). *Professionalism and the early childhood practitioner.* New York: Teachers College Press.

Spodek, B., Saracho, O.N., & Peters, D.L. (1988b). Professionalism, semi-professionalism, and craftmanship. In B. Spodek, O.N. Saracho, & D.L. Peters (Eds.), *Professionalism and the early childhood practitioner* (pp. 3–9). New York: Teachers College Press.

Sroufe, A., Fox, N.E., & Pancake, V.R. (1983). Attachment and dependency in developmental perspective. *Child Development, 54,* 1615–1627.

Sroufe, L.A., Egeland, B., & Kreutzer, T. (1990). The fate of early experience following developmental change: Longitudinal approaches to individual adaptation in childhood. *Child Development, 61,* 1363–1373.

Stamp, R.M. (1982). *The schools of Ontario, 1876–1976.* Toronto: University of Toronto Press.

Stapleford, E. (1987). The challenge of good child care. *International Journal of Early Childhood, 19* (1), 14–20.

Stapleford, E. (1992). Daycare: A historical perspective as a basis for policy issues. *Canadian Journal of Research in Early Childhood Education, 3* (2), 119–121.

Stapleford, E.M. (1976). *History of the day nurseries branch.* Toronto: Ministry of Community and Social Services.

Statistics Canada. (1993). *Basic facts on families in Canada: Past and present* (Catalogue No. 89–516). Ottawa: Author.

Statistics Canada. (1996). Nation Series - Complete Edition. [CD-ROM] (Catalogue No. 93F0020XCB96004). Ottawa: Author. [p23]

Statistics Canada. (1997a). *Census families by presence of children, 1996 Census* [On-line]. Available: http://www.statcan.Pgdb/People/Families/famil54c.htm

Statistics Canada. (1997b). *A national overview - population and dwelling counts (data products : 1996 Census of Population).* (Catalogue No. 93–357–XPB). Ottawa: Author. [On-line]. Available: http://www.statcan.ca/english/census96/table15.htm

Statistics Canada. (1997c, July 29). Age and sex, 1996 Census. *The Daily* [On-line]. Available: http://www.statcan.ca/Daily/English/970729/d970729.htm

Statistics Canada. (1997d, August 26). Earning characteristics of two-partner families, 1995. *The Daily* [On-line]. Available: http://www.statcan.ca/Daily/English/970826/d970826.htm

Statistics Canada. (1997e, October 14). 1996 Census: Marital status, common-law unions and families: Marriage a fragile bond for more people. *The Daily* [On-line]. Available: http://www.statcan.ca/Daily/English/971014/d971014.htm

Statistics Canada. (1997f, November 4). 1996 Census: Immigration and citizenship. *The Daily* [On-line]. Available: http://www.statcan.ca/Daily/English/971104/d971104.htm

Statistics Canada. (1998a). *Census families, number and average size* (Catalogue No. 91–213–XPB) [On-line]. Available: http://www.statcan.ca/english/Pgdb/People/Families/famil40.htm

Statistics Canada. (1998b). *Census families in private households by number of persons, 1971–1996 Censuses, Canada* [On-line]. Available: http://www.statcan.ca/english/Pgdb/People/Families/famil50a.htm

Statistics Canada. (1998c). *Census families in private households by number of persons, 1996 Census* [On-line]. Available: http://www.statcan.ca/english/Pgdb/People/Families/famil50d.htm

Statistics Canada. (1998d). *Population estimates for 1996 and projections for the years 2001, 2006, 2011, 2016, 2021 and 2026, July 1* [On-line]. Available: http://www.statcan.ca/english/Pgdb/People/Population/demo23a.htm

Statistics Canada. (1998e). *Work absence rates, 1980–1997.* [Analytic Report No. 9, Catalogue No. 71–535–MPB, no. 9]. Ottawa: Author.

Statistics Canada. (1998f, January 13). 1996 Census: Aboriginal data. *The Daily* [On-line]. Available: http://www.statcan.ca/Daily/English/980113/d980113.htm

Statistics Canada. (1998g, March 17). 1996 Census: Labour force activity, occupation and industry, place of work, mode of transportation to work, unpaid work. *The Daily* [On-line]. Available: http://www.statcan.ca/Daily/English/980317/d980317.htm

Statistics Canada (1998h, April 14). 1996 Census: Education, mobility and migration. *The Daily* [On-line]. Available: http://www.statcan.ca80/Daily/English/980414/d980414.htm

Statistics Canada. (1998i, May 12). 1996 Census: Sources of income, earnings and total income, and family income. *The Daily* [On-line]. Available: http://www.statcan.ca/Daily/English/980512/d980512.htm

Statistics Canada. (1998j, June 9). 1996 Census: Private households, housing costs and social and economic characteristics of families. *The Daily* [On-line]. Available: http://www.statcan.ca/Daily/English/980609/d980609.htm

Statistics Canada. (1998k, June 24). Demographic situation in Canada: Substantial decline in natural growth since 1991. *The Daily* [On-line]. Available: http://www.statcan.ca/Daily/English/980624/d980624.htm

Statistics Canada. (1999a, May 18). Divorces. *The Daily* [On-line]. Available: http://www.statcan.ca/DAily/English/990518/d990518b.htm

Statistics Canada. (1999b, September 1). Employment after childbirth.

The Daily [On-line]. Available: http://www.statcan.ca/Daily/English/990901/d990901a.htm

Statistics Canada. (1999c, October 12). Computer technology in schools. *The Daily* [On-line]. Available: http://www.statcan.ca/Daily/English/991012/td991012.htm

Statistics Canada. (1999d, October 14). National Longitudinal Survey of Children and Youth: School component. *The Daily* [On-line]. Available: http://www.statcan.ca/Daily/English/991014/d991014a.htm

Statistics Canada. (1999e, October, 28). Marriages. *The Daily* [On-line]. Available: http://www.statcan.ca/Daily/English/991028/d991028c.htm

Statistics Canada. (1999f, November, 9). General Social Survey: Time use. *The Daily* [On-line]. Available: http://www.statcan.ca/Daily/English/991109/d991109a.htm

Steedman, C. (1990). *Childhood, culture and class in Britain: Margaret McMillan, 1860-1931.* London: Virago Press.

Steffy, B.E. (1989). *Career stages of classroom teachers.* Lancaster, PA: Technomic Publishing.

Steinberg, S.R., & Kincheloe, J.L. (Eds.) (1997). *Kinderculture.* Boulder, CO: Westview Press.

Steinhauer, P.D. (1999). How a child's early experiences affect development. *Interaction, 13* (1), 15–21.

Stevenson, J.H. (1990). The cooperative preschool model in Canada. In I.M. Doxey (Ed.), *Child care and education: Canadian dimensions* (pp. 221–239). Scarborough, ON: Nelson Canada.

Stevenson, M. (1999, December 9). Web site lets parents keep eye on children at daycare centres. *National Post*, p.A3.

Stipek, D., Daniels, D., Galluzzo, D., & Milburn, S. (1992). Characterizing early childhood education programs for poor and middle-class children. *Early Childhood Research Quarterly, 7,* 1–19.

Stoiber, K.C., Gettinger, M., & Goetz, D. (1998). Exploring factors influencing parents' and early childhood practitioners' beliefs about inclusion. *Early Childhood Research Quarterly, 13,* 107–124.

Stone, S.J. (nd). *The Multiage classroom: A guide for parents* [Brochure]. Olney, MD: Association for Childhood Education International.

Stoney, L. (1996). The role of accreditation in public policy. In S. Bredekamp & B.A. Willer (Eds.), *NAEYC Accreditation: A decade of learning and the years ahead* (pp. 113–128). Washington, DC: National Association for the Education of Young Children.

Stott, F., & Bowman, B. (1996). Child development knowledge: A slippery base for practice. *Early Childhood Research Quarterly, 11,* 169–183.

Stott, F., & Musick, J.S. (1994). Supporting the family support worker. In S.L. Kagan & B. Weissbourd (Eds.), *Putting families first: America's family support movement and the challenge of change* (pp. 189–215). San Francisco: Jossey-Bass.

Stremmel, A.J. (1991). Predictors of intention to leave child care work. *Early Childhood Research Quarterly, 6,* 285–298.

Strong-Boag, V. (1982). Intruders in the nursery: Childcare professionals reshape the years one to five, 1920–1940. In J. Parr (Ed.), *Childhood and family in Canadian history* (pp. 160–178). Toronto: McClelland and Stewart.

Strother, D.B. (1984). Latchkey children: The fastest-growing special interest group in the schools. *Phi Delta Kappan, 66,* 290–293.

Stuart, B., Brophy, K., Lero, D., Callahan, J., & deVoy, A. (1998). Developing a collaborative mode of child care and student learning: Notes on process and outcome at the University of Guelph. *Canadian Journal of Research in Early Childhood Education, 6,* 299–311.

Stubbs, E. (1988). Continuity: A working model. *Australian Journal of Early Childhood Education, 13* (3), 12–14.

Sub-Committee on Poverty, Standing Committee on Health and Welfare, Social Affairs, Seniors and the Status of Women. (1991). *Canada's children: Investing in our future.* Ottawa: Queen's Printer.

Super, G. (1991a). *What is a family?* Frederick, MD: Twenty-First Century Books.

Super, G. (1991b). *What kind of family do you have?* Frederick, MD: Twenty-First Century Books.

Swap, S.M. (1992). Parent involvement and success for all children: What we know now. In S.L. Christenson & J.C. Conoley (Eds.), *Home-school collaboration: Enhancing children's academic and social competence* (pp. 53–80). Silver Spring, MD: National Association of School Psychologists.

Swartz, M. (1999). A win/win intergenerational program: Baycrest Centre for Geriatric Care and Esther Exton Childcare Centre. *Interaction, 13* (2), 32–34.

Swick, K.J. (1999). Empowering homeless and transient children/families: An ecological framework for early childhood teachers. *Early Childhood Education Journal, 26,* 195–201.

Sykes, B., Wolfe, R., Gendreau, L., & Workman, L. (1998). Rhymes that bind: Adapting the Parent Child Mother Goose program model. In A. Thomas (Ed.), *Family literacy in Canada: Profiles of effective practices* (pp. 127–138). Welland, ON: éditions Soleil publishing.

Szanton, E.S. (1998). Infant/toddler care and education. In C. Seefeldt & A. Galper *Continuing issues in early childhood education* (2nd ed., pp. 62–86). Upper Saddle River, NJ: Merrill/Prentice-Hall.

Tapscott, D. (1998). *Growing up digital: The rise of the net generation.* New York: McGraw-Hill.

Taylor, A. (1999). Providing home child care for a living: Summary of the national surveys. *Interaction, 12* (4), 21–28.

Taylor, K.W. (1967). *Parents and children learn together.* New York: Teachers College Press.

Taylor, K.W. (1981). *Parents and children learn together* (3rd ed.). New York: Teachers College Press.

Tegano, D.W., & Burdette, M.P. (1991). Length of activity periods and play behaviors of preschool children. *Journal of Research in Childhood Education, 5* (2), 93–99.

Tertell, E.A., Klein, S.M., & Jewett, J.L. (Eds.). (1998). *When teachers reflect: Journeys toward effective, inclusive practice.* Washington, DC: National Association for the Education of Young Children.

The 10 best schools in the world, and what we can learn from them. (1991, December 2). *Newsweek,* 50–59.

Theemes, T. (1999). *Let's go outside! Designing the early childhood playground.* Ypsilanti, MI: High/Scope Press.

Theilheimer, R. (1993). Something for everyone: Benefits of mixed-age groups for children, parents, and teachers. *Young Children, 48* (5), 82–87.

Thomas, A. (Ed.). (1998). *Family literacy in Canada: Profiles of effective practices.* Welland, ON: éditions Soleil publishing.

Thomson, M., & Caulfield, R. (1998). Teen pregnancy and parenthood: Infants and toddlers who need care. *Early Childhood Education Journal, 25,* 203–205.

Thorne, B. (1993). *Gender play: Girls and boys in school.* New Brunswick, NJ: Rutgers University Press.

Tieleman, B. (2000, January 4). Moving poverty line doesn't end poverty. *Financial Post.* p. C7.

Tietze, W., Cryer, D., Bairrão, J., Palacios, J., & Wetzel, G. (1996). Comparisons of observed process quality in early child care and education programs in five countries. *Early Childhood Research Quarterly, 11,* 447–475.

Tipper, J. (1997). *The Canadian girl-child: Determinants of the health and well-being of girls and young women.* Ottawa: Canadian Institute of Child Health.

Tobin, J.J., Wu, D.Y.H., & Davidson, D.H. (1989). *Preschool in three cultures: Japan, China, and the United States.* New Haven, CT: Yale University Press.

Trawick-Smith, J. (1998). Why play training works: An integrated model for play intervention. *Journal of Research in Childhood Education, 12* (2), 117–129.

Tremblay, R.E. (2000). The development of aggressive behaviour during childhood: What have we learned in the past century? *International Journal of Behaviour Development, 24* (2), 129-141.

Trostle, S.L. (1984). Play therapy and the disruptive child. In T.D. Yawkey & A.D. Pellegrini (Eds.), *Child's play and play therapy* (pp. 157–169). Lancaster, PA: Technomic Publishing.

Turner, D. (1998). Child hunger in Canada. *Perceptions, 22* (3), 5–7.

Turner, J.S. (1992). Montessori's writings versus Montessori practices. In M.H. Loeffler (Ed.), *Montessori in contemporary American culture* (pp. 17–47). Portsmouth, NH: Heinemann.

Ulrey, G.L., Alexander, K., Bender, B., & Gillis, H. (1982). Effects of length of school day on kindergarten school performance and parent satisfaction. *Psychology in the Schools, 19,* 238–242.

UNICEF/United Nations Children's Fund. (1998). *The progress of nations: 1998.* New York: Author.

United Nations. (1991). *Convention on the rights of the child.* Ottawa: Human Rights Directorate/Department of Multiculturalism and Citizenship.

United Nations. (1994). United Nations Proclamation of the International Year of the Family. *Early Childhood Educator, 9* (4), p. 5.

United Nations. (1996). *Family: Challenges for the future.* Geneva: United Nations Publications.

Van der Eyken, W. (1982). *The education of three-to eight year olds in Europe in the eighties.* Windsor, Berks: NFER-Nelson.

Vandell, D., Henderson, V.K., & Wilson, K.S. (1988). A longitudinal study of children with day care experiences of varying quality. *Child Development, 59,* 1286–1292.

Vandell, D.L., & Shumow, L. (1999). After-school child care programs. *Future of Children, 9* (2), 64–80. [On-line]. Available: http://www.futureofchilren.org/wso/wso_07.pdf

Vandell, D.L., & Su, H. (1999). Child care and school-age children. *Young Children, 54* (6), 62–71.

Vander Ven, K. (1988). Pathways to professional effectiveness for early childhood educators. In B. Spodek, O.N. Saracho, & D.L. Peters (Eds.), *Professionalism and the early childhood practitioner* (pp. 137–160). New York: Teachers College Press.

Vander Ven, K. (1997). Chaos/complexity theory, constructivism, inter-disciplinarity and early childhood teacher education. *Journal of Early Childhood Teacher Education, 18* (3), 43–48.

Vander Wilt, J.L., & Monroe, V. (1998). Successfully moving toward developmentally appropriate practice: It takes time and effort! *Young Children, 53* (4), 17, 24.

Vandewalker, N.C. (1908). *The kindergarten in American education.* New York: Macmillan.

Vanier Institute of the Family. (1992). *Canadian families in transition: The implications and challenges of change.* Ottawa: Author.

Vanier Institute of the Family. (1993). *Canadian families.* Ottawa: Author.

Vanier Institute of the Family. (1994). *Profiling Canada's families.* Ottawa: Author.

Vanier Institute of the Family. (1996). *Canada's families: They count.* Ottawa: Author.

Varga, D. (1993). From service for mothers to the developmental management of children: Day nursery care in Canada, 1890–1960. *Perspectives in Developmentally Appropriate Practice, 5,* 115–143.

Varga, D. (1997). *Constructing the child: A history of Canadian day care.* Toronto: James Lorimer Publishers.

Varga, D. (2000). A history of early-childhood-teacher education. In L. Prochner & N. Howe (Eds.), *Early childhood care and education in Canada* (pp. 66–95). Vancouver: UBC Press.

Vartuli, S. (1999). How early childhood teacher beliefs vary across grade level. *Early Childhood Research Quarterly, 14,* 489–514.

Vernon, J., & Smith, C. (1994). *Day nurseries at a crossroads: Meeting the challenge of child care in the nineties.* London: National Children's Bureau.

Vogel, N. (1997). *Getting started: Materials and equipment for active learning preschools.* Ypsilanti, MI: High/Scope Press.

Vygotsky, L.S. (1962). *Thought and language* (E. Haufmann & G. Vakar, Eds., Trans). Cambridge, MA: MIT Press.

Vygotsky, L.S. (1966). Play and its role in the mental development of the child. *Soviet Psychology, 1,* 16–18.

Vygotsky, L.S. (1967). Play and its role in the mental development of the child. *Soviet Psychology, 5* (3), 6–18 (Original work published 1933)

Walmsley, S., & Walmsley, B.B. (1996). *Kindergarten: Ready or not? A parent's guide.* Portsmouth, NH: Heinnemann.

Walsh, D.J. (1991). Extending the discourse on developmental appropriateness: A developmental perspective. *Early Education and Development, 2,* 109–119.

Walsh, D.J. (1992). Us against them: A few thoughts on separateness. *Early Education and Development, 3* (2), 89–91.

Walsh, D.J., Smith, M.E., Alexander, M., & Ellwein, M.C. (1993). The curriculum as mysterious and constraining: Teachers' negotiations of the first year of a pilot programme for at-risk 4–year-olds. *Journal of Curriculum Studies, 25,* 317–332.

Wandersman, L.P. (1987). New directions of parent education. In S.L. Kagan, D.R. Powell, B. Weissbourd, & E.F. Zigler (Eds.), *America's family support programs: Perspectives and prospects* (pp. 207–380). New Haven, CT: Yale University Press.

Washington, V., & Andrews, J.D. (Eds.). (1999). *Children of 2010.* Washington, DC: National Association for the Education of Young Children.

Washington, V., Johnson, V., & McCracken, J.B. (1995). *Grassroots success! Preparing schools and families for each other.* Washington, DC: National Association for the Education of Young Children.

Waterland, L. (1995). *The bridge to school: Entering a new world.* York, ME: Stenhouse Publishers.

Waters, J. (1998). *Helping young children understand their rights.* Victoria, Australia: World Organization for Early Childhood Education.

Waxler-Morrison, N., Anderson, J.M., & Richardson, E. (Eds.). (1990). *Cross-cultural caring: A handbook for health professionals in Western Canada.* Vancouver: UBC Press.

We are all related: A celebration of our cultural heritage (1996). Vancouver, BC: G.T. Cunningham Elementary School.

Weber, E. (1984). *Ideas influencing early childhood education: A theoretical analysis.* New York: Teachers College Press.

Weber, L. (1971). *The English infant school and informal education.* Englewood Cliffs, NJ: Prentice-Hall.

Weber, L. (1984). *Ideas influencing early childhood education: A theoretical analysis.* New York: Teachers College Press.

Weikart, D.P. (1989). *Quality preschool programs: A long-term social investment.* New York: The Ford Foundation.

Weikart, D.P. (Ed.). (1999). *What should young children learn? Teacher and parent views in 15 countries.* Ypsilanti, MI: High/Scope Press.

Weikart, D.P. & Schweinhart, L.J. (1993). The High/Scope curriculum for early childhood care and education. In J.L. Roopnarine & J.E. Johnson (Eds.), *Approaches to early childhood education* (2nd ed., pp. 195–208). New York: Merrill.

Weikart, D.P., Rogers, L., Adcock, C., & McClelland, D. (1971). *The cognitively oriented curriculum: A framework for preschool teachers.* Urbana, IL: ERIC-National Association for the Education of Young Children.

Weininger, O., & Fitzgerald, D. (1988). Symbolic play and interhemispheric integration: Some thoughts on a neuropsychological model of play. *Journal of Research and Development in Education, 21* (4), 23–40.

Weinreb, M.L. (1997). Be a resiliency mentor: You may be a lifesaver for a high-risk child. *Young Children, 52* (2), 14–20.

Weiss, L. (1984). *My teacher sleeps in school.* New York: Puffin Books.

Weissbourd, B. (1991). Family resource and support programs: Changes and challenges in human services. In D.G. Unger & D.R. Powell (Eds.) *Families as nurturing systems: Support across the life span* (pp. 69–85). New York: Haworth Press.

Weissbourd, B., & Patrick, M. (1988). In the best interest of the family: The emergence of family resource programs. *Infants and Young Children, 1* (2), 46–54.

Weissbourd, R. (1996). *The vulnerable child: What really hurts America's children and what we can do about it.* Reading, MA: Addison-Wesley Publishing.

Welken, M. (1993). Washington Elementary School Valley City, North Dakota. *Reading Today, 10* (3), 30.

Werner, E.E. (1989). High-risk children in young adulthood: A longitudinal study from birth to 32 years. *American Journal of Orthopsychiatry, 59* (1), 72–81.

Werner, E.E., & Smith, R.S. (1982). *Vulnerable but invincible: A study of resilient children.* New York: McGraw-Hill.

Werner, E.E., & Smith, R.S. (1992). *Overcoming the odds: High risk children from birth to adulthood.* Ithaca, NY: Cornell University Press.

Westman, J.C. (Ed.). (1991). *Who speaks for the children? The handbook of individual and class child advocacy.* Sarasota, FL: Professional Resource Exchange.

Whipple, G.M. (Ed.). (1929). *The twenty-eighth yearbook of the National Society for the Study of Education: Preschool and parent education.* Bloomington, IL: Public School Publishing Company.

White, D., & Mill, D. (2000). The child care provider. In L. Prochner & N. Howe (Eds.), *Early childhood care and education in Canada* (pp. 236–251). Vancouver: UBC Press.

White, S.H., & Buka, S.L. (1987). Early education: Programs, traditions, and policies. In E.Z. Rothkopf (Ed.), *Review of research in education* (Vol.14, pp. 43–91). Washington, DC: American Education Research Association.

Whitebook, M. (1996). NAEYC Accreditation as an indicator of program quality: What research tells us. In S. Bredekamp & B.A. Willer (Eds.), *NAEYC Accreditation: A decade of learning and the years ahead* (pp. 31–46). Washington, DC: National Association for the Education of Young Children.

Wien, C.A. (1995). *Developmentally appropriate practice in 'real-life': Stories of teacher practical knowledge.* New York: Teachers College Press.

Wien, C.A. (1997). Time, work, and developmentally appropriate practice. *Canadian Children, 22* (2), 30–38.

Wiggin, K.D., & Smith, N.A. (1896). *Kindergarten principles and practice.* Cambridge, MA: Riverside Press.

Wildman, T.M., Magliaro, S.G., Niles, R.A., & Niles, J.A. (1992). Teacher mentoring: An analysis of roles, activities, and conditions. *Journal of Teacher Education, 43,* 205–213.

Willer, B. (1994). A conceptual framework for early childhood professional development. In J. Johnson & J.B. McCracken (Eds.), *The early childhood career lattice: Perspectives on professional development* (pp. 4–23). Washington. DC: National Association for the Education of Young Children.

Williams, L.R. (1992a). The Froebelian kindergarten. In L. R. Williams & D.P. Fromberg (Eds.), *Encyclopedia of early childhood education* (pp. 49–51). New York: Garland Publishing.

Williams, L.R. (1992b). The McMillan nursery school. In L. R. Williams & D.P. Fromberg (Eds.), *Encyclopedia of early childhood education* (p. 53). New York: Garland Publishing.

Williams, L.R. (1992c). Nursery school (prekindergarten). In L.R. Williams & D.P. Fromberg (Eds.), *Encyclopedia of early childhood education* (p. 152). New York: Garland Publishing.

Williams, L.R. (1994). Developmentally appropriate practice and cultural values: A case in point. In B.L. Mallory & R.S. New (Eds.), *Diversity and developmentally appropriate practices: Challenges for early childhood education* (pp. 166–165). New York: Teachers College Press.

Williams, M.L. (1998). Day care as intervention: An update of day care effects on child development. *Canadian Journal of Research in Early Childhood Education, 7,* 31–49.

Williams, P. (1998, October). The last company town. *The Financial Post Magazine, 56,* 52–59.

Wilson, D.J., Stamp, R.M., & Audet, L.P. (Eds.). (1970). *Canadian educa-*

tion: A history. Scarborough, ON: Prentice-Hall.

Wing, L.A. (1995). Play is not the work of the child: Young children's perceptions of work and play. *Early Childhood Research Quarterly, 10,* 223–247.

Winn, M., & Porcher, M.A. (1967). *The playgroup book.* New York: Macmillan.

Winter, S.M. (1999). *The early childhood inclusion model: A program of all children.* Olney, MD: Association for Childhood Education International.

Witkin, B.R. (1984). *Assessing needs in educational and social programs.* San Francisco: Jossey-Bass Publishers.

Wolery, M., & Bredekamp, S. (1994). Developmentally appropriate practices and young children with disabilities: Contextual issues in the discussion. *Journal of Early Intervention, 18,* 331–341.

Wolery, M., Holcombe, A., Venn, M.L., Brookfield, J., Huffman, K., Schroeder, C., Martin, C.G., & Fleming, L.A. (1993). Mainstreaming in early childhood programs: Current status and relevant issues. *Young Children, 49* (I), 78–84.

Wolfe, P., & Brandt, R. (1998). What do we know from brain research? *Educational Leadership, 56* (3), 8–13.

Wood, L., & Attfield, J. (1996). *Play, learning and the early childhood curriculum.* London: Paul Chapman.

Woodhead, J., & Woodhead, M. (1990). *All our children: A window on the world of childhood.* Crowsnest, NSW: ABC Enterprises for the Australian Broadcasting Company

Woodhead, M. (1979). *Preschool education in Western Europe: Issue, policies and trends.* London: Longman.

Woodhead, M. (1989). "School starts at five … or four years old?" The rationale for changing admission policies in England and Wales. *Journal of Education Policy, 4* (I), I–21.

Woodill, G.A., Bernhard, J., & Prochner, L. (Eds.). (1992). *International handbook of early childhood education.* New York: Garland Publishing.

Woolfolk, A.E., & Brooks, D.M. (1985). The influence of teachers' non-verbal behaviors on students' perceptions and performance. *The Elementary School Journal, 85,* 513–528.

World Organization for Early Childhood Education (OMEP) and Association for Childhood Education International. (1999). *Early childhood education and care in the 21st century: Global guidelines and papers from an international symposium hosted by the World Organization for Early Childhood Education (Organisation Mondiale pour L'Éducation Préscolaire) and the Association for Childhood Education International.* Olney, MD: Association for Childhood Education International and World Organization for Early Childhood Education (Organisation Mondiale pour L'Éducation Préscolaire).

Worth, B. (1997). *I can go to preschool.* New York: Golden Books.

Wortham, S. (1992). *Childhood 1892–1992.* Wheaton, MD: Association for Childhood Education International.

Wortham, S.C. (1995). Reconsidering developmentally appropriate practices. *ACEI Exchange, 71,* 224–A, 224D.

Wright, F.L. (1995). *Frank Lloyd Wright collected writings* (B.B. Pleiffer, Ed.). New York: Rizzoli International Publications. (Original work published 1957)

Wright, J.L., & Shade, D.D. (Eds.). (1994). *Young children: Active learners in a technological age.* Washington, DC: National Association for the Education of Young Children.

Wright, M.J. (1983). *Compensatory education in the preschool: A Canadian approach: The University of Western Ontario Preschool Project.* Ypsilanti, MI: The High/Scope Press.

Wright, M.J. (1999). The history of developmental psychology in Canada. *Canadian Journal of Research in Early Childhood Education, 8* (I), 31–36.

Wright, M.J. (2000). Toronto's Institute of Child Study and the teachings of W.E. Blatz. In L. Prochner & N. Howe (Eds.), *Early childhood care and education in Canada* (pp. 98–114). Vancouver: UBC Press.

Wrobleski, L.C. (1990). The writer's briefcase. *Young Children, 10* (3), 69.

Yang, H. (1993). Confucius (K'ung Tzu) (551–479 B.C.). *Prospects, 23,* 211–219.

Yardley, A. (1976). *The organisation of the infant school.* London: Evans Brothers.

Yardley, A. (1989). *The teacher of young children.* Oakville, ON: Rubicon Publishing.

Yeom, J.S. (1998). Children's transition experiences from kindergarten to grade one. *Canadian Children, 23* (I), 25–33.

Young, M.E. (1997). Policy issues and implications of early child development. In M.E. Young (Ed.), *Early child development: Investing in our children's future* (pp. 323–330). New York: Elsevier.

Youth rate families at top in UNICEF-sponsored poll. (1999, November 20). *Times-Colonist,* p.A8.

Zakaluk, B. (1998). Book Bridges. In A. Thomas (Ed.), *Family literacy in Canada: Profiles of effective practices* (pp. 73–82). Welland, ON: éditions Soleil publishing.

Zeanah, C.H., & Scheeringa, M.S. (1997). The experience and effects of violence in infancy. In J.D. Osofsky (Ed.), *Children in a violent society* (pp. 97–123). New York: The Guildford Press.

Zelizer, V.A. (1985). *Pricing the priceless child: The changing social value of children.* New York: Basic Books.

Zetlin, A. (1995). Commentary: Lessons learned about integrating services. In L.C. Rigsby, M.C. Reynolds, & M.C. Wang (Eds.), *School-community connections: Exploring issues for reseach and practice* (pp. 421–426). San Francisco: Jossey-Bass.

Zigler, E., & Muenchow, S. (1992). *Head Start: The inside story of America's most successful educational experiment.* New York: Basic Books.

Zigler, E., & Styfco, S.J. (Eds.). (1993). *Head Start and beyond: A national plan for extended childhood intervention.* New Haven, CT: Yale University Press.

Zigler, E., & Valentine, J. (1979). *Project Head Start: A legacy of the war on poverty.* New York: Macmillan.

Zigler, E., Styfco, S.J., & Gilman, E. (1993). The national Head Start program for disadvantaged preschoolers. In E. Zigler & S.J. Styfco (Eds.), *Head Start and beyond: A national plan for extended childhood intervention* (pp. I–4I). New Haven, CT: Yale University Press.

Zigler, E.G., Finn-Stevenson, M., & Marsland, K.W. (1995). Child day care in the schools: The School of the 21st Century. *Child Welfare, 74,* 301–326.

Zimiles, H. (1986). The social context of early childhood education in an era of expanding preschool education. In B. Sopdek (Ed.), *Today's kindergarten* (pp. I–14). New York: Teachers College Press.

Zoehfeld, K. (1997). *Pooh's first day of school.* New York: Disney.

Zolotow, C. (1972). *William's doll.* New York: Harper.

Author Index

Subject Index